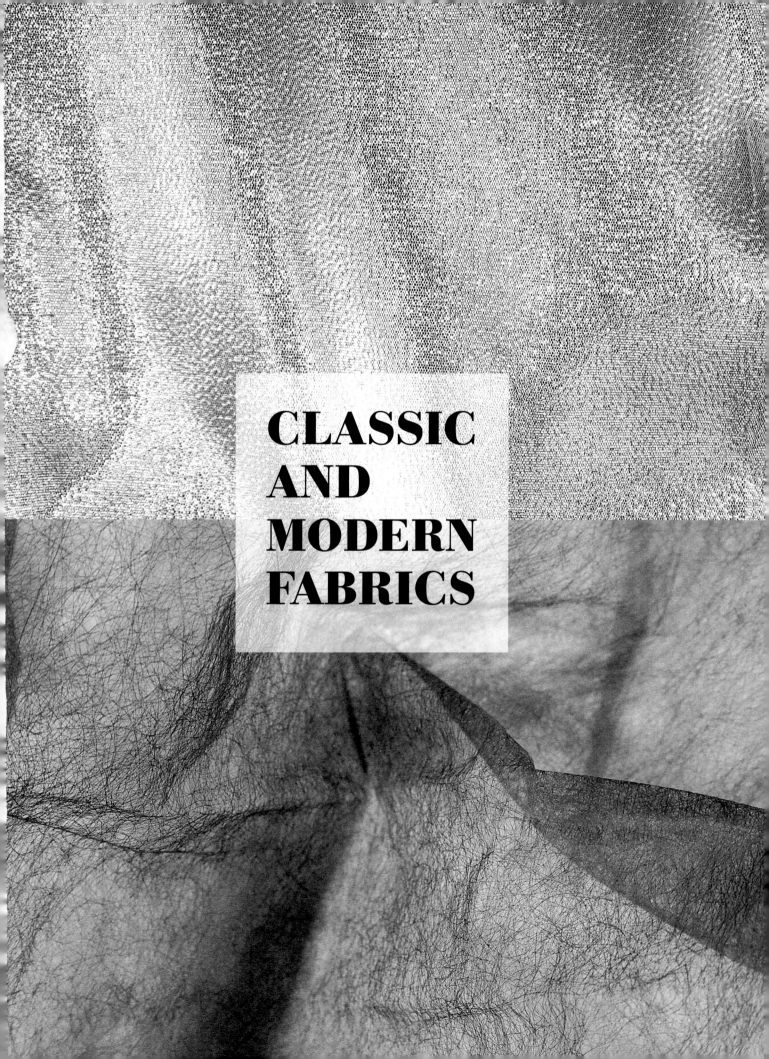

CLASSIC AND MODERN FABRICS

Thames & Hudson

JANET WILSON

CLASSIC AND MODERN FABRICS

THE COMPLETE ILLUSTRATED SOURCEBOOK

With 834 colour illustrations

I would like to dedicate this book to my partner, Phil Wong, and to my parents, Doreen and Tony Wilson, for their constant love and support.

First published in the United Kingdom in 2010 by
Thames & Hudson Ltd, 181A High Holborn, London WC1V 7QX

thamesandhudson.com

British Library Cataloguing-in-Publication Data
A catalogue record for this book is available from the British Library

ISBN 978-0-500-51507-5

Printed and bound in China by Toppan Leefung Printing Limited

God Loveth Sinners,

Dyers and Spinners.

Weavers even

May hope for Heaven.

When Nought is left

Of Warp and Weft

With Spindle and Loom

They will meet their Doom.

The Lamb's White Fleece

Has brought their Peace.

From a charter granted to Cirencester
weavers by Philip and Mary, dated 1558.

This book has a dedicated website for comments and suggestions:
please visit www.classicandmodernfabrics.com.

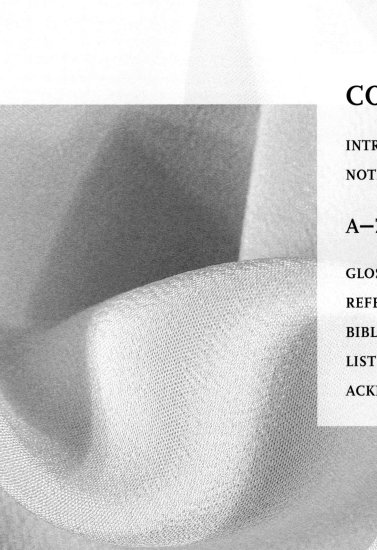

CONTENTS

INTRODUCTION Since the earliest times, textiles of all kinds have been produced by cultures and societies all over the world. Textiles play a very important role in our daily lives, fulfilling both practical and cultural requirements.

Many fabrics do not have a specific name, but there are numerous others that do. These tend to be the 'classic fabrics' that have been reproduced time and again throughout history, either because they are of great practical value or because they are exquisitely beautiful, and sometimes for both of these reasons. Fabrics such as canvas, flannel, tartan and velvet have been widely used for many centuries and continue in their popularity today. Others, such as bridal satin, tend to be used more rarely, only for special occasions. Others again, like tapestry and ornamental batik, are expressions of an artistic or technical excellence in craftsmanship. In this respect, they fulfil a cultural need. They are essentially works of art, and are more likely to be collected and displayed on walls than put to any functional use. All these are examples of true classic fabrics.

More recently, there have been a great many new developments and technical innovations in the field of fabrics – microencapsulated textiles and moisture transport textiles, for instance – that are making a great impact on our lives and changing the way we think about and use textile materials. The technology of microencapsulation has led to a variety of new products, including perfumed fabrics that gradually release a fragrance over time. Moisture transport textiles, with their increased ability to wick perspiration, have also prompted the creation of many novel products, such as 'breathable' sportswear and rainwear; and the use of microfibres in particular has yielded a whole new range of strong, breathable, lightweight garments that are comfortable to wear and often water-repellent.

Changing markets make it vital that professionals involved in the textile and clothing industries should be familiar with the vast range of fabrics that can be produced. In today's commercial climate, in which economics usually dictate which fabrics are manufactured and sold, it is important that the wide diversity of fabrics that have been produced historically should not be lost or forgotten. These fabrics have proven their value over time and can be adapted to create new products that meet the requirements of the present day. It is therefore in everyone's best interest that our knowledge of this cultural heritage should be retained.

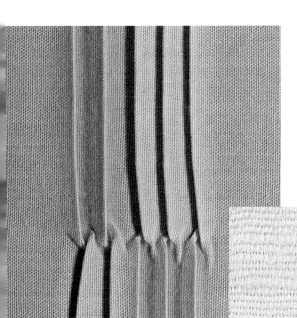

Classic and Modern Fabrics: The Complete Illustrated Sourcebook has been written to fulfil a need for a book that comprehensively catalogues and describes a wide variety of fabrics, from well-known classics such as denim to an ever increasing range of innovative products like microfibre fabrics. The book documents over six hundred different classic and modern fabrics alphabetically, most with construction details and a photograph to aid recognition. Some background history and information on typical end uses have also been provided. Most of the fabrics described are in current use, but a number that appear to be obsolete are also included. The aims of this book are:

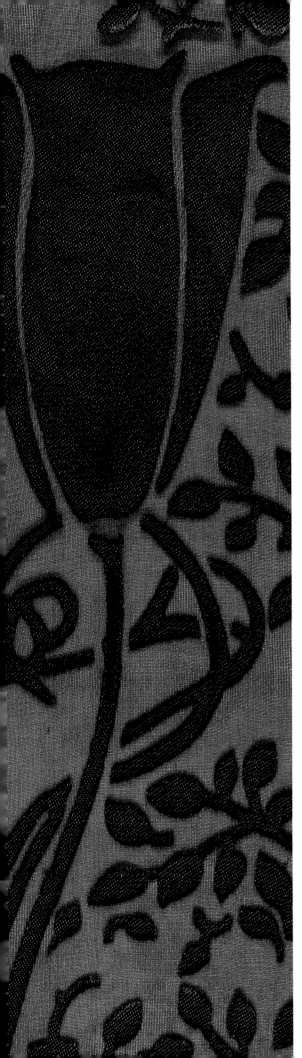

- to preserve our knowledge of the diversity of classic fabrics, which form part of our cultural heritage
- to provide information on a range of new developments in fabrics
- to inform professionals involved in the textile and clothing industries about the construction and production of the various classic and modern fabrics
- to explain the characteristics of different types of fabric, thus allowing readers to assess their suitability for particular end uses
- to promote an appreciation of the variety of fabrics and textile materials currently available
- to provide information about particular fabrics that could be produced for special niche markets

It is my hope that anyone working in the textile and clothing industries, those who use textiles in interior design, textile and fashion historians, fashion and textile students, and anyone with a general interest in the field will find *Classic and Modern Fabrics* a useful resource.

The book encompasses a diverse range of textiles, fabrics and related materials. Great care has been taken in researching the different items to be included, and every effort has been made to produce a comprehensive and accurate description of each fabric. There are, however, a number of considerations that the reader should take into account: the variation in fabrics over time and across different regions; fluctuating trends in production; and the rapid pace of recent technological developments.

As they have evolved over the years, many of the classic fabrics have undergone significant changes to their qualities and characteristics. Today many variations on original, traditional fabrics are produced, and in a greater number of different fibres than ever before. Perhaps the greatest change occurred with the introduction of man-made fibres, which now account for a significant part – and sometimes all – of the content of many fabrics. The inclusion of man-made fibres has led to the design of many new qualities of classic fabrics.

At the same time, much of the beauty and integrity of the original classic fabrics discussed here stems from the fact that they were made with raw materials produced in the areas where the fabrics originated. For example, in England and Scotland many of the classic tweed fabrics were produced from the wool of the local Cheviot breed of sheep. This type of wool produces unique fabrics that are very warm and hard-wearing (some Harris tweed jackets have been known to last more than a generation). It is not possible to achieve the same quality by using wool from other breeds of sheep or by including man-made fibres, and any fabrics containing these elements will inevitably differ from the original fabric.

The same is true of classic fabrics produced elsewhere in the world. India, China and other countries in the Far East traditionally have specialized in fine silk fabrics made from locally produced silk that is natural to the area. Examples of classic fabrics made in these regions include pongee, shantung and tussore, each with its own unique characteristics. The southern states of the United States, the West Indies, Egypt and parts of India all have climates that are ideal for the production of cotton, and historically they have produced a great variety of cotton fabrics. Much of Europe, including Ireland, France, Belgium and Russia, has a climate that is perfectly suited to the production of flax, used to make linen fabrics. Classic fabrics produced in these countries include Irish linen and Holland. Thus the production and the quality of the majority of original classic fabrics worldwide are closely linked to the raw materials from which they are made, and ultimately to their regions of origin, giving these textiles a unique look and character that are impossible to match with materials from elsewhere.

Another change that has occurred over the last fifty years or so is a general trend for fabrics to become gradually lighter in weight. This is partly due to the arrival of central heating in modern homes, partly due to changes in lifestyle (for example, much clothing currently produced is classified as 'fast fashion' and seen as disposable after only one season), and partly the result of economics (textile goods are sold by weight, and lightweight fabrics are therefore often considered more cost-effective).

For all these reasons, many of the classic fabrics produced today have changed a great deal when compared to their historical equivalents. It also should be noted that, because some classic fabrics have been produced in more than one part of the world, they may have evolved in different ways in different places. The text has included these various interpretations as far as possible, but there may be countries and regions that have a slightly different understanding and perception of how certain fabrics should be. This should be taken into account when working with suppliers overseas.

Another consideration is that fabrics are constantly coming in and going out of popularity in response to changes in fashion and to market demands. There are also regional trends, so that fabrics may be available in some countries but

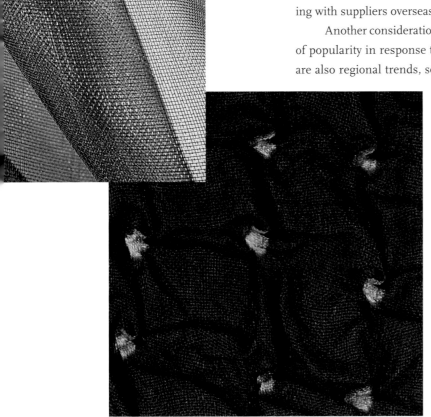

not in others. This makes it difficult to decide which fabrics are in production and which are currently obsolete. Where it seems that a fabric is obsolete, this has been indicated in the text; but it should be noted that any of these fabrics could be reproduced at any time, and some could even be in current production. In addition, there are many ancient fabrics that have not been included in the main text, but that may be found in publications cited in the bibliography.

Lastly, one should be aware of the rapid pace at which fabrics are changing. New man-made fibre technology, new construction techniques and processes, and recent developments in finishing have not only led to the design of many new qualities of existing fabrics, but have also inspired a wide range of completely new textiles. Many of these are discussed in this book, but the reader should also note that this is an area that is constantly evolving.

NOTES TO THE READER

PRESENTATION OF FABRIC NAMES

- At the beginning of each entry, the main fabric name is given in bold, with the most important alternative names, spellings or forms following in parentheses, e.g. DOUPION (dupion); HOPSACK (basket cloth); DEVORÉ FABRIC (burn-out fabric, burnt-out fabric).
- Some names are given in inverted order: this is done to distinguish between sub-types of a fabric that are important and distinct enough to be treated separately. Warp-knitted satin and woven satin, for instance, will be found under SATIN, WARP-KNITTED and SATIN, WOVEN, respectively.
- Sometimes cross-references direct the reader to the main entry under which that fabric or subtype is discussed: e.g. IRISH LINEN *see* LINEN FABRIC; BURN-OUT FABRIC *see* DEVORÉ FABRIC. In a few instances there are pointers to more than one entry, such as when a term has two different uses.
- Fabric names appear in alphabetical order letter by letter, so that INDIAN LAWN comes before INDIA SILK.
- Where a fabric is believed to be obsolete, this is indicated by the abbreviation *obs.* in parentheses, e.g. COUPURE (*obs.*).

CONSTRUCTION OF ENTRIES

Each entry begins with a definition setting out the principal features by which a fabric can be identified. The remainder of the entry provides more detailed information about fibres, yarns, construction, finishes, characteristics, history, origins of the name, alternative names, variant types of the fabric, similar fabrics, and other fabrics with which it might be confused. Typically, a list of cross-references and a list of end uses is given at the end. Several fabrics – e.g. CRÊPE – have more complex entries listing subtypes.

CROSS-REFERENCES

Cross-references to other entries are indicated by *see* or *see also* in italics. The *See also* list that appears at the end of most entries refers the reader to related fabrics, usually mentioned in the entry, that will broaden his or her understanding of the fabric being discussed. Cross-references may also be given within the entry.

GLOSSARY

Technical terms – for fibres, yarns, techniques, processes or other mechanisms – that are not covered in the main text are explained in the glossary on pp. 310–16.

REFERENCES

Sources are indicated by means of superscript numbers, which refer to the numbered list of books and articles on p. 316.

SPECIAL CONVENTIONS

- Fabric weights are quoted in grams per square metre (g/m^2).
- The yarn count, or yarn number, is a way of designating a yarn's 'size' or thickness. Historically, various count systems have been used; they are classified as either 'direct systems' (which refer to the number of mass units per defined length unit) or 'indirect systems' (which refer to the number of length units per unit mass).

This book, however, follows the internationally recognized system of designating the count of a yarn in tex units. The tex system is a direct yarn count system, in which the higher the count number, the coarser the yarn. The basic tex unit is the mass in grams of one kilometre of yarn, whereas decitex (dtex) is the mass in decigrams of one kilometre of yarn. In a few instances the resultant yarn number is given; this is indicated by the prefix R. For example, R40/2 is descriptive of a yarn where 40 is the resultant count of a 2-fold yarn composed of 2 × 20 tex singles yarns (ignoring folding twist contraction).

- Where construction details are given for woven fabrics, the count of the warp yarns, and the number of warp yarns per centimetre, are given first, followed by the count of the weft yarns and the number of weft yarns per centimetre. The weave structure is usually given separately.

- In all weave diagrams, coloured squares represent a warp yarn lifted over a weft yarn:

- In all diagrams illustrating machine-produced weft-knitted fabrics, dots represent the site of needles. One double row of alternating dots indicates the needles of a rib machine, while one double row of aligned dots represents the needles of an interlock or purl machine (see examples below). In all these cases, a double row of dots represents one cycle or knitted course, but it is possible, and sometimes desirable, to build up more than one cycle on one set of dots. The order of a sequence of knitted courses is indicated by a number at the side of each double row of dots, starting at the bottom with the first course knitted.[25]

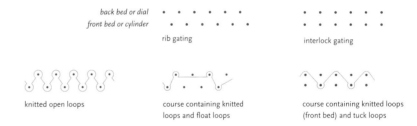

- In the diagrams of warp-knitted fabrics, dots represent the position of the needles on successive courses. Vertical rows of dots represent wales, and horizontal rows of dots represent courses. The lowest row of dots represents the first course. The grey line shows the path of the yarn as it progresses from course to course throughout the fabric. Each guide bar is shown separately.[25]

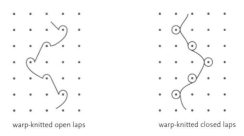

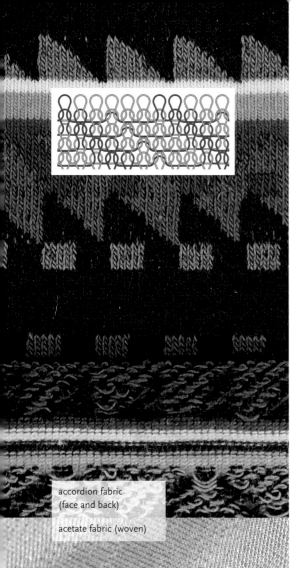

accordion fabric
(face and back)

acetate fabric (woven)

ABBOT CLOTH *see* MONK'S CLOTH.

ABBOTSFORD (*obs.*) A term used for a variety of dress-weight fabrics woven in muted check designs and slightly napped on one side. They may be made from cotton, wool, viscose, modal or acrylic.[2]

ABERCROMBIE *see* TARTAN.

ACCORDION FABRIC A weft-knitted jacquard fabric that is knitted in a plain knit construction and incorporates figured designs in two or more colours.

Accordion fabric may be hand-knitted or knitted by machine. The pattern is made by knitting different areas of the design in different colours by a knitting and missing process. When a yarn is not being knitted into the face of the fabric to form the pattern, it is floated on the back. The face of the fabric is therefore normally outermost in use. Any long floats on the back of the fabric are secured by extra tuck loops that are arranged to create minimum distortion, but that tend to grin through to the face side of the fabric.[25] Accordion fabric is similar to fairisle but can be made in any jacquard pattern, whereas fairisle patterns have recognizable characteristics.

See also FAIRISLE; FIGURED FABRIC; JACQUARD FABRIC, KNITTED; KNITTED FABRIC; PLAIN KNIT FABRIC; WEFT-KNITTED FABRIC.

End uses: sweaters and cardigans.

ACCORDION PLEATS *see* PLEATED FABRICS.

ACETATE FABRIC A general term for any fabric that has been constructed using acetate fibres or yarns. Acetate is the generic term for a regenerated man-made material chemically reprocessed from cellulose.[25] It may be produced either in sheet form or in fibre form. It is usually the fibres that are used to make clothing and furnishing fabrics.

The fibres may be used in continuous filament form, or they may be chopped into shorter staple lengths and respun into yarns with different characteristics, sometimes blended with other staple fibres. The term 'acetate fabric' is used for fabrics of various weights and constructions that are composed of 100% acetate fibres or yarns. Where acetate is used together with other fibres, the percentage of each should be stated.

Characteristically, acetate fabrics have excellent drape and a soft handle. However, they have poor abrasion resistance and low wet and dry strength; they also crease fairly easily. They are used mainly as lining fabrics. Acetate fibres can also be given a range of different properties by varying the manufacturing parameters. Modified acetate fibres are marketed under different brand names.

End uses: linings, lingerie and dress fabrics.

ACRYLIC FABRIC A general term for any fabric that has been constructed using acrylic fibres or yarns. Acrylic is the generic term for a synthetic man-made material.[25] It may be produced in sheet form or in continuous filament fibre form. It is usually the fibres that are used to make clothing and furnishing fabrics.

The term 'acrylic fabric' is used for fabrics of various weights and constructions composed of 100% acrylic fibres or yarns. Where acrylic is used together with other fibres, the percentage of each should be given. Acrylic fibres are thermoplastic or heat-sensitive and may be used in continuous filament form, or chopped into shorter staple lengths and spun into more natural-looking yarns.

aeroplane fabric

acrylic fabric (knitted)

Afgalaine

Characteristically, acrylic fabrics are soft, warm and quite strong, but they are not very absorbent and can be prone to static build-up. Acrylic fibre can be given a wide range of different properties by varying the manufacturing parameters, but it is usually made in staple form and given properties similar to those of wool. Acrylic fabric is usually knitted and is used for a wide range of knitted apparel. Acrylic and modified acrylic fibres (modacrylic) can also be used to make fake fur and sliver knitted fleece fabrics. These fabrics are brushed to produce a fur-like surface and are used for items such as jackets, toys and trims. Modified acrylic fibres, which are inherently flame-resistant, are marketed under different brand names.

See also FLAME-RESISTANT TEXTILES, FLEECE FABRIC, FUR FABRIC, STITCH-BONDED FABRIC.

End uses: knitted sweaters, sweatshirts, T-shirts, dress fabrics, underwear, fleece fabrics and simulated fur fabrics (casual jackets, dressing-gowns, toys, and collar and cuff trims).

ADMIRALTY CLOTH *see* MELTON.

AEROPLANE FABRIC (airplane fabric) A coated fabric used in light aircraft manufacture and for products such as protective clothing. It was originally used in the construction of early aircraft: the fabric was stretched over the wooden frame and given a waterproof coating. Nowadays aeroplane fabrics coated with a thin polymer film or films are used on light and microlight aircraft, gliders and hang-gliders.[25] These are medium- to lightweight fabrics that also have a wide range of other end uses (see below).

The original aeroplane fabric was a strong fabric made from high-twist, two-fold cotton or linen yarns that had been combed and mercerized. It was coated with cellulose acetate lacquer to shrink and strengthen the fabric, making it less air-permeable and more waterproof.[3] Nowadays aeroplane fabrics are usually made of nylon, polyester or blends. They are woven in a closely sett, balanced plain weave (square cloth) and coated with thin films of a polymer such as polyurethane. Sometimes ripstop yarns are included to enhance their resistance to tearing.

See also BALLOON CLOTH, COATED FABRIC, POLYURETHANE, RIPSTOP.

End uses: component for microlight aircraft, gliders and hang-gliders; also used for sportswear, shirts, rainwear, protective clothing, uniforms and luggage.

AERTEX® *see* CELLULAR FABRIC.

AFGALAINE (Afghalaine) A woven, all-wool dress fabric with a crisp handle and a slightly crinkled appearance. It is a medium-weight fabric, with a typical weight of 250–285 g/m².[25]

Afgalaine is woven in plain weave using highly twisted 'S' and 'Z' twist yarns. These are arranged alternately in the warp, and the fabric is woven with 'S' twist yarns only in the weft. This produces the characteristic crisp handle and crinkled appearance. There are two main qualities: woollen warp with woollen weft, and worsted warp with woollen weft. Less expensive qualities may also be made, using a mixture of wool and a cheaper fibre.

See also COATING FABRIC, PLAIN WEAVE FABRIC.

End uses: dresses, suits and coats.

AIDA (aida canvas) *see* JAVA.

AILESHAM (*obs.*) A term used in England in the Middle Ages for a fine, plain weave linen fabric.[36]

airloop fabric

albatross

Albert cloth

AIRLOOP FABRIC A warp-knitted fabric that is usually made from nylon or polyester yarns, in a construction that produces a low loop pile on one side of the fabric. This gives a soft, fluffy surface.

Airloop fabrics were originally developed as a cheaper method of producing loopraise for sheeting fabrics, and these two fabrics can therefore be very similar. The fabric is knitted on a two-bar tricot warp-knitting machine using fine filament nylon or polyester yarns. The front guide bar knits a 1 and 1 tricot stitch under high tension, and the back guide bar knits a longer lap (reverse locknit or sharkskin) over two or three needle spaces, lapping in the opposite direction. Yarn is fed to the back bar at a very high rate (overfeed) so that the excess yarn forms a low loop pile on the technical reverse of the fabric.

Airloop fabric is not as soft as loopraise and is prone to irregularities; however, it does not require brushing (unlike loopraise) and is very economical to produce. Plush and velour are also similar to airloop fabric, but they are heavier and usually superior in both appearance and quality. Airloop fabrics are also made using different yarns and modified constructions to produce bouclette, suede fabrics and various other outerwear fabrics.

See also BOUCLETTE, KNITTED FABRIC, LOOPRAISE, PILE FABRICS, PLUSH, SHEETING FABRIC, SUEDE FABRICS, VELOUR, WARP-KNITTED FABRIC.

End uses: sheeting, furnishings and outerwear.

ALAMODE (*obs.*) A lightweight silk fabric woven in plain weave and used for silk scarves. It was usually dyed black and given a soft, glossy finish.[36]

ALBATROSS A fine, soft, lightweight fabric that is woven in plain weave; there are wool and cotton versions.

Wool albatross is a soft woollen fabric woven in plain weave. It is a crêpe fabric made using highly twisted worsted crêpe yarns. This gives it a characteristic crinkled crêpe appearance and a textured handle. Less expensive fabrics may use blended yarns. The fabric is traditionally piece-dyed, usually in pale colours or black. Cotton albatross is a similar soft, plain woven fabric. It was originally made from Egyptian cotton and had a napped face, but is now also made with man-made fibres. It is a lightweight, semi-sheer fabric.

See also CRÊPE, NAPPED FABRICS, PLAIN WEAVE FABRIC.

End uses: dresses, blouses, children's wear and nuns' habits.

ALBERT CLOTH A heavy, reversible, woven fabric of good quality, made from wool and used for overcoating. It frequently has a different pattern on the face and back. It has traditionally been used for men's overcoats, recognizable by their characteristic velvet collars.

Albert cloth is a centre- or self-stitched double cloth fabric made with good quality woollen yarns. Sometimes a different design of stripes or checks, often in different colours, is used on one side of the fabric. It may be napped during finishing. The fabric construction and thickness of the yarns make it particularly warm.

See also COATING FABRIC, DOUBLE CLOTH, NAPPED FABRICS.

End uses: coats and jackets.

ALBERT TWILL A lustrous fabric with a smooth face, woven in twill weave.

Albert twill was originally an alpaca union fabric, made from a cotton warp and an alpaca weft. There was also an all-cotton version.[36]

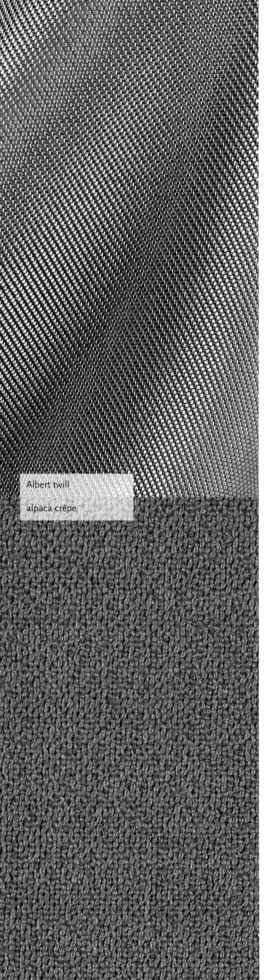

Albert twill

alpaca crêpe

It was traditionally dyed in dark colours and given a special finish to produce a lustrous, smooth-faced fabric that was used mainly for linings. Nowadays the fabric is more usually woven with various man-made fibres. It is woven in a left-hand 1/3 twill weave structure with the weft predominating. Albert twill is similar to Italian and to cotton Venetian.

Albert twill

See also ALPACA FABRIC, LINING FABRIC, TWILL FABRICS, UNION FABRIC.

End uses: linings and pocketings.

ALCANTARA® *see* SUEDE CLOTH.

ALEXANDRIA (*obs.*) A fine, lightweight dress fabric made of cotton and wool with a small woven design.[2]

ALHAMBRA QUILTING (*obs.*) A thick, heavy, colour-woven jacquard fabric with elaborate patterns, traditionally made in cotton and used for bed quilts.[4, 25]

ALLSPORT *see* COVERT CLOTH.

ALMA (*obs.*) A silk fabric with a distinct diagonal twill weave, originally made in black or purple for mourning. The name derives from an Egyptian word meaning 'mourner'.[9]

ALPACA CRÊPE A woven crêpe fabric produced as a relatively inexpensive imitation of an alpaca union fabric. It is usually made from acetate, viscose or polyester, so the use of the term 'alpaca' is misleading. It is woven to resemble a coarse wool fabric and is flat and dull in appearance with a soft handle.

Alpaca crêpe is woven in plain weave from two-fold moss crêpe yarns. These yarns are made by doubling a normal-twist yarn (e.g. acetate singles yarn) with a high-twist yarn (e.g. crêpe viscose singles yarn); all twists are made in the same direction ('S' or 'Z'). The crêpe effect is produced by alternating 'S' and 'Z' twist moss crêpe yarns in both the warp and the weft.

See also ALPACA FABRIC, CRÊPE.

End uses: dresses.

ALPACA FABRIC A general term for any fabric constructed with yarns made from the fleece of the alpaca (*Lama pacos*), a relative of the llama. Alpaca is a natural animal fibre, classed as a speciality hair fibre.

Strictly speaking, the term 'alpaca fabric' should be used only for fabrics made from 100% alpaca fibre. However, as alpaca fibre is expensive, most alpaca fabrics are union fabrics containing alpaca mixed with other fibres. When there is a mixture of fibres, the percentages of each should be stated. Characteristically, alpaca is a warm, soft fibre, with a high natural lustre. It may be used in woven or knitted fabrics. It is often used to make soft, lightweight, lustrous, pile-weave coating fabrics. Alpaca is often blended with other fibres, usually wool; sometimes a small percentage of nylon is also added for extra strength.

Alpaca union fabrics are usually fine, springy, lustrous woven fabrics. They are frequently black, and resemble mohair fabrics. The fabric may be made with a dyed wool, silk or cotton warp (often black) and natural-coloured alpaca weft yarns. The alpaca yarns may be white, brown, grey or black, and are often mixed. Alternatively the fabric may be cross-dyed after weaving. The fabric is usually woven in a closely sett, simple weave construction, often either a weft-faced twill weave or plain weave. Some Albert twill fabrics are alpaca union fabrics. *See also* ALBERT TWILL.

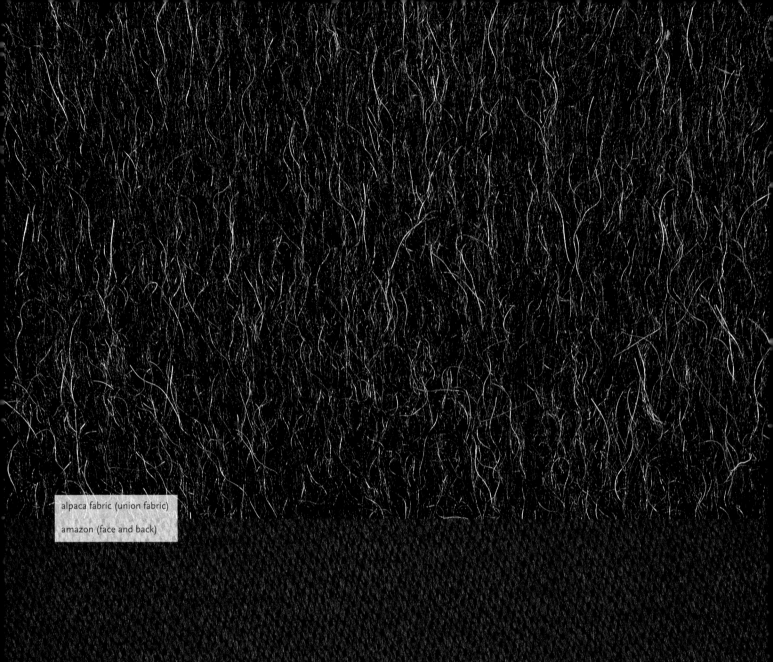

alpaca fabric (union fabric)

amazon (face and back)

Alpaca yarns are also used to make knitted fabrics. The fabric may be weft-knitted on knitting machines or knitted by hand. They are usually knitted in simple structures like plain knit in order to best accentuate the soft, hairy fibres.

See also Bradford lustre fabrics, coating fabric, hair fabrics, pile fabrics, union fabric, wedding ring fabrics.

End uses: (woven fabrics) coats, jackets, men's suitings, dresses, pile fabrics and linings; (knitted fabrics) cardigans, jackets, coats, jumpers, shawls and scarves.

ALTAR LINEN *see* linen fabric.

AMABOUK (*obs.*) A half-bleached, coarse Irish linen fabric, woven in plain weave and used for sailors' shirts.[3, 36]

AMAZON A soft, fine, dress-weight woven fabric. It is a woollen fabric with a warp-faced, fibrous surface.

Amazon has a worsted warp (usually merino) and a slightly thicker woollen or soft-spun worsted weft. It is usually woven in a 5-end warp-faced satin weave, or sometimes in a 2/1 warp-faced twill. The twist of the warp yarns is designed to emphasize the twill lines of the satin weave. A typical amazon fabric construction is 24 to 22 tex worsted warp sett at 28 to 36 ends per cm and 72 to 48 tex woollen weft woven at 14 to 18 picks per cm.[26] After weaving, the fabric is lightly milled and raised, which slightly obscures the weave structure and gives the fabric its soft handle. Amazon is similar to wool Venetian.

See also napped fabrics; satin, woven; twill fabrics.

End uses: ladies' and men's suiting fabrics.

ANACOSTA (*obs.*) A worsted dress fabric woven in 2/2 twill, with a pronounced weft twill caused by the picks predominating. It was woven grey and piece-dyed.[36]

ANCELIA (*obs.*) A woven dress fabric made with a hard-twist cotton warp and a wool and cotton weft. When it is piece-dyed, interesting colour effects are produced.[3, 36]

ANDALUSIANS (*obs.*) The term given to a variety of fancy woven dress fabrics made in England from the finest Spanish merino wools. The name comes from the Andalucia region of Spain.[3]

ANGOLA FLANNEL *see* flannel.

ANGORA FABRIC (rabbit-hair fabric) A general term for any fabric constructed with yarns made from the hair of the angora rabbit (*Oryctolagus cuniculus*).[25] Angora fibre or hair is a natural animal fibre and it is classed as a speciality hair fibre. Characteristically, it is a warm, extremely soft fibre that has a high natural lustre. Strictly speaking, the term 'angora fabric' should be applied only to fabrics made from 100% angora; however, it is sometimes also applied to fabrics composed partly of angora and partly of another fibre. In such cases, the percentages of each fibre should always be stated. Angora fabric is sometimes also called 'rabbit-hair fabric'. Angora fabrics should not be confused with mohair fabrics, which are made with hair from angora goats (*see* mohair fabric).

Angora may be used in woven, knitted or nonwoven fabrics. Whatever the fabric construction, the main characteristic of angora fabric is its very soft, luxurious handle. Since angora is quite an expensive fibre, it is often mixed with other fibres, usually wool. Sometimes a small percentage of nylon may also be added for extra strength. Examples of different kinds of angora fabric are described below.

angora fabric (knitted)

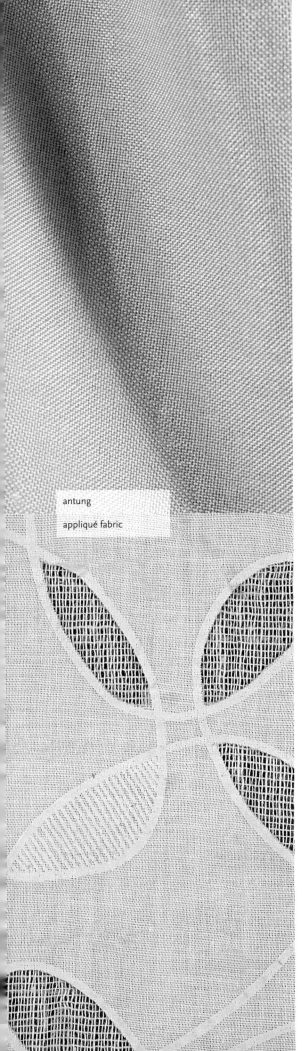

antung

appliqué fabric

Woven angora coating or jacketing fabrics are made in a variety of different weights, ranging from lightweight to heavyweight. The angora is usually combined with wool yarns (typically 70% angora and 30% wool, or 60/40, or 50/50), or wool and man-made fibres (typically 70% angora, 20% wool and 10% nylon). The fabric is usually woven in a closely sett, simple weave construction, like plain weave, twill or satin. The fabrics are typically soft, warm and lustrous, with good drape. Sometimes angora is used to make soft, lustrous, pile-weave coating fabrics. *See also* COATING FABRIC, PILE FABRICS.

Knitted angora fabrics may be made on weft-knitting machines and, since the yarns are so soft and hairy, they are also sometimes hand-knitted. Simple structures like plain knit are usually used, in order to best accentuate the soft, hairy fibres.

See also HAIR FABRICS.

End uses: (woven angora fabrics) coats, jackets and suits; (knitted angora fabrics) cardigans, jackets, jumpers, shawls and scarves.

ANTERINE (anterne) (*obs.*) An 18th-century woven fabric made of worsted and silk or of mohair and cotton.[3, 36]

ANTIMICROBIAL FABRIC A fabric that has had bioactive chemicals incorporated into it. Either antibacterial or antifungal chemicals may be used.

Antibacterial chemicals diffuse out into the atmosphere surrounding the textile and act as an antiseptic barrier, inhibiting or killing bacteria. Antifungal chemicals either kill or inhibit the growth of a wide range of micro-organisms, including skin bacteria, fungi, mould and yeast. In order to effectively destroy odour-causing bacteria, a minimum content of bioactive material must be present.

Antimicrobial agents may be incorporated into the fabric in several different ways. (i) *Antimicrobial finishes.* Bioactive chemicals may be applied to the surface of the fabric during finishing. Both natural and man-made fabrics may be given an antimicrobial finish. This is a semi-durable finish that will wear off in time.
(ii) *Modified man-made fibres.* Antimicrobial additives may be incorporated into the fibre structure of man-made fibres during their manufacture. Since the chemicals are bonded into the fibre structure, they remain functional throughout the lifespan of the fibre. Antimicrobial additives can be incorporated into acrylic, acetate and polypropylene fibres, but not into nylon or polyester fibres, with which they are chemically incompatible. However, antimicrobial fibres can be blended with nylon and polyester fibres effectively.
(iii) *Microencapsulation.* Antimicrobial chemicals may be encapsulated and incorporated into textiles. *See also* MICROENCAPSULATED TEXTILES.

End uses: socks, workwear (healthcare industry, food industry, hygiene sectors), contract textiles (e.g. hand towels in public places), military textiles, nursery items and baby wear.

ANTIQUE SATIN *see* SATIN, WOVEN.

ANTIQUE TAFFETA *see* TAFFETA.

ANTUNG A woven fabric made from silk yarns. The name means 'silk fabric' in Chinese.[25] Antung is usually a medium- to heavyweight fabric without slubs. It is woven in a simple plain weave construction, using wild 'net' tussah silk yarns.

See also PLAIN WEAVE FABRIC, SILK FABRIC.

End uses: dresses and blouses.

aramid fabric

Aran fabric (detail)

APPLIQUÉ FABRIC A complex double or triple layer fabric in which a (usually) dense woven fabric has been either sewn or embroidered onto a (usually) finer woven ground fabric and afterwards cut away around the stitched sections to reveal the contrasting character of the different layers. Contrasting colours and textures accentuate the effect. Typically the figured effect of an opaque image is produced against a light, transparent ground fabric once areas of the densely woven fabric have been cut away. Sometimes pre-cut fabric shapes are sewn onto a ground fabric. Appliqué fabrics are usually delicate, highly decorative fabrics that are used for occasion wear.

See also EMBROIDERED FABRICS, FIGURED FABRIC, HOLOGRAPHIC FABRICS, VEILING.

End uses: bridal wear, evening wear, dresses, blouses, veiling and curtains.

ARAMID FABRIC A general term for any fabric constructed with aramid fibres or yarns. Aramid is the generic name of a synthetic man-made material derived from polyamide (nylon). It may be produced in sheet or fibre form. It is usually the fibres that are used to make clothing and furnishing fabrics.

The term 'aramid fabric' is used for fabrics of various weights and constructions composed of 100% aramid. Aramid fibres may be used in continuous filament form, or they may be cut into shorter staple lengths and spun into yarns. The staple fibres may also be blended with other fibres to produce different qualities. Characteristically, aramid fibres are immensely dense and stiff; they have extremely high abrasion resistance and are highly flame-resistant (they ignite with difficulty at 538 °C).[10] They are therefore used to make specialist fabrics for end uses requiring extreme strength, stiffness and/or flame-resistant properties, such as protective clothing.

Different types of aramid fibres and fabrics are produced, each with a slightly different emphasis on the inherent properties. These are marketed under different brand names. For example, Kevlar® is the registered brand name of a particularly strong aramid fibre used to make various kinds of protective clothing, including bullet-resistant vests. Nomex® is the registered brand name of a flame-resistant type of aramid fibre that is used for items such as suits for racing drivers.

See also CARBON-FIBRE TEXTILES, FLAME-RESISTANT TEXTILES, GLASS-FIBRE TEXTILES.

End uses: bullet-resistant vests, protective body armour clothing, firemens' uniforms, industrial clothing, workwear, motor sports clothing, footwear, motorcycle helmets, aircraft furnishings, outdoor equipment, luggage, car tyre reinforcement material and industrial textiles.

ARAN FABRIC A term denoting a range of chunky, weft-knitted fabrics, traditionally made from wool and knitted by hand into thick, warm sweaters. Machine-knitted garments are also produced. The wool is traditionally used in its natural, undyed state, and the sweaters are therefore characteristically ecru in colour.

Aran garments were first knitted on the island of Aran off the west coast of Ireland. The traditional garments are hand-knitted using pure new home-spun wool from the local sheep. The wool is spun on the woollen system. A range of traditional knitted stitches and patterns are used in various combinations, producing the distinctive Aran look. These include cable stitch, diamond pattern, honeycomb pattern, zigzag pattern, trellis pattern, ladder patterns (two ribs joined by horizontal lines), moss stitch and chain stitch.

See also CABLE STITCH FABRIC, KNITTED FABRIC, MOSS-STITCH FABRIC, WEFT-KNITTED FABRIC.

End uses: hats, scarves, sweaters, cardigans and socks.

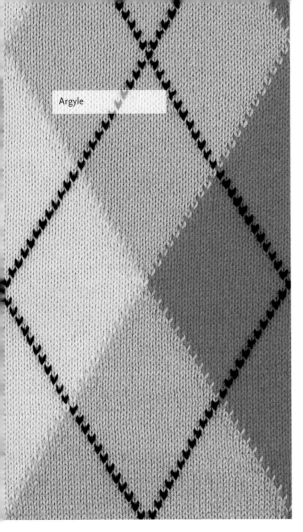

Argyle

ARESTE (*obs.*) A gold cloth with elaborate figured patterns, made in England from the 11th century.[3, 36]

ARGENTINAS (Austria's, Austrian twill) (*obs.*) A woven fabric similar to jean. It was woven in a 2/1 twill and piece-dyed, usually black.[3, 4, 36]

ARGENTINE CLOTH *see* TARLATAN.

ARGYLE A weft-knitted fabric that is patterned with a diamond-shaped design in two or more different colours (usually three). In order to be a true Argyle, the fabric must be knitted using the intarsia method. Argyle was first produced in Scotland, and its design is based on the woven tartan pattern worn by the dukes of Argyle and the Campbell clan in the Western Highlands. It is from this that the fabric takes its name.

See also INTARSIA, KNITTED FABRIC, WEFT-KNITTED FABRIC.

End uses: sweaters, cardigans, T-shirts, dresses and hosiery (socks and tights).

ARMOZINE (armozeen, armazine) (*obs.*) A heavy French corded silk fabric, usually black, used for waistcoats, dresses and mourning clothes during the 17th and 18th centuries.[3, 9]

ARMURE A woven fabric with an all-over pebbly surface texture produced by using armure weave structures. This effect resembles chain mail (the name derives from the French for 'armour'). The pebbly effect is similar to a crêpe weave but more pronounced. Armure is a medium dress-weight fabric.

Armure was originally woven only in silk and cotton.[3] Another traditional quality was made with a warp composed of alternate ends of two-fold mohair and worsted wool and a weft of singles worsted wool.[36] Today armure may be made from any fibre or fibre blend; a wool version is particularly common. Armure royale is made from 100% worsted yarn.

A number of different weave constructions may be used to produce the pebbly effect, but armure is usually woven in wavy or broken warp rib weaves, typically running in the weft direction. The pattern is made by floating warp yarns on the surface and weft yarns on the back. This produces a raised, embossed effect. If the warp floats on the surface are long, they may be back-stitched in plain weave. The weave effect may also be accentuated by arranging two different types of warp yarn 'end and end', or alternately: for example cotton and viscose, and/or 'S' and 'Z' twist yarns. Sometimes armure has small repeating motifs rather than an all-over effect; it may therefore be either dobby or jacquard woven. Common patterns include birdseye, diamonds, and stripe and rib effects in one or more colours. The term 'armure' is also sometimes applied to metallic evening wear fabrics.

See also BARATHEA, COATING FABRIC, DOBBY FABRIC.

End uses: dresses, coats, men's neckties, curtains and bedspreads.

ARMY CLOTH (*obs.*) A term denoting either a fabric used in army uniforms or a low-grade grey woollen fabric made in Yorkshire, England.[9]

ARRAS FABRIC An open-sett, coarse, linen or jute fabric, which may be embroidered with simple designs. The name comes from the town of Arras in northern France, which since the 14th century has produced many different types of fabrics, notably lace, worsted fabrics and tapestries used for wall hangings.

Arras fabric is woven in an open-sett plain weave construction using either flax or jute yarns. It is woven in wide widths and may be piece-dyed or embroidered.

End uses: curtains, cushion covers and tablecloths.

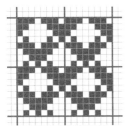

example of armure weave

Arras fabric

P pile warp threads
W wire insertion
■ ground weave
✕ pile warp interlacing

astrakhan fabric (woven)

atlas, warp-knitted
(double atlas)

ARROWHEAD TWILL *see* HERRINGBONE.

ARTILLERY CLOTH *see* WHIPCORD.

ART LINEN *see* LINEN FABRIC.

ASSAM SILK *see* SILK FABRIC.

ASTRAKHAN FABRIC A thick, lustrous curly pile fabric made in imitation of the fleece from young or stillborn karakul lambs, originally from the Astrakhan region of Russia.[25] It is also known as 'karakul cloth'.[9] There are woven and knitted versions, and it is usually a heavyweight fabric.

Astrakhan fabrics may be constructed in four different ways; however, in all cases a specially curled astrakhan yarn is either formed into loops or floated against a base fabric in which it is firmly held. The base fabric may be woven or knitted, and the loops formed may be cut or uncut.

(i) *Woven warp pile astrakhan.* The pile warp is lifted over wires at regular intervals during weaving against a firmly woven ground of plain weave. When the wires are removed, a mass of curly loops are formed on the surface of the fabric.

(ii) *Woven weft pile astrakhan.* Extra weft yarns are floated at regular intervals across the surface of a firmly woven ground of plain weave. The texture may be emphasized by using a non-shrink extra weft yarn, such as mohair, and a yarn that shrinks in the ground fabric, such as botany wool. When the cloth is finished after weaving, the botany fabric shrinks but the mohair does not. The mohair yarns therefore form longer loops on the surface of the fabric. *See also* EXTRA WARP AND EXTRA WEFT FABRICS.

(iii) *Warp-knitted astrakhan.* In one version, a thick, curly yarn is attached to the surface of a ground fabric by the fine yarns on one set of guide bars, while the ground fabric is knitted on different guide bars. Alternatively, a loop pile fabric may be knitted on a 'Pol' (pile-sinker) machine and subsequently finished to produce a curly effect.

(iv) *Weft-knitted astrakhan.* A thick, curled or crimped yarn is laid-in in the horizontal direction against a plain knit base fabric. This is also sometimes known as 'astrakhan stockinette'.[38] *See also* LAID-IN FABRIC.

Mohair, worsted or woollen yarns are normally used as the pile yarns, with mohair being used in the higher-quality fabrics as it gives the most lustre. The ground fabric may be made from a wide variety of fibres, including man-made fibres, cotton, worsted, wool and silk. Some astrakhan fabrics are therefore union fabrics. Similar fabrics to astrakhan include bouclé fabric, éponge, frisé, Montagnac, poodle cloth, ratiné and terry fabric.

See also COATING FABRIC, FUR FABRIC, PILE FABRICS, UNION FABRIC.

End uses: overcoats, jackets, collars, hats and bags.

ATLAS, WARP-KNITTED A warp-knitted fabric with a characteristic vertical zigzag construction. If different coloured yarns are used, vertical zigzag stripes are formed.

There are several variants, constructed in different ways.

(i) *Single atlas.* One full set of warp yarns is traversed progressively by one needle space for 'single-needle atlas' (or by two needle spaces for 'two-needle atlas') in a diagonal direction for a few consecutive courses, and then traversed back again for a few consecutive courses. This gives the characteristic zigzag effect. As the fabric is made with one guide bar only, it is quite fine and prone to laddering. However, unlike virtually all other single-bar warp-knits, it will not 'split' and is therefore useful as a lightweight ground construction – for example, for warp-knitted crêpe fabrics. *See also* CRÊPE.

(ii) *Double atlas.* Two full sets of warp yarns on two guide bars are each traversed as in single atlas but in opposite directions. Since the fabric is made with two guide bars, this produces a fabric construction that is much more stable than single atlas and is ladder-proof. This fabric was traditionally made in cotton but nowadays is very rare.

(iii) *Fancy atlas*. This term is given to a single or double atlas with variable thread movements or irregular changes in the zigzag direction throughout the repeat.

Atlas is similar to warp-knitted milanese but simpler. Modified atlas structures are also used to make various mesh fabrics.

See also KNITTED FABRIC, MESH FABRICS, WARP-KNITTED FABRIC.

End uses: ground fabric construction for more complex fabrics, and base fabric for printed fabrics.

ATLAS, WOVEN A very rich, lustrous fabric that is woven using atlas silk yarns in a satin weave construction. The term 'atlas' originated in India and refers to the type of silk produced from the cocoon of the wild silkworm *Attacus atlas*. This type of silk is similar to tussah silk but darker in colour.[3]

The fabric is woven in a 5-end or 8-end warp satin weave. Although it is traditionally made of 100% silk, some less expensive versions are made with a silk warp and cotton or man-made fibres in the weft. This shows only on the reverse of the fabric. There are also less expensive imitations made entirely from man-made fibres. The term 'atlas' is also used in several languages to refer to the satin weave construction.[36]

See also SATIN, WOVEN; SILK FABRIC.

End uses: evening wear, dresses and linings.

ATLAS SILK *see* SILK FABRIC.

AUSTRIA'S, AUSTRIAN TWILL *see* ARGENTINAS.

AVIGNON (*obs.*) A lightweight silk taffeta lining fabric woven in twill weave.[9, 36]

AWNING CLOTH A fabric, usually duck (or sometimes canvas), that is used for awnings, beach umbrellas and outdoor furniture, and that may be solid in colour or striped. If striped, it is either colour-woven or printed with stripe designs. *See also* CANVAS, DUCK.

AXMINSTER *see* CARPET.

BABY CORD *see* CORDUROY.

BABY FLANNEL *see* FLANNEL.

BACKED FABRIC A single cloth woven fabric in which extra warp or extra weft yarns are interlaced into the back without altering the appearance of the face. This is done for one or more of the following reasons: to add thickness, weight, stability or strength to a fabric; to produce a warmer fabric; or to make a fabric more opaque. Similar effects may also be achieved by laminating a fabric to a backing fabric (*see* LAMINATED FABRIC), by lining a fabric (*see* LINING FABRIC), or by 'back-coating' fabrics with adherent substances in order to give them special properties (*see* COATED FABRIC).

Backed fabrics provide the opportunity for different colours or weave structures to be used on the face and the back of the fabric, and double-sided or reversible fabrics may therefore be produced. 'Warp-backed' fabrics have an extra set of warp yarns that do not appear on the face, while 'weft-backed' fabrics have an extra set of weft yarns that do not appear on the face. The binding points for the extra warp and extra weft yarns are carefully arranged so that they are invisible on the face of the fabric. Examples of backed

awning cloth

backed fabric (face and back)

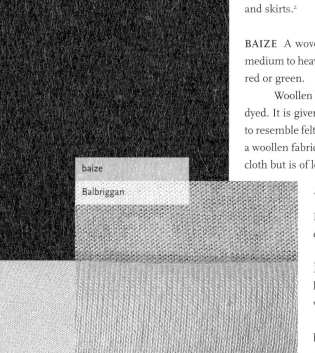

baize

Balbriggan

balloon cloth

fabrics include some cotton blanket cloths, charmante satin, Frenchback, Frenchback serge (*see* SERGE), some molleton fabrics and some vicuña fabrics.

See also DOUBLE CLOTH, EXTRA WARP AND EXTRA WEFT FABRICS.

End uses: coating fabrics, suiting fabrics, evening wear, curtains and window blinds.

BAD (*obs.*) An ancient Egyptian linen fabric used by high priests and mentioned in the Bible.[36]

BAININ (*obs.*) A hand-woven, woollen homespun fabric from Ireland, used for coats and skirts.[2]

BAIZE A woven fabric made from wool that has been heavily milled and felted. It is medium to heavy in weight, has a slightly rough handle, and is usually piece-dyed in bright red or green.

    Woollen baize fabric is loosely woven in plain weave. It may be yarn-dyed or piece-dyed. It is given a special finish in which it is fulled, napped and sheared on both sides to resemble felt. The term 'baize' has been used in England since at least 1605 to describe a woollen fabric made in Sandwich, Colchester and Norwich.[36] Baize is similar to billiard cloth but is of lower quality and is not as smooth or dense.

See also FELTED FABRIC, NAPPED FABRICS.

End uses: wall coverings, billiard table coverings, lining for cutlery drawers and screens.

BALBRIGGAN A fine, lightweight, weft-knitted fabric, knitted in a plain knit construction. It is inherently stretchy and is used mainly for underwear, including long johns.

    Balbriggan is usually knitted using fine-spun cotton or cotton blends. It is knitted in a plain knit structure, usually in tubular form on circular knitting machines. It is normally given a light nap finish on the back. It was originally made at Balbriggan in Ireland, which became known for its production of the first bleached hosiery.[5]

See also KNITTED FABRIC, NAPPED FABRICS, PLAIN KNIT FABRIC, WEFT-KNITTED FABRIC.

End uses: underwear, long johns, hosiery, lingerie, pyjamas, sportswear, lightweight sweaters and gloves.

BALLOON CLOTH A very closely sett woven fabric made in a square cloth, plain weave construction. It was originally a very strong, fine, lightweight fabric made from combed, mercerized cotton, silk or linen, but is now also made of viscose, polyester or nylon.

    As the name suggests, balloon cloth was originally used for hot-air balloons. The fabric was given a special rubber coating to make it waterproof and less permeable to gas. Nowadays fabrics for hot-air balloons are made from polymer-coated nylon or polyester, while balloon cloth made from other fibres, usually fine pima cotton, is produced mainly as an apparel fabric with a wide range of end uses (see below).

See also AEROPLANE FABRIC, PLAIN WEAVE FABRIC.

End uses: apparel, dresses, blouses, shirts and downproof interlinings for cushions.

BALLYMENA (*obs.*) An Irish linen fabric woven in plain weave and used for linen shirts. It was originally hand-woven in Ballymena, Ireland.[36]

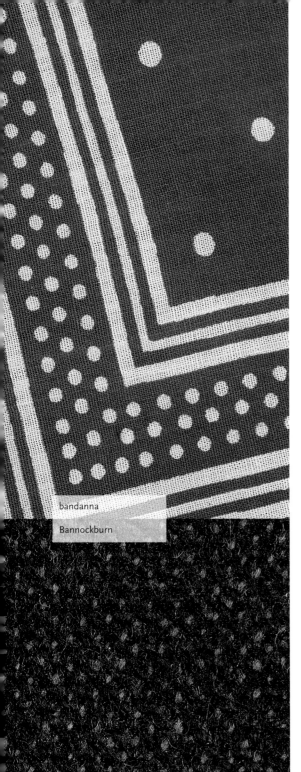

bandanna

Bannockburn

BALZARINE (balzarine brocade) (*obs.*) A woven cotton brocade fabric. It was jacquard woven with a fine gauze ground and elaborate figured patterns.[36]

BAMBOO *see* PLANT-FIBRE FABRICS.

BANBURY PLUSH (*obs.*) An English woven pile fabric with a cotton warp and a woollen weft, used for upholstery. It is named after the town of Banbury in Oxfordshire.[17, 36]

BANDANNA A fabric square, usually woven in cotton and tie-dyed or printed to obtain a regular pattern of small white dots or other bold designs against a ground of bright red, yellow, dark blue, brown or black. Bandannas are traditionally used as head or neck scarves.

Bandannas were originally produced in India. The word *bandha* in Sanskrit means 'to knot, bind or tie'. The traditional bandanna is a resist-dyed fabric. Small areas of the fabric are tightly bound with thread to resist the dye. When the ties are removed after dyeing, undyed areas of fabric form the pattern against the dyed ground. Mass-produced bandanna fabric is also made by printing or discharge printing, giving a similar effect to the tie-dyed fabrics – small, white dot motifs against a coloured ground.

See also DISCHARGE PRINTED FABRIC, DYED FABRICS, POLKA DOT FABRIC, PRINTED FABRIC, RESIST-DYED FABRICS, TIE-DYED FABRIC.

End uses: head and neck scarves, dresses and saris.

BANDLE (*obs.*) A coarse, plain weave linen fabric, hand-woven in narrow widths in southern Ireland from around 1760.[3, 36]

BANNIGAN *see* MOLESKIN FABRIC.

BANNOCKBURN A thick, firmly woven, half woollen, half worsted fabric. It is a type of tweed, sometimes called 'pepper and salt tweed' because of the characteristic speckled effect produced by the arrangement of yarn colours.

Traditionally Bannockburn is woven either in a 2/2 twill or a herringbone weave from Cheviot woollen-spun yarns (from the British Cheviot breed of sheep). The fabric is composed of two-fold yarns with solid colour yarns and marl or grandrelle yarns (two singles yarns in contrasting colours twisted together) alternating in both the warp and weft directions. This gives the fabric its characteristic speckled appearance. The marl yarns are usually woollen-spun yarns and the solid colour yarns are usually worsted spun yarns. Bannockburn can be made in a variety of colours from light to dark. The fabric is given a light nap finish. Nowadays it may be composed of wool fibre other than Cheviot, or of man-made fibre, but the visual effect remains the same. Bannockburn is named after the Scottish town where the fabric has traditionally been produced. It is similar to thornproof tweed.

See also COATING FABRIC, HERRINGBONE, MARL FABRIC, NAPPED FABRICS, TWEED, TWILL FABRICS, WOOL FABRIC.

End uses: suits, jackets and lightweight overcoats.

BARATHEA A closely woven fabric with a smooth but pebbly surface texture that is created with the use of special weave constructions based on a hopsack weave structure. The name 'barathea' was originally a registered trade name for an armure silk tie fabric made with a silk warp and a worsted weft. Now the term has been adopted to describe a range of different pebbly-surfaced fabrics, most of which are worsted suiting fabrics usually produced in dark colours.[3, 36]

The weave construction is usually a broken-rib weave or a twilled hopsack, which gives the appearance of a twill effect in both right and left directions.[25] Square blocks of hopsack are arranged to make these diagonal lines in the fabric. Baratheas can be classified into four different types, according to the different qualities woven (a range of different weights are produced in each quality):

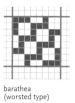

barathea
(worsted type)

- A fine, rich-looking dress fabric with a silk warp and a fine botany worsted weft. It is woven with a broken weft rib weave. In cheaper versions, a cotton or man-made fibre warp may be used in place of the silk. This fabric is used for dresses, men's neckties and cravats.
- A fine dress fabric made from 100% silk filament or man-made fibre in a broken rib weave structure. This too is used for dresses, men's neckties and cravats.
- A cotton shirting fabric made in a broken warp rib weave.
- A smooth-faced worsted fabric of medium to heavy weight. It is woven in a twilled hopsack weave, with fine, two-fold botany worsted yarns in both warp and weft. Less expensive fabrics may be produced by using wool or wool mixes in the weft. This type of barathea is used for men's suits and evening wear (usually in black), uniforms, women's coats, suits and skirts. *See also* COATING FABRIC.

barathea (cotton type)

barathea (silk type)

Another version of barathea was formerly used for army uniforms: it was woven from fine, two-fold cross-bred worsted yarns in both warp and weft and constructed as a stitched double cloth for extra strength, with a broken twill on the surface and plain weave on the back. It was vat-dyed indigo.[16]

See also ARMURE, HOPSACK, SUITING FABRICS, TIE FABRIC.

End uses: dresses, men's neckties, cravats, shirts, men's suits, men's evening wear (usually in black), tuxedo lapels, uniforms, trousers, women's coats and skirts.

BARBOUR® *see* OILSKIN.

BARÈGE (barrège) (*obs.*) A sheer, lightweight gauze fabric, with a raw silk warp and a worsted weft, woven in a leno weave. It was originally made in Barèges in the Pyrenees and was used mainly for veilings.[3, 9, 17]

BARK CLOTH (tapa cloth) A nonwoven fabric, similar to felt in its construction. It is made from the inner bark of certain tropical trees, which is treated to make the fibres mat together to form a fabric.

Suitable bark comes from the paper mulberry tree (*Broussonetia papyrifera*) in Hawaii and the south Pacific, the wild fig tree (*Ficus thonningii*) in Mozambique and the breadfruit tree (*Artocarpus altilis*) native to the Malay Peninsula and western Pacific islands. The cedar bark tree was also used in a similar manner by American Indians. The softer, inner bark of the tree or shrub is treated by soaking (to soften the fibre) and beating to cause the fibres to mat together into a web-like fabric. The fabrics may be beaten to any thickness, from very fine muslin-like qualities to thick, leathery qualities. Afterwards they may be bleached, painted, dyed or printed. In Hawaii, bark cloth is also known as 'tapa' or 'kapa cloth'; in Fiji, it is called 'masi'. It is not often used outside the areas in which it is produced.

See also NONWOVEN FABRIC, PLANT-FIBRE FABRICS.

End uses: clothing and decorative wall hangings.

barathea (ties)

barathea (wool suiting)

bark cloth

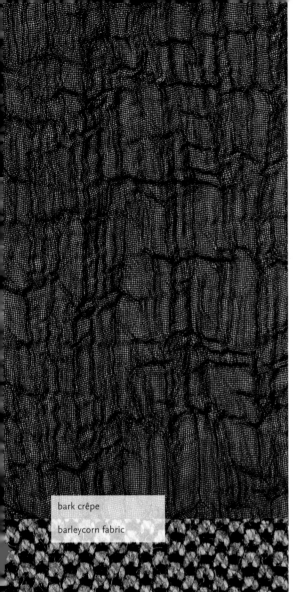

bark crêpe

barleycorn fabric

BARK CRÊPE A stiff, heavy, woven fabric with a rough 'crêpe' texture similar to that of tree bark. The characteristic grainy texture runs in the warp direction.

Bark crêpe is woven in plain weave and was originally a union fabric, woven with a silk or man-made fibre warp and a wool weft. It is now also woven in other fibres. The crêpe effect is produced by using ordinary twist yarns in the warp and high-twist crêpe yarns in the weft. The crêpe-twist yarns all have the same twist direction ('S' or 'Z'). Bark crêpe may therefore be termed a 'half crêpe' fabric. Bark crêpe fabrics may also be made by applying a chemical treatment to a woven fabric to produce an imitation of the woven bark crêpe effect. Bark crêpe is a similar heavy crêpe fabric to crepon.

See also CRÊPE, CREPON, PLAIN WEAVE FABRIC, UNION FABRIC.

End uses: evening wear, dresses, coats, upholstery and curtains.

BARLEYCORN FABRIC A fabric woven in a barleycorn weave structure. There are several variations, but all are a simple, small-scale, geometric weave structures that resemble grains of barley. Barleycorn fabric is firmly woven and has a matt, grainy appearance.

Any type of fibre or yarn may be used to make barleycorn fabrics. The barleycorn weave structure is a firmer variation of a hopsack weave. The size of the geometric motifs may be varied, and typical designs may be repeated over 6 × 6, 6 × 8 or 8 × 8 ends and picks. Barleycorn weave structures are also frequently used as ground weaves in more complex dobby and jacquard fabrics.

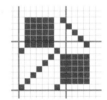

example of barleycorn weave

See also HOPSACK.

End uses: dresses, blouses, suiting fabrics and men's neckties.

BASKET CLOTH (basket weave) *see* HOPSACK.

BATIK A resist-dyed fabric that has an intricate, colourful pattern. Selected areas of the fabric that is to be dyed are treated with wax, a protective resist material, in a predetermined pattern. When the fabric is subsequently dyed, the areas protected by the wax remain undyed. The result is usually a pale-coloured pattern against a darker dyed background. Sometimes the wax resist is made to crack on purpose, so that the dye will seep into the unprotected areas underneath, producing a characteristic 'veining' pattern.

Any fabric may be batik dyed, but cotton and silk fabrics are probably the most frequently used. The wax resist in the form of a pattern is applied to the (usually) initially white fabric, using a brush or a *tjanting* – a metal tool from which the hot liquid wax is poured. After dyeing, the wax is removed by ironing, by boiling the fabric or by applying a solvent. The result is a white pattern against a coloured ground. More complex patterns may be produced with further applications of wax and further overdyeings using different colours. The batik process has been used since antiquity. The best known batiks come from Indonesia, particularly Java, where they are still produced by the traditional hand methods described. Nowadays batik-effect fabrics are also mass-produced by printing. Other resist-dyed fabrics that can have similar effects to batik include chiné fabrics, ikat and tie-dyed fabric.

See also DYED FABRICS, RESIST-DYED FABRICS.

End uses: lightweight summer clothing, curtains, wall hangings and artworks.

BATISTE A fine, lightweight but opaque fabric that is woven in plain weave. Its finish makes it smooth, soft and lustrous with good drape. Batiste fabrics typically weigh 80–100 g/m².

batik

batik (Java)

batik (China)

batiste

beaded fabric

Batiste is named after a 13th-century French linen weaver, Jean Baptiste from Cambrai, and the fabric was originally woven in flax.[3, 5] The term 'batiste' was used to describe the type of soft, lustrous finish that the fabric was given (i.e. a batiste finish). Nowadays, although a linen batiste may still be found, the most common batiste fabric is a cotton batiste made from 100% cotton or, more usually, a cotton blend, typically cotton/polyester. Occasionally batiste may be made from wool, silk, polyester or viscose, or blends of these, producing fabrics of similar weight and quality to cotton batiste. Tamise, now obsolete, was a batiste fabric woven with fine worsted wool yarns,[3] similar to worsted wool voile.

Traditionally the best-quality cotton batiste is made from long staple, combed cotton yarn. These high-twist singles yarns may be used in both the warp and the weft; sometimes, when a two-fold yarn is used in the warp only, a characteristic lengthwise streakiness may be apparent in the fabric. Batiste is usually woven in a balanced plain weave. The resulting fabric is of a high quality and is strong and hard-wearing, with excellent launderability. It is usually produced as grey cloth and afterwards bleached, mercerized and calendered. Batiste fabrics are often dyed (traditionally in light colours) or printed. Sometimes they are embroidered, as with Swiss batiste (see EMBROIDERED FABRICS). Two other variations are nelo batiste, a very fine batiste produced in Switzerland, and glacé batiste, a lustrous cotton batiste that is made transparent and stiff with a parchmentizing finish. The latter is used for trimmings and evening wear.

Cotton batiste is very similar to lawn, nainsook and organdie. It is possible to produce cotton batiste, lawn and organdie from the same grey goods, giving each a different finish. Both lawn and organdie are usually given a crisper handle than batiste, with organdie being given the stiffest finish of the three.

End uses: dresses, blouses, men's shirts, lingerie, nightwear and linings.

BATTING *see* WADDING.

BAY (bayes) (*obs.*) A woven fabric with a worsted warp and a wool weft, often mixed with silk, that was made in England from the 16th to the 18th centuries. It was woven in plain weave and napped on one side, and resembled coarse flannel.[36]

BAYADÈRE (*obs.*) A woven fabric of silk, wool, cotton, man-made fibres or mixes, with horizontal stripes in brilliant colours. The stripes were colour-woven or printed; the fabric was woven in plain or twill weaves. It originated in India.[1, 3, 5]

BEADED FABRICS Any fabrics embroidered with beads as a decorative dress trimming.

Any kind of fabric may be decorated with beads, including woven, knitted, nonwoven and lace fabrics. However, the fabrics chosen are normally fine, costly ones that are typically used for glamorous occasion wear garments. The beads may be made in any size and shape from a wide variety of different materials, including glass, plastic, pearl, enamel, wood and metal. They are usually threaded onto a strong yarn or thread before being embroidered (by hand or machine) onto the backing fabric. A fabric or garment may be decorated with beads over its whole surface, making a very elaborate, expensive product; more often only selected areas are decorated.

See also EMBROIDERED FABRICS, SEQUINNED FABRICS.

End uses: evening wear, bridal wear, wedding veils, theatrical costumes, shoes and evening bags.

BEAVER CLOTH A heavy woollen fabric with a dense, firm texture. It is given a special finishing sequence to make it resemble beaver fur and is usually used as a coating fabric.

Beaver cloth is woven from soft, high-quality woollen yarns in a variety of weights, usually medium to heavy (400–800 g/m²). It may be woven as single cloth, as double cloth or as a 'backed' fabric, normally using satin or twill weaves. Traditionally a 4-end satin is used. Beaver cloth undergoes a special finishing routine that causes the fabric to shrink considerably in both warp and weft directions, making it dense and firm. It is heavily milled, raised and sheared closely on the face side and then given a dress-face finish. This lays all the fibres on the surface of the fabric in one direction, giving it a fine, smooth, lustrous face and a rougher back. It was originally made in the west of England and belongs to a group of fabrics collectively known as 'West of England fabrics'. Beaver cloth is similar to wool broadcloth, wool doeskin fabric and wool duvetyn; however, the broadcloth has a longer nap, giving it a softer handle, and both doeskin and duvetyn are lighter and finer in construction.

See also BACKED FABRIC; COATING FABRIC; DOUBLE CLOTH; FACED CLOTH; FELTED FABRIC; FUR FABRIC; NAPPED FABRICS; SATIN, WOVEN; SUEDE CLOTH; WEST OF ENGLAND FABRICS.

End uses: winter-weight overcoats and jackets, uniforms and hats.

BEAVERTEEN A strong, smooth, weft-faced cotton fabric woven in a sateen-type weave structure. It belongs to the group of fabrics known as 'fustians'.

Beaverteen is woven using cotton yarns in a number of different sateen-type weave structures. The fabric has a very high weft sett, of up to 160 weft picks per centimetre. The weft forms short floats over (usually) four ends on the face of the fabric. The fabric is normally piece-dyed and may also be printed. In finishing, the back of the fabric is slightly raised, producing a short, soft nap. One of the possible weave structures is the same as the one used for moleskin fabric. Typical beaverteen fabric constructions include:

- 18 tex warp sett at 13 ends per cm and 20 tex weft woven at 110 picks per cm[25]
- 18 tex warp sett at 13 ends per cm and 16 tex weft woven at 160 picks per cm[25]
- 60/2 tex warp sett at 13 ends per cm and 33 tex weft woven at 90 to 120 picks per cm[26]

Beaverteen is similar to moleskin, imperial sateen and swansdown, but lighter in weight than moleskin and heavier than the other two.

See also FUSTIAN, NAPPED FABRICS, SATEEN, SUEDE CLOTH.

End uses: heavy-duty trousers, suitings and sportswear.

BEDFORD CORD A firm, hard-wearing woven fabric with prominent rounded cords or ribs running in the warp direction and sunken lines in-between.

Bedford cords were originally made from worsted fibre. Nowadays, although frequently found in cotton, they may be woven in any fibre. The cords, which are normally of a uniform size, are produced by a special weave construction. The warp is very closely sett and predominates on the face of the fabric. Two or more weft picks float the width of the cords on the back of the fabric to every one pick woven into the face of the fabric. This causes the fabric to buckle into the characteristic cords or ribs without the need for any extra threads. The cords may be made more prominent by using especially bulky, low-twist warp yarns as wadding yarns that float vertically, between the face cords and the back weft floats.

The yarns on the face of the fabric are usually dyed a solid shade and woven in plain weave. However, twilled cords and coloured warp stripes may be woven as variations. Twill-faced cotton Bedford cords are termed 'London cord'. Some Bedford cords are woven on a jacquard loom, where they are combined with figured patterns; the result is sometimes called 'crocodile cloth'. Bedford cord was originally called 'cord broadcloth' and was woven in Britain during the 14th century by Flemish weavers. In the late 15th century it was used by the duke of Bedford in uniforms for his troops, and from this time it became known as 'Bedford cord'.[3]

beaver cloth

beaverteen

F – face pick
B – back pick

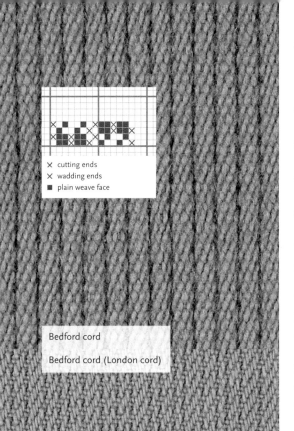

cutting ends
wadding ends
plain weave face

Bedford cord

Bedford cord (London cord)

bengaline

Bedford cords are made in many weights and qualities. Typical examples are: [26]
- 25 to 50 tex warp sett at 35 to 40 ends per cm and 12 to 25 tex weft woven at 30 picks per cm
- lightweight worsted Bedford cord: 28/2 tex botany warp sett at 36 ends per cm and 32 tex botany weft woven at 32 picks per cm
- cotton London cord: 42 tex warp (plus wadding ends) sett at 34 ends per cm and 30 tex weft woven at 31 picks per cm
- military Bedford cords: 100 tex woollen warp (50/2 tex cotton warp for plain ends) sett at 26 ends per cm and 100 tex woollen weft woven at 27 picks per cm

The lighter qualities, particularly those made from cotton, are sometimes termed 'piqué fabrics' (*see* PIQUÉ, WOVEN).

See also COATING FABRIC, CORD FABRICS.

End uses: (heavier qualities) trousers, riding breeches, uniforms, coats and upholstery; (lighter qualities) dresses, suits, women's outerwear, children's clothes and curtains.

BEIGE (*obs.*) A fine, soft dress fabric made in 100% worsted wool and woven in a 2/2 twill weave. It has a mixed colour appearance due to the use of printed, mélange or colour twisted yarns. Cotton imitations were also made.[26]

BELGIAN DOUBLE PIQUÉ *see* PIQUÉ, WEFT-KNITTED.

BELL-ISLES (*obs.*) A woollen dress fabric woven in Norwich, England, in the 18th century.[36]

BENGALINE A stiff, lustrous, warp-faced woven fabric in which the warp threads create a rib effect that runs across the width of the fabric. It is a strong, durable fabric with good drape. Bengaline is similar to poplin or faille in appearance but heavier and stiffer. It is a medium- to heavyweight fabric. A different, lighter-weight fabric, also called bengaline, is used for men's suitings. Although it has a slight texture, it differs in construction from bengaline rib.

Bengaline rib is firmly woven in a plain or rib weave using more threads in the warp than the weft. The warp-rib effect is produced by the fine, highly sett warp yarns that completely hide the thicker, softer weft yarns. Sometimes two warps are woven simultaneously to give the required high sett. Originally this fabric was produced using silk and cotton or silk and wool, and also as an all-silk quality called 'bengaline de soie'. Nowadays, however, it may be made of many different fibres, the warp yarns often being man-made filament yarns. At one time bengaline was widely used as a mourning fabric and so was often black. Now it has other end uses (see below). The name 'bengaline' comes from Bengal in India, where the fabric was first produced.

There is a range of warp rib fabrics characterized by the size and prominence of their ribs. In increasing order of rib size, these are: broadcloth, poplin, taffeta, poult, faille, bengaline and grosgrain. However, as many of them are woven in a variety of different weights, it is sometimes difficult to distinguish between them. 'Ondine' is the term for a thick bengaline fabric in which every rib is crinkled.

Bengaline suiting fabric has a very slight 'crêpe' look. It is woven in plain weave with alternating 'S' and 'Z' twist yarns in both the warp and the weft. Wool or worsted yarns are normally used, sometimes with a small percentage of man-made fibres or elastane added for ease of fit.

See also RIB FABRICS, WOVEN; SILK FABRIC; SUITING FABRICS.

End uses: dresses, coats, men's suits, tuxedo lapels, hats, ribbons, trimmings and curtain fabrics.

bengaline (suiting fabric)

billiard cloth

BERBER *see* CARPET.

BERLIN CANVAS (*obs.*) A cotton fabric woven in a 2 × 2 hopsack weave structure and used as a base fabric for embroidery. The fabric was originally made from silk union yarns (yarns with a cotton core around which silk was wrapped).[36]

BILLIARD CLOTH A very high-quality woollen fabric that is woven and heavily milled to make it smooth and even. It is usually dyed green or red and is used for covering billiard or card tables. It is similar in appearance to felt, but is a much stronger, higher-quality fabric.

    Billiard cloth is made from the finest high-grade merino wool. The best quality fabric is woven in plain weave, while other qualities are woven in a 2/1 twill weave structure. It is very heavily milled, shrunk and cropped to produce a compact, even fabric with a very smooth, fibrous finish. Billiard cloth is similar to baize, but is smoother, denser and of higher quality.

See also FELTED FABRIC, NAPPED FABRICS.

End uses: covering for billiard and card tables.

BINCA (boldwork cloth) A woven fabric that is used as a base for embroideries. Characteristically, it has fairly large square holes between groups of warp and weft yarns. It is particularly suited to cross stitch since the weave provides regularly spaced holes for each stitch, and so it is frequently used as a beginners' or children's embroidery base fabric. It is sometimes also known as 'boldwork cloth'. Binca is usually woven with cotton yarns in either white or ecru, and the fabric is often piece-dyed. It is woven in a small-scale dobby weave structure and afterwards given a soft finish.

See also EMBROIDERED FABRICS.

End uses: base fabric for embroideries.

BIOMIMETICS *see* HIGH-TECH TEXTILES.

BIRDIES (*obs.*) A plain weave, coarse linen fabric from Kirriemuir, Scotland, dating from about 1790.[3, 36]

BIRDSEYE A fine fabric that is patterned with tiny, uniform geometric dots or indentations resembling the eye of a bird. The birdseye pattern may be produced in a woven fabric using colour and weave effects, or it may be produced as a weft-knitted fabric using a jacquard technique.

    The woven fabric is dobby woven using an arrangement of two or more contrasting colours in the warp and the weft. A simple plain or twill weave is normally used. The pattern is a result of the combination of weave and colour. The fabric was traditionally made from worsted yarn, linen or cotton, but nowadays any fibre combination may be used. Many cotton birdseye fabrics are traditionally woven in a small diamond pattern with a small birdseye dot in the centre of each diamond. The pattern is created by weft floats woven in diamond formation against a contrasting ground colour. The cotton yarns used are carded and loosely spun from short staple fibres. They produce soft, absorbent fabrics, at one time widely used for towelling and nappies. Worsted birdseye fabrics characteristically have small indentations on the face of the fabric and are given a 'clear' finish to accentuate the pattern. They are usually employed as suiting fabrics and are sometimes called 'birdseye suitings'. A larger-scale birdseye pattern is sometimes called 'fisheye cloth'.[2]

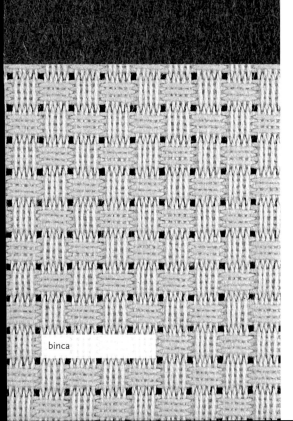

binca

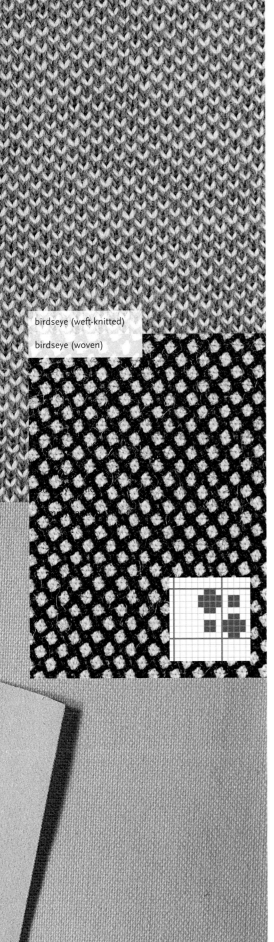

birdseye (weft-knitted)

birdseye (woven)

blackout fabric (back and face)

In weft-knitted birdseye fabric, the effect is produced on double-bed jacquard knitting machines by knitting one colour on all needles of one knit bed and a second contrasting colour on alternate needles of the second knit bed. The speckled effect is produced on the technical back of the fabric. Knitted birdseye is a popular backing structure used on many rib jacquard (double jersey) fabrics (*see* JERSEY).

See also COLOUR AND WEAVE EFFECTS; DOBBY FABRIC; JACQUARD FABRIC, KNITTED; SUITING FABRICS; TOWELLING.

End uses: (woven birdseye) kitchen and hand towels (in cotton or linen), babies' nappies (cotton), napkins (linen) and worsted suiting fabrics; (knitted birdseye) all kinds of knitted fabrics and garments.

BISHOP'S CLOTH *see* MONK'S CLOTH.

BISHOP'S LAWN *see* LAWN.

BISSO LINEN *see* LINEN FABRIC.

BLACKOUT FABRIC A term for a range of opaque fabrics that block out light to varying degrees. They are therefore used as window treatments. Most blackout fabrics are very closely sett woven fabrics, and are usually firm and hard-wearing.

Blackout fabrics are used mainly for window blinds. Any fibres may be used, and they are usually woven in a very closely sett plain weave, warp-faced twill or satin weave. Some blackout fabrics are given a special finish to make them opaque, and this gives them a characteristic stiff, hard handle. For example, natural fibre fabrics may be beetled or heavily sized with oil, starch or pyroxylin. They may also be calender glazed, treated with resins or back-coated with synthetic polymers or fire-resistant finishes. After finishing, the fabric is usually rolled rather than folded. Window blind fabrics are often made in plain dark colours such as black, grey, dark blue and dark green; alternatively, they may be back-coated white or ecru fabrics. Treated Holland is an example of a blackout fabric. Similar fabrics include awning cloth, book cloth, canvas, duck, hopsack and sailcloth.

See also CASEMENT CLOTH, COATED FABRIC.

End uses: window blinds and other blackout treatments.

BLANKET A thick fabric with good thermal insulation, chiefly used as bedding. Blankets may be produced by weaving or knitting, or as needlefelt. Most traditional blankets are made from wool, and are usually heavily raised and milled to give a thick nap on both sides. This obscures the warp and weft yarns and may blur colours together.

Woven blankets may be produced as single cloths in one colour or as colour-woven fabrics with stripe and check designs. More elaborate reversible designs may be woven as stitched double cloths. Plain or twill weaves are normally used, and the weft is usually soft-spun. Some blankets have borders all around or at the ends. Traditionally most blankets are made from wool or wool/cotton or wool/nylon blends, but they may also be made from acrylic, polyester, cotton and blends of these fibres. They are often raised on both sides during finishing to produce a heavy nap surface (*see* NAPPED FABRICS). There are also needlefelted blankets, such as horse blankets, which are heavily felted woollen fabrics (*see* FELT). The name 'blanket' is said to derive from Thomas Blanket of Bristol, England, who is thought to have been the first to produce these fabrics, in the mid-14th century.[36]

There are many traditional types of blanket produced worldwide. Examples include:
- Ayrshire blankets (Scotland): all-wool blankets, woven in a 2/2 twill weave with a dark blue border and milled but not raised[36]

- Bath or Cheviot blankets (England): Cheviot wool blankets woven in a 2/2 twill weave with a dark blue border and heavily raised[36]
- Yorkshire blankets (England): woven in plain weave and finished with a dense nap[36]
- Witney blankets (England): wool blankets with one or more coloured stripes at both ends
- Navajo blankets (Mexico): brightly coloured blankets
- buffalo check (United States): a checked blanket fabric (*see* BUFFALO CHECK)

blanket (Witney)

blanket (needlefelted)

blazer cloth

blanket cloth

End uses: bed coverings.

BLANKET CLOTH A woven fabric, characteristically raised during finishing to give a soft, brushed nap. There are two main types: one made from wool and used as an overcoating fabric, and the other made from cotton and used for bathrobes.

Woollen blanket cloth is a heavy overcoating fabric traditionally made from West of England wool in both the warp and the weft. It is woven in a 2/1 twill weave structure and given a soft raised finish on the face of the fabric, which produces a wavy line effect.[2] One such fabric is Witney, a thick, soft and hard-wearing blanket cloth that is used for overcoats. Its name comes from the town in Oxfordshire, England, where it was originally produced. *See also* COATING FABRIC, WEST OF ENGLAND FABRICS.

Cotton blanket cloth, sometimes called 'bathrobe blanketing' or 'bathrobe cloth', is used mainly for bathrobes. The fabric is woven with thick cotton yarns. The weft yarn is soft-spun and sometimes a 'bump' yarn is used. It may be woven as a single cloth in a plain or twill weave structure, or it may be a weft-backed reversible fabric. It is given a similar finish to flannelette, in which it is raised on both sides. Other bathrobe fabrics are woven in cellular leno constructions or honey-comb weave and are unbrushed. *See also* BACKED FABRIC, BUMP CLOTH, NAPPED FABRICS.

End uses: (woollen blanket cloth) overcoats; (cotton blanket cloth) bathrobes.

BLATTA (*obs.*) A purple silk fabric ornamented with gold threads, made in the 15th century.[3, 36]

BLAZER CLOTH A woven fabric made from wool, traditionally striped but now also produced in solid colours. A blazer is a traditional type of jacket that was originally made from vertically striped, woven fabrics in a wide variety of colour combinations, to associate the wearer with membership of a particular school, club or college.

Traditional blazer cloth is a striped, colour-woven, woollen or worsted fabric woven in a 5-end satin weave construction. The traditional fabric is woven with a wool warp and a cotton weft; the warp completely covers the weft. Other qualities are also made, including wool and man-made fibres and blends. Sometimes the fabric is woven in plain weave. The stripes may also be printed, and the fabric is also produced in solid colours. For instance, blazers are often made from plain woven flannel fabric. Blazer cloth is milled and raised and finished with a fibrous surface. It is similar to a wool Venetian. Blazer stripe is sometimes also called 'Venetian stripe' because both fabrics use the same satin weave structure. *See* VENETIAN.

See also FELTED FABRIC; FLANNEL; NAPPED FABRICS; SATIN, WOVEN; STRIPES.

End uses: lightweight jackets, suits, sports jackets and caps.

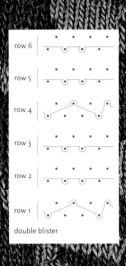

row 6
row 5
row 4
row 3
row 2
row 1

double blister

blister cloth (jacquard knitted double blister)

blister cloth (woven)

BLISTER CLOTH A general term for a range of different fabrics with a puckered or blistered appearance. The term is used for both knitted and woven fabrics. The French term 'cloqué' (meaning 'blistered') is also used to describe 'figured' blister fabrics; it is used mainly for woven fabrics, but also sometimes for figured weft-knitted blister fabrics. *See also* CLOQUÉ.

Knitted blister cloth, also known as 'relief fabric', may be produced in a number of different ways. One example is a weft-knitted double jersey fabric produced by knitting a double fabric construction on the two needle-beds of a rib jacquard machine. There is both a single and a double version of this blister fabric, but in both cases there are more stitches on the effect side than on the back. This produces a fabric with a blistered relief effect over the surface of an underneath fabric.[38] In single blister fabrics of this type, the knit construction comprises four courses

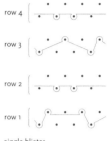

row 4
row 3
row 2
row 1

single blister

that repeat throughout the fabric. In row 1, alternate needles are knitted on the reverse side of the fabric and selected needles only are knitted on the effect side. In row 2, only the needles on the effect side that were not knitted in row 1 are knitted. In row 3, the opposite alternate needles from row 1 are knitted on the reverse side of the fabric, together with the same needles as row 1 on the effect side. Row 4 is a repeat of row 2.[38] The double blister fabric has a more pronounced blister effect than single blister. This fabric is the same as the single blister except that the knit construction repeats over six courses rather than four. There are two extra rows on the effect side. Rows 2 and 5 are repeated, creating extra bulk for the blister effect.[38] *See also* JACQUARD FABRIC, KNITTED; JERSEY; WEFT-KNITTED FABRIC.

Woven blister cloths are also sometimes known by the collective term 'crimp fabrics', as are crepon fabrics.[36] There are various ways to produce blistered effects in a woven fabric:

(i) The fabric may be woven with alternating groups of yarns (warpways and/or weftways), with different shrinkage properties (i.e. yarns of different twist, count or fibre content). When wet-finished, the fabric will contract in the areas where the high-shrink yarns were placed, causing the fabric to pucker only in certain areas (differential shrinkage).

(ii) A blister effect may be woven into a fabric using a special weave structure. This fabric is often a compound or double cloth fabric woven using two sets of yarns of different character. In one example, the face fabric is woven using fine botany wool yarns in both warp and weft, and the back fabric is woven with mohair yarns in both warp and weft. These yarns are alternated 1 end botany and 1 end mohair in the warp. During weaving, the back fabric is interchanged with the face fabric in a predetermined pattern. When the fabric is finished, the botany yarns shrink and the mohair bulges, forming blisters on the face of the fabric.[36]

(iii) A blister effect may be obtained on cellulosic fibre fabrics (e.g. cotton and linen) by printing a sodium hydroxide solution (caustic soda) onto localized areas. This causes these areas to shrink and the adjacent areas to pucker.

(iv) A resist may be printed onto cellulosic fibre fabrics that are then treated in a sodium hydroxide solution (caustic soda). The areas that were protected from the chemical by the resist material will be the areas that pucker.

(v) Thermoplastic fibre fabrics (e.g. polyester and nylon) may be given a permanent blister effect by embossing the fabric with hot rollers. *See* CRÊPE, EMBOSSED FABRICS.

Examples of woven blister fabrics include blister crêpe, cloqué and crinkle crêpe. Similar fabrics to woven blister cloth include embossed crêpe, jacquard crêpe, some embossed fabrics, matelassé, matelassé crêpe and seersucker.

See also CLOQUÉ, DOUBLE CLOTH, FIGURED FABRIC.

End uses: (knitted blister cloth) ladies' sweaters, cardigans, T-shirts and dresses; (woven blister cloth) shirts, blouses, dresses, skirts, summer jackets, trousers, shorts, beachwear, pyjamas, nightgowns, lingerie, aprons, children's wear, tablecloths, bedspreads and curtains.

BLISTER CRÊPE *see* CRÊPE.

BLUETTE A strong, weft-faced, woven fabric, traditionally made in blue cotton and used for overalls. It takes its name from its characteristic blue colour.

Bluette is woven in a 'reclining' 2/2 twill weave structure with more than twice as many weft picks as warp ends. This makes it a weft-faced fabric. Traditionally bluette was a colour-woven fabric made with blue-dyed cotton yarns. Nowadays, although still made in cotton, it is more likely to be made in cotton/man-made fibre blends and piece-dyed blue. Bluette fabrics typically weigh about 250 g/m². An example of a bluette fabric construction is 30 tex warp sett at 17 ends per cm and 37 tex weft woven at 43 picks per cm.[25] The same fabric dyed in colours other than blue is sometimes called 'twillette'. Bluette is similar to denim, drill, dungaree, florentine, hickory cloth and jean.

See also TWILL FABRICS.

End uses: overalls, protective clothing, trousers, jackets and casual wear.

BOBBIN NET (bobbinet, bobbinette) *see* NET.

BOLDWORK CLOTH *see* BINCA.

BOLIVIA A soft, thick and firm woven fabric with a cut weft pile surface. It is usually made from wool and characteristically has a soft, velvet-like pile surface, where the pile runs in lines.

Bolivia is usually made from 100% worsted wool and sometimes also contains a speciality hair fibre such as mohair or alpaca. It is a weft pile fabric, the base of which is closely woven, often in a 3/3 twill weave structure. After weaving, the weft pile is cut into tufts that run in lines, either in the warp direction or diagonally along the twill lines. This gives the soft, velvet-like pile surface.

See also COATING FABRIC, PILE FABRICS.

End uses: coats and suitings.

BOLTING CLOTH (miller's gauze) A sheer, open fabric, woven in an open-sett plain weave (gauze) or a leno construction. It belongs to the muslin family of fabrics.

Originally bolting cloth was made from wool, linen or gummed silk yarns and was used to sift flour. The term 'bolting' derives from French *blutage*, meaning 'sifting'.[3] Bolting cloth was also known as 'miller's gauze'. The gauze fabric was heavily stiffened during finishing. Nowadays bolting cloth is more likely to be made from filament polyester or nylon and used as a mesh for screen printing. Fabrics similar to bolting cloth and that also belong to the muslin family include book muslin, buckram, bunting, butter muslin, cheesecloth, crinoline, étamine, gauze, mull, scrim and tarlatan.

See also GAUZE, LENO FABRIC, MUSLIN, SHEER FABRICS.

End uses: screen printing mesh, dress trimmings and foundation fabric for wigs.

BOLTON SHEETING *see* SHEETING FABRIC.

BOMBAZINE (bombasine) A traditional woven, black-dyed mourning cloth. It is a soft, fine, dress-weight fabric woven in plain or twill weave.

Bombazine was first woven in Norwich, England, in the 16th century.[36] It was originally made with silk and cotton and it is named after the 'bombasine' cotton from Brazil

bluette

Bolivia

bolting cloth

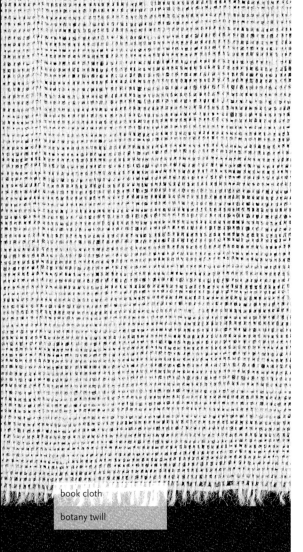

book cloth

botany twill

from which the fabric was originally made.[36] The fabric was piece-dyed in black or other colours. Later qualities included an all-silk version and a version woven with a silk warp and a worsted weft. Bombazine is rarely made nowadays; when it is made, it is more likely to be woven using viscose, cotton or man-made fibres. It is woven in a plain or twill weave construction.

See also SILK FABRIC.

End uses: mourning fabric and formal clothes.

BOOK CLOTH A coarse, stiff woven fabric that is used mainly for bookbinding, but also for stiffening items such as belts, hats and bags. It is made from a variety of different qualities of base cloth, which may be finished in different ways.

Most book cloth fabrics are inexpensive plain weave cotton fabrics that are either very heavily sized to make them stiff or treated with pyroxylin to make them waterproof and washable. Sometimes they are also embossed. The different qualities of base cloth include buckram, canvas, duck, Holland, osnaburg and sheeting fabric. The base cloths may be dyed or undyed. Book muslin is a bookbinders' fabric made from a softer, finer quality cotton muslin base cloth. Book cloth belongs to the muslin family of fabrics. Similar fabrics include bolting cloth, buckram, bunting, butter muslin, cheesecloth, crinoline, étamine, gauze, mull, scrim and tarlatan.

See also MUSLIN, PLAIN WEAVE FABRIC.

End uses: bookbinding, and stiffening for belts, hats and bags.

BOTANY TWILL A general term for dress fabrics that are woven in twill weave structures using botany worsted yarns in both the warp and weft. These are high-quality, smooth fabrics that are made in a variety of different weights.

Since botany wool is the top-quality worsted yarn made from merino wool, botany twill fabrics are usually quite expensive. They are normally woven in balanced 2/2, 3/3 or 4/4 twill weaves in various weights, or sometimes in fancy twill weave structures. They are then lightly milled and given a clear finish to show up the twill effect. Examples of botany twill fabrics include some gaberdine fabrics, imperial cloth and serge.

See also TWILL FABRICS, WOOL FABRIC, WORSTED FABRIC.

End uses: men's and women's worsted suits and dresses.

BOUCHE (bluché) (*obs.*) A plain weave, undyed woollen fabric, originally used as a shirting fabric, particularly by the clergy in southern France.[17]

BOUCLÉ FABRIC A fabric with a looped, textured surface that is woven or knitted using fancy 'bouclé' yarns. Loops inherent in the yarn protrude from the surface of the fabric in an all-over irregular manner to form a loop pile on the surface of the fabric.

The word 'bouclé' comes from the French meaning 'buckled, curled or looped'. Bouclé yarns are fancy yarns made by wrapping an effect yarn of irregular semi-circular loops around a central twisted core. Any fibres may be used, but common ones include mohair or wool and cotton. A wide range of fabric weights are produced but, because the bulky texture traps air, even fine bouclé fabrics are quite warm.

Woven bouclé fabrics normally use plain twist yarns in the warp and bouclé yarns in the weft. They are usually woven in loose, open weave structures like leno or basket weaves in order to accentuate the yarn effect. Knitted bouclé fabrics are made by inlaying bouclé yarns into the weft-knitted fabric structure. Other examples of loop yarn fabrics include éponge and frotté. Fabrics similar to bouclé fabrics include astrakhan fabric, poodle cloth, ratiné and terry fabric.

See also COATING FABRIC, PILE FABRICS.

End uses: (woven bouclé fabrics) ladies' coats, suits and dresses; (knitted bouclé fabrics) sweaters, jackets, sweater dresses and sportswear accessories.

BOUCLETTE A warp-knitted fabric knitted in a construction that produces a low loop pile on one side of the fabric. This produces a lightweight, fine fabric with a fine, textured surface.

The fabric is knitted on a three-bar tricot warp-knitting machine. Fine filament nylon or polyester yarns are usually knitted on the front and back bar to form the ground fabric. The centre guide bar, usually containing a different fibre yarn (e.g. triacetate), mislaps in order to form the pile. The yarn floats form a low loop pile on the technical reverse of the fabric. This construction is similar to an airloop fabric construction. Airloop fabric and terry fabric are similar to bouclette; terry fabric, however, is usually heavier.

See also AIRLOOP FABRIC, KNITTED FABRIC, PILE FABRICS, WARP-KNITTED FABRIC.

End uses: dresswear and casual wear.

BOURETTE A lightweight, rough, neppy fabric woven in plain or twill weave using silk noil yarns. The name comes from the French term for silk noil yarns,[36] which are spun with the short fibres discarded from the manufacture of higher-quality silk yarns. This waste silk produces an irregular textured fabric with neps.

See also SILK FABRIC.

End uses: mainly curtain fabric and furnishings, but also dresses, blouses, shirts, jackets and skirts.

BOURRELET A knitted fabric that may be either warp- or weft-knitted. Characteristically, both kinds have ridges or raised ribs running horizontally across the face side of the fabric.

Weft-knitted bourrelet can be made on an interlock basis, a rib basis or a knit-tuck basis. A classic interlock bourrelet is a double jersey fabric composed of ten courses that repeat throughout the fabric, although there are variations on this depending on the height of rib required. Two full courses of interlock, knitted on both needle-beds, are followed by six half-gauge, plain knit courses knitted on one set of needles only on the effect side of the fabric. This produces the ribbed effect in the fabric.[25, 38]

Warp-knitted bourrelet is usually knitted on a double-bar raschel machine. More courses per unit length are knitted on one side of the fabric than on the other.[38] This produces a kind of ridged crêpe effect in the fabric (*see* CRÊPE). Warp-knitted bourrelet can also be produced on a two-guide-bar tricot machine, by blind lapping on the front bar while producing stitches with the back guide bar. A more exaggerated version of this fabric is sometimes termed 'plissé' (*see* PLEATED FABRICS).

See also INTERLOCK, JERSEY, KNITTED FABRIC, WARP-KNITTED FABRIC, WEFT-KNITTED FABRIC.

End uses: fancy knitwear.

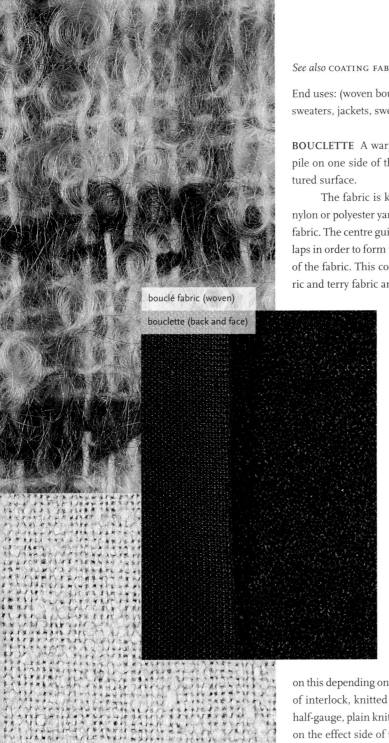

bouclé fabric (woven)

bouclette (back and face)

bourette

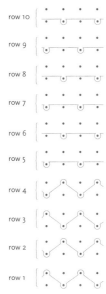

row 10
row 9
row 8
row 7
row 6
row 5
row 4
row 3
row 2
row 1

interlock bourrelet

box cloth

broadcloth (cotton)

broadcloth (silk)

BOX CLOTH A thick, firm, woven fabric made with wool. Characteristically, it is heavily milled so that it resembles dense felt.

Box cloth is traditionally woven from dyed woollen-spun wool yarns in a broken 2/2 twill weave. Lighter-weight box cloths may be woven in other weave structures. Traditionally it is often buff or tan in colour. In finishing, the heavy milling allows the fabric to shrink and compact in a controlled manner, completely obscuring the yarns. This is followed by a dress-face finish in which a high lustre is obtained by raising and cropping the surface of the cloth and laying the fibres flat in one direction. Box cloth is usually quite water-repellent. Its name may have originated from the 'mill box' of the milling machine in which it is finished. Box cloth is similar to melton, but it is slightly heavier, and melton has a soft, fibrous finish in which the fibres are not laid flat after raising.

See also COATING FABRIC, FACED CLOTH, FELTED FABRIC.

End uses: overcoats, suits, horse-riding jackets, uniforms and billiard cloth.

BRADFORD LUSTRE FABRICS The collective term for a group of woven fabrics characterized by the high lustre of their weft yarns and traditionally used as men's suiting fabrics.

Bradford lustre fabrics are so called because they have traditionally been woven in the English town of Bradford, Yorkshire, or in the surrounding areas. They are usually woven in plain weave, with a cotton or man-made fibre warp and weft yarns that have a high lustre, such as mohair, worsted or alpaca. A special finishing process brings the weft yarns to the surface of the fabric, thereby accentuating the lustrous effect. For examples of Bradford lustre fabrics, *see* BRILLIANTINE, GRANADA, MÉLANGE LUSTRE FABRIC and PEKIN.

See also ALPACA FABRIC, MOHAIR FABRIC, SHADOW STRIPES AND CHECKS, WORSTED FABRIC.

End uses: lightweight suiting fabrics.

BREATHABLE FABRICS *see* MOISTURE TRANSPORT TEXTILES, POLYMER MEMBRANE LAMINATES.

BRIDGEWATER (*obs.*) A light woollen broadcloth made in England in the 16th century.[3, 36]

BRIGHTON HONEYCOMB *see* HONEYCOMB.

BRILLIANTINE A fine, lustrous union fabric, with a cotton or man-made fibre warp and a lustrous worsted or mohair weft. It belongs to the group of fabrics known as 'Bradford lustre fabrics'.

Brilliantine is usually woven in a plain or twill weave, but sometimes it may have small weft figures (usually floral) on a plain ground. These may be jacquard or dobby woven. The weft yarns are much thicker than the warp yarns, and the fabric is woven so that the warp is almost completely hidden by the lustrous weft yarns. The weft predominance is also increased with a special finishing process in which the fabric is extended along its length and shrunken across its width. The warp may be pre-dyed black so that in piece-dyeing only the weft would need to be dyed, or a bleached warp may be used with light-coloured fabrics. Brilliantines are lightweight fabrics in which the weft is 38 tex worsted or finer and the warp is sett at 20 to 28 ends per cm in the loom.[26] 'Sicilian' is the term given to a slightly heavier brilliantine-type fabric in which the weft is thicker than 38 tex worsted and the warp is set at 14 to 19 ends per cm.[26] Sicilian was first made in Sicily from cotton and mohair and used as a lining fabric. It is now woven in plain weave and has heavy weft ribs.[2] It too is a type of Bradford lustre fabric.

See also MOHAIR FABRIC, UNION FABRIC.

End uses: dresses, women's and men's summer suits, nuns' habits and linings.

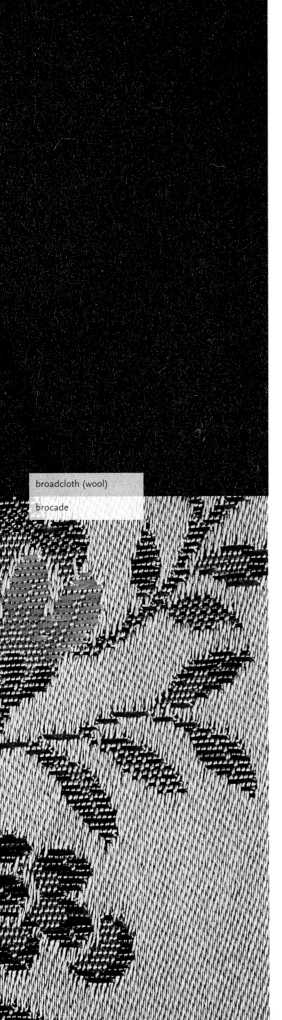

broadcloth (wool)

brocade

BROADCLOTH A very fine, high-quality fabric that is woven in wide widths in the weaving loom (hence the name). There are three main traditional types: cotton broadcloth, silk broadcloth and woollen broadcloth.

Cotton broadcloth is a lightweight cotton or cotton blend fabric with a very fine warp rib effect across the width of the fabric. In fact, cotton broadcloth has the finest ribs of all woven rib fabrics. It is woven in plain weave, usually with 100% bleached, mercerized cotton yarns or cotton/man-made fibre blends (usually polyester). The fine warp yarns are closely sett with nearly twice as many warp as weft yarns. The weft yarns are either the same thickness as or slightly thicker than the warp yarns and this gives the fine-ribbed effect. Cotton broadcloth is usually piece-dyed and it is also often printed. The fabric may be sanforized to give a soft, lustrous finish. There is a range of warp rib fabrics characterized by the size and prominence of their ribs. In increasing order of rib size, these are: broadcloth (cotton), poplin, taffeta, poult, faille, bengaline and grosgrain. *See also* SILK FABRIC. Cotton broadcloth is similar to, but finer than, poplin, percale and Fuji. *See also* PRINT CLOTH; RIB FABRICS, WOVEN.

Silk broadcloth is similar in appearance and construction to cotton broadcloth, but is usually woven using continuous filament warp yarns and staple weft yarns. It may be made from 100% silk yarns, 100% man-made yarns or a combination of these.

Woollen broadcloth is completely different from either cotton or silk broadcloth. It is a soft, smooth, slightly felty but lustrous woollen or wool blend fabric with a velvety handle and good drape. It is a very high-quality fabric. It is usually woven in a 2/1 or a 2/2 twill weave (or occasionally plain weave) and uses fine, high-quality woollen yarns such as merino or wool/man-made fibre blends. Woollen broadcloth is sett extra wide in the loom to allow for shrinkage during the finishing process, and it is from this that the name 'broadcloth' originated. For example, a 230 cm fabric in the loom is finished at 140 cm wide. The fabric is heavily milled to shrink it in a controlled manner. It is then given a fine dress-face finish in which the nap is flattened and laid in one direction so that it obscures the weave structure. As the nap lies in one direction, pattern pieces cut in different directions will reflect light differently. The fabric is therefore normally cut with the nap in the downward direction. Woollen broadcloth is usually dyed in dark colours. It is a similar fabric to beaver cloth, kersey and melton.

See also COATING FABRIC, FACED CLOTH, FELTED FABRIC.

End uses: (cotton and silk broadcloth) shirts, blouses, dresses, undergarments and curtains; (woollen broadcloth) coats, jackets, suits, tailored clothes and traditional ecclesiastical garments.

BROCADE A true brocade is a luxurious, jacquard woven fabric in which multicoloured figured patterns, often floral, are woven with supplementary weft yarns on the face of the fabric against a (usually) simple ground weave. The figured areas often stand slightly proud from the surface of the fabric. However, the term 'brocade' is also used nowadays to include fabrics in which the pattern is formed by supplementary warp yarns, either alone or with the addition of supplementary weft yarns, floating on the fabric surface. Characteristically, the pattern is only visible on the face side of brocade fabrics, so they are not reversible. Brocade is a luxurious, often heavyweight fabric, but it is made in a wide variety of weights and qualities.

Originally brocades were always woven in silk and figured with gold and silver threads,[36] but now they may be woven in any fibre/blend combinations. The supplementary warp or weft yarns float on the back of the fabric and are only brought to the surface to form the figure. The figured patterns are usually formed by floating the supplementary yarns on the fabric surface in an irregular satin or sateen-type weave structure against the simple ground weave (plain, rib, twill or satin). Contrasting colours are also often used in the figured and ground areas. Brocades tend to fray easily due to the floats

brocatelle

broché (face and back)

on the back of the fabric. The name 'brocade' comes from the Spanish and Portuguese *brocado* and the Italian *broccato,* meaning 'figured with threads'. Brocade is similar to damask, but it is heavier and not reversible like damask. It is also similar to lampas. There is also a brocade velvet (*see* VELVET) and an épingle brocade (*see* ÉPINGLE).

See also FIGURED FABRIC; JACQUARD FABRIC, WOVEN; SILK FABRIC.

End uses: ladies' evening wear, accessories, curtains and upholstery.

BROCATELLE A firm, patterned fabric, very similar to brocade but heavier. Like brocade, it is jacquard woven, but its figures are constructed so that they have a much more pronounced relief effect than in a brocade. Brocatelles are therefore recognizable by their distinctive three-dimensional embossed or quilted quality.

Brocatelles are often constructed with two sets of warp and weft yarns: one fine set and one thicker set. The thicker yarns are used to weave the figured areas and the finer yarns are used for the ground weave. The contrast between the two thicknesses is what produces the relief effect in the fabric. The figured areas are tightly woven in a satin or other warp-faced weave construction. The background weave is also tightly woven in a simple weave structure (e.g. plain, rib, twill or sateen), which is often weft-faced. The relief effect may also be further accentuated by using thick, soft extra weft backing yarns to pad out the figured areas. This causes the figures to stand out in very high relief against the simple, closely woven background. As the supplementary weft yarns float on the back of the fabric, brocatelles are also prone to fraying like brocades. Sometimes, however, a higher-quality brocatelle is woven as a double cloth in which an extra binder warp is used to secure the yarns floating on the back of the fabric. Like brocades, brocatelles were originally all-silk fabrics, but now they may be woven in any fibre/blend combinations and in a variety of medium- to heavyweight qualities.

See also FIGURED FABRIC; JACQUARD FABRIC, WOVEN; SILK FABRIC.

End uses: evening wear, accessories, curtains and upholstery.

BROCHÉ (swivel fabrics, swivels) A brocade fabric that is hand-woven on a swivel loom. The figured pattern is made by extra weft yarns that are not integrated into the whole of the base fabric – that is, they do not travel from selvedge to selvedge but are woven into the background fabric by hand to form the patterned areas only. Broché fabrics are therefore lighter-weight fabrics than either brocades or brocatelles. As their manufacture is very labour-intensive and requires a skilled weaver, they are very expensive and are usually produced only to special order. Visually they are similar to embroidered fabrics. They are sometimes called 'swivel fabrics' or 'swivels'.

The extra or supplementary weft yarn is woven into the areas where the pattern is required using a series of small swivel shuttles mounted over the top of the weaving surface. Each weft pick of the background fabric that travels from selvedge to selvedge is alternated with a weft pick of the figure that is inserted across the width of the figure only. The weft figures are therefore bound around the edges, which distinguishes the fabric from other similar-looking ones, such as clip spot and some dotted Swiss fabrics, which have cut edges. The yarns used to weave the figure are usually thicker than, and in a contrasting colour to, the yarns used for the ground weave. They will therefore completely cover the ground fabric. The term 'broché' comes from the French, meaning 'figured'.

See also BROCADE, CLIP SPOT, DOTTED SWISS, EMBROIDERED FABRICS, EXTRA WARP AND EXTRA WEFT FABRICS, FIGURED FABRIC, LANCÉ.

End uses: exclusive bed linen, drapes, upholstery, hangings, lingerie, ribbons and trimmings.

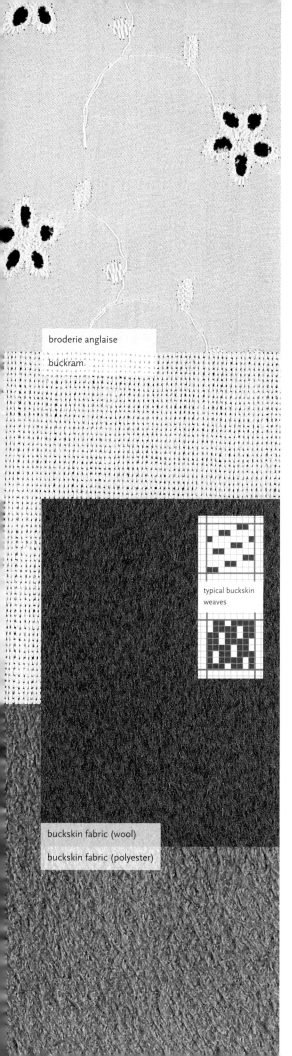

broderie anglaise

buckram

typical buckskin weaves

buckskin fabric (wool)

buckskin fabric (polyester)

BRODERIE ANGLAISE (Madeira, Madeira work) A lightweight woven cotton fabric in which a pattern is made by cutting shaped holes into the fabric and embroidering around their edges. True broderie anglaise fabrics are made in pure white with white embroidered edges. Coloured versions of this fabric are normally called 'eyelet'. Some broderie anglaise fabrics have an all-over design, but most have border designs; some have a scalloped edge.

The base fabric is usually a cotton, polyester/cotton or linen fabric woven in plain weave, for example batiste, (cotton) broadcloth, cambric, poplin, dimity or organdie. Broderie anglaise used to be made by hand using hand embroidery techniques. Nowadays the design is embroidered on a Schiffli embroidery machine using a buttonhole stitch outline. The centres are then cut away, leaving a pattern of holes in the fabric. The term 'broderie anglaise' is French, meaning 'English embroidery', but this fabric is most frequently made in Austria or Switzerland. Broderie anglaise is also sometimes called 'Madeira work' or 'Madeira', since many fine examples come from this Portuguese island. Hand embroidery was established as an industry there by the daughter of an English wine importer in 1856.[23]

See also EMBROIDERED FABRICS, EYELET, LASER-CUT FABRICS.

End uses: lingerie, blouses, dresses, children's formal wear, nightwear, trimmings, table linen and bed linen.

BRUSHED COTTON FABRIC *see* COTTON FABRIC.

BRUSHED NYLON *see* LOOPRAISE.

BRUSHED POLYESTER *see* LOOPRAISE.

BUCKRAM A coarse, stiff fabric made by impregnating a lightweight woven fabric or a two-fabric laminate with size or resin. Buckram is used as a stiffening fabric for a wide range of goods. It belongs to the muslin family of fabrics.

The base fabric is woven in an open-sett plain weave construction using carded cotton yarns or occasionally linen yarns. 'Cheesecloth' grey goods are often used. The stiffening solution, or size, was traditionally made with a flour paste, china clay and glue. Nowadays synthetic resins are more likely to be used. Thicker, stiffer buckram fabrics are made by laminating two stiffened fabrics together. The two fabrics may be different: one woven in an open-sett plain weave using thicker yarns (like cheesecloth) and one woven with finer yarns in a more closely sett plain weave, for instance. Coloured buckram fabrics are stiffened after piece-dyeing. When making up, the fabric is often cut on the cross to allow easing of shapes. The name 'buckram' is derived from the early English word *bokeram*, used to describe fabrics originally from Bukhara in South Russia.[3] Buckram is similar to crinoline but it is stiffer and heavier.

See also BOLTING CLOTH, BOOK CLOTH, BUNTING, BUTTER MUSLIN, CHEESECLOTH, ÉTAMINE, GAUZE, LAMINATED FABRIC, MULL, MUSLIN, SCRIM, STRAW FABRICS, TARLATAN.

End uses: interlining or support fabric in tailoring, millinery, bookbinding, lampshades and pleated drapes.

BUCKSKIN FABRIC A durable woven fabric made in imitation of the skin of a male fallow deer. It is usually made in cream, brown or beige colours, like the colour of real deerskin. Buckskin fabric may be made from wool, or it may be a type of woven suede cloth fabric made with man-made fibres, often polyester.

Wool buckskin fabric is woven from fine merino wool in a number of different closely sett satin weave variations. After weaving, the fabric is usually piece-dyed and given

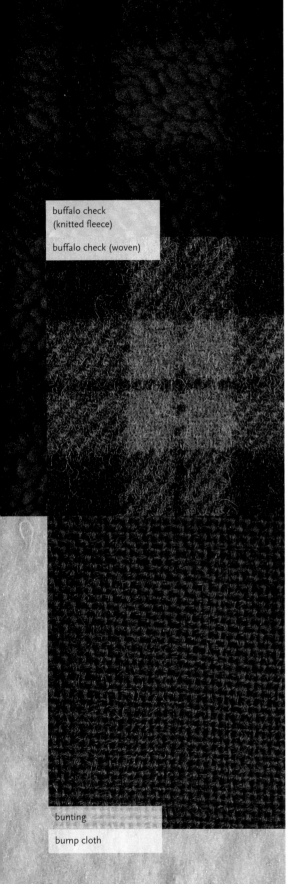

buffalo check
(knitted fleece)

buffalo check (woven)

bunting

bump cloth

a dress-face finish in which it is heavily milled, raised and cropped to make it firm and smooth. Buckskin produced with man-made continuous filament fibres, including microfibres, is usually sanded or emerized during the finishing process in order to break the surface filaments in a manner that resembles the surface of real buckskin. Real buckskin was used for riding breeches by American soldiers during the American Civil War,[3] and buckskin fabric is still used today for riding breeches and similar end uses. Buckskin fabric is similar to doeskin fabric but heavier.

See also FACED CLOTH, NAPPED FABRICS, SUEDE CLOTH.

End uses: riding breeches, trousers, jackets, curtains and upholstery.

BUFFALO CHECK (mackinaw) Traditionally a thick, heavy colour-woven fabric, originally woven in wool and used for coats, jackets and blankets. Characteristically, it has a bold, large-scale check pattern all over the fabric, often in black and red. It is a strong, durable and warm fabric. Today the buffalo check pattern is also used in fabrics of other constructions, for example knitted fleece fabrics.

Traditional buffalo check fabric is also known as 'mackinaw' or 'mackinac'. This was the name given to the double-breasted jackets made from this fabric worn by lumberjacks. The name comes from Mackinaw City, in Michigan, United States, where buffalo check coats and blankets were once traded with American Indians.[3] In the traditional fabric, the yarns are coarse wool yarns or wool blend yarns. Sometimes cotton is used in the warp. The checks are formed by alternating large groups of red and black yarns (or other contrasting colours) in both the warp and the weft directions. The fabric is produced either as a single cloth woven in a 2/2 twill weave structure or as a double cloth construction. With the double cloth version, both the face and back cloths are woven in twill weaves, but the fabric is traditionally checked on one side only, while the other side is a solid colour. After weaving, the fabric is heavily milled and brushed on both sides, which produces a long nap and gives the fabric a felted appearance. This obscures the weave structure underneath. Sometimes a lighter quality buffalo check fabric is made in a similar coloured check pattern, but in a plain weave structure and using cotton yarns. The buffalo check pattern is also sometimes used to pattern knitted fleece fabrics (*see* FLEECE FABRIC). Buffalo check is similar to melton, but unlike melton it is checked and uses coarser yarns.

See also BLANKET, CHECKS, COATING FABRIC, DOUBLE CLOTH, FELTED FABRIC, MELTON, NAPPED FABRICS.

End uses: (wool fabric) blankets, lumber jackets and coats; (cotton fabric) casual shirts and dresses.

BUMP CLOTH (bump) A heavy, low-quality cotton woven fabric that is used principally as a backing fabric by the printing industry.[25] The fabric is thick, absorbent and warm but not very stable.

Bump is woven in plain weave using low-quality, medium-sized cotton yarns in the warp and thick 'bump' cotton yarns in the weft. Bump yarns are made from the waste fibres produced in the making of higher-quality cotton yarns. The term 'bump' comes from the cotton fibre industry, where it refers to a hard lump in cotton bales.[3] Bump is a similar fabric to batting (*see* WADDING).

End uses: backing fabric, curtain interlinings and cleaning cloths.

BUNTING (ensign fabric, tammy) A loosely woven, plain weave fabric used for flags, banners and outdoor decorations. It is a semi-sheer fabric and belongs to the muslin family of fabrics.

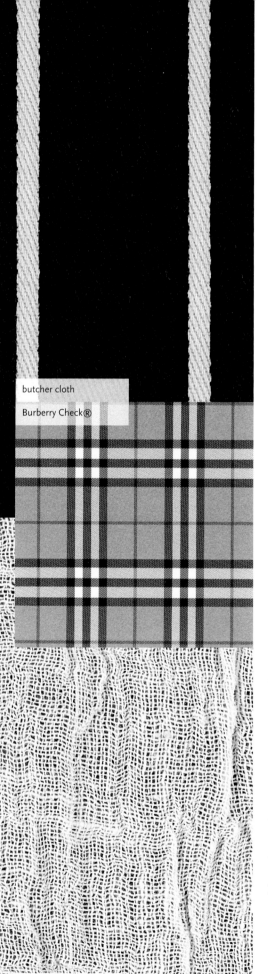

butcher cloth

Burberry Check®

butter muslin

Originally bunting was woven from woollen or worsted yarns and cheaper versions were woven in carded cotton. Nowadays it is likely to be woven with a blend of nylon and wool. It is usually piece-dyed and/or printed in basic, bright colours. Bunting is also known as 'ensign fabric' or 'tammy'. In France it is known as 'étamine' (which is the source of 'tammy'). Bunting is similar to cheesecloth, gauze and scrim.

See also ÉTAMINE, MUSLIN, PLAIN WEAVE FABRIC.

End uses: flags, banners, outdoor decorations, curtains and hangings.

BURBERRY CHECK® A well-known check recognizable from its characteristic red, black, white and camel colours. The pattern is used for fabrics made in a variety of different weights and qualities for different end uses.

Burberry Check was first created in 1924 by the English clothing company Burberry for use as a lining fabric in trench coats. Although still employed for this purpose, it is also widely used in its own right for all kinds of clothing and accessories. The check design is usually colour-woven, but it is also sometimes printed.

See also CHECKS.

End uses: lining fabric (for trench coats, coats and jackets), scarves, bags, luggage and umbrellas.

BURLAP *see* HESSIAN.

BURN-OUT FABRIC *see* DEVORÉ FABRIC.

BUTCHER CLOTH A strong, stiff, hard-wearing woven fabric. It was originally manufactured for butchers' aprons. Traditionally it is navy blue in colour with bleached white stripes.

This fabric was originally woven using linen yarns and was formerly known as 'butcher linen'. Now it is woven in a variety of different fibres, but most often in cotton or cotton blends. The weave structure is usually plain weave, but twill weave is also sometimes used. The fabric is often given a stiff, crease-resistant resin finish in imitation of linen. Butcher cloth for aprons was traditionally colour-woven in navy blue with bleached white stripes. Nowadays the blue is often printed onto the bleached white fabric. 'Fodens' was a term formerly used for a similar but lighter-weight fabric that was also woven in blue and white stripes and traditionally used as aprons for butchers, fishmongers, milkmen and domestic householders.[3, 4]

See also STRIPES.

End uses: aprons and overalls.

BUTTER MUSLIN A soft, lightweight woven fabric constructed in an open plain weave using cheap cotton yarns. It belongs to the muslin family of fabrics.

Butter muslin is woven as grey cloth with cotton yarns. The weave is normally an open, square-sett, plain weave construction, and the fabric usually weighs less than 68 g/m². Butter muslin was traditionally used in its grey state in the production of dairy products, hence its name. It is a similar fabric to cheesecloth.

See also MUSLIN.

End uses: a household fabric used in jam-making and for cleaning and ironing cloths.

BUTTERNUT (*obs.*) A heavy woollen homespun fabric from the United States, used for trousers. It was dyed brown with extracts from the butternut tree.[36]

cable stitch fabric

calico

CABLE CORD *see* CORD FABRICS.

CABLE STITCH FABRIC A weft-knitted fabric that contains cable stitches. Characteristically, these form a three-dimensional cable effect – a pattern of ridges that cross over and under one another in the vertical direction.

Cable stitch is a rib-based construction in which small groups of two or more adjacent wales, knitted in rib structure, cross over and under one another, producing a cable effect. The fabric is often knitted using thick woollen yarns and used for heavy sweaters and jackets. Finer cable stitch fabrics are knitted with cotton yarns and are used mainly for summer sweaters. Cable stitch is often used in Aran garments (*see* ARAN FABRIC).

See also KNITTED FABRIC; RIB FABRICS, KNITTED; WEFT-KNITTED FABRIC.

End uses: sweaters and jackets.

CADET CLOTH A heavy, durable fabric woven in wool and used for overcoats and uniforms at military schools and academies. It is usually made in blue-grey, grey or dark blue colours. It is an all-wool fabric woven as a double cloth, usually with a 2/2 twill on both sides. It is a napped fabric that is heavily milled, raised and cropped to produce a dense, weatherproof fabric similar to flannel.

See also COATING FABRIC, DOUBLE CLOTH, FELTED FABRIC, FLANNEL, NAPPED FABRICS, TWILL FABRICS.

End uses: overcoats and uniforms.

CALICO A generic term applied to various qualities of plain woven cotton fabric heavier than muslin. Calico is known for its strength and durability, but it has poor crease resistance.

Calico is a firm fabric, closely woven in a balanced plain weave and made from carded cotton or sometimes cotton/polyester blends. It is often sold in its unbleached state, sometimes retaining small flecks of seed matter from the cotton. It is also often heavily sized with starch to give it weight and stiffness. Frequently, however, calico is either dyed or printed after further finishing processes. Printed calicoes are very common, especially in the United States, where it is typical for small bright prints, often floral, to be shown against a contrasting background. 'Calico' was formerly the name given to all types of cotton cloth coming from Calicut on the south-west coast of India. The term was known in 1604,[36] but calico itself is one of the oldest types of known textile.[2] It was formerly called 'pintadores' and was brought from India to Europe by Vasco da Gama in about 1497.[5] Calico may be made from the same grey cloth as chintz, cretonne, percale and plissé, each being given a different finish.[19]

See also COTTON FABRIC, PLAIN WEAVE FABRIC, PRINT CLOTH.

End uses: (heavier qualities, usually unbleached) furnishings and mattress covers; (lighter qualities) sheets, shirts, dresses, rag dolls, patchwork quilts and toiles in the making of dress patterns.

CAMBRIAN TWEED *see* TWEED.

CAMBRIC A lightweight, firm, closely woven plain weave fabric traditionally made from cotton. It is usually given a finish that stiffens it and gives it a slight lustre on one side.

Cambric gets its name from Cambrai in northern France, where it was originally produced. It was originally made from linen, and it is still possible to obtain an 'Irish cambric' woven in linen. However, most cambric is now made from good-quality cotton yarns, often Egyptian; it is also sometimes made in man-made fibres or blends. It is usually piece-dyed in solid colours. In the finishing process, the fabric is coated on one side with a special size or resin and calendered to make it lustrous. Sometimes it is given a heavier waxed or glazed finish so that it becomes impenetrable to feathers or down. This 'down-proof cambric' is usually white or cream in colour and is used as a covering for pillows, cushions, duvets and mattresses.

Cotton cambric is woven in a wide range of qualities. It is similar to cotton batiste, chambray, jaconet, lawn, longcloth, nainsook, organdie and percale. These fabrics are all woven in plain weave using high-quality cotton yarns and look very similar in the grey state, differing only in their finish. Cambric, longcloth and nainsook are often converted from the same grey goods and given different finishes.

See also COTTON FABRIC, PLAIN WEAVE FABRIC.

End uses: children's clothes, baby clothes, nightwear, dresses, blouses, shirts, aprons, tablecloths, underwear, linings, pillowcases, cushion covers, duvet covers and mattress covers.

cambric (downproof)

cambric

camel-hair fabric

CAMEL-HAIR FABRIC A general term for any fabric constructed with yarns made from camel hair, a natural animal fibre from either the Bactrian camel (*Camelus bactrianus*) or the dromedary camel (*Camelus dromedarius*). It is classed as a speciality hair fibre. Both the strong, coarse outer hair and the soft, fine undercoat are used. For clothing, it is usually the undercoat fibres that are used: these are warm and extremely soft fibres that have a high natural lustre. Strictly speaking, the term 'camel-hair fabric' should be applied only to fabrics made from 100% camel hair; however, since camel hair is very expensive, such fabrics are rare. More commonly the camel hair is blended with other fibres to reduce the cost, in which case the percentages of each fibre should be stated.

Because it is so expensive, camel hair is usually mixed with other fibres, especially wool. Sometimes a small percentage of nylon may also be added for extra strength. Most camel-hair fabrics are used as coating fabrics. They are usually medium- to heavyweight woven fabrics, and are characteristically soft, warm and lustrous. They are normally woven in plain weave or other simple weave structures, and are raised during finishing to produce a soft, napped surface. The natural colours of the camel hair give the fabric its characteristic colour, which ranges from light tan to dark brown. Sometimes the names 'camel cloth' and 'camel fabric' are used incorrectly to describe a fabric that has a camel colour but contains no camel-hair fibre. Using the term 'camel-hair fabric' helps to avoid such confusion. Camlet and Montagnac are examples of fabrics that are sometimes woven from camel hair.

See also CAMLET, COATING FABRIC, HAIR FABRICS, NAPPED FABRICS.

End uses: coats, scarves, suits, dressing gowns and rugs.

CAMELOT *see* CAMLET.

candlewick

cannelle (face and back)

CAMLET A fine, thin plain weave fabric made from wool or hair fibres, sometimes with silk added, or with 'camlet' yarns. The original version was made in India from camel hair,[36] but most camlet fabrics are made with wool, goat hair or mixed hair fibres. Camlet yarn is made with lustrous wool from the English Leicester and Lincoln breeds of sheep.[36] The fabric is woven in a range of different qualities for suiting fabrics and furnishings. It was first woven in Wales on the banks of the river Camlet in the 17th century. It was highly prized, and was dyed in various colours, including bright red.[36] 'Camelot', or 'camelott', is the term for an imitation camlet fabric made in cotton and wool.[25]

See also CAMEL HAIR FABRIC, HAIR FABRICS, SUITING FABRICS.

End uses: suiting fabrics and furnishings.

CAMPBELL TWILL *see* TWILL FABRICS.

CANDLEWICK A soft, thick, warm tufted pile fabric that is characteristically very absorbent and does not crease. It was originally produced using candle wicks made from cotton string or yarn (hence the name). These were threaded by hand into a loosely woven cotton muslin base fabric to form loops. The thicker 'wick' yarns were threaded into the base fabric in straight lines or in patterns, but with spaces left in-between. The loops were then cut to form fluffy tufts on the surface of the fabric. Today's candlewick looks similar but is mass-produced on tufting machines, where the tufts are secured in a base cloth that is usually woven in plain weave. Carded cotton yarns are still used most frequently in both the base fabric and the pile, but viscose is also sometimes employed. Candlewick is similar to chenille fabric.

See also MUSLIN, TUFTED FABRIC.

End uses: bedspreads, dressing gowns, bathrobes, bath mats and rugs.

CANNELLE (cannele) A woven fabric with fine ribs running in the weft direction. It is a 'repp' fabric, in which the horizontal ribs are alternated with flat sections of the ground weave. Typically, the ribs are prominent on the face side only. Cannelle is traditionally made from silk.[25,36] There are several different variants of cannelle, which are described in greater detail below.

Cannelle simpleté is the classic cannelle fabric. It is made with two warps, one of fine singles yarn and the other of thicker doubled yarn.[36] The finer warp is woven in plain weave and forms the ground weave. The second, supplementary pattern warp floats over approximately eight picks of the ground weave to form the rib effect. It is then bound with the ground weave by one or two picks of the weft.[1,25]

Cannelle des Indes is the same as cannelle simpleté, except that only alternate ends of the supplementary pattern warp float over the ground weave to form the rib effect, while the remaining ends are bound in with the ground weave. The ribs are therefore less prominent.[1]

Cannelle alternatif is made with one warp only. The even-numbered ends float on the face of the fabric to form the ribs, while the odd-numbered ends are woven in a plain weave ground construction. The ends are then interchanged so that the odd-numbered ends float on the face of the fabric to form the ribs, while the even-numbered ends are woven to form the ground weave.[1]

Fabrics similar to cannelle include cannetille and woven rib fabrics.

See also EXTRA WARP AND EXTRA WEFT FABRICS, REPP, SILK FABRIC.

End uses: curtains and furnishing fabrics.

cannetille
(fancy repp weave)

Canton

CANNETILLE A woven 'repp' fabric (that is, a fabric in which horizontal ribs are alternated with flat sections of ground weave) traditionally made from cotton. It is a further variant of the classic cannelle simpleté.

Cannetille may be woven in the traditional cotton or in other fibres. Like cannelle simpleté, it is made with two warps: a ground warp and a supplementary pattern warp. The fabric is woven with alternate ends under very low and very high tension: the supplementary pattern warp is slackly tensioned and the ground warp is tightly tensioned. The slack ends of the supplementary pattern warp float over eight picks of the ground weave to form the rib effect.[25, 36] The supplementary pattern warp may also be floated in small alternating blocks over the ground fabric to form a pattern of small ribbed checks. Each group of floating ends is bound at intervals with the ground weave.[1] Fabrics similar to cannetille include cannelle and woven rib fabrics.

See also EXTRA WARP AND EXTRA WEFT FABRICS, REPP.

End uses: curtains, furnishing fabrics, women's suiting fabrics and coats.

CANTON (Canton flannel) Traditionally a strong, woven, all-cotton fabric; it is also made in other qualities, including a wool fabric and a cotton/wool union fabric. The name refers to Canton in China, where it was originally made.[3] It was also made in Britain and exported to Canton.[36]

Traditional Canton is a strong, medium- to heavyweight woven fabric made from cotton or a cotton blend. It is woven in a warp-faced twill weave that is apparent on the face of the fabric. It is made in two main qualities: a heavier-weight fabric, woven in 2/2 twill, and a lighter-weight fabric, woven in 2/1 twill. The weft yarns are thicker than the warp yarns and are made from soft, loosely spun, carded cotton. After weaving, the weft yarns on the back of the fabric are raised (brushed) to produce a long, soft, heavy nap on one side, similar to a flannel fabric. The fabric is produced as grey cloth and it may be unbleached, bleached, dyed (usually bright colours) or printed.[36] Characteristically, cotton Canton flannel is a soft, warm, strong and absorbent fabric. It is similar to swansdown, flannelette and winceyette.

Other fabrics called 'Canton' are also made, including a wool version made from botany wool yarns in both warp and weft, and a union fabric made with a cotton warp and a botany wool weft. These fabrics are both woven in plain weave.[26] An example of a plain weave Canton fabric construction is 12 tex combed cotton warp sett at 26 ends per cm and 15 tex botany weft woven at 30 to 36 picks per cm.[26]

See also COTTON FABRIC, NAPPED FABRICS, TWILL FABRICS, UNION FABRIC.

End uses: (cotton Canton) linings, interlinings, pockets, work gloves, baby clothes, nightgowns and pyjamas; (wool Canton) dresses, suits and blouses.

CANTON CRÊPE A lightweight, woven crêpe fabric with a distinctive rough, crinkled appearance.

Canton crêpe was originally an all-silk fabric from Canton in China. Nowadays it is woven with coarse yarns of silk, viscose or polyester. The fabric is woven in plain weave using warp yarns that are finer than the weft yarns. The crêpe effect is produced by the use of high-twist crêpe yarns either in the weft only, or in both the warp and the weft. 'S' and 'Z' crêpe-twist yarns are alternated in groups of two, four or six. Canton crêpe may therefore be produced as a half crêpe or a full crêpe fabric. It is often made in white, or it may be piece-dyed. It is durable and has good washability. Canton crêpe is similar to crêpe de chine but slightly heavier.

See also CRÊPE.

End uses: dresses, suits and blouses.

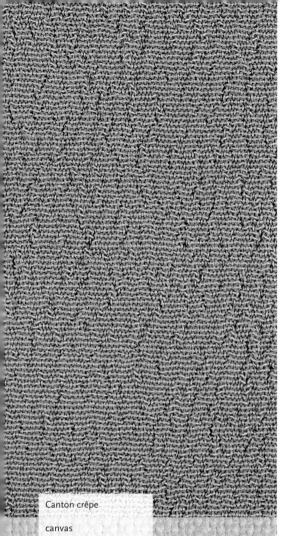

Canton crêpe

canvas

CANTOON A heavy, weft-faced woven fabric made from cotton. It has a distinct diagonal cord effect on the face of the fabric, whereas the back remains smooth.

Cantoon is woven in irregular, 'reclining' twill weaves, which have a much larger number of weft picks per centimetre than warp ends. The weft yarns that form the twill diagonals therefore run at a low angle in the fabric. After weaving, the back of the fabric is given a slight nap finish. The name derives from Canton in China. Cantoon belongs to the group of fabrics known as 'fustians'.

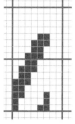

cantoon

See also NAPPED FABRICS, TWILL FABRICS.

End uses: riding breeches and sports clothing.

CANVAS A term used for a wide range of strong, durable, cotton-type fabrics. These are firm, heavy fabrics, closely woven in plain weave or plain weave variations. Canvas is very similar to duck, and the terms are sometimes used interchangeably, but canvas is generally a smoother and more tightly woven fabric than duck, which is usually slightly heavier and rougher.

Although unbleached, carded cotton or linen yarns are mainly used to make traditional canvas fabrics, hemp, jute, nylon, polyester and blends are also sometimes employed. The fabric is woven in plain weave or double-end plain weave (hopsack). The warp ends are densely sett and outnumber the weft picks per centimetre. Canvas is therefore a warp-faced fabric in which the warp yarns have a high degree of crimp around more or less straight weft yarns. The name derives from 'cannabis', the Latin word for hemp, from which canvas-type fabrics for tents and sails were originally made.[3]

When the fabric becomes wet, the fibres typically swell, filling any gaps in the construction and making the fabric naturally resistant to water. This effect can be increased by treating it with wax or resin-based finishes. Other finishes vary according to the end use, ranging from heavy sizing to a soft finish. Traditional tarpaulin fabric is produced by treating a canvas fabric with tar or oil, although many tarpaulins today are also made with nylon or other man-made fibres.[23]

Canvas is produced in a wide variety of different weights according to end use, traditionally ranging from 200 to 2,000 g/m².[25] Some examples of different qualities follow. Artist's canvas is a cotton or linen canvas that is stretched onto wooden frames and treated with white primer for painting. Awning stripes is a canvas or duck fabric that is either colour-woven or printed with stripes (*see* AWNING CLOTH). Embroidery canvas comes in many types, such as Berlin canvas, Hardanger, Java (aida, bincarette), panama and Penelope canvas; they are all open-mesh canvas fabrics made from hard-twisted yarns[3] (*see also* EMBROIDERED FABRICS). Lock thread canvas is an open-mesh canvas woven in a leno or mock leno weave construction and used for embroidery. Hair canvas is a firm, stiff canvas fabric woven with a wool, cotton or viscose warp and a mohair or horsehair weft; it is often grey and is used as interfacing for the collars and lapels of tailored suits and coats. Tailor's canvas, used for the same purposes, is a firm, stiff linen canvas, often beige or dark brown in colour; it is cut on the cross and does not fray, and may be 'sewn in' or 'ironed on'. Fabrics similar to canvas include book cloth, duck, Holland, hopsack and sailcloth.

See also COATING FABRIC, COTTON FABRIC, HOPSACK, PLAIN WEAVE FABRIC, WATERPROOF AND WATER-REPELLENT FABRICS.

End uses: tents, sails, tarpaulins, awnings, blinds, curtains, deckchairs, directors' chairs, garden furniture, shoes, luggage, bags, workwear, sportswear, coats, jackets, embroidery canvas, artist's canvas, interlining and lining fabrics.

canvas (plain weave variation)

carbon-fibre textile (woven)

cardigan rib (full cardigan, face and back)

cardigan rib (half cardigan, face and back)

CARBON-FIBRE TEXTILES (carbon cloth) Textiles made from carbon fibres. They can be produced in woven, knitted and nonwoven form, and are characteristically very strong, lightweight textiles, suitable for many industrial uses. Graphite is one kind of carbon fibre, and the terms 'graphite fibre' and 'carbon fibre' are sometimes used interchangeably. Carbon in granular or powder form can also be incorporated into textiles to produce carbon cloth or charcoal cloth.

Carbon fibres have similar end uses to glass and aramid fibres. They are particularly strong and are widely used to reinforce all kinds of structures, such as buildings, bridges, tennis racquets, skis and bicycles. Characteristically, carbon fibres and particles do not burn or ignite, and they are highly efficient at adsorbing a wide range of gases, vapours, odours and solvents. They are therefore used to make lightweight, strong textiles for many different industrial and military uses. Their anti-static properties make them a useful component in carpets and they are also the base unit for all kinds of nanomaterials[6] (*see* NANOMATERIALS). Carbon and other fibres can be blended to make epitropic fibres, which conduct electricity and can be used to make products such as static-resistant carpeting.[6]

See also ARAMID FABRIC, CARPET, FLAME-RESISTANT TEXTILES, GLASS-FIBRE TEXTILES, NANOMATERIALS.

End uses: static-resistant carpeting; industrial textiles; water filtration and purification; filters; and nanomaterials, including wound dressings, bandages and protective clothing for industrial and military purposes (including protection against chemical warfare).

CARDIGAN RIB A weft-knitted fabric based on a 1 × 1 rib structure. There are two kinds: full cardigan (polka rib) and half cardigan (royal rib). They can be made with knitting yarns made from any fibre.

Full cardigan, also known as 'polka rib', is knitted on two needle-beds. The knit structure repeats over two courses. In the first course, all the needles on one bed knit and all those on the other bed tuck. The second course is the same but on reverse needle-beds.

Half cardigan, or royal rib, is also knitted on two needle-beds. One side of the fabric consists entirely of knitted loops. The other side is composed of alternating wales of all knitted loops and all tuck loops. The knit structure repeats over two courses. In the first course, all the needles on one bed knit and all those on the other bed tuck. In the second course, all the needles on both needle-beds knit.[25, 38]

See also KNITTED FABRIC; RIB FABRICS, KNITTED; WEFT-KNITTED FABRIC.

End uses: general knitwear.

CARMELITE CLOTH (*obs.*) A loosely constructed, plain woven woollen fabric that was heavily fulled and used for habits by the nuns of the Carmelite order of the Roman Catholic church.[9]

CARPET A heavyweight textile floor covering that is strong and durable; it either has a surface composed of a fibre web (nonwoven carpet), or is a pile fabric that has been tufted or woven.

The pile yarns for carpets may be of wool, wool/nylon or manufactured fibres; some very luxurious carpets and rugs are even made with silk yarns. Carpets may be produced by hand-knotting, tufting or weaving, or they may be nonwoven.

Nonwoven carpets are formed directly from fibres that are laid in a loose web and then bonded or interlocked together, usually by the mechanical process known as

carpet (Axminster)

carpet (tufted, back and face)

carpet (Wilton, face and back)

'needle-punching' (*see* NONWOVEN FABRIC). Nonwoven carpets are less durable than those produced by other methods, but they are usually cheaper.

Originally all pile carpets were produced by knotting lengths of yarn very densely into a warp by hand. Some very elaborately patterned carpets are still produced by this method today. However, the vast majority of carpets are now produced by machine and most are tufted carpets, as this is currently the cheapest production method.

Tufted carpets are pile fabrics that are made on tufting machines by inserting the pile yarns with needles into a primary backing fabric. A secondary backing fabric, such as hessian or foam, is then bonded or laminated onto the back of this to secure the tufts more firmly. Tufting is a cheaper method of producing a pile carpet than weaving, as it is extremely quick and less labour-intensive. However, the tufts may not always be as firmly secured in the base fabric as in woven carpets. *See also* HESSIAN, LAMINATED FABRIC, MULTI-COMPONENT FABRICS, TUFTED FABRIC.

Woven carpets are generally more hard-wearing than tufted carpets, with the pile yarns being more securely anchored into the backing fabric. There are two main types of woven carpet, Wilton and Axminster, which are named after the two West Country towns in England where the fabrics were originally made. Wilton is a warp pile carpet and is woven with the warp pile yarns fed continuously into the structure as it is woven, so that they form an integral part of the fabric. There are three warps: one to form the pile, and two, known as the 'stuffer' and 'chain' warps, to form the ground structure. The stuffer warp, which is usually jute, lies straight under the pile warp and in the centre of the chain warp, which is usually cotton. The structure of the ground prevents the pile warp from appearing on the back, which minimizes abrasion in use. To make the pile, the pile warp yarns are lifted over wires or hooks at regular intervals during weaving. When the wires are removed, a mass of loops is formed on the surface of the fabric. This produces a loop pile fabric. Cut pile Wilton carpet is made in a similar manner, but the wires have blades attached to them. When the wires are removed after weaving, the blades cut the pile loops and the cut pile is formed. Cut pile carpets may also be made on the 'face-to-face principle', like some velvet fabrics. In this method, two carpet fabrics are woven face to face simultaneously. The warp pile ends are interchanged between both base fabrics and the connecting yarns are cut in the middle while the fabric is still on the loom, producing two separate carpets.[25]

Axminster carpets are made by inserting successive weft-wise rows of cut pile during weaving in a pre-arranged colour sequence. As with Wilton carpets, a stuffer warp and a chain warp form the ground structure. The pile yarns may be inserted by gripper or spool. In 'gripper' Axminster carpets, tufts of yarn are inserted at the point of weaving by grippers, which are fed the appropriate colours by jacquard-operated carriers before the tufts are severed. In 'spool' Axminster carpets, the yarn for each weft-wise row is wound onto separate spools. Unlimited colours may therefore be used in the design. The tufts are severed at the point of weaving after insertion into the base fabric. With both methods, the tufts of yarn are firmly interwoven and anchored into the base fabric.[25] Both Wilton and Axminster carpets may be produced in a single colour or in multiple colours, or they may be woven on a jacquard loom and have fancy figured designs. Different pattern effects may also be obtained in the pile surface of carpets. *See also* FIGURED FABRIC, PILE FABRICS.

'Berber' is a term that was originally used to describe hand-woven carpets produced in Africa using wool in natural colours from the local breeds of sheep. More recently the use of the term has been extended to include manufactured carpets woven with natural-coloured wools or dyed wools that have a homespun appearance.[25]

See also CARBON-FIBRE TEXTILES, HESSIAN, KILIM, LAMINATED FABRIC, MULTI-COMPONENT FABRICS, TUFTED FABRIC.

End uses: floor coverings, including wide-width carpets, stair carpets and rugs; also hangings, bags and luggage.

casement cloth

cassimere

cashmere cloth (100%, woven)

cashmere cloth (blended, woven)

CASEMENT CLOTH A general term for a variety of fine woven fabrics that may be used as window coverings, curtains or blinds. (A casement is a hinged window or part of a window.) Casement cloths are woven in weights ranging from light to heavy, although most are fine to medium. They are usually soft and opaque, with good drape, and white or cream in colour.

Originally casement cloth was woven as a natural cotton grey cloth fabric, but nowadays, although white and cream are the most common, it may also be woven in any colour and from any fibre. Casements are usually plain weave fabrics and they are often weft-faced. The finer casements are woven with one end per dent. Cotton casements may be given a mercerized finish.[36] Similar fabrics to casement cloth include limbric and Wigan.

See also PLAIN WEAVE FABRIC.

End uses: window coverings, curtains and blinds.

CASHA *see* KASHA.

CASHMERE CLOTH (cashmere fabric) A general term for any fabric constructed with cashmere yarn or fibre. Cashmere is a natural animal fibre from the undercoat of a range of different Asiatic goat breeds, including *Capra hircus laniger*.[25] It is classed as a speciality hair fibre.

Most cashmere is produced in China; however, hair with a similar average diameter from other breeds of goat selectively bred in Australia, New Zealand and Scotland may also be regarded as cashmere.[25] Cashmere cloth is known for its extreme softness, and it is luxurious and expensive when made from 100% cashmere fibre. However, such fabrics are rare. Since it is such an expensive fibre, slightly cheaper, more durable fabrics may be made by mixing other fibres with the cashmere. Cashmere is therefore usually blended with wool or worsted yarns; botany wool is the most frequently used. Sometimes silk is also included to increase lustre, and sometimes a small percentage of nylon is added for extra strength. The percentages of each fibre should always be stated for these blends.

Cashmere cloth may be woven or knitted. Woven cashmere cloth is usually constructed in a simple plain or twill weave and given a nap finish, which produces a smooth, soft handle and an appearance similar to that of flannel. Most woven cashmere fabrics are used as coating or suiting fabrics. They are usually medium to heavy in weight, and characteristically soft, warm and lustrous. Montagnac is a coating fabric sometimes woven from cashmere, while pashmina is a very fine, soft woven cashmere cloth used for scarves and shawls. Coburg and Henrietta are less expensive fabrics that are woven in imitation of cashmere cloth.

Knitted cashmere cloth may be weft-knitted on knitting machines or, as the yarns are so soft and hairy, hand-knitted. Simple structures such as plain knit are normally used to accentuate the soft, hairy fibres.

See also COATING FABRIC, HAIR FABRICS, KASHA, MONTAGNAC, NAPPED FABRICS, PASHMINA, SUITING FABRICS, WEDDING RING FABRICS.

End uses: (woven cashmere cloth) overcoats, and also, in lighter weights, suits, dresses, shawls and scarves; (knitted cashmere cloth) cardigans, jackets, coats, jumpers, shawls and scarves.

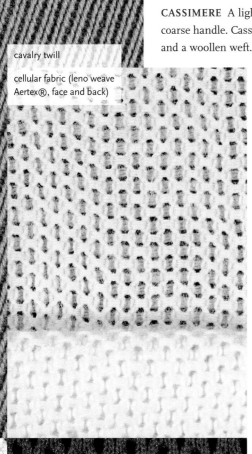

cavalry twill

cellular fabric (leno weave Aertex®, face and back)

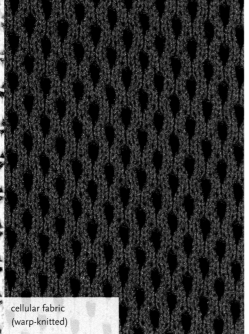

cellular fabric (warp-knitted)

cellular fabric (woven)

CASSIMERE A light- to medium-weight woven fabric made from wool, with a slightly coarse handle. Cassimere is woven in a closely sett 2/2 twill weave with a worsted warp and a woollen weft. The yarns are tightly twisted, and after weaving the fabric is fulled and sheared to give a smooth surface and a slight lustre to the face. Cassimere is a slightly coarser version of a serge fabric. Lightweight kersey fabrics are similar, and are sometimes called 'kerseymere' to indicate the similarity (*see* KERSEY).

See also SERGE, TWILL FABRICS.

End uses: men's suits and trousers.

CAVALRY TWILL A strong, hard-wearing fabric with steep, pronounced double twill lines running from bottom left to top right (twill right). The fabric was originally used for riding breeches for the cavalry, hence the name, but it has many other end uses as well. The term is also now used more generally for any fabric with steep double twill lines.

Traditionally cavalry twill was a medium- to heavyweight fabric made from woollen or worsted yarns. Nowadays it may also be made from cotton, viscose or other man-made fibres. Whichever fibre is used, the yarns have a very high twist that accentuates the diagonal cords on the face side of the fabric. Cavalry twill is firmly woven in a fancy twill weave structure with closely sett warp yarns to produce a warp-faced fabric. The steep, double twill diagonals are formed by the warp yarns and are separated by deep grooves filled with weft yarns. A smooth, hard surface is produced during finishing. Cavalry twill is also known as 'elastique' or 'tricotine' in the United States.[3] It is similar to covert cloth, gaberdine and whipcord.

See also COATING FABRIC, TWILL FABRICS.

End uses: riding breeches, trousers, coats, raincoats, suits, jackets, sportswear and uniforms.

CELLULAR FABRIC A general term for a range of usually light- to mid-weight fabrics that have a regular cell-like construction and small perforations in-between. The construction allows air to pass through the fabric, making it cool and comfortable to wear next to the skin.

Cellular fabrics may be made in various woven or knitted constructions, although the term tends to be used more for woven fabrics, while similar knitted fabrics are more likely to be described as 'mesh fabrics'. Woven cellular fabrics are usually constructed in leno, mock leno or honeycomb weaves. Yarns typically used include cotton, polyester and polyester/cotton mixes, which give clear definition to the cellular structure. The fabric is usually given a soft finish. Aertex® is the well-known brand name of a cellular fabric used for casual wear, underwear and sports clothing.

See also HONEYCOMB; JAVA; LENO FABRIC; MESH FABRICS; MOCK LENO; PIQUÉ, WARP-KNITTED; PIQUÉ, WEFT-KNITTED.

End uses: sports shirts, T-shirts, casual shirts, school clothing, blouses, underwear and furnishing fabrics.

challis

chambray

chamois cloth (nonwoven)

CEYLON (*obs.*) A colour-woven stripe or solid colour fabric woven with a cotton warp and a wool mixture weft, used for plain woven shirtings.[36]

CHALK STRIPE *see* pin stripe.

CHALLIS A soft, light, dress-weight fabric woven in a slightly open-sett plain weave. It is a particularly fine, high-quality fabric, noted for its softness and drape. When woven in wool, it is the finest type of delaine fabric. Wool challis is the softest and finest of all wool sheer fabrics.

Characteristically, challis is woven in plain weave using very fine yarns and it frays easily. It was first produced in the 1830s in Norwich, England, from silk and worsted wool yarns.[5] Nowadays it is found in a variety of qualities. The classic quality is made from worsted wool using singles worsted spun yarns in both the warp and the weft. Other qualities are made in: fine 100% wool; 80% wool/20% silk; wool/polyester; wool/nylon; 100% cotton; and various man-made fibres. Challis is given a soft nap finish. It may be undyed, dyed solid colours or printed, often with small floral designs or Paisley prints. For men's neckties, wool challis is normally printed, often with 'country-style' motifs such as horse heads and game birds. A typical challis construction is 24 tex worsted warp sett at 22 ends per cm and 24 tex worsted weft woven at 22 picks per cm.[26]

The term 'challis' comes from the Anglo-Indian word 'shalee' meaning 'soft to the touch'.[3] Before this name came into general use, a very similar fabric, which was slightly lighter in weight and called 'nun's veiling' or 'convent cloth', was produced specifically for religious gowns and mourning garments,[5] being dyed black, brown or grey. The French term for challis is 'étamine glacé'[3] (*see* ÉTAMINE). Challis is a similar fabric to worsted wool voile.

See also DELAINE, PLAIN WEAVE FABRIC, SHEER FABRICS.

End uses: dresses, blouses, shirts, men's neckties and scarves.

CHAMBORD (*obs.*) A rib woven dress fabric of wool, silk and cotton, used in France for mourning clothes.[9]

CHAMBRAY A light- to medium-weight plain weave fabric that has a coloured warp and a white weft. This use of colour gives the fabric its characteristic mottled appearance. Sometimes it has additional stripes or checks and in this form it may be called 'chambray gingham'.

Chambray is traditionally an all-cotton fabric, but synthetic yarns and cotton blends are also sometimes used. Some finer chambrays are made with a cotton warp and a silk weft. The fabric is usually woven in a fairly balanced plain weave. It is a durable, easy-care fabric. Iridescent chambray is also sometimes produced with one colour in the warp and a second colour in the weft. Chambray takes its name from the town of Cambrai in the north of France, where the fabric originated.[3] It is very similar to a soft-finished cambric fabric.[36]

See also COTTON FABRIC, OXFORD, PLAIN WEAVE FABRIC, SHIRTING FABRICS.

End uses: pyjamas, children's clothes, shirts, blouses, dresses, lightweight trousers, aprons, overalls and curtains.

CHAMELEON FABRIC An iridescent fabric in which the colour changes as the fabric moves and catches the light . This effect may be produced in any quality and in any type of fabric, either woven or knitted. The term therefore refers more to the type of effect than a particular kind of fabric. Perhaps the best-known chameleon fabric is chameleon taffeta.

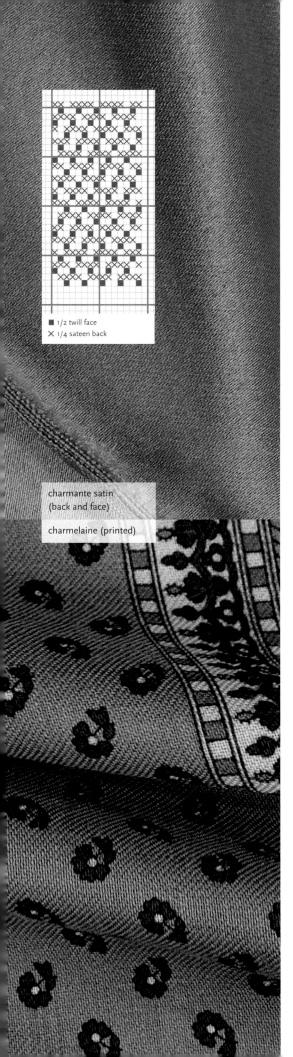

■ 1/2 twill face
X 1/4 sateen back

charmante satin
(back and face)

charmelaine (printed)

The term 'chameleon' comes from the chameleon lizard, noted for its ability to change colour. The colour effect is produced by weaving three different contrasting colours together, one in the warp and two in the weft, which are woven together in the same shed. This gives a three-colour 'shot' effect, which is a variation of the two-colour shot effect produced in shot fabrics. Silk or man-made fibre filament yarns accentuate this effect more than staple fibre yarns, and simple weave structures like plain weave are usually the most effective.

See also DYED FABRICS, SHOT FABRICS, TAFFETA.

End uses: dresses, evening dresses, women's suits, blouses, trimmings, lingerie, theatrical costumes, hats, bags, curtains and upholstery.

CHAMOIS CLOTH (shammy cloth) A woven, knitted or nonwoven fabric made to imitate chamois leather. Chamois leather is the skin of the chamois, a species of antelope, and is naturally a very soft material, more similar to suede than most leather (*see* LEATHER). Chamois cloth is usually a woven cotton fabric that is given a fine, soft nap in the finishing process and cropped close to the fabric surface to produce a fine, soft surface texture similar to that of chamois leather. Chamois cloth is a type of suede cloth.

See also LEATHER, NAPPED FABRICS, SUEDE, SUEDE CLOTH.

End uses: polishing cloths and dusters, coat and jacket linings.

CHAMOIS LEATHER *see* LEATHER.

CHANGEANT *see* SHOT FABRICS.

CHARCOAL CLOTH *see* CARBON-FIBRE TEXTILES.

CHARMANTE SATIN A woven fabric that was traditionally made from silk and woven in a variation of the satin weave structure. This produces a thicker, stronger and more durable fabric than most other satin fabrics.

Although it was originally an all-silk fabric, charmante satin is more likely nowadays to be woven with man-made fibres. Charmante satin is a double-wefted satin fabric in which two sets of weft yarns are interlaced with the warp yarns. Traditionally the warp is made from high-twist net silk yarns. The face of the fabric is woven in a 1/2 twill with lower-twist silk yarns, and the fabric is backed with extra weft silk yarns that have hardly any twist. The extra weft backing yarns alternate with the face picks and are interwoven in a sateen weave structure. The binding points of the backing weft are invisible on the face.

See also EXTRA WARP AND EXTRA WEFT FABRICS; SATIN, WOVEN; SILK FABRICS.

End uses: dresses, ladies' suits and jackets.

CHARMELAINE A soft worsted wool fabric woven in twill weave, with a lustrous textured face and a matt back. It has good drape.

Charmelaine is woven in a 1/2 twill weave using botany wool in both the warp and the weft. The fine, two-fold yarns in the warp are highly sett and the thicker, low sett weft yarns are hard-twisted. This gives a ribbed effect to the twill lines. In finishing, the face of the fabric is sheared and pressed to form a lustrous surface. Charmelaine is usually produced in light colours. The name is French for 'charming wool fabric'.

See also TWILL FABRICS, WOOL FABRIC.

End uses: dresses, scarves and women's outerwear.

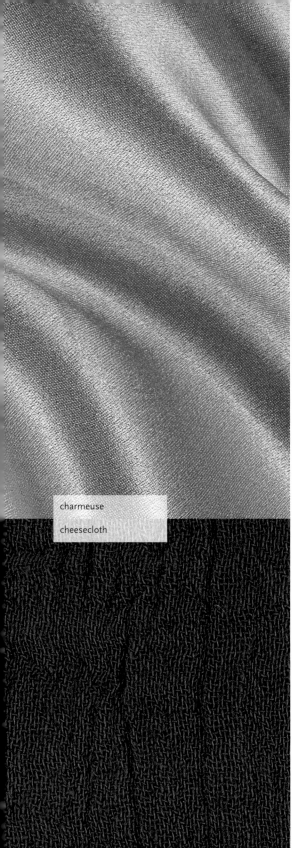

charmeuse

cheesecloth

CHARMEUSE A soft, lightweight crêpe fabric woven in a satin weave structure. It has a smooth, semi-lustrous face and a matt crêpe back, and is known for its soft lustre, excellent drape and slightly clinging quality. The name is French for 'charming fabric'. Charmeuse is sometimes also called 'crêpe charmeuse'.

Charmeuse is traditionally woven with grenadine silk in both the warp and the weft. Grenadine silk is a thrown silk yarn similar to organzine but with a higher twist. Nowadays, however, charmeuse may be woven in any fibre or mixture of fibres, including cotton, viscose, polyester and other man-made fibres. It is woven in satin weave with hard-twisted yarns in the warp and high-twist crêpe yarns in the weft. This produces a soft-lustre satin face and a dull crêpe back. Charmeuse may therefore be termed a 'half crêpe' fabric. It may be produced in solid colours or printed. It is usually not very hard-wearing and frays and creases easily. Some warp-knitted locknit fabrics are knitted in imitation of woven charmeuse. In Europe, warp-knitted locknit is sometimes termed 'charmeuse'.

See also CRÊPE; LOCKNIT; SATIN, WOVEN; SILK FABRIC.

End uses: evening wear, dresses, blouses, lingerie, nightwear and linings.

CHECKS Fabrics with a characteristic pattern of squares, rectangles or lines crossing at right angles to one another. Checks may be woven or knitted into a fabric or printed onto the surface of a fabric.

When constructed in a fabric, checks may be created in several different ways that may be used singly or in combination.
(i) *Colour effects.* Two or more contrasting colours in the warp and weft directions form the check pattern.
(ii) *Contrasting yarns.* Different yarns in the warp and weft directions form textural check patterns. Fancy yarns or different yarn counts may be used.
(iii) *Structural effects.* Fabric structural effects in the warp and weft directions form textural check patterns.

Many check fabrics also have an 'overcheck', or a secondary check design over the top of a ground check. The overcheck is usually in contrasting colours to the ground. Many tartan fabrics have this feature. A fabric with a fine outline check against a plain ground is usually called 'window-pane check'. 'Plaid' is a general term, used especially in the United States, for elaborate check patterns (*see* TARTAN). There is a great variety of classic check patterns. For the best-known check fabrics, *see* BUFFALO CHECK, BURBERRY CHECK®, CRANKY CHECKS, DICED WEAVES, DISTRICT CHECKS, DORIA STRIPES, FOUR-POINTED STAR CHECK, GINGHAM, GLEN URQUHART CHECK, GUARDS CHECK, GUN-CLUB CHECK, HARVARD SHIRTINGS, HORSE-BLANKET CHECK, HOUNDSTOOTH CHECK, HUCKABACK, MADRAS, PINHEAD CHECK, PRINCE OF WALES CHECK, PYJAMA FABRIC, SHADOW STRIPES AND CHECKS, SHEPHERD'S CHECK, SHIRTING FABRICS, TARTAN, TATTERSALL CHECK, ZANZIBAR, ZEPHYR.

See also COLOUR AND WEAVE EFFECTS, CRANKY CHECKS.

End uses: all kinds of fashion and furnishing fabrics.

CHEESECLOTH A soft, lightweight, semi-sheer fabric woven in an open-sett plain weave structure, usually with carded cotton yarns. It has a characteristic wrinkled appearance and belongs to the muslin family of fabrics.

Cheesecloth is an inexpensive, rough fabric that was named after its principal use, as a soft cloth for wrapping cheese. In this form, it is also used for cleaning cloths or as a lining fabric. Sometimes it is used for packing tobacco leaf, but in this case is more likely to be called 'tobacco cloth'. Cheesecloth is usually woven as grey cloth, but it may also be bleached, dyed, printed or colour-woven with stripes or checks. It is usually given

checks (overcheck)

checks

checks

checks (window pane)

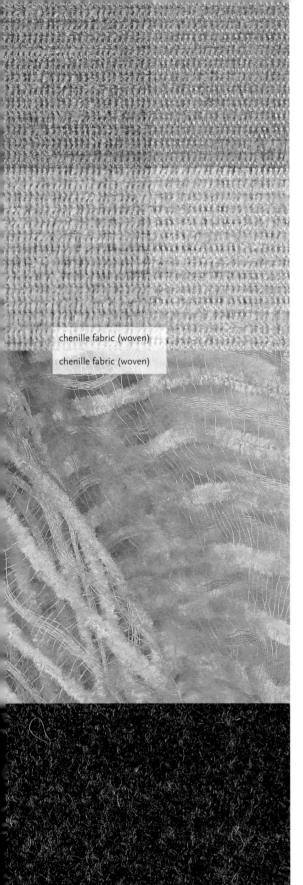

chenille fabric (woven)

chenille fabric (woven)

Cheviot

a rough finish and sometimes it is heavily sized and stiffened for end uses such as inter-linings. When used for fashion fabrics, it may be slightly more closely sett and woven with slightly better-quality yarns, although it still retains its wrinkled appearance. Cheese-cloth is similar to bolting cloth, book muslin, buckram, bunting, butter muslin, crinoline, étamine, gauze, mull, scrim and tarlatan. Buckram and crinoline may be made from cheesecloth fabric by stiffening it with size or resin. Scrim is also either a cheesecloth or a cheesecloth-like fabric that has been given a stiffening finish.

See also MUSLIN, PLAIN WEAVE FABRIC.

End uses: blouses, shirts, skirts, dresses, nightwear, curtains, interlinings, cleaning cloths, surgical bandages and coverings.

CHENILLE FABRIC A soft, bulky woven or knitted fabric that contains chenille yarn, usually in the weft. It is recognizable from the short tufts of fibre standing proud of the surface on one or both sides of the fabric.

Chenille yarn is a fancy yarn that has small tufts of fibre protruding all around its central core, so that it resembles a caterpillar (*chenille* is the French word for caterpillar). When chenille yarn is woven or knitted into a fabric, it forms a soft fibrous surface on one or both sides according to the fabric construction used. Chenille yarns may be made from any fibres, including cotton, silk, viscose, wool, man-made fibres or mixtures. They are traditionally used in many furnishing fabrics or as decorative yarns in many other textiles. Chenille fabric does not crease, but it frays easily and is subject to seam slippage, and lint may be shed from the pile during use. It is a similar fabric to candlewick. Visu-ally, it is also similar to some velour, velvet and velveteen fabrics.

See also COATING FABRIC.

End uses: curtains, upholstery, cushion covers, bedspreads, rugs, towels, bathmats, bathrobes, casual wear, sweaters, dresses, jackets and coats.

CHEVIOT A medium- to heavyweight tweed fabric that is traditionally woven using Cheviot wool. It is a coarse, rough, fibrous-surfaced fabric that is very warm and hard-wearing.

Cheviot wool is wool from the Cheviot breed of sheep, which originated in the Cheviot Hills in the Scottish Borders region of Great Britain. The classic Cheviot fabric is woven using Cheviot wool. It is normally woven with woollen-spun yarns, but finer, more expensive Cheviot fabrics are woven with worsted yarns. Imitation Cheviot fabrics are also made, using wools of a similar quality. Similar cross-bred worsted yarns may be used instead of worsted wool, and sometimes man-made fibres are included, but the char-acteristic rough, uneven surface of the fabric is retained. Since the yarns used in Cheviots are finer than those used in most other tweed fabrics, Cheviot is one of the finest qual-ity tweed fabrics.

Cheviot fabric is usually woven in plain or twill weave, or occasionally in a her-ringbone. It may be woven in plain colours, or colour-woven to produce fancy patterns, including stripes and checks. It is usually fulled and napped in finishing, which produces a fairly clean surface and clearly shows the weave structure. If used for overcoatings, it may be heavily milled to produce a firm, compact fabric in which the weave structure is less clearly seen. Cheviot is a similar fabric to fearnought.

See also COATING FABRIC, NAPPED FABRICS, TWEED, WOOL FABRIC.

End uses: men's casual suits and jackets, sports jackets and overcoats.

CHICKEN'S-FOOT CHECK *see* FOUR-POINTED STAR CHECK.

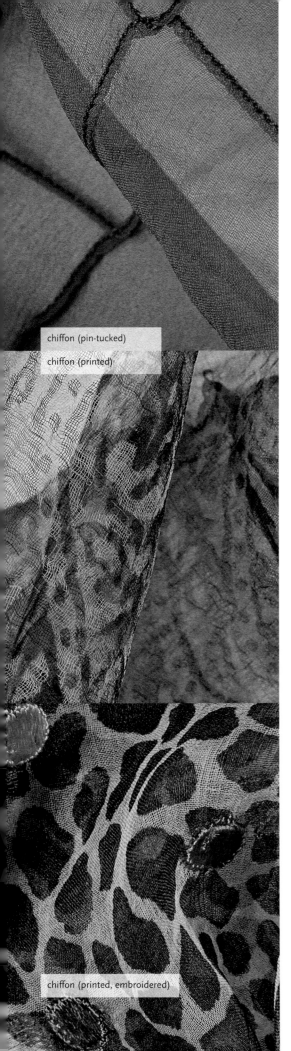

chiffon (pin-tucked)

chiffon (printed)

chiffon (printed, embroidered)

CHIFFON A soft, flimsy, transparent sheer fabric woven in plain weave. It is probably the finest and most lightweight of all woven fabrics, but although delicate, it is still relatively strong. It has excellent handle and drape.

Originally chiffon was always woven in silk, but nowadays it may be woven in nylon, viscose, cotton, polyester or wool. Silk chiffon, however, is the softest. In its classic form, it is woven in a balanced plain weave with singles yarns made from highly twisted continuous filament fibres in both the warp and the weft. If the yarns are very highly twisted, a crêpe chiffon with a characteristic crinkled appearance will be produced. Chiffon is usually found in plain colours, but occasionally it is decorated with satin stripes or spots, printed, or embroidered with cotton, viscose or metal threads. It is usually given a soft finish but for some end uses is stiffened with size. As it is such a fine, light fabric, chiffon is difficult to sew, frays easily and is prone to seam slippage. *Chiffon* is a French word meaning 'rag' or 'wisp', an apt description of this limsy fabric.[9] Silk chiffon is similar to silk mousseline (mousseline de soie) and ninon, but lighter; it is smoother and more lustrous than georgette. The term 'chiffon' is also frequently used to describe the most lightweight versions of many other fabrics (e.g. chiffon batiste, chiffon crêpe, chiffon net, chiffon taffeta, chiffon velour and chiffon velvet).

See also CRÊPE, EMBROIDERED FABRICS, PLAIN WEAVE FABRIC, SHEER FABRICS, SILK FABRIC.

End uses: lingerie, nightwear, scarves, blouses, dresses, bridal wear and evening wear.

CHINA SILK A very fine, lightweight lustrous fabric woven in plain weave from raw silk yarns. It is recognizable from its soft surface texture caused by the slight imperfections in the yarn. It is often used as a lining fabric.

China silk was originally hand-woven in China from fine, raw silk yarns as long ago as 1200 BC, hence the name.[9] Nowadays it is woven in various countries from raw silk yarns and it is usually slightly heavier than the original hand-woven fabrics. Low-twist yarns are used for softness, and the fabric is woven in a balanced plain weave. Imitations of the fabric are also made using man-made fibre yarns. China silk is a similar fabric to habotai but is slightly lighter in weight. It is also similar to jappe (or jappe silk).

See also LINING FABRIC, PLAIN WEAVE FABRIC, SILK FABRIC.

End uses: scarves, women's dress and suit linings, dresses, blouses, soft suits and lingerie.

CHINCHILLA FABRIC A thick, soft, spongy fabric made from wool with a curly textured surface; it may be woven or knitted. In its woven form it is one of the warmest and most durable coating fabrics.

When woven, chinchilla fabric is usually a tightly woven, weft pile, double cloth fabric. It is woven in twill weave with a cotton warp and a woollen weft. Extra weft yarns made from softly twisted wool are woven as long floats on the surface of the fabric. These floats are teazled during finishing to produce a long nap, which is then rubbed to form curly nubs on the face of the fabric. Knitted chinchilla fabric is knitted in wool and given a nap finish. Chinchilla fabric is usually piece-dyed in solid colours. It is a similar fabric visually to ratiné. It bears no resemblance to the fur of the chinchilla rodent found in Peru and Chile.

China silk

See also COATING FABRIC, DOUBLE CLOTH, EXTRA WARP AND EXTRA WEFT FABRICS, PILE FABRICS.

End uses: coats, uniforms and hats.

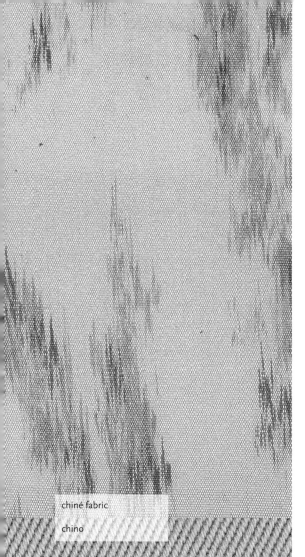

chiné fabric

chino

CHINÉ FABRICS Warp-patterned woven fabrics that have characteristic diffuse, shadowy motifs with feathered edges. They are costly, since the production method is complex and time-consuming and very expensive raw materials are frequently used.

The term 'chiné' comes from the French verb meaning 'to mottle'. Chiné fabrics were produced in Europe from about the 16th century onwards. At this time, the chiné effect was achieved by patterning groups of warp yarns prior to weaving, using various tie-dyeing and resist-dyeing techniques, similar to those used for producing ikat fabrics. The patterned warp yarns move slightly during the subsequent weaving process, producing a diffuse pattern with slightly blurred edges, which is also partially obscured by the weft yarns. As modern printing processes evolved, the patterns were often printed onto the warp yarns prior to weaving. Although these warp-printed fabrics are slightly different visually from true chiné fabrics, they are sometimes also called 'chiné'.[29] Chiné fabrics may be woven in any weave structure, although plain and satin weaves are the most frequently used as these accentuate the dyed pattern most effectively. Chiné fabrics are frequently woven in silk, although yarns made from any fibre may be used. Similar effects may also be produced in fabrics by space-dyeing.

See also DYED FABRICS, IKAT, RESIST-DYED FABRICS, SPACE-DYED FABRIC, TIE-DYED FABRIC, WARP-PRINTED FABRIC.

End uses: furnishing fabrics, ribbons, men's neckties, exclusive dresses, blouses and evening wear.

CHINO A firm, hard-wearing cotton fabric with a slight sheen. It is woven in a warp-faced twill weave and produced in different weights, from medium to heavy.

Chino is woven in a steep twill weave using two-fold, combed, mercerized cotton, or sometimes polyester/cotton yarns in both warp and weft. The close sett of the warp yarns makes it a very strong and durable fabric. Chino is usually either piece-dyed (often khaki) or white in colour.

See also COTTON FABRIC, TWILL FABRICS.

End uses: military uniforms, sportswear, work clothes and trousers.

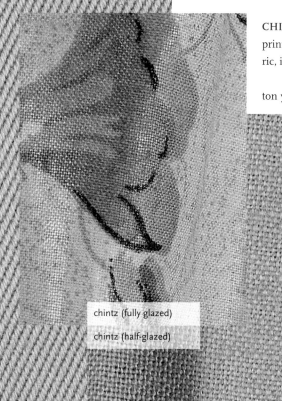

chintz (fully glazed)

chintz (half-glazed)

CHINTZ A highly lustrous plain woven cotton fabric that is usually printed and is given a glazed finish on the face side. This stiffens the fabric, increases its durability and ensures good drape.

The fabric is closely woven in plain weave using good-quality cotton yarns or occasionally polyester/cotton blends. The warp yarns are highly twisted and the weft yarns are slightly thicker with less twist. This produces a cotton fabric that is usually slightly lighter in weight than cretonne. Chintz is usually printed in bright colours, frequently with floral motifs or other large-scale patterns, but fabrics that have been piece-dyed one colour and highly glazed are also sometimes called 'chintz fabrics'.

The glaze finish makes the fabric thicker, stiffer and more durable, and produces a high lustre that is better able to resist soiling. There are different degrees of glaze finish. Semi-glazed or half-glazed chintz is finished by friction-calendering alone. This produces a subtle sheen on the fabric surface that is a semi-permanent finish and that will be lost with washing. Fully-glazed chintz is stiffened with starch or resin and then friction-calendered. This produces a more durable fabric with a high

ciré

clip spot

lustre. It is a more permanent finish that will not wash out easily; however, most chintz fabrics are generally dry-cleaned to protect the finish. Chintz may be made from the same grey cloth as calico, cretonne, percale and plissé, each fabric being given a different finish.[19]

The term 'chintz' is derived from the Sanskrit word *citra*, which evolved into *chit* or *chint* (singular) and *chintes* (plural) in Hindi and means 'coloured', 'spotted' or 'variegated'.[3] Hand-painted chintz fabrics were originally imported to Britain from India in the 17th century by the East India Company. They achieved huge popularity at this time and have been produced in the West ever since, first using block printing techniques and later screen printing.[28]

See also COTTON FABRIC, PRINT CLOTH, PRINTED FABRIC.

End uses: curtains, cushions, upholstery, loose covers and bedspreads.

CIRÉ A fabric given a high gloss by a ciré finishing process. Both knitted and woven fabrics may be given a ciré finish, also sometimes called a 'patent leather' or 'wet look' finish.

Silk and nylon woven fabrics are those most commonly given a ciré finish. The fabrics are coated with resin and friction-calendered with heat to produce the highly lustrous surface. This presses the fabric flat and closes up any gaps in the weave structure. The heat tends to melt thermoplastic fibres like nylon slightly, producing a smooth shiny surface and making the fabric water-repellent. Ciré fabrics are therefore often used as water-repellent fabrics. Ciré-finished nylon fabrics, for example, are lightweight plain weave fabrics, woven from filament nylon fibres and produced in bright colours; they are used for all kinds of items that protect against rain. Typical silk fabrics to be given a ciré finish include silk taffetas or satin fabrics woven with silk yarns. These fabrics may be dyed black or in metallic colours such as gold, steel and copper.[36] The term 'ciré' comes from the French word for 'waxed', since wax finishes were used prior to the development of resin finishes.

See also TAFFETA; SATIN, WOVEN; WATERPROOF AND WATER-REPELLENT FABRICS.

End uses: (ciré-finished nylon) anoraks, cagoules, raincoats, protective clothing, sportswear, tents, umbrellas and children's rainwear; (ciré-finished silk) hat and dress trimmings; (ciré-inished knitted fabrics) swimwear and lingerie.

CLIP SPOT A woven fabric in which extra warp and/or extra weft yarns are interwoven with the ground fabric, usually at regular intervals, to form a spotted or figured design on the surface. After weaving, the extra yarns floating between the motifs are cut away, sometimes leaving a small fringe around the edge of the motif. Many different qualities are made.

In extra warp clip spot fabrics, the motifs or figures are produced by the extra warp yarns along the fabric length. In extra weft clip spot fabrics, they are produced by the extra weft yarns across the fabric width. The two effects can also be combined. This method of producing woven motifs creates a much finer fabric overall than if the same pattern were produced as a conventional jacquard weave. It is therefore frequently used where a very fine pattern-woven fabric is required. Typical weave constructions are plain weave for the ground fabric (although twill or satin is also sometimes used) and satin or sateen weave for the motif. This gives a good contrast between the ground and patterned areas. The extra warp or extra weft yarns stand out from the ground weave due to the interlacings, but also because they are usually in a contrasting yarn count, colour, fibre type or lustre.

In some classic examples of clip spot fabrics, the background fabric is sheer and the clip spot areas are more dense. For example, Madras muslin and one type of dotted Swiss are woven as clip spot fabrics. Voile is also a suitable ground fabric for clip spot structures. Clip spot is a similar fabric to lancé, but the extra yarns floating between the motifs or figured patterns in clip spot fabrics are cut after weaving, whereas those in lancé

cloqué (knitted)

cloqué (woven)

coated fabric
(resin back-coated)

fabrics are not. Clip spot is also visually similar to broché, but the extra weft yarns in broché are continuously interwoven into the figured areas and bound around the edges. Some clip spot fabrics also look very similar to embroidered fabrics.

See also EXTRA WARP AND EXTRA WEFT FABRICS, FIGURED FABRIC, SHEER FABRICS.

End uses: ladies' evening wear, scarves, dresses, blouses and furnishing fabrics.

CLOQUÉ A figured blister cloth with a characteristic puckered or blistered appearance (*cloqué* means 'blistered' in French). The term 'cloqué' is used mainly for woven fabrics, but may also be used to describe weft-knitted fabrics with figured effects (*see* BLISTER CLOTH).

Woven cloqué is a compound jacquard or double cloth fabric woven with figured blister effects. The blistered effect may be produced by the weave structure or by using yarns with different shrinkage properties, or both of these combined.[26] When the fabric is woven using yarns of different character or twist, the blister effect is caused by the differential shrinkage of these yarns during finishing. In one example, the face cloth is woven using fine yarns with normal twist, while the back cloth is woven with crêpe yarns that are stitched to the face cloth in a predetermined pattern. During finishing, the crêpe yarns in the back cloth shrink, causing the face cloth to buckle and form blisters.

Most woven cloqué fabrics were originally woven with silk yarns, but nowadays various fibres are used. The blistered surface texture of cloqué makes it an easy-care fabric as it will not show any other creases. Woven cloqué fabrics are similar to matelassé crêpe but they have smaller raised blisters.

See also BLISTER CLOTH; CRÊPE; DOUBLE CLOTH; FIGURED FABRIC; JACQUARD FABRIC, WOVEN.

End uses: ladies' evening wear, dresses, blouses, lingerie, outerwear and hats.

row 2

row 1

cloqué (knitted)

CLOQUÉ CRÊPE *see* CRÊPE.

COATED FABRIC A fabric (woven, knitted or nonwoven) finished by the application of one or more layers of an adherent substance to one or both sides. Textiles may be coated with rubber, linseed oil, synthetic resins, metallic particles, or vinyl or polymer compounds.

The coating is usually applied to the textile in the form of a fluid. It may be applied to the face ('face-coating'), to the back ('back-coating'), or to both sides (for which the more general term 'coated fabric' is normally used). The coating may be applied by a blade, by roller, by immersing the fabric in a solution, or by spraying. Both the amount of coating applied and the degree of penetration of the mixture are controlled in order to produce various effects. After coating, the fabric may also be printed or embossed.

Fabrics are coated for many reasons, including the following:

- to increase strength or stability (*see* CARPET, TUFTED FABRIC)
- to enable them to block out light (e.g. for window blinds; *see* BLACK-OUT FABRIC)
- to make them waterproof (*see* PLASTIC TEXTILES, RUBBER, TEFLON®, UMBRELLA FABRIC, WATERPROOF AND WATER-REPELLENT FABRICS)
- to give the appearance of leather (*see* LEATHER-CLOTH)
- for decorative effect (*see* METALLIC FABRICS)
- to give them protective properties (*see* AEROPLANE FABRIC, NEOPRENE, OIL CLOTH, POLYURETHANE, PVC, TEFLON®)
- to give them flame-resistant properties (e.g. coating with flame-retardant chemicals; *see* FLAME-RESISTANT TEXTILES)
- to enable them to be laminated to other surfaces (coating with adhesive; *see* HOLOGRAPHIC FABRICS, LAMINATED FABRIC)

coated fabric
(PVC face-coated)

coated fabric

coating fabrics

- for insulation or as a safety feature (coating with reflective material), e.g. for outerwear garments for police, firefighters and ambulance workers (*see* METALLIC FABRICS, REFLECTIVE FABRICS)
- to give them other special features (e.g. coating with microcapsules; *see* MICROENCAPSULATED TEXTILES)

See also BACKED FABRIC, FLAME-RESISTANT TEXTILES, LINING FABRIC, TEFLON®.

End uses: a very wide range of uses, including waterproof, protective and decorative apparel, upholstery, window blinds and awnings, floor coverings, wall coverings, vinyl car hoods, luggage, shoe uppers and linings, bandages, acoustic barriers, filters, and pond and ditch liners.

COATING FABRIC (coatings) Any fabric (woven, knitted or nonwoven) that may be made into coats or overcoats. Coating fabrics are worn mainly for protection against the weather. Most, therefore, are very warm and hard-wearing for use in cold weather, and/or waterproof, water-repellent or windproof for protection against those elements. Some, however, are purely fashion fabrics.

Most classic coating fabrics used for cold weather protection are made from animal fibres, including wool, cashmere, camel hair, mohair, alpaca and (more rarely) vicuña. They are usually napped or brushed during finishing to produce a more compact, and therefore warmer, structure. *See* ALPACA FABRIC, CAMEL-HAIR FABRIC, CASHMERE CLOTH, FUR FABRIC, MOHAIR FABRIC, VICUÑA FABRIC. Warm fleece fabrics made from man-made fibres are also used: see FLEECE FABRIC, POLAR FLEECE. A variety of fabrics are used for rain and wind protection: *see* CANVAS, GABERDINE, MICROFIBRE FABRIC, PLASTIC TEXTILES, WATERPROOF AND WATER-REPELLENT FABRICS.

Coating fabrics include: Afgalaine, Albert cloth, alpaca fabric, angora fabric, armure, astrakhan fabric, Bannockburn, barathea, beaver cloth, Bedford cord, blanket cloth, Bolivia, bouclé fabric, box cloth, broadcloth (woollen), buffalo check, cadet cloth, camel-hair fabric, canvas, cashmere cloth, cavalry twill, chenille fabric, Cheviot, chinchilla fabric, covert cloth, Donegal, duffel, éponge, Eskimo cloth, fleece fabric, flushing, frieze, fur fabric, gaberdine, granada, Harris tweed, imperial cloth, kersey, loden cloth, marengo, melton, microfibre fabric, mohair fabric, molleton, Montagnac, pilot cloth, plush, polar fleece, polo cloth, poodle cloth, quilted fabric, ratiné, Saxony, serge, suede cloth, some tartan fabrics, Tattersall check, thornproof tweed, tweed, Ulster, velvet, velveteen, wool Venetian, vicuña fabric, West of England fabrics, whipcord and zibeline.

See also NAPPED FABRICS, PILE FABRICS, WADDING.

End uses: coats and jackets of all kinds.

COBURG (Cobourg) A woven fabric that is made in imitation of cashmere cloth, being considerably less expensive; however, it is much coarser and heavier, and not as soft. Coburg is a union fabric made with a cotton warp and a worsted wool weft. It is woven in a 2/1 twill weave structure, and may be piece-dyed or printed. It is a similar fabric to Henrietta.

See also CASHMERE CLOTH, UNION FABRIC.

End uses: linings, overcoats, suits and dresses.

COCO MATTING *see* PLANT-FIBRE FABRICS.

COIR *see* PLANT-FIBRE FABRICS.

Coburg

colour and weave effects

cord fabric

COLOUR AND WEAVE EFFECTS Patterns created in woven fabrics by the combination of a simple weave structure and the arrangement of small groups of contrasting colours in the warp and/or weft. The interaction of these two elements produces a wide range of interesting geometric patterns.

Two or more colours may be alternated in the weft, to give widthways stripes; in the warp, to give lengthwise stripes; or in both warp and weft, to give checks. The fabric is woven in various simple weave structures, such as plain weave or twills. The weave structure interacts with the colour order and, when aligned with the coloured warp and weft stripes, produces different, more complex geometric patterns. The colours usually contrast strongly or are arranged in a dark/light sequence in order to emphasize the pattern. Fabrics in which dark and light yarns alternate in the warp are sometimes called 'end-and-end' fabrics; those where they alternate in the weft are sometimes called 'pick-and-pick' fabrics. The French-derived term 'fil-à-fil' is also sometimes used for fabrics with alternating dark and light yarns in either warp or weft.

Fabrics woven with colour and weave effects include birdseye, chambray, cranky checks, district checks, four-pointed star check, Glen Urquhart check, Guards check, gun-club check, hairline, hopsack, houndstooth check, houndstooth stripe, panama (shirting fabrics), pinhead check, pinstripe, Prince of Wales check, shepherd's check, tartan and Zanzibar. Many worsted fabrics also have designs produced in this manner; they are typically used as suiting fabrics.

See also CHECKS, STRIPES, TWILL FABRICS.

End uses: suiting fabrics, coats, jackets, trousers, dresses, blouses, shirts, men's neckties and furnishing fabrics.

COMPOUND FABRIC *see* DOUBLE CLOTH.

CONSTITUTIONAL CORD *see* CORDUROY.

CONVENT CLOTH *see* CHALLIS.

CORAH SILK *see* SILK FABRIC.

CORD FABRICS A general term for fabrics with pronounced ridges or cord effects that run down the length of the fabric parallel to the selvedge. The term includes both woven and knitted fabrics, but most cord fabrics are woven. For woven fabrics, the term 'weft rib fabric' is also sometimes used (*see* RIB FABRICS, WOVEN).

For an example of a weft-knitted cord fabric, *see* SINGLE JERSEY CORD. Woven cord fabrics are made in many different weights and qualities, from lightweight to heavy. All kinds of fibres and weave structures are used, but cord fabrics are typically strong, hard-wearing fabrics with closely sett warp and weft yarns. Several examples of woven cord fabrics are described below;[26] *see also* BEDFORD CORD, CORDUROY, FUSTIAN, HAIR CORD, OTTOMAN, PIQUÉ FABRICS, ROYAL RIB, RUSSIAN CORD.

Cable cord is woven in plain weave with a cotton warp and a worsted weft. One quality is woven as follows: 38/2 tex cotton warp sett at 17 ends per cm and 16 tex botany weft woven at 52 picks per cm. Gordon cord and Metz cord are both woven in a fancy cord weave structure with a cotton warp and a botany worsted weft. Persian cord is woven in a 2 and 2 weft rib construction with a cotton warp and a botany worsted weft. It is woven with 2 ends per dent, with the ends, which run in pairs, separated by the reed wires. One quality is woven as follows: 24/2 tex cotton warp sett at 30 ends per cm and 18 tex botany weft woven at 48 picks per cm. Russell cord (or Russel cord) is similar in structure to Persian cord but woven with a mohair or lustre worsted weft.

End uses: trousers, jackets, skirts, shirts, dresses, workwear and children's clothing.

Metz cord

Gordon cord

cord (2 and 2 weft rib construction)

corduroy

corduroy (uncut and undyed)

corduroy (pincord)

corduroy (needlecord)

corduroy (weft-knitted)

corduroy (elephant cord)

CORDUROY A woven fabric that has a cut-weft pile on the face side; the tufts of weft pile form ribs or cords that run down the length of the fabric parallel to the selvedge. Sometimes called 'rib velvet', corduroy is hard-wearing but is also soft and comfortable.

The name 'corduroy' comes from the French *cord du roi*: the fabric was widely used for servants' uniforms in the royal households of France during the 17th and 18th centuries.[3] At one time, the fabric was extensively produced in Lancashire in England, and in many parts of Europe it is still called 'Manchester', after the main trading centre of that region. Corduroy is woven in a similar manner to velveteen. The pile is produced by supplementary weft yarns that float over the top of a tightly woven ground weave. The ground weave that makes the base cloth is usually plain or twill weave in construction. The supplementary weft is interlaced with the ground weave at binding points arranged in columns up the length of the fabric (unlike velveteen, in which the binding points are spread throughout the fabric). When the floats between the binding points are cut after weaving, they form the pile cords in the longitudinal direction. Differently sized cords or ribs may be produced according to the length and density of weft floats used. Fabrics with wide cords have a deeper pile and are heavier than fabrics with narrow cords.

Traditionally corduroy was woven with cotton yarns, and this is often still the case today, although some are made from cotton and man-made fibre blends. The best-quality corduroy is woven with a supplementary weft of combed, mercerized cotton yarns. Most corduroy fabrics, however, are woven with carded cotton yarns. Corduroy may be piece-dyed, colour-woven and/or printed. During finishing, the cut weft is usually brushed to raise the pile and is usually laid in one direction.

Many different weights and qualities of corduroy are produced today. The classic corduroy fabric typically has 10 to 14 cords per inch. Finer or thicker qualities are usually given different names; some examples follow. Needlecord is of the same construction as classic corduroy, but the cords are finer, with 14 to 18 cords per inch. This gives a lighter-weight fabric with a shorter pile than regular corduroy. It is used for skirts, dresses, children's clothes and shirts. Pincord or baby-cord is also constructed in the same way, but is even lighter and finer than needlecord, with 18 to 22 cords per inch. It has similar end uses to needlecord. Constitutional cord (also called 'jumbo' or 'elephant' cord) is a good-quality, thick, heavy corduroy fabric with broad, heavily-wefted cords. Made in the same way as other corduroy fabrics, it is the broadest corduroy fabric made, with 3 to 10 cords per inch. An example of one quality is: 2/30's cotton count (20/2 tex) warp set at 36 to 44 ends per inch and 1/16's to 1/20's cotton count (37 tex to 30 tex) weft with 400 to 500 picks per inch.[4] Corduroy belongs to the group of fabrics known as 'fustians'. Knitted fabrics are also made in imitation of woven corduroy fabric; these are usually lightweight fabrics with stretch, which tend to be not very durable.

See also CORD FABRICS, COTTON FABRIC, FUSTIAN, PILE FABRICS, VELVETEEN.

End uses: casual trousers, jeans, coats, jackets, skirts, dresses, shirts, children's clothes and upholstery.

CORKSCREW FABRIC A woven fabric, usually made from worsted wool, with a diagonal rib effect running across the fabric at a very low angle. This corkscrew rib is produced by a special corkscrew weave structure based on a twill rib construction.

Warp corkscrew fabrics are warp-faced fabrics, with the twill ribs formed by the warp yarns, while weft corkscrew fabrics are weft-faced fabrics in which the twill ribs are formed by the weft yarns. A variety of different 'corkscrew' weave structures may be used. One typical quality of corkscrew fabric is: 28/2 tex botany warp set at 48 ends per cm and 30 tex botany weft woven at 36 picks per cm.[26] Some fabrics that are woven using fancy corkscrew or spiral yarns are also called 'corkscrew fabric' or 'corkscrew repp'.

weft corkscrew weaves

End uses: fine coatings, suitings and dresses.

CORONATION CLOTH (*obs.*) A medium-weight suiting fabric woven from wool and unfinished worsted yarns, with warp-wise single thread stripes about one inch apart and made with gold or metallic yarns. It was first made in England for the coronation of King Edward VII in 1901.[9]

COTTON FABRIC A general term for any fabric constructed with cotton fibres or yarns. Cotton is a natural plant fibre, the seed hair of a wide variety of plants of the genus *Gossypium* (part of the mallow family).[25] Cotton fibres are staple fibres that are spun into yarns; they are sometimes blended with other staple fibres. The term 'cotton fabric' is used for fabrics of a range of different weights and constructions composed of 100% cotton fibres or yarns. Where cotton is used together with other fibres, the percentage of each should be stated. Fabrics containing both cotton yarns and yarns made from a different fibre or fibres are described as 'cotton union fabrics' (*see* UNION FABRIC).

Cotton fabrics are known for their excellent moisture absorption, which makes them cool and comfortable to wear next to the skin. They are strong, with good abrasion resistance, and have good launderability, although they can crease fairly easily. Cotton fabrics may be brushed on one or both sides to make them warmer. Examples of brushed cotton fabrics include Canton, flannelette and winceyette.

Cotton is grown in many parts of the world, most notably in Egypt, the United States, the West Indies, Peru, Africa, Israel, India, China and elsewhere in Asia. After being graded according to quality (whiteness, fineness, regularity, etc.), cotton fibres are divided into two main groups according to their staple length. The longer staple fibres produce the strongest, finest combed cotton yarns and fabrics, and are used for high-quality woven shirtings, for example. Regions known for producing this type of cotton include Egypt and the Sea Islands, located off the south-eastern coast of the United States. The shorter staple cotton fibres are used to make carded cotton yarns and fabrics. They are carded prior to spinning; the resulting yarns are generally less strong and slightly 'hairier' than combed cotton yarns, but they are usually warmer. They can be woven or knitted and are used mainly for casual clothing.

The following are commonly used terms for kinds of cotton. Egyptian cotton is a top-quality long-staple fibre cotton, grown in Egypt and used to make shirts and dress goods. Pima cotton is a variety of American–Egyptian cotton developed in 1910 and grown in the southern United States and in Mexico. Its staple length is not quite as long as that of Egyptian or Sea Island cotton, but it is a high-quality long-staple fibre cotton, used to make shirts and dress goods. It is named after Pima County in Arizona.[9] Sea Island cotton is a top-quality long-staple fibre cotton grown on the Sea Islands and on some islands in the West Indies, such as Barbados. Their distinctive climate provides the ideal growing conditions for the highest-quality cotton fibres. Sea Island cotton is used to make shirts and dress goods.

warp corkscrew weaves

corkscrew fabric

cotton fabric (woven)

'Brushed cotton fabric' is a general term for any fabric made from cotton in which the surface fibres have been raised, napped or brushed during finishing to produce a soft, warm surface. Flannelette and winceyette are examples. *See also* NAPPED FABRICS.

There are hundreds of classic fabrics traditionally made from cotton. Examples include cotton batiste, Bedford cord, calico, cambric, Canton flannel, canvas, chambray, chino, chintz, clip spot, corduroy, cretonne, denim, dimity, dotted Swiss, drill, duck, eyelet, flannelette, gauze, gingham, jean, lawn, Madras, moleskin fabric, mull, muslin, organdie, osnaburg, Oxford, percale, piqué, poplin, print cloth, sheeting fabric, Tattersall check, terry fabric, ticking, velveteen, voile and winceyette.

See also PLANT-FIBRE FABRICS.

End uses: an extremely wide range of uses, including casual wear, underwear, dresses, T-shirts, suits, rainwear, overalls, sewing threads, and curtain and upholstery fabrics.

COUPURE (*obs.*) A cashmere fabric woven in twill weave, diagonally cut and used on the bias, so that the diagonal twill makes a lengthwise line. The name derives from the French for 'crack' or 'gash'.[9]

COUTIL (coutille) A very heavy, strong cotton fabric that is closely woven, either in a narrow striped herringbone or reverse twill weave. Its main use is for corsetry, and it is therefore a firm, durable fabric.

Weave structures that may be used are a 2/1 warp-faced twill or a 2/2 warp-faced twill weave, usually arranged in herringbone stripes. Coutil may be bleached or piece-dyed or sometimes it may be patterned. One way of achieving this is to alternate colour stripes in the warp so that they match up with the vertical stripes formed by the herringbone weave pattern. One typical quality of coutil is 46 tex warp set at 21 ends per cm and 27 tex weft woven at 30 picks per cm; weave structure 2/1 twill; fabric weight 175 g/m².[25] Coutil is sometimes also used as a strong lining or tropical suiting fabric.[2] *See* LINING FABRIC, TROPICAL SUITING.

See also HERRINGBONE, TWILL FABRICS.

End uses: corsets, foundation wear, lining fabric and tropical suiting fabric.

COVERT CLOTH (allsport) A firm, durable wool fabric that is usually woven in a warp-faced twill weave with fancy grandrelle yarns in the warp and a solid-colour weft yarn. This gives the fabric a characteristic mottled appearance. Covert cloth was originally made in England for hunting garments, and it is traditionally made in colours that allow the wearer to blend in with the natural colours of the British countryside. It takes its name from 'covert', meaning a thicket or hiding-place for game.[5, 7] Sometimes this fabric is known as 'allsport'.

Traditional covert cloth is made using worsted or woollen yarns and is tightly woven in a 2/1 twill, other steep twill weave structures, or herringbone weave. This produces a firm, rugged, hard-wearing fabric that is thornproof and water-resistant. Most covert cloths are still made in this quality today, but lighter-weight covert fabrics are also produced. These are made in the same manner but using cotton or man-made fibre yarns. This produces a fabric similar in weight to denim, but with the characteristic mottled appearance of the original covert cloth.

The mottled appearance is produced by the closely sett grandrelle yarns in the warp. These are two-fold yarns composed of two singles yarns in different colours that have been twisted together. Traditionally the two colours used were different shades of brown, producing a mottled beige fabric when woven. Other traditional colours include olive, fawn, brown and grey. These could be combined with a different shade of the same colour or with a black or white yarn. Nowadays a variety of contrasting colours are used

coutil

covert cloth (face and back)

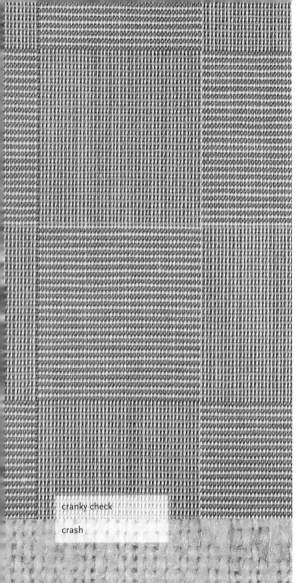

cranky check

crash

to make the grandrelle yarns, often with a strong dark/light contrast. Sometimes mock grandrelle yarns are used instead; these are singles yarns with an inherent speckled grandrelle effect achieved by combining a mixture of dyed and undyed fibres together. Occasionally the grandrelle effect is produced by twisting an undyed singles worsted yarn and an undyed singles cotton yarn together. After weaving, the grey cloth is piece-dyed with wool dyes. The cotton portion of the yarn remains white, unaffected by the wool dye. Covert cloth is usually showerproofed and either napped or given a clear finish. Examples of typical qualities of this fabric include:

- warp: 35/2 to 30/2 tex botany wool or worsted/cotton sett at 34 to 38 ends per cm; weft: 45 to 38 tex botany wool woven at 22 to 26 picks per cm
- warp: 90 tex woollen mixture sett at 22 ends per cm; weft: 120 tex wool woven at 14 picks per cm[26]

Covert cloth is similar to cavalry twill, gaberdine, whipcord, some tweed fabrics (such as gamekeeper tweed) and some heavyweight Venetian fabrics.

See also COATING FABRIC, TWILL FABRICS.

End uses: (wool and worsted covert cloth) men's lightweight coats, jackets, suits and caps; (cotton and man-made fibre covert cloth) suits, raincoats, workwear and overalls.

CRANKY CHECK A woven checked fabric in which the pattern is made by using a colour and weave effect. The classic cranky check is a blue and white square checked fabric in which the squares are filled with blue and white hairline stripes.[36] Most cranky checks are lightweight cotton or polyester/cotton fabrics used for shirts and dresses.

Thin stripes of coloured yarns are alternated in both the warp and the weft directions. The fabric is typically woven in a plain weave structure which, when combined with the coloured warp and weft stripes in a certain order, produces the checked pattern. Originally the checks were two inches square, but smaller checks are probably more common nowadays.[36] The warp and weft yarns may be woven individually, or woven together in pairs in order to emphasize the colour and weave effect. Zanzibar is an example of a cranky check fabric that is woven with double ends and picks.[36] Cranky check fabrics are sometimes used for Harvard shirtings.[4]

See also CHECKS, COLOUR AND WEAVE EFFECTS, HAIRLINE, HARVARD, SHIRTING FABRICS, ZANZIBAR.

End uses: shirts, dresses and blouses.

CRASH A woven fabric with a coarse, irregular, rough surface texture created by the use of thick, uneven yarns, particularly in the weft. It was originally made from 100% linen.

Today crash is made using linen, cotton, viscose, other man-made fibre yarns or unions of any of these. It is woven either in a balanced but fairly open-sett plain weave, or in fancy crêpe weave structures such as oatmeal crêpe (especially when cotton yarns are used). Traditionally it is unbleached and creamy beige in colour, but it may also be bleached, dyed or printed. The fabric is usually finished to give it a soft, lustrous appearance (it may be beetled), although sometimes the rough surface texture is accentuated by giving it a finish that fixes creases into the fabric. Crash is produced in a variety of weights and qualities, but most are medium- to heavyweight fabrics. Crash is similar to osnaburg.

See also PLAIN WEAVE FABRIC, PRINT CLOTH, TOWELLING, UNION FABRIC.

End uses: towels, curtains, upholstery, table linen, bookbindings and embroidery fabrics; also (in lighter qualities) suits and dresses.

CRÊPE A type of fabric with a distinctive crinkled surface texture that is rough and grainy (the name comes from French *crêper*, 'to crinkle'). Such an effect may be produced in both woven and knitted fabrics. Woven crêpe fabrics are characteristically springy to handle and fray easily.

Crêpe effects may be produced in fabrics in a variety of different ways.

(i) *Crêpe yarns.* Crêpe yarns may be used in the fabric. They are high-twist yarns that are 'twist-lively'. When woven, they cause the fabric to distort as they partially relax after a wet-finishing treatment. 'Full crêpe' woven fabrics have crêpe yarns in both the warp and weft, while 'half crêpe' woven fabrics have crêpe yarns in one direction only (usually weft). Different crêpe textures may also be made in a woven fabric by alternating yarns of 'S' and 'Z' crêpe twists, either in both directions or one direction only.

(ii) *Crêpe weaves.* Special crêpe weave structures, such as **oatmeal crêpe**, granite and **moss crêpe** weaves, may be used to emphasize the effect of fabrics woven with crêpe yarns. These are irregular weave structures with a random distribution of floats and interlacings, which produce an all-over textured effect in the fabric, making it difficult to discern the pattern repeat. Although crêpe weave structures emphasize the crêpe effect produced by using high-twist yarns, they cannot create this effect on their own. Special knitted fabric constructions are discussed below under **warp-knitted crêpe** and **weft-knitted crêpe**.

(iii) *Chemical finishing.* Chemical finishing treatments may be applied to produce differential shrinkage in the finished fabric, giving it a crêpe-like appearance. For example, a chemical paste may be printed onto the fabric in a pattern, causing the treated areas to shrink and pucker.

(iv) *Mechanical finishing.* Mechanical finishing treatments may be applied to non-crêpe fabrics in order to create a crêpe-like appearance. The fabric is thermally embossed by running it between revolving heated rollers that have been engraved with the desired pattern. Sometimes resins are added as well. Embossing may be a permanent treatment (especially for thermoplastic fibre fabrics) or an impermanent treatment, depending on the type of fibre and the process used.

Crêpe fabrics shrink significantly as they relax during finishing, and this should be taken into account when planning the fabric dimensions before manufacture. Crêpe can be made from any fibre, whether natural or synthetic, or from blends of fibres. Many crêpe fabrics take their name from the fibre from which they are made (e.g. 'polyester crêpe', 'silk crêpe', 'cotton crêpe', 'linen crêpe'), and exist in a wide variety of weights and qualities. Many crêpe fabrics are also noted for having particular characteristics or qualities. A number of these are discussed below; *see also* ALBATROSS, ALPACA CRÊPE, BARK CRÊPE, CANTON CRÊPE, CHARMEUSE, CREPON, CREPON GEORGETTE, CRINKLE CRÊPE, GEORGETTE, GRANITE CLOTH, MATELASSÉ, PEAU DE CYGNE, RADIUM.

crêpe weave

BLISTER CRÊPE (cloqué crêpe) A crêpe fabric made with crêpe yarns in which small sections have been woven in a dobby or jacquard double cloth structure, creating small blistered motifs. This fabric is also called 'cloqué crêpe' or, when jacquard woven, 'jacquard crêpe' (*see* **jacquard crêpe** below). *See also* BLISTER CLOTH, CRINKLE CRÊPE, CLOQUÉ.

CLOQUÉ CRÊPE see **blister crêpe** above.

CRÊPE-BACK SATIN A lightweight double-faced fabric, woven in a satin weave construction, usually with silk or polyester yarns. It is made with continuous filament yarns in the warp, which dominate one side of the fabric, and high-twist crêpe yarns in the weft, which dominate the other side. This produces a lustrous satin face and a dull crêpe back, either of which may be used as the face side of the fabric. Crêpe-back satin is a half crêpe fabric. It is used for evening wear, bridal wear, dresses, blouses, linings and lingerie. *See also* SATIN, WOVEN.

CRÊPE CHARMEUSE *see* CHARMEUSE.

crêpe (woven)

blister crêpe

crêpe-back satin
(face and back)

crêpe chiffon (printed)   crêpe de chine
crêpe meteor   embossed crêpe

CRÊPE CHIFFON A soft, flimsy, sheer woven fabric, like ordinary chiffon but with the distinctive crinkled appearance of a crêpe fabric. It is woven in silk or any man-made fibre in a balanced plain weave. High-twist crêpe yarns made from continuous filament fibres are arranged in an alternating sequence of two 'S' and two 'Z' twist yarns in both the warp and the weft. Crêpe chiffon may therefore be termed a 'full crêpe' fabric. It is used for lingerie, nightwear, scarves, blouses, dresses, bridal wear and evening wear. *See also* CHIFFON, SHEER FABRICS.

CRÊPE DE CHINE A fine, soft, lightweight woven crêpe fabric with a medium to high lustre. Characteristically, it has a fine rib effect in the weft direction. It has a fairly crisp, luxurious handle and very good drape. It was originally made in China (hence the name). Crêpe de chine is traditionally woven in plain weave using silk yarns, but is now also made with man-made continuous filament fibres. The warp is more highly sett than the weft and is composed of normal flat filament or 'Z' twist yarns. The weft consists of very high-twist filament crêpe yarns, which are arranged in an alternating sequence of two 'S' and two 'Z' twist yarns to produce the crêpe effect. Crêpe de chine is therefore a half crêpe fabric. It may be piece-dyed or printed. It is a strong fabric with good washability, and is used for dresses, blouses, lingerie, scarves and linings. One quality is woven with 6.4 tex warp, sett at 60 ends per cm, and 9 tex weft, woven at 34 picks per cm.[26] Crêpe de chine façonné is a jacquard woven brocade fabric.

CRÊPE DE LAINE see **wool crêpe** below.

CRÊPE GEORGETTE *see* GEORGETTE.

CRÊPE LAVABLE see **warp crêpe** below.

CRÊPE MAROCAIN A heavy woven crêpe fabric with characteristic slightly wavy ribs running across the width of the fabric (weftway ribs). It was originally made in French Morocco (hence the name).[3] Crêpe marocain is woven in plain weave, normally using filament yarns in both warp and weft. These may be of silk or any man-made fibre; wool, cotton or natural/man-made fibre blends are also sometimes used. The crêpe effect is produced by the use of normal flat filament or 'Z' twist yarns in the warp, and thicker, high-twist crêpe yarns in the weft. The warp yarns are closely sett and the crêpe yarns in the weft are arranged in an alternating sequence of two 'S' and two 'Z' twist yarns. Crêpe marocain is therefore a half crêpe fabric. The rib effect may be accentuated by embossing the fabric during finishing. Crêpe marocain is used for evening wear, bridal wear, dresses, women's suits and blouses. It is similar to Canton crêpe but slightly heavier.

CRÊPE MATELASSÉ *see* MATELASSÉ.

CRÊPE METEOR A soft, lightweight, lustrous crêpe fabric that is woven in silk and has excellent drape. It is woven in satin weave with normal twist yarns in the warp and high-twist crêpe yarns in the weft. This produces a lustrous satin face and a dull crêpe twill back. Crêpe meteor is therefore a half crêpe fabric.

CRÊPE ROMAINE A lightweight, semi-sheer woven crêpe fabric in which crêpe warp yarns are arranged alternately with ordinary warp yarns. It was originally woven with silk yarns, but nowadays it is also woven in viscose, acetate, wool and other man-made fibres and blends. Crêpe romaine is woven in a 2/1 hopsack weave, which gives the fabric an uneven, dull-lustre surface texture. It is used for evening wear, bridal wear, dresses and linings. Crêpe romaine is similar to georgette but heavier and less transparent.

jacquard crêpe

French crêpe

moss crêpe

EMBOSSED CRÊPE A fabric that has been given an embossed finish, producing a crêpe-like texture. A variety of natural and man-made fibre fabrics may be embossed. The fabric is passed between revolving heated rollers that have been engraved with the desired pattern (usually one that imitates a woven crêpe effect). The crinkle effect produced is impermanent with lightweight cotton fabrics, but permanent with thermoplastic man-made fibre fabrics. *See also* CRINKLE CRÊPE, CRINKLE FABRIC, EMBOSSED FABRICS, PLEATED FABRICS, SEERSUCKER.

FAILLE CRÊPE A smooth, rich, dull crêpe fabric woven with crêpe yarns in the weft only. Faille crêpe is therefore a half crêpe fabric. It has a characteristic fine horizontal rib on the face and a satin back. It resembles crêpe de chine but is heavier. Faille crêpe may be silk or synthetic, and is used for evening wear, dresses, blouses and lingerie. It is a lighter-weight fabric than faille. *See also* FAILLE.

FRENCH CRÊPE A very soft, flat, lightweight and inexpensive crêpe fabric, used for lingerie (and also known as 'lingerie crêpe'). It is made from crêpe twisted yarns. Originally it was a woven fabric made with silk yarns in France. Nowadays it is made in various countries and may be woven or tricot knitted using any fibre (including nylon, viscose, acetate and blends).

JACQUARD CRÊPE A crêpe fabric woven with jacquard patterns. Crêpe yarns are used, and small areas of the fabric or motifs are woven in either a single or double cloth jacquard weave, which can sometimes produce blister effects (see **blister crêpe** above). *See also* BLISTER CLOTH; CLOQUÉ; JACQUARD FABRIC, WOVEN.

LINGERIE CRÊPE see **French crêpe** above.

MOSS CRÊPE A woven crêpe fabric with a characteristic soft, spongy handle (like moss) and good drape. True moss crêpe is produced by using a combination of moss crêpe weave structure and alternating 'S' and 'Z' twist moss crêpe yarns in both warp and weft. Moss crêpe yarn is a two-fold yarn made by doubling a normal-twist yarn with a high-twist yarn. All twists are made in the same direction ('S' or 'Z'). The moss crêpe weave structure has a characteristically large repeat area. Made in wool, cotton, polyester, viscose or acetate, moss crêpe is used for dresses and blouses.

weft-knitted crêpe (face and back) oatmeal crêpe

warp-knitted crêpe

sand crêpe

wool crêpe

OATMEAL CRÊPE A woven fabric with a characteristic rough crêpe texture, a soft, spongy handle and good drape. The crêpe effect is produced by using an oatmeal crêpe weave structure. This is an irregular weave structure with a random distribution of floats and interlacings, producing an all-over textured effect in the fabric and making it difficult to discern the pattern repeat. Oatmeal crêpe may be woven in wool, cotton, linen, polyester, viscose or acetate; the warp yarns are usually finer in count than the weft yarns. The weft is soft-spun, and sometimes condenser cotton is used. A typical oatmeal crêpe fabric construction is 30 tex cotton warp, sett at 26 ends per cm, and 38 tex cotton weft, woven at 28 picks per cm.[26] Oatmeal crêpe is used for dresses and blouses, and is also one of the base fabrics used for cretonne printed fabrics. *See also* CRE-TONNE, PRINT CLOTH.

oatmeal crêpe

SAND CRÊPE A woven fabric with a characteristic rough, grainy, sand-like texture. The crêpe effect is sometimes produced by using a crêpe weave structure. Usually, however, the fabric is woven in plain weave and the crêpe effect is produced by using normal twist yarns in the warp and high-twist crêpe yarns in the weft. The crêpe yarns in the weft are arranged in an alternating sequence of two 'S' and two 'Z' twist yarns. Sand crêpe may therefore be termed a 'half crêpe' fabric. It is usually made in silk or man-made fibres. Sand crêpe is similar to crêpe de chine, but it is heavier and has a rougher handle. It is used for dresses and blouses. One quality is made with 15.6 tex acetate warp sett at 40 ends per cm and 22.2 tex viscose crêpe weft woven at 18 picks per cm (2 'S'/2 'Z'); the fabric weight is 136 g/m².[25]

SATIN CRÊPE see **crêpe-back satin** and **crêpe meteor** above.

SERPENTINE CRÊPE A woven crêpe fabric made with cotton yarns. It is woven in plain weave, and the crêpe effect is produced by using high-twist crêpe yarns (all with the same twist direction) in the weft only. Serpentine crêpe may therefore be termed a 'half crêpe' fabric. It is produced in a wide variety of weights and qualities, and has almost the appearance of a crepon. One quality is woven with 10 tex warp sett at 23 ends per cm and 23 tex weft woven at 20 picks per cm.[26]

WARP CRÊPE A plain woven crêpe fabric in which the crêpe effect is produced by using filament crêpe yarns in the warp and normal filament yarns in the weft. Warp crêpe is therefore a half crêpe fabric. It is used for dresses and blouses. It is also known by the French name 'crêpe lavable'.

WARP-KNITTED CRÊPE A warp-knitted crêpe fabric with an irregular surface texture. Lightweight warp-knitted crêpe fabrics are usually made on a two-guide-bar tricot machine using overfeed on an atlas ground. Alternatively, a textured monofilament yarn may be used on the back bar; this will create the crêpe effect when the fabric is relaxed. *See also* ATLAS, WARP-KNITTED; WARP-KNITTED FABRIC.

WEFT-KNITTED CRÊPE An irregular-surfaced fabric, either plain or rib based, usually constructed from knit-float or knit-tuck loops introduced in a predetermined random order. *See also* WEFT-KNITTED FABRIC.

WOOL CRÊPE A soft, lightweight woven fabric with good drape and a typical crêpe appearance. It is also known by the French name 'crêpe de laine'. Wool crêpe is loosely woven either in plain weave or a crêpe weave structure. High-twist worsted crêpe yarns are used in the warp, arranged in an alternating sequence of 'S' and 'Z' twist yarns, and normal twist yarns are used in the weft. Wool crêpe may therefore be termed a 'half crêpe' fabric. It is often piece-dyed and is available in a variety of weights. It is used for ladies' suits and dresses.

ALL WOOL

crepon

crepon georgette

cretonne

CREPON A soft, absorbent, crêpe-type woven fabric that is heavier and more prominently textured than most other crêpe fabrics. The characteristic deep-crêpe texture forms wavy ridges in the warp direction.

Crepon is woven in plain weave, often with cotton yarns, but also in polyester, viscose and mixes. The ridged crêpe effect may be produced in different ways. Usually ordinary twist yarns are used in the warp and high-twist crêpe yarns in the weft, all with the same twist direction ('S' or 'Z'). Alternatively, crepon may be woven using weft yarns with different amounts and/or directions of crêpe-twist. Sometimes chemically crimped yarns are used in the weft rather than crêpe yarns. The effect may also be produced on a plain woven fabric by giving it a special finishing treatment (thermal embossing or chemical finishing). Crepon may be bleached, dyed and/or printed. It is a similar heavy crêpe fabric to bark crêpe. Crepon is sometimes also called by the collective term 'crimp fabric' (*see* BLISTER CLOTH).[36]

See also BARK CRÊPE, CRÊPE, ÉPINGLE CREPON.

End uses: blouses, dresses, casual shirts, nightwear, scarves and curtains.

CREPON GEORGETTE A very fine, lightweight, transparent woven dress fabric like georgette, but with a characteristic crêpe-type, grainy texture in the warp direction. Crepon georgette is a variation of a georgette fabric; however, unlike georgette, in which crêpe yarns are used in both the warp and weft, crepon georgette is woven with high-twist crêpe yarns in the weft only, all of which have the same twist direction. This gives the fabric its characteristic warpway texture. It is often given a permanent crêpe-like finish.

See also CRÊPE, GEORGETTE.

End uses: dresses, blouses and lingerie.

CRETONNE A medium- to heavyweight fabric that has been printed, typically with large-scale floral patterns. The base cloth is a fairly stiff woven fabric traditionally made from 100% cotton. Cretonne derives its name from the French village of Creton in Normandy, where the fabric was first made.[3, 5]

The base fabric used for cretonne prints may be any firmly woven cotton fabric, but it is often osnaburg or oatmeal crêpe. Both these fabrics have a fine cotton warp and thicker weft yarns spun from coarse waste cotton. In osnaburg the weave structure is usually plain weave, while oatmeal crêpe is woven in an oatmeal weave structure. After printing, cretonne fabric is given a dull surface finish. Cretonne is similar to an unglazed chintz fabric but heavier in weight. It is a durable fabric with good washability. Nowadays it is also available in linen, man-made fibres and blends. Cretonne may be made from the same grey cloth as calico, chintz, percale and plissé, each fabric being given a different finish.[19]

Shadow cretonne is a cretonne fabric in which the pattern has been printed onto the warp yarns prior to weaving. The warp yarns are usually quite highly sett and the fabric woven in plain weave. This produces a diffuse, shadow printed effect in the fabric. *See* WARP-PRINTED FABRICS, CHINÉ FABRICS.

See also COTTON FABRIC, CRÊPE, OSNABURG, PRINT CLOTH, PRINTED FABRIC.

End uses: curtains, upholstery, loose covers, bedspreads and aprons.

CRIMP FABRICS *see* BLISTER CLOTH.

CRIMPS *see* SEERSUCKER.

crinkle crêpe

crinkle fabric (weft-knitted)

crinoline

CRINKLE CRÊPE A term applied to a variety of woven fabrics, in different weights and qualities, that have been given a puckered or crinkled surface by a special finishing treatment to make them resemble a woven crêpe fabric. Characteristically, most crinkle crêpe fabrics are soft, lightweight fabrics with good drape, which emphasizes the crinkled effect. Since that effect is intended, they are easy-care fabrics that do not usually require ironing.

The crêpe-like appearance is produced by applying a chemical treatment to the finished woven fabric, which is usually a plain weave cotton or a polyester/cotton fabric. A crinkled effect may be obtained on cellulosic fibre fabrics (e.g. cotton and linen) by printing a sodium hydroxide solution (caustic soda) directly onto the fabric either in stripes or in an all-over pattern. The printed areas will shrink in relation to the unprinted areas, which stay the same, causing the fabric to pucker. Alternatively, a protective resist material (usually a gum) may be printed onto cellulosic fibre fabrics. The fabric is then immersed in caustic soda, causing the unprotected areas to shrink. The areas that were protected from the chemical by the resist material, which is afterwards removed, will be the areas that pucker. Caustic soda treatments may be either permanent or semi-permanent finishes. They may be given to piece-dyed fabrics, printed fabrics or colour-woven fabrics, but images printed with caustic soda paste onto some piece-dyed fabrics tend to be darker in colour because the chemicals increase dye absorbency.[19] A permanent crinkle effect may also be achieved on man-made, thermoplastic fibres (e.g. nylon and polyester) by embossing the fabric with hot rollers. *See* CRÊPE, EMBOSSED FABRICS.

Some crinkle crêpe fabrics look similar to seersucker fabrics, but in a true seersucker the crinkled effect is achieved with the fabric construction. Crinkle crêpe is also sometimes called by the more general terms 'blister crêpe', 'blister cloth' or 'plissé'.

See also BLISTER CLOTH, CRÊPE, CRINKLE FABRIC, PLEATED FABRICS, SEERSUCKER.

End uses: casual clothing (including blouses, skirts, dresses and beachwear), lingerie and curtains.

CRINKLE FABRIC A general term applied to both knitted and woven fabrics that have a crinkled surface. The crinkle effect is usually multi-directional and distributed randomly throughout the fabric.

The crinkles are usually ironed or pressed into the fabric using heat during finishing. These treatments are impermanent on cellulosic fabrics (e.g. cotton and linen), but a permanent crinkle effect may be achieved on man-made thermoplastic fibre fabrics (e.g. nylon and polyester) by embossing the fabric with hot rollers. (*See* CRÊPE, EMBOSSED FABRICS.) The term 'crinkle fabric' is sometimes used to describe seersucker fabrics, but seersucker is made by quite a different method (*see* SEERSUCKER). Some plissé fabrics are also similar to crinkle fabrics, but the term 'plissé' is used mainly for fabrics in which the folds are in the vertical direction (*see* PLEATED FABRICS). Other fabrics similar to crinkle fabrics include crêpe and crinkle crêpe.

End uses: casual clothing, shirts, T-shirts, blouses, dresses, sweaters, cardigans, skirts, summer jackets, trousers, shorts, beachwear, pyjamas, nightgowns, lingerie and children's wear.

CRINOLINE A dull, coarse fabric made stiff by impregnating a lightweight woven fabric with size or resin. It is best known for its use as a stiff underskirt fabric in the 19th century to make skirts full. It is also used as a stiffening fabric for a wide range of other goods. Crinoline belongs to the muslin family of fabrics.

Crinoline fabrics were originally woven with a linen or cotton warp and a horsehair weft, which gave them their stiffness. Nowadays the base fabric is usually woven in an open-sett plain weave construction using carded cotton yarns or occasionally yarns made

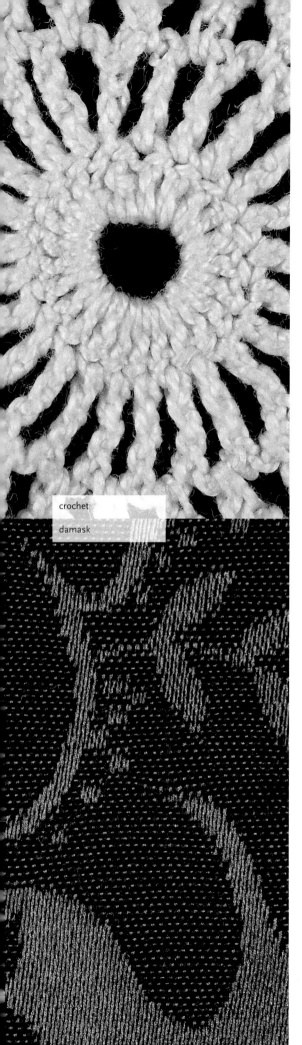

crochet

damask

with linen, man-made fibres or blends. Cheesecloth grey goods are often used. The fabric is then stiffened either with starch, which is a non-durable finish, or with synthetic resin, which provides a more durable finish. Crinoline is usually made in black, white or grey. It is similar to buckram but less stiff and lighter in weight.

See also MUSLIN, PLAIN WEAVE FABRIC.

End uses: interlining or support fabric in tailoring, millinery, bookbinding, lampshades and pleated drapes.

CRISTALE (*obs.*) A term used in Europe around 1850 for a white worsted dress fabric.[36]

CROCHET An openwork fabric that is similar to lace but usually coarser. It is made by crocheting, a very similar process to making lace by hand or tatting. The loop structure produced is also similar to the structure of a warp-knitted fabric.

    Crochet is made by hand using a crochet hook, which is like a hooked needle. Crocheted fabrics may be made from any fibres, including wool, cotton, silk, flax or man-made fibres, but the yarns or threads are usually tightly twisted in order to accentuate the loop structure of the fabric. The crochet hook is used to chain the yarns or threads, which may be of varying thicknesses, into a continuous loop structure. Different elements of the design are made separately and then joined together by linking threads. The name derives from the French for 'hook'.

See also KNITTED FABRIC, LACE, TATTING, WARP-KNITTED FABRIC.

End uses: cardigans, sweaters, jackets, dresses, hats, scarves, tablecloths, table mats and trims.

CROCODILE CLOTH *see* BEDFORD CORD.

CROISÉ *see* TWILL FABRICS.

CRYSTAL (crystalline) (*obs.*) A dress fabric with alternating fine and heavy cords, made with a silk or viscose warp and a wool weft.[9]

CURTRIKE (*obs.*) A fine worsted dress fabric, originally made in Belgium.[36]

DAMASK A firm, reversible woven fabric with a figured, jacquard woven pattern. It is usually lustrous and woven in a single colour only.

    Damask is a jacquard woven fabric, made using one warp and one weft, usually both the same colour. The figured pattern is formed by the subtle contrast between two reversible weave structures woven in different areas of the fabric. In a classic damask, a warp-faced weave structure (usually satin) produces a lustrous surface that is contrasted against a matt surface produced by a weft-faced weave structure (usually sateen). This creates a pattern on the face of the fabric, which appears in exact reverse on the back. The patterns are often floral, usually with the floral figure in the weft sateen weave structure and the background in the warp satin weave structure.[26] The most frequently used weave structures are 5-end or 8-end satin weaves, sometimes distinguished as 'single damask' and 'double damask' respectively, although the latter term is usually applied only to the higher-quality 8-end damask fabrics in which there are approximately 50% more weft picks per centimetre than there are warp ends.[26]

    Damasks are considered to have originated in China;[5] however, they take their name from Damascus in Syria, from where silk damasks were traded with Europe as long ago as the 13th century.[3] Nowadays damask is probably best known as a hard-wearing fabric used for tablecloths and traditionally woven in linen. Damasks are also produced in cotton,

delaine

delaine (printed)

silk, wool, man-made fibres and blends. The fabric is usually compressed during finishing (linen damask is beetled, for example) and damask is probably the flattest-looking of all jacquard fabrics.[19] It can also be given a schreiner finish to make it lustrous. Damask is similar to brocade but flatter, smoother, lighter in weight and reversible.

Damas or *damassé* is the French word for damask.[3] Damasquette is a damask woven with more than one weft, to provide extra colour. The terms 'damassin' or 'damassé brocat' are sometimes used for a damask that has been woven with metallic threads in the weft.[3, 8]

See also FIGURED FABRIC; JACQUARD FABRIC, WOVEN; SATEEN; SATIN, WOVEN; SILK FABRIC; TICKING; TOWELLING.

End uses: (light- to medium-weight damasks) tablecloths, napkins, towels and evening wear; (medium- to heavyweight damasks) curtains, upholstery and mattress covers.

DARYA (*obs.*) A natural-coloured wild silk fabric made in India.[9]

DELAINE A term used for a range of fine, soft, lightweight, all-wool woven fabrics, often printed with small-scale patterns. The finest delaine fabrics are usually called 'challis' (*see* CHALLIS). Characteristically, delaine fabrics have excellent drape.

The term 'delaine' derives from 'mousseline de laine', which is French for wool muslin. It was first woven in France in 1826.[5, 9] Delaine fabrics are usually quite expensive. They are woven in plain weave using high-quality botany worsted yarns made from merino wool. Less expensive delaine fabrics are also made in cotton, in imitation of wool delaine, and are sometimes called 'delainette'. Delaine may be made in plain colours or printed, and occasionally it is warp-printed. One quality made is: 20 tex botany warp, sett at 26 ends per cm, and 13 tex botany weft, woven at 27 picks per cm.[26] Delaine is a similar fabric to étamine.

See also MOUSSELINE, PLAIN WEAVE FABRIC, WARP-PRINTED FABRIC.

End uses: dresses, blouses and scarves.

DENIM A strong, stiff, durable woven fabric, usually woven in a warp-faced twill weave. In the classic denim fabric, the warp yarns are dyed an indigo blue colour and the weft yarns are undyed. As the dyed warp yarns are predominant on the face of the fabric, this is darker than the back, where the undyed weft yarns predominate. Denim was originally woven in the French town of Nîmes for overalls and sailcloth. It was known as 'serge de Nîmes', and it is from 'de Nîmes' that it takes its name.[3]

Denim is traditionally made from 100% cotton with high-twist, two-fold warp yarns and a softer, slightly thicker, singles weft yarn. It is also made from other fibres and fibre combinations, for example lyocell, polyester/cotton blends, cotton/viscose, or cotton mixed with other man-made fibres. If elastane fibres are included, a stretch denim is produced. The classic denim fabric is woven in a firm, 3/1 warp-faced twill weave, but some denim variations are woven in other weave structures. Originally the warp yarns were dyed blue with natural indigo dyestuffs, but nowadays synthetic dyestuffs are normally used. Although the indigo blue colour is still by far the most popular, denim is also produced in a wide range of other colours.

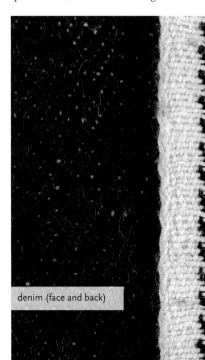

denim (face and back)

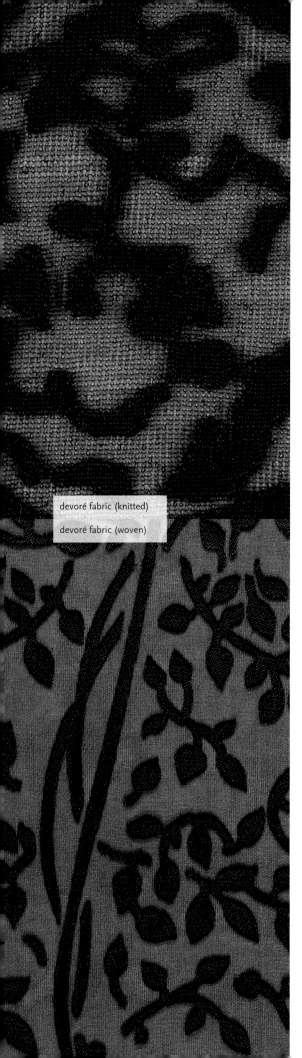

devoré fabric (knitted)

devoré fabric (woven)

Although denim has very good washability, it will naturally fade with age and use to a streaky pale blue, which is considered desirable. there are many different finishes for denim, therefore, most of which are designed to give the fabric a 'worn' look. The fabric is usually pre-shrunk and is sometimes brushed to give it a soft handle. Other finishes include the following.

(i) *Bleaching*. Denim may be bleached to make it pale and streaky.

(ii) *Enzyme treatments*. Denim fabrics made from cotton, viscose and lyocell may be given enzyme treatments. An enzyme is a complex protein that creates a chemical reaction, which partially destroys the fabric surface. This results in a denim fabric with a soft, smooth handle, but reduced weight and strength.

(iii) *Sanding or sueding*. The surface of the fabric is abraded with an abradant similar to sandpaper in order to produce a soft, smooth surface. This treatment also reduces the strength of the fabric, sometimes by as much as 60%.[6]

(iv) *Stonewashing*. Stonewashed denim fabrics or garments are tumble-washed with pumice stone to abrade the fabric surface and accentuate its worn look.

(v) *Acid-washing*. Although acid is not used, denim fabrics or garments may be washed in chemicals such as alkalis and oxidizing agents that partially destroy the surface of the fabric to produce a soft, smooth handle. The treatment reduces the fabric weight and strength.[6]

Denim is available in a wide variety of weights and qualities, but most range from 200 to 320 g/m². One example is made with 33 tex warp sett at 36 ends per cm and 42 tex weft woven at 24 picks per cm.[26] Another quality is made with 45 tex warp sett at 32 ends per cm and 54 tex weft woven at 19 picks per cm; the cloth weight is 310g/m².[25] Denim is similar to bluette, drill, dungaree, florentine, hickory cloth and jean.

See also COTTON FABRICS, TWILL FABRICS.

End uses: casual wear, including jeans, jackets, skirts, dresses, shorts, children's clothes, accessories, workwear, overalls and protective clothing.

DEVORÉ FABRIC (burn-out fabric, burnt-out fabric) A fabric that has been printed with a chemical paste to burn out or dissolve some of the fibre from the printed areas. This usually produces a transparent pattern that contrasts against an opaque ground (or vice versa). Visually the effect is quite lace-like. Woven, knitted or nonwoven fabrics that have a suitable fibre content may be patterned in this way.

The fabric is normally constructed with yarns or fibres made from a blend of natural and man-made fibres, such as silk/viscose or polyester/cotton. The chemical print will usually destroy the natural component. It is therefore is important that the man-made component should be stucturally sound once the natural fibres have been removed. Devoré fabrics are often lightweight sheer fabrics, usually in one colour only. However, they may be piece-dyed or subsequently printed with a coloured pattern. An example of a devoré fabric is façonné velvet (*see* VELVET).

See also SHEER FABRICS.

End uses: evening wear, dresses, blouses, lingerie, scarves and curtains.

DHURRIE *see* KILIM.

DIAGONALS *see* TWILL FABRICS.

DIAPER *see* DICED WEAVES.

DICED WEAVES (dice checks) Any woven fabrics constructed with a diced weave structure, which produces a small-scale check effect in the fabric. There are numerous different variations. Diced weaves are characteristically absorbent and are mainly used as towelling fabrics.

Fabrics woven in diced weave structures are mostly made with linen or cotton yarns since these are highly absorbent. A diced weave is produced by quartering and reversing a design element along both the vertical and the horizontal axis and then repeating this across the fabric. This produces a small-scale check effect in the fabric. Many diced weaves are diamond-based in character. Huckaback is an example of a fabric made using diced weaves. In the United States, diced weaves are perhaps better known by the term 'diaper'. Originally diaper was a woven linen fabric with a small diamond-shaped twill weave pattern,[4] but nowadays the term is used for all kinds of diced weave structures that produce a small-scale check effect in the fabric.

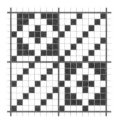

examples of diced weaves

See also CHECKS, DOBBY FABRIC, GLASS CLOTH, HUCKABACK, TEA TOWELLING, TOWELLING.

End uses: tea cloths, towels, napkins and babies' nappies.

DIMITY A light- to mid-weight woven fabric, usually made from cotton. It is woven in plain weave and has a characteristic stripe or check pattern made with thicker corded yarns.

Dimity is usually made from good-quality combed cotton yarns, sometimes mercerized. The corded effect is produced by weaving either thicker yarns, or two or more yarns as one, at regular intervals in a simple, fine, plain woven fabric. The yarns are usually all the same colour, and this produces a solid-colour fabric textured with ridges. If the cords are in the warp, the fabric will have a vertical stripe effect and may be termed a 'stripe fabric'. If cords are used in both the warp and the weft, the fabric will have a checked effect and may be termed a 'check fabric'. Cord yarns may be individual or they may be grouped together to produce a more pronounced rib effect. Dimity may also be colour-woven with multicoloured stripe and check patterns, or it may be piece-dyed and/or printed after weaving. It is usually given a stiff finish and is a durable fabric that tends to fray easily.

The name 'dimity' is thought to come from the Greek word *dismitos*, meaning 'double warp threads'.[3] One quality is made with 18 tex warp, sett at 28 ends per cm, and 18 tex weft, woven at 26 picks per cm.[26] Pyjama fabric or pyjama check is a similar fabric to dimity, but it is usually woven with soft, carded cotton yarns and is given a soft finish.

See also CHECKS, COTTON FABRIC, STRIPES.

End uses: dresses, blouses, children's clothes, nightwear, curtains, bedspreads and napkins.

DISCHARGE PRINTED FABRIC A fabric that has been dyed and subsequently printed with a special print paste. Characteristically, it has small, light-coloured motifs against a large area of dark background colour. Unlike a conventional printed fabric, in which the printed colours seldom penetrate completely to the back of the fabric, a discharge printed fabric has an equal amount of colour on both sides of the fabric.

The fabric is first piece-dyed using a dye that is known to discharge. Then a chemical discharge print paste is printed onto the fabric in a predetermined pattern. The print paste is a chemical compound that removes the colour from the areas where it is printed. The pattern will therefore be apparent usually in white or ecru against the dyed background colour; alternatively, a different, non-dischargeable coloured dye,

diced weave

dimity

discharge printed fabric

district check

called an 'illuminating colour', may be incorporated into the chemical paste and deposited in place of the ground colour. The background colour is completely removed from the fabric but, if desired, a whitish halo effect may be left visible around the edges of the design.

Piece-dyed fabrics have better colour-fastness properties than printed fabrics, so where a small-scale design against a large area of dark background colour is required, discharge printing is a more efficient and cheaper option than printing large expanses of dark colour. A good example of a discharge printed fabric is a polka dot fabric. Similar effects to discharge printing may also be produced by resist-dyeing.

See also BANDANNA, FOULARD, POLKA DOT FABRIC, PRINTED FABRIC, RESIST-DYED FABRICS.

End uses: dresses, blouses, scarves and men's neckties.

DISTRICT CHECKS Woven fabrics traditionally made in the Highlands of Scotland. They were originally designed for the livery of big Scottish landowners and the districts where they lived, so there are numerous different patterns. Characteristically, they are all-wool fabrics with distinctive, bold, block check patterns.

District checks are colour-woven fabrics, and it is the groupings of contrasting colours into stripes and bands, in both the warp and the weft directions that produce the check pattern. The yarns are usually arranged in a sequence of alternating dark and light colours in both the warp and the weft. The light colour is frequently ecru or white. The fabric is then usually woven in a 2/2 twill weave structure and may include sections of houndstooth or shepherd's checks. Some district checks additionally have a fine windowpane overcheck on top of this.

The different district check patterns include the following: Ardtornish, Arndilly, Bateson, Benmore, Brooke, Carnegie, Carnousie, Coigach, Dacre, Dalhousie, Fannich, Forest, Gairloch, Glencoe, Glenfeshie, Glenmorrison, Glen Urquhart, Gordon, Guisachan, Hay (or Dupplin), Highlanders' tweed, Horse Guards, Ing, King's Own, Kinlochewe, Kintail, Lochmore, Mar, Minmore, Russell, Scottish Borderers, Scotsguard, Seaforth, small Glen Urquhart, Strathmashie, Strathspey, Welsh Guards, Wyvis.[3]

See also CHECKS, COLOUR AND WEAVE EFFECTS, GLEN URQUHART CHECK, HOUNDSTOOTH CHECK, SHEPHERD'S CHECK.

End uses: men's and women's suits, jackets, trousers, skirts, coats, caps and hats.

DOBBY FABRIC (dobby weave) A general term for a woven fabric that is characteristically patterned with small-scale geometric designs or motifs created by the interlacings of the weave structure.

The dobby patterns are woven using a dobby patterning mechanism on a weaving loom (as opposed to a tappet or a jacquard mechanism). The fabrics all have distinctive small-scale geometric motifs or patterns formed by warp/weft floats and/or fancy weave structures. An unlimited number of patterns and combinations is possible. Fabrics may be a single colour throughout, or they may be colour-woven with various colours in addition. Many shirting and tie fabrics are woven in small-scale dobby weaves. Typical examples of dobby fabrics include armure, birdseye, diced weaves, dotted Swiss, honeycomb, hopsack, huckaback, Java, Madras shirting, marcella, mock leno, monk's cloth, natté, Oxford, piqué, some Saxony fabrics, many shirting fabrics, some suiting fabrics and many different tie fabrics.

See also WOVEN FABRIC.

End uses: shirts, blouses, men's neckties, suits, dresses, skirts, trousers, scarves and furnishing fabrics.

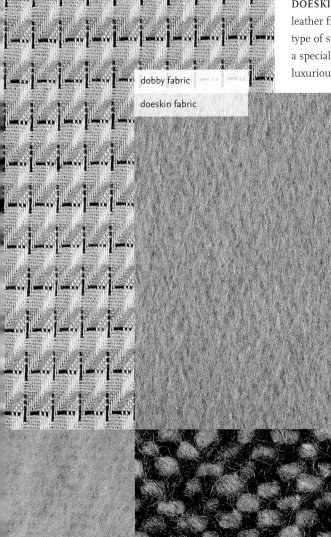

dobby fabric

doeskin fabric

Donegal

domet (interlining)

DOESKIN FABRIC A fine, medium-weight woven fabric made in imitation of the suede leather from the hide of a doe, or female deer. It may be made from wool, or it may be a type of suede cloth made with man-made fibres, often polyester. Doeskin fabric is given a special finish to make it smooth, soft and lustrous, like suede. In its best qualities, it is luxurious and quite expensive.

Wool doeskin fabric is traditionally woven from high-quality merino wool or from a wool blend. It is woven in a densely sett 5-end satin weave, or in another warp-faced weave structure such as a 2/1 warp twill or a 3/1 broken crow. The twist of the warp yarns runs in the same direction as the twill of the satin weave. Wool doeskin is given a dress-face finish that shrinks the fabric and obscures the weave structure: that is, it is heavily milled, raised and given a short, napped finish on the face side. The nap is cut and laid in one direction, and it is therefore preferable that the nap should run from top to bottom when the fabric is made up. One quality is made with 95 to 75 tex warp, sett at 20 to 26 ends per inch, and with 180 to 135 tex weft, woven at 12 to 14 picks per inch.[26]

Doeskin was originally made in the west of England and belongs to the group known as 'West of England fabrics'. Doeskin fabric made with man-made continuous filament fibres, including microfibres, is usually sanded or emerized during the finishing process in order to break the surface filaments, thus creating a resemblance to the surface of real doeskin. Doeskin fabric is similar to both buckskin and beaver cloth but lighter and finer. It is also similar to wool duvetyn.

See also FACED CLOTH; NAPPED FABRICS; SATIN, WOVEN; SUEDE CLOTH.

End uses: tailored suits, dresses, trousers, jackets, overcoats, cushions and upholstery.

DOGSTOOTH CHECK *see* HOUNDSTOOTH CHECK.

DOMET (domett, domette) A very soft fabric with a long nap on both sides, woven in imitation of flannel. It is traditionally woven using cotton and wool yarns and is therefore a low-grade flannel union fabric. There is also an all-cotton version.

Domet is a medium- to heavyweight fabric. It is woven in an open-sett twill or plain weave with a hard-twisted cotton warp and either wool or a mixture of cotton and wool in the weft. Domet may be dyed a solid colour or it may be woven in stripes or checks. It is slightly milled and raised on both sides of the fabric during finishing. This brings the wool fibres to the surface and produces a nap that hides the cotton yarns. Domet is an inexpensive version of a flannel fabric, but it soon becomes threadbare as the nap is quickly rubbed away during wear. It is a similar fabric to outing flannel but it has a longer nap.[9]

See also FLANNEL, NAPPED FABRICS, UNION FABRIC.

End uses: shirts, pyjamas, skirts, linings, wadding, coat/jacket interfacings and interlining for quilted fabrics.

DONEGAL A type of woven tweed, originally made on hand-looms in County Donegal, Ireland. The traditional Donegal is a thick, rough woollen fabric with characteristic random flecks or slubs in bright colours. It is a medium- to heavyweight fabric that is used for both men's and women's clothing. It is perhaps more suited to women's garments than some of the other tweed fabrics.

doria checks

doria stripes

True Donegal fabrics are woven with coarse woollen Cheviot yarns (wool from the Cheviot breed of sheep), but imitations may be woven using other fibres and blends. The warp is a solid colour, usually light grey, brown or natural, and the weft is similar in colour but has been specially spun with uneven fibre-dyed slubs containing brightly coloured flecks at random intervals. This gives a speckled or flecked appearance to the fabric. Donegal is usually woven in plain weave, or sometimes in a 2/2 twill. Nowadays it is normally woven on power looms rather than hand-looms. The fabric is finished with little or no milling, which maintains the rough handle. The warp and weft yarns can be from 400 to 240 tex and sett 4 to 8 ends and picks per cm.[26]

See also COATING FABRIC, TWEED.

End uses: coarse wool suiting, sports jackets, coats, trousers and skirts.

DORIA CHECKS *see* DORIA STRIPES.

DORIA STRIPES Light plain woven cotton fabrics (such as muslin) in which stripe patterns are formed by lengthways cords running through the fabric at intervals.

In the traditional fabric, the warp yarns are arranged so that there is only one end per dent in the reed. The cords are produced by entering two or more ends per dent of the fine cotton warp yarns at intervals across the ground fabric.[36] This produces raised warp-wise stripes in the fabric. Alternatively, the cords are produced by using slightly thicker yarns than the ground yarns. The fabric is traditionally woven in plain weave. Doria checks are made in a similar manner, with extra yarns inserted at intervals in both the warp and weft directions.

See also CHECKS, PLAIN WEAVE FABRIC, STRIPES.

End uses: dresses, blouses and curtains.

DOTTED SWISS A fine, lightweight woven fabric, usually of cotton, with a characteristic small dot pattern woven into the fabric at regular intervals.

The ground fabric is usually a crisp lawn, voile or batiste fabric woven in plain weave. Cotton yarns are traditionally used, but polyester/cotton or other fibre blends may also be used. The dot pattern may be made in several different ways.
(i) *Swivel loom*. The fabric may be woven on a swivel loom. The dots are individually woven into the fabric at regular intervals by using slightly thicker extra weft yarns contained on small shuttles. This is the most expensive type of dotted Swiss fabric, but the dots are the most securely anchored. This type was originally woven in Switzerland, hence the name.
(ii) *Clip spot technique*. A clip spot technique may be used. Slightly thicker extra weft yarns are woven into the fabric at regular intervals to form the dots. After weaving, the floats of extra weft between the dots are cut away.
(iii) *Lappet attachment*. The fabric may be woven with a lappet attachment to the loom. This weaves in slightly thicker extra warp yarns at regular intervals to form the dots. After weaving, the floats of extra warp between the dots are cut away.
(iv) *Flock printing*. Imitation dotted Swiss fabrics are sometimes also made by flock printing. Dots of glue are printed onto the ground fabric and covered with short cotton, wool or viscose fibres. This is the quickest, cheapest method, but also the least durable, since the fibres wear off in a relatively short time.

Whichever method is used to make dotted Swiss, the dotted effect may be the same colour as the ground fabric or it may be in contrasting colours. The fabric may be given a soft finish, or it may be given a permanent resin finish that makes it fairly stiff. Lancé and Madras muslin are made in a similar manner to dotted Swiss.

dotted Swiss

double cloth (woven)

See also BROCHÉ, CLIP SPOT, COTTON FABRIC, DOBBY FABRIC, EXTRA WARP AND EXTRA WEFT FABRICS, FLOCKED FABRIC, LAPPET.

End uses: wedding dresses, bridesmaids' dresses, ladies' evening wear, dresses, blouses and curtains.

DOUBLE CLOTH A general term for woven fabrics composed of two component fabrics, each with its own warp and weft (as opposed to single cloth, which is a single layer of woven fabric). The two layers are interlaced in a single weaving process, in several different ways (described below). Double cloth is classed as a two-layer (or two-ply) compound fabric (compound fabrics are woven layered fabrics consisting of any number of layers). Double cloth fabrics are typically heavy fabrics with a fine surface texture or reversible fabrics in which either side can be used as the face side. They may be alike on both sides or they may have different colours, structures or designs on each side. They are sometimes also called 'double-faced fabrics' or 'reversibles'.

Double cloths are woven in a wide variety of weights and qualities and may be woven in any fibre. The two fabrics are woven separately, with face ends and face picks for the face fabric and back ends and back picks for the back fabric. The two fabrics may be woven in the same or contrasting colours. 'Janus cloth' is an obsolete term for a reversible worsted fabric woven with different colours on either side.[9] Double cloths may be constructed in several different ways.

(i) *Self-stitched double cloths.* The face fabric may be attached to the back fabric by occasionally weaving one of the back warp ends with the face ends and picks or by weaving one of the face warp ends together with the back ends and picks. This produces a very stable double cloth whose two layers cannot normally be separated. An example of a self-stitched double cloth is double-face satin: the two fabric layers are both woven in a warp satin weave and stitched together as described. This fabric requires a large number of warp ends; it is often woven in narrow width and used for ribbons (*see* NARROW FABRICS, SATIN, WOVEN).

(ii) *Centre-stitched double cloths.* Extra warp yarns, independent of the two fabric warps, may be employed as binding threads to link the face and back fabrics together. These are contained between the two fabric layers and do not show on either side. Alternatively, the two fabrics may be attached to one another by extra weft yarns, which are also contained between the two fabric layers and do not show on either side. Fabrics joined by this stitching method may usually be pulled apart.

(iii) *Interchanging double cloths.* The two fabrics can be made to interchange with one another, which not only binds them together but creates a wide range of pattern possibilities. The pattern is the same on both sides of the fabric, but usually in reverse. The two sides may also be coloured differently. Interchanging double cloths may be left unstitched between the interchanges to form small pockets (sometimes called 'pocket cloth'), or they may be stitched.

Probably the majority of double cloths are composed of two fabrics both woven in plain weave. These fabrics are termed 'double plain'. They may be stitched together or they may interchange. Examples of fabrics that may be woven as double cloths include Albert cloth, blankets, blister cloth, buffalo check, cadet cloth, chinchilla fabric, cloqué, Eskimo cloth, fur fabric, hairline, kersey, lampas, Marseilles, matelassé, matelassé crêpe (*see* MATELASSÉ), some melton fabrics, woven piqué, woven plush, silence cloth and some vicuña fabrics. Double satin, satin-back and satin royale are examples of double cloth fabrics woven in a satin weave structure on either one or both sides (*see* SATIN, WOVEN).

See also BACKED FABRIC, EXTRA WARP AND EXTRA WEFT FABRICS, LAMINATED FABRIC, MULTI-COMPONENT FABRICS, PILE FABRICS.

End uses: coats, jackets, dresses and furnishings.

DOUBLE JERSEY (double-knit fabric) *see* JERSEY.

DOUBLE PLAIN *see* DOUBLE CLOTH.

DOUPION (dupion) A general term for woven silk fabrics made using doupion yarns. Doupion fabrics are rough-textured, medium-weight fabrics with a characteristic slubby texture. They are usually woven in plain weave.

Doupion yarns are silk yarns obtained from double cocoons. The silk is spun by two silkworms in close proximity, and the strands of fibre become mixed with each other. When the strands are reeled, an irregular, rough silk yarn with slubs is produced. Imitation doupion fabrics are also made using synthetic yarns that have been manufactured with an uneven thickness to resemble silk doupion yarns. Doupion tends to fray easily. Doupion shantung (*see* SHANTUNG) and antique taffeta (*see* TAFFETA) are examples of fabrics that are made with doupion yarns.

See also SILK FABRIC.

End uses: women's lightweight suiting fabrics, bridal wear, occasion wear, cushions and furnishing fabrics.

DOWLAS (*obs.*) Originally a coarse, half-bleached linen fabric from Daoulas in Brittany.[3] It was later imitated in cotton, as a low-quality fabric woven in plain weave and used for towels and aprons.

DRILL A strong, thick, durable woven fabric, usually woven in a warp-faced twill weave. Characteristically, the twill lines run from bottom right to top left (left-hand twill) – that is, in the opposite direction to most twill weaves. Drill is a similar fabric to denim, but it is usually piece-dyed, smoother in appearance and of better quality.

Traditionally, drill is made from 100% carded cotton using good-quality, high-twist, two-fold warp yarns and a softer, slightly thicker, singles weft yarn. Other fibre combinations are available, for example polyester/cotton blends or cotton mixed with other man-made fibres. Elastane fibres are also sometimes included to produce a stretch fabric. Drill is woven in a firm 3-, 4-, or 5-end warp-faced twill weave (usually a 3/1 warp-faced twill). The twill lines run in the opposite direction to the twist direction of the warp yarns in order to accentuate the twill effect. Sometimes drill is woven in a 5-end satin weave, in which case it is termed a 'satin drill'.

Drills may be undyed, bleached, piece-dyed, warp-striped or printed. The fabric is usually pre-shrunk and it is sometimes brushed to give it a soft handle. Drill is a medium- to heavyweight fabric and is available in a wide range of qualities. One example of a 3/1 drill fabric is: 37 tex warp sett at 39 ends per cm and 50 tex weft, woven at 18 picks per cm; cloth weight 260 g/m².[25] Typical 5-end satin drill fabrics are: 14 tex cotton warp sett at 50 ends per cm and 16 tex cotton weft, woven at 32 picks per cm;[26] or 27 tex cotton warp sett at 44 ends per cm and 46 tex cotton weft, woven at 28 picks per cm.[26]

Khaki is a type of drill fabric that is piece-dyed a khaki colour and used for army uniforms. Florentine, which is similar to drill, is piece-dyed navy blue and was traditionally used for policemen's uniforms. The term 'drillette' was previously used for a grey cloth fabric woven in sateen weave and used as a lining fabric;[4] nowadays the term tends to be used (if at all) for lightweight drill fabrics. Drill is a similar fabric to bluette, denim, dungaree, some gaberdine fabrics, hickory cloth, jean and ticking.

See also COTTON FABRIC; SATIN, WOVEN; TWILL FABRICS.

End uses: (lighter weights) shirts, skirts and dresses; (heavier weights) uniforms, trousers, suits, shorts, children's clothes, workwear, overalls, protective clothing, bags, shoes, mattress covers and furnishing fabrics.

doupion

drill (back and face)

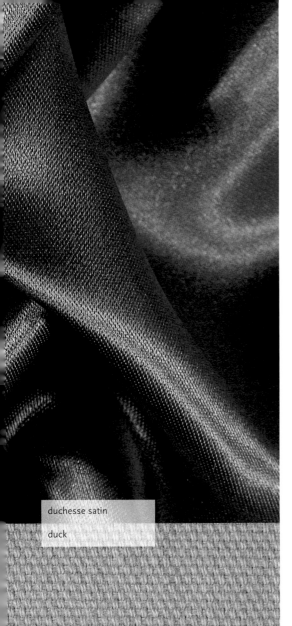

duchesse satin

duck

DRILLETTE *see* DRILL.

DRUID'S CLOTH *see* MONK'S CLOTH.

DUCAPE (*obs.*) An all-silk fabric woven in plain weave with heavy cords. It is a heavy poplin-type fabric.[36]

DUCHESSE SATIN A thick, heavy fabric woven in satin weave, traditionally using 100% silk yarns. Characteristically, it is a smooth, rich, luxurious fabric with a very high lustre. It is an expensive fabric.

   Although duchesse satin is still made in silk, cheaper versions, made from viscose filament or other man-made filament fibres, are also available. It is usually yarn-dyed in solid colours. The warp is very closely sett, and the fabric is woven in a 7-, 8-, 10- or 12-end warp satin weave structure. This produces a heavy, warp-faced fabric. One quality is made with 2 tex filament silk warp sett at 144 ends per cm and with 18 tex spun silk weft woven at 36 picks per cm.[26] Duchesse satin is a stiff fabric and frays easily. It is similar to shoe satin (used for ballet shoes). Duchesse mousseline is a variation of duchesse satin, but it is woven in a fancy twill weave (*see* MOUSSELINE).

See also SATIN, WOVEN; SILK FABRIC.

End uses: wedding and evening dresses, occasion wear, blouses and dresses.

DUCK A term used to describe a wide range of strong, durable cotton- or linen-based fabrics. Duck fabrics are firm, heavy fabrics, closely woven in plain weave or plain weave variations. Duck is very similar to canvas, and the terms tend to be used interchangeably; however, duck is usually slightly heavier and rougher, while canvas is smoother and more tightly woven.

   Duck was originally made in linen. The name is derived from the Dutch word *doek*, meaning a linen canvas used for sailors' clothing.[3] Nowadays duck is more likely to be made in cotton or cotton/polyester. Both warp and weft yarns are highly sett, and the fabric is usually tightly woven in a simple hopsack weave structure (plain weave with the warp yarns weaving in pairs and either single or double weft yarns). This gives the fabric a characteristic grainy texture.

   Duck is available in a wide range of weights and qualities. It may be undyed, bleached, dyed or printed. Finishes vary according to the end use, ranging from heavy sizing to a soft finish. An example of a heavyweight duck fabric construction is 250/6 tex cotton warp sett at 13 ends per cm and 250/6 tex cotton weft woven at 10 picks per cm.[26] An example of a medium-weight duck fabric construction is 170/5 tex cotton warp sett at 18 ends per cm and 120/3 tex cotton weft woven at 12 picks per cm.[26] The term 'duck' may also be applied to a tropical suiting fabric woven in hopsack weaves.[26] Sailcloth is a similar fabric to duck, but slightly lighter in weight.

See also AWNING CLOTH, BOOK CLOTH, CANVAS, HOPSACK, LINING FABRIC, SAILCLOTH, TROPICAL SUITING.

End uses: uniforms (army duck), awnings (awning duck or awning cloth), driving belts (belting duck), shoe and boot linings (shoe, boot or bootleg duck), tennis and basketball shoes (enamelling duck, a fabric coated to imitate leather), hosepipes (hosepipe duck), linen (linen duck), plimsolls and casual shoes (plimsoll duck), sails (sailcloth duck), tents (tent duck), tarpaulins, blinds, curtains, deckchair seats, directors' chairs, garden furniture, luggage, bags, workwear, sportswear, coats, jackets, (heavyweight) interlining and lining fabrics.

DUFFEL (duffle) A very heavy, low-quality woven fabric made from low-grade wool. It has a dense nap on both sides and is known for its principal use – as a hard-wearing, weatherproof fabric employed in a style of short coat with a hood, called a 'duffel coat'.

Duffel is woven in wool, in a 2/2 twill weave. After weaving, it is heavily milled and raised to give it a dense nap on both sides. It takes its name from the small town of Duffel, near Antwerp in Belgium, where it was first woven.[3] Flushing is a similar fabric to duffel, but of slightly higher quality. Melton is also similar, but of much higher quality.

See also COATING FABRIC, FELTED FABRIC, NAPPED FABRICS.

End uses: duffel coats, jackets and blankets. (Duffel bags are not made of duffel; they are drawstring bags that were first used by sailors to carry their duffel blankets.[3])

DUNGAREE A strong, hard-wearing woven fabric, usually woven in a warp-faced twill weave. It is similar to denim, but the warp and weft yarns are dyed the same colour, making it a solid-colour fabric. The fabric is synonymous with its principal use – for durable workwear trousers or bib and brace overalls.

Dungaree is traditionally made from 100% cotton, but other fibre combinations are also available, for example polyester/cotton blends or cotton mixed with other man-made fibres. Dungaree is woven in a 3/1 or a 2/1 warp-faced twill weave structure. Some dungaree fabrics are piece-dyed, but the better-quality fabrics are yarn-dyed, with both the warp and weft yarns dyed the same colour. As with denim, the most popular colour for dungaree fabrics is indigo blue, but it is also woven in other colours.

Dungaree was first woven in Goa in India,[3] and its the name originates from the Hindi word *dungri*. An example of one quality of dungaree fabric is: 38 tex warp sett at 32 ends per cm and 27 tex weft woven at 26 picks per cm.[26] Dungaree is similar to bluette, denim, drill, florentine, hickory cloth and jean.

See also TWILL FABRICS.

End uses: casual and workwear, including dungarees, jeans, overalls, protective clothing, jackets, skirts, dresses, shorts and children's clothes.

DUPION *see* DOUPION.

DUVETYN (duvetine) A thick, smooth woven fabric that is given a special finish to produce a characteristic soft suede-like appearance and handle. The fabric was first woven in France and takes its name from the French *duvet*, meaning 'down'.[5]

Duvetyn is woven in a variety of fibres including cotton, wool, silk, man-made fibres and combinations of these. It is therefore available in a range of different weights and qualities, but they are all given the characteristic suede-effect finish. Duvetyn may be yarn-dyed or piece-dyed. The fabric is closely woven in a 3/1 twill or a satin weave, but this is partially obscured by the heavy nap finish given to the face side of the cloth. The smooth, suede-like surface is achieved by raising the surface fibres with emery rollers, closely shearing and brushing the fabric and then pressing it to give it softness and good drape.

Duvetyn is similar to suede cloth, but usually lighter in weight and with more drape. Cotton duvetyn, cotton suede cloth and flannelette can all be converted from the same grey goods, but duvetyn and suede cloth are more closely sheared, to give a smoother, flatter surface.[19] Duvetyn is sometimes also called 'suede flannel', 'suede duvetyn' or 'mouse skin' (*peau de souris*). All-wool duvetyn can resemble a compact velvet and is more like a mock velvet fabric. Wool duvetyn is similar to beaver cloth and doeskin fabric, but lighter in weight and smoother. It is also similar to a napped velour fabric but differs in having a shorter, less dense nap and an obscured weave structure.

See also NAPPED FABRICS.

End uses: women's suits, coats, dresses, jackets, hats, handbags, collars, trimmings and curtains.

duffel

dungaree

duvetyn

dyed fabric (fibre-dyed)

dyed fabric (piece-dyed)

DYED FABRICS A general term for fabrics that have been coloured with natural or synthetic dyes. Dyeing is the process of applying and fixing a dye to a textile substrate. Dye may be applied to the fibres and yarns from which the fabric is composed or directly to the fabric itself.

Dyeing is a very ancient art or science that has been practised in many cultures, and today a huge variety of colours is available. Throughout most of history, textiles were dyed with natural dyestuffs made from plants, roots, bark and berries. Examples include indigo (from indigo plants), saffron (from crocus stamens) and madder (from plant roots). These were often combined with different chemical mordants (e.g. alum, tin or chrome) to make the colours fast. It was only relatively recently, in the mid-19th century, that synthetic dyestuffs made from chemicals were developed; these are now used very widely to dye textiles of all kinds. There are hundreds, if not thousands, of different synthetic dyestuffs, all with different characteristics and fastness properties.

Dyeing is achieved by immersing the textile in a (usually hot) solution of chemical dyes in water, sometimes in pressurized containers in order to facilitate the process. The textile will usually require subsequent after-treatments in order to fix the dye. The dye may be applied to the textile at the fibre, yarn, fabric or garment stage, or it may be applied in thickened form to print patterns onto fabric (*see* PRINTED FABRIC). Many different tweed fabrics – to give an example – are dyed at the fibre stage. The majority of fabrics, however, are dyed either at the yarn stage (woven fabrics are called 'colour-woven') or at the fabric stage (when the fabrics are called 'piece-dyed'). Fabrics with interesting dyed effects include bandanna, batik, chameleon fabric, chiné fabrics, ikat, marble cloth, marl fabric, mélange fabric, ombré, resist-dyed fabrics, shot fabrics, space-dyed fabric, tie-dyed fabrics and tweed.

See also PRINTED FABRIC.

End uses: all kinds of fashion and furnishing fabrics.

EGYPTIAN COTTON *see* COTTON FABRIC.

EGYPTIAN LAWN *see* LAWN.

EIGHT-LOCK A light- to medium-weight weft-knitted fabric that consists of two layers of rib-based fabric that are joined together in the middle. It is a type of double jersey fabric. The fabric is reversible, and either side may be used as the face side.

The two fabric layers are both closely knitted using fine yarns, in a 2 × 2 rib structure. They are joined together by interlocking sinker loops. The vertical wales on one side of the fabric are alternated with the vertical wales on the other side (i.e. the pattern repeat is over four wales), and this produces an intermeshed double 2 × 2 rib fabric. When knitted in colour, check or stripe effects can be produced.[38] Eight-lock is a similar fabric to interlock, but it is based on a 2 × 2 rib structure rather than a 1 × 1 rib structure. It also has a greater widthways extensibility, and usually a softer handle, than interlock.

See also INTERLOCK; JERSEY; KNITTED FABRIC; RIB FABRICS, KNITTED; WEFT-KNITTED FABRIC.

End uses: underwear, sweaters, T-shirts, polo shirts, sportswear, leisure wear, pyjamas and dresses.

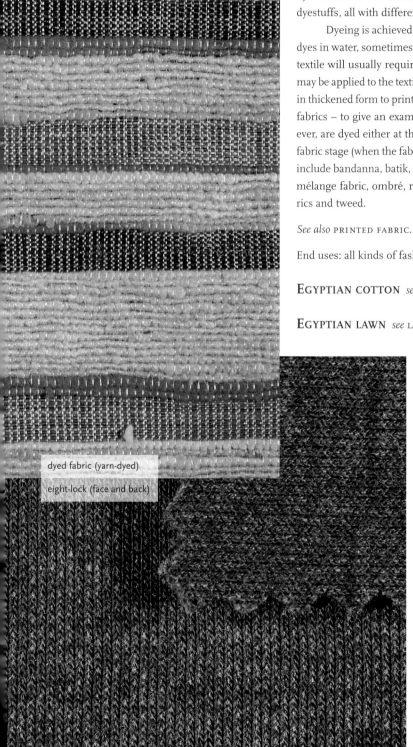

dyed fabric (yarn-dyed)

eight-lock (face and back)

elastane fabric
(containing elastane fibre)

elastane fabric
(showing elastane fibre)

ELASTANE FABRIC A general term for any fabric in which elastane fibres or yarns have been incorporated; the term may be used for fabrics of all different weights and constructions, including woven, knitted and lace fabrics. Elastane is the generic name of a rubber-like, man-made synthetic fibre composed of segmented polyurethane (as defined by the International Organization for Standardization in ISO 2076:1999E).[25] Elastane is stronger and more flexible than rubber, which loses its stretch and becomes brittle with age. Characteristically, elastane fabrics are extremely stretchy fabrics with very good recovery. Elastane is also known by the name LYCRA®, which is perhaps the best-known brand of elastane. In the United States, spandex is the generic name (as approved by the US Federal Trade Commission) of a very similar fibre to elastane.

Elastane fibres have an exceptionally high degree of stretch and rapid recovery, with an elongation to break within the range of 400% to 600%. They are produced by a block co-polymer process, in which long flexible blocks of polyurethane alternate with shorter, more crystalline segments. The long flexible portions provide the stretchiness, while the stiff segments act as re-enforcing points.

Elastane is usually produced in two colours, black and white. As the fibres are so fine, they are rarely seen when incorporated into a fabric. Fabrics are not usually made solely with elastane; instead it is incorporated into fabrics along with other yarns and fibres. Elastane is used in all kinds of fabric constructions, but it is widely employed in warp-knitted and single jersey fabrics in particular. With fine fabrics (mostly single jersey fabrics), very fine, bare elastane yarns are usually 'plated' together with other non-stretchy yarns. These fabrics are knitted on conventional single jersey weft-knitting machines, sometimes modified to use bare elastane, which is cheaper than covered elastane. Very fine elastane yarns are knitted together with a (usually) thicker, non-stretchy yarn, which can be made from most fibre types. The fabric may be knitted in different single jersey knit structures, but most fabrics are knitted in a plain knit structure, with the elastane being plated at every course. The elastane is therefore mainly hidden behind the other yarn within the construction and does not grin through. In some fabrics the elastane yarn is plated at every other course to reduce cost, but this usually produces a lower-quality fabric, with reduced warpways stretch in particular. The elastane is invisible within the fabric structure. These fabrics may then be piece-dyed. It is not possible to dye the elastane, but the surrounding yarns and fibres may be dyed. Care must be taken since too long an exposure to high temperatures can weaken elastane.

With chunkier fabrics, the elastane is either wrapped with an outer covering of other fibres (e.g. cotton) or is core-spun with an outer covering of other fibres (usually nylon or polyester). Elastomeric single jersey jacquards are also produced, and a wide range of patterns are possible, but these fabrics often use float stitch patterning to give a 'satin' pattern effect.

Since elastane is normally used in conjunction with other fibres, the percentage of each should always be stated. The inclusion of elastane in a fabric gives it excellent stretch and recovery properties. Elastane fabrics therefore find a very wide range of end uses where a degree of stretchiness is desirable. Depending on the fabric construction and how the elastane is incorporated, it is possible to achieve either one-way or two-way stretch. If a garment containing elastane loses its shape during use, it can be returned to its original dimensions in steam or hot water. Examples of fabrics that often incorporate elastane are: double jersey (*see* JERSEY), lace, locknit, micromesh, power net, raschel lace, raschel stretch fabrics, raschel warp-knitted fabric, simplex, single jersey (*see* JERSEY), spacer fabrics and tricot (stretch tricot).

See also ELASTOMERIC FABRIC, JERSEY, PLAIN KNIT FABRIC, PLATED FABRICS, POLYURETHANE, RUBBER, STRETCH FABRIC.

End uses: sportswear, leisure wear, swimwear, T-shirts, socks, tights, lingerie, bras, corsetry, furnishings, accessories, medical and industrial textiles.

elastique

elastomeric fabric

elastomeric fabric
(gypsy cloth)

ELASTIC FABRIC *see* STRETCH FABRIC.

ELASTIQUE A term now used mainly in the United States for a range of strong, durable woven fabrics characterized by steep double twill lines.[3] These include cavalry twill and tricotine. In the 19th century elastique was an overcoating fabric woven in a steep double twill weave using fine merino wool.

Elastique fabrics are usually made from high-twist wool or worsted yarns and they have a very close warp sett. When woven in a steep twill weave, this accentuates the double twill lines, which are apparent only on the face side of the fabric. The back is smooth and is sometimes given a nap finish. Elastique fabrics are usually dyed in natural fawn colours.

See also CAVALRY TWILL, TRICOTINE, TWILL FABRICS.

End uses: trousers, jackets, coats, uniforms and riding jodhpurs.

ELASTOMERIC FABRIC A general term for any fabric, whether woven, warp-knitted or weft-knitted, that has been constructed using elastomeric yarns or fibres such as elastane. Characteristically, elastomeric fabrics are very stretchy.

Elastomeric yarns are made with elastomers, which are inherently stretchy polymers characterized by high extensibility and rapid, virtually complete recovery. Elastomeric yarns may be incorporated in a fabric in their bare state, or they may be wrapped in other fibres for the aesthetic enhancement of the fabric. Depending on the fabric construction and how the elastomeric yarns are incorporated, it is possible to achieve either one-way or two-way stretch in the fabric. The degree of stretch depends on the fabric construction and the types of yarn used.

Many elastomeric fabrics are weft-knitted, single jersey constructions (*see* JERSEY). A large number are also warp-knitted. These fall into two groups: tricot and raschel knitted products. The stretch fabric trade uses the term 'tricot' to describe elastomeric locknits with elastane, to distinguish them from elastomeric raschel fabrics (*see* LOCKNIT, RASCHEL STRETCH FABRICS, TRICOT).

Elastomeric yarns inserted at intervals into a fabric, either regularly or randomly, produce a puckered or ruched effect. A woven fabric with this effect is sometimes called 'gypsy cloth'.

See also ELASTANE FABRIC, STRETCH FABRIC.

End uses: Sportswear, leisure wear, swimwear, casual wear, socks, tights, corsetry, lingerie, blouses, furnishings, accessories, industrial textiles and medical textiles.

ELECTRONIC TEXTILES (e-textiles) *see* SMART TEXTILES.

ELEPHANT CORD *see* CORDUROY.

EMBOSSED CRÊPE *see* CRÊPE.

EMBOSSED FABRICS Fabrics that have had a relief engraving pressed into them using heat and pressure in order to produce a pattern or texture in the fabric. Both flat and pile fabrics may be embossed. The embossing may produce a flat, glazed design on the fabric (flat-embossed fabric) or, if pressed more deeply into the fabric, a three-dimensional, raised or relief effect (relief-embossed fabric).

Embossing is a type of fabric finish, and fabrics are processed using an embossing calender. The fabric is passed between two rotating metal rollers that press against

embossed fabric

embroidered fabric
(machine-embroidered)

one another. One roller is heated and has been engraved with the desired pattern. The second is covered with compressed paper or cotton fabric to make it soft. When the fabric is passed between the two rollers, the pattern from the engraved roller is pressed into the fabric.

Both natural and man-made fibre fabrics may be embossed. With natural fibre fabrics, however, the embossing is usually less permanent and may come out with washing. Natural fibre fabrics may be treated with resins to increase the lifespan of embossed finishes. With synthetic man-made fibre fabrics, the embossing is usually permanent. This is because the heat softens the thermoplastic fibres and, on cooling, they remain fixed in the embossing position. Embossing onto man-made fibre fabrics can create effects similar to crinkle crêpe or seersucker fabrics. The 'watermark' effect on some moiré fabrics is also produced by embossing (see MOIRÉ FABRIC). Fabrics that are suitable for embossing include brocade, crêpe, leather-cloth, plush, satin (see SATIN, WOVEN), velour and velvet.

See also CRINKLE CRÊPE; CRINKLE FABRIC; HOLOGRAPHIC FABRICS; PIQUÉ, WOVEN; PLEATED FABRICS; REFLECTIVE FABRICS; SEERSUCKER.

End uses: women's wear, scarves, accessories and furnishing fabrics.

EMBOSSED VELVET *see* VELVET.

EMBROIDERED FABRICS Traditionally a term for fabrics that have been decorated on the face side with threads applied either by hand-sewing or by machine stitching. Traditional embroidery techniques may be used on any existing fabric, whether it be woven, knitted or nonwoven. Beads, sequins and ribbons may also be attached to enhance the decorative effect of the stitching. As embroidery stitching is a fairly lengthy process, embroidered fabrics are usually quite expensive. They are sometimes difficult to care for, since many are delicate, often having long floats, and they may not be washable. The term 'embroidery' is also sometimes used in a much wider sense, to include fabrics, art works or constructions that incorporate threads, yarns or fabrics as a major component.

Embroidery has been practised for centuries in many parts of the world. There are references to gold thread embroidery from the 12th century.[5] The early embroideries were all worked by hand and were therefore quite exclusive. It was not until the 1860s, when the first embroidery machine was developed, that embroidered fabrics became more affordable.[5] This was the Schiffli embroidery machine, and much machine embroidery today is made on modern Schiffli machines. 'Schiffli embroidery' is a term used to describe many fine machine-embroidered fabrics. The embroidery takes the form of closely stitched zigzag stitches of varying lengths. Many lace fabrics are also produced on Schiffli embroidery machines (see LACE). The other main machine is the multihead embroidery machine, which is capable of creating flat or pile embroidery designs, stitching crests and logos, and working with ribbons, beads and sequins.

The embroidery threads may be of any fibre (or sometimes metallic), and they are usually in contrasting colours to the base fabric. Embroidery is often done on lightweight fabrics with thicker threads than the yarns used in the base fabric. Suitable base fabrics for embroidery include Assam silk (see SILK FABRIC), binca, embroidery canvas (see CANVAS), chiffon, gazar, Hardanger, Java, mousseline, mull, net, ninon, organdie, organza, panama canvas (see PANAMA), pashmina, percale, pina cloth (see PLANT-FIBRE FABRICS), satin (woven), tulle and voile. Examples of embroidered fabrics include Swiss batiste, broderie anglaise, eyelet, needlepoint lace, Richelieu and some veiling fabrics. Broché, clip spot and lappet are woven fabrics that sometimes look like embroidered fabrics.

See also APPLIQUÉ FABRIC, BEADED FABRICS, LAMÉ, METALLIC FABRICS, SEQUINNED FABRICS.

End uses: ladies' evening wear, blouses, dresses, lingerie, veils, saris and ecclesiastical robes.

embroidered fabric
(hand-embroidered)

embroidered fabric
(hand-embroidered)

épingle

épingline

éponge

EMPRESS CLOTH (*obs.*) A double-faced woollen fabric with a twill face (2/1 weft twill) and a ribbed back. It was originally made with a cotton warp and a worsted wool weft. It was made popular by Empress Eugénie of France in the 19th century.[8, 36]

END-AND-END FABRICS *see* COLOUR AND WEAVE EFFECTS.

ENSIGN FABRIC *see* BUNTING.

EOLIENNE (*obs.*) A lightweight woven fabric made with a silk or man-made fibre warp and a thicker, hard-twisted botany wool or cotton weft. It has a fine warp rib, is piece-dyed and is made lustrous in finishing. The name refers to Aeolus, the ancient Greek god of the winds.[3, 5, 26]

ÉPINGLE A lustrous, lightweight woven fabric, constructed in plain weave. It may be a warp rib or a weft rib fabric, and characteristically large and small ribs or cords alternate with each other to produce a fine, textured fabric, an effect that may be enhanced by using contrasting colours for the different ribs. Épingle frays quite easily.

Épingle is quite an ancient fabric, originally woven in silk. Now it is made from any of many different fibres, including worsted, cotton or man-made fibres. The name 'épingle' is French for 'pin', which describes the fine pin-like warp ribs. There are a number of variations of this fabric. Épingle brocade is a figured jacquard fabric with an épingle-ribbed background across the width of the fabric; épingle crepon is similar, but with silk and worsted yarns alternating in the weft; and épingle façonné also resembles épingle brocade, but has a silk warp and a worsted weft. Épingline also has a silk warp and a worsted weft, but it is a weft rib fabric in which the cords run in the warp direction. Épingle velvet is a fine, soft velvet fabric, patterned with pin-like velvet cords; *see* VELVET.

See also REPP; RIB FABRICS, WOVEN; SILK FABRIC.

End uses: women's tailored dresses and suits, men's ties, furnishing fabrics and ribbons.

ÉPONGE A general term for a range of thick but lightweight open-textured woven fabrics that feel sponge-like (the name is French for 'sponge'). The texture is made by weaving the fabric with either loop yarns or other fancy textured yarns.

There are several main types of woven éponge:
- A soft, open-sett woollen fabric that is woven in plain weave with smooth warp yarns (often hard-twisted) and loosely spun, thick fancy yarns (often bouclé yarns) in the weft only. If bouclé yarns are used, the loops from the yarn stand up from the main body of the fabric to form a loop pile on the surface of the fabric.
- A soft, open-sett woollen fabric that is woven in plain weave with fancy warp and weft yarns (often bouclé yarns).
- Cotton éponge, a soft, open-sett cotton fabric that is woven in plain weave with soft, irregular spiral or gimp yarns in both the warp and the weft. A typical construction is as follows: 140 tex cotton warp sett at 7 ends per cm and 140 tex cotton weft woven at 7 picks per cm. This produces a fabric that is very similar to ratiné but softer.[26]
  See RATINÉ.
- Man-made fibre éponge, which is soft, loose and spongy, rather like terry fabric.
  See TERRY FABRIC.

Éponge is a particular type of sponge cloth and is sometimes also called by that name (*see* SPONGE CLOTH). Astrakhan fabric, poodle cloth and terry fabric are similar to éponge. Other examples of loop yarn fabrics include bouclé fabric and frotté.

See also COATING FABRIC, PILE FABRICS, RATINÉ.

End uses: dresses, ladies' suits, lightweight coats and jackets, and furnishing fabrics.

Eskimo cloth
(face and back)

étamine

ESKIMO CLOTH A thick, heavyweight, all-wool woven fabric that is extremely warm and is used for overcoats; it is double-faced and therefore reversible. Eskimo cloth is a double cloth fabric, woven in wool with a 5-end satin face weave and a twill back. It is usually piece-dyed or sometimes colour-woven with bold, wide stripes (usually in the weft direction). It is given a thick nap finish.

See also COATING FABRIC; DOUBLE CLOTH; NAPPED FABRICS; SATIN, WOVEN; TWILL FABRICS.

End uses: heavy overcoats and jackets.

ESTAMENE (*obs.*) A woven fabric made with cross-bred worsted yarns; it is usually woven in 2/2 twill, piece-dyed, milled and finished with a rough fibrous surface.[26]

ESTRELLA (*obs.*) A woven crêpe fabric woven in plain weave with a silk warp and a hard-twisted botany weft. Two 'S' twist yarns and two 'Z' twist yarns are alternated in the weft.[26]

ÉTAMINE A lightweight, open, porous woven fabric. It was originally a coarse, gauze-like fabric used to sift flour (the name is French for 'sieve'); it was sometimes also used as a bunting fabric and as such was known as 'tammy'. Today étamine is usually of a higher quality and is used for apparel. It belongs to the muslin family of fabrics.

Étamine was originally made from wool and continues to be woven mainly from worsted wool today; however, it is also made in coarse cotton and linen qualities, man-made fibres and blends. Thick, high-twist yarns are woven in a variety of open weave structures, including plain weave, 2/2 twill, leno and mock leno. The fabric is finished with a short nap.

Étamine glacé is a finer fabric than ordinary étamine; the term is the French one for challis (*see* CHALLIS).[3] Étamine à bluteau was the quality made specifically for flour sifting. Étamine à voile was a fine worsted fabric used for church vestments. Étamine is a similar fabric to cheesecloth, delaine, gauze and scrim.

See also BUNTING, LENO FABRIC, MOCK LENO, MUSLIN.

End uses: (coarse qualities) flags, banners, outdoor decorations, curtains and hangings; (finer qualities) dresses, blouses, shirts and sportswear.

EXTRA WARP AND EXTRA WEFT FABRICS Woven fabrics that have an extra set of either warp or weft yarns interwoven into a base fabric. The extra yarns are sometimes termed 'supplementary warp' or 'supplementary weft' yarns.

Extra yarns may be used to provide additional properties, as the following examples illustrate.

(i) *Thickness, weight or strength.* Fabrics may be woven with extra warp or weft yarns in order to add thickness, weight or strength, as with backed fabrics (*see* BACKED FABRIC). Extra yarns may also be used with some rib and cord fabrics in order to emphasize the rib or cord effect. Where two warps are used, the ribs may be padded out by inserting extra yarns between the face and the back fabrics, making the fabric more three-dimensional. Fabrics that use extra warp or extra weft yarns in this way include cannelle, cannetille, charmante satin and woven piqué fabrics (*see* PIQUÉ, WOVEN).

(ii) *Pile.* Extra warp or extra weft yarns may be employed to form a pile on one side, or sometimes both sides, of a woven fabric (*see* PILE FABRICS). With most fabrics where the pile is made in this way, the extra yarns are usually positioned regularly throughout the width or length of the fabric. The base fabric is usually woven in a simple, firm weave structure like plain weave or twill. Weft pile fabrics are made by floating the extra weft yarns on the surface of the base fabric. Warp pile fabrics are made by looping the extra warp yarns over wires that are removed after weaving. Whether the pile is made from extra warp or extra weft yarns, the loops formed may either be cut to form tufts (cut pile

extra weft fabric
(back and face)

extra warp fabric

eyelash fabric

fabrics), or left uncut to form loop pile fabrics. Fabrics that use extra warp and extra weft yarns in this way include astrakhan fabric, chinchilla fabric, eyelash fabric, fustian fabrics and poodle cloth.

(iii) *Patterns*. Extra warp and extra weft yarns may be used to enable figures or patterns to be woven into the fabric. With most fabrics patterned in this way, the yarns are introduced only into small sections of the fabric where the pattern is required. In some fabrics, such as broché, extra weft yarns contained on small swivel shuttles are woven into the base fabric across the width of each individual figure. With most extra warp and extra weft fabrics, however, the extra yarns travel the whole length or width of the fabric. When the extra yarns are not required to make the pattern, they are either floated on the back of the fabric or floated on the surface of the fabric and cut off after weaving.

Extra warp fabrics typically have vertical stripes of woven pattern. The extra warp yarns in these areas are usually arranged end-and-end with the warp yarns of the ground fabric. The ground fabric is usually woven in a simple weave structure like plain weave, hopsack or twill. The extra warp yarns are typically woven in a warp-faced weave structure, such as a satin weave or a warp-faced twill weave, in order to accentuate the woven pattern against the surface of the ground fabric.

Extra weft patterned fabrics typically have horizontal stripes of woven pattern. In the patterned areas, each weft pick of the background fabric is alternated with an extra weft pick. As with extra warp fabrics, the ground fabric is usually woven in a simple weave structure, and the extra weft stripes are usually woven in a structure such as a weft sateen, that allows them to predominate on the surface of the fabric.

Extra warp and weft yarns are often thicker than, and in a contrasting colour to, the yarns used for the ground weave. Patterned fabrics woven with extra warp or extra weft include clip spot, dotted Swiss and voile (woven striped voile); those woven with extra warp include lappet; and those woven with extra weft include broché, lancé, Madras muslin, some molleton fabrics, Montagnac and some paisley woven fabrics.

See also DOUBLE CLOTH, FIGURED FABRIC.

End uses: apparel and furnishings.

EYELASH FABRIC A woven or knitted fabric that has a decorative surface of fringing, composed of cut yarns or threads that float freely over the surface of the fabric.

Eyelash fabrics are made using many fibre types, although fine man-made fibres or metallic or plastic yarns are often used for the fringing in order to make it a feature. In woven fabrics, the fringes are sometimes made with extra warp or extra weft yarns. The fringing yarns are usually securely woven or knitted into the backing fabric in parts and floated across its surface, usually at regular intervals. Afterwards these floats are cut to form relatively long fringes. According to the nature of the yarns used, the fringes may hang downwards like tassels, or they may form a surface of wiry threads all over the fabric surface.

See also EXTRA WARP AND EXTRA WEFT FABRICS.

End uses: ladies' evening wear, occasion wear, theatrical costumes and (more rarely) cushion covers and drapes.

EYELET, WEFT-KNITTED A weft-knitted fabric with intricate patterns of ornamental holes.

The ground fabric is most commonly knitted in a plain knit construction and occasionally in rib (rib eyelet). The holes are created by means of eyelet stitches. Usually

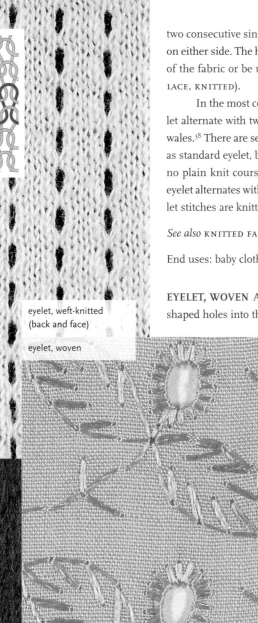

eyelet, weft-knitted
(back and face)

eyelet, woven

faced cloth

two consecutive sinker loops are transferred, one onto each of the two adjacent needles on either side. The holes may be spaced any distance apart, and may decorate large areas of the fabric or be used as border details. Eyelet is a similar fabric to knitted lace (*see* LACE, KNITTED).

In the most common eyelet fabric, known as 'standard eyelet', two courses of eyelet alternate with two courses of plain knit, and the eyelet holes are separated by three wales.[38] There are several common variations. Fine eyelet is constructed in the same way as standard eyelet, but the holes are separated by two wales. Close eyelet is knitted with no plain knit courses and the holes are staggered. In pin-point eyelet, one course of eyelet alternates with two plain knit courses. For patterned eyelet, patterns knitted in eyelet stitches are knitted into a (usually) plain knitted ground fabric.

See also KNITTED FABRIC, PLAIN KNIT FABRIC, WEFT-KNITTED FABRIC.

End uses: baby clothes, fashion knitwear and lingerie.

EYELET, WOVEN A lightweight woven fabric in which a pattern is made by cutting small shaped holes into the fabric and stitching around their edges with embroidery threads. It is a coloured, embroidered fabric; white versions are normally called 'broderie anglaise'. Eyelet fabrics may be patterned along the border or in an all-over design.

Eyelet used to be embroidered by hand, but nowadays it is usually machine-embroidered on a Schiffli embroidery machine using a buttonhole stitch outline. The base fabric is usually a cotton, polyester/cotton or linen fabric woven in plain weave. Typical base fabrics used include batiste (eyelet batiste), broadcloth (eyelet broadcloth), organdie (eyelet organdie) and linen fabrics (eyelet linen). The fabric is usually piece-dyed in pale pastel colours. The shapes, which are frequently round, are typically embroidered with thread of the same colour as the fabric. More rarely, they are embroidered with a contrasting thread colour. Afterwards their centres are cut away or punched out, leaving a pattern of holes in the fabric.

See also BRODERIE ANGLAISE, EMBROIDERED FABRICS, LASER-CUT FABRICS.

End uses: blouses, dresses, children's dresses, nightwear, lingerie, trimmings, curtains, table linen and bed linen.

FACED CLOTH A general term used for any woven fabric that has been given a dress-face finish. In this finish, which is given mainly to wool fabrics, the fabric is milled and then the nap on the face side of the fabric is raised, cropped and laid in one direction. This gives the fabric a characteristic smooth, flat surface with a high lustre. It is therefore advisable that all pattern pieces should be cut in the same direction when the fabric is made up. Usually the nap runs from top to bottom.

The best-quality faced cloths are made of wool; however, fabrics made from other fibres and blends may also be given a similar finish. With wool fabrics, the finish shrinks the fabric and obscures the weave structure underneath. The fabric is milled, and then the surface fibres are raised on the fabric face, closely cropped, and laid all in one direction. Examples of faced cloths include beaver cloth, box cloth, wool broadcloth, buckskin fabric and doeskin fabric.

End uses: mainly coats and jackets.

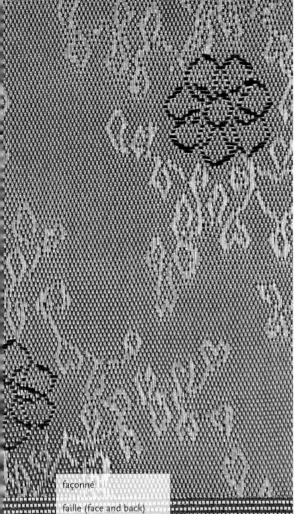

faҫonné

faille (face and back)

FAÇONNÉ A general term used to describe woven jacquard or dobby fabrics patterned with small figures or motifs. The term comes from the French, meaning 'figured' or 'patterned'.

Although 'faҫonné' is essentially a French term for 'figured fabric',[25] it is normally used to describe single colour-woven figured fabrics with good drape, particularly those that are woven with shiny, slippery yarns, such as viscose, acetate, polyester, and blends or mixtures. These fabrics are typically soft crêpe-type fabrics woven with reversible satin, sateen or taffeta figures, producing shiny figures on a dull background.[2] The fabrics are slippery to handle and fray easily.

See also CRÊPE; DOBBY FABRIC; ÉPINGLE; FIGURED FABRIC; JACQUARD FABRIC, WOVEN; LINING FABRIC; SATIN, WOVEN; SATEEN; VELVET.

End uses: blouses, dresses, evening wear and linings.

FAILLE A fine, soft woven fabric that has characteristic flattish ribs running either horizontally across the width of the fabric or vertically down the length of the fabric parallel to the selvedge (as is traditional for tie fabrics). It generally has a slight lustre and drapes well but it may crease easily. It is a medium-weight fabric.

Faille was originally woven in silk, but nowadays it is usually woven with man-made, continuous filament yarns like acetate, viscose or polyester. It can also be made in cotton, wool or blends. Ribs in the horizontal direction are made with highly sett warp yarns and slightly thicker weft yarns. The fabric is woven in plain weave and the warp yarns more or less completely cover the weft yarns, resulting in a warp-faced fabric. Ribs in the vertical direction are made with fine, highly sett weft yarns and slightly thicker warp yarns. When woven in plain weave, the weft yarns cover the warp yarns more or less completely to produce a weft-faced fabric. The ribs are slightly flattened during finishing and are therefore not very prominent.

Faille can be given a moiré finish to make a moiré fabric (*see* MOIRÉ FABRIC). There are several variations of the basic faille fabric: faille crêpe (*see* CRÊPE), faille taffeta (*see* TAFFETA) and tissue faille. Tissue faille is the lightest-weight faille fabric and is woven in plain weave using fine silk yarns. Characteristically, this fabric is highly lustrous and semi-transparent. The weft yarns are slightly thicker than the warp yarns, which gives the faille effect, but it is the open sett that produces the diaphanous quality. The handle is smooth and soft, and it is usually woven in plain colours.

There is a range of warp rib fabrics characterized by the size and prominence of their ribs. In increasing order of rib size, these are: broadcloth, poplin, taffeta, poult, faille, bengaline and grosgrain. However, as many of them are woven in a variety of different weights, they are sometimes difficult to distinguish. Faille is a similar fabric to Mogador.

See also RIB FABRICS, WOVEN; SILK FABRIC; TIE FABRIC.

End uses: dresses, bridal wear, evening dresses, women's suits, men's neckties (particularly formal ties and bow ties), tuxedo lapels, lining, trimmings, hats and bags.

FAILLE CRÊPE *see* CRÊPE.

FAIRISLE A type of weft-knitted jacquard pattern that is knitted for sweaters and cardigans. Characteristically, fairisle fabrics are highly patterned with horizontal bands composed of elaborate geometric shapes and forms in many colours. Fairisle knitwear was originally hand-knitted on the island of Fair Isle, midway between Shetland and Orkney off the north-east coast of Scotland. There are many different traditional pattern variations.

Traditional fairisle garments are knitted with dyed wool yarns; originally the wool came from local Scottish sheep. Fairisle patterns are also knitted with other fibres, such

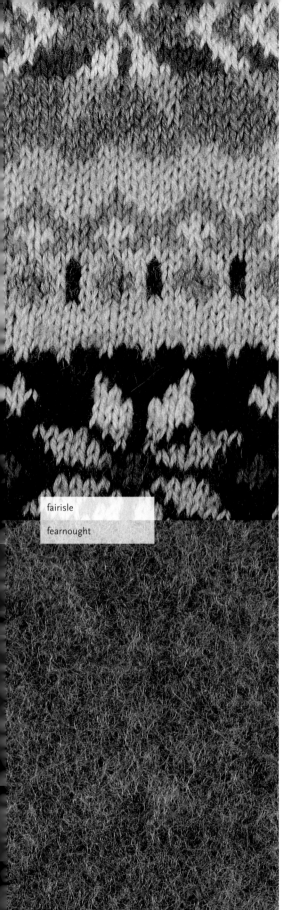

fairisle

fearnought

as acrylic and mixes. The fabric may be hand-knitted or knitted by machine and it is usually knitted in a plain knit structure. The pattern is made by knitting different areas of the design in different colours by a knitting and missing process. The needles are individually selected for knitting and mis-knitting. When a yarn is not being knitted into the face of the fabric to form the pattern, it is floated on the back. The pattern is gradually built up by the combination and sequence of colours used in each weft course. The face of the fabric is therefore normally outermost in use.[25] Fairisle is similar to accordion fabric, but the intricacy of the patterns usually ensures that the yarns floating on the back of the fabric are adequately secured, making additional tuck loops unnecessary.

row 3

row 2

row 1

fairisle

See also ACCORDION FABRIC; FIGURED FABRIC; KNITTED FABRIC; JACQUARD FABRIC, KNITTED; WEFT-KNITTED FABRIC.

End uses: sweaters and cardigans.

FAKE FUR *see* FUR FABRIC.

FEARNOUGHT (fearnaught) A term given to a number of different thick, heavy woven fabrics that are woven from recycled wool and wool shoddy combined and used as coating fabrics. Fearnought is napped during finishing to produce a long-haired, rough, shaggy face. Some qualities are made from Cheviot wool and these fabrics are similar to Cheviot.

See also NAPPED FABRICS, RECYCLED TEXTILES.

End uses: overcoating and scarves.

FEATHER CLOTH (*obs.*) A soft novelty fabric made with wool yarn mixed with feathers (chicken or ostrich) sewn onto fabric. It was popular in the 1960s for evening dresses, trousers, jackets, stoles and shawls.[9]

FEATHER TWILL *see* HERRINGBONE.

FELT A nonwoven fabric composed of a web of entangled fibres. Felting is one of the oldest known methods of making a fabric.[5, 19] It is also one of the cheapest. Felt is characteristically quite a stiff, weak fabric, with poor drape and no elasticity. It does not wear well and loses its shape easily. Felt may be made with any fibre, but some of the best qualities are made from wool.

There are two main kinds of felt, constructed in different ways.
(i) *Pressed felt*. Pressed felt is a nonwoven fabric. It is made chiefly from staple animal fibres, in particular wool. These fibres have the natural characteristic of surface scales, which cause them to interlock and mat together with the application of heat, moisture and a mechanical pressing action. Chemicals or bonding agents are sometimes also added. The pressure compacts the fibres into place. Felt made from animal fibres other than wool is sometimes called 'fur felt'. Wool or hair fibres that can felt are sometimes mixed with cheaper non-felting fibres, such as viscose; in this case the felting fibre should make up approximately 50% of the mix.
(ii) *Needlefelt*. Needlefelt is a nonwoven fabric formed by the mechanical bonding of fibres using needles. The needles are mounted in a needleloom and have barbed edges. The process of punching the needles into the web of fibres is called 'needling'. This causes the fibres to become entangled with one another. Using this method, felts may be made

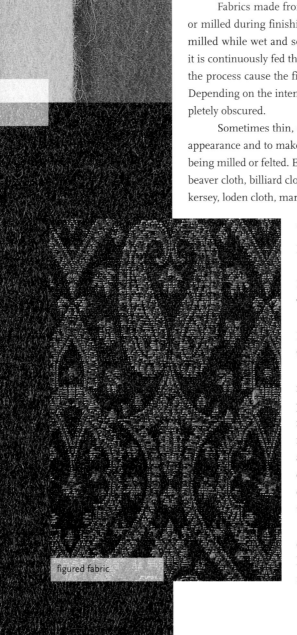

felt

felted fabric

figured fabric

from any fibre or fibre blends, for example cotton, wool, viscose, synthetic or waste fibres. The felts that are made from manufactured fibres, however, are stronger than the natural fibre felts. Needlefelts may be produced as flat fabrics or may have either a cut pile or a loop pile texture (*see* PILE FABRICS). Sometimes, especially with very fine needlefelts, a scrim fabric is used as a support fabric in order to aid the punching operation and to provide greater strength and dimensional stability.

True felt is always nonwoven. However, other fabrics – especially woven – may be given a special finish to produce a felt-like appearance. These fabrics are called 'felted fabrics'. Woven fabrics finished in this way have not only the appearance of felt, but also the strength and durability that true felt lacks.

See also FELTED FABRIC, NONWOVEN FABRIC, RECYCLED TEXTILES, SCRIM.

End uses: hats, appliqué, slippers, handicrafts, bags, fancy dress, theatrical costumes, coats, interlining, upholstery, curtains, table and floor coverings, insulation, padding, soundproofing, filtering and other industrial end uses.

FELTED FABRIC A fabric given a special finish to produce a felt-like appearance. Most felted fabrics are woven fabrics, but knitted fabrics may also be felted. The finish is called 'milling', 'felting' or 'fulling' (the terms are synonymous).

Fabrics made from staple animal fibres, especially wool or blends, may be felted or milled during finishing to make them fuller and denser. The woven fabric is heavily milled while wet and soapy. The wet fabric is alternately extended and compressed as it is continuously fed through rollers. The heat, moisture and mechanical action used in the process cause the fibres on the surface of the fabric to interlock and matt together. Depending on the intensity of the process, the fabric structure underneath may be completely obscured.

Sometimes thin, cheap fabrics are given a felted finish to improve their cover and appearance and to make them warmer. Fabrics are often raised or napped in addition to being milled or felted. Examples of fabrics that are milled during finishing include baize, beaver cloth, billiard cloth, blazer cloth, box cloth, broadcloth (woollen), duffel, flushing, kersey, loden cloth, marengo, melton and molleton.

See also NAPPED FABRICS.

End uses: coats, jackets, blazers, suits, skirts and trousers.

FERRANDINE (*obs.*) A lightweight plain weave fabric with a silk warp and a wool or cotton weft, similar to challis.[36]

FIGURED FABRIC A general term for any fabric, woven or knitted, that has been constructed with motifs, figures or patterns.

A dobby or jacquard patterning mechanism is normally required to produce figured designs in woven fabrics, and a jacquard patterning mechanism to produce figured designs in knitted fabrics. The figured effects are usually formed by the use of two or more visually contrasting weave or knit structures in different areas of the fabric. The fabrics can be solid in colour or the figuring can be emphasized with contrasting colours. 'Façonné', though essentially the French term for 'figured fabric', is normally used to describe a particular type of woven figured fabric (*see* FAÇONNÉ).

Examples of woven figured fabrics include brocade, brocatelle, some carpets, clip spot, damask, grenadine, jaspé, lampas, lappet, Madras muslin, Marseilles, matelassé, woven paisley fabrics, tapestry, tapestry jacquard, ciselé velvet, cut velvet and tapestry

fishnet (fishing net)

fishnet (micronet tights)

fishnet (tights)

velvet (for the last three, *see* VELVET). Examples of knitted figured fabrics include accordion fabric, fairisle, intarsia and knitted jacquard fabric.

See also APPLIQUÉ FABRIC; BROCHÉ; DOBBY FABRIC; EXTRA WARP AND EXTRA WEFT FABRICS; JACQUARD FABRIC, KNITTED; JACQUARD FABRIC, WOVEN.

End uses: (woven figured fabric) dress fabrics, blouses, shirts, men's neckties, curtains and upholstery; (knitted figured fabric) sweaters, cardigans, T-shirts and dresses.

FIL-À-FIL *see* COLOUR AND WEAVE EFFECTS.

FISHEYE CLOTH *see* BIRDSEYE.

FISHNET An open-mesh net fabric. Characteristically, it has a large, diamond-shaped net structure and it is traditionally used for fishing nets. Textiles with a fishnet construction are also made in a wide range of different mesh sizes and qualities for a variety of other end uses (see below). Fishnet is particularly known for its use in tights and stockings.

Fishnet fabrics are made mostly with nylon or polyester, together with elastane if stretch is a requirement. They are also sometimes made with cotton. A range of different warp-knitted and weft-knitted fabric structures are used.

(i) *Warp-knitted fishnet.* Warp-knitted fishnet is a type of knotless netting. 'Knotless netting' is a generic term for warp-knitted net fabrics in which the mesh is constructed with pillar stitches and tricot stitches forming the joints rather than knots. String vest mesh is made in a similar manner but with thicker yarns.[38] Lightweight fishnets for apparel are typically made on a tricot machine, while heavier, industrial weights and tubular fabrics are knitted on a raschel machine.

(ii) *Weft-knitted fishnet.* Weft-knitted fishnet is a float-plated fabric. It is made by plating a thick and a thin yarn to make a fine mesh net construction. The thick yarn is floated across the thin yarn to produce a wide range of patterned openwork structures, which are used mainly as hosiery fabrics.[25]

See also KNITTED FABRIC, MESH FABRICS, NET, PLATED FABRICS, TULLE, WARP-KNITTED FABRIC, WEFT-KNITTED FABRIC.

End uses: tights, stockings, millinery, net curtains, mosquito netting, fishing nets, fruit and vegetable sacks, and trimmings.

FLAME-RESISTANT TEXTILES Textiles with the ability to resist flaming combustion, by slowing, terminating or preventing it.[25] Some textiles are inherently flame-resistant and others are treated to make them so. These textiles have a range of end uses where non-flammable properties are required, such as protective clothing and upholstery fabrics.

Textiles that are inherently flame-resistant include modacrylic, aramid fibre, carbon fibres, glass fibre and wool. (*See* ACRYLIC FABRIC, ARAMID FABRIC, CARBON-FIBRE TEXTILES, GLASS-FIBRE TEXTILES, WOOL FABRIC.) Other fabrics, such as some upholstery fabrics and some pyjama fabrics, may be given a flame-retardant finish in order to improve their flame resistance. This usually involves coating them with a flame retardant, a chemical substance. Flame-retardant finishes may be given to cotton, viscose, nylon and polyester fabrics. Fabrics treated with such finishes are normally less expensive than those made with inherently flame-resistant fibres or fibre variants; however, they are usually less durable and the finish can be lost through repeated washing. *See* COATED FABRIC, PYJAMA FABRIC.

End uses: protective clothing, firemen's uniforms, industrial clothing, motor sports clothing, some pyjama fabrics, upholstery fabrics, furnishing fabrics, carpets and industrial textiles.

FLANNEL A woven, wool-based fabric that is given a special finish to raise the nap, producing a characteristically dull fabric with a slightly fuzzy appearance and a soft handle. It was traditionally an all-wool fabric, but wool blends and wool union fabrics are now also made. Flannel fabrics are available in a wide variety of weights, ranging from light to heavy. The fabrics vary in density of yarns and degree of nap finish.

Traditional flannel fabrics are made from 100% woollen or worsted yarns. Other qualities are also made by blending wool with other fibres, such as nylon, polyester or cotton. An addition of 15% to 20% of nylon or polyester blended with the wool, for example, will improve the strength of the fabric. Flannel union fabrics are also produced, using yarns made with different fibres in both the warp and the weft (see **zephyr flannel** below). With both flannel blends and union fabrics, the percentage of each fibre should always be stated.

Flannel is usually loosely woven in plain weave or sometimes in a 2/2 or 2/1 twill weave structure. The weft yarns are usually thicker than the warp yarns and they are given a low twist to facilitate the nap finish. The fabric is lightly milled and raised during finishing, on one or both sides. This raises the fibres on the surface of the fabric in a random, non-directional manner and either partially or fully obscures the weave structure. Flannel is usually woven in plain colours, but it can also be striped. It may be yarn-dyed, piece-dyed or, as with **grey flannel**, fibre dyed.

Particularly when made from top-quality wool, flannel has excellent tailorability and is therefore widely used. It is soft, warm and elastic, drapes well and does not fray. Flannel originated in Wales, and the name derives from the Welsh term *gwlanan* (*gwlan* is Welsh for wool).[3] It was originally made for underwear, which was coarse and scratchy. It is also the red petticoat fabric that forms part of the Welsh national costume.[3] An example of a typical, ordinary plain woven flannel fabric construction is 95 to 80 tex warp sett at 10 to 11 ends per cm and 84 to 74 tex weft woven at 11 to 14 picks per cm.[26] There are, however, many different types of flannel fabric, each with their own unique characteristics, as discussed below. Other fabrics similar to flannel include blazer cloth, cadet cloth, domet, kasha, melton, molleton and wincey.

ANGOLA FLANNEL A type of flannel that is usually woven in plain or twill weave using angola yarns (blended yarns of recycled wool and cotton). The best angolas are produced with yarns composed of at least 80% wool and 20% cotton. The wool is either shoddy or mungo. A low-grade version with a cotton warp and angola weft yarns is also made, but the raised nap in this fabric wears quickly, leaving the fabric threadbare.[16] *See* RECYCLED TEXTILES.

BABY FLANNEL A fine, lightweight flannel fabric that is used for children's garments.

FRENCH FLANNEL A soft, very fine twill weave fabric that is woven in wool and slightly napped on the face side only. It may be dyed a solid colour or it may be woven in stripes or checks.

GREY FLANNEL A flannel fabric that is fibre dyed in varying shades of grey, producing a characteristic mottled appearance. Fabrics with a similar mottled effect are also produced in colours other than grey.

OUTING FLANNEL (outing cloth) A light- to medium-weight, part-wool part-cotton flannel fabric, woven in plain weave and napped on one or both sides. It may be dyed a solid colour or it may be woven in stripes or checks. The nap rubs away during wear. It is similar to both domet and flannelette, but it has a shorter nap than domet[9] and is heavier and stiffer than flannelette. It is used for winter pyjamas and nightwear, shirts, dresses, cricket trousers, blazers, lightweight jackets and linings.

SALISBURY FLANNEL A British wool flannel, white in colour and sometimes called 'Salisbury white'.[36]

grey flannel

flannel (heavy)

Salisbury flannel

SHAKER FLANNEL A soft, plain weave flannel fabric usually woven in white using cotton or wool yarns. It is napped on both sides and is thought to have been first made in grey by Shakers.[9]

SUEDE FLANNEL A wool flannel that is raised on both sides, sheared and firmly pressed to produce a fabric with a soft, smooth handle like that of a close felted fabric. *See* FELTED FABRIC, SUEDE CLOTH.

WEST OF ENGLAND FLANNEL A flannel fabric woven in a twill weave and napped on both sides. *See also* WEST OF ENGLAND FABRICS.

WORSTED FLANNEL A lightweight but strong and soft flannel fabric, usually woven in a 2/2 twill weave structure. The best worsted flannels are woven with fine, two-fold worsted wool yarns. Worsted flannels have less nap than wool flannels, and the fabric structure underneath is only partially obscured. They also wear better than wool flannels and can hold sharp creases more easily. Worsted flannel is used to make men's suits and furnishing fabrics.

ZEPHYR FLANNEL A lightweight wool union fabric with good drape. It is woven with a worsted wool warp and a weft of spun silk. *See* UNION FABRIC, ZEPHYR.

See also NAPPED FABRICS, TWILL FABRICS, UNION FABRIC, WOOL FABRIC.

End uses: trousers, jackets, blazers, men's and women's suits, skirts, dresses and coats.

worsted flannel

flannelette

FLANNELETTE A light- to medium-weight cotton fabric that was originally woven in imitation of wool flannel. Characteristically, it has a soft, fibrous surface and it is known for its warmth and comfort.

Flannelette is traditionally woven with cotton yarns in the warp and thick, low-twist cotton yarns in the weft. Sometimes other fibres, such as viscose, are included in the weft, but such fabrics should be labelled accordingly, for example as 'cotton/viscose flannelette'. Flannelette may be woven in plain weave, double-end plain weave or twill weave. In finishing, the surface of the fabric is raised on both sides, which obscures the weave structure beneath and gives the fabric its soft, warm handle. The nap is produced almost entirely from the soft, low-twist weft yarns. Flannelette is usually woven as grey cloth and subsequently bleached and dyed. It may also be colour-woven with dyed yarns, either in solid colours or with stripes and checks. Sometimes it is also printed.

Flannelette typically weighs 180 to 200 g/m².[10] It is prone to pilling, creasing and abrasion, but it is relatively cheap and has good washability and warmth. Examples of typical constructions include:[26]

- 25 tex warp sett at 20 ends per cm and 50 tex weft woven at 19 picks per cm (plain weave)
- 27 tex warp sett at 38 ends per cm and 46 tex weft woven at 16 picks per cm (double-end plain weave)
- 25 tex warp sett at 27 ends per cm and 40 tex weft woven at 28 picks per cm (2/2 twill weave)

Similar fabrics to flannelette include Canton, cotton duvetyn (*see* DUVETYN), outing flannel (*see* FLANNEL), cotton suede cloth (*see* SUEDE CLOTH), swansdown, wincey and winceyette. Flannelette is heavier than winceyette and lighter in weight and less stiff than outing flannel. Cotton duvetyn, cotton suede cloth and flannelette can all be converted from the same grey goods, but duvetyn and suede cloth are more closely sheared, to give a smoother, flatter surface.[19]

fleece fabric (weft-knitted)

fleece fabric (weft-knitted, face and back)

See also COTTON FABRIC, NAPPED FABRICS, PYJAMA FABRIC.

End uses: pyjamas, nightgowns, sheets, pillowcases, shirts, underwear, children's clothes, linings and gloves.

FLAX *see* LINEN FABRIC.

FLEECE FABRIC A soft, warm fabric with a lofty, fibrous napped surface and good insulating properties. Fleece fabrics were originally made in imitation of animal fleece, a fleece being a complete hair coat shorn in a single piece from a live animal (e.g. a sheep or goat). Nowadays there are many different types of fleece fabric, which may be warp-knitted, weft-knitted or woven using many different types of natural or man-made fibres. Fleece fabrics are either made in imitation of all kinds of real animal fleeces, or they may have distinctive characteristics of their own. Fleece fabrics are warm and comfortable to wear, but they are prone to pilling and, with the lower qualities, the nap will wear away quite quickly.

Fleece fabrics are produced in a wide variety of thicknesses and weights. The spaces between the fibres in the raised surface of the fabric trap air, giving the fabric its characteristic warm handle. Fleece fabrics may be made from cotton, cotton blends, wool, nylon, polyester, acrylic and modacrylic. Lighter-weight fleeces are also made using microfibres. There are two main ways of obtaining the fibrous surface:

(i) Loose fibres or 'slivers' are firmly fixed to a flexible backing fabric to create a pile by weaving or knitting them into the fabric structure.

(ii) The fleece effect is produced by the finishing process. Both knitted and woven fabrics are heavily raised, cropped and steamed to produce a dense nap. This raises the fibres on the surface of the fabric in a random, non-directional manner and obscures the fabric structure underneath. The nap or pile surface may be on one or both sides of the fabric and it may be of any length – long and brushed or cut short.

Warp-knitted fleece fabrics are commonly made with continuous filament microfibre yarns and are knitted on two- or three-bar tricot machines. After construction, they are heavily brushed, on either one or both sides. Most weft-knitted fleece fabrics are single jersey fabrics knitted in a plain knit structure with extra 'laid-in' yarns on the back of the fabric. The extra yarns are low-twist yarns that are usually slightly thicker than the ground yarns. The fabric is raised and steamed on the technical back and this will sometimes be used as the face side of the fabric. However, with garments like sweatshirts and tracksuits, the fleecy side is used on the inside of the garment. Woven fleece fabrics are usually woven in a weft-faced twill or a sateen weave structure using a low-twist, carded weft yarn. It is the fibre from this yarn that will form the nap surface when finished.

See also ACRYLIC FABRIC, COATING FABRIC, FUR FABRIC, JERSEY, KNITTED FABRIC, LAID-IN FABRIC, MICROFIBRE FABRIC, NAPPED FABRICS, PLUSH, POLAR FLEECE, WARP-KNITTED FABRIC, WEFT-KNITTED FABRIC.

End uses: coats, jackets, waistcoats, insulating linings (especially for coats and jackets), knitted sweatshirts, tracksuits, sportswear, hats, gloves, scarves and toys.

FLOCKED FABRIC A fabric in which a velvet-like relief effect is produced on a base fabric by printing it with adhesive and applying finely cut fibre fragments called 'flock' to this surface. The whole of the fabric may be coated with adhesive to produce an all-over flocked fabric or the adhesive may be printed onto the fabric in localized areas only. The fibres will adhere only to the printed areas, and thus a flocked pattern will be produced. Flocked fabric is made in imitation of pile fabric.

The flock is made by cutting or grinding fibres into small fragments, usually from 0.5 mm to 3 mm long. It may be the same colour as the base fabric or a contrasting colour.

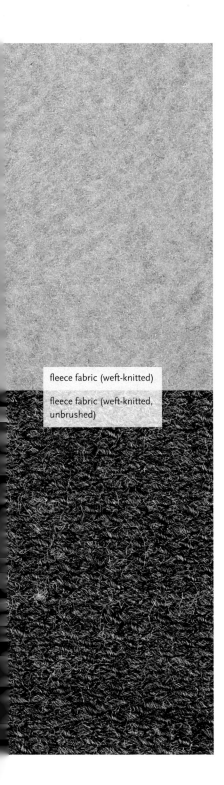

fleece fabric (weft-knitted)

fleece fabric (weft-knitted, unbrushed)

flocked fabric

flushing

florentine

The type of fibre used can also be the same as, or different from, that in the base fabric. Viscose, nylon, acrylic, polyester and wool are the fibres most frequently used for flocking. The adhesive that is used to print the base fabric is usually an aqueous-based acrylic resin that has good flexibility and durability. The flock fibres are applied to the base fabric either by shaking them on using mechanical agitation or by electrostatic attraction. In both methods the flock fibres are orientated to stand vertically, which allows the fibres to fully penetrate the adhesive. Afterwards the fabric is heated in an oven to dry the adhesive, and the surplus flock fibres are blown off.

Flock may be applied to a wide range of base materials, including cloth, foam, paper, wood and metal. It may be applied to materials of any weight or quality; it can also be applied to an adhesive film that is laminated to a base fabric (this would be a laminated flock fabric and could also be termed a 'multi-component fabric'; *see* LAMINATED FABRIC, MULTI-COMPONENT FABRICS). Flocked fabrics can usually be washed or dry-cleaned, but the flock will eventually wear off. Fabrics that may be flock-printed include imitation dotted Swiss fabrics, some net fabrics (point d'ésprit), suede cloth (flocked) and some veiling fabrics.

See also DOTTED SWISS, NET, VELVET.

End uses: evening dresses, evening wear, dresses, blouses, blankets, bedspreads, curtains, wall coverings, carpets, upholstery fabrics, toys, books, shoes and hats.

FLORENTINE A heavy, strong, thick and durable woven fabric that is made in a warp-faced twill weave. It is similar to drill, but the weft yarns in florentine are thicker than those used in drill.

Florentine is traditionally made from 100% carded cotton using good-quality, high-twist two-fold warp yarns and a softer, thicker singles weft yarn. Other fibre combinations are also available, such as polyester/cotton blends or cotton mixed with other man-made fibres. Florentine is woven as grey cloth in a 3/1 warp-faced twill weave structure. Afterwards it is usually piece-dyed – this is done in navy blue for police uniforms and in khaki for army uniforms. A typical florentine fabric is woven with 37 tex warp sett at 38 ends per cm and with 49 tex weft woven at 19 picks per cm.[25] Florentine is a similar fabric to bluette, denim, dungaree, jean, some gabardine fabrics, hickory cloth and ticking.

See also DRILL, KHAKI, TWILL FABRICS.

End uses: overalls, trousers, jackets and uniforms.

FLUSHING A heavy woven fabric made from wool. It has a dense nap on both sides and is used mainly as a coating fabric. It is similar to duffel but of slightly higher quality. Flushing is woven in wool in a 2/2 twill weave structure. After weaving, it is heavily milled and raised to give it a dense nap on both sides. The term comes from the English name for Vlissingen, the small town in the Netherlands where it was first woven.[25]

See also COATING FABRIC, DUFFEL, FELTED FABRIC, NAPPED FABRICS.

End uses: coats, jackets and blankets.

FOAM A spongy material made by modifying stretch materials such as polyurethane and rubber. Certain chemicals mixed with these materials will cause tiny air pockets to form, creating a thicker, more sponge-like material. Foam is not very strong and is therefore generally used in conjunction with other materials. It is most often laminated to at least one other material and used as padding or for insulation. Usually it is fused to a face fabric and sometimes also to a backing fabric, so that it is sandwiched between the two layers. Foams vary in their thickness and degree of sponginess.

See also LAMINATED FABRIC, POLYURETHANE, RUBBER, SPACER FABRICS.

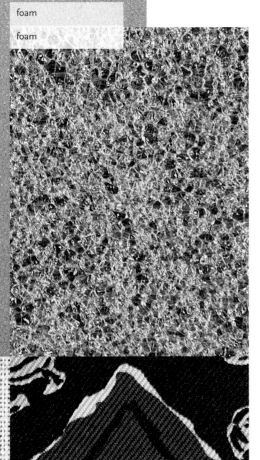

foam

foam

foulard (printed)

folk weave

End uses: carpet backings; mattresses; padding for upholstery, cushions, shoes and luggage; stuffing for pillows, cushions and toys; foam laminates for coats and sportswear; protective coverings; automotive textiles, aerospace textiles and a large range of industrial end uses.

FODENS *see* BUTCHER CLOTH.

FOLK WEAVE A general term for a woven fabric patterned with folk weaves – simple woven designs and motifs in several colours. Most are loosely woven fabrics made with coarse yarns, and the fabric usually has a rough, irregular surface. Folk weaves come from the tradition of weaving fabrics by hand, an occupation practised for centuries by peasants living in rural areas in all parts of the world. There are many traditional regional patterns. Weftway and/ or warpway stripes are among the most common patterns; small-scale geometric motifs are also sometimes used. Folk weaves are normally used as furnishing fabrics.

See also HARDANGER, HOMESPUN, KHADI.

End uses: furnishing fabrics.

FOULARD A lightweight woven fabric, originally made from silk yarns and woven in twill weave. It is usually printed in classic small-scale geometric designs appropriate for use as neckties and scarves. Characteristically, it is a very soft, smooth fabric with good drape and a lustrous face and dull back.

Although originally woven in silk, foulard is also woven from viscose, polyester, acetate or triacetate yarns. The fabric is woven in a balanced 2/2 twill weave structure. It may be piece-dyed, but more often it is printed with small-scale motifs and patterns against contrasting backgrounds. One classic pattern that is printed onto foulard fabrics by discharge printing gives the effect of a white spot against a coloured ground.[26] A typical foulard fabric is woven with 5 tex filament warp sett at 51 ends per cm and with 9 tex filament weft woven at 54 picks per cm.[26] Foulard was originally woven in India[3] and it was used as a handkerchief fabric.[5] The name is French for neck scarf or tie.[23] Foulard is similar to surah, but lighter in weight.

See also DISCHARGE PRINTED FABRIC, SILK FABRIC, TIE FABRIC, TWILL FABRICS.

End uses: men's neckties, scarves, dresses, blouses and linings.

FOUR-POINTED STAR CHECK A colour-woven fabric with a characteristic pattern of small-scale checks shaped like stars with four points. The pattern is made with a colour and weave effect, which is created by combining a plain or hopsack weave structure with narrow, yarn-dyed stripes of alternating dark and light colours in both the warp and the weft. This pattern is woven in a wide range of different weights and qualities.

four-pointed star check

Frenchback (face and back)

Fresco®

The four-pointed star pattern may be woven using any fibre. The yarns are arranged in a sequence of two dark and two light in both the warp and the weft. The light colour is frequently ecru or white, and the fabric is woven either in a balanced plain weave or a hopsack weave structure. The four-pointed star pattern is also sometimes printed onto fabrics. 'Chicken's-foot check' (or *pied à poule* in French) is the name given to an enlarged four-pointed star pattern in which the colour sequence is four dark and four light in both the warp and the weft and the fabric is woven in a hopsack weave structure. The four-pointed star pattern should not be confused with the houndstooth check pattern, which looks similar; *see* HOUNDSTOOTH CHECK.

See also CHECKS, COLOUR AND WEAVE EFFECTS, HOPSACK, PLAIN WEAVE.

End uses: casual jackets, trousers, skirts, suits, coats, shawls, caps and furnishing fabrics.

FRED PERRY FABRIC *see* PIQUÉ, WEFT-KNITTED.

FRENCHBACK A woven backed fabric that has a characteristic corded twill on the face of the fabric and a different weave structure, usually a smooth one like a satin weave, on the back of the fabric. Frenchback is woven in a similar manner to a stitched double cloth fabric, usually with two warps, but with one weft only, linking the two fabrics together. Sometimes the face and back fabrics are woven in different fibre yarns. For example, the face fabric may be woven in worsted yarn and the back in less expensive cotton yarn.

See also BACKED FABRIC, DOUBLE CLOTH, EXTRA WARP AND EXTRA WEFT FABRICS, SERGE, TWILL FABRICS.

End uses: suits and jackets.

FRENCH CRÊPE *see* CRÊPE.

FRENCH DOUBLE PIQUÉ *see* PIQUÉ, WEFT-KNITTED.

FRENCH FLANNEL *see* FLANNEL.

FRENCH MERINO *see* MERINO FABRIC.

FRESCO® A lightweight woven suiting fabric made from specially twisted worsted wool yarns; it is lustrous, firm and durable. Characteristically, its construction gives it a porous quality, which allows air to pass through and makes it cool and comfortable to wear in hot weather. Fresco is a hard-wearing fabric with good drape and very good crease recovery.

The specially twisted worsted wool yarns give Fresco its distinctive porous quality. Hard-twisted, two-fold worsted yarns are twisted together with a singles yarn. The yarns may be solid-coloured or marl yarns and they are used in both the warp and the weft. The fabric is usually colour-woven in plain weave and it is given a finish that accentuates the crisp handle created by the high-twist yarns. The name 'Fresco' comes from the Italian *al fresco*, meaning 'in the fresh air'. This fabric is intended to be worn in the summer or in hot climates and so may be described as a tropical suiting fabric.

See also MARL FABRIC, PLAIN WEAVE FABRIC, TROPICAL SUITING.

End uses: men's lightweight summer suits.

FRIAR'S CLOTH *see* MONK'S CLOTH.

frieze

frisé

frotté

FRIEZE A thick, heavyweight woven overcoating fabric that is made from wool. It is a very durable, waterproof fabric that has a rough appearance and handle.

Frieze is woven from thick woollen yarns in a balanced 2/2 or an irregular twill weave structure. During finishing, the fabric is very heavily milled and raised on the face of the fabric. It undergoes two raising treatments, first with wires and then with teazles. This lays the fibres in one direction and produces a fibrous, felted surface that completely obscures the weave structure underneath. On some frieze fabrics, the nap is raised and then rubbed into small curls or balls, which produce a fabric with a rough, pebbly surface that is called a 'nap frieze'. A typical 2/2 twill frieze fabric is woven with 270 tex warp sett at 8 or 9 ends per cm and with 270 tex weft sett at 8 or 9 picks per cm. Contraction would be about 25% to 30% in the width and 20% in the length.[26]

Frieze was woven in Ireland as far back as the 14th century, although it may have been of French origin.[3] A similar fabric woven in England and mentioned in Chaucer was called 'falding', while the equivalent Scottish fabric was called 'kelt'.[3] These fabrics are not known today. Frieze is a similar fabric to kersey and melton.

See also COATING FABRIC, FELTED FABRIC, NAPPED FABRICS.

End uses: overcoats and sports jackets.

FRISÉ A thick, heavy, woven loop pile fabric. It is very strong, durable and hard-wearing, and does not crease. It has a lower pile and is also less dense than most other pile fabrics.

Traditionally the loops of frisé were made of wool or mohair, but nowadays frisé is more likely to be woven using cotton or man-made fibres. Cotton/acrylic, cotton/viscose or cotton/modal yarns may also be used. Most frisé fabrics are constructed in the following manner. A base fabric is woven in a firm, plain weave ground construction. The pile is made by inserting wires to lift particular pile-warp yarns above the surface of the base fabric at regular intervals during weaving. When the wires are removed, a dense pile of small, closed loops is formed on the surface of the fabric. Some frisé fabrics are also made in a similar way to terry towelling. Some of the warp yarns are slack-tensioned at regular intervals. During weaving, the slack warp yarns will loop up to make pile loops on the face of the fabric.

Patterns may be made in the pile loops, either by raising them to different heights or by shearing them at different heights. The pattern may contain both areas that have been cut and areas that are left uncut. Frisé may also be woven in more than one colour. It is a very resilient, hard-wearing fabric that does not crease, but it tends to fray easily. Its name comes from the French verb *friser*, meaning 'to curl'.[3] Frisé is constructed in a similar manner to astrakhan fabric and terry fabric, but it is much more closely sett than either. It is also a similar fabric to grospoint and moquette.

See also PILE FABRICS.

End uses: upholstery and curtains.

FROCS (*obs.*) A coarse woollen twill made for French peasants' garments.[3]

FROTTÉ A soft, voluminous, loop yarn fabric that is woven in imitation of terry fabric and used as towelling. It is a cheaper but less durable version of terry fabric (*frotté* is the French term for towelling).[36] The loops from the yarn stand up from the main body of the fabric to form a loop pile on the surface. The fabric is usually woven from cotton yarns, using plain twist yarns in the warp and fancy loop yarns in the weft. Other examples of loop yarn fabrics include bouclé fabric and éponge.

See also PILE FABRICS, TERRY FABRIC.

End uses: towels and bathrobes.

Fuji

fur (real fur)

FUJI A smooth, lightweight woven fabric made from silk or man-made fibre yarns and woven in plain weave. Originally Fuji was a trade name for a 100% silk fabric woven in Japan. Nowadays Fuji may be woven anywhere and is more likely to be made from viscose, acetate or triacetate yarns. The fabric is woven in plain weave with continuous filament warp yarns and spun weft yarns. It is similar to cotton broadcloth.

See also PLAIN WEAVE FABRIC, SILK FABRIC.

End uses: dresses, blouses and undergarments.

FULL MILANO RIB *see* MILANO RIB.

FUR FABRIC A fabric made in imitation of real fur; it is also called 'imitation fur' or 'fake fur'. Real fur is the skin or hide of an animal with the hair still attached. Both fur fabrics and real fur are characteristically very warm materials and so are used principally in garments for warmth, for example coatings. Fur fabric is a pile fabric, in which long staple fibres are attached to a backing fabric. The 'fur' pile may vary in colour or length; the fabric may be printed with animal markings (e.g. leopard spots) or given a special textural finish to make it resemble real fur.[38] Alternatively, it may be made to look unlike real fur. There is a wide variety of colours and types available. Fur fabric is a fairly expensive fabric.

With fur fabric, a pile, usually made from synthetic staple fibres, is secured in a firmly constructed base fabric, which may be woven, knitted, stitch-bonded or tufted. The 'fur' pile is usually made from acrylic, modacrylic, polyester, nylon or polypropylene fibre. Different construction methods are outlined as follows.
(i) *Woven fur fabrics.* Woven fur fabrics are usually warp pile fabrics woven as double cloths. They have a cut pile surface, produced in a similar manner to velvet; *see* VELVET.
(ii) *Knitted fur fabrics.* Knitted fur fabrics may be either warp- or weft-knitted. The weft-knits are usually knitted in a firm plain knit base structure. Staple fibres or 'slivers' with little or no twist are 'laid-in' into the weft courses and knitted in at each loop. Bound by the intermeshing, the fibres produce a fur-like pile on the technical back of the fabric. The fibres are brushed and raised during finishing, and this surface usually then becomes the face side in use. The technical name for this fabric is a 'sliver high-pile fabric'.[38] Warp-knitted fur fabrics are made by binding together a fibrous web with knitted stitches, reinforced with warp and weft inlay yarns. Special pointed compound needles are used to stitch through all the layers. The fabric is heavily brushed after knitting.[38] *See* LAID-IN FABRIC.
(iii) *Stitch-bonded fur fabrics.* Stitch-bonded fur fabrics are usually made by forming the warp direction yarns into pile loops. These loops are simultaneously stitched into a base fabric that may be woven, knitted, nonwoven or stitch-bonded. The loop pile is then brushed to form the fur effect. *See* STITCH-BONDED FABRIC.
(iv) *Tufted fur fabrics.* Tufted fur fabrics are made by inserting pile yarns with needles into a backing fabric. The pile is secured during finishing by the shrinkage of the backing fabric, by the opening out (blooming) of the pile yarns and, with some fabrics, by back-coating the fabric with latex or a similar material. *See* TUFTED FABRIC.

All fur fabrics, no matter how they are constructed, may be finished by curling, embossing, shearing, sculpturing and printing. The back of the fabric is sometimes resin-bonded for extra pile security. Examples of real furs imitated by printed fur fabrics include fox, giraffe, sheepskin, leopard, lynx, mink, ocelot, rabbit, raccoon, sable, seal, skunk, tiger and zebra. Examples of fur fabrics or fur-like fabrics include astrakhan, beaver cloth, fleece fabric, plush, polar fleece, poodle cloth and zibeline.

See also ACRYLIC FABRIC, COATING FABRIC, DOUBLE CLOTH, KNITTED FABRIC, LAID-IN FABRIC, LEATHER, PILE FABRICS, PLAIN KNIT FABRIC, SCRIM, WARP-KNITTED FABRIC, WEFT-KNITTED FABRIC.

End uses: coats, jackets, hats, collars, cuffs, gloves, trims, slippers, soft toys and rugs.

fur fabric

fur fabric

fur fabric

fustian (uncut and
undyed corduroy)

gaberdine

FUR FELT *see* FELT.

FUSTIAN A general term applied to a group of woven fabrics that have a very high weft count (that is, a much greater number of weft picks per centimetre than warp ends per centimetre). The term is used for all types of heavily wefted fabrics, including weft-corded fabrics and weft pile fabrics. Characteristically, fustian fabrics are very strong, hard-wearing fabrics that are usually made from cotton.

Fustian fabrics are usually composed of a firmly constructed ground fabric woven in plain or twill weave. Extra (or supplementary) weft yarns are interlaced with the ground weave at binding points arranged in columns up the length of the fabric. This produces vertical columns of crosswise floats that float over the top of the ground weave. Originally all fabrics produced in this manner with uncut floats were called 'fustians'. Now, however, the term may also be used to include fabrics that are woven in this manner but have had the floats cut after weaving. This produces pile fabrics with pile cords in the longitudinal direction. Cut weft pile fustian fabrics include constitutional cord, corduroy and velveteen.

Fustian fabrics were originally woven with linen warps and cotton wefts.[3] They are ancient fabrics, thought originally to have been made in Egypt in Roman times.[2] The name comes from the Old English *fustane* or *fustyan* (derived from Latin *fustis*), meaning 'stick' or 'club', and was probably used because the fabric was beetled (beaten) with a wooden stick during finishing.[3] In the past fustian was used extensively by the clergy, and the name is often associated with ecclesiastical garments. At one time Cistercian monks were not allowed to weave any other type of cloth.[3] Fustian fabrics include beaverteen, cantoon, constitutional cord, corduroy, imperial sateen, moleskin fabric, swansdown and velveteen.

See also CORD FABRICS, SUEDE CLOTH.

End uses: (lighter weights) ladies' wear, skirts and children's wear; (heavier weights) riding breeches, trousers and jackets.

GABERDINE (gabardine) A closely sett, warp-faced woven fabric that is woven in a steep twill weave. The twill lines, which run from bottom left to top right (twill right), form prominent diagonal ribs on the face of the fabric but are not evident on the back. Because of the close sett and steep twill angle, gaberdines are particularly water-repellent and they are very hard-wearing.

Originally gaberdine fabrics were union fabrics, woven with a worsted wool warp and a cotton weft.[4] These union gaberdines are still made, but the best-quality gaberdines are usually botany twill fabrics made from 100% worsted wool using two-fold or three-fold yarns in both warp and weft. Very high-quality gaberdines are also made from 100% cotton. Gaberdine fabrics are also made in polyester/cotton, polyester, viscose and (more rarely) silk.

Characteristically, gaberdines have a much greater number of warp ends per centimetre than weft picks per centimetre. The fabric is usually woven in a 2/1 or a 2/2 twill weave. Occasionally it is woven in a fancy twill weave. Because of the high warp sett, the warp yarns produce a steep twill angle and cover the weft yarns almost entirely. The fabric may be piece-dyed or colour-woven. Gaberdine is given a clear finish and sometimes it is napped on the back. If the fabric is to be used for rainwear, it is given a showerproof finish.

Gaberdine fabrics are available in light, medium and heavy weights. For men's suiting fabrics, the twill angle is usually 63°; for women's suiting fabrics it is usually 45°.[5, 17] Typical examples of different types of gaberdine fabrics include:[26]

- 27/2 tex botany worsted warp sett at 42 ends per cm and 20/2 tex cotton weft woven at 35 picks per cm (gaberdine union)
- 36/2 tex botany worsted warp sett at 40 ends per cm and 24 tex botany or cross-bred weft woven at 25 picks per cm, woven in 3/1 twill (all-worsted gaberdine)
- 15/2 tex cotton warp sett at 64 ends per cm and 15/2 tex cotton weft woven at 42 picks per cm, woven in 3/1 twill (cotton gaberdine)

gauze (printed)

gauze

Gaberdine was originally woven during the Middle Ages in Spain, where it was used for cloaks and capes.[5] In Shakespeare's *The Merchant of Venice*, there is a reference to Shylock wearing a 'gabardine', suggesting a cassock-type garment.[36] A fabric very similar to gaberdine is paddock, a lightweight worsted coating fabric that is woven in twill weave and piece-dyed in shades of brown. It is given a water-repellent finish and is traditionally worn at horse race meetings, hence the name. Gaberdine is also similar to Poiret twill (but thicker and less smooth), serge (but with a more pronounced twill) and whipcord (but with a less pronounced twill).

See also BOTANY TWILL, CAVALRY TWILL, COATING FABRIC, COVERT CLOTH, TWILL FABRICS, UNION FABRIC, WATERPROOF AND WATER-REPELLENT FABRICS.

End uses: outerwear, raincoats, overcoats, jackets, anoraks, trousers, skirts, tailored suits, uniforms and sportswear.

GALATEA A hard-wearing cotton fabric that is woven in twill weave. Most galateas have a characteristic blue ground with white or coloured stripes printed onto them. Occasionally they are dyed solid colours.

Galatea is usually woven in cotton in a 2/1 (or sometimes a 3/1) warp-faced twill weave structure. The fabric is given a stiff, lustrous finish to repel dirt. A typical galatea fabric construction is 23 tex warp sett at 36 ends per cm and 28 tex weft woven at 26 picks per cm.[26] The name comes from the British warship HMS *Galatea*.[9] Galatea is a similar fabric to regatta but lighter in weight.

See also SHIRTING FABRICS, STRIPES, TWILL FABRICS.

End uses: nurses' uniforms, children's clothes, shirts and linings.

GALLOON (*obs.*) A narrow fabric or ribbon of wool, silk or cotton, sometimes patterned with gold or silver threads. It was used for garment trims.[36]

GAUZE A very lightweight woven fabric in which both the warp and weft yarns are spaced apart (open sett) to produce an open mesh-like construction. Gauze fabrics are woven either in a balanced plain weave (square cloth) or in a simple leno construction. There are various qualities, ranging from sheer, open-sett fabrics like net, to heavier semi-sheer fabrics. Gauze belongs to the muslin family of fabrics.

Gauze is thought to have originated in Gaza in Palestine, where a fine, sheer fabric called 'gazzatum' was woven.[3] It is from this that it takes its name. There are many different types of gauze fabric. Gauze may be woven in a variety of weights and qualities, and from any fibre. It may be soft and limp, or it may be given a size finish to make it stiff. When the fabric is woven in plain weave, it is not very stable: the yarns tend to slip out of position quite easily, and the fabric is prone to fraying and shrinkage. A much more stable gauze construction, in which the yarns do not slip so readily, is created by weaving the entire fabric in a leno weave construction. In this construction, some warp ends (called 'doup ends') are made to cross over other warp ends (called 'fixed ends'), trapping the weft yarns in-between and preventing them from slipping. The terms 'gauze' and 'leno' are often used synonymously to describe any fabric in which the doup principle of weaving is employed. *See* LENO FABRIC.

Gauze fabrics and fabrics similar to gauze include bolting cloth, bunting, cheesecloth, étamine, gossamer, (woven) marquisette, some mock leno fabrics, scrim and (woven) tulle. Stiffened gauze fabrics include buckram, crinoline and tarlatan.

See also LENO FABRIC, MUSLIN, NET, PLAIN WEAVE FABRIC, SCRIM, SHEER FABRICS.

End uses: curtains, theatrical scenery, veiling, trims, backing fabrics and gauze bandages (called 'surgical gauze').

gazar (face and back)

georgette

GAZAR A very fine, semi-sheer and stiff lightweight woven fabric that is usually made with silk yarns. It is a crisp fabric with a high sheen on the face side, and it tends to crease easily.

Gazar is woven in an open-sett plain weave, usually with double silk yarns woven as one. It is also sometimes made with continuous filament man-made fibre yarns such as viscose, polyester or nylon. Gazar may be white, dyed, printed or embroidered. It is given extra stiffness by sizing. Gazar is a similar fabric to organza, but is slightly more open sett and stiffer. It is also similar to, but stiffer than, organdie, (silk) mousseline, ninon and voile.

See also EMBROIDERED FABRICS, SILK FABRIC.

End uses: wedding dresses, bridal wear, evening wear, dresses and blouses.

GEORGETTE A fine, lightweight woven crêpe fabric, sometimes also called 'crêpe georgette' or 'georgette crêpe'. Characteristically, it is a crisp, grainy crêpe fabric with a dull surface texture. Georgette is a durable fabric with a springy handle and does not crease easily (polyester georgette hardly creases at all). It has excellent drape but frays easily. Garments made with georgette are often lined.

Originally georgette was made using silk. Nowadays it is made in silk, polyester, cotton, wool, nylon and viscose. It is therefore available in a wide range of qualities, including sheer and semi-sheer qualities. Most georgette fabrics are woven in a fairly open-sett, balanced plain weave. High-twist crêpe yarns are arranged in an alternating sequence of two 'S' and two 'Z' twist yarns in both the warp and the weft. Georgette may therefore be termed a 'full crêpe' fabric. It is the yarns that produce the crêpe texture in the fabric. Some georgette fabrics, however, are not only woven with crêpe yarns, but also woven in a crêpe weave structure: this produces an even more grainy texture. Georgette is usually piece-dyed in plain colours, or it may be printed.

One example of a silk georgette fabric construction is 1.7 tex silk filament warp (2 or 3 threads) sett at 43 ends per cm and 1.7 tex silk filament weft (2 or 3 threads) woven in plain weave at 43 picks per cm; yarns with 20 to 32 turns per cm.[26] An example of a cotton georgette fabric construction is 17/2 tex warp sett at 20 ends per cm and 17/2 tex weft woven in plain weave at 18 picks per cm (the fabric will contract about 25% in both width and length).[26]

The name 'georgette' was originally a trademark for a silk crêpe fabric named after Madame Georgette de la Plante, a French milliner.[3] Georgette is a similar fabric to both chiffon and crêpe chiffon, but it has no lustre and is grainier and more opaque.

See also CRÊPE, CREPON GEORGETTE, SHEER FABRICS, SILK FABRIC.

End uses: women's dresses, blouses, evening wear, bridal wear, suits, nightwear, lingerie, scarves, millinery and curtains.

GEOTEXTILES A general term for a variety of woven, knitted and nonwoven textiles that are characteristically permeable and used for a range of agricultural and industrial end uses (such as those listed below).

Geotextiles are usually made from man-made fibres, including polyester, nylon and polyolefin (a synthetic man-made polymer). Although they may be woven or knitted, many are nonwoven textiles made by heat fusion or entanglement, since these are the least expensive production methods. Geotextiles are also often custom-made to fit the specific requirements of their end use.

See also LAID-IN FABRIC, MESH FABRICS, NONWOVEN FABRIC, POLYPROPYLENE TEXTILES.

End uses: textiles for crop and soil protection; industrial textiles for filtration, drainage, layer separation; and reinforcement and stabilization structures in civil engineering and construction materials.

gingham

gingham (crêpe)

glass cloth

GINGHAM A classic woven check fabric (occasionally a variation is also made in narrow stripes). It is usually a crisp, lightweight cotton fabric that is colour-woven with alternating bands of white and coloured yarns. Ginghams are available in a wide variety of weights and colours, but the checks are usually quite small.

Ginghams are usually woven with cotton yarns, which may be carded or combed. Sometimes fabrics made from other fibres are also called 'gingham'; in this case they should be labelled accordingly (e.g. as polyester gingham). The fabric is traditionally composed of two colours only, one of which is white. The yarns are fairly closely sett, and a regular check pattern is created with equal numbers of dyed yarns and undyed yarns in both the warp and the weft. Gingham is woven in a balanced, plain weave, square cloth construction. Some gingham fabrics have thicker yarns outlining the checks in both the warp and the weft directions. This creates corded checks in the fabric, which makes it similar to a dimity fabric. Gingham is usually lightly sized during finishing to give it a crisp handle. The fabric is quite hard-wearing and has excellent washability, because very fast dyes are normally used to dye the yarns.

Gingham is thought to have been first woven in north-eastern India from cotton and tussah silk. *Guingan* in Hindi and *gingan* in Malay mean 'striped or checked cloth'.[3] Gingham is a similar fabric to Madras but is more subtly coloured. Very lightweight gingham fabrics made from fine singles combed-cotton yarns are sometimes called 'zephyr', 'zephyr gingham' or 'tissue gingham'. These fabrics are similar in weight to chambray, lawn and batiste. Variations of gingham fabric include crêpe gingham and seersucker gingham, which combine the gingham check pattern with a crinkled and a puckered surface texture respectively.

See also CHECKS, COTTON FABRIC, CRÊPE, PLAIN WEAVE FABRIC, SEERSUCKER, ZEPHYR.

End uses: blouses, shirts, dresses, children's clothes, pyjamas, aprons, tablecloths, napkins and curtains.

GIVRENE (*obs.*) A silk, acetate or polyester fabric, very similar in appearance to grosgrain.[2]

GLASS CLOTH A slightly stiff woven fabric that was designed specifically for drying glasses and crockery. Characteristically, therefore, it is a very absorbent, strong and hard-wearing fabric. Glass cloth should not be confused with fabric made from the material glass (*see* GLASS-FIBRE TEXTILES below). It is sometimes called 'tea cloth' or 'tea towel' in order to avoid such confusion.

The highest-quality, traditional glass cloth is made with twisted and bleached linen yarns in a plain or twill weave construction. It is usually woven in narrow widths and given a smooth, flat finish. It may be woven as grey cloth, it may be colour-woven in stripes or checks, or it may be printed. Sometimes it has a jacquard woven stripe down either side with a name or pattern on it. A medium-quality glass cloth is also made as a linen/cotton union fabric, and the cheapest quality is made with cotton yarns only. These fabrics become damp more quickly and are not as hard-wearing as the linen glass cloth. An example of a typical glass cloth fabric construction is 50 tex linen or cotton warp sett at 18 ends per cm and 50 tex linen or cotton weft woven at 18 picks per cm.[26]

See also DICED WEAVES, HUCKABACK, TEA TOWELLING, TOWELLING, UNION FABRIC.

End uses: tea towels, and roller towels in public buildings.

GLASS-FIBRE TEXTILES Textiles that incorporate glass fibres. Glass fibres, also known as 'fibreglass', are very fine filaments of glass. They may be incorporated into woven structures and plastics and are used mainly for industrial textiles.

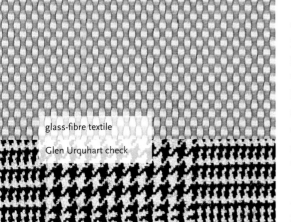

glass-fibre textile

Glen Urquhart check

Glass fibres are incorporated into many different industrial textiles for various purposes: to provide extra strength; for thermal insulation; for electrical insulation; to provide non-flammable properties in curtains and blinds; and as an essential element of fibre optics. In fibre optics, fine glass filaments can transmit beams of light over long distances.[6] Glass in powdered form may also be used as a coating for textiles and other materials.

See also ARAMID FABRIC, CARBON-FIBRE TEXTILES, FLAME-RESISTANT TEXTILES, MALIMO, NANOMATERIALS.

End uses: moulded plastics for sporting goods such as boats, and flame-resistant curtains, blinds and wall coverings.

GLEN CHECK *see* GLEN URQUHART CHECK.

GLENSHEE (*obs.*) A coarse, plain woven fabric made from mercerized cotton or cotton mixed with linen. It was used for curtains and loose covers and as a base for embroidery.[2]

GLEN STRIPE *see* GLEN URQUHART CHECK.

GLEN URQUHART CHECK (Glen check) A woven fabric traditionally made in wool in a distinctive check pattern; it was originally woven in Scotland and is one of the best-known and most common district check fabrics. It is also known by the shortened form 'Glen check'. The pattern is made with a colour and weave effect, which is created by combining a 2/2 twill weave structure with yarn-dyed stripes of alternating dark and light colours in both the warp and the weft. Similar fabrics with stripes rather than checks are called 'Glen stripes'; the stripes are normally in the warp direction. Glen Urquhart check is sometimes mistaken for Prince of Wales check, which is exactly the same except that the Prince of Wales check has a fine outline overcheck in addition.

Glen Urquhart check is usually woven with either wool or worsted wool yarns in a 2/2 twill weave structure. The yarns are arranged 4 dark / 4 light in sections that alternate with sections arranged 2 dark / 2 light in both the warp and weft directions. This produces alternating panels of houndstooth check and Guards check. Glen Urquhart check is woven in a variety of weights, ranging from light suiting weights to heavy overcoating weights. The design originates from the district near Loch Ness in the Highlands of Scotland, where Castle Urquhart overlooks Loch Ness.[3]

See also CHECKS, COLOUR AND WEAVE EFFECTS, DISTRICT CHECKS, GUARDS CHECK, HOUNDSTOOTH CHECK, PRINCE OF WALES CHECK.

End uses: men's and women's suits, jackets, trousers, skirts, coats, caps and hats.

GLISSADE (*obs.*) A cotton fabric, closely woven in satin weave, polished in finishing and used as a lining fabric.[2]

GLORIA *see* UMBRELLA FABRIC.

GOBELIN *see* TAPESTRY.

GORDON CORD *see* CORD FABRICS.

GORE-TEX® FABRICS *see* POLYMER MEMBRANE LAMINATES.

GOSSAMER An extremely fine, sheer, gauze-like woven fabric. Gossamer is the name for spider silk, and humans have long sought to imitate the fine mesh constructions of cobwebs. Gossamer is a very soft, lightweight and flexible fabric, chiefly used for veils.

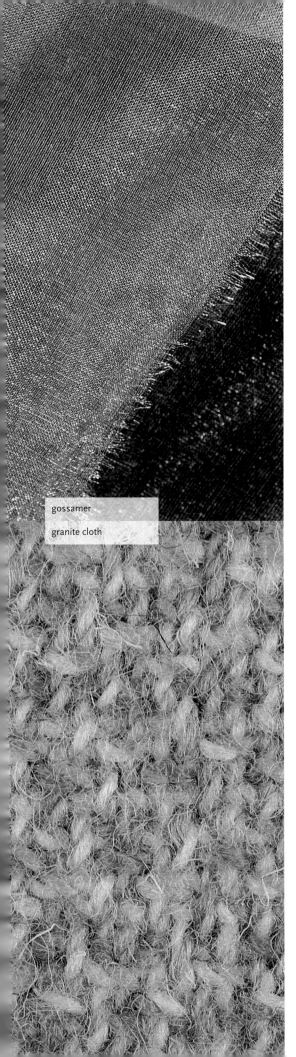

gossamer

granite cloth

Gossamer is usually made from very fine silk yarns and sometimes also with very fine man-made continuous filament fibres. It is woven in plain weave or leno weave constructions. A typical gossamer fabric construction is 2.5 tex warp sett at 18 ends per cm and 4 tex weft woven at 32 picks per cm.[26]

See also GAUZE, LENO FABRIC, PLAIN WEAVE FABRIC, SHEER FABRICS, SILK FABRIC, VEILING.

End uses: bridal veils, millinery trims and trims for evening wear and lingerie.

GRANADA (grenada) A fine worsted woven fabric with a high lustre; it belongs to the group known as 'Bradford lustre fabrics'. The weave structure gives the fabric a characteristic grainy surface texture.

Granada is a union fabric, traditionally woven with a cotton warp and a lustrous worsted wool weft. The weft yarn is much thicker than the warp yarn. The fabric is woven in a weft-faced broken twill weave structure that produces a weft-faced surface and gives the fabric its grainy texture. Sometimes alpaca or mohair is added to the weft yarns to increase both softness and lustre. The fabric is given a fine, face finish that accentuates the lustre on the face of the fabric. The cotton warp is usually yarn-dyed black, and the lustre weft yarn is usually coloured by piece-dyeing. By means of this cross-dyeing, the weft may be dyed any contrasting colour.[36] Granada is also made in black throughout. The fabric's name comes from the Latin *granum*, meaning 'grain'.

granada

See also BRADFORD LUSTRE FABRICS, COATING FABRIC, MOHAIR FABRIC, SUITING FABRICS, UNION FABRIC.

End uses: men's and women's coats and suits.

GRANDRELLE SHIRTING A woven fabric containing grandrelle yarns, which give it a slightly speckled appearance. This fabric is used mainly for casual work shirts.

A grandrelle yarn is a two-fold or two-ply yarn composed of two singles yarns of either different colours or contrasting lustre. For grandrelle shirting, cotton grandrelle yarns are used in the warp, together with single twist solid-colour yarns. The fabric is woven in a 5-end warp satin weave structure using white cotton weft yarns. A typical grandrelle shirting fabric construction is 30/2 tex grandrelle and 30 tex single warp sett at 36 ends per cm and 60 to 49 tex weft woven at 26 picks per cm.[26]

See also SATIN, WOVEN; SHIRTING FABRICS.

End uses: casual and work shirts.

GRANITE CLOTH (momie cloth) A woven fabric with a characteristic crinkled surface texture that is rough and grainy. It is a type of crêpe fabric in which the texture has been created by the weave structure. It has a matt, dull surface appearance, is springy to handle and frays easily.

Originally granite cloth was woven with a silk warp and a wool weft.[18] Nowadays it is most frequently woven with wool yarns, but sometimes also with cotton, silk or viscose. It is woven in a granite weave structure that is based on a restructured satin weave to form small, broken effects. This irregular weave structure produces an all-over pebbly texture in the fabric. Granite cloth may be bleached, dyed or printed. Granite weave structure is also used in other fabrics: for example, it may be employed in furnishing tweeds and in some crêpe fabrics, and is often used as a ground weave in jacquard fabrics (*see* JACQUARD FABRIC, WOVEN).

See also CRÊPE.

End uses: women's suits, jackets, dresses and furnishing fabrics.

grosgrain

Guards check

GRASS CLOTH *see* PLANT-FIBRE FABRICS.

GRENADINE A fine, sheer, lightweight, loosely woven leno fabric. It is an open gauze or net-like fabric that has figured sections, usually arranged in vertical (warpways) stripes or check designs. It is therefore either transparent or semi-transparent, depending on the yarn count and figured pattern used. It is a springy fabric with good drape.

Grenadine may be woven in silk, worsted wool, cotton, polyester, nylon, viscose or blends. The fabric is woven in a leno weave construction with more densely woven, figured sections that may be woven in twill or satin weaves. The fabric is often given a finish that lends it a stiff quality. Grenadines are colour-woven fabrics. At one time they had a black ground and were called 'black lenos',[4] but they may be woven in a wide variety of colours. Grenadine is a similar fabric to (woven) marquisette.

See also LENO FABRIC, FIGURED FABRICS, SHEER FABRICS.

End uses: dresses, blouses, scarves, men's neckties and curtains.

GRENFELL CLOTH (*obs.*) A closely woven reversible twill fabric made from worsted, polyester or blends. It was used mainly for raincoats and is similar to gaberdine.[2]

GREY FLANNEL *see* FLANNEL.

GROS DE LONDRES *see* GROSGRAIN.

GROS DE TOURS *see* GROSGRAIN.

GROSGRAIN A woven fabric with prominent, rounded, warp-faced ribs running either horizontally across the width of the fabric or vertically down the length of the fabric parallel to the selvedge (as is traditional for tie fabrics). In comparison to other similar rib fabrics (listed below), the ribs of grosgrain are the most prominent, hence its name (from French *gros* 'large', *grain* 'cord').[3] It is a fairly stiff, lustrous and hard-wearing fabric.

Like faille, grosgrain was originally woven in silk; it still is, but, being quite a heavy fabric, it is expensive. More usually, grosgrain is woven with man-made continuous filament yarns in both warp and weft, or with a man-made continuous filament warp and either man-made or cotton staple yarns in the weft. It can also be made in cotton or blends. Ribs in the horizontal direction are made with highly sett warp yarns and slightly thicker weft yarns. The fabric is woven in plain weave, and the warp yarns completely cover the weft yarns, which lie straight, without crimp, resulting in a warp-faced fabric. Ribs in the vertical direction are weft-faced fabrics in which the warp yarns are slightly thicker and the fine weft yarns are very highly sett. The fabric is woven in plain weave, and the weft yarns completely cover the warp yarns. Grosgrain is usually made only in plain colours and it frays easily.

An example of a good-quality grosgrain fabric construction weighing 170 g/m² is 8.3 tex warp sett at 76 ends per cm and 6 tex weft woven at 11 picks per cm.[25] Grosgrain is a suitable fabric from which to make moiré fabrics by using a moiré finish. Gros de Tours is a variation of grosgrain that is woven with two picks in each shed, producing chunkier, more prominent ribs. Another variation is gros de Londres, a lightweight woven fabric with either alternating heavy and fine flat ribs, or ribs of different colours running in the weft direction. It is a stiff fabric and in this respect is similar to taffeta. Gros de Londres is usually woven with shiny yarns such as viscose, acetate, polyester or silk. It is woven in plain weave or plain weave variations with highly sett warp yarns and thicker weft yarns. The heavy and fine ribs are not always alternated in a regular sequence. The fabric may be piece-dyed or warp-printed and it is usually given a lustrous finish.

See TAFFETA, WARP-PRINTED FABRIC.

guernsey

gunclub check

There is a range of warp rib fabrics characterized by the size and prominence of their ribs. In increasing order of rib size, these are: broadcloth, poplin, taffeta, poult, faille, bengaline and grosgrain. However, since many of them are woven in a variety of different weights, they are sometimes difficult to distinguish.

See also RIB FABRICS, WOVEN; SILK FABRIC.

End uses: dresses, men's neckties, evening dresses, women's suits, church vestments, trimmings, ribbons, millinery and bags.

GROSPOINT A thick, heavy woven loop pile fabric. It has a rough handle, does not crease and characteristically has a higher loop pile than other similar fabrics.

Grospoint is woven using all kinds of cotton or man-made fibres. A base fabric is woven in a firm plain weave ground construction. The pile is made by inserting wires to lift particular pile-warp yarns above the surface of the base fabric at regular intervals during weaving. When the wires are removed, a dense pile of small, closed loops is formed on the surface of the fabric. Grospoint is a similar fabric to frisé but has larger loops. It is also similar to moquette and terry fabric.

See also PILE FABRICS.

End uses: upholstery and curtains.

GUARDS CHECK A woven check fabric that has a vertical line effect. The pattern is made with a colour and weave effect, which is created by combining a 2/2 twill weave structure with narrow yarn-dyed stripes of alternating dark and light colours in both the warp and the weft.

Guards check may be made using any fibre; however, the traditional wool is still the most popular and the most commonly used. The yarns are arranged in a sequence of two dark and two light in both the warp and the weft. The light colour is frequently ecru or white. The fabric is woven in a 2/2 twill weave structure. Variations of Guards check may be made by slightly changing the relationship between the weave structure and the colour order; larger outline checks in different colours may also be overlaid on top of this. Guards check is used in conjunction with houndstooth check to make the pattern in Glen Urquhart check.

See also CHECKS, COLOUR AND WEAVE EFFECTS, TWILL FABRICS.

End uses: men's and women's suits, jackets, trousers, skirts, coats, caps and hats.

GUERNSEY A type of chunky weft-knitted fabric used for sweaters. As with the better-known term 'jersey', the name comes from one of the Channel Islands between England and France. The fabric is used on Guernsey for fishermen's sweaters (or 'guernseys', as they are commonly known). Guernsey sweaters are very heavy, warm and hard-wearing garments. They are usually knitted by hand using coarse local wools. They are characteristically knitted 'in the round' – as seamless tubes – and therefore have no side seams. They are usually knitted in simple structures like plain knit or rib structures.

See also JERSEY; KNITTED FABRIC; PLAIN KNIT FABRIC; RIB FABRICS, KNITTED; WEFT-KNITTED FABRIC.

End uses: sweaters.

GUNCLUB CHECK A woven fabric that is a variation of houndstooth check. It has the same characteristic small houndstooth-shaped pattern, but instead of using a dark/light colour sequence, two different dark colours are alternated against a light ground colour.

habotai

haircloth

Gunclub check may be made using any fibre; the traditional wool is still the most commonly used, however. The houndstooth pattern is made with a colour and weave effect. The yarns are arranged in a sequence of four dark and four light in both the warp and the weft, with the two different dark colours alternating with the one light colour. The light colour is frequently ecru or white. The fabric is woven in a 2/2 twill weave structure. Gunclub checks are usually woven in greens, browns and blues. Sometimes they are overlaid with a larger outline check. Gunclub check is usually a medium- to heavy-weight woven fabric.

See also CHECKS, COLOUR AND WEAVE EFFECTS, HOUNDSTOOTH CHECK, TWILL FABRICS.

End uses: men's and women's suits, jackets, trousers, skirts, coats, caps and hats.

GYPSY CLOTH *see* ELASTOMERIC FABRIC.

HABIT CLOTH (*obs.*) A fine woven fabric made from good-quality wool yarns, woven in satin weave and given a dress-face finish. It was usually made in dark colours and used for ladies' riding habits (hence the name).[26]

HABOTAI (habutae) A soft, fine silk fabric that was originally woven on hand-looms in Japan and used for lining kimonos;[25] the name is the Japanese one for the fabric. It is a lightweight but opaque fabric with a characteristic soft surface texture caused by slight imperfections in the raw silk yarns. Habotai is usually woven in natural ecru colour.

Habotai fabrics are woven using yarns comprised of 12 to 16 filaments of raw silk, slightly twisted and 'in the gum', or still coated in the natural gum sericin produced by the larvae of the silk moth when they spun the fibre.[3] Nowadays habotai is woven on power looms in many different Far Eastern countries. The fabric is woven in plain weave and then de-gummed by boiling. It is often used in its ecru form or it may be piece-dyed. Habotai is a similar fabric to China silk but is slightly heavier. It is also similar to jappe (or jappe silk).

See also PLAIN WEAVE FABRIC, SILK FABRIC.

End uses: lightweight lining fabric for evening and wedding dresses, dresses, blouses, curtains, scarves and lingerie.

HAIRCLOTH A strong, stiff woven fabric that is made either with horsehair in the weft or with horsehair mixed with other fibres. It is a very hard-wearing fabric.

The horsehair used is the wiry hair from the tails and manes of horses. When it is woven in the weft, single fibres of horsehair are inserted into a (usually high-twist) cotton or linen warp, using a special weaving loom that is capable of inserting discontinuous fibres. The fabric width is determined by the length of the horsehair (usually between 47 and 76 cm).[25] Other haircloth fabrics are made with yarns that are composed of horsehair mixed with other fibres, such as cotton, polyester or linen. The weave structure will vary according to the end use but is often plain weave.

Traditionally haircloth was used for interlinings in coats and suits, but less expensive, bonded fibre fabrics are normally used for this purpose nowadays. At one time it was also widely employed as the base fabric in upholstered furniture; although it is rarely found today, it may still sometimes be used when renovating antique furniture. The term 'haircloth' is sometimes also used to describe the rough shirts formerly worn by monks doing penance; in this case it refers to any rough, scratchy fabric that might have been made from wool, goat's hair or horsehair.

End uses: interlinings, stiffening fabric used in tailoring, furnishing fabrics, upholstery, and sieve and press cloths.

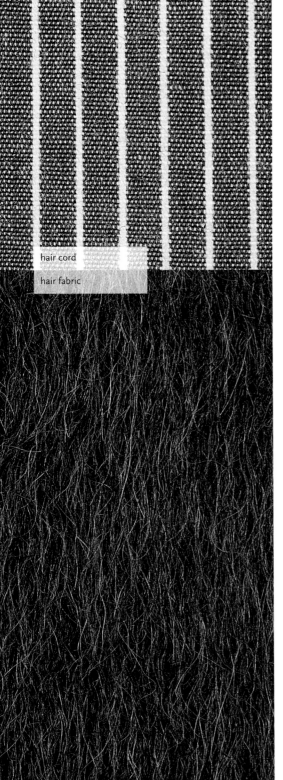

hair cord

hair fabric

HAIR CORD A lightweight woven cord fabric that has characteristic fine, weft-faced cords that run longitudinally down the fabric in the warp direction, parallel to the selvedge.

Hair cord is usually woven with cotton yarns. The cord effect is produced either by alternating fine and thick warp ends or by weaving two or more ends as one and alternating them with one or more single ends. The fabric is then woven in plain weave or simple plain weave variations. Alternatively, warp ends all of the same count may be woven in a 1 and 2 rib construction. Hair cords are usually either yarn-dyed or piece-dyed. One example of a hair cord fabric construction is 2 ends of 18 tex / 1 end of 21 tex cotton warp sett at 28 ends per cm and 21 tex soft-spun cotton weft woven at 26 picks per cm.[25]

See also CORD FABRICS; RIB FABRICS, WOVEN.

hair cord

End uses: dresses and blouses.

HAIR FABRICS A general term for any fabrics constructed in part or in whole with natural animal hair fibres. Wool is the most common hair fibre, but the term 'hair fabrics' is normally used for those that contain more unusual animal fibres or speciality hair fibres, for example alpaca (hair from the alpaca, a relative of the llama), vicuña (hair from the vicuña, another relative of the llama), camel hair, cashmere (goat hair), mohair (hair from the angora goat), horsehair and angora (hair from the angora rabbit).

These speciality hair fibres are usually quite expensive, and they are therefore often blended with, or used together with, other less expensive fibres, usually wool. Hair fibres are staple fibres that are spun into yarns. 'Hair fabric' is a general term used for fabrics of all different weights and constructions composed either of 100% speciality hair fibres or yarns, or a blend of speciality hair fibre with another fibre. In the latter case, the percentage of each should always be stated. Characteristically, most hair fabrics are luxurious fabrics, known for their warmth, natural high lustre and soft handle. For examples of hair fabrics, *see* ALPACA FABRIC, ANGORA FABRIC, CAMEL-HAIR FABRIC, CAMLET, CASHMERE CLOTH, KASHA, MOHAIR FABRIC, SHATUSH, WOOL FABRIC, VICUÑA FABRIC and WEDDING RING FABRICS.

End uses: coats, jackets, suits and knitted apparel of all kinds.

HAIRLINE A woven fabric that is patterned with very fine solid-colour stripes, hair-width in size. The stripes may be in the warp direction (warp hairline) or the weft direction (weft hairline). The lines may be either printed onto the fabric or woven into the fabric using colour and weave effects.

In true colour-woven hairline fabrics, the colours of the warp and weft yarns are arranged so that each colour in the warp intersects only with the same weft colour. This produces solid lines of colour in the fabric. The fabric is woven in simple weave structures, including plain weave, plain weave variations, double plain and double twill weaves.[26]

See also COLOUR AND WEAVE EFFECTS, CRANKY CHECKS, DOUBLE CLOTH, STRIPES.

End uses: shirts, blouses, dresses, men's and women's suitings, trousers and skirts.

HALF-MILANO RIB *see* MILANO RIB.

hairline (warp hairline)

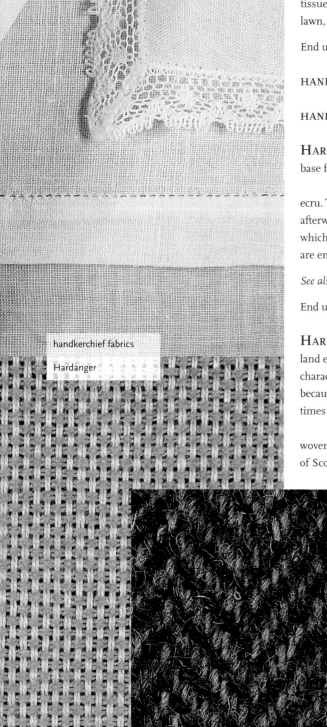

handkerchief fabrics

Hardanger

Harris tweed

HANDKERCHIEF FABRIC A general term for a range of fine cotton-type fabrics that are used for handkerchiefs. Most are lightweight woven fabrics. They may be bleached white, yarn-dyed, piece-dyed or printed. They may also be embroidered or have decorative lace incorporated into them. Nowadays handkerchiefs have largely been replaced by paper tissues. Traditional handkerchief fabrics include bandanna, batiste, chambray, foulard, lawn, linen fabric, Madras, malabar, nainsook and surah.

End uses: handkerchiefs, head squares and scarves.

HANDKERCHIEF LAWN *see* LAWN.

HANDKERCHIEF LINEN *see* LINEN FABRIC.

HARDANGER A woven fabric constructed in a hopsack weave structure and used as a base fabric for embroidery.

Hardanger is traditionally woven with mercerized cotton yarns, often in white or ecru. The fabric may also be piece-dyed. It is woven in a 2 × 2 hopsack weave structure and afterwards given a soft finish. The name comes from the Hardanger region in Norway, which has a tradition of folk weaving and where coarse, bleached linen or cotton fabrics are embroidered with coloured threads in traditional patterns.

See also CANVAS, EMBROIDERED FABRICS, FOLK WEAVE, HOPSACK.

End uses: base fabric for embroideries.

HARRIS TWEED (Hebridean tweed) A woven tweed fabric traditionally made in Scotland entirely from Scottish wool. It is known as a very warm, hard-wearing fabric, and is characteristically rough and hairy. Harris tweed is fibre-dyed in soft, natural colours and, because it is produced mainly by hand, is an exclusive, expensive fabric. It is also sometimes called 'Hebridean tweed' or 'Hebridean fabric'.[36]

Harris tweed is probably the best-known Scottish tweed fabric. It is a traditional woven fabric from the Outer Hebridean islands of Harris and Lewis, off the west coast of Scotland, where it has been produced by the local cottage industry for at least three hundred years.[5] In 1909 the islanders formed the Harris Tweed Association and registered 'Harris Tweed' as their trademark. Therefore only fabrics that have been spun, woven, dyed and finished in this region can carry the trademark that shows that they are authentic. The fabrics also carry labels stating that they have been hand-woven from pure virgin Scottish wool.[10] The wool used to make Harris tweed is Scottish Cheviot wool.[10]

Both fibres and yarns are dyed with natural dyestuffs that are found locally, including lichen and heather. Fibres that have been fibre-dyed are often blended together to give the characteristic soft tones for which Harris tweeds are known. Sometimes the dyes are heated over peat and this smell can remain in the fibres and yarns, becoming more noticeable when the fabric is damp.[18] At one time the fabric was made entirely from hand-spun yarns and was hand-woven. Nowadays machines are used in some of the processes. Harris tweed is woven in simple plain, twill or herringbone weave structures. An example of a Harris tweed fabric construction is 250 tex warp sett at 7 ends per cm and 250 tex weft woven at 7 picks per cm.[26]

See also COATING FABRIC, TWEED.

End uses: suits, sports jackets, coats, caps, hats and upholstery.

hemp fabric

herringbone

HARVARD (Harvard shirting) A strong, hard-wearing cotton woven fabric that is used for shirts. The fabric is colour-woven and usually has coloured stripes in the warp direction.

Harvards are woven in a 2/2 twill weave base structure using coarse singles yarns. The weft yarn is quite soft, with a low twist, giving the fabric a soft, fluffy surface texture. Harvard shirtings usually have coloured warp yarns and a white weft. The warpways stripes may be colours alternating with white stripes; they may be different coloured stripes; or they may be composed of simple weave effects. Traditional colours used include red, white, navy, sky blue and pink.

Examples of Harvard fabric constructions are: 30 tex warp sett at 64 ends per cm and 49 tex weft woven at 56 picks per cm;[25] or 38 to 33 tex warp sett at 28 ends per cm and 38 to 33 tex weft woven at 26 to 29 picks per cm (with both warp and weft yarns twisted warpways).[26] Sometimes cranky check patterns are also used for Harvard shirtings (*see* CRANKY CHECK). Harvard is a similar fabric to regatta in both texture and weight.

See also SHIRTING FABRICS, STRIPES, TWILL FABRICS.

End uses: shirts.

HEBRIDEAN TWEED *see* HARRIS TWEED.

HEMP FABRIC A general term for any fabric constructed from hemp yarns or fibres. Hemp is a natural bast fibre obtained from the hemp plant, *Cannabis sativa*.[25] It is a long, very strong, pale-coloured, semi-lustrous fibre.

Hemp fibres are staple fibres that are spun into yarns; sometimes they are blended together with other staple fibres. The term 'hemp fabric' is used for fabrics of all different weights and constructions composed of 100% hemp fibres or yarns. In fabrics where hemp is used together with other fibres, the percentage of each should be stated. Characteristically, hemp fabrics are strong and have good lustre. Hessian is an example of a fabric that is sometimes made from hemp yarns (*see* HESSIAN). Hemp is a very similar fibre to flax fibre, which is used to make linen fabric, and microscopically it is difficult to distinguish between the two.[45]

See also LINEN FABRIC, PLANT-FIBRE FABRICS.

End uses: shirts, trousers, T-shirts, jeans, jackets, socks, floor coverings, bags, shoes, sacking, tents, rope and string.

HENRIETTA A fine, soft, lustrous woven fabric that is particularly noted for its drape. Traditionally it is a union fabric, woven with a fine silk warp and a fine botany wool weft, and it is made in imitation of the more expensive cashmere cloth. It may also be produced in a variety of different weights, sometimes using other fibre blends.

Henrietta is named after Henrietta Maria, the consort of King Charles I, who reigned in England from 1625 to 1649.[5] The fabric is woven in a 1/2 twill weave structure. An example of a Henrietta fabric construction is 10/2 to 8/2 tex spun silk warp sett at 26 to 29 ends per cm and 12 to 11 tex botany weft woven at 62 to 66 picks per cm.[26] Henrietta is a similar fabric to Coburg but it is usually finer.

See also CASHMERE CLOTH, TWILL FABRICS, UNION FABRIC.

End uses: dresses, blouses and skirts.

HERRINGBONE A general term for woven fabrics constructed in a distinctive herringbone pattern, which is a reversed broken twill.[2, 25, 26] Visually the fabric resembles the backbone structure of a herring, hence the name. Herringbone is sometimes also called 'feather twill' or 'arrowhead twill'.[12] Herringbone should not be confused with a waved or reverse twill weave, which produces a zigzag effect in the fabric (*see* TWILL FABRICS).

Herringbone fabrics are made in all weights and using all kinds of fibre or fibre combinations. The herringbone pattern is made by 'cutting and reversing' alternate vertical sections of a broken twill weave. The twill diagonals are arranged into vertical columns and are staggered along the vertical line

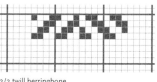

2/2 twill herringbone

at the point where they reverse. This produces a characteristic vertical 'break' or 'cut' in the fabric. There are two main ways in which a herringbone pattern may be produced in a woven fabric. The first is by weaving the fabric in a herringbone weave structure. The second is by using special drafting arrangements when setting up the warp for weaving; the fabric is then woven in twill weave or a combination of different twill weaves, and the drafting arrangement automatically changes the direction of the twill line at regular intervals to form the herringbone pattern.

The herringbone diagonals are usually all the same size and arranged in columns of equal width, which may be wide or narrow. 'Pin-feather' is the name given to a herringbone fabric with narrow columns of herringbone. Irregular herringbone patterns are also produced, by varying both the width of diagonal and the column width. Herringbone fabrics are usually colour-woven fabrics. They often use contrasting colours in the warp and the weft in order to accentuate the pattern, and the contrast may be bold or very subtle. Examples of fabrics woven in a herringbone construction include some Bannockburn fabrics, some Cheviot fabrics, coutil, some covert cloth fabrics, some jean fabrics, some mohair fabrics, many suiting fabrics, surah chevron, some ticking fabrics, some tie fabrics and some tweeds.

See also SHADOW STRIPES AND CHECKS, TWILL FABRICS.

End uses: men's and women's suitings and coats (perhaps the best-known uses); all kinds of fashion and furnishing fabrics.

HESSIAN (burlap) A coarse, rough woven fabric made from bast fibres (usually jute) and woven in a fairly open-sett plain weave. Hessian is a heavyweight fabric, known for its strength and durability, but it frays easily. It is traditionally used for sacking and carpet backings. It is also known as 'burlap', especially in the United States.

Bast fibres from which hessian may be woven include jute and hemp. Singles yarns of approximately the same count in both the warp and the weft are used, mainly in their natural unbleached and undyed form. The fabric is woven in a square-sett plain weave construction. In this form the fabric is used as sacking and as carpet backing. However, hessian is sometimes piece-dyed after weaving, and with special finishing treatments it becomes a smooth, attractive fabric that can be used for furnishings.

See also CARPET, HEMP FABRIC, PLAIN WEAVE FABRIC, PLANT-FIBRE FABRICS, TUFTED FABRIC.

End uses: sacking, curtains, blinds, wall coverings, upholstery, bags, carpet and linoleum backings.

HICKORY CLOTH An American term for a strong, durable woven fabric made from cotton or polyester/cotton. The fabric often has coloured stripes in the warp direction and is used for workwear in the United States.[36]

Hickory cloth is a colour-woven fabric, usually having stripes of coloured yarns alternating with white yarns in the warp, and white weft yarns. The most common colour

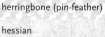

herringbone (pin-feather)

hessian

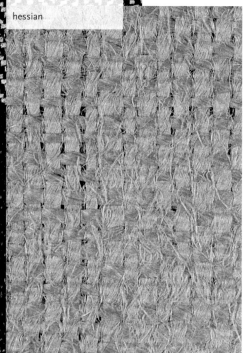

hickory cloth

high-tech textile
(face and back)

Holland (calender-glazed)

combinations are blue and white and brown and white. It is woven in a 2/2 twill weave structure or twill variation and given a soft finish. Hickory cloth is a similar fabric to ticking, but it is lighter in weight and less closely sett. Other similar fabrics include bluette, denim, drill, dungaree, florentine and jean.

See also STRIPES, TWILL FABRICS.

End uses: protective clothing, overalls, work shirts, jackets and trousers.

HIGH-TECH TEXTILES (high-performance textiles) A general term for textiles constructed with special features that enable them to exceed the performance normally expected in similar textiles. For example, a nylon anorak fabric is not in itself high-tech, but becomes so when it is laminated to a thin polymer membrane: this makes it both waterproof and windproof while still allowing water vapour (perspiration) to pass through, thus rendering it breathable and comfortable to wear next to the skin.

Some of the special features incorporated by high-tech fabrics include new fibre developments, new fabric developments, special colour effects and innovative finishes. Many high-tech fabrics have been developed as a result of studying and imitating naturally occurring mechanisms to see how they react with and respond to stimuli in their external environment (the science of imitating nature is called 'biomimetics'). There have been a number of developments in clothing and textile materials where inspiration has been drawn from nature. For example, the textured surface of a shark's skin has been replicated in swimwear fabrics to make them more hydrodynamic. For further examples of high-tech fabrics, *see* ANTIMICROBIAL FABRIC, HOLOGRAPHIC FABRICS, MICROENCAPSULATED TEXTILES, MICROFIBRE FABRIC, MOISTURE TRANSPORT TEXTILES, NANOMATERIALS, NEOPRENE, POLYMER MEMBRANE LAMINATES, SMART TEXTILES.

End uses: all kinds of fashion and furnishing fabrics and technical textiles.

HIMALAYA *see* SHANTUNG.

HOLLAND A fine, smooth, medium-weight woven fabric that is woven in plain weave; it was originally made from linen yarns but may now be made with cotton or linen yarns. Holland is a firm, hard-wearing fabric that is used mainly for window blinds or as a stiffening interlining in dressmaking. It is given a special finish to make it opaque, which lends the fabric a characteristic stiff, hard handle.

The fabric was first produced in Holland, hence the name. Originally it was made from unbleached flax and in this form was sometimes called 'brown Holland'.[3] It may also be bleached and dyed. After weaving in plain weave, the fabric is either beetled or heavily sized with oil, starch or pyroxylin.[17] It may be calender-glazed as well. After finishing, the fabric is usually rolled rather than folded.

Holland used as a window blind fabric is usually made in plain, dark colours such as black, grey, dark blue and dark green. An example of a Holland fabric construction is 51 tex warp sett at 17 ends per cm and 51 tex weft woven at 17 picks per cm.[26] Similar fabrics to Holland include awning cloth, book cloth, canvas, duck, hopsack and sailcloth.

See also BLACKOUT FABRIC, PLAIN WEAVE FABRIC.

End uses: window blinds, blackout fabric and interlinings for dressmaking.

HOLOGRAPHIC FABRICS Fabrics decorated with holographic films, either in sheet form, as novelty trims, in sequin form or in thread form. Characteristically, the films are highly reflective and they are used as decorative dress trimmings in order to give the fabrics sparkle.

Any fabrics may be decorated with holographic films, including woven, knitted, nonwoven, lace and stretch fabrics of all kinds. To make the holographic film, light from a laser beam is split and projected onto the film like a photographic image. The image is then transferred from the film negative to a metal die, which is used to stamp the image onto very thin, shiny polyester foil or film. To make holographic sewing threads, the hologram film is cut into very fine, flat film threads. For use on fabrics, the film is back-coated with a heat-sensitive adhesive. It may then be cut into novelty trim shapes, logos or sequins, or may be used in sheet form and laminated to the fabric by heat transfer. Holographic films are sometimes also appliquéd onto fabrics by sewing. Fabrics and garments may be decorated with holographic films over the whole of their surface, which produces a very shiny effect similar to a lamé fabric, or the films may be used on selected areas only.

See also APPLIQUÉ FABRIC, COATED FABRIC, EMBOSSED FABRICS, LAMÉ, LAMINATED FABRIC, METALLIC FABRICS, REFLECTIVE FABRICS, SEQUINNED FABRICS.

End uses: swimwear, leotards, evening wear, bridal wear, wedding veils, theatrical costumes, ballet costumes, shoes, purses and evening bags.

HOMESPUN A general term for any coarse-looking woven fabric that has an irregular, rustic appearance, as if it had been hand-woven; the term is most often applied to fabrics woven in wool that have a tweed-like appearance. At one time, homespun was clearly defined as 'cloth, the wool of which was hand spun and woven on hand-looms at home', and this seems to have been enforced by law,[16, 36] but the term now has the more general application described above. Homespun fabrics are characteristically very hard-wearing, practical fabrics.

Homespun fabrics originated in Britain,[5] where they were woven by hand in the individual homes of local communities using hand-spun yarns. Similar fabrics, however, have also been woven in most countries of Europe and in the United States. True homespun fabrics are made in narrow widths, according to the width of the hand-weaving loom. Nowadays homespun fabrics are usually machine-woven in wider widths, but they still retain a hand-woven appearance. They are typically woven in a loose plain weave or 2/2 twill, using thick, irregular wool yarns with low twist. Natural or dyed yarns may be used, or yarns blended from differently coloured fibres (natural fibres or fibres that are dyed with natural colours). Homespun fabrics are woven in a variety of different weights and qualities, but most are heavyweight fabrics.

See also FOLK WEAVE, KHADI, TWEED.

End uses: jackets, suits, coats and furnishing fabrics.

HONAN A light- to medium-weight woven fabric with a rough, irregular texture, traditionally woven from wild 'net' tussah silk yarns in plain weave. Nowadays honan fabrics are also made using man-made fibres (often polyester), which are textured to imitate the wild silk yarns.

Traditional honan is woven from a wild silk yarn that comes from the Honan area of China. Characteristically, the yarn has an uneven slub texture, and it is the only type of wild silk that accepts dye evenly. The same yarns are used in both the warp and the weft, and the slub effect is therefore apparent in both directions. The fabric is woven in plain weave and it may be dyed or printed. Honan is a similar fabric to silk pongee and silk shantung, but it has slub yarns in both warp and weft directions (pongee and shantung use slub yarns in the weft only).

See also PLAIN WEAVE FABRIC, SILK FABRIC.

End uses: dresses, blouses and furnishings.

holographic fabric

honan

homespun

honeycomb

honeycomb

HONEYCOMB A woven fabric constructed in a honeycomb weave structure. It is easily recognizable from its characteristic three-dimensional cellular structure, which resembles a bee's honeycomb. Honeycomb is made in many different weights and qualities and is used mainly for towels and bedspreads.

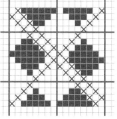
Brighton honeycomb

In ordinary honeycomb weave structures, the warp and weft threads are interlaced and floated in a manner that produces a regular pattern of small square ridges and hollows in the fabric. This cellular effect is produced equally on both the face and the back of the fabric. The fabric may be patterned all over with the honeycomb weave structure, or sometimes honeycomb weaves are used in conjunction with other, usually simpler weave structures (e.g. twill or plain weave). The three-dimensional honeycomb structure gives honeycomb fabrics a large surface area, making them

honeycomb weave

either very absorbent (especially if made with cotton) or warm (especially if made with wool or with thick yarns).

Other weave structures that produce similar effects to honeycomb weaves are Grecian weaves and sponge weaves. Brighton honeycomb is a variation of ordinary honeycomb weave, in which the cellular structure is more prominent on the face of the fabric than on the back. The effect is also less regular than ordinary honeycomb, and it consists of a mixture of large and small square cell structures. Honeycomb is a dobby fabric that is woven on a dobby loom. Honeycomb fabric is sometimes also called 'waffle' or 'waffle fabric' (especially in the United States).[5, 13]

See also CELLULAR FABRIC; DOBBY FABRIC; PIQUÉ, WOVEN; SPONGE CLOTH; TEA TOWELLING; TOWELLING.

End uses: towels, bathrobes, bedspreads, tea towels, blankets, quilts, tablecloths, curtains, children's clothes, dresses, blouses, sportswear and thermal underwear.

HOPSACK (basket cloth) A general term for any woven fabric that is woven in a hopsack weave structure. This is a larger-scale variation of a plain weave fabric structure, in which two or more warp and weft yarns are woven as one in a plain weave construction. This produces a small geometric pattern or texture in the fabric. Hopsack fabrics usually crease less than plain weave fabrics, but they are more prone to fraying and snagging. The terms 'basket cloth' or 'basket weave' are also sometimes used to describe hopsack weaves, as are the general terms 'mat (matt) weaves' or 'panama' (the latter being the German word for a hopsack weave structure).

Hopsack was originally a coarse, durable fabric that was woven in hopsack weave structure from jute or hemp yarns and used to make sacks for hop growers. At that time it was known as 'hop pocketing', but this was gradually replaced by the name 'hopsack'. Nowadays the term is used to describe any fabric that is woven in a hopsack weave structure. Hopsack fabrics are made in a wide variety of weights from many different fibres, including cotton, wool, silk, man-made fibres and man-made fibre/natural fibre mixes.

Hopsack is a dobby fabric that is woven on a dobby loom. Most hopsack fabrics are balanced fabrics that are made by weaving two, three or four yarns as one, in both warp and weft directions (2 × 2 and 4 × 4 are the most common). The 2 × 2 hopsack, or 'Celtic' weave, is perhaps

hopsack 2/2

hopsack (weft-knitted)
hopsack (woven 4 × 4)
hopsack (woven 2 × 2)

horse-blanket check

the most common of all.[36] There are also a large number of variations on the basic hopsack weave structure; some examples follow.

(i) Unbalanced hopsack fabrics may be made by weaving two, three or four warp ends as one with a single weft pick, or vice versa (e.g. Oxford).

(ii) A stitched hopsack may be woven with additional interlacings in order to produce a more stable fabric (e.g. barleycorn fabric and natté).

(iii) Twilled hopsack patterns may be produced by arranging square blocks of hopsack to make diagonal lines in the fabric (e.g. barathea).

(iv) Some interesting colour and weave effects may be produced in conjunction with hopsack weaves. Alternatively, hopsack fabrics may be piece-dyed or printed.

Examples of fabrics that are woven in hopsack weave structure include some barathea fabrics, crêpe romaine (*see* CRÊPE), some duck fabrics, Hardanger, louisine, monk's cloth, natté, Oxford, panama, panama canvas (*see* PANAMA), sailcloth and some sharkskin fabrics. Knitted fabrics are also made in imitation of woven hopsack fabric. There are many variants, but they are usually weft-knitted single jersey fabrics.

See also DOBBY FABRIC, MOCK LENO, PLAIN WEAVE FABRIC.

End uses: men's and women's suits, jackets, coats, skirts, blouses, shirts, curtains and upholstery fabrics.

HORSE-BLANKET CHECK A thick, woven blanket fabric made from wool that has a fine outline over-check design woven into it. As the name suggests, this fabric is traditionally used for horse blankets. Thin warpways and weftways stripes in a bright colour typically form a large-scale outline over-check pattern against a light background colour. Often two different check patterns in different colours overlap one another against the light ground. Tattersall check fabrics are frequently copies of horse-blanket checks.

See also BLANKET, CHECKS, TATTERSALL CHECK.

End uses: horse blankets and blankets.

HOSE *see* MICROMESH.

HOUNDSTOOTH CHECK (dogstooth check) A colour-woven fabric with a characteristic pattern of small-scale pointed checks shaped like hounds' teeth. The pattern is made with a colour and weave effect, which is created by combining a 2/2 twill weave structure with narrow, yarn-dyed stripes of alternating dark and light colours in both the warp and the weft. Houndstooth is woven in a wide range of different weights and qualities.

houndstooth stripe

houndstooth check

Houndstooth check may be made using any fibre; however, the traditional wool is probably still the most common. The yarns are arranged in a sequence of four dark and four light in both the warp and the weft. The light colour is frequently ecru or white, and the fabric is woven in a balanced 2/2 twill weave structure. The houndstooth check pattern is also sometimes printed onto fabrics.

Houndstooth check is a type of shepherd's check and is also frequently used in sections of other district check fabrics in conjunction with other patterns. A houndstooth stripe is a variation of the houndstooth check in which the weft is all one colour, creating a houndstooth stripe in the warp direction instead of a check. Gunclub check is another variation of a houndstooth check fabric (*see* GUNCLUB CHECK). The houndstooth check pattern should not be confused with four-pointed star check or chicken's foot check, both of which look similar (*see* FOUR-POINTED STAR CHECK).

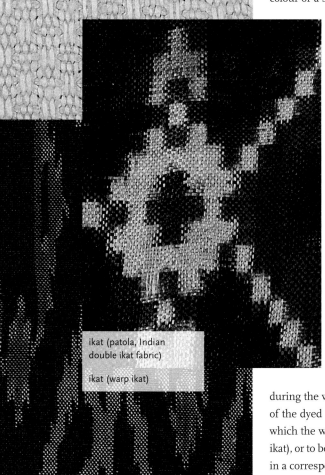

huckaback

ikat (patola, Indian double ikat fabric)

ikat (warp ikat)

See also CHECKS, COLOUR AND WEAVE EFFECTS, DISTRICT CHECKS, GLEN URQUHART CHECK, SHEPHERD'S CHECK, TWILL FABRICS.

End uses: casual jackets, trousers, skirts, suits, coats, shawls, caps and furnishing fabrics.

HOUNDSTOOTH STRIPE *see* HOUNDSTOOTH CHECK.

HUCKABACK A heavy, slightly stiff woven fabric that is woven in a huckaback weave structure. Huckaback is used mainly as a towelling or tea towelling fabric and is often woven in narrow widths. It is characteristically very absorbent, strong and hard-wearing.

Huckaback is usually made with low-twist linen or cotton yarns as these are highly absorbent. The huckaback weave structure is a type of diced weave or diaper weave structure in which a small-scale check effect is produced on both sides of the fabric. The weave structure itself is a variation of plain weave. On one side of the fabric, short warp floats create a small-scale check effect against a plain ground weave. On the other side of the fabric, short weft floats create a similar effect against the plain ground weave. These floats increase the absorbent qualities of the fabric.

Huckaback is usually white in colour and sometimes has a woven stripe in a different colour or a stripe with a name woven on it. An example of a huckaback fabric construction is 74 tex warp sett at 16 ends per cm and 74 tex weft woven at 38 picks per cm.[26] Huckaback is a dobby fabric that is woven on a dobby loom.

See also CHECKS, DICED WEAVES, DOBBY FABRIC, GLASS CLOTH, TEA TOWELLING, TOWELLING.

End uses: towels, roller towels in public buildings, tea cloths, curtains and shirts.

example of huckaback weave

IKAT A woven fabric in which either the warp yarns, the weft yarns or both have been partially dyed (resist-dyed) prior to weaving. When the fabric is then woven, the undyed sections form patterns in the fabric that have characteristic feathered or blurred edges in the direction of the ikat-dyed yarns. Ikat is usually an expensive fabric, since ikat dyeing is mainly a hand-dyeing process that is both complex and time-consuming.

The ikat dyeing process is usually applied to natural fibre yarns that are easy to dye by hand. The yarns may be of any thickness. Protective bindings are wrapped around the yarns in a predetermined pattern. When the yarns are dyed the sections that were wrapped preserve their original colour. The resist-dyed yarns may then be woven using a variety of different weave structures, but simple ones like plain weave and satin are best, so that the pattern is not obscured. The ikat-dyed yarns will unavoidably slip and twist during the weaving processes, and it is this that produces the feathered effect at the edges of the dyed sections. The ikat technique may be applied to the warp only (warp ikat), for which the warp yarns are wrapped in a resist. It may also be applied to the weft only (weft ikat), or to both warp and weft (double ikat), in which case both warp and weft yarns are dyed in a corresponding pattern and are aligned to overlap each other in the finished fabric.

The ikat process is a very ancient one. The earliest known specimens date back to the 7th or 8th centuries AD.[29] The word 'ikat' derives from the Malay–Indonesian language, where it forms the stem of the verb *mengikat*, meaning 'to bind', 'to knot', 'to wind around'.[29] Ikat is called 'kasuri' in Japan and 'mudmee' or 'matmee' in Thailand; Indian double ikat fabrics are called 'patola'. Early chiné fabrics were produced by resist-dyeing techniques similar to ikat techniques. Similar effects may also be produced in fabrics by space-dyeing and warp printing.

See also CHINÉ FABRICS, DYED FABRICS, RESIST-DYED FABRICS, SPACE-DYED FABRIC, TIE-DYED FABRIC, WARP-PRINTED FABRIC.

End uses: furnishing fabrics, ribbons, men's neckties, exclusive dresses, blouses and evening wear.

ILLUSION *see* MALINES, TULLE.

IMITATION FUR *see* FUR FABRIC.

IMPERIAL CLOTH A heavy, durable woven fabric made from worsted wool yarns and used mainly as a coating fabric. The lighter-weight qualities are botany twill fabrics.

Imperial cloth is traditionally woven with fine botany worsted wool yarns in a 2/2 twill weave structure. The fabric is piece-dyed, usually navy blue. An example of an imperial cloth fabric construction is 35/2 to 30/2 tex botany warp sett at 27 to 30 ends per cm and 24 to 18 tex botany weft woven at 32 to 28 picks per cm.[26] Imperial serge is a similar fabric, but it is more loosely woven and softer (*see* SERGE).

See also BOTANY TWILL, COATING FABRIC, TWILL FABRICS, WOOL FABRIC, WORSTED FABRIC.

End uses: coats and jackets.

IMPERIAL SATEEN A woven cotton fabric that has a very heavily wefted face side. It belongs to the group of fabrics known as 'fustians'.

Imperial sateen is usually woven with cotton yarns in a weave structure based on an 8-end sateen. This gives a long weft float of six on the surface. Traditionally it is woven as grey cloth and piece-dyed, and the underside of the fabric is given a soft nap finish. Alternatively, the face side of the fabric may be raised to form a very soft napped surface. An imperial sateen fabric finished in this way is called 'lambskin', since the surface is smooth and soft like a lamb's skin.[26]

'Reversible imperial' is also produced, by using a special 4 and 4 weave structure based on an 8-end sateen. This structure, combined with a large number of weft picks per centimetre, produces a fabric with a dense weft-faced structure on both sides, which may be either raised to form a soft napped surface on both sides of the fabric or left smooth.[26]

Examples of imperial sateen fabric constructions are 66/2 to 49/2 tex warp sett at 19 to 25 ends per cm, and 38 to 21 tex weft woven at 120 to 170 picks per cm.[26] Imperial sateen is similar to beaverteen but lighter in weight. It is also similar to moleskin fabric and swansdown but is heavier.

See also FUSTIAN, NAPPED FABRICS, SATEEN, SUEDE CLOTH.

End uses: heavy-duty trousers, suitings and jackets.

INDIAN LAWN *see* LAWN.

INDIA SILK *see* SILK FABRIC.

INLET *see* TICKING.

INTARSIA A weft-knitted fabric in which two or more coloured yarns and/or textures are incorporated into the fabric construction in the weft direction in sections, to form a pattern without floats. This produces a fine, reversible fabric.

imperial cloth

imperial sateen (brushed)

imperial sateen (unbrushed)

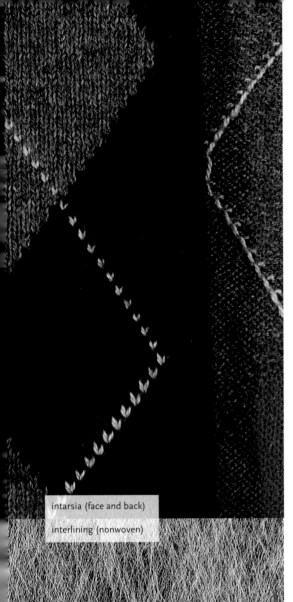

intarsia (face and back)

interlining (nonwoven)

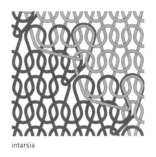

intarsia

Each colour in the intarsia pattern is knitted using a separate yarn. Within the same weft course, each colour is knitted only in the sections where it is required to form the pattern and is not floated on the back of the fabric. In terms of construction, intarsia is therefore the knitted equivalent of a tapestry weave. Intarsia fabrics may be knitted in any weft-knit structure, including plain, rib or purl structures.

The term 'intarsia' comes from the Italian word for 'inlaid'.[5] Argyle is an example of an intarsia fabric. Intarsia fabrics produce the look of a weft-knitted jacquard fabric but without any floats or backing stitches. Unlike the jacquard fabric, intarsia is a much finer, more lightweight reversible fabric.

See also ARGYLE; FIGURED FABRIC; JACQUARD FABRIC, KNITTED; KNITTED FABRIC; WEFT-KNITTED FABRIC.

End uses: sweaters, cardigans, T-shirts and dresses.

INTERLINING A fabric that is used between the inner and outer layers of a garment in order to improve shape retention, strength, warmth or bulk. Interlinings come in a wide variety of weights and qualities. They may be woven, knitted or nonwoven, and are available with or without a fusible adhesive coating.[25]

Woven interlinings are mainly woven in a plain weave structure using cotton, linen, polyester or blended yarns. Knitted interlinings are usually warp-knitted fabrics that are produced quite cheaply using filament nylon or polyester yarns. Nylon is often used since it drapes well and has a soft handle (*see* WARP-KNITTED FABRIC). Nonwoven interlinings may be thermal-bonded, chemical-bonded, water-entangled or stitch-bonded fabrics. They are usually the cheapest interlinings and are available in very fine to heavy qualities (*see* NONWOVEN FABRIC). All interlinings, whether woven, knitted or nonwoven, are either sewn in to the fabric or, if they have a fusible adhesive coating, fused to the fabric by means of heat and pressure.

Many different types of thermoplastic resin are used to coat the fusible interlinings, including polyethylene, polypropylene, polyamides, polyesters, polyvinyl chloride (PVC) and plasticized polyvinyl acetate (PVA). There are two main ways in which the resin may be applied to the interlining base. One is dry dot printing, in which dots of resin are printed onto the interlining in a regular manner, for flexible reinforcement. The other is paste coating, in which the entire surface of the interlining is coated for strong, stiff reinforcement. Vilene® is the well-known brand name of a range of different interlining fabrics.

See also LINING FABRIC, NONWOVEN FABRIC, STITCH-BONDED FABRIC.

End uses: tailoring, suits, coats, jackets and shirts; interfacing reinforcements for coat fronts, collars, cuffs, buttoned openings, pocket flaps, waistbands, pleats, appliqué and hems.

INTERLOCK A general term for any weft-knitted fabric that is knitted in an interlock structure. Interlock consists of two layers of rib-based fabric joined together in the middle; it is a type of double jersey fabric. Interlock is one of the four primary weft-knit base structures (the others are plain knit, purl and rib). The construction produces a firm fabric that has a smooth, flat face on both sides and a controlled stretch in the crosswise direction only. The fabric is therefore reversible, and either side may be used as the face side. Interlock is a more stable fabric construction than the 1 × 1 rib from which it is derived. It is usually a light- to medium-weight fabric.

The two fabric layers are both closely knitted using fine yarns, in 1 × 1 rib structure. They are joined together by interlocking sinker loops, which are not visible on the face of the fabric, to form a double-faced rib construction. The vertical wales on one side of the

interlock
interlock

Italian

fabric are aligned immediately behind the vertical wales on the other side. This requires the fabric to be knitted on knitting machines that have two sets of opposed needles, by a 'gating' process. In terms of construction, interlock is the knitted equivalent of a self-stitched woven double cloth fabric.

Interlock was originally knitted from cotton and used for underwear,[25] but nowadays it is knitted using a wide range of different fibres, including cotton and blends, polyester, nylon and acrylic. Elastane is also often added for extra stretch. It may be in plain colours, striped or printed, and it is used for a wide variety of different products (see below). Interlock is a similar fabric to eight-lock. Both are double fabrics composed of two fabric layers joined together in the middle: the two fabric layers of interlock knitted in 1 × 1 rib structure and the two fabric layers of eight-lock knitted in 2 × 2 rib structure. Examples of other knitted fabrics that contain interlock structure in part include bourrelet, weft-knitted piqué (cross-tuck interlock; see PIQUÉ, WEFT-KNITTED), piquette, punto-di-Roma and texi-piqué.

See also EIGHT-LOCK; JERSEY; KNITTED FABRIC; RIB FABRICS, KNITTED; WEFT-KNITTED FABRIC.

End uses: underwear, sweaters, T-shirts, polo shirts, sportswear, leisure wear, pyjamas, dresses and casual trousers.

IRIDESCENT FABRICS *see* SHOT FABRICS.

IRISH LAWN *see* LAWN.

IRISH LINEN *see* LINEN FABRIC.

IRISH POPLIN *see* POPLIN.

IRISH TWEED *see* TWEED.

ITALIAN A woven fabric that is usually made in cotton, in a weft-faced, sateen weave structure. It is given a special finish to produce a lustrous, smooth-faced fabric that is used mainly for linings.

Italians were originally made with a dyed cotton warp and a grey botany wool weft, wool-dyed in the piece and given a lustrous finish.[26] Nowadays they are made with cotton in both the warp and the weft. Mercerized cotton is sometimes used to ensure a high lustre. The fabric is woven grey, in a 5-end sateen weave structure in which the twill lines of the weave run in the same direction as the weft twist in order to promote a smooth fabric face. Italian fabrics are usually piece-dyed in dark colours, often black. The face of the fabric is made particularly lustrous in the finishing process, mainly by schreinering.

An example of an Italian fabric construction is 17 to 14 tex cotton warp sett at 34 to 38 ends per cm and 14 tex combed and gassed Egyptian weft woven at 52 to 64 picks per cm.[26] Italian is sometimes confused with cotton Venetian. They are very similar and both are lining fabrics, but Italian is woven in a sateen weave structure and Venetian in a satin weave structure. Italian is also similar to Albert twill.

See also LINING FABRIC, SATEEN, VENETIAN.

End uses: lining fabric.

JACOB TWEED *see* TWEED.

JACONET (jaconette) A thin, lightweight woven fabric made with fine cotton yarns. It is woven in plain weave and given a finish that produces a smooth but slightly stiff fabric with a high lustre on the face side.

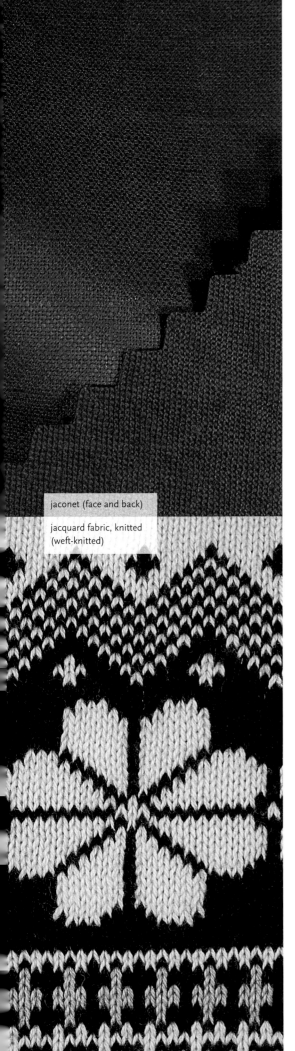

jaconet (face and back)

jacquard fabric, knitted
(weft-knitted)

Jaconet was traditionally made with 100% cotton yarns, but nowadays polyester/ cotton versions are also available. It is woven in a closely sett plain weave construction in a variety of different lightweight qualities. The fabric is usually woven as grey cloth and afterwards piece-dyed in solid colours. More rarely it may have a stripe or check pattern, either woven in or printed on. Afterwards the fabric is usually glazed to produce a high lustre on the face side.

Jaconet was originally woven in eastern India.[3] The name is a French word derived from Hindi *jagannath*, meaning 'light cotton fabric'.[23] Variant spellings are sometimes used (jaconette, jacconette, jaconnette, or jaconnet). Jaconet is a similar fabric to cambric but is slightly heavier. It is also similar to batiste, lawn, nainsook, organdie and percale. These fabrics are all woven in plain weave using high-quality cotton yarns and look very similar in the grey state; it is their various finishes that distinguish them.

End uses: men's shirts, dresses, children's clothes and pyjamas.

JACQUARD CRÊPE *see* CRÊPE.

JACQUARD FABRIC, KNITTED A general term for a knitted fabric that is produced on a machine fitted with a jacquard patterning mechanism. This device enables the machine to select individual yarns and colours, allowing patterns and motifs to be produced. Typically, therefore, knitted jacquard fabrics are fabrics with multicoloured patterns.

Knitted jacquard fabrics may be knitted from any fibre and are made in a wide range of weights and qualities according to their end use. There are two different groups: weft-knitted and warp-knitted.

'Weft-knitted jacquard fabric' is a general term applied to any weft-knitted fabric that has been knitted using a jacquard patterning mechanism on a weft-knitting machine. In some weft-knitted jacquards the design motifs are formed by tuck stitches. In these 'knit-tuck' jacquards, the ground fabric may be knitted in any knit structure: plain knit, rib or purl. These fabrics are often produced in a single colour.[38] Other, 'knit-miss' jacquards are knitted by a knitting and missing process. The needles are individually selected for knitting and miss-knitting. Yarns of any colour or texture are selectively fed to different needles in order to produce knitted motifs or designs. Needle selections and colours are changed on each course to build up the pattern. In this manner, complex multicoloured patterns may be machine-knitted. When a yarn is not being knitted into the face of the fabric, it is either floated on the back or knitted into a backing (rib jacquard) – for example birdseye backing, striped backing or ladderback. The face of the fabric is therefore normally outermost in use.

Weft-knitted jacquard fabrics that have characteristic weft floats on the back of the fabric sometimes lack stretch as a result; however, the patterns are clear and the colours pure. Accordion fabric and fairisle are examples of fabrics produced in this manner.[38] Although jacquards with a backing do not have long weft floats on the back of the fabric, the extra stitches, and sometimes the colours used, can tend to grin through to the face side of the fabric, making the colours less pure, particularly when the fabric is stretched. Intarsia fabrics, on the other hand, produce the look of a weft-knitted jacquard fabric but without any floats or backing stitches. Unlike most other jacquard fabrics, intarsia is a reversible fabric (*see* INTARSIA). Examples of plain knit, weft-knitted jacquard fabrics include accordion fabric, knitted birdseye (*see* BIRDSEYE), fairisle, knitted paisley (*see* PAISLEY) and Scandinavian 'snowflake' design. The most common double jersey jacquard is a flat jacquard with a 1 × 1 birdseye backing. Another example of a double jersey jacquard fabric is knitted blister cloth (*see* BLISTER CLOTH).

'Warp-knitted jacquard fabric' is a general term applied to any warp-knitted fabric that has been knitted using a jacquard patterning mechanism on a warp-knitting machine. This is a device that is able to select individual guides within a guide bar, allowing

jacquard fabric, knitted
(warp-knitted)

jappe

different sections of the fabric to be patterned differently. The pattern is made by knitting a greater or lesser amount of lap in selected areas of the fabric.

See also FIGURED FABRIC, JERSEY, KNITTED FABRIC, WARP-KNITTED FABRIC, WEFT-KNITTED FABRIC.

End uses: (weft-knitted jacquard fabric) jackets, skirts, sweaters, waistcoats, cardigans and tights; (warp-knitted jacquard fabric) car upholstery fabrics, household upholstery fabrics, curtains, mattress ticking, luggage and lingerie.

JACQUARD FABRIC, WOVEN A general term for a woven fabric that is produced on a weaving loom fitted with a jacquard patterning mechanism (as opposed to a dobby or tappet mechanism). This device enables the individual selection and lifting of any of the warp ends, allowing a wide variety of complex patterns and designs to be produced. Typically, therefore, woven jacquard fabrics are multicoloured fabrics figured with intricate designs. The fabrics are named after the Frenchman Joseph Marie Jacquard (1752–1834), who is credited with inventing this patterning mechanism in 1801.[5]

Woven jacquard fabrics may be made from any fibre and in a wide range of weights and qualities for different end uses. However, they are often expensive, as they are usually highly sett fabrics that are complex and time-consuming to produce. The control of the jacquard warp-lifting mechanism may be by pegs, punch cards, punched tape or microchip. This allows each warp yarn to be controlled individually for each weft insertion. Different weave structures, yarn types and colours may be woven in different parts of the fabric and interchanged in an unlimited number of ways. The designs may be geometric or figured, and large or small in scale. Woven jacquards often have curvilinear motifs and sometimes have pictorial designs.

Examples of jacquard woven fabrics include brocade, brocatelle, damask, some façonné fabrics, jacquard taffeta (*see* TAFFETA), lampas, Marseilles, some matelassé fabrics, some pashmina fabrics, tapestry jacquard and many tie fabrics. Fabrics that are visually similar to jacquard woven fabrics include broché, clip spot and extra warp and extra weft fabrics.

See also FIGURED FABRIC.

End uses: upholstery fabrics, curtains, mattress ticking, luggage, men's neckties and formal wear.

JACQUARD LACE see LACE.

JANUS CLOTH (*obs.*) A reversible worsted fabric with different colours on either side, woven in twill or satin weave and used for dress goods or coatings.[9, 36]

JAPPE A very fine, lightweight woven fabric, woven in plain weave. It is woven with continuous filament yarns, traditionally in silk and nowadays also in man-made fibre yarns. Jappe is such a fine fabric (at approximately 70 g/m²) that it has an almost papery quality.[10] It is a lustrous fabric, with a soft surface texture caused by slight imperfections in the yarn.

Low-twist continuous filament fibre yarns are used for softness, and the fabric is woven in a plain weave square cloth construction. Jappe is usually piece-dyed in solid colours. As it is so fine, jappe is used mainly as a lining fabric. If printed, it may be used for fine outerwear fabrics. Jappe is also sometimes called 'jappe silk'. It is a very similar fabric to China silk and habotai.

See also LINING FABRIC, PLAIN WEAVE FABRIC, SILK FABRIC.

End uses: lining fabric, women's dress and suit linings, dresses, blouses, scarves and lingerie.

jacquard fabric, woven

jacquard fabric, woven

jaspé

Java

jean

JASPÉ (jasper) A woven fabric in which the warp yarns have been dyed in different colours or in different tones of the same colour. This produces narrow vertical stripes in the fabric, giving an overall shaded effect. Jaspé is a hard-wearing fabric that is usually woven in cotton, although it is available in different weights and qualities.

The warp yarns may be dyed different tones of one colour or they may be multi-coloured. These yarns are then positioned in a random order of ones and twos throughout the warp. It is this that produces the shaded effect in the fabric. Alternatively, the effect is sometimes also produced by the random printing of warp yarns, or by twisting together two singles yarns, in contrasting tones of the same colour. Jaspé is woven with a single-colour weft yarn, either in plain weave or in a figured design.

'Jaspé silk' is a term used for silk jaspé fabrics, in which the silk contains coloured slubs or nubs.[3] Novelty jaspé is a fabric with vertical stripes and with small dots woven into the fabric.[5] The term 'jaspé' (derived from French) means randomly mottled or variegated, like the stone jasper. Curtains made of jaspé are often left unlined in order for the light to shine through and accentuate the colour effect.[2]

See also FIGURED FABRIC, PLAIN WEAVE FABRIC, STRIPES, WARP-PRINTED FABRIC.

End uses: bedspreads, curtains and upholstery.

JAVA (Java canvas, aida) A woven fabric that is used as a base for embroideries and needle-work. It is a loose, open dobby fabric that is woven in a mock leno weave construction on a dobby loom. It is a type of cellular fabric. Java is similar in weight to a medium-weight canvas fabric. It is also known as 'Java canvas', 'aida' (or 'ada') or 'aida canvas'.

Java is usually woven with hard-twist cotton yarns in both the warp and weft. Sometimes man-made fibres are also used. The yarns are spaced apart to produce a fabric with an open mesh-like construction, with holes in-between and woven in a mock leno weave. The mesh size can be varied according to the yarn count used. The fabric is usually bleached or dyed and it is given a fairly stiff finish.

See also CANVAS, CELLULAR FABRIC, DOBBY FABRIC, EMBROIDERED FABRICS, MOCK LENO.

End uses: base fabric for embroidery and needlework.

JEAN (middy twill) A strong, thick, durable woven fabric, usually woven in a warp-faced twill weave. It is a similar fabric to denim but is produced in solid colours, whereas denim has a dyed warp and an undyed weft. Jean was used before denim, from the 18th century onwards, for workwear, overalls and casual wear. Jean is also similar to drill, but it is usually softer and lighter in weight. It is sometimes also called 'middy twill'.[18, 22]

Most jean fabrics are made from 100% carded cotton, using good-quality, high-twist two-fold warp yarns and a softer, slightly thicker singles weft yarn. Other fibre combinations are also available: for example cotton/linen blends, cotton/wool blends, polyester/cotton blends or cotton mixed with other man-made fibres. Jean is woven in a fairly steep 2/1 warp-faced twill weave structure. (Sometimes it is also woven in a her-ringbone weave structure.) Jean was formerly colour-woven with warp and weft yarns of the same colour. Nowadays it is usually piece-dyed in solid colours, and sometimes it is bleached. It is a medium-weight fabric and is available in a number of different qualities. Two examples are: 30 tex warp sett at 36 ends per cm and 30 tex weft woven at 26 picks per cm;[26] and 32 tex cotton warp sett at 35 ends per cm and 21 tex cotton weft woven at 24 picks per cm.[25]

The name 'jean' comes from the town of Genoa in northern Italy, where the fabric was first made and used as a lining fabric.[3] The plural form 'jeans' is nowadays widely used to refer to many different qualities of highly durable work and leisure trousers. The term 'blue jeans' refers to a typical jean fabric, woven in a twill weave from carded cotton yarns and dyed blue.[5] The term 'jeanette' is sometimes applied to the lighter-weight jean fabrics. Jeanette fabrics are used mainly as linings. Jean is a similar fabric to bluette, denim, drill, dungaree, some gaberdine fabrics, hickory cloth and ticking.

See also COTTON FABRIC, HERRINGBONE, TWILL FABRICS.

End uses: overalls, workwear, protective clothing, boiler suits, bags, boot and shoe linings, linings, children's clothes, sportswear, jeans, workmen's trousers and all kinds of casual wear.

JERSEY A generic term that is applied to all types of weft-knitted fabric, whether knitted by hand or machine. The name 'jersey' (like that of the similar guernsey) comes from one of the Channel Islands between Britain and France, where thick weft-knitted fabrics were originally hand-knitted for fishermen's sweaters (or jerseys). Jersey fabric was made popular by the Edwardian actress Lillie Langtry, who was the daughter of the dean of Jersey. She became known as 'Jersey Lily' for her habit of wearing a long, tight jersey garment with her long, tight skirt.[3] *See also* GUERNSEY.

There are two categories of machine-knitted jersey fabrics: single jersey, which is knitted with a single set of needles on a single needle-bed of a weft-knitting machine, and double jersey, which is knitted with two sets of needles on a double needle-bed weft-knitting machine. These two categories are discussed below.

'Single jersey' is a generic term applied to a range of weft-knitted fabrics that are knitted with one set of needles on a single needle-bed of a weft-knitting machine. Single jersey is a single layer fabric, and is sometimes also called 'single-knit fabric'. Single jersey fabrics are usually more extensible but less stable than most double jersey fabrics. Single jersey fabrics may be knitted using any fibre type or thickness of knitting yarn, and a very wide range of weights and qualities are produced. The fabric may be knitted in a wide variety of both jacquard and non-jacquard knit structures. Elastane fibres are frequently incorporated into the fabric to produce elastomeric fabrics with greater stretch and recovery properties.

Examples of single jersey knitted fabrics or fabrics that incorporate single jersey in part are accordion fabric, Balbriggan, fairisle, fleece fabric, fur fabric, laid-in fabric (weft-knitted), micromesh, plain knit fabric, plush (weft-knitted), polar fleece, single jersey cord and terry fabric (weft-knitted).

'Double jersey' is a generic term applied to a range of weft-knitted fabrics that are knitted with two sets of needles on a weft-knitting machine with two needle-beds. Double jersey is a double-layer fabric and is sometimes also called 'double-knit fabric'. Characteristically, most double jersey fabrics are firmer, less extensible and more stable than most single jersey fabrics. Double jersey may be knitted in any weight and using any fibre or yarn type. Patterns can be formed by interchanging yarns between the face and back needles. The fabrics are therefore often reversible and are knitted in double-knit, rib or interlock structures. They may be patterned on one or both sides with multicoloured jacquard patterns or they may be knitted in single colours on both sides.

Examples of non-jacquard double jersey fabrics include bourrelet, eight-lock, interlock, weft-knitted piqué (including cross-tuck interlock, Belgian double piqué, French double piqué and Swiss double piqué; see PIQUÉ, WEFT-KNITTED), piquette, punto-di-Roma and texi-piqué. Knitted blister cloth is an example of a jacquard double jersey fabric (*see* BLISTER CLOTH).

See also ELASTANE FABRIC, ELASTOMERIC FABRIC, KNITTED FABRIC, STRETCH FABRIC, WEFT-KNITTED FABRIC.

End uses: (single jersey): T-shirts, sweaters, cardigans, dresses, sportswear, jackets, scarves, hats, gloves, nightwear, children's wear, lingerie, underwear, stockings, tights and socks; (double jersey) tailored garments such as fitted or semi-fitted jackets, dresses, skirts, trousers and sportswear.

jersey (single jersey, face and back)

jersey (patterned double jersey, face and back)

jersey (double jersey, face and back)

kasha
kersey

JUMBO CORD *see* CORDUROY.

JUTE *see* PLANT-FIBRE FABRICS.

KAPOK *see* PLANT-FIBRE FABRICS.

KARAKUL CLOTH *see* ASTRAKHAN FABRIC.

KARAMINI (*obs.*) A lightweight woollen cloth with a napped surface.[3]

KASHA (casha) A woven fabric that was originally an extremely soft, luxurious fabric made from vicuña hair.[5] Since vicuña is such an expensive fibre of limited availability, kasha is nowadays usually made either from very fine wool (typically merino) or from a blend of cashmere and wool.[5] It is a type of flannel fabric.

Kasha is woven in twill weave and given a soft nap finish on the face side. In the traditional fabric the weft yarns produced a slightly streaky effect, since they were composed of the varying natural tones of the animal fibre. This mottled appearance is simulated nowadays when the fabric is piece-dyed: the sized warp yarns readily accept the dye, whereas the natural lanolin weft yarns tend to resist it. The slightly uneven dyeing produces a streaky effect resembling that of the original vicuña fabric. Tan or brown shades are the most frequently used. Kasha is a similar fabric to cashmere cloth and pashmina.

See also FLANNEL, HAIR FABRICS, NAPPED FABRICS, TWILL FABRICS, VICUÑA FABRIC.

End uses: dresses, suits and jackets.

KASURI *see* IKAT.

KERSEY A soft, thick, heavy woven fabric made from wool that is fulled and felted during finishing; this compacts it and prevents fraying. It has a short nap that is very lustrous. Most kersey fabrics are coating fabrics, although finer qualities are also made.

Kersey is a traditional all-wool fabric woven using strong Cheviot or cross-bred wools (small amounts of man-made fibres are sometimes also included). The fabric is usually woven either in a 2/2 twill weave or a diagonal rib structure. However, some kersey fabrics, especially the heavyweight qualities, may be woven as double cloth fabrics. Kersey is heavily milled on the face side and finished to give a short lustrous nap. This completely obscures the weave structure underneath.

The name of the fabric comes from the small village of Kersey in Suffolk, England, where the fabric was originally made.[3] The earliest records of kersey date back to 1262, and the fabric has been produced since this time in many different weights and qualities.[5] Nowadays, however, it is usually woven as a heavyweight fabric and used as a coating fabric. Lighter-weight kersey fabrics may be used for suits and dresses, and some kersey fabrics are very fine. Lighter-weight qualities are sometimes called 'kerseymere' after the similar cassimere fabrics,[9] and are used for men's suits and trousers. *See also* CASSIMERE.

An example of a typical heavyweight kersey fabric construction is 190 tex warp sett at 10 ends per cm and 190 tex weft woven at 10 picks per cm. Contraction is about 25% in width and 15% to 20% in length.[26] Kersey is a similar fabric to melton, although kersey is heavier, has a little more nap and is more lustrous. It is also similar to woollen broadcloth (*see* BROADCLOTH), frieze and Tattersall check. It is given a similar finish to pilot cloth.

See also COATING FABRIC, DOUBLE CLOTH, FELTED FABRIC, NAPPED FABRICS.

End uses: overcoats, military uniforms, dresses, men's suits and trousers.

khadi (printed)

khaki

khaki (printed)

KETTLE CLOTH (*obs.*) A fairly stiff plain weave fabric with a slight slub. It was made in cotton and polyester and used for casual trousers and jackets.[2]

KEVLAR® *see* ARAMID FABRIC.

KHADI (khaddar) An inexpensive woven cotton fabric from India. It is made with coarse, hand-spun cotton yarns and is hand-woven in plain weave.[3] The fabric may be undyed, dyed or printed.

Khadi is a homespun fabric, woven by hand from hand-spun cotton yarns in the individual homes of local communities in India. It is usually woven in narrow widths according to the width of the hand-weaving loom. The fabrics may be undyed, piece-dyed or block printed by hand using wooden blocks.

See also FOLK WEAVE, HOMESPUN, PLAIN WEAVE FABRIC, PRINTED FABRIC.

End uses: casual clothing, blouses, dresses, children's clothes, curtains and cushion covers.

KHAKI A term applied to a wide range of hard-wearing fabrics used by armies worldwide and also widely employed for general workwear and casual wear. 'Khaki' is a Hindi word meaning 'dust-coloured', and it was first used to describe the colour of the uniforms of Indian army soldiers during the mid-19th century.[3] Khaki is a dull, yellowish brown, green/brown or tan colour. Khaki fabrics are traditionally produced to act as camouflage in natural environments.

The fabrics may be made of cotton, wool, worsted or man-made fibres and blends, as appropriate to the climate in which they will be used. Khaki fabrics are often produced by piece-dyeing hard-wearing fabrics a khaki colour. Drill, florentine, serge and whipcord are all appropriate qualities. The fabric may also be made with khaki-coloured man-made microfibres, and sometimes the fabric is printed with a camouflage pattern.

See also MICROFIBRE FABRIC.

End uses: army uniforms, workwear and casual clothing (including trousers, dungarees, shorts and jackets).

KILIM A woven fabric that is a type of flat tapestry woven in a weft-faced plain weave from hand-spun wool or goat hair. Kilims are usually colour-woven fabrics patterned with simple geometric designs. They are traditionally woven in Turkey and the Middle East, often by hand, and are used for rugs. A kilim is a very similar fabric to a dhurrie. Dhurries are woven in exactly the same manner, but are traditionally made in the Indian subcontinent from hand-spun or power-spun cotton.

Both kilims and dhurries usually consist of one plain-coloured warp and a series of different-coloured weft yarns. The fabric is woven in plain weave with more weft picks per centimetre than warp ends. This produces the characteristic weft-faced fabric. The patterns are formed using traditional tapestry weaving techniques whereby the weft yarns do not pass from selvedge to selvedge but are interlaced with the warp yarns only in the areas where they are required to form the pattern.

The edges between the different blocks of woven colour may be formed in a number of different ways.

(i) *Slit tapestry*. The weft yarns of adjacent colours are each woven into separate groups of warp yarns, leaving a slit in the warp direction between the two areas of colour. Since there

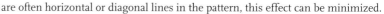

kilim (antique Persian rug)

kilim (detail)

kilim (Indian dhurrie)

knitted fabric

are often horizontal or diagonal lines in the pattern, this effect can be minimized.

(ii) *Toothed tapestry or single dovetailed tapestry*. The weft yarns of adjacent colours are turned alternately around the same warp end. This results in a neat integration of the two colours at the point where they meet.

(iii) *Interlocked tapestry*. The weft yarns of adjacent colours are interlocked around each other, either around the same warp end or around adjacent warp ends. The lock made between the two weft yarns can be either a single interlock or a double interlock. This construction produces a strong bond between the adjacent areas of colour.

(iv) *Dovetailed tapestry*. The weft yarns of adjacent colours are turned, in groups of two or more, alternately around the same warp end. This produces a visual dovetailed effect at the edges of adjacent colour areas, which can be a characteristic feature of these fabrics.

(v) *Reinforced tapestry*. Kilims can be made stronger and more stable by every so often weaving one weft pick across the entire fabric, from selvedge to selvedge.

(vi) *Inserted tapestry*. Woven motifs are inserted, in sections only, into a fabric that is woven in a plain weave structure throughout, from selvedge to selvedge. When the warp yarns are not required to weave the patterned sections on the face of the fabric, they are left to float on the back of the fabric.

See also CARPET, TAPESTRY.

End uses: rugs, floor coverings, prayer mats, wall hangings and ceiling hangings.

KILMARNOCK (*obs.*) A coarse serge fabric made in Scotland in the 18th century.[36]

KNITTED FABRIC The generic name for a fabric in which the yarn is formed into an interconnecting loop construction; a woven fabric, by contrast, maintains the relatively straight nature of the yarn by interweaving two sets of yarns at right angles to one another. Many knitted fabrics have the characteristics of great extensibility and recoverability.

In knitting, yarn is looped through a series of previously formed loops. A column of loops along the length of the fabric, parallel to the selvedge, is called a 'wale', and a row of loops across the width of a fabric (or, in circular knitted fabrics, around the circumference) is called a 'course'.

There are two generic groups of knitted fabrics: warp-knitted fabrics and weft-knitted (or jersey) fabrics. Warp-knitted fabrics are made on a warp-knitting machine, and the loops, made with the warp yarns or threads, are formed substantially along the length of the fabric.[25] Weft-knitted fabrics may be constructed by hand, using hand knitting needles, or on a weft-knitting machine. In weft-knitted fabrics the loops made with the weft yarns or threads are formed substantially across the width of the fabric.[25] Both warp- and weft-knitting machines may be fitted with a jacquard patterning mechanism in order to knit complex jacquard patterns and designs.

See also JACQUARD FABRIC, KNITTED; JERSEY; WARP-KNITTED FABRIC; WEFT-KNITTED FABRIC.

End uses: all kinds of fashion and furnishing fabrics.

LACE A fine, delicate openwork or mesh fabric (usually transparent) that is made of fine yarns, by looping, twisting or knotting them together in a variety of different lace constructions. Typically a lace fabric is composed of a net-like ground fabric, upon which all manner of intricate and elaborate patterns are inter-worked in thread. Lace may be constructed both in piece form (as a wide fabric) and as narrow fabric edgings. With both types, the intricate patterning on the fabric may be inter-worked simultaneously with the ground fabric, or it may be applied later. Any fibre may be used to make lace fabrics, but the most common are nylon, viscose, cotton and flax (linen). Elastane is often added for stretch. Silk was traditionally used for many lace fabrics and it is still used today for more exclusive items. *See also* ELASTANE FABRIC, NARROW FABRICS.

Historically, lace-making can be dated as far back as the Bronze Age.[2] All lace fabrics were originally constructed by hand with bobbins or a needle. Nowadays, although some lace is still produced by hand in the traditional manner, the vast majority of fabrics are produced by machine (as discussed below).

Handmade lace is among the most complex of all textile constructions. It is time-consuming to produce and requires skilled labour. It is therefore one of the most expensive fabrics. Many different types of handmade lace have been produced over the centuries in many different countries and areas, and these have gradually developed their own particular styles and characteristics. There are two main groupings of handmade lace: bobbin or pillow lace and needlepoint lace.

Bobbin or pillow lace is a handmade lace which was developed by twisting threads around pins to form the pattern. The yarns, contained on many bobbins, are twisted and plaited around a series of pins arranged in a pattern sequence on hard cushions or pillows, hence the name. Handmade lace fabrics usually take their name from the area where they were first made. Among the best-known bobbin or pillow lace fabrics are Bruges lace, Brussels lace, Chantilly lace, Cluny lace, duchesse lace, Honiton lace, Irish lace, Maltese lace, Nottingham lace, shadow lace, Spanish lace, tulle and Valenciennes.

Needlepoint lace is a handmade lace that evolved from threadwork and cutwork techniques developed in Italy during the 16th century.[23] Needlepoint laces are constructed by embroidering complex designs with an embroidery needle in buttonhole stitch onto a parchment or fabric base. Fine flax or silk threads are normally used. Some of the best-known needlepoint lace fabrics are: Alençon, gros point, guipure, point de neige, point plat, rose-point and Venetian point. *See also* EMBROIDERED FABRICS, MESH FABRICS, VEILING.

Machine-made lace is made on various machines, by twisting, by embroidery techniques or by knitting.

(i) *Machine-twisted lace.* The first lace-making machine was the bobbinet machine, invented in 1808 by John Heathcoat in Nottingham, England.[5] This machine could twist yarns together in imitation of handmade bobbin lace. It could very quickly produce a wide net base fabric, which was subsequently embroidered by hand. In 1813 the bobbinet machine was further developed and adapted by John Leavers, also in Nottingham, and thus the Leavers lace machine was invented. The Leavers machine was capable of constructing lace patterns with or without a net background and could construct a wide variety

lace (machine-made)

lace (edging, machine-made)

lace (machine-made)

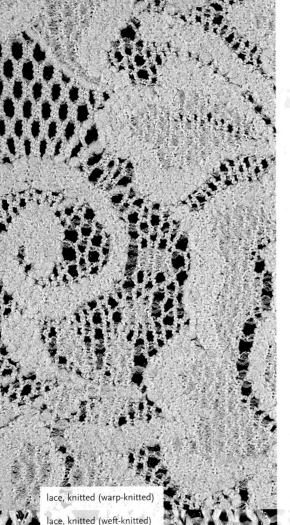

lace, knitted (warp-knitted)

lace, knitted (weft-knitted)

of fine, intricate fabrics.[2, 3, 5, 23] The modern Leavers machine developed from these two original machines. The machine imitates handmade bobbin lace by twisting yarns carried on thin bobbins around vertical threads moved by guide bars. The pattern is usually controlled by a jacquard mechanism and is often very complex but, of all machine methods of producing lace fabrics, the Leavers machine can imitate the depth of texture found in handmade laces the most accurately.[23] A wide variety of complex patterns and motifs are produced in these jacquard lace fabrics. Lace fabrics produced on the Leavers machine are usually called either 'Leavers lace' or 'Nottingham lace'. *See also* MALINES, NET, TULLE.

(ii) *Machine-embroidered lace*. Lace fabrics may be constructed on Schiffli embroidery machines that apply lace patterning to a previously constructed net or fabric background. An all-over design is embroidered onto net or a fine base fabric. Afterwards the base fabric is either cut away or dissolved away in a process called 'aetzing', leaving a delicate, openwork, lacy fabric.[5] This construction method is most suited to reproducing the look of handmade needlepoint lace made using a heavy buttonhole stitch, such as guipure or rose-point lace.[23] *See also* EMBROIDERED FABRICS.

(iii) *Machine-knitted lace*. Lace fabric may be made on raschel warp-knitting machines. Warp-knitted lace fabric is also called 'raschel lace'. All manner of patterns may be produced by laying in the patterning yarns against the vertical columns of loops or wales. With this method, the background net and the patterned areas are constructed simultaneously.[11] Warp-knitting is therefore the cheapest method of producing a lace fabric and it is also one of the most frequently used methods. Characteristically, however, warp-knitted lace fabrics are flat and lack the depth of texture it is possible to achieve on either a Schiffli or a Leavers machine. *See also* RASCHEL LACE, WARP-KNITTED FABRIC.

Fabrics with a similar appearance to lace may also be produced by other construction methods, including crochet, embroidery, knitting (*see* LACE, KNITTED), laser-cutting (*see* LASER-CUT FABRICS), tatting and weaving. *See also* RICHELIEU.

End uses: lingerie, wedding gowns and veils, evening wear, dresses, blouses, nightwear, curtains, tablecloths, edgings and trims.

LACE, KNITTED A knitted fabric that has an open mesh or net-like lacy structure similar to that of traditional lace. Knitted lace fabrics may be weft- or warp-knitted and are made in a range of weights, from light to medium.

Knitted lace fabrics may be made using yarns of any fibre or blend. In weft-knitted lace fabrics, the open lace effect is created by interspersing lace stitches in among a base structure, which is usually in plain knit. Rib or purl base structures are also possible but are less common. The lace stitch intermeshes the yarns together in such a way as to produce holes or openings in the structure as a feature. The openings may be regular throughout the fabric or arranged to form motifs or patterns. A wide variety of lacy designs and effects are possible.[38] Similar effects may also be obtained by stitch transfer, in which loops are transferred from the needles on which they were knitted onto adjacent needles. *See* EYELET, WEFT-KNITTED.

Warp-knitted lace fabric, also known as 'raschel lace fabric', is a generic name for warp-knitted fabrics in which decorative threads are superimposed on a mesh-like ground structure to form motifs and decorative effects (*see* RASCHEL LACE). The ground structure can be locknit, marquisette, pillar inlay net or tulle. The decorative threads can be knitted-in, laid-in or tucked-in by means of a fall-plate (a thin metal blade attached to a bar and capable of extending the full width of the machine).[31, 38]

See also KNITTED FABRIC; LACE; LAID-IN FABRIC; LOCKNIT; MARQUISETTE, WARP-KNITTED; MESH FABRICS; NET; PLAIN KNIT FABRIC; RASCHEL LACE; TULLE; WARP-KNITTED FABRIC; WEFT-KNITTED FABRIC.

End uses: lingerie, hosiery, sweaters, cardigans, T-shirts, evening wear and trims.

laid-in fabric, weft-knitted
(technical back and face)

laid-in fabric (weft-knitted)

LACOSTE® FABRIC *see* PIQUÉ, WEFT-KNITTED.

LAHAR (*obs.*) A soft, lightweight crêpe fabric, woven in plain weave on hand-looms in India with a cotton warp and a silk weft.[36]

LAID-IN FABRIC A generic term for a knitted fabric that has extra non-knitting yarns 'laid-in' or incorporated into its structure. It may be either warp-knitted or weft-knitted; these two kinds are discussed below.

In warp-knitted laid-in fabrics, extra yarns may be laid-in in the following ways: in a horizontal direction (weft inlay); in a vertical direction (vertical inlay); diagonally (diagonal inlay); in both vertical and horizontal directions (biaxial fabric); and in all three directions, vertical, horizontal and diagonal (multiaxial fabric).[38] All these constructions are used mainly to stabilize regular warp-knitted fabric structures, although weft inlay and vertical inlay are sometimes also used as a design feature to pattern the fabric, or to incorporate stretch elastane yarns into the fabric structure (*see* RASCHEL STRETCH FABRICS). The different constructions are described below.[38]

(i) Weft inlay fabric is produced by laying-in extra weft yarns into the fabric horizontally. These are held in position by the knitted structure, which traps them between the face loops and the underlaps of the ground construction (back loops). The extra weft yarns may be laid-in between two or more wales, or they may be laid-in across the full width of the fabric (weft-insertion). See *also* WARP-KNITTED FABRIC.

(ii) Vertical inlay fabric is produced by laying-in extra warp yarns into the fabric in a vertical direction over its length. These are held in place by parts of the fabric stitches.

(iii) Diagonal inlay fabric is produced by laying-in extra yarns into the fabric in both diagonal directions, usually at a 45° angle. The diagonal yarns are held in place by pillar stitches.

(iv) In biaxial fabric, extra yarns are laid-in in both vertical and horizontal directions, throughout both the length and width of the fabric.

(v) Multiaxial fabric is made by laying-in extra yarns vertically, horizontally and diagonally, throughout both the length and width of the fabric.

See also MARQUISETTE, WARP-KNITTED; MESH FABRICS; NET; RASCHEL STRETCH FABRICS; RASCHEL WARP-KNITTED FABRIC; TERRY FABRIC; TULLE; WARP-KNITTED FABRIC.

Weft-knitted laid-in fabrics are known by the generic name 'laid-in jersey fabric'.[38] In these fabrics, extra yarns may be laid-in in the following ways: in a horizontal direction (weft inlay); in a vertical direction (vertical inlay); or in both vertical and horizontal directions (biaxial fabric).[38] Details of these constructions follow.

(i) In weft inlay fabrics, extra, non-knitting yarns are laid-in or floated on the technical back of a weft-knitted fabric. The base fabric is usually knitted in a plain knit structure, but may also be knitted in rib structure. The extra yarns are linked into the main structure every so often at regular intervals on a tuck-and-miss basis, so that they form a surface of loops on the technical back of the fabric. Usually the laid-in yarn is coarser than the ground yarn, so the fabric typically has a smooth technical face and a bulky looped back. The technical back is often raised (napped) to produce a fleecy effect. In this case, the laid-in yarns will be low-twist in order to facilitate the brushing. Either side of the fabric may be used as the actual face side.

(ii) In vertical inlay fabrics, extra ornamental yarns are laid-in in localized areas to form figured designs of restricted width. The extra yarns interlace horizontally and vertically on a tuck-and-miss basis.[38]

(iii) In biaxial fabrics, extra yarns are laid-in in both vertical and horizontal directions, throughout both the length and width of the fabric.[38]

Weft-knitted laid-in fabric is a similar fabric to knitted plush, but the loops are shorter and flatter. *See*

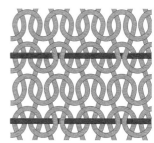

weft-knitted laid-in fabric (weft inlay)

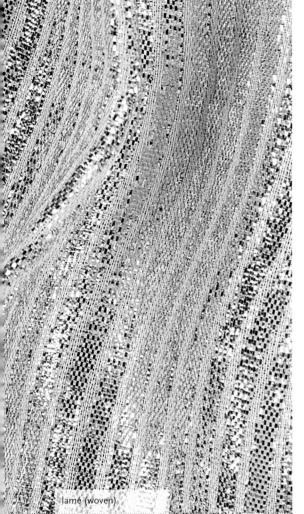

lamé (woven)

lamé (woven, silver)

also FLEECE FABRIC; NAPPED FABRICS; PLAIN KNIT FABRIC; RIB FABRICS, KNITTED; TERRY FABRIC; WEFT-KNITTED FABRIC.

End uses: (warp-knitted laid-in fabric) curtains, upholstery, window blinds, geotextiles and composite material substrates (e.g. incorporating carbon fibre and glass fibre); (weft-knitted laid-in fabric) sweatshirts, T-shirts, tracksuits, leisure wear, children's wear and socks.

LAMBSKIN *see* IMPERIAL SATEEN.

LAMÉ A general term for any fabric, woven or knitted, that contains a substantial amount of metallic yarn or thread. Lamé fabrics are characteristically very shiny, glittery fabrics that give a glamorous, showy effect.

Originally the term 'lamé' was used for fabrics containing flattened gold or silver threads only.[25] Nowadays it is applied to fabrics containing metallic threads of all kinds. Aluminium is the metal most frequently used since it is economical and light in weight. Occasionally gold and silver are also used. The metal yarns or threads are made in a number of different ways; the types include plastic-coated metal, metal wound around a core yarn, and metal-coated plastic.[5] The metallic yarns may be an integral part of the fabric (i.e. warp or weft yarns) or they may be applied to a fabric (i.e. embroidered or sewn onto it). Woven lamé fabric usually has metallic yarns in the weft.

See also EMBROIDERED FABRICS, HOLOGRAPHIC FABRICS, METALLIC FABRICS, SEQUINNED FABRICS.

End uses: evening wear, evening dresses, ball gowns, boleros, fancy dress, theatrical costumes, knitted sweaters and tops, shoes, bags and accessories.

LAMINATED FABRIC A material composed of two or more layers, at least one of which is a fabric, joined together and used as one.[25] The fabric layers are adhered or bonded together, either through the adhesive properties of one or more of the component layers, or with an added adhesive.[25] Woven, knitted and nonwoven fabrics – or any combinations of these – may be laminated. Laminated fabrics either consist of a face fabric joined to one or more backing fabrics, or are double-faced fabrics where there is a different colour, structure or design on each side and where either side could be used as the face side.

The fabric layers may be joined with an adhesive, fused together with heat or chemicals, laser-welded or heat-fused to other components. Laser-welding is a process used for fully or partially synthetic materials that are thermoplastic in nature, for example nylon, polyester, polypropylene, PVC or polyurethane (PU). It is a thermal process whereby the surface of one of the materials being joined is melted by an infrared laser beam. The fabrics are pressed together so that the melted surface adheres to the other material. The outer surfaces of both fabrics or materials are unaffected by the process. The two materials to be welded need to be compatible or of a similar nature. Warp-knitted fabrics such as locknit, sharkskin and tricot are frequently used as backing fabrics, since these give the greatest flexibility to the face fabric(s). Acetate and nylon tricot are used most often due to their low cost. Note that 'multi-component fabrics' and 'multiplex fabrics' are general terms for a wide range of fabrics that may or may not be laminated, but that combine several layers or constructions together to form a single layer. *See* LOCKNIT, MULTI-COMPONENT FABRICS, SHARKSKIN, TRICOT.

Laminated fabrics offer a number of advantages. They are thicker, stronger and more stable than a single fabric layer. The laminating process is less expensive than producing a backed fabric, a woven double cloth or a knitted double cloth fabric. Laminating allows cheaper fabrics to be upgraded; it can increase the warmth of a fabric, without necessarily adding much weight; and it allows finer fabrics to be used for outerwear (e.g. microfibre fabrics). Finally, laminating can eliminate the need for linings, interfacings,

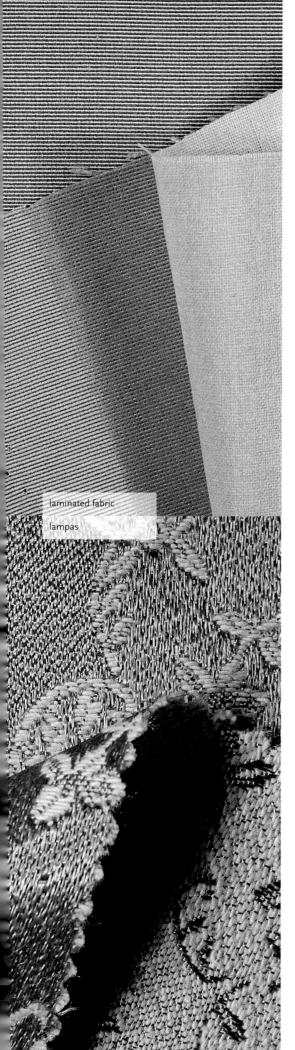

laminated fabric

lampas

stay-stitching and seam finishing. However, there are also disadvantages to laminated fabrics. They may de-laminate; uneven shrinkage between the laminated layers may occur; and the fabric may be bonded off-grain. Laminated fabrics are also stiffer, with reduced drape, and they do not hold sharp creases.

Many laminated fabrics are laminated with materials that give them special features. Examples are listed as follows:

- A scrim, which is used as a backing fabric, especially for fine fabrics, to give them extra dimensional stability and strength. *See* SCRIM.
- A thin layer of foam, usually made from polyurethane (PU) laminated to a fabric by heat fusing. The foam is extremely light in weight, acts as an effective insulator and provides cushioning. This type of laminate is particularly useful for shoes and accesssories. *See* FOAM, POLYURETHANE.
- Thin metal films, laminated onto another fabric with adhesive for insulation or light reflection. *See* METALLIC FABRICS.
- Transfer films composed of light-reflective lenses bonded with heat-activated adhesives, laminated onto backing fabrics to form reflective fabrics. *See* REFLECTIVE FABRICS.
- Rubber or synthetic rubber, laminated onto woven fabrics to make them waterproof. *See* NEOPRENE, RUBBER.
- A thin polymer film or membrane laminated onto a fabric with adhesive, to make the fabric both waterproof and windproof while allowing moisture vapour (perspiration) to pass through. *See* PLASTIC TEXTILES, POLYMER MEMBRANE LAMINATES.

See also BACKED FABRIC, CARPET, COATED FABRIC, DOUBLE CLOTH, FLOCKED FABRIC, HOLOGRAPHIC FABRICS, LINING FABRIC, MICROFIBRE FABRIC, MOISTURE TRANSPORT TEXTILES, PLASTIC TEXTILES, POLYMER MEMBRANE LAMINATES, QUILTED FABRIC, SCRIM, SPACER FABRICS, SUEDE CLOTH, TRICOT.

End uses: suits, coats, rainwear, anoraks, protective clothing, furnishing fabrics, blinds, shoes and accessories.

LAMPAS A heavy jacquard woven fabric composed of a ground fabric against which figured patterns are formed by weft floats bound by a secondary binding warp. Contrasting colours are often used in the figured and ground areas.

Lampas may be woven in any fibre or blend combinations, although silk, cotton and viscose are often used. Lampas is constructed with two warps, which are usually dyed the same colour. A main warp and weft are used to make the ground weave, which is normally a simple construction (plain, rib, twill or satin). The secondary warp is used as a binding warp to interlace with the patterning weft yarns (usually in contrasting colours) and to form the figured areas. The figured or patterned areas may make up the bulk of the fabric, or they may be just minor details. The patterning weft yarns float on the surface of the fabric, as required by the pattern, and they are bound by the binding warp ends, usually in a plain or twill construction. The fabric is therefore prone to fraying. Lampas is a similar fabric to brocade. Lampas taille-douce is a French variation of a lampas fabric. It was a silk textile developed at the beginning of the 19th century. In addition to the main and binding warps, a third supplementary warp (termed *chaîne poil* or *chaîne taille-douce*) was introduced to modify the colour of the weft floats.[1]

See also DOUBLE CLOTH; FIGURED FABRIC; JACQUARD FABRIC, WOVEN.

End uses: curtains and upholstery.

LANCÉ A woven fabric in which extra weft yarns are interwoven with just a few warp ends of a ground fabric, usually at regular intervals across its width, to form tiny dots on the surface of the fabric. When the extra weft yarns are not interwoven, they float on the back of the fabric (usually) or sometimes on the face side as a feature.

lancé (back and face)

lappet

Typical weave constructions are plain weave or satin for the ground fabric and sateen-type weaves at the interlacing points of the extra weft yarns. If there are large spaces between the interlacing points, then the floats may have additional binding points in-between that are not visible on the face of the fabric. Lancé made in various qualities and is similar to clip spot, dotted Swiss and broché. None of those three, however, have floating yarns between the motifs as lancé does. The extra weft yarns floating between the motifs or figured patterns in clip spot fabrics and some dotted Swiss fabrics are cut away after weaving, and the extra weft yarns in broché and some dotted Swiss fabrics are continuously interwoven into the figured areas and bound around the edges.

See also EXTRA WARP AND EXTRA WEFT FABRICS.

End uses: ladies' evening wear, scarves, dresses, blouses and furnishing fabrics.

LAPPET A woven fabric in which extra warp yarns are floated on the surface of a usually plain woven base fabric to form figured effects. The figured patterns are usually simple geometric effects, for example zigzag stripes against a plain weave ground fabric. The figured patterns look as if they have been embroidered onto the fabric.

Lappet may be woven with any fibres or fibre combinations. The ground fabric, however, is usually a fine, lightweight fabric woven in plain weave, often muslin or voile. Lappet weaving is done on a special loom that has a lappet attachment in the form of one or more needlebars between the reed and the fell of the cloth. The extra warp figuring threads are arranged in the needlebar(s), and a pattern wheel controls its sideways traverse to form the pattern.[25] The base fabric and the figured patterns are woven simultaneously, with the extra warp threads being carried across the back of the fabric when not in use. After weaving, excess yarns are cut away on the reverse side, after being secured at the pattern edges. Lappet weaving can also be used to form woven spots on the surface of a fabric. After weaving, the floating yarns between the spots are cut away. One type of dotted Swiss fabric is made by lappet weaving.

See also CLIP SPOT, EMBROIDERED FABRICS, EXTRA WARP AND EXTRA WEFT FABRICS, FIGURED FABRIC.

End uses: ladies' evening wear, scarves, dresses, blouses and furnishing fabrics.

LASER-CUT FABRICS Fabrics into which shaped holes have been cut to form decorative patterns; they are usually lightweight woven fabrics. Some laser-cut fabrics have all-over designs; others have border designs, sometimes with a scalloped edge.

The fabric is usually a fine polyester fabric woven in a very closely sett plain weave construction. It may be a single colour, it may be patterned with colour-woven stripes or checks, or it may be printed. A pattern of holes is cut into the fabric by a laser cutter. As polyester is thermoplastic, the process automatically heat-seals the edges and there is no need for further treatments. Laser-cut fabrics are similar to broderie anglaise, eyelet and some lace fabrics.

See also POLYESTER FABRIC.

End uses: evening wear, blouses, dresses, lingerie and trimmings.

LASTING (*obs.*) A strong woven fabric used for shoe uppers and other purposes. It was at one time composed of worsted yarns, but was later made from cotton or synthetic materials. It was woven in various single and weft-backed weaves to produce a strong, hard, smooth surface.[26]

LATEX FABRIC *see* RUBBER.

laser-cut fabric

lawn (printed)

LAWN A very fine, lightweight but opaque fabric that is woven in plain weave, with either cotton or linen yarns. It is a smooth, cool, absorbent and hard-wearing fabric that has good drape and excellent washability, but it creases quite easily.

Lawn was originally made from linen yarns;[4] although linen lawn is still produced, high-quality cotton (usually combed cotton) yarns are now more likely to be used, sometimes in combination with polyester. The fabric is woven in a tightly woven plain weave using singles yarns in both the warp and the weft. Lawn fabrics are often printed, normally with delicate floral patterns, but they may also be bleached, yarn-dyed or piece-dyed. They may be given either a soft or a slightly crisp (light-starch) finish, which may be permanent.

The name 'lawn' comes from the town of Laon in northern France, where the fabric was originally woven in linen and used for garments for the clergy.[3] Today lawn is woven in a variety of lightweight qualities, with the finest lawn fabrics being used for handkerchiefs (called 'handkerchief lawn'). Other lawn fabrics include bishop's lawn (bleached, given a bluish-white tint and traditionally used for ecclesiastical vestments), Egyptian lawn, Indian lawn, Irish lawn (produced using fine linen yarns), opaline (a fine-quality, white cotton lawn fabric with a soft finish), Persian lawn (also a soft-finish fabric) and Victoria lawn (a closely woven cotton lawn with a slightly stiff finish, used as an interfacing fabric).[26] Perhaps the best-known lawn fabric is Liberty Tana lawn, which is the registered trademark of Liberty Plc. Their Tana lawn fabrics are characteristically printed with small-scale floral designs and were first manufactured in the 1920s. Tana lawn is named after Lake Tana in the Sudan, where the raw cotton used to be grown;[3] nowadays Egyptian cotton is used.

An example of a typical lawn fabric construction is 8 to 6 tex warp sett at 32 to 36 ends per cm and 8 to 6 tex weft woven at 32 to 36 picks per cm.[26] Lawn is very similar to cotton batiste and organdie. It is possible to produce all three from the same grey goods, with each fabric being given a different finish.[19] Lawn is usually given a crisper handle than batiste, but not as crisp as organdie. Lawn is also similar to cambric, longcloth, nainsook and percaline (*see* PERCALE). It is lighter in weight, more closely woven and slightly stiffer than cambric. Lawn is also lighter in weight than longcloth and lighter and finer than nainsook.

See also COTTON FABRIC, PLAIN WEAVE FABRIC, PRINT CLOTH.

End uses: blouses, dresses, shirts, scarves, nightwear, lingerie, children's and baby's clothing, curtains and table linen.

LEATHER The natural skin or hide of an animal, for example cowhide, pigskin, sheepskin or snakeskin. Animal skin with the hair left attached is usually known as 'fur'.

The skin from a large animal is termed a 'hide', and that from a smaller animal a 'skin'. To make leather, any hair is removed, and the skin is preserved and softened in the tanning process. The outside layer of the skin, or 'top grain', is what is called leather. It is very tough and hard-wearing. It shows the grain or pores of the animal skin or any other characteristic features, such as the scales of snakeskin. Leather may be dyed, coated and/or embossed to give it a wide range of different characteristics. Patent leather is leather that has been varnished to give it a very high gloss.

Chamois leather (or shammy leather) is the skin of the chamois, a species of antelope native to the mountainous regions of Western Europe and Asia. It is naturally a very soft type of leather. Nowadays the term 'chamois' is sometimes also used to describe the soft inner layer of the natural skin or hide of other animals, for example cowhide, goatskin, pigskin or sheep/lambskin. Thick animal hides can be split into layers. The outer layer of an animal skin or hide is the top-grain leather, also called 'leather'. The inside split layer or flesh side is called 'suede'. It is the softest, innermost split layer from cowhide, mountain goat or sheepskin that is sometimes also known as 'chamois' (*see also* SUEDE).

leather (face and back)

leather-cloth (back and face)

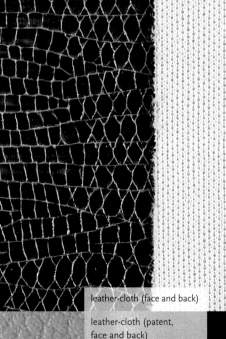

leather-cloth (face and back)

leather-cloth (patent, face and back)

See also CHAMOIS CLOTH, FUR FABRIC, LEATHER-CLOTH, SUEDE, SUEDE CLOTH.

End uses: boots, shoes, jackets, coats, trousers, belts, gloves, luggage, bags, upholstery and furnishings.

LEATHER-CLOTH (leatherette) A woven or warp-knitted fabric that is given a special finish so that it resembles real leather.

Leather-cloth is usually a medium- to heavyweight woven or warp-knitted fabric that is coated and then embossed with a texture resembling that of the animal skin being imitated. This makes the fabric waterproof, but coated leather-cloth does not wear as well as real leather and may be more easily damaged or torn. The coating is usually polyurethane (PU) or polyvinyl chloride (PVC). Leather-cloth is often coated with expanded vinyl (PVC), which is softer and more flexible than ordinary PVC. Heavyweight melton fabrics, woven with a two-fold cotton warp and a thick woollen weft, were also sometimes called 'leather cloth'.[16]

See also CHAMOIS CLOTH, COATED FABRIC, EMBOSSED FABRICS, KNITTED FABRIC, LEATHER, MELTON, OIL CLOTH, POLYURETHANE, PVC, SUEDE CLOTH, WARP-KNITTED FABRIC, WATERPROOF AND WATER-REPELLENT FABRICS.

End uses: jackets, trousers, shoes, handbags, accessories and upholstery fabrics.

LENO FABRIC A woven fabric that is woven in a special leno fabric construction, either in whole or in part, to form a stable open-mesh fabric construction. This is achieved by a special weaving technique called 'leno weaving'. In the leno woven areas, warp yarns are made to cross over one another between the weft picks. This produces an open mesh-like construction with spaces between the consecutive warp and weft yarns. Leno weaving is often employed to produce decorative, openwork structures in specific areas of a fabric, which form a contrast against a usually simple woven ground structure, such as plain weave.

Leno fabrics may be woven in a wide range of weights and qualities and from any fibre, although cotton or man-made fibres are probably those most often used. Leno weaves require a doup attachment on a weaving loom. This is a device that facilitates the crossing of the warp yarns. The warp yarns are arranged in pairs. One of the pair, called a 'doup', 'crossing' or 'leno end', is passed from side to side, crossing over the other warp end, called a 'standard' or 'fixed' end. The warp ends are thus crossed rather than twisted: that is, one yarn of the pair is always above the other, and they are bound in that position by the weft. The weft picks are also trapped tightly between the warp yarn crossings and therefore, although they are spaced apart, they do not slip easily.

Many different fabrics are woven in leno weaves. The simpler types of lightweight fabric produced by leno weaving are known as 'gauze'.[25] In gauze fabrics, the entire fabric is woven in a leno fabric construction rather than just sections of the fabric. It is possible to create a much more stable open-mesh fabric construction by leno weaving than could be produced by other weaving methods. The terms 'leno' and 'gauze' are often used synonymously to describe any fabric in which the doup principle of weaving is employed. Leno is also sometimes

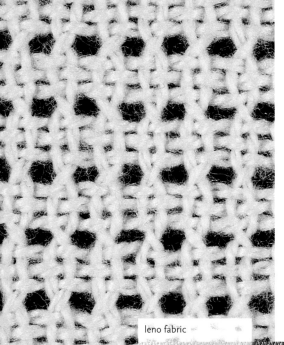

leno fabric

limbric

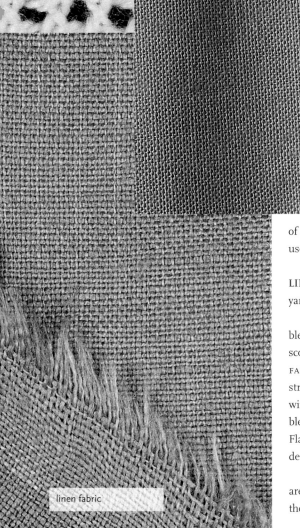

linen fabric

called 'doup weave'.[5] Other fabrics that are woven in a leno fabric construction throughout the entire fabric include leno woven bolting cloth, leno woven cellular fabric, leno woven étamine fabric, leno woven gossamer fabric, woven marquisette, leno woven mosquito netting, leno woven muslin, leno woven ondulé fabric, Russian cord and leno woven scrim.

Fabrics with leno structures in some areas of the fabric only are usually made purely for their decorative effect. Examples of fabrics in which the leno effect is used in combination with other weave structures include some cellular fabrics, grenadine, leno voile (*see* VOILE) and some Madras muslin. The leno fabric construction is also often used as the weave construction along the selvedges of many woven fabrics.

See also GAUZE, MOCK LENO, NET.

End uses: curtains, blankets, laundry bags, fruit and vegetable bags, evening wear, bridal wear, trims and millinery.

LIMBRIC   A lightweight to medium-weight fabric (weighing approximately 100 g/m²) that is closely woven in plain weave using cotton yarns. It is usually woven as grey cloth.

Limbric is woven from good-quality cotton yarns, usually Egyptian. The weft yarns are soft-spun and lustrous. They are thicker than the warp yarns, and traditionally there are more weft picks per centimetre than warp ends. This produces a soft fabric in which the weft yarns predominate on both sides. An example of a typical limbric fabric construction is 12 tex warp sett at 14 ends per cm and 16 tex weft woven at 27 picks per cm.[25] The name is derived from the village of Limbrick in Lancashire, England, where the fabric was first made.[4] Limbric is a similar fabric to casement cloth, but it is much finer.

See also COTTON FABRIC, PLAIN WEAVE FABRIC.

End uses: curtains and dresses.

LIMOGES   *see* TICKING.

LINCOLN GREEN (*obs.*)   A stout woollen fabric made with wool from the Lincoln longwool sheep, native to the Lincolnshire region of England. The fabric was originally woven in this area and traditionally dyed green for use by archers, huntsmen and foresters.[3, 36]

LINEN FABRIC   A general term for any fabric that has been constructed using flax (linen) yarns or fibres from the plant *Linum usitatissimum*.[25]

Flax fibres are staple fibres that are spun into yarns, and sometimes they are blended with other staple fibres. (Note that flax is a very similar fibre to hemp, and microscopically it is difficult to distinguish between the two;[45] *see also* HEMP FABRIC, PLANT-FIBRE FABRICS.) The term 'linen fabric' is used for fabrics of all different weights and constructions that are composed of 100% flax fibres or yarns. Where flax is used together with other fibres, the percentage of each should be stated. Fabrics made from yarns of flax blended with other fibres are usually described as 'linen blends' or 'linen-look fabrics'. Flax yarns woven together with yarns of different fibres (usually cotton) produce fabrics described as 'linen union fabrics'; *see* UNION FABRIC.

Most linen fabrics are woven in a closely sett plain weave construction. Linen yarns are characteristically slightly slubby and uneven, and this quality is carried through into the fabric, both warpways and weftways. Characteristically, most woven linen fabrics are very strong and hard-wearing. They have excellent washability; they may be boiled, bleached and starched and they dye well. Linen fabric is prone to creasing but may be given a crease-resistant finish. Some of the best-known linen fabrics are described below. Altar linen, also called 'bisso linen', is a very fine, sheer linen fabric that has traditionally been used in churches. It is a highly sett plain weave fabric that has a firm, crisp handle. Art linen is a heavy, plain woven linen fabric used for embroidery, dresses and table linens; it may be unbleached, bleached or dyed.[17, 18] Handkerchief linen is a very fine linen fabric woven in plain weave; it is similar in weight and lustre to batiste. Irish linen is a fine linen fabric woven in Ireland from Irish flax. Linen twill is a lightweight linen fabric woven in twill weave and used mainly for embroidery. Other traditional linen fabrics include linen batiste, some butcher cloth, linen cambric, crash, dowlas, Holland and linen lawn.

End uses: tablecloths, serviettes, bed linen, tea towels, suits, jackets, dresses, blouses, shirts, trousers, furnishing fabrics and sewing threads.

LINGERIE CRÊPE *see* CRÊPE.

LINING FABRIC A general term for any fabric that is used on the inside or back of apparel, curtains or other products. Lining fabrics may be used for a variety of reasons, for instance to provide greater strength, durability or stability; to make the item more opaque; to provide added comfort, warmth or insulation; or to provide special protective features. Woven, knitted or nonwoven fabrics may be used as lining fabrics, depending on the product that needs to be lined. The weight of the lining fabric and its colour should suit the top fabric. Lining fabrics are normally fine, lightweight fabrics that have good drape and are substantially cheaper than the top fabric. Lining fabrics for apparel are usually smooth, soft and slippery to facilitate the putting on and removal of the garment.

Lining fabrics may be made from any fibre, but the most frequently used are probably viscose, acetate, triacetate, polyester, nylon, cupro and lyocell, while silk may be used for more exclusive items. The yarns are normally low-twist filaments and they are often shiny. Most woven lining fabrics are woven in plain, satin, sateen or twill weaves. Most knitted lining fabrics are warp-knitted. The lining fabric is usually attached to the top fabric along one or more edges.

Fabrics that may be used as lining fabrics include acetate fabric, Albert twill, woven atlas, balloon cloth, batiste, bump cloth, cambric, Canton, chamois cloth, charmeuse, cheesecloth, China silk, Coburg, coutil (heavyweight lining), crêpe-back satin (*see* CRÊPE), domet, duck (heavyweight lining), façonné, flannel, flannelette, fleece fabric, foulard, galatea, haircloth, Holland, interlining, Italian, jappe, jeanette (*see* JEAN), warp-knitted locknit, longcloth, loopraise, louisine, mesh fabrics, metallic fabrics, moiré fabric, moleskin fabric, mull, sateen, nonwoven fabric, organza, osnaburg, percaline (*see* PERCALE), polar fleece, poult, radium, sarsenet, sateen, satin, shot fabrics, various different silk fabrics, silesia, stitch-bonded fabric, suede cloth, surah, swansdown, tarlatan, tufted fabric, cotton Venetian, viscose fabric, Wigan and winceyette.

See also BACKED FABRIC, COATED FABRIC, LAMINATED FABRIC, SHOT FABRICS.

End uses: inner or backing fabric for all kinds of apparel, curtains, shoes, luggage and many other products.

LINSEY (*obs.*) A union fabric with a coarse linen or cotton warp and a weft of cotton blended with waste wool.[26] Originally made in Lindsey in Suffolk, England,[3] it was also known as 'linsey-wolsey' or 'linsey-woolsey'.

LISLE (*obs.*) A very fine single jersey knitted fabric made from mercerized cotton yarns. Before the invention of nylon, it was used for women's stockings.[2, 23]

lining fabrics
lining fabric

locknit (warp-knitted, back and face)

locknit (weft-knitted, face and back)

loden cloth

LOCKNIT A firm, closely knitted fabric. There is both a weft-knitted and a warp-knitted version.

Weft-knitted locknit is a variation of a plain knit fabric. It is a half-gauge jersey fabric, knitted on alternate needles in the first course, on all needles in the second course, on the opposite (to course one) alternate needles in the third course and again on all needles in the fourth course. These four courses are then repeated throughout the fabric. The fabric may be knitted on flat or circular knitting machines.[38] Weft-knitted locknit is made in a variety of different fibres for many different end uses.

Warp-knitted locknit is the most popular of all warp-knitted structures, accounting for 70% to 80% of total output.[31] It is usually made with man-made fibres and often includes elastane to give stretch. The fabric will not ladder or split. It has good extensibility, cover, opacity and drape, with a smooth soft handle, making it highly suitable for all comfort stretch fabrics, including lingerie and swimwear. Weights range typically from 70 to 200 g/m². A typical fabric for swimwear, sportswear or lingerie is 185 g/m² with a fibre content of approximately 82% nylon and 18% elastane.

Warp-knitted locknit is knitted on a tricot warp-knitting machine on two full-set guide bars that make closed lap movements in opposition to each other. The front guide bar underlaps two needle spaces, and the back guide bar underlaps one needle space.[25] The technical face of the fabric is formed by both systems of yarns. The technical back is formed by the front bar underlaps that lie on the surface, covering the other stitches underneath. A wider, more stable warp-knitted locknit fabric is produced using a 'reverse locknit' structure, in which the front guide bar underlaps one needle space and the back guide bar underlaps two needle spaces. This fabric is widely used for linings and scrims for laminating. Other similar, two-bar warp-knitted fabrics include warp-knitted sharkskin and queenscord. Warp-knitted locknit is sometimes also called 'jersey stitch' in the United States, and some warp-knitted locknit fabrics are known as 'charmeuse' in Europe since they are knitted in imitation of woven charmeuse (*see* CHARMEUSE).

See also ELASTANE FABRIC, ELASTOMERIC FABRIC, KNITTED FABRIC, SCRIM, STRETCH FABRIC, TRICOT, WARP-KNITTED FABRIC, WEFT-KNITTED FABRIC.

End uses: (weft-knitted locknit) general knitwear; (warp-knitted locknit) lingerie, sportswear, swimwear (with elastane), linings and scrims for laminating.

LOCKSTITCH *see* RASCHEL STRETCH FABRICS.

LODEN CLOTH A heavy, coarse woven fabric made from wool. It is a thick, felt-like fabric that is traditionally made in a dark green colour. Loden cloth is a very warm fabric and it is naturally water-repellent, making it an ideal coating fabric.

Loden cloth has been made in Austria in a similar manner for about a thousand years. The term 'loden' comes from the Old German *loda*, meaning 'hair cloth', traditionally woven in the Austrian Tyrol.[3] Loden cloth was traditionally woven with wool from the local mountain sheep, which was naturally coarse in texture but also very hardwearing. Nowadays the fabric is made from a blend of different wools. The fabric is woven in a modified plain weave double cloth structure. After weaving, the fabric is heavily milled during finishing, which shrinks and compacts it by about a third of its original width in the loom. Then it is raised, sheared and brushed.[3] Loden cloth may be either piece-dyed or yarn-dyed; although dark green has become the most popular colour, it is also traditionally produced in black, red and white.

See also COATING FABRIC, DOUBLE CLOTH, FELTED FABRIC, NAPPED FABRICS.

End uses: coats, jackets and capes.

LONDON CORD *see* BEDFORD CORD.

longcloth

loopraise (face and back)

louisine

LONGCLOTH A fine, soft, closely sett woven cotton fabric; it may also be made in cotton blends.

Longcloth was originally woven in the Chennai (Madras) area of India.[3] It was one of the first fabrics to be woven in long pieces, hence the name.[5] Longcloth is woven as grey cloth, using good-quality, fine combed cotton yarns that are loosely twisted. It is woven in a tight plain weave construction. After weaving, the fabric is usually bleached white, and it may be dyed. It is lightly sized and calendered during finishing, which gives it a slight lustre.

An example of a typical longcloth fabric construction is 20 to 16 tex warp sett at 28 to 32 ends per cm and 20 to 16 tex weft woven at 28 to 40 picks per cm.[26] Indian longcloth is a finer, softer fabric, more like cambric, and typically constructed as follows: 12 to 9 tex warp sett at 36 to 40 ends per cm and 12 to 9 tex weft woven at 38 to 54 picks per cm.[26] Longcloth is a similar fabric to lawn, nainsook and percale, but it is heavier than lawn and nainsook, and the weave is more dense than in percale. Cambric, longcloth and nainsook are often converted from the same grey goods and given different finishes.[14]

See also PLAIN WEAVE FABRIC.

End uses: dresses, blouses, shirts, children's clothes, lingerie, lining and sheeting.

LOOPRAISE (unbroken loop) A warp-knitted fabric that is knitted using nylon or polyester yarns and then brushed, usually on one side only, to produce a soft, fluffy surface. This makes the fabric much warmer than unbrushed versions, but it is prone to static build-up. Loopraise is an easy-care fabric that does not crease and has good launderability. It is sometimes also called 'brushed nylon', 'brushed polyester' or, in the US, 'unbroken loop' (UBL).

Loopraise is traditionally knitted on a two-bar tricot warp-knitting machine using fine filament nylon or polyester yarns. The back bar knits a 1 and 1 tricot stitch and the front bar knits a longer lap over three or four needle spaces, depending on the required pile height and fabric weight. Normally both bars lap in the same direction, producing distinctive racked stitches. After knitting, the fabric is raised by brushing, usually on one side only. The knit construction allows easy brushing with very little filament breakage or reduction in the fabric width. An alternative warp-knitted construction is also made, in which the guide bars lap in opposite directions, which is effectively a satin construction. This produces a softer, fluffier fabric, but the fabric becomes narrower when brushed, there is much higher filament breakage, and the fabric is prone to curling at the edges.

Similar fabrics to loopraise include airloop fabric, plush, suede cloth and velour. Airloop fabric is a cheaper way of making a similar fabric to loopraise. Plush, suede cloth and velour, however, are all heavier fabrics, and they are usually superior in both appearance and quality.

See also KNITTED FABRIC, LINING FABRIC, NAPPED FABRICS, SHEETING FABRIC, SUEDE CLOTH, WARP-KNITTED FABRIC.

End uses: nightwear, sheeting, slippers, linings, textiles for car interiors, and liner for laminated fabrics.

LOUGHREAS (*obs.*) A plain woven Irish linen fabric from Galway, Ireland, made with locally grown flax.[36]

LOUISINE Traditionally a very fine, lustrous, lightweight silk fabric that resembles taffeta but is woven in a weave structure that gives it a small-scale surface texture. It is a hardwearing fabric but it frays easily. Although originally woven in silk, louisine may also be woven with synthetic fibres. It is woven in a 2/2 hopsack weave structure.

See also HOPSACK, LINING FABRIC.

End uses: dresses and coat linings.

lyocell fabric

macramé

LUMBERDINE (*obs.*) A sheer black woven gauze fabric used for women's dresses and veils.[3, 36]

LUREX® *see* METALLIC FABRICS.

LUSTRE FABRIC *see* BRADFORD LUSTRE FABRICS.

LYCRA® *see* ELASTANE FABRIC.

LYOCELL FABRIC A general term for any fabric that has been constructed using lyocell fibres or yarns. 'Lyocell' is the generic term for a man-made material made from cellulose.[25] It may be produced in sheet form or in fibre form. For textiles, it is usually the fibres that are used.

The fibres may be used in continuous filament form, or they may be chopped into shorter staple lengths and respun into yarns with different characteristics, sometimes blended with other staple fibres. The term 'lyocell fabric' is used for fabrics of all different weights and constructions that are composed of 100% lyocell fibres or yarns. Where lyocell is used together with other fibres, the percentage of each should be stated. Most lyocell fabrics have properties similar to cotton fabrics. They are strong, with good abrasion resistance and a cool, natural handle. It is also possible to give lyocell fibres a range of different properties by varying the manufacturing parameters. Modified lyocell fibres are marketed under different brand names.

End uses: blouses, dresses and jeanswear.

LYRE (*obs.*) A 15th-century woollen fabric of good quality.[3, 36]

MACCLESFIELD SILK *see* SILK FABRIC.

MACINTOSH FABRIC *see* WATERPROOF AND WATER-REPELLENT FABRICS.

MACKINAW *see* BUFFALO CHECK.

MACRAMÉ A craft that produces decorative fabrics by various knotting techniques rather than by weaving or knitting. It is sometimes also called 'Chinese knotting'.

Macramé is believed to have originated during the 13th century in Arabia, where weavers knotted the excess threads and yarns along the edges of hand-loomed fabrics into decorative fringes. The word 'macramé' is derived from the Arabic *migramah*, believed to mean 'striped towel', 'ornamental fringe' or 'embroidered veil'. In modern macramé fabrics, the entire fabric is usually constructed from knots throughout. The main knots used are the square knot and various forms of hitch knot (full hitch and double half hitches). Common materials used to construct macramé fabrics include cord, cotton twine, hemp, leather and yarns of various types and thicknesses. At one time, decorative macramé fabrics and forms were made by sailors to embellish items such as knife handles and bottle holders. Various craft-based products continue to be made by macramé today.

End uses: wall hangings, table coverings, table mats, drapes, plant hangers, bags and furnishings.

MADAPOLAM (*obs.*) A plain woven bleached cotton fabric, coarser than cambric, nainsook and lawn, but given a soft finish like nainsook.[26]

MADEIRA *see* BRODERIE ANGLAISE.

MADRAS A fine, lightweight woven check or stripe fabric made with soft cotton yarns. It is a bright multicoloured fabric that usually has a bold, irregular check pattern.

Madras is woven in plain weave, traditionally using carded cotton yarns. It is a colour-woven fabric that has checks or stripes in varying proportions. It is woven in a wide range of weights and qualities suitable for a diverse range of end uses (see below). Madras was the previously the name of the city in south-eastern India now called Chennai. A true Madras fabric is a hand-woven fabric produced in this region. Traditionally it is dyed with vegetable dyes that characteristically bleed when the fabric is washed ('bleeding Madras'). This can produce some interesting shaded effects, but it is not always desirable. Nowadays, therefore, Madras is also machine-woven with colour-fast yarns. Although similar fabrics to Madras are produced in many different countries, only those made in the Chennai region of India are allowed to be labelled 'Madras'.[5] Madras is a similar fabric to gingham but is multicoloured. It is also similar to zephyr, but it is heavier in weight.

See also CHECKS, COTTON FABRIC, STRIPES, SHIRTING FABRICS.

End uses: dresses, blouses, shirts, skirts, curtains and upholstery fabric.

MADRAS MUSLIN An open weave fabric with a gauze ground, figured with patterns woven into it at intervals using extra weft yarns. It is a clip spot fabric.

The base fabric is traditionally woven with cotton yarns. It is woven in an open-sett plain weave or leno fabric construction that is transparent. The figured patterns are interwoven into the base fabric using thick, soft-spun extra weft yarns, which makes the patterned areas opaque. When the extra weft yarns are not required to make the pattern, they are floated either on the surface or on the back of the fabric and cut off after weaving, sometimes leaving a small fringe around the edge of the motif. Madras muslin is often produced as a single-colour fabric, but in more expensive versions two or more colours may be used. Like cotton Madras fabric and Madras shirting, Madras muslin was also originally produced in the Madras (now Chennai) region of south-eastern India.

See also CLIP SPOT, COTTON FABRIC, EXTRA WARP AND EXTRA WEFT FABRICS, FIGURED FABRIC, GAUZE, LENO FABRIC, MUSLIN.

End uses: curtains.

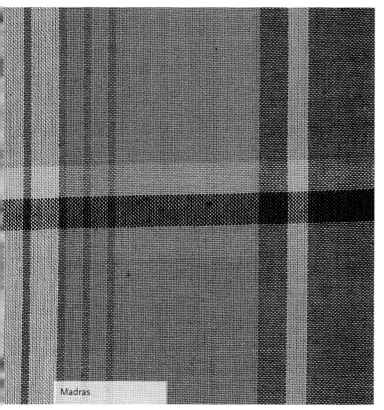

Madras

MADRAS SHIRTING A fine, lightweight woven fabric that is woven with cotton yarns and that has a small dobby design woven into it.

Madras shirting is a better-quality cotton fabric than an ordinary Madras cotton fabric, and is more like a zephyr fabric. Madras shirting is woven in plain weave but has stripes (usually vertical) of highly sett yarns crammed together and woven in satin weave. It is a colour-woven fabric and may be woven using one or more colours. Like cotton Madras fabric and Madras muslin, Madras shirting was also originally produced in the Madras (now Chennai) region of south-eastern India.

See also COTTON FABRIC; DOBBY FABRIC; SATIN, WOVEN; SHIRTING FABRICS; STRIPES; ZEPHYR.

End uses: shirts and blouses.

MALABAR (*obs.*) A cotton fabric from eastern India, made in very bright colours and used for handkerchieves.[2]

Madras muslin

Madras shirting

Malimo (glass filament
and polyester)

Malimo (glass roving
and polyester)

Malines

marble cloth (warp-printed)

MALIMO The generic term for a variety of stitch-bonded textiles that are constructed on Malimo stitch-bonding machines. Stitch-bonding is a special form of warp-knitting that is used mainly for the manufacture of technical textiles, particularly composite and nonwoven textiles (*see* STITCH-BONDED FABRIC).

Three sets of yarn are used to make Malimo fabrics: warp yarns, weft yarns that are laid across the warp yarns at a slight angle to them, and a third set that stitches them both together in vertical columns with a stitch like a warp-knitted loop. The special Malimo machines that construct Malimo fabrics operate at high speeds, and therefore the fabric is usually made with strong synthetic yarns. One type of Malimo fabric is made from glass fibre and used for industrial filters.[23] Malimo was developed by Heinrich Mauersberger in 1958 in the former East German towns of Limbach and Oberfrohna. The name 'Malimo' is formed from the first two letters of Mauersberger, the first two letters of Limbach and the first two letters of Molton.[43]

Malimo (glass filament and polyester)

See also GLASS-FIBRE TEXTILES, KNITTED FABRIC, NONWOVEN FABRIC, STITCH-BONDED FABRIC, WARP-KNITTED FABRIC.

End uses: base materials for fibre-reinforced plastics, vertical blinds, semi-sheer curtains, tablecloths, blankets, bedspreads, interlining, upholstery fabrics, dishcloths and vegetable bags.

MALINES An extremely fine, lightweight, plain net fabric with a hexagonal mesh. Characteristically, it is a fine, sheer, soft, transparent fabric with excellent drape. However, it is also sometimes stiffened with starch, for use in millinery. Malines is not as widely available as some of the other net fabrics on the market today.

Malines is a very ancient type of net fabric. It originated in Malines in Belgium, hence the name. It is traditionally made with fine silk yarns, but it is also produced using fine nylon filaments. Malines is produced on a lace machine and it has a distinctive fine hexagonal mesh. It is a very similar fabric to tulle. Like tulle, Malines is also sometimes called 'illusion', since it is so fine that it can barely be seen.[9]

See also LACE, NET, SHEER FABRICS, VEILING.

End uses: veiling and millinery trims.

MARABOUT (*obs.*) A delicate, thin silk fabric made from twisted raw silk and used for blouses and linings.[2]

MARBLE CLOTH Traditionally a soft, lightweight woven silk fabric that is woven with multicoloured yarns, in either the warp or the weft. This gives the fabric a variegated or iridescent quality.

Marble cloth was first produced in England and was originally made with silk and wool yarns. Nowadays it is woven using all kinds of different fibres.[5] Usually marble cloth is woven with variegated colours in the weft. The yarns may be made multicoloured by space-dyeing or ikat dyeing them prior to weaving. The fabric is usually woven in a simple weave construction like plain weave. A similar effect may also be produced in fabric by printing the warp yarns prior to weaving (warp printing). This is less common, however, since it is a more expensive production method.

See also CHINÉ FABRICS, DYED FABRICS, IKAT, RESIST-DYED FABRICS, SPACE-DYED FABRIC, WARP-PRINTED FABRIC.

End uses: dresses, blouses and furnishing fabrics.

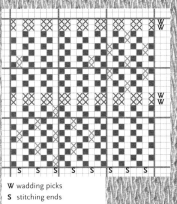

W wadding picks
S stitching ends
■ plain weave ground
✕ stitching end interlacings
✕ wadding pick interlacings

marcella

marengo

marl fabric (weft-knitted)

MARCELLA A fine woven fabric constructed in a fancy geometric weave structure, which gives it a three-dimensional surface texture. It has an embossed or quilted surface appearance and is traditionally used for dress shirt fronts.

Marcella is usually woven with bleached white cotton yarns. It is a dobby weave fabric, woven in a piqué weave structure. An example of a typical marcella fabric construction is warp, 15 tex face ends sett at 28 ends per cm and 21 tex stitching ends sett at 14 ends per cm; weft, 10 face picks of 12 tex / 2 wadding picks of 30 tex, woven at 38 picks per cm.[25] The name 'marcella' is probably derived from Marseilles fabrics, which are similar visually but much larger in scale.[16] Marcella is sometimes also called 'waffle piqué'.

See also COTTON FABRIC, DOBBY FABRIC, MARSEILLES, PIQUÉ, WOVEN, SHIRTING FABRICS.

End uses: dress shirt fronts and waistcoats.

MARENGO A mid- to heavyweight woven fabric made from wool. It is made in dark colours with 2% to 5% of white fibres mixed in, so that the fabric does not show fluff or dirt.[13]

'Marengo' was originally the term for a now obsolete French overcoating fabric, made from wool with a black warp and a predominantly black weft, and with occasional white weft yarns. The fabric was woven in plain or twill weave.[36] The term is now used for a similar-looking wool fabric in which the dark and light fibres are blended together; it is also usually woven in a plain or twill weave. Marengo is normally milled and raised during finishing, which obscures the weave structure underneath and produces a type of felted fabric.

See also COATING FABRIC, FELTED FABRIC, NAPPED FABRICS, WOOL FABRIC.

End uses: coats, suits and jackets.

MARL FABRIC A general term for a knitted or woven fabric that has been either constructed with fancy marl yarns or dyed by a differential dyeing technique. Marl fabrics characteristically have a speckled appearance produced by the interaction of two or more colours.

Marl yarns may be made from any fibres but wool is often used. A marl yarn can be made by twisting together two or more single yarns of different colours. Woollen spun marls are usually made in this way. Worsted spun marls, however, are produced in a variety of different ways to create different effects:[25] single marl yarns are made from rovings containing two strands of different colours; double marl yarns are made by twisting two single marl yarns together to produce a yarn containing four colours; and half-marl yarns are made by twisting a single marl yarn together with either a solid-colour yarn or a mixture yarn.

Marl effects are also produced by the differential dyeing of fabrics that have been constructed with yarns or fibres of different types. When dyed, different shades of colour are obtained on the different fibres, thus producing the characteristic speckled effect. Examples of fabrics that may be woven as marl fabrics include some Bannockburn fabrics and some tweed fabrics.

See also DYED FABRICS, WOOL FABRIC.

End uses: (woven marl fabrics) suits, jackets, trousers, skirts and coats; (knitted marl fabrics) sweaters and cardigans.

MARLY (marli) (*obs.*) A lightweight French linen fabric used for dresses and furnishings.[36]

MAROCAIN *see* CRÊPE.

MARQUISETTE, WARP-KNITTED An open mesh or net type of fabric that has square holes. Warp-knitted marquisette is a lightweight, fine, sheer, transparent fabric, and looks very similar to woven marquisette.

The warp yarns that run the length of the fabric are simultaneously formed into pillar stitches by separate machine needles. These are reinforced with two sets of laid-in weft yarns, which are lapped in opposite directions, usually every third course. This inter-links the pillar stitches together and forms the open mesh knitted structure.[38] As a variation, oblong holes are produced when the laid-in yarns are lapped every five or seven courses rather than every three.[38] Jacquard marquisette is produced by laying-in extra yarns on additional guide bars to 'fill in' selected areas of a warp-knitted marquisette ground fabric. This produces areas of solid design against an open mesh background.[38]

See also KNITTED FABRIC; LACE, KNITTED; LAID-IN FABRIC; MESH FABRICS; NET; SHEER FABRICS; WARP-KNITTED FABRIC.

End uses: net curtains, dresses, ladies' evening wear and blouses.

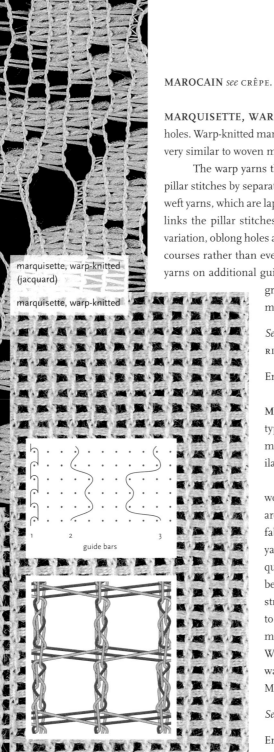

marquisette, warp-knitted (jacquard)

marquisette, warp-knitted

guide bars

marquisette, woven

MARQUISETTE, WOVEN A fine, sheer, open mesh gauze or net type of fabric that is woven in a leno fabric construction. Woven marquisette is a lightweight, transparent fabric that looks very similar to warp-knitted marquisette.

Originally marquisette was woven from silk, but it may be woven in any type of fibre and nowadays filament polyester or nylon are most often used. Occasionally it is woven with glass fibres.[2] The fabric is produced in a range of different colours, either by using yarn-dyed yarns or by piece-dyeing the fabric after weaving. Marquisette may be woven in a simple leno fabric construction or it may be patterned with a simple dobby or jacquard pattern. The leno construction makes it a very stable open weave fabric that is not prone to fraying. The name 'marquisette' comes from French *marquise*, meaning the canopy or awning at the entrance of a tent or marquee. Woven marquisette was originally used to drape across entrance-ways and it was also frequently used as mosquito netting.[3] Marquisette is a similar fabric to grenadine.

See also GAUZE, LENO FABRIC, NET, SHEER FABRICS, SILK FABRIC.

End uses: curtains, dresses, ladies' evening wear and blouses.

MARRY-MUFF (*obs.*) A coarse plain weave fabric, hand-woven with woollen yarns and worn by the peasantry in medieval England.[36]

MARSEILLES A thick, reversible double cloth or compound woven fabric, with characteristic raised woven patterns that give it a quilted appearance. It is usually woven on a jacquard loom, but it may also be woven on a dobby loom.

Marseilles fabrics are traditionally made with good-quality Egyptian cotton yarns and woven on a jacquard weaving loom. Marseilles is a double cloth fabric that is composed of two separate fabric layers, each woven in a simple ground weave structure such as plain weave. In-between the two fabric layers, very thick weft yarns are inserted as wadding, and the fabric is figured, either by passing figuring warp ends from one fabric to the other or by floating the thick wadding weft yarns onto the surface of the fabric. This produces the characteristic raised figured effects.

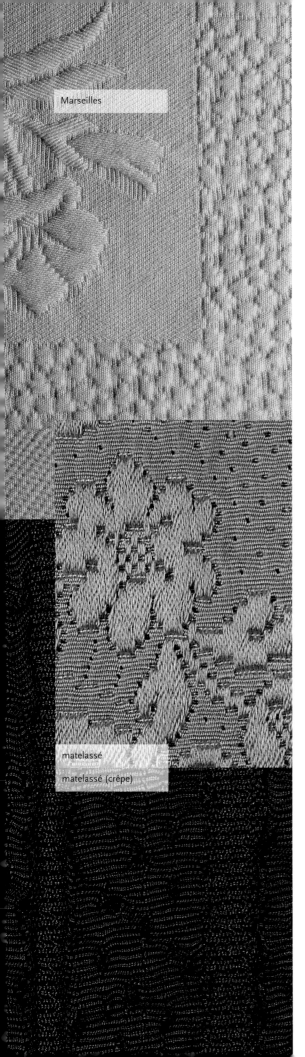

Marseilles

matelassé

matelassé (crêpe)

The best-known Marseilles fabrics are all-white fabrics that have elaborate stitched patterns in different white yarns, but coloured fabrics may also be produced. The name derives from the city of Marseilles in the south of France, where this fabric originated. Marseilles is a similar fabric to matelassé but is finer. It is also visually similar to marcella but is much larger in scale.

See also DOUBLE CLOTH; FIGURED FABRIC; JACQUARD FABRIC, WOVEN; QUILTED FABRIC.

End uses: quilts and bedspreads.

MARVELLA (marvello) (*obs.*) A high-quality, high-lustre, heavyweight pile fabric, traditionally made with a worsted warp and a mohair and silk weft, and used for coats.[5, 17]

MATELASSÉ A thick double cloth or compound woven fabric with a characteristic three-dimensional, quilted or puckered appearance on the face side. It is usually woven on a jacquard loom, but it may also be woven on a dobby loom.

Matelassé may be woven with any fibre, in any colour and in a wide range of different weights and qualities. It was originally a very heavyweight fabric, but nowadays it is produced in much lighter weights too. Those woven in silk, viscose, acetate, polyester, nylon and blends tend to be used as dress fabrics. Metallic threads are also sometimes added. Those woven in cotton and blends tend to be used for furnishing fabrics and are usually thicker and heavier in weight.

Matelassé is a double cloth fabric that is composed of two separate fabric layers. The top fabric is usually composed of fine yarns and is woven in a closely sett, simple ground weave structure such as plain weave. The back fabric is usually a more open-sett fabric than the top fabric (often the ratio is 2:1, i.e. 2 face ends and picks to 1 back end and pick, in both warp and weft). In-between the two fabric layers, very thick weft yarns, usually soft cotton, are inserted as wadding picks. These are not visible on either side of the fabric, but they accentuate the quilted effect. The fabric layers are held together by the figuring threads, which form the figures or pattern on the face of the fabric. This is achieved either by raising back ends from the back fabric onto the face of the top fabric or by lowering face warp ends from the face fabric and interweaving them with the back ends and picks.

During wet-finishing, there may be differential shrinkage of the face and back fabrics. Greater shrinkage of the back fabric causes the face fabric to pucker, giving the characteristic quilted appearance. This effect may be further accentuated by using crêpe yarns in one of the sets of warp and weft yarns. The crêpe yarns are arranged so that they are woven mainly on the back of the fabric. When the fabric is wet-finished, the crêpe yarns shrink greatly, causing the face fabric to pucker. These half crêpe fabrics are sometimes called 'matelassé crêpe'. They are a type of blister cloth and are similar in appearance and construction to woven cloqué fabrics, but they have larger raised blisters. *See* BLISTER CLOTH, CLOQUÉ, CRÊPE.

The term 'matelassé' comes from the French verb *matelasser*, meaning 'to quilt, pad, stuff or cushion'.[3] Matelassé is also sometimes called *fourré* in France. Matelassé is a very similar fabric to Marseilles and it is made in the same way, but it is a thicker, heavier fabric. Matelassé is also similar in appearance to some piqué fabrics, but it is usually much larger in scale.

See also DOUBLE CLOTH; FIGURED FABRIC; JACQUARD FABRIC, WOVEN; QUILTED FABRIC.

End uses: formal dresses, coats, jackets, waistcoats, ladies' evening wear, curtains, upholstery and bedspreads.

MATMEE *see* IKAT.

mélange fabric (woven)

mélange fabric (woven)

mélange lustre fabric

MAUD (*obs.*) A checked woollen fabric, woven in different shades of grey to make the pattern. It is used for travelling rugs.[2, 26]

MAYO TWILL *see* TWILL FABRICS.

MECKLENBURGH (*obs.*) A heavy English woollen damask with floral patterns, made in Norwich in the early 18th century.[3, 36]

MEDLEY (*obs.*) A 17th-century wool fabric dyed in the raw wool state.[36]

MÉLANGE FABRIC Any fabric, knitted or woven, that has been constructed with multi-coloured mélange yarns. The term 'mélange' is French for 'mixture'. Mélange fabrics are coloured at the fibre stage.

Mélange yarns are made by colour-printing the fibres while they are in combed sliver or tops form. Bands of thickened dye paste are printed at intervals across the fibre slubbings by a process called 'vigoureux printing' or 'mélange printing'. After steaming and washing, the printed fibres are subsequently spun into yarn. A very even blend of dyed and undyed fibres is produced by this method. For example, if black has been printed onto undyed fibre, a grey yarn will result.[10] Mélange yarns differ from mixture yarns, since the individual fibres are of more than one colour. The yarns may be composed of any number of contrasting colours that, when knitted or woven into fabrics, will produce subtle multicoloured effects. Many tweed fabrics, such as Shetland tweed, are mélange fabrics.

See also DYED FABRICS, MÉLANGE LUSTRE FABRIC, SHETLAND TWEED, TWEED.

End uses: all kinds of fashion and furnishing products.

MÉLANGE LUSTRE FABRIC A woven fabric made from (usually worsted) wool or fine cashmere yarns; it is woven with a lustrous mélange weft yarn, producing a subtle mixed colour effect. Mélange lustre fabric belongs to the group of fabrics known as 'Bradford lustre fabrics'.

The fibres for the weft yarns are printed in different colours while in combed sliver or tops form. The fabric is usually woven in plain weave or twill weave, and afterwards it is given a special finishing process that accentuates the effect of the mélange weft yarns and brings out their natural lustre.

See also BRADFORD LUSTRE FABRICS, MÉLANGE FABRIC.

End uses: lightweight suiting fabrics.

MELROSE (*obs.*) A woven fabric made with a silk warp and a wool weft and woven in a double twill weave. It was first woven in Melrose, Scotland, in the 18th century.[9, 36]

MELTON A thick, firm, heavy woven fabric that is traditionally made in wool. It is given a special finish that makes it into a felted fabric. It therefore has a characteristic dull, felt-like appearance, with a short, dense, non-directional nap. It does not fray.

Melton is woven in a wide range of different weights and qualities, but the best qualities are made entirely from wool that is of merino quality. Most melton fabrics are woven in the traditional manner, using wool in both the warp and weft. Cheaper versions include a union fabric woven with a cotton warp and a woollen weft, and fabrics woven with wool/man-made fibre blends. Melton is traditionally woven in a broken 2/2 twill weave structure,[26] but sometimes also in 2/2 twill, plain weave, or in other simple weave structures. Some melton fabrics, especially the heavyweight qualities, are sometimes also woven as double cloth fabrics.

melton
(broken 2/2 twill)

melton

melton (meltonette)

merino fabric

During finishing, melton is heavily milled, raised and closely sheared on both sides of the fabric. This compacts the fabric, prevents fraying and gives the fabric a smooth, felted surface with little or no lustre. In a well-made melton fabric, the short, dense nap produced by the finish will completely obscure both the yarns and the weave structure underneath. Melton may be yarn-dyed or piece-dyed but is usually available only in solid colours.

An example of a typical melton fabric construction is 160 to 95 tex warp sett at 10 to 14 ends per cm and 160 to 95 tex weft woven at 10 to 14 picks per cm in the loom. After finishing, contraction is approximately 35% in the width and 25% in the length.[26] Admiralty cloth is the name given to a particularly heavy type of melton fabric that was originally used for the uniforms and coats of British naval officers.[9] A cheaper, heavy-weight melton fabric is woven with a two-fold cotton warp and a thick woollen weft; this is sometimes called 'leather cloth',[16] presumably because the finish gives the fabric a leather-like or suede-like handle. The term 'meltonette' is sometimes given to lighter-weight melton fabrics, which are normally used for women's suits and coats.

The name 'melton' comes from Melton Mowbray in Leicestershire, England, where the fabric originated.[3] Melton is most similar to kersey, but it is smoother and lighter in weight. It is also similar to box cloth, woollen broadcloth, buffalo check, duffel, flannel, frieze and pilot cloth.

See also COATING FABRIC, DOUBLE CLOTH, FELTED FABRIC, NAPPED FABRICS, TWILL FABRICS, UNION FABRIC.

End uses: coats, military uniforms, jackets, horse-riding jackets, and in tailoring for lining the undersides of collars.

MELTONETTE *see* MELTON.

MERINO FABRIC A general term for a range of light- to medium-weight, good-quality woven fabrics that are made from fine merino wool.

Merino wool comes from the merino breed of sheep; it originated in Spain and is noted for its fineness and whiteness. Merino wool in tops, yarn and fabric form is sometimes also called 'botany wool'. Merino fabric may be made in a variety of different weights and qualities, but two classic merino fabrics are as follows:
• A plain-back worsted fabric, made from fine merino wool yarns, with 23 to 28 tex warp and 17 to 22 tex weft. A plain-back fabric is a weave structure that has a twill face and a plain weave back. It is woven with fine singles worsted yarns. This fabric was developed in England in the 1820s.[25]
• French merino, a fabric made using fine botany wool yarns in both the warp and the weft, with 15 tex botany warp sett at 24 ends per cm and 11 tex botany weft woven at 76 picks per cm. The fabric is woven in a 2/2 twill weave structure. Because of the ratio of ends to picks, the twill runs at a very flat angle in the fabric, with the weft predominating on the face. It is an example of a 'reclining twill' fabric.[26]

See also TWILL FABRICS, WOOL FABRIC.

End uses: men's and women's suiting fabrics, dress fabrics, blouses, shawls and scarves.

MERVEILLEUX (*obs.*) A woven fabric made in all silk (net silk), silk and cotton, or viscose. It is woven in a satin weave with a twill back and is used as a lining fabric for men's outerwear. The name comes from the French for 'marvellous'.[9, 17, 36]

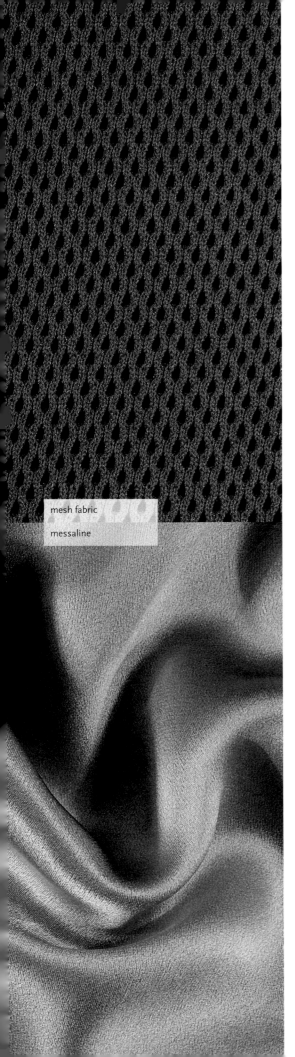

mesh fabric

messaline

MESH FABRICS A general term given to a wide range of fabrics, knitted, woven or lace, that have an open mesh structure characterized by holes or spaces between the yarns used in their construction. This allows air to pass through the fabric, making it cool and comfortable to wear next to the skin.

Mesh fabrics may be made using various knitted, woven or lace constructions, although the term is probably used more for knitted and lace fabrics. (Similar woven fabrics are more likely to be described as 'cellular fabrics.) Any natural or man-made yarns may be used, but common examples include nylon, polyester or polyester/cotton mixes and cotton, all of which give the mesh structure a clear definition. Knitted mesh fabrics are mostly warp-knitted fabrics, which may be made on either raschel or tricot warp-knitting machines. They are usually knitted using two guide bars with part-set threading to produce the holes. The constructions are based on either modified atlas structures or pillar and inlay techniques (*see* ATLAS, WARP-KNITTED; LAID-IN FABRIC). The holes may be made in a wide variety of shapes and sizes. Examples of mesh fabrics include fishnet, lace, knitted lace (*see* LACE, KNITTED), marquisette (warp-knitted), net (warp-knitted), piqué (warp-knitted and weft-knitted), power net, raschel lace, straw fabrics and tulle (warp-knitted).

See also CELLULAR FABRIC, KNITTED FABRIC, WARP-KNITTED FABRIC.

End uses: sportswear, sports shirts, linings, curtains, automotive fabrics, fishing nets, vegetable bags, safety nets, nets for crop protection, industrial textiles and geotextiles.

MESSALINE A highly lustrous, lightweight woven fabric, constructed in satin weave and traditionally made from soft, fine silk yarns. It is a very soft, luxurious fabric with excellent drape, but it frays easily.

As well as the more expensive silk yarns, messaline is also woven with other continuous filament yarns, such as polyester, acetate and triacetate. It is usually woven in a closely sett, 5-end warp-faced satin weave. When woven in silk, two-fold organzine yarns are used in the warp, and three-fold tram yarns in the weft.[17] It is usually woven in plain colours. Messaline is named after Messalina, the third wife of the Roman emperor Claudius, who was fond of wearing this type of silk fabric.[2] It was later woven in France from the end of the 19th century.[5] Messaline is a very similar fabric to peau de cygne.

See also SATIN, WOVEN; SILK FABRIC.

End uses: ladies' evening wear, dresses, gowns and lingerie.

MESSELLAWNY (*obs.*) A 17th-century woollen fabric of unknown construction.[36]

METALLIC FABRICS A general term for any fabrics that have metal as a component. Metal may be integrated into a fabric in a number of different ways: fabrics may have metallic yarns knitted or woven into them or embroidered onto them, for example, or they may have metallic particles deposited onto them. Any type of metal may be used. For decorative applications, aluminium is probably the most frequently used metal since it is economical and light in weight. Occasionally gold and silver may also be used. For some fabrics, including many technical textiles, fine metal yarns or fibres (often steel) are added to provide extra strength.

One way of constructing metallic fabrics is by using metal yarns. The metal yarns employed for decorative textiles are usually highly lustrous. When included as part of the fabric construction, they produce a glittering or sparkling effect in the fabric. Woven, knitted or embroidered fabrics may be constructed using metal yarns. The fabrics produced are usually fine, costly fabrics that are typically used for glamorous evening wear. Lamé is an example of a fabric that is made from metallic yarns (*see* LAMÉ). There are a number of different types of metallic yarns, the most common of which are as follows.

metallic fabric (89% man-made; 11% metal added for strength)

metallic fabric (decorative)

(i) *Flat metal yarns*. These yarns take the form of paper-thin continuous lengths of (usually lustrous) metal strip. An example of this type is the single metal yarn found in banknotes. It is also possible to insert twist into flat metal yarns in order to vary the light reflection properties for decorative effect.[25]

(ii) *Metal fibres or filaments*. Metal may be made into fibres or filaments that are even finer than flat metal yarns. These may then be used individually in a fabric, in groups of two or more fibres together, or in combination with other types of textile fibre.[25]

(iii) *Plastic-coated metal yarns*. Flat metal yarns may be coated or laminated with a transparent or coloured film made from materials such as viscose, acetate, butyrate or polyester.[25] A thin sheet of metal foil is laminated between two layers of plastic film, which prevents the metal from tarnishing. This may then be cut into fine yarns of any width.[26] An example of a plastic-coated metal yarn is Lurex®. Lurex® is the brand name of a fine aluminium yarn that is coated on both sides with a thermoplastic resin in a variety of different colours.[2]

(iv) *Metal-coated plastic yarns*. Metal particles may be attached to yarn fibres by chemical means, by electric arc or by adhesive.[25]

(v) *Metal-covered core yarn*. A core yarn, usually of man-made fibre, is covered with a metal strip by wrapping.

The use of metallic particles is another way of constructing metallic fabrics. Fabrics made from any fibre types may be given a special finish whereby metallic particles are deposited or applied onto them in the form of a coating. Any metal that flakes may be used to make metallic particles, but aluminium is most frequently used owing to its light weight and comparatively low cost. There are a number of different ways to deposit metallic particles onto a fabric. The most common of these are as follows:

- By chemical means.
- By printing. Metallic particles may be mixed into a printing paste and printed on to a fabric.
- By electric arc.
- By plasma treatment. This is an electrical discharge treatment carried out under vacuum.
- By lamination using an adhesive. Thin metal films may also be laminated onto another fabric with adhesive for the purposes of insulation or light reflection.
- By spraying. Metallic particles, usually dispersed in a resin, are sprayed onto the fabric surface.

Metal-coated or reflective lining fabrics are fabrics that have had metallic particles sprayed onto them during finishing. They are used to line the inside of garments, usually for protective wear.[7] Fabrics may also be insulated by back-coating them with aluminium metal flakes. These fabrics are used mainly as curtain linings. They are heat-insulating but breathable, reflective fabrics that keep out the cold in winter and the heat in summer. MILIUM® fabric is the brand name of such a fabric.[2, 3] Sequinned fabrics and holographic fabrics also sometimes use components made from metal.

See also COATED FABRIC, EMBROIDERED FABRICS, HOLOGRAPHIC FABRICS, LAMÉ, LAMINATED FABRIC, SEQUINNED FABRICS.

End uses: ladies' evening wear, ball gowns, boleros, fancy dress, theatrical costumes, saris, knitted sweaters, tops, curtain linings, insulation materials, protective wear (e.g. jackets for emergency services personnel) and industrial textiles.

METZ CORD *see* CORD FABRICS.

MEXICAIN (mexicaine) (*obs.*) A colour-woven fabric, traditionally made from silk, that has coloured vertical stripes alternating with stripes figured with small-scale patterns made with extra warp yarns. The stripes are of equal width, as in a pekin fabric. It was originally woven in France.[1, 36]

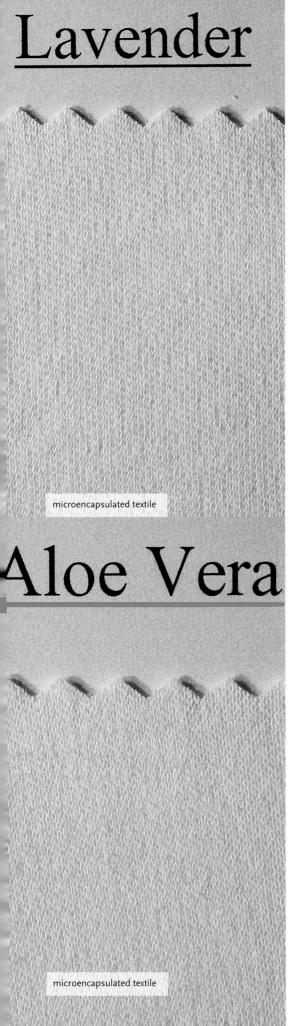

Lavender

microencapsulated textile

Aloe Vera

microencapsulated textile

MICROENCAPSULATED TEXTILES Textiles given a variety of special features by the process of microencapsulation. Fabrics may be dyed, printed, impregnated or coated with microcapsules (tiny, microscopic capsules) containing various liquids, solids, liquid dispersions or gases. Microcapsules containing any of these may also be manufactured as an inherent component within the structure of man-made fibres.

The microcapsules act as minute containers for a wide range of substances. They are so small that approximately one thousand microcapsules could fit onto a single pinhead. Microcapsule coverings may be made from gelatin, ethyl cellulose, yeast cells, polyamide or polyester, and they may be hard or soft. Soft microcapsules are made to contain substances that are intended to be released gradually over time. The capsules gradually break during use, when touched or under pressure. Hard microcapsules are used to protect substances that are intended to remain intact, such as the phase-change materials discussed below.

Microencapsulation is used for a wide range of applications; some of the most important are as follows.[41]

(i) *Dyeing and printing.* Microencapsulation in dyeing and printing is used to obtain various novel colour effects on fabrics. For example, disperse dyes contained in water-insoluble wax or resin microcapsules may be used in dyeing and printing processes to achieve speckled colour effects. Another example is the creation of colour-change effects: microencapsulated hydrochromic dyes change colour on exposure to water, and are used in swimwear; microencapsulated piezochromic dyes change colour in response to pressure; and some microencapsulated temperature-sensitive dyes are used to coat fabrics in a layer that changes colour (reversibly) in different temperatures.

(ii) *Fragrances.* Various scents, including aromatherapy fragrances, may be microencapsulated. This facilitates a controlled release of the fragrance over time, unlike sprayed garments that may lose their fragrance in domestic washing. This means that the fabric remains fresher for longer. End uses include lingerie, hosiery, socks and novelty applications.

(iii) *Health-promoting finishes.* Microcapsules containing substances such as vitamins, skin moisturizers and anti-ageing creams may be incorporated into fabrics and garments that come into contact with the skin. The contents of the capsules are gradually released and absorbed by the skin.

(iv) *Antimicrobial and deodorizing finishes.* Antimicrobial chemicals or deodorant may be encapsulated. The contents of the capsules are gradually released, eliminating bacteria and keeping textiles fresher for longer. End uses include household textiles, transport textiles, medical textiles, socks, lingerie, shoes and trainers. *See* ANTIMICROBIAL FABRIC.

(v) *Insect-repellent treatments.* Microencapsulated insect-repellent chemicals are used in textiles and garments to provide resistance to mosquito or moth attack.

(vi) *Medical applications.* Microcapsules containing various drugs may be incorporated into fabrics or clothing for the slow, controlled, constant release of medication. Active drugs, microencapsulated in yeast cells, may also be incorporated into items such as wound dressings or targeted drug delivery to specific areas.

(vii) *Thermoregulation using phase-change materials.* A paraffin hydrocarbon-based phase-change material may be microencapsulated into hard microcapsules; these are then incorporated into textiles and clothing in any of the ways described above. The phase-change material is ultra-sensitive to changes in temperature. When the temperature is 37 °C (body temperature) or above, the paraffin changes into a liquid state and absorbs surplus body heat, keeping the body cool. When the temperature drops below 37 °C, the paraffin reverts to a solid state, releasing stored heat back to the body. Thus a constant body temperature is regulated and maintained. The state of phase-change materials may change an unlimited number of times.[42] End uses include ski wear, outerwear, bedding, mattresses and duvets. Other thermoregulated materials include some smart textiles; *see* SMART TEXTILES.

See also HIGH-TECH TEXTILES, NANOMATERIALS, SMART TEXTILES.

End uses: as described above for the various applications.

MICROFIBRE FABRIC (microfabric) A general term for a woven, knitted or nonwoven fabric that is made using microfibres. Microfibres are very fine man-made fibres or filaments that have a linear density of below (approximately) 1 decitex.[25] Because the fibres are so fine, they produce a fabric that is characteristically very strong but extremely fine and light in weight. Microfibre fabrics usually have a very smooth, soft handle and good drape. They are used for a wide variety of end uses that require strong, lightweight fabrics.

Any man-made fibre may be produced as a microfibre, including viscose, acetate, polyester, nylon and acrylic. The fibres may be engineered to have a wide range of specific aesthetic and/or performance characteristics appropriate to their end use. Microfibres may be used in woven, knitted or nonwoven fabrics. Knitted microfibre fabrics may be made into lightweight but warm fleece garments and ultra-fine hosiery fabrics. Closely woven microfibre fabrics can be highly water-repellent but still breathable or vapour-permeable. They are therefore often used in showerproof rainwear garments.

See also FLEECE FABRIC, MICROMESH, WATERPROOF AND WATER-REPELLENT FABRICS.

End uses: raincoats, rainwear, jackets, trousers, outdoor wear, hiking equipment, casual wear, hats, sportswear, tents, awnings, bags and luggage.

MICROMESH A very fine, sheer fabric that is weft-knitted in a special ladder-resistant construction and used for women's hosiery.

Extremely fine yarns made from inherently stretchy fibres such as nylon and silk are used for most hosiery fabrics, in combination with elastane for added stretch and comfort fit. The fibres may be in continuous filament form, or thicker fabrics (e.g. for winter tights) may use a core-spun elastane fibre covered with cotton or polyester staple fibres. Man-made microfibres are also used in the production of the finest fabrics. Micromesh is a very fine-gauge single jersey fabric. An openwork effect is produced by means of tuck stitches in seamless hose fabrics.[38] The tuck stitches occur at every alternate course and, with 3 × 1 micromesh, at every fourth wale. This spacing ensures that the tuck stitches spiral around the leg, reducing light reflectance.[25]

See also ELASTANE FABRIC, JERSEY, KNITTED FABRIC, MICROFIBRE FABRIC, SHEER FABRICS, WEFT-KNITTED FABRIC.

End uses: women's tights and stockings.

MIGNONETTE (*obs.*) A fine, lustrous weft-knitted fabric made from silk or viscose and used for underwear and lingerie.[2, 9]

MILANESE, WARP-KNITTED A fine, lightweight, sheer, warp-knitted fabric. It is a strong fabric that is run-resistant or ladder-proof.

Originally milanese was knitted using fine silk filament fibres, but it may be made using any filament fibre yarns and in a variety of different weights. Milanese fabrics are knitted on a milanese warp-knitting machine (either straight-bar or circular), which was especially designed for the purpose. To make the fabric construction, two sets of warp threads, each contained on a separate guide bar, move continuously in opposite directions to one another. Each set of warp threads is traversed one step with each course, towards opposite edges of the fabric, until they reach the selvedge, at which point they travel back again to the other selvedge. This makes a very stable type of double fabric construction that is ladder-proof. Milanese was originally knitted on machines in Milan, Italy, hence the name. Milanese is similar to warp-knitted atlasbut is a more intricate fabric.

See also KNITTED FABRIC, SHEER FABRICS, SILK FABRIC, WARP-KNITTED FABRIC.

End uses: underwear, lingerie, gloves, dresses, blouses and ladies' evening wear.

microfibre fabric (suede, warp-knitted, face and back)

micromesh

row 8
row 7
row 6
row 5
row 4
row 3
row 2
row 1

3 × 1 micromesh

microfibre fabric (woven)

milanese, warp-knitted

Milano rib (full Milano, face and back)

Milano rib (half-Milano, face and back)

mock leno

MILANESE, WOVEN (*obs.*) A low-quality woven fabric traditionally made from cotton.[25]

MILANO RIB A weft-knitted double-knit fabric. It is a double layer fabric composed of a special rib-based structure. Characteristically, therefore, it is a firm, stable knitted construction that has good extensibility in the weft direction. There are two variations: full Milano rib and half-Milano rib.

Milano is the Italian name for the city of Milan, which has a tradition of producing fine knitted fabrics. Milano rib fabrics are knitted in many weights and qualities, using all kinds of fibres and yarns. Elastane is frequently included to increase stretch.

Full Milano rib is a non-jacquard rib-based double-knit structure that is usually knitted on a modified interlock knitting machine.[31] The machine has two needle-beds. The knit construction is composed of three different weft courses that repeat throughout the fabric. The first row is of 1 × 1 rib, knitted on both needle-beds; the second row is of plain knit structure, knitted on the front bed only; and the third row is of plain knit structure, knitted on the back bed only (i.e. rows 2 and 3 form a tubular knit). Visually this makes a reversible fabric in which courses of small stitches alternate with courses of larger stitches on both sides. The top arcs of the larger stitches adjacent to one another are in perfect alignment, as in a 1 × 1 rib fabric.[38] This fabric is very similar to punto-di-Roma.

Half-Milano rib is a variation of the full Milano fabric. It is also a weft-knitted, rib-based double-knit structure. The knit construction is composed of two different weft courses only, which repeat throughout the fabric. The first row is of 1 × 1 rib, knitted on both needle-beds. The second row is of plain knit structure, knitted on one bed only. There are twice as many courses on one side of the fabric as on the other, and the fabric has a tendency to curl towards the side with fewer courses.[38]

See also JERSEY; KNITTED FABRIC; RIB FABRICS, KNITTED; WEFT-KNITTED FABRIC.

End uses: general knitwear and fully fashioned collars.

MILIUM® FABRIC *see* METALLIC FABRICS.

MILLER'S GAUZE *see* BOLTING CLOTH.

MILLINERY MATERIALS *see* STRAW FABRICS.

MISSION CLOTH *see* MONK'S CLOTH.

MISTRAL (*obs.*) A crêpe-effect worsted cloth woven with highly twisted warp and weft yarns.[2]

MOCK LENO A loose, open dobby woven fabric (usually lightweight) that has the appearance of a leno fabric. It is a type of cellular fabric. The yarns are spaced apart to produce a fabric with an open mesh-like construction with holes in between. Unlike in a leno fabric, however, in a mock leno the warp yarns do not cross one another and the result is a much less stable fabric in which the yarns tend to slip quite easily.

Mock leno fabrics may be woven in any weight and using any type of fibre, although cotton and man-made fibres are probably most often used. The gaps in the fabric are created by alternating small groups of warp yarns with spaces when denting the reed. This may be done in a regular or an irregular manner. This, in conjunction with a mock leno weave structure, produces the open weave fabric. The fabric is often bleached or dyed. Mock leno fabrics include some hopsack fabrics, Java and natté. Some mock leno fabrics are similar to gauze.

mock leno

See also CELLULAR FABRIC, DOBBY FABRIC, LENO FABRIC.

End uses: shirts, blouses, dresses, curtains and dishcloths.

mock leno

Mogador

MODACRYLIC *see* ACRYLIC FABRIC.

MOGADOR A lustrous woven fabric with characteristic prominent weft-faced ribs running in the warp direction parallel to the selvedge. It is a reversible fabric that is traditionally woven in silk and used for men's neckties and cravats.

Mogador is traditionally woven with thick cotton warp yarns and fine silk weft yarns. Less expensive qualities might use man-made, continuous filament yarns such as acetate, viscose or polyester. Mogador is usually a colour-woven fabric woven with striped patterns. It is constructed in plain weave, and the weft yarns are so densely woven that they completely cover the warp yarns to form the warpway ribs or cords. The thickness of the cotton yarns both emphasizes the ribs and gives the fabric strength. The name comes from the Moroccan seaport town of Mogador, where similar fabrics were traditionally made.[9] Mogador is a similar fabric to faille.

See also RIB FABRICS, WOVEN; SILK FABRIC; TIE FABRIC.

End uses: men's neckties and cravats.

MOHAIR FABRIC A general term for any fabric, woven, knitted or nonwoven, that has been constructed, either in whole or in part, with mohair. Mohair is a natural animal fibre that comes from the angora goat (*Capra hircus aegagrus*).[25] It is classed as a speciality hair fibre. Strictly speaking, the term 'mohair fabric' should be applied only to fabrics made from 100% mohair; however, since it is quite an expensive fibre, it is often used together with other fibres, in which case the percentages of each fibre should be stated. Mohair fabrics should not be confused with angora fabrics, which are made from the hair of angora rabbits (*see* ANGORA FABRIC).

The name 'mohair' comes from the Arabic *mukhayyar*, meaning 'goat's hair fabric'.[9] Characteristically, mohair is quite a long fibre that is warm and hard-wearing, with a high natural lustre. It is also a versatile fibre that can be used to make a wide range of very different fabrics. Some of the best-known examples, discussed below, are mohair suiting fabrics, woven mohair coating fabrics, open weave mohair fabrics, woven pile mohair fabrics and knitted mohair fabrics.

Mohair suiting fabrics are lightweight woven fabrics in which mohair is either woven by itself or combined with worsted yarns. Simple weave structures (like plain weave, twills and herringbones) are used and the fabrics are typically warm and lustrous, with good drape. They are used for men's lightweight suits and dinner jackets. Examples of suiting fabrics that may be woven with mohair yarns include brilliantine, granada and Sicilian. *See also* BRADFORD LUSTRE FABRICS, SUITING FABRICS.

Woven mohair coating fabrics are thick, medium- to heavyweight woven fabrics in which mohair is usually combined with wool yarns (typically 70% mohair and 30% wool) or with wool and man-made fibres. They are usually woven in a closely sett, simple weave construction, such as plain weave, twill or satin. Mohair coating fabrics are raised during finishing, which produces a soft, thick, compact, warm fabric with a very hairy texture that is used for coats and jackets. An example of a coating fabric that may be woven with mohair yarns is zibeline. *See also* BRADFORD LUSTRE FABRICS, COATING FABRIC.

Open weave mohair fabrics are light- to medium-weight woven fabrics in which mohair is usually combined with wool yarns or wool and man-made fibres. They are usually woven in a simple, fairly open plain weave construction and brushed or raised during finishing. This produces soft, thick, bulky, warm fabrics with a very hairy texture. They are used for jackets, shawls and scarves. Sometimes mohair bouclé yarns are used, which creates a fabric with a looped surface texture.

Woven pile mohair fabrics are thick, medium- to heavyweight woven fabrics in which mohair is usually combined with wool yarns or wool and man-made fibres. The

mohair fabric (coating)

mohair fabric (suiting)

fabric is woven as a double cloth construction with mohair yarns connecting the two fabrics. After weaving, the mohair yarns are cut to produce two separate fabrics. End uses include coats, curtains and upholstery. An example of a pile fabric woven with mohair yarns is astrakhan fabric. *See also* DOUBLE CLOTH, PILE FABRICS.

Knitted mohair fabrics are usually hand-knitted, since mohair knitting yarns are usually very hairy. They may be knitted in a wide variety of hand-knitted structures, but simple structures are most often used. End uses include cardigans, jackets, coats, jumpers, shawls and scarves.

See also HAIR FABRICS.

End uses: as described above for the various kinds of mohair fabric.

MOIRÉ FABRIC A rib or cord woven fabric that has been given a moiré finish after weaving. 'Moiré' is a French term applied to a finishing process that produces a characteristic wavy, watermark effect on the surface of the fabric, similar to wood grain. Silk fabrics with a moiré finish are also known as 'watered silk'.

The moiré effect may be obtained by two different finishing methods.

(i) In a true moiré fabric, two layers of a rib or cord fabric are placed face to face, so that the ribs of the two layers are slightly off-grain to one another. The two layers are either stitched together or held together along the selvedge. The fabrics are then passed between the two smooth, heavy, heated metal rollers of a calender. The heat and pressure of the calender rollers causes the fabric to become flattened at the points where the pressure is greatest (i.e. where the rib lines of the two fabrics are against one other). Where the rib lines of one fabric come between the rib lines of the other fabric, the threads remain round. The flattened areas of the fabric reflect light differently from the rest of the fabric and this gives rise to the random watermark effect.

(ii) A rib or cord fabric may also be embossed by metal calender rollers with the moiré pattern engraved onto them. This method flattens the ribs according to the engraved design.

In addition, the moiré effect may also be imitated by printing a watermark-style design onto a fabric.

The moiré finish was originally developed for silk taffeta fabrics,[5] but it is also a very effective finish on cotton and man-made fibre fabrics. Moiré fabric is made in a wide range of different weights for both dress and furnishing fabrics. The best results are obtained in fine warp and weft rib structures in which the face threads are very closely sett and the straight threads are hard and stiff.[26] Highly sett filament yarns, either warp or weft, usually form the surface of the fabric. They are usually composed of highly lustrous fibres such as viscose, acetate, triacetate or silk, since these fibres reflect the light well and therefore accentuate the watermark effect. The weft yarns are best if they are hard and stiff, and cotton is often used. If the face yarns of the fabric are composed of thermoplastic fibres such as nylon or polyester, and the fabric passes between heated rollers, the finish will be permanent. Fabrics made from other fibres must be cleaned with great care or the markings may be lost when the fabric is washed. Woven rib fabrics or cord fabrics that are suitable for a moiré finish include faille, grosgrain, poplin, poult, repp, ribbed satin (*see* SATIN, WOVEN) and taffeta.

The moiré finishing process may be modified to produce many different pattern variations or patterns other than the traditional watermark design; some examples follow.

- Moiré antique: a silk moiré fabric with a pronounced irregular effect.
- Moiré français: a striped moiré effect produced by an engraved metal roller.
- Moiré retours: a fabric in whcih the moiré pattern is mirror-imaged down the centre of the fabric. This is achieved by folding the fabric down the centre during the finishing process.

moiré fabric

moisture transport
textile (face and back)

- Moirette: a yarn-dyed moiré fabric that is plain woven in either a warpway or a weftway rib structure using cotton yarns. A typical warpway rib moirette fabric construction is 20/2 tex cotton warp sett at 45 ends per cm and 30/2 tex polished cotton weft woven at 25 picks per cm.[26] (Moreen is a similar fabric to moirette, except that it is piece-dyed while moirette is yarn-dyed; *see* MOREEN.)

See also CORD FABRICS; EMBOSSED FABRICS; MOREEN; PERCALE; RIB FABRICS, WOVEN.

End uses: curtains, upholstery, dresses, jackets, coats, blouses, ladies' eveningwear, men's neckties, linings and trimmings.

MOISTURE TRANSPORT TEXTILES 'High-tech' clothing fabrics developed to transport moisture or perspiration away from the skin of the wearer and through the fabric, either to the next layer of clothing or to the outside air, where it can evaporate. It is this property that makes the fabric comfortable to wear. Fabrics with this characteristic are sometimes described as 'breathable'.

Moisture transport textiles seek to exploit the natural ability of a fibre to 'wick' moisture along its length. Wicking is the inherent ability that all fibres have (some more than others) to transport moisture droplets (water and perspiration) through the fabric to the outside. The moisture is transported along the capillaries running through the individual fibres. Absorbent fibres that naturally attract moisture are called 'hydrophilic' fibres. They are comfortable to wear next to the skin and include all natural fibres and viscose. Non-absorbent fibres that resist moisture are called 'hydrophobic'. Hydrophobic fibres include nylon, polyester and polypropylene. Fabrics made with regular versions of these fibres tend to be less comfortable to wear next to the skin.

In moisture transport textiles, hydrophobic fibres and fabrics are modified to increase their ability to wick moisture so that it can evaporate much more quickly and effectively. This feature is achieved with modifications to man-made fibres and/or with special fabric constructions.

(i) *Man-made fibres*. A range of different man-made fibres have been specially developed to facilitate moisture evaporation more quickly than other natural or man-made fibres. These modified fibres may be used to make woven, knitted or nonwoven fabrics. The modified fibres include hydrophobic (or naturally moisture-resisting) fibres such as polyester, nylon and polypropylene. Polypropylene was the original moisture transport fibre since it is the most hydrophobic of all commercial fibres. These generic fibres may be modified in a number of different ways:

- polymer modification prior to extrusion through the spinneret
- modifications to fibre shape and size at the spinneret to enhance moisture movement along the fibre capillaries
- a combination of the two methods above
- co-polymers or two polymers with different properties extruded as one
- chemical grafting of hydrophobic fibres

In the chemical grafting process, hydrophilic (moisture-attracting) molecules are permanently grafted around the surface of hydrophobic fibres such as nylon, polyester or acrylic. Moisture vapour is then drawn away from the hydrophobic core by the hydrophilic layer and transported and spread along this layer, enhancing its evaporation rate to the outside air.

(ii) *Special fabric constructions*. Fabric constructions that promote the transport of moisture from one side of the fabric to the other are usually made with hydrophobic (moisture-resisting) fibres or yarns on one side and hydrophilic (moisture-attracting) fibres or yarns on the other. The fabrics may be woven, knitted or nonwoven in construction. The composite layers may be integrally constructed; they may be loosely sewn together; or they may be laminates, consisting of two or more layers. The hydrophobic side is worn next to the skin. The perspiration is not absorbed by the hydrophobic fibres, but pulled through

F - face pick
B - back pick

moleskin fabric

molleton

this layer as it is absorbed into the hydrophilic fibres; it then evaporates into the outside air. Such fabric constructions are sometimes called 'push/pull fabrics'.

See also HIGH-TECH TEXTILES, LAMINATED FABRIC, POLYMER MEMBRANE LAMINATES.

End uses: outdoor clothing, rainwear, sports clothing, fleece garments, sweatshirts, T-shirts, thermal underwear and socks.

MOLESKIN FABRIC A thick, dense woven cotton fabric that is very strong and hard-wearing. It is given a special nap finish that produces a smooth, dense fibrous surface, similar to the skin of a mole (hence the name). Moleskin fabric looks like a heavy suede fabric. It belongs to the group of fabrics known as 'fustians' (*see* FUSTIAN).

Moleskin fabric is traditionally made using cotton in both the warp and the weft. The weave structure is a special weave, based on a sateen weave structure, that allows a large number of thick weft picks to be inserted – two on the face and one on the back. This gives the fabric a very high weft sett and produces a very closely woven fabric with short weft floats on the face. This fabric construction is the same as for an uncut cotton vel-veteen fabric.[26] During finishing, the fabric is raised and sheared on the back, which gives it its suede-like appearance. Moleskin fabric is usually piece-dyed.

Moleskin fabric was originally an uncut corduroy fabric,[25] and it was a particularly warm, durable fabric that was made especially for protective work clothing such as dun-garees and trousers. Nowadays moleskin fabrics are also available in a range of different weights, including lighter-weight qualities. A typical moleskin fabric construction is as follows: 72/2 to 60/2 tex cotton warp sett at 14 to 16 ends per cm and 38 to 33 tex cotton weft woven at 96 to 160 picks per cm, with shrinkage in width of about 20%.[26] 'Banni-gan' is an old term that was given to a moleskin fabric used to make work suits for the Staffordshire potters in England.[3, 4] Moleskin fabric is similar to beaverteen but is heav-ier in weight. It is also similar to imperial sateen and swansdown.

See also CORDUROY, COTTON FABRIC, NAPPED FABRICS, SATEEN, SUEDE CLOTH, VELVETEEN.

End uses: workwear, dungarees, heavy-duty trousers, cotton suitings, winter coat linings and casual trousers and jackets.

MOLLETON A heavy, reversible woven fabric that is given a felt-like finish. It is a type of flannel fabric that has a nap on both sides.

Molleton was originally made entirely from wool, but now it is also made from wool blended with man-made fibres. The fabric may be woven in a 2/2 twill[26] or a plain weave structure.[4] Some molleton fabrics are also made especially thick by the insertion of an additional set of soft, low-twist weft yarns in the back of the fabric; these are extra weft or weft-backed fabrics.[13] After weaving, the fabric is heavily milled, raised and finished with a dense fibrous nap on both sides. Traditionally molleton was dyed in pale, delicate colours and used for dressing gowns. A typical molleton fabric construction is 62 tex warp sett at 15 ends per cm and 62 tex weft woven at 17 picks per cm.[26]

See also BACKED FABRIC, COATING FABRIC, EXTRA WARP AND EXTRA WEFT FABRICS, FELTED FABRIC, FLANNEL, NAPPED FABRICS.

End uses: dressing gowns, jackets and coats.

MOMIE CLOTH *see* GRANITE CLOTH.

MONK'S CLOTH (abbot cloth, bishop's cloth, druid's cloth, friar's cloth, mission cloth, oatmeal) A heavy cotton woven fabric that is constructed in a loose, open hopsack weave structure. It is a homespun-like fabric and is thick and soft, with a coarse, rough handle. Visually it has a distinctive dobby woven pattern that resembles a basket construction.

monk's cloth

moquette (cut pile)

Traditionally monk's cloth is woven using thick two-fold carded cotton yarns, but sometimes flax, jute or hemp yarns are used in the weft. Nowadays it is also made with man-made yarns. Monk's cloth is usually woven in a 4 × 4 hopsack weave structure, but it may also be woven in a 2 × 2, 3 × 3, 6 × 6 or 8 × 8 hopsack weave. Because of its loose open weave construction, monk's cloth is prone to snagging, shrinkage and unravelling. It may also lose shape if stretched. Monk's cloth is usually woven in either a natural oatmeal or a brownish-white colour. Sometimes it is dyed in natural colours like brown, blue or green, and occasionally it is printed. It is thought that monk's cloth takes its name from the coarse sackcloth that was once used by monks doing penance.[3] Monk's cloth is sometimes called 'oatmeal' because of its mottled beige colour.[5] It is also sometimes known as 'abbot cloth', 'bishop's cloth', 'druid's cloth', 'friar's cloth' or 'mission cloth'.

See also DOBBY FABRIC, HOMESPUN, HOPSACK.

End uses: curtains and loose covers.

MONTAGNAC A heavy, warm woven fabric that is used for overcoats. It is made with wool yarns or other luxurious animal fibres and it has a curly pile, like astrakhan fabric. It is a soft, lustrous and hard-wearing fabric.

Montagnac was originally made in France. It is woven with wool yarns and often contains cashmere, camel hair or vicuña yarns as well. This makes it a luxurious, high-quality fabric. Montagnac is woven in a twill weave and it has an extra set of weft yarns that float on the face of the fabric. After weaving, some of the weft floats are cut and others are left uncut. It is then brushed to form the long curly pile.

See also ASTRAKHAN FABRIC, CAMEL-HAIR FABRIC, CASHMERE CLOTH, COATING FABRIC, EXTRA WARP AND EXTRA WEFT FABRICS, PILE FABRICS, POODLE CLOTH, VICUÑA FABRIC.

End uses: overcoats and jackets.

MOQUETTE A woven pile fabric that is used mainly as an upholstery fabric. It is a heavy and very durable fabric whose pile does not flatten in use.

There are three main types of moquette fabric: one with a cut pile, one with an uncut pile and one that contains both cut and uncut pile. Moquette is a warp pile fabric, and the pile is usually made with worsted, mohair or nylon warp yarns. The base fabric is usually woven with wool, cotton or man-made yarns in a firmly woven ground of plain weave. To make the pile, the warp yarns are lifted over wires at regular intervals during weaving. When the wires are removed, a mass of loops is formed on the surface of the fabric. This produces an uncut pile fabric. Cut pile moquette is made in a similar manner, but the wires have blades attached to them. When the wires are removed after weaving, the blades cut the pile loops and the cut pile is formed. Cut pile moquettes may also be made on the 'face-to-face' principle, like some velvet fabrics. With this construction method, two moquette fabrics are woven face to face simultaneously. The warp pile ends are interchanged between both fabrics, and these connecting yarns are cut in the middle while the fabric is still on the loom, producing two separate moquette fabrics.

Moquette may be produced in a single colour only or as a multicoloured fabric. It may also be woven with a jacquard pattern. The name is from the French, meaning 'tufted fabric'. Moquette is a similar fabric to frisé, grospoint and terry fabric.

See also PILE FABRICS.

End uses: upholstery, luggage, table coverings and curtains.

moquette (uncut pile)

moss-stitch fabric

mousseline (silk)

MOREEN (morine) A woven rib fabric that is made from cotton yarns. It is recognizable from its prominent warp- or weftway ribs and from a watermark effect that is produced by a moiré finish.

In the 18th and early 19th centuries, 'moreen' was a term given to a worsted furnishing fabric that had horizontal ribs and was given a moiré-type finish.[25] Nowadays the term is used for an all-cotton woven fabric that has a coarse cotton warp and a fine cotton weft. The fabric is woven as grey cloth in plain weave and has either a warpway or a weftway rib effect. After weaving, moreen is piece-dyed and given a moiré finish.

A typical warpway rib moreen fabric construction is 16/2 tex cotton warp sett at 50 ends per cm and 60/3 tex cotton weft woven at 18 picks per cm.[26] A typical weftway rib moreen fabric construction is 60/3 tex cotton warp sett at 17 ends per cm and 11 tex cotton weft woven at 56 picks per cm.[26] Moreen is a similar fabric to moirette, except that moreen is piece-dyed and moirette is yarn-dyed (for moirette, *see* MOIRÉ FABRIC). It is also a similar fabric to royal rib.

See also COTTON FABRIC; MOIRÉ FABRIC; RIB FABRICS, WOVEN.

End uses: lining fabric.

MORNING STRIPE *see* PIN STRIPE.

MOSCOW (*obs.*) A heavyweight woollen overcoating fabric woven in a double plain weave, piece-dyed and given a napped finish. The fabric has a shaggy surface similar to that of Shetland fabric.[9, 17, 36]

MOSS CRÊPE *see* CRÊPE.

MOSS-STITCH FABRIC A weft-knitted fabric that is knitted in a purl-based, moss-stitch knit construction. Moss-stitch fabrics are typically fairly chunky fabrics with a fancy surface texture on both sides. This fancy construction can be knitted by hand or by a special purl knitting machine.

Moss-stitch is a purl-based fabric construction that repeats over two courses. Face and back stitches are knitted alternately in the first course and then reversed in the second course.[38] In double moss-stitch fabric, the structure repeats over four courses. Face and back stitches are knitted alternately for two courses and then reversed for courses 3 and 4.[38] The complex nature of purl knitting machines makes them unsuited to high-speed production, so they are normally used for knitting garments rather than continuous lengths of fabric. Moss-stitch is also often used in Aran garments.

See also ARAN FABRIC, KNITTED FABRIC, PURL FABRIC, WEFT-KNITTED FABRIC.

End uses: sweaters, cardigans, jackets, scarves and hats.

MOUFFLIN (*obs.*) A thick double-faced coating fabric woven in wool or in wool mixed with acrylic or mohair.[2]

MOUSSELINE A general term for a range of fine, semi-opaque plain woven fabrics that are finer and of a better quality than most muslin fabrics (even though 'mousseline' is the French term for muslin). Mousseline fabrics are produced in a range of different weights and qualities, and they may be made from silk, wool, cotton or man-made fibres.

Silk mousseline (mousseline de soie) is traditionally made with good-quality highly twisted silk yarns, but is also imitated with man-made fibres. It is a fine, lightweight, sheer fabric that is woven in plain weave. It is usually treated with size, which gives it a crisp, slightly stiff handle. If the size is applied to the yarns before weaving, this will be more permanent than if the size is applied to the fabric as a finish after weaving. Silk mousseline

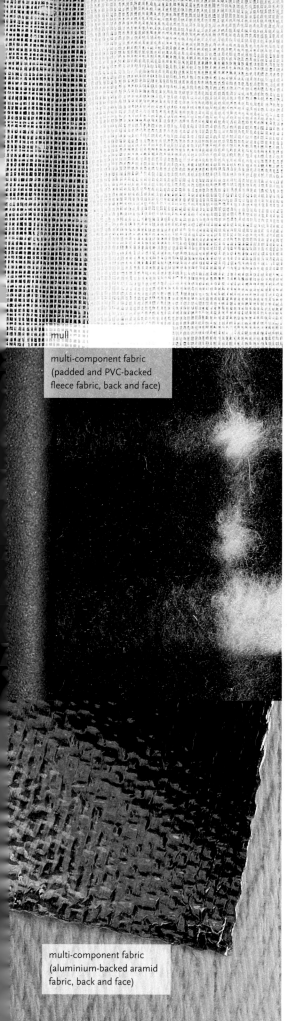

mull

multi-component fabric
(padded and PVC-backed
fleece fabric, back and face)

multi-component fabric
(aluminium-backed aramid
fabric, back and face)

is usually produced in plain colours. It is a similar fabric to gazar, organza, chiffon, organdie and voile. It is more closely woven and slightly stiffer than chiffon, and it is softer than organdie and less soft than voile. *See also* DUCHESSE SATIN, SHEER FABRICS, SILK FABRIC.

Wool mousseline (mousseline de laine) is woven with good-quality worsted yarns made from merino wool. It is probably better known as 'delaine'. The term 'delaine' derives from 'mousseline de laine', which is French for wool muslin. Cotton mousseline was made as a cheaper version of wool mousseline and is sometimes called 'delainette'.

See also DELAINE, MUSLIN.

End uses: (silk mousseline) evening dresses, formal dresses, blouses, scarves, ribbons and millinery; (wool mousseline) dresses, blouses and scarves; (cotton mousseline) dresses, scarves, blouses and shirts.

MOZAMBIQUE (*obs.*) A fine, lightweight gauze fabric woven with a combed and gassed cotton warp and a mohair weft. It was sometimes colour-woven with patterns and checks.[9, 36]

MUDMEE *see* IKAT.

MUGA SILK *see* SILK FABRIC.

MULL A fine, soft, lightweight woven fabric that is constructed in an open plain weave, traditionally using cotton yarns. It is a sheer fabric with good drape and it belongs to the muslin family of fabrics.

Mull is traditionally woven as grey cloth with fine cotton yarns. The weave is normally an open, square-sett plain weave construction, and the fabric usually weighs about 50 g/m². After weaving, the fabric may be bleached white or piece-dyed in pale colours, and it is given a soft finish. Typical mull fabric constructions are within the following range: 6 to 10 tex cotton warp sett at 25 to 31 ends per cm and 6 to 10 tex cotton weft woven at 25 to 31 picks per cm.[25]

The name 'mull' comes from the Hindi *mulmull*, which means 'muslin'; and it was originally a hand-woven fabric from Bengal in India.[3] In the 17th century, mull was used as a dress fabric and it was often embroidered and used for petticoats.[3] Nowadays it has different end uses, such as those listed below. Fabrics similar to mull that belong to the muslin family include: bolting cloth, book muslin, buckram, bunting, butter muslin, cheesecloth, crinoline, étamine, gauze, scrim and tarlatan.

See also COTTON FABRIC, EMBROIDERED FABRICS, LINING FABRIC, MUSLIN, SHEER FABRICS.

End uses: lining fabric, turban fabric, bookbinding fabric and fabric for making toiles.[2]

MULTI-COMPONENT FABRICS (multiplex fabrics) A general term for a wide range of fabrics that combine several layers or different constructions to form a single layer. At least one of the components should be a recognized textile structure. Woven, knitted and nonwoven fabrics may be used as one or more of the components.

The fabric layers may be adhered or bonded together, as with a laminated fabric, or they may be combined during fabric construction. Multi-component fabrics are often double-faced – that is, double fabrics – with a different colour, structure or design on each side, either of which could be used as the face side. Examples of multi-component fabrics include carpet, some double cloth fabrics, flocked fabric, laminated fabric, polymer membrane laminates, quilted fabric, spacer fabrics, stitch-bonded fabric and tufted fabric.

End uses: suits, coats, rainwear, anoraks, sportswear, protective clothing, furnishing fabrics, carpets, floor coverings, blinds, shoes and accessories.

muslin

muslin
(with metallic threads)

MUNGO *see* RECYCLED TEXTILES.

MUSLIN A generic term for any fine, soft, lightweight woven fabric made from cotton and woven in an open-sett plain weave or simple leno fabric construction. There are many different qualities, ranging from sheer open-sett fabrics to heavier semi-sheer fabrics, but they do not normally weigh more than about 68 g/m².[25]

Muslin fabrics are usually woven as grey cloth, but afterwards may be bleached, dyed or printed. They are traditionally all-cotton fabrics, made in a wide range of different widths, weights and qualities, and they are given a variety of different finishes. Muslin was the name given to a variety of plain woven cotton fabrics that were originally woven in Mosul, in northern Iraq, during the 13th century.[3, 5] These early muslins were traditionally decorated with metallic threads. The term 'muslin' has also been used in India for at least three hundred years, and many Indian muslins were printed with gold and silver.[3]

Fabrics that belong to the muslin family of fabrics include bolting cloth, book muslin, buckram, bunting, butter muslin, cheesecloth, crinoline, étamine, gauze, mull, scrim and tarlatan. In the United States, the term 'muslin' is used to describe a much wider group of more closely woven cotton fabrics, which also includes batiste, cambric, cretonne, lawn, longcloth, organdie, percaline, print cloth, sheeting fabric and cotton voile.

See also COTTON FABRIC, LENO FABRIC, MADRAS MUSLIN, MOUSSELINE, PLAIN WEAVE FABRIC, SHEER FABRICS.

End uses: dresses, scarves, blouses, shirts, bookbinding fabric, household fabric and packing material.

NAINSOOK A fine, soft, lightweight woven fabric that is constructed in plain weave, traditionally using cotton yarns. The fabric is often mercerized and in this form has a soft lustre.

Nainsook is woven in a square-sett plain weave structure, using fine carded or combed cotton yarns. Nainsook fabrics are usually woven as grey cloth, but afterwards they may be bleached, dyed or printed. Pale, pastel colours are often used for this lightweight fabric. After weaving, the fabric is traditionally given a soft finish in the UK and a hard, crisp finish in France. Sometimes a novelty version of nainsook is woven with a satin or twill stripe at intervals across the fabric, or occasionally with a satin or twill check. The stripes or checks form slight ridges or cords in the fabric. Nainsook is woven in a range of different weights and qualities. Typical nainsook fabric constructions are as follows: 8 tex warp sett at 36 ends per cm and 8 tex weft woven at 34 picks per cm; and 6 tex warp sett at 44 ends per cm and 6 tex weft woven at 56 picks per cm.[26]

The name 'nainsook' is composed of two Hindi words: *nain*, meaning 'eye', and *sukh*, meaning 'delight'; nainsook fabrics have been woven in India since at least the 17th century.[3] Nainsook is a similar fabric to cotton batiste, cambric, longcloth, jaconet, lawn and percale. Nainsook is not as transparent as cotton batiste, it is slightly heavier and coarser than lawn, and it is lighter in weight than longcloth. Cambric, longcloth and nainsook are often converted from the same grey goods and given different finishes.[14]

See also COTTON FABRIC, PLAIN WEAVE FABRIC.

End uses: bias binding, lingerie, baby clothes, blouses and dresses.

NANKEEN (*obs.*) A durable cotton fabric woven in 2/1 warp-face twill and dyed in drab colours suitable for pocket linings and corsets.[26] It was originally hand-loomed in Nanking, China, from local cotton with a natural yellowish tint.[36]

NANOMATERIALS Materials produced using nanotechnology. The constituent materials are so small that they are invisible to the human eye. Nanotechnology is a new science that explores the concept of restructuring nature's basic building blocks in the form of

nainsook

nainsook (printed)

atoms and molecules, and thus permanently changing their inherent properties. Research has focused on two main areas: the manipulation of existing materials and products, and the creation of new materials and products. This technology is finding applications in numerous areas, including computers, sports equipment, foodstuffs, medical supplies, military equipment, space flight applications and textiles. In the textile sector, research and development have produced innovations of three main kinds, discussed below: nanofibres, nanotubes and nanoparticles.

(i) *Nanofibres.* A nanofibre is a man-made material that can be made from a variety of different existing materials, simply by reducing their size through the application of new production technologies. Materials used include polyamide (nylon), polypropylene, carbon and ceramics. Characteristically, nanofibres are so small that they are measured in nanometres. A nanometre (US spelling nanometer) is a measure of length, signifying one billionth of a metre (or one millionth of a millimetre). Nanosized molecules may be custom-designed to suit specific needs. Nanofibres may be produced in the form of non-woven sheets or as structured webs or mats; they may be incorporated into the surface fibres of standard yarns in order to give both the yarns and the subsequent fabric particular properties; or they may be sprayed onto other materials. These methods, and examples of their applications, are discussed in the following text.

(a) Nonwoven sheets of nanofibres. These are ultra-fine sheets of nanofibres that are extremely light in weight and capable of being folded into very small spaces. They can be used as breathable membranes in active sportswear and performance wear, making the fabric to which they are attached both waterproof and windproof, at the same time as allowing moisture vapour (perspiration) to pass through. *See* MOISTURE TRANSPORT TEXTILES.

(b) Nanofibre webs. Nanofibres may be made into fibre webs that are used as filters. Their sub-micron fibre diameters and the high surface area created make them effective filters of viruses, air impurities, smoke and odours, which are employed for industrial purposes such as dust collection, turbines and heavy-duty engines.

(c) Nanofibre mat. Wound dressings and bandages may be produced from a nanofibre mat, formed of nanofibres made from fibrinogen, a soluble protein present in blood. Fibrinogen thickens blood and increases the stickiness of the clotting blood cells, thus encouraging them to clot.

(d) Nanofibres incorporated into yarns. The nanofibres may be of the same generic material as the rest of the yarn fibres or they may be different. Nanofibres may be given special properties to neutralize various chemical agents and then be incorporated into yarns and fabrics used in protective clothing for industrial or military end uses. Nanoclays are incorporated into synthetic fibres to improve their flammability performance.

(e) Nanofibre sprays. Nanofibres may be sprayed onto other materials from an aerosol. Applications include bonding, lining, repairing, layering, covering and moulding.[34]

(ii) *Nanotubes.* A nanotube is a new material that is intrinsically nanosized. Nanotubes are miniscule, long, thin cylinders that have a hollow centre, thus making them very light in weight. The first nanotubes were carbon nanotubes, discovered in 1991 by Sumio Iijima, consisting of long, thin cylinders of graphite. Graphene is the basic structural element of carbon nanotubes. Carbon nanotubes have a unique range of properties. They are particularly known for their great strength, which is a hundred times the tensile strength of steel, even though they are six times lighter than steel. They are as stiff as diamond; they also have excellent thermal conductivity, and electrical conductivity similar to that of copper, but with the ability to carry much higher currents. They are therefore suited to applications where strength and light weight are desirable. Nanotubes may also be made from other materials, including boron nitride and various kinds of proteins. It is also possible to engineer nanotubes to have a range of different properties by varying the manufacturing parameters. Textile applications for carbon nanotubes include featherweight bullet-resistant uniforms for military personnel and astronauts' clothing.

napped fabric

narrow fabric (Petersham)

(iii) *Nanoparticles.* Nanoparticles are too small to be visible to the human eye. They are usually applied to a textile in solution form, as either a finish or a coating. Because the nanoparticles are so miniscule, they can be applied to the fabric without changing its inherent appearance, properties or handle. Thus fabrics remain soft and breathable. The following text describes their application as finishes and coatings.

(a) Nano-finishes. Nanoparticles may be incorporated into various finishing treatments, which may then be applied to fabrics in order to give them a range of different properties. The nanoparticles permanently attach themselves to the fibres of the textile, either by adhering to the fibre surface or by wrapping around the fibres. Nanoparticles may also be microencapsulated and then padded onto the fabric as a finish. *See* MICROENCAPSULATED TEXTILES.

(b) Nano-coatings. Using plasma or ionized gas, nanoparticles can be deposited in layers only molecules thick over any surface. The particles are so fine that they form part of the molecular structure, creating an invisible barrier that can be water- or stain-repellent or have other properties.

Various properties may be engineered into nanoparticles, such as superior strength and durability, or high rates of absorption that enable them to soak up liquids like sponges. Nanoparticles can also be engineered for superior resistance to liquids, enabling them to repel water, grease, dirt or other spills; such nanoparticles can be incorporated into fabrics for end uses such as protective clothing, workwear, sports clothing, furnishing fabrics, and hospital and catering textiles. Nanoparticles can also be engineered to allow free movement between the different molecules so that stains can be shed readily.

See also CARBON-FIBRE TEXTILES.

End uses: sportswear, performance wear, protective clothing for industrial or military usage, bullet-resistant uniforms for military personnel, astronauts' clothing, furnishing fabrics, industrial filters, wound dressings and bandages.

NAPPED FABRICS Fabrics that have a characteristic raised or fibrous surface texture. This is produced by the finishing process of napping or raising (the two terms are synonymous), where a layer of protruding fibres is lifted from the fabric ground onto the surface of the fabric by brushing, teazling or rubbing. This completely changes the appearance and texture of the original fabric. Woven, knitted or nonwoven fabrics may be given a nap finish. Napped fabrics should not be confused with pile fabrics, where the fabric is constructed so that some of the yarns stand up from the main body of the fabric; *see* PILE FABRICS.

The best fabrics for napping are constructed using good-quality, loosely spun, wool or cotton yarns or multifilament man-made yarns. Most raising machines have a series of rollers covered with a heavy fabric into which bent wires are embedded. These rollers are mounted around a large drum or cylinder that rotates against the surface of the fabric being finished at a faster rate than the fabric is moving through the machine. Many coating fabrics in particular are given a nap finish.

Examples of woven fabrics that are given a nap finish include: (cotton) albatross, Albert cloth, amazon, baize, Balbriggan, Bannockburn, beaver cloth, beaverteen, billiard cloth, blanket, blanket cloth, blazer cloth, box cloth, broadcloth (woollen), buckskin fabric, buffalo check, cadet cloth, camel-hair fabric, Canton (the back), cantoon (the back), cashmere cloth, chamois cloth, cheviot, doeskin fabric, domet, duffel, duvetyn, Eskimo cloth, fearnought, flannel, suede flannel, flannelette, fleece fabric, flushing, frieze, gaberdine, imperial sateen, kasha, kersey, loden cloth, marengo, melton, moleskin, molleton, Montagnac, pilot cloth, polar fleece, polo cloth, pyjama fabric, Saxony, silence cloth, suede cloth, swansdown, some tartan fabrics, Ulster, velour (napped velour), cotton whipcord (the back), wincey, winceyette and zibeline. *See also* COATING FABRIC, FELTED FABRIC.

narrow fabric (VELCRO®)

natté (tie fabric)

Examples of knitted fabrics that are given a nap finish include fleece fabric, laid-in fabric (weft-knitted), loopraise, plush and velour. Examples of nonwoven fabrics that are given a nap finish include blanket (nonwoven), felt and suede cloth (nonwoven).

End uses: mainly coats, jackets, suits and outerwear garments, and fleecy surfaced items including pyjamas and shirts.

NARROW FABRICS A general term for any fabrics with finished edges that do not exceed a certain width. In the UK the maximum width is 45 cm; in the United States, and for tariff purposes in the EU, it is 30 cm.[25]

Narrow fabrics may be woven, knitted, nonwoven or lace in construction and they are made from all types of fibre. There is a wide range of different kinds. Woven narrow fabrics may be woven singly on a narrow loom, or several may be woven together, side by side, on a broad loom. Petersham is an example of a woven narrow fabric; it is made for stiffening waistbands (especially on skirts) and for hatbands. It may be made from cotton, viscose or polyester yarns, and it is usually woven in plain weave, in a firm, stiff rib structure. This is created by using a fine, closely sett warp and thick weft yarns (*see* RIB FABRICS, WOVEN). Tulle may also be woven as a narrow fabric. VELCRO® is the well-known brand name of a hook-and-loop narrow fabric used as a fastening material.

See also LACE, NET.

End uses: ribbons, tapes, braids, belts, hatbands, bindings, elastic webbing, zipper tapes, vertical blinds, labels, pipings, trims, safety belts and industrial fabrics.

NATTÉ A dobby woven fabric that is woven in a fairly open, mesh-like construction with holes in-between. This construction gives the fabric a characteristic basket-like or plaited texture (*natté* means 'plaited' in French).

Originally natté fabrics were colour-woven fabrics, woven with a silk warp and mercerized cotton weft.[36] Now they are woven in any weight and using any type of fibre, although cotton and man-made fibres are probably most often used. The holes in the fabric are created by spacing both the warp and weft yarns apart. Small groups of warp yarns are alternated with spaces when denting the reed. The fabric is then loosely woven in a complex dobby weave structure that is a variation of a hopsack weave. This weave structure is a 'stitched' hopsack weave, which holds the yarns in place much more firmly than an ordinary hopsack weave structure. The yarns are much less likely to slip, and natté is therefore a more stable fabric than most other hopsack fabrics. Natté is also a type of mock leno fabric. The fabric may be bleached, dyed, or colour-woven with different-coloured yarns in both the warp and the weft.

See also DOBBY FABRIC, HOPSACK, MOCK LENO.

End uses: shirts, men's neckties, blouses, dresses and curtains.

NEEDLECORD *see* CORDUROY.

NEEDLEFELT *see* FELT.

NEEDLEPOINT *see* LACE.

NEOPRENE A generic name for a lightweight synthetic rubber material. It is chiefly known for its flexibility and its insulating and protective properties. Characteristically, it has very good tensile strength, abrasion strength and elasticity. It is also resistant to many chemicals and oil, and it is waterproof and buoyant. It is available in sheet form and may also be applied as a coating to other fabrics and materials.

Neoprene was developed in the 1930s. It was originally developed as an oil-resistant substitute for natural rubber. Neoprene is a synthetic elastomer composed of polychloroprene. It is used in fabrics in two forms:

(i) *Neoprene sheets.* In sheet form, neoprene is produced in a variety of thicknesses, and it may be smooth or textured. In this form it is normally laminated between two backing fabrics in a similar manner to foam, but its unique characteristics offer significant advantages over plastic foam materials. The backing fabrics are usually warp-knitted tricot fabrics, often made from nylon or polyester.

(ii) *Neoprene coating.* Neoprene may be applied in the form of a liquid dispersion as a coating to a fabric that may be woven, knitted or nonwoven. It is normally used to give a fabric protective properties, and it may be applied to either one or both sides of the fabric. The neoprene coating is applied to the textile in the form of a fluid mixture by either a blade or a roller. Both the amount of coating applied and the degree of penetration of the mixture are controlled in order to produce different fabrics for different end uses. In some fabrics used for protection against chemicals, for example, the coating will completely block the penetration of any outside agents. In other fabrics – those used for wet suits, for example – the coating will allow controlled amounts of water to penetrate. Neoprene-coated fabric is similar to a plastic- or rubber-coated fabric.

See also COATED FABRIC, FOAM, LAMINATED FABRIC, PLASTIC TEXTILES, RUBBER, TRICOT, WATERPROOF AND WATER-REPELLENT FABRICS.

End uses: protective clothing, including wetsuits, chemical-proof gloves, waders, sports gloves, elbow and knee pads; also orthopaedic supports, protective covers and mouse mats.

NET A sheer, open mesh fabric (usually transparent) that is made of fine yarns, by looping, twisting or knotting them together into a firm construction. Net fabrics may be made by a number of different construction methods, including gauze weaving, construction on a lace machine, leno weaving, nonwoven fabric construction methods or warp-knitting. The various construction methods all produce slightly different kinds of net fabric. *See also* SHEER FABRICS.

Any fibre may be used to make net fabrics, but the most commonly employed are nylon, viscose, polyester, cotton and silk. Net fabrics are made in a very wide range of weights and qualities, ranging from very sheer to very heavy. The mesh may also be made in a variety of different sizes and thicknesses according to the end use. The holes in the mesh may be square, diamond, hexagonal or octagonal in shape. The various types of net produced by different construction methods are described below.

(i) *Net fabrics made by gauze weaving.* A type of net fabric may be made by weaving a fabric in a very open-sett plain weave construction using fine yarns. This is not a very stable fabric construction. A much more stable, open type of net fabric is a gauze fabric woven in a leno weave construction. *See also* GAUZE, LENO FABRIC, SARSENET, TARLATAN, TULLE.

(ii) *Net fabrics constructed on lace machines.* Plain net fabric may be produced in piece form (as a wide fabric) on lace machines. For example, mosquito netting is mass-produced on Leavers lace machines, and is also warp-knitted (plain netting, including mosquito netting, was formerly called 'bobbin net').[25] In addition, the ground construction of most handmade and machine-made lace fabrics is usually a net construction. The bobbinet machine characteristically produces a hexagonal-shaped net mesh. This may be simultaneously or subsequently interworked with intricate thread patterns to form a wide variety of complex lace fabrics. These fabrics may be constructed both in piece form and as narrow fabric edgings. *See also* LACE, Malines, NARROW FABRICS, TULLE.

(iii) *Leno woven net fabrics.* A transparent net-type fabric may be produced by weaving fine cotton or man-made fibre yarns in a leno fabric construction. In leno woven fabrics, warp threads are made to cross over one another in-between the weft picks. This crossing of the warp yarns produces a mesh-like construction with holes in-between. Leno

neoprene (back and face)

net (gauze woven, leno)

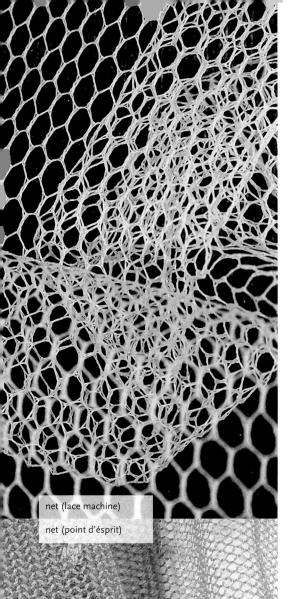

net (lace machine)

net (point d'ésprit)

woven net fabrics may be woven in a wide range of weights and qualities. *See also* LENO FABRIC; MARQUISETTE, WOVEN.

(iv) *Nonwoven net constructions.* Nonwoven net fabrics are made using fibre-forming polymers, in the form of either a film or a mass of fibre strands. The film is embossed with a (usually geometric) pattern while still molten. This produces a mesh structure when the polymer cools and sets. This type of net fabric is typically used for fruit and vegetable bags, garden and agricultural netting and plastic fencing. *See also* NONWOVEN FABRIC.

(v) *Warp-knitted net fabrics.* Net fabrics may be knitted on both raschel and tricot warp-knitting machines. A wide variety of different net constructions are possible using this method, but usually adjacent wales are connected at predetermined intervals, leaving spaces or openings in-between. Power net is an example of a raschel warp-knitted net fabric. Tubular net fabrics are also made on double needlebar raschel warp-knitting machines for fruit and vegetable bags. The bags are sometimes formed on the machine with a closed base and incorporated drawstring top. Mosquito netting is also made on warp-knitting machines (and on Leavers lace machines). *See also* FISHNET; LACE, KNITTED; LAID-IN FABRIC; MARQUISETTE, WARP-KNITTED; MESH FABRICS; POWER NET; RASCHEL LACE; RASCHEL STRETCH FABRICS; STRETCH FABRIC; TRICOT; TULLE; WARP-KNITTED FABRIC.

warp-knitted net

    Point d'ésprit is a net fabric that has small dots of yarns or fibres interlaced at intervals all over it. The dots may be embroidered or flocked, or they may be simultaneously interworked in thread as the net itself is constructed. *See also* EMBROIDERED FABRICS, FLOCKED FABRIC, VEILING.

End uses: bridal wear, evening wear, veiling, ballet costumes, millinery, tights, stockings, net curtains, mosquito netting, fruit and vegetable bags, fishing nets and trimmings.

NET SILK (nett silk) *see* SILK FABRIC.

NETTLE-FIBRE FABRIC *see* PLANT-FIBRE FABRICS.

NINON A very fine woven sheer fabric that is woven in plain weave with either two or three ends weaving as one in the warp and two or three picks weaving as one in the weft. Ninon fabrics are therefore sometimes also called 'double' or 'triple ninon', or 'double' or 'triple voile' (ninon is a variation of a voile fabric). 'Ninon voile' is a term sometimes given to a cotton voile fabric that is woven in this manner. Ninon is a smooth, crisp, lightweight fabric that has good drape but is fairly slippery and frays easily.

    Ninon was originally made from very fine high-twist silk yarns in the warp and a silk weft yarn composed of either two or three threads twisted together very loosely. Nowadays, although the twist is usually the same, the fibres used are more likely to be viscose, acetate, polyester or nylon filaments. If the fabric is to be used as curtaining, polyester is normally used because of its strength, good resistance to sunlight and good washability. Ninon is woven in plain weave with groups of either two or three yarns weaving as one in both the warp and the weft. Sometimes every third warp yarn is omitted in order to increase transparency. The fabric is usually either white or yarn-dyed in solid colours. Occasionally it is printed.

    Ninon is woven in a range of different weights and qualities; however, a typical ninon fabric construction is as follows: 20 dtex warp sett at 130 ends per cm and resultant count 60 dtex/3 weft woven at 44 picks per cm.[25] Ninon is a similar fabric to chiffon but heavier and not as soft. It is also similar to gazar and organza, but softer.

See also SHEER FABRICS, SILK FABRIC, VOILE.

End uses: sheer curtains, scarves, evening dresses, blouses and lingerie.

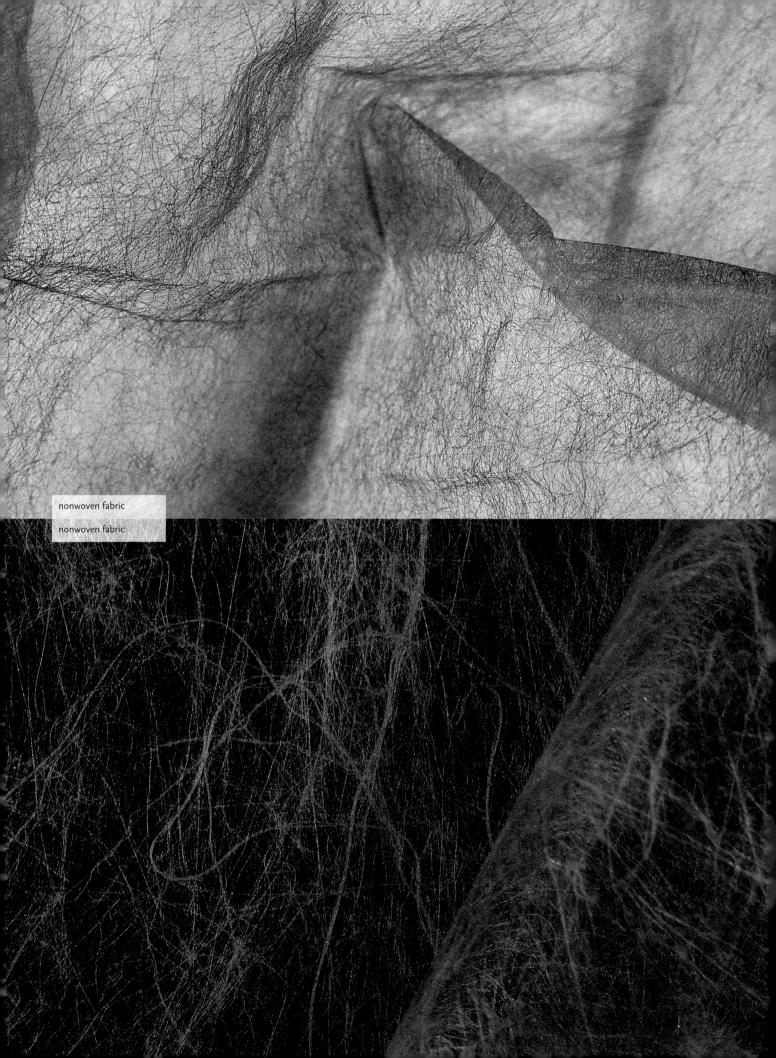

nonwoven fabric

nonwoven fabric

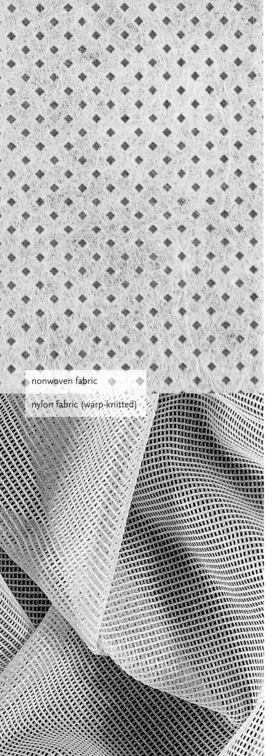

nonwoven fabric

nylon fabric (warp-knitted)

NOIL *see* SILK FABRIC.

NOMEX® *see* ARAMID FABRIC.

NONWOVEN FABRIC A fabric that is formed directly from the fibre rather than being constructed from yarns as woven, knitted, knotted and lace fabrics are. Nonwoven fabrics are typically stiff fabrics with little or no drape. They are usually less strong than constructed fabrics, but they do not stretch or fray and may be designed for specific end uses.

Nonwoven fabrics may be made from any fibre, including natural and man-made fibres, staple fibres and continuous filament fibres. Continuous man-made fibres may be 'spunbonded' together during their manufacture to make nonwoven fabric; however, most nonwoven fabrics are formed from preformed fibres. The fibres are normally laid in a loose web (or batt) and then bonded or interlocked together. This may be achieved in several different ways.

(i) Mechanical interlocking by needle-punching (needling) is one method. Fine barbed needles are punched in and out of a fibre web until the fibres become entangled. Nonwoven blankets and carpets are made by this method, as are some waddings and some very soft nonwoven imitation suede fabrics that have microfibres on their surface. *See* SUEDE CLOTH.

(ii) Mechanical interlocking by high-pressure jets of water (fluid jet entanglement) is another method.

(iii) Adhesives or chemicals may be used (adhesive bonding; chemical bonding).

(iv) Heat (thermal bonding) may be used. Synthetic fibres are often thermally bonded together, using heat to melt the surface of the fibre and pressure to fuse the fibres together where they overlap. Examples of fibre webs bonded by this method include Tyvek, nylon and polyester interlinings, household cleaning cloths and tablecloths. *See* TYVEK®.

(v) Stitching fibres together (stitch bonding) is another method. A web of fibres (often multifilament man-made fibres) is interlocked together by the stitches of a special Malimo machine. Malimo fabrics are examples of fabrics made by this method. *See* MALIMO, STITCH-BONDED FABRIC.

Examples of nonwoven fabrics include: Alcantara®, bark cloth (tapa cloth), felt, interlining, Malimo, net (nonwoven), some stitch-bonded fabrics, Tyvek® and wadding. There are a number of other fabrics that (strictly speaking) are also nonwoven fabrics, for example films, foam and leather; however, the term 'nonwoven' is used mainly for fabrics constructed from fibres.

End uses: nonwoven blankets, carpets, imitation suede fabric, interlinings, household cleaning cloths and tablecloths.

NORFOLK SUITING (*obs.*) A woollen or worsted fabric made in Norfolk, England. It was introduced in the 1880s and used for Norfolk jackets.[9]

NORWICH CRÊPE (*obs.*) A fabric woven in a crêpe weave structure with a silk warp and a cotton weft; it was similar to georgette.[36]

NUN'S VEILING *see* CHALLIS.

NYLON FABRIC A general term for any fabric constructed using nylon fibres or yarns. Nylon (generic name 'polyamide') is a synthetic man-made material,[25] which may be produced in sheet form or in fibre form. It is usually the fibres that are used for textiles.

The term 'nylon fabric' is used for fabrics of all different weights and constructions that are composed of 100% nylon fibres or yarns. Where nylon is used together with other fibres, the percentage of each should be given. Nylon fibres are thermoplastic or heat-sensitive by nature, and they may be used in continuous filament form or chopped into shorter staple lengths and spun into yarns with different characteristics. Nylon fabrics are known for their strength and good abrasion resistance. However, they have low absorbency and can be prone to static build-up.

'Industrial nylon' is a term used for a very strong, stiff, plain woven nylon fabric that is used for overalls, protective clothing and pocket linings.[2] It is also possible to give nylon fibres a range of different properties by varying the manufacturing parameters. Modified nylon fibres are marketed under different brand names.

End uses: sportswear, leisure wear, socks, tights, stockings, rainwear, umbrella fabrics, overalls, protective clothing, pocket linings, upholstery, net curtains, furnishings, carpets, luggage, shoes, outdoor equipment and industrial textiles.

OATMEAL *see* MONK'S CLOTH.

OATMEAL CRÊPE *see* CRÊPE.

OIL CLOTH Traditionally a plain woven, (usually) cotton fabric that is coated on one side with a drying oil to make it water-resistant. This gives the fabric a shiny surface appearance. Oil cloth was one of the first waterproof fabrics, and it was widely used before laminated plastics and other more durable, modern coated fabrics began to replace it. Nowadays similar fabrics are made by coating with synthetic resins, polyurethane or PVC. Oil cloth is cleaned by gently sponging its surface.

Most oil cloth is made from a closely sett plain woven cotton fabric. Traditional oil cloth is coated on one side with a linseed oil and pigment mixture. The pigment may be white or tinted with a colour. The fabric is then given a glazed finish to make it waterproof. The main disadvantage of this fabric is that the coated surface is prone to cracking, which allows water to penetrate. The coated surface also wears off relatively quickly. Traditional oil cloth has therefore largely been replaced by waterproof fabrics coated with synthetic resins, polyurethane or PVC. Teflon-coated fabric is perhaps the most similar to the original oil cloth. Teflon® is the brand name of a fluoropolymer treatment that can be applied as a coating to fabrics to make them waterproof and stain-resistant. Traditional oil cloth is similar to leather-cloth and oilskin.

See also COATED FABRIC, OILSKIN, PLAIN WEAVE FABRIC, PLASTIC TEXTILES, POLYURETHANE, PVC, TEFLON®, WATERPROOF AND WATER-REPELLENT FABRICS.

End uses: raincoats, jackets, bags, waterproof covers, kitchen tablecloths, aprons and covers.

OILSKIN A plain woven fabric, usually made from cotton, that has been thoroughly impregnated throughout with a drying oil to make it waterproof. This treatment makes the fabric stiff and gives it a smooth, translucent appearance, sometimes with a characteristic yellowish tinge. The fabric also smells of the oil used to treat it.

Most oilskin is made from a closely sett plain woven cotton fabric, such as lawn, percale or taffeta.[23] The fabric is thoroughly impregnated throughout with linseed oil, dried and oxidized to make it waterproof. Like oil cloth, oilskin was one of the first waterproof fabrics. It was used as a heavy-duty waterproof fabric for such end uses as seamen's clothing before the invention of man-made fibres and plastics. Although oilskin is still made, nowadays most waterproof fabrics incorporate synthetic resins, polyurethane or PVC. Barbour® is the brand name of a well-known oilskin fabric that is used for weather protection garments.

oil cloth (Teflon-coated)

oilskin

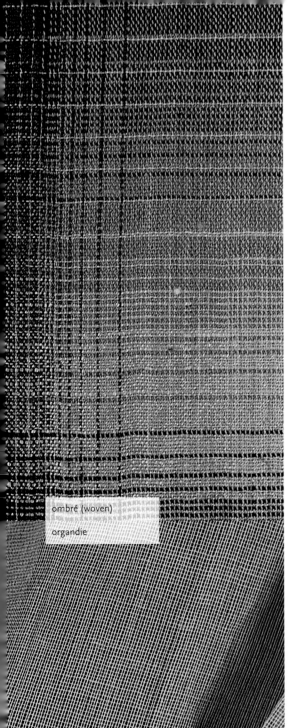

ombré (woven)

organdie

See also OIL CLOTH, PLAIN WEAVE FABRIC, PLASTIC TEXTILES, POLYURETHANE, PVC, WATER-PROOF AND WATER-REPELLENT FABRICS.

End uses: heavy-duty waterproof clothing, including slickers, sou'westers, jackets and raincoats.

OMBRÉ A general term used to describe any fabric, whether woven, knitted, printed, dyed or nonwoven, in which the colour is graduated from light to dark to produce a shaded effect. 'Ombré' is a French word that means 'shaded'.

Then shaded effect may be a gradual all-over shading, or it may be produced using stripes of colour. Ombré patterns may be produced using different tones of the same colour or various tones of different colours. Ombré fabrics can be made in any weight and from any kind of fibre, and so have a very wide range of end uses. Ombré was especially popular on wool challis and cotton textiles in the mid-19th century.

See also DYED FABRICS, SHADOW STRIPES AND CHECKS.

End uses: all kinds of fashion and furnishing fabrics.

ONDINE *see* BENGALINE.

ONDULÉ A woven fabric that has a wavy yarn effect, usually in the warp direction, produced by a special weaving technique. It is also possible to have a weftway ondulé fabric, but this is less common. 'Ondulé' is a French word meaning 'wavy' or 'undulating'.

A warpway ondulé effect is produced in the fabric by a special reed called an 'ondulé' reed. This reed has alternate groups of dents that are spaced widely at the top and closely at the bottom, and vice versa. The reed is continually raised and lowered during the weaving of the fabric, which pushes groups of warp ends from side to side to create the wavy effect. Ondulé fabrics may be woven from any fibres, but the weave structure used is normally either plain weave or a leno fabric construction, which binds the wavy warp yarns more firmly. Weftway ondulé effects are produced by arranging the warp into alternate sections. The odd sections are gradually tightened while the even sections are gradually slackened, and then vice versa. Where the warp is tighter, the weft picks are closer together than in the slacker areas. This causes the picks to form a horizontal wavy effect. Ondulé effects may be produced across the whole width of the fabric or in certain sections only.

See also LENO FABRIC.

End uses: furnishing fabrics of all kinds, especially curtains.

OPALINE *see* LAWN.

ORGANDIE (organdy) A very thin, fine, lightweight woven fabric made from high-twist cotton yarns. It is a sheer, transparent fabric that undergoes a special finishing treatment to give it a characteristically crisp to stiff handle. The best-quality organdie fabrics have an almost wiry handle. Organdie is the finest woven cotton fabric made. It is prone to creasing.

Organdie is made from high-twist combed cotton singles yarns in both the warp and weft. The fabric is woven in plain weave, often as grey cloth that is then bleached white. Although white is probably the most common colour, organdie fabric is also available in a wide range of other colours and also in printed and embroidered qualities. The special finish that gives organdie its crisp handle may be either permanent or temporary. The permanent finish was originally developed in Wattwil, Switzerland, for Heberlein & Co.[5] The fabric is 'parchmentized', or treated with a strong solution of sulphuric acid.

organza

osnaburg

This partially dissolves the surface of the fabric, which then hardens, giving a permanent stiff finish that can withstand repeated laundering without its character being changed.[10, 11] Organdie fabric finished in this manner is sometimes called 'Swiss organdie', and it has a characteristic translucent appearance. Less expensive organdie fabrics are given a temporary stiffening finish by treatment with starch, size or resin. These impermanent finishes will eventually wash out.

A typical organdie fabric construction is 7.5 tex warp sett at approximately 30 ends per cm and 6 tex weft, twisted warpway and woven at approximately 30 picks per cm.[26] Shadow organdie is an organdie fabric that is printed with a pattern in the same colour as the base fabric (e.g. white on white); this produces a shadowy effect in this very fine fabric (see also SHADOW STRIPES AND CHECKS). Organdie is a very similar fabric to cotton batiste and lawn. It is possible to produce all three from the same grey goods, with each fabric being given a different finish.[19] Organdie is usually given the stiffest, crispest handle of all three, followed by lawn and then batiste. Other similar fabrics to organdie include gazar, silk mousseline (see MOUSSELINE), organza and voile.

See also COTTON FABRIC, EMBROIDERED FABRICS, PLAIN WEAVE FABRIC, SHEER FABRICS.

End uses: dresses, blouses, scarves, evening dresses, bridal wear, millinery, curtains and as a stiffening fabric; also often used as trims in small areas of garments (e.g. collars, cuffs, bows and sashes).

ORGANZA A very thin, fine, lightweight woven fabric that is very similar in appearance to organdie, but is made from high-twist silk or man-made fibre yarns rather than cotton. It is a stiff but sheer transparent fabric with a pearl-like lustre. Organza creases easily.

Organza is woven in an open-sett plain weave with high-twist yarns. Originally it was woven with fine continuous filament gummed silk yarns (called 'organzine'), which were first twisted and then folded or plied together in the opposite direction to the singles twist. Silk qualities like this are still available, but organza is also made with continuous filament man-made fibre yarns such as viscose, polyester or nylon. Organza may be white, dyed, printed or embroidered. It is made stiff by finishing it with natural gums or resin. Organza is a similar fabric to gazar, organdie and silk mousseline (see MOUSSELINE). It is also similar to, but stiffer than, ninon and voile.

See also EMBROIDERED FABRICS, PLAIN WEAVE FABRIC, SHEER FABRICS, SILK FABRIC.

End uses: evening wear, bridal wear, dresses, blouses, lingerie, scarves, millinery, curtains, panels and trims in small areas of garments, lightweight facings and linings.

ORLÉANS (lustre Orléans) (obs.) A plain Bradford lustre fabric woven with a fine cotton warp and a worsted weft and mostly used as a lining fabric.[3, 26]

OSNABURG A coarse woven cotton fabric with uneven weft yarns spun from low-grade cotton. Sometimes the weft yarns are spun from cotton waste and so contain slubs of cellulosic matter. It is a medium- to heavyweight utility fabric that is characteristically very strong and durable.

Osnaburg originated in the city of Osnabruck in Germany, where it was originally woven with coarse flax yarns and used in its unbleached state for grain and cement sacks.[3] Nowadays it is typically woven in coarse cotton yarns with uneven, condenser-spun yarns in the weft. Sometimes it is woven in man-made fibres or cotton blends. It is woven in plain weave. There are many different qualities of osnaburg. It may be unbleached, bleached, piece-dyed or printed, or it may incorporate stripes and checks. Blue and white or dark brown and white are traditional colours for osnaburg stripes and checks. The fabric is available with or without a finish. If left without a finish, it is prone to shrinkage the first time it is washed.

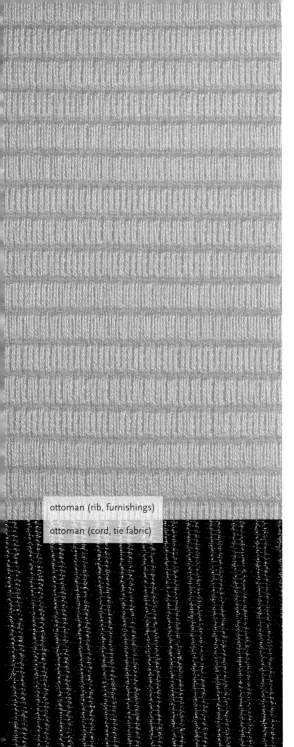

ottoman (rib, furnishings)

ottoman (cord, tie fabric)

A typical osnaburg fabric construction is 37 tex warp sett at 22 ends per cm and 74 tex weft woven at 14 picks per cm (2 ends per heald and 2 healds per dent).[26] Osnaburg is similar in appearance to crash, and it is one of the base fabrics used to make book cloth and cretonne. It may also be used as a sheeting fabric.

See also CHECKS, COTTON FABRIC, PLAIN WEAVE FABRIC, PRINT CLOTH, STRIPES.

End uses: curtains, upholstery, work shirts, overalls, sheeting, mattress covers, tie linings, boot and shoe linings, and formerly bags for sugar, grain or cement.

OTTOMAN A thick, heavy woven fabric that has bold, wide, flattish ribs running either horizontally across the width of the fabric (called 'ottoman rib') or vertically down the length of the fabric parallel to the selvedge (called 'ottoman cord' and traditionally used for tie fabrics). The ribs are apparent on both the face and back of the fabric. Characteristically, ottoman fabrics have alternating narrow and wide ribs. This is achieved using alternate thick and thin weft yarns. Ottoman is typically a lustrous, stiff fabric that creases easily. It is woven in a range of different rib sizes, weights and qualities appropriate to the end uses. Soleil is the name given to an ottoman-like fabric that is composed of narrower ribs than a normal ottoman.

Ottoman is an ancient fabric that originated in Turkey as far back as the 13th century, if not earlier.[3] It was originally woven with a silk warp and a worsted wool weft. Nowadays ottomans may be woven in any fibres, but for suiting fabrics, wool is normally used; for shirts, cotton is usually used; and for other end uses, viscose, acetate, triacetate, silk or cotton yarns may be used. The two main kinds of ottoman, ottoman rib and ottoman cord, are described below.

Ottoman rib has ribs in the horizontal direction, which are made with highly sett warp yarns and slightly thicker weft yarns. Fine lustrous yarns are normally used in the warp, and thick (three-fold to six-fold) cotton or worsted yarns are used in the weft to make the ribs. The fabric is woven in plain weave, and the fine warp yarns completely cover the weft yarns to produce a warp-faced rib in the horizontal direction.

Ottoman cord has ribs in the vertical direction. It is a weft-faced fabric in which the warp yarns are slightly thicker than the fine weft yarns, which are very highly sett. The fabric is woven in plain weave, and the weft yarns completely cover the warp yarns to produce vertical weft-faced cords down the length of the fabric, parallel to the selvedge.

See also RIB FABRICS, WOVEN.

End uses: dresses, shirts, coats, jackets, suits, men's neckties, ladies' evening wear, curtains, upholstery and trims.

OUTING FLANNEL *see* FLANNEL.

OVERCHECK *see* CHECKS.

OXFORD A medium-weight woven fabric made with good-quality cotton yarns or cotton and man-made fibre yarns. It is traditionally used as a casual shirting fabric. It is an inexpensive, soft, slightly lustrous fabric that wears well and has good washability.

Usually Oxford is woven with 100% combed cotton yarns, which may or may not be mercerized. Sometimes a cotton/viscose or cotton/polyester mix is used. The warp yarns are finer and have more twist than the weft yarns. Characteristically, Oxford is woven in a hopsack weave structure with two warp ends weaving as one and a single weft yarn. This is a variation of plain weave. Oxford is a colour-woven fabric that is usually woven with coloured warp yarns and a white weft yarn. When coloured in this manner

Oxford (Royal Oxford)

Oxford (shirting)

it is sometimes termed 'Oxford chambray'. Oxford fabrics may also be made in white or striped with different-coloured warp yarns ('Oxford stripes'). Some also incorporate small dobby woven fancy weave effects. The finishing process gives the fabric a slight lustre, and special crease-resistant finishes are also sometimes used.

A typical Oxford fabric construction is 20 tex warp sett at 35 ends per cm and 30 tex weft woven at 20 picks per cm.[25] Oxford fabric was first woven in Scotland during the late 19th century.[5] The name arose because shirts made from the fabric were often worn by the undergraduates of Oxford University in England, not because it was ever made in Oxford.[3]

See also CHAMBRAY, COTTON FABRIC, DOBBY FABRIC, HOPSACK, SHIRTING FABRICS, STRIPES.

End uses: shirts, blouses, dresses, lightweight suits, pyjamas and curtains.

PADDOCK *see* GABERDINE.

PAHPOONS (papoons) (*obs.*) Plain cotton woven fabrics made with a warp of one colour and a weft of a different colour, so as to produce 'shot' effects.[4, 26]

PAILLETTE SATIN *see* SATIN, WOVEN.

PAISLEY A type of intricate, exotic, decorative pattern that has what is sometimes described as a stylized pine cone motif as its characteristic feature. It is one of the best-known and most widely used textile patterns and is available in a wide range of variations.

From the beginning of the 19th century until about the 1870s, designs based on this motif became very popular as a shawl decoration, which was extensively hand-woven in the town of Paisley, near Glasgow in Scotland.[26] This is how the name arose; however, paisley designs originated in Kashmir, where they have been used for centuries to decorate fine, hand-woven shawls made from soft cashmere. These shawls, known as 'pashminas' (pashmina is a breed of goat), were either hand-woven with jacquard designs or embroidered.[23] The source of the Indian design motifs is uncertain. It could be a stylized version of the growing shoot of the date palm,[23] or it could have been inspired by the cashew fruit with its seed pod, which looks similar to a pine cone and which has been a symbol of fertility and abundance in India for thousands of years.[3]

The original Scottish paisley designs for shawls were jacquard woven using fine, soft woollen yarns. In some designs the pattern covered the entire surface of the fabric, while in others the centre of the shawl was left as a single solid colour. The woven pattern was usually woven into the fabric using different colours of extra weft yarns. Most paisley shawls of this type had a face and a back, and the figuring threads would float on the back of the fabric when not being used to make the face pattern. Some woven paisley fabrics, however, were completely reversible. Nowadays the paisley design has become a classic design motif and paisley patterns are used to decorate many different types of fabrics made from all fibre types and for a wide variety of end uses. However, since woven paisley designs are very expensive to produce, most paisley patterns today tend to be printed onto fabric (usually a woven fabric, sometimes a knitted fabric), which is a much cheaper method of production. Paisley patterns may also be incorporated into a jacquard knitted fabric.

See also CASHMERE CLOTH; EMBROIDERED FABRICS; EXTRA WARP AND EXTRA WEFT FABRICS; FIGURED FABRIC; JACQUARD FABRIC, KNITTED; JACQUARD FABRIC, WOVEN; PASHMINA; TAPESTRY.

End uses: Paisley patterns are used on a very wide variety of textile goods, including shawls, scarves, dressing gowns, dresses, blouses, bags, casual wear, underwear, outerwear, furnishing fabrics and household textiles.

paisley (woven)

paisley (printed)

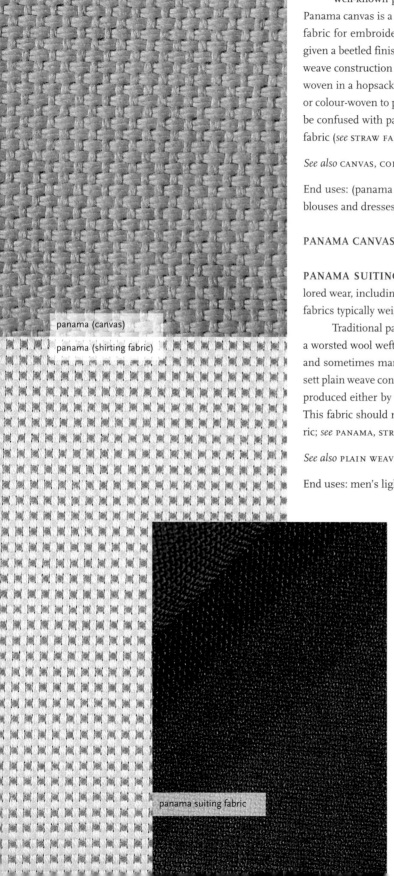

panama (canvas)

panama (shirting fabric)

panama suiting fabric

PALMYRENNE (*obs.*) A wool and silk union fabric with a shot effect.[3]

PANAMA A term used for a range of woven fabrics in different weights and qualities that are woven in a hopsack weave structure. 'Panama' is the term for hopsack weave structure in German.

Well-known panama fabrics include panama canvas and panama shirting fabric. Panama canvas is a cotton fabric woven in a hopsack weave structure and used as a base fabric for embroidery. The fabric is traditionally woven with dyed cotton yarns and is given a beetled finish to soften it. At one time a panama canvas woven in a 3 × 3 hopsack weave construction was used as sacking.[36] Panama shirting fabric is a fine cotton fabric woven in a hopsack weave structure and used for shirts. It may be dyed in solid colours or colour-woven to produce various colour and weave effects. Panama fabrics should not be confused with panama suiting fabric (*see* PANAMA SUITING FABRIC) or panama straw fabric (*see* STRAW FABRICS).

See also CANVAS, COLOUR AND WEAVE EFFECTS, EMBROIDERED FABRICS, HOPSACK.

End uses: (panama canvas) base fabric for embroidery; (panama shirting fabric) shirts, blouses and dresses.

PANAMA CANVAS *see* PANAMA.

PANAMA SUITING FABRIC A lightweight woven fabric that is used mainly for tailored wear, including men's summer-weight suits and tropical suitings. Panama suiting fabrics typically weigh 170–240 g/m².

Traditional panama suiting fabric is a union fabric, woven with a cotton warp and a worsted wool weft yarn. Some panama fabrics are also woven in 100% worsted yarns, and sometimes man-made fibres are included as well. The fabric is woven in a square-sett plain weave construction and given a 'clear' finish. It is usually found in solid colours produced either by yarn-dyeing or by piece-dyeing. It is prone to fraying and creasing. This fabric should not be confused with panama, panama canvas or panama straw fabric; *see* PANAMA, STRAW FABRICS.

See also PLAIN WEAVE FABRIC, SUITING FABRICS, TROPICAL SUITING, UNION FABRIC.

End uses: men's lightweight suits, tailored garments, women's dresses and suits.

PANNE SATIN *see* SATIN, WOVEN.

PANNE VELVET *see* VELVET.

PARACHUTE SILK *see* SILK FABRIC.

PARAMATTA (*obs.*) A fabric with a worsted warp and a cotton or silk weft, like bombazine; it was woven in a 2/1 twill weave, dyed, waterproofed and used for overcoat linings.[3, 4]

PARASISAL *see* STRAW FABRICS.

PASHMINA A very lightweight, soft and lustrous fabric that is woven with fine cashmere fibre from the undercoat (of the neck and belly) of the pashmina goat, a breed indigenous to the Himalayas. This is a luxurious, expensive fabric that is extremely fine, but also very warm. Pashmina has been traditionally hand-woven in India and Nepal for centuries and is used for blankets and shawls.

pashmina (jacquard woven paisley design)

patchwork

Pashmina fabrics may be woven with 100% cashmere yarns, or with cashmere yarns in combination with silk yarns in the weft. The whole process of making pashmina fabric is carried out by hand. The cashmere fibre is collected by hand, and is then hand-spun, hand-woven and hand-finished. Pashmina is usually woven in simple weave structures like plain, twill or reverse twill weaves. It is either yarn-dyed or piece-dyed. More expensive pashmina fabrics are then printed or embroidered.

The most expensive pashminas are jacquard woven with very intricate patterns. It was these patterns that influenced the classic paisley design motifs. The traditional design motif used for jacquard woven pashmina fabrics is an exotic motif that to the Western eye looks like a stylized pine cone. The source of this motif is uncertain. It could be a stylized version of the growing shoot of the date palm,[23] or it could have been inspired by the cashew fruit with its seed pod, which looks similar to a pine cone and has been a symbol of fertility and abundance in India for thousands of years.[3] Pashmina is similar to cashmere cloth and kasha but is softer.

See also CASHMERE CLOTH; EMBROIDERED FABRICS; JACQUARD FABRIC, WOVEN; KASHA; PAISLEY.

End uses: shawls, blankets and scarves.

PATCHWORK A fabric constructed by sewing together many smaller pieces of fabric, usually woven, into a larger overall piece. The smaller fabric pieces are usually geometric shapes that are arranged to fit together to create an interesting pattern. Complex, beautiful patchwork fabrics may be produced. Many are so elaborate that they are used as works of art to decorate walls. Others are traditionally used as quilts for bed coverings.

It is possible to use all kinds of fabric pieces to make patchwork, and historically this has been a way of using up even the smallest scraps of fabric. The fabric pieces are usually selected for their colour or pattern. Printed fabrics are frequently used and fabrics of different fibre types are often mixed together. The fabric pieces are usually cut into simple geometric shapes such as squares or hexagons.

patchwork (detail)

They are carefully cut to size, so that their edges align with the adjacent pieces for sewing. They may be sewn together by hand or they may be machine-stitched. When used to make a quilt, the patchwork fabric forms the top layer; there are usually two other layers, the middle layer being the wadding and the bottom layer the backing. *See* QUILTED FABRIC, WADDING.

End uses: bed quilts, bedspreads, cushions, baby quilts, baby clothes, wall hangings, floor coverings, upholstery fabrics, bags, dresses and jackets.

PATENT LEATHER *see* LEATHER.

PATOLA *see* IKAT.

PEACH-SKIN FABRIC (peau de pêche) A general term for any smooth, light- to medium-weight fabric that has a slight nap and a soft handle similar to the feel of a peach skin. Most peach-skin fabrics are fine woven fabrics that are given a special finish to produce the characteristic soft handle.

peach-skin fabric
(back and face)

peau de cygne

peau de soie

peau d'ange

Peach-skin fabrics may be woven in silk, cotton, polyester or other man-made fibres. Most peach-skin fabrics are woven in a simple weave structure, such as a plain or twill weave, and given a special emerizing finish in which the fabric is passed over a series of rotating emery-covered rollers to produce a suede-like or peach-skin finish.[25]

End uses: lingerie, ladies' evening wear, dresses, blouses and furnishing fabrics.

PEAU D'ANGE A light- to medium-weight woven fabric that is smooth, very soft and highly lustrous; the name is French for 'angel skin'. Peau d'ange is a luxurious fabric with excellent drape. It is woven with fine, soft silk yarns in a closely sett 12-end warp-faced satin weave construction, usually in solid colours.

See also SATIN, WOVEN; SILK FABRIC.

End uses: lingerie, ladies' evening wear, dresses and gowns.

PEAU DE CYGNE A light- to medium-weight woven crêpe fabric that is highly lustrous and has a very soft, crinkled texture; the name is French for 'swan skin'. Peau de cygne is woven with fine, soft silk yarns in a satin weave construction. It is a very soft, luxurious fabric with excellent drape.

Peau de cygne is woven with high-twist silk crêpe yarns. It is usually woven in a closely sett 8-end warp-faced satin weave structure in solid colours. It is a very similar fabric to messaline.

See also CRÊPE; SATIN, WOVEN; SILK FABRIC.

End uses: lingerie, ladies' evening wear, dresses and gowns.

PEAU DE SOIE A fine, heavy, closely woven fabric, originally made from silk; it has a slightly matt or grainy appearance on both sides of the fabric. The name is French for 'silk skin'. Peau de soie has good drape, a dull lustre and a tendency to fray easily. It is sometimes made as a reversible fabric.

Peau de soie was originally made from 100% silk, but nowadays it may be made from synthetic fibres, such as polyester and acetate, and woven to look like the original silk fabric. In such cases the name of the fibre should be stated. The fabric is woven in a modified 5-end or 8-end satin weave construction in which satin floats are produced on both sides of the fabric. It is the fabric construction that produces the slightly dull surface appearance. In 15th-century England, this fabric was also known as 'paduasoy'. It was a silk fabric originally made in Padua, Italy.[36]

See also SATIN, WOVEN; SILK FABRIC.

End uses: dresses, ladies' evening wear, wedding dresses and shoes.

PEKIN (pekin stripes) Woven fabrics with characteristic wide stripes of equal width. The stripes run vertically throughout the fabric parallel to the selvedge. Pekin stripes may be made in different ways, as outlined below.

Pekin fabrics are woven in all kinds of fibres and in a wide variety of different weave structures, although many are woven in plain weave. Simple pekin stripes are made by alternating two or more different colours in wide vertical stripes. More complex pekin stripes are made by alternating different weave structures: for example wide velvet stripes with satin woven stripes of equal width. Other pekin stripe fabrics are woven with shadow stripe effects. This is achieved in plain woven fabrics by varying the denting of the warp yarns in alternate sections: to give an example, one section dented with two ends per dent alternating with sections dented with one end per dent. One pekin fabric belonging to the Bradford lustre fabrics group is an example of a suiting fabric with a shadow stripe

pekin (self-stripe, Bradford lustre fabric)

pekin

percale

percaline

woven in a different weave structure from the ground structure.

See also SHADOW STRIPES AND CHECKS, STRIPES, VELVET.

End uses: both furnishing and fashion fabrics, according to the quality of the fabric.

PENELOPE CANVAS (*obs.*) A cotton fabric with a stiff finish used as a base fabric for embroidery. It is woven in an unbalanced hopsack weave structure. Three ends are woven as one in the warp, and four picks are woven as one in the weft.[36]

PEPITA *see* SHEPHERD'S CHECK.

PERCALE A closely woven plain weave cotton fabric with a smooth, firm surface. It is medium-weight, hard-wearing and washes well. It is widely used as a sheeting fabric.

Percale is usually woven with good-quality Egyptian cotton singles yarns, the better qualities with combed cotton yarns. Some qualities are blended with polyester. It is woven in a plain weave, approximately square cloth construction. Percale may be bleached, piece-dyed in a wide variety of solid colours, printed or used as a base fabric for embroidery. It may be given a matt finish or glazed with synthetic resins to make it lustrous.

The name 'percale' is thought to come from the Persian *pargalah*, a term for a cotton fabric of Persian origin.[3] Percale may be made from the same grey cloth as calico, chintz, cretonne and plissé, each being given a different finish.[19] It is also similar to broadcloth, longcloth, nainsook and poplin, but it is finer than broadcloth, less closely woven than longcloth and similar in weight to poplin.

Percaline is a lighter-weight version of a percale fabric. It is a lightweight, closely woven plain weave cotton fabric with a smooth, soft surface. It has a characteristic lustre that comes from the use of combed and mercerized (usually Egyptian) cotton yarns or a synthetic resin finish. Some qualities are polyester/cotton blends. Percaline may be bleached, piece-dyed or printed, and sometimes it is calendered to give it a moiré finish (*see* MOIRÉ FABRIC). Percaline is a similar fabric to lawn and is used for summer-weight clothes and linings.

See also COTTON FABRIC, EMBROIDERED FABRICS, PLAIN WEAVE FABRIC, PRINT CLOTH, SHEETING FABRIC.

End uses: sheets, duvet covers, shirts, blouses, dresses, children's clothes, curtains and bedspreads.

PERCALINE *see* PERCALE.

PERFUMED FABRICS *see* MICROENCAPSULATED TEXTILES.

PERSIAN CORD *see* CORD FABRICS.

PERSIAN LAWN *see* LAWN.

PETERSHAM *see* NARROW FABRICS.

PHASE-CHANGE MATERIALS *see* MICROENCAPSULATED TEXTILES.

PICK-AND-PICK FABRICS *see* COLOUR AND WEAVE EFFECTS.

PILE FABRICS A woven or knitted fabric that is constructed in such a way that particular yarns stand up from the main body of the fabric. Collectively these yarns form what is

pile fabric

pile fabric (loop pile)

called the 'pile'. The pile is normally composed of tufts or loops of yarn. Pile fabrics are typically thick, heavy, warm and durable fabrics. They should not be confused with napped fabrics, where the fibre is raised up from the surface of the fabric (*see* NAPPED FABRICS).

Pile fabrics may be constructed with yarns made from any fibres, either natural or man-made. Pile yarns may be incorporated into a woven, knitted or stitch-bonded base fabric, or they may be tufted into a pre-made backing fabric. Woven pile fabrics and tufted pile fabrics are discussed below. For knitted pile fabrics, *see* AIRLOOP FABRIC, ASTRAKHAN FABRIC, BOUCLETTE, FLEECE FABRIC, FUR FABRIC, PLUSH, POLAR FLEECE, TERRY FABRIC, VELOUR. For stitch-bonded pile fabrics, *see* STITCH-BONDED FABRIC.

In a woven pile fabric, the pile is incorporated into the actual structure of the fabric. The pile is usually made with extra warp or extra weft yarns that are formed into loops, usually on one side but sometimes on both sides of the fabric. Weft pile fabrics are made by floating the extra weft yarns on the surface of the fabric. Warp pile fabrics are made by looping the extra warp yarns over wires that are removed after weaving. Warp pile fabrics may also be woven as a double cloth. With this construction method, two fabrics are woven face to face simultaneously. The warp pile ends are interchanged between both fabrics, and these connecting yarns are cut in the middle while the fabric is still on the loom, producing two separate fabrics. Some moquette fabrics and some velvet fabrics are made in this way. Whether the pile is made from warp yarns or weft yarns, the loops formed may either be cut to form tufts (cut pile fabrics) or may be left uncut to form loop pile fabrics. Examples of cut pile fabrics include alpaca fabric, angora fabric, Bolivia, carpet, constitutional cord, corduroy, fur fabric, mohair fabric (woven pile), some moquette fabrics, some needlefelts (*see* FELT), plush, terry velour, velour, velvet and velveteen. Examples of loop pile fabrics include airloop fabric, astrakhan fabric, bouclé fabric, bouclette, carpet, chinchilla fabric, éponge, frisé, frotté, grospoint, Montagnac, some moquette fabrics, some needlefelts (*see* FELT), poodle cloth and terry fabric. See *also* DOUBLE CLOTH, EXTRA WARP AND EXTRA WEFT FABRICS.

A tufted pile fabric (or tufted fabric) is made by inserting pile yarns with needles into a backing fabric. The pile is secured during finishing by the shrinkage of the backing fabric, by the opening out (blooming) of the pile yarns and, with some fabrics, by backcoating the fabric with latex or a similar material. Examples of tufted pile fabrics include candlewick and carpet. See *also* TUFTED FABRIC.

Different pattern effects may be obtained in pile fabrics, including the following.

(i) *Carved pile*. Patterns may be created in cut pile fabrics by cutting the pile to different levels.

(ii) *Curled pile*. A curled pile effect may be obtained in loop pile fabrics by the use of high-twist pile yarns.

(iii) *Cut and loop pile*. A fabric may contain areas of both cut pile and loop pile. The tufts and loops may be the same or different heights.

(iv) *Sculptured pile*. Patterns may be created in cut pile fabrics either by varying the height of the pile in certain areas or by omitting the pile in certain areas.

(v) *Shag pile*. Extra long tufts of cut pile are used to create a shag pile. These tufts fall over one another in random directions to form a mass of yarns lying all over the surface of the fabric.

(vi) *Textured pile*. Different textures may be created across the surface of a pile fabric, for example by using different types of yarn.

(vii) *Tip-sheared pile*. A tip-sheared pile fabric is produced by cutting the tips off the tallest pile loops of a loop pile fabric that has been constructed with loops of different heights.

With pile fabrics, all pattern pieces should be laid in the same direction for cutting and making up.

End uses: a very wide range of both fashion and furnishing end uses; also carpets and luggage.

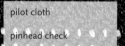

pilot cloth

pinhead check

PILOT CLOTH A heavy woven fabric that is traditionally made from wool. It is most commonly made in navy blue and used for coats, jackets, overcoats and uniforms.

Pilot cloth was originally made as a heavy overcoating fabric for seamen's coats and was dyed indigo blue.[36] It is traditionally woven in wool, but some qualities may contain man-made fibres as well. It is woven in a range of different weights for its different end uses. However, it is usually woven in a 2/2 twill weave structure, dyed navy blue, brown, green or black, and heavily milled and raised on the face side during finishing to give it a dense nap.[36] A typical pilot cloth fabric construction is 200 to 140 tex warp sett at 11 to 13 ends per cm and 300 to 230 tex weft woven at 9 to 10 picks per cm in the loom; the contraction up to 35% in width and 20% to 25% in length.[26] The finish given to pilot cloth is very similar to that given to kersey.

See also COATING FABRIC, FELTED FABRIC, NAPPED FABRICS.

End uses: coats, jackets, overcoats, suits and uniforms.

PIMA COTTON *see* COTTON FABRIC.

PINA CLOTH *see* PLANT-FIBRE FABRICS.

PIN CORD *see* CORDUROY.

PINEAPPLE FIBRE *see* PLANT-FIBRE FABRICS.

PIN-FEATHER *see* HERRINGBONE.

PINHEAD CHECK (pinhead) A small-scale colour-woven check pattern that is typically found in worsted suiting fabrics. The pinhead check pattern is produced in a woven fabric using colour and weave effects.

The small-scale check pattern is formed by the colour sequence of the warp and weft yarns, which are composed of contrasting colours of usually pale and dark yarns, in conjunction with the weave structure. Any contrasting colours may be used, but a common example is navy blue and white. To use this colour combination as an example, navy blue and white yarns are alternated in the warp, and the fabric is woven in plain weave using navy blue weft yarns only. This produces small white pinhead dots that run both vertically and horizontally, alternating with continuous vertical and horizontal navy blue hairlines.[36]

See also CHECKS, COLOUR AND WEAVE EFFECTS, PIN STRIPE, SUITING FABRICS.

End uses: men's and women's suits, jackets, trousers and women's skirts.

PIN STRIPE A woven fabric that is patterned with very fine (pin-width) vertical stripes in the warp direction. The stripe may be printed onto the fabric but more usually is colour-woven. This type of pattern is used particularly for men's worsted suiting fabrics.

Pin stripe worsted suitings are traditionally woven with worsted wool yarns in either a plain or twill weave fabric construction. The fine pin stripes are usually formed by placing single light-coloured warp yarns (usually white) at regular intervals among a ground of darker yarns. The stripes may become partially obscured when the fabric is raised during finishing.

'Chalk stripe' is the term given to a slightly wider stripe, made by using two or three light-coloured warp yarns against a darker background. The effect of the stripe is thought to resemble the mark made by tailors' chalk. 'Morning stripe' is the term given to a wider stripe than chalk stripe. This fabric is traditionally used as a men's suiting fabric for weddings and funerals.

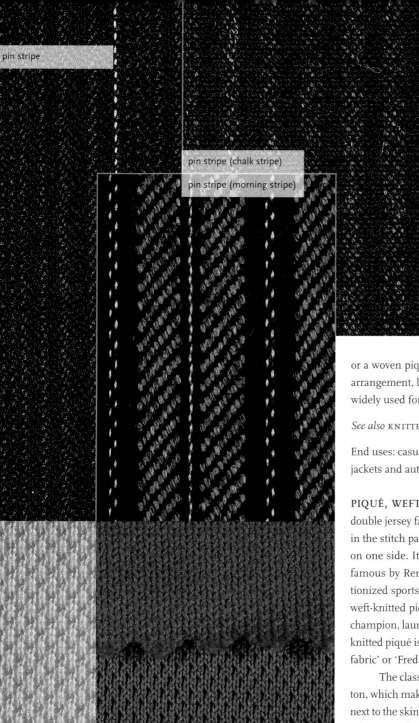

pin stripe

pin stripe (chalk stripe)

pin stripe (morning stripe)

piqué, warp-knitted
(back and face)

piqué, warp-knitted
(automotive textile)

See also PINHEAD CHECK, STRIPES, SUITING FABRICS.

End uses: men's suits, trousers and jackets; women's skirts, trousers and jackets.

PIQUÉ, WARP-KNITTED A type of open mesh fabric with pronounced cord effects in the warp direction.

Warp-knitted piqué is normally made using two guide bars. The sunken lines between the cords are made by omitting one or more yarns from the back guide bar that is making the smaller tricot laps. The fully threaded front guide bar makes the cord laps.[25, 38] A mesh fabric with a diamond piqué effect, similar to a weft-knitted or a woven piqué fabric, is also produced with a similar threading arrangement, but by making mesh or atlas-type laps. This fabric is widely used for football shirts and sportswear.

See also KNITTED FABRIC, MESH FABRICS, WARP-KNITTED FABRIC.

End uses: casual wear, T-shirts, football shirts, sportswear, dresses, jackets and automotive textiles.

PIQUÉ, WEFT-KNITTED A generic term for a range of single or double jersey fabrics that characteristically have small perforations in the stitch pattern, producing a textured or 'piqué' effect, usually on one side. It is a mesh or cellular fabric. The fabric was made famous by René Lacoste, a French tennis champion who revolutionized sportswear by designing his own tennis shirt made from weft-knitted piqué in 1933. In 1952 Fred Perry, the English tennis champion, launched a similar piqué shirt called a 'polo shirt'. Weft-knitted piqué is therefore also known as 'Lacoste fabric', 'polo shirt fabric' or 'Fred Perry fabric'.

The classic piqué fabric is traditionally made from 100% cotton, which makes it a cool, comfortable, absorbent material to wear next to the skin as sportswear or casual clothing. Weft-knitted piqué fabrics can be made on single or double jersey base structures, although most are double jersey fabrics made on a rib basis, using a selection of knitted and float loops to produce the piqué effect. This is a very firm, stable fabric construction, similar to a woven fabric, that may be used for dresses, trousers and jackets. There are many different types of piqué fabric, but the most important, described below, are single jersey cross-tuck, cross-tuck interlock, Swiss double piqué, French double piqué and Belgian double piqué.

Single jersey cross-tuck is the classic polo shirt fabric. It is a non-jacquard single jersey fabric knitted in a double cross-tuck stitch. The knit construction is composed of four different weft courses that repeat throughout the fabric. Rows 1 and 2 are both the same, composed of knit and tuck loops on alternate needles. Rows 3 and 4 are also both the same, composed of alternate knit and tuck loops on the intervening needles. This produces a clear piqué effect on the technical face side of the fabric. There is also a cross-tuck stitch, which produces a piqué fabric with a less pronounced texture. This fabric construction repeats over two weft courses only, knitting alternate knit

piqué, weft-knitted (single
piqué, face and back)

piqué, weft-knitted (single
jersey pintuck, face and back)

row 4

row 3

row 2

row 1

piqué, weft-knitted (Swiss
double piqué, face and back)

and tuck loops in row 1 and alternate knit and tuck loops on the intervening needles in row 2. Variations of both these fabrics can be made by knitting any number of courses of plain knitting between the knit-tuck courses.

Cross-tuck interlock is a non-jacquard double jersey fabric made on an interlock basis. The knit construction is composed of six different weft courses that repeat throughout the fabric. Courses 1, 2, 4 and 5 are knitted in interlock structure on both needle-beds. Course 3 is knitted in tuck loops on alternate needles, on one needle-bed only. Course 6 is knitted in tuck loops on the intervening needles of the same needle-bed. This produces a clear piqué effect on one side of the fabric.[38]

Swiss double piqué is a non-jacquard double jersey fabric knitted on a circular rib machine. The knit construction is composed of four different weft courses that repeat throughout the fabric. Rows 1 and 3 are knitted on all needles on the effect side of the fabric and on alternate, staggered needles on the reverse side. Rows 2 and 4 are knitted in a half-gauge plain knit structure on the reverse side only, on the same needles that have knitted the preceding course.[38] French double piqué is the same as Swiss double piqué except that the half-gauge, plain knit courses (rows 2 and 4) are knitted on the intervening needles rather than the same needles that have just knitted the preceding course.[38] Belgian double piqué is the same as Swiss double piqué except that two half-gauge, plain knit courses (rows 2 and 3, and rows 5 and 6) are knitted rather than one. Rows 1 and 4 are knitted on all needles on the effect side of the fabric and on alternate, staggered needles on the reverse side. The knit construction is therefore composed of six different weft courses that repeat throughout the fabric.[38]

See also CELLULAR FABRIC; INTERLOCK; JERSEY; KNITTED FABRIC; MESH FABRICS; PIQUETTE; RIB FABRICS, KNITTED; TEXI-PIQUÉ; WEFT-KNITTED FABRIC.

End uses: casual wear, sportswear, polo shirts, T-shirts, dresses, trousers and jackets.

row 4

row 3

row 2

row 1

piqué, weft-knitted
(French double piqué)

PIQUÉ, WOVEN A fine, stiff, three-dimensional fabric that has an embossed or quilted surface appearance created by the weave structure. The term 'piqué' comes from the French *piquer*, meaning 'to quilt'. Piqué is dobby woven and is traditionally an all-white fabric woven using cotton yarns. Woven piqué fabrics are very hard-wearing, absorbent fabrics that have a definite face and back. Marcella is an example of a woven piqué fabric (*see* MARCELLA).

The traditional piqué fabric is woven using cotton yarns. Other qualities are also made, in a variety of both natural and man-made fibres. When woven in wool, piqué is sometimes also known as 'waffle' or 'waffle piqué'. Most woven piqué fabrics are bleached white or piece-dyed. Occasionally they are printed. Originally piqué fabrics were fabrics that had rounded ribs running in the weft direction. This fabric is also known as a 'welt' or 'weft' piqué. Nowadays some lightweight Bedford cord fabrics that have narrow cords running in the warp direction are also called 'piqué', 'corded piqué' or 'warp piqué'. Various geometric patterns may be made on the face of the fabric, for example squares or diamonds. This fabric is usually called 'birdseye piqué'.

Woven piqué is a stitched double cloth fabric, composed of one warp of fine yarns and one warp of yarns approximately twice as thick. The fine warp is woven in a plain weave structure on the face of the fabric, while the thicker warp yarns are woven on the back of the fabric in a much looser weave structure. The thick warp yarns are raised onto the surface of the fabric at intervals, which both stitches the two fabrics together and forms either horizontal ribs or vertical cords in the fabric. To emphasize this effect, extra warp or weft yarns may be inserted between the face and the back fabrics: this pads out the fabric, making it more three-dimensional. There is also a range of fabrics woven with small

piqué, woven (weft piqué)

piqué, woven

plain knit fabric
(face and back)

piquette (face and back)

dobby weave structures that resemble the raised, embossed look of a piqué fabric, but they are not true piqué fabrics. Cheaper imitations of the fabric may be made by embossing techniques, using either resin or synthetic man-made fibres.

See also BEDFORD CORD, CORD FABRICS, COTTON FABRIC, DOBBY FABRIC, DOUBLE CLOTH, EMBOSSED FABRICS, EXTRA WARP AND EXTRA WEFT FABRICS, HONEYCOMB, MATELASSÉ, QUILTED FABRIC.

End uses: tennis clothes, sportswear, children's clothes, dresses, blouses, hats, men's dress shirts, suits, waistcoats, curtains and tablecloths.

PIQUETTE A weft-knitted, non-jacquard double jersey fabric based on an interlock structure. The structure is the same on both sides of the fabric.

Piquette is usually knitted on an interlock knitting machine with two needle-beds. The knit construction is composed of six different weft courses that repeat throughout the fabric. Rows 1 and 4 are knitted in interlock structure on both needle-beds; rows 2 and 5 are knitted in a half-gauge plain knit structure on one needle-bed only; and rows 3 and 6 are knitted in a half-gauge plain knit structure on the other needle-bed.[38]

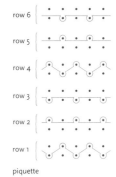

piquette

See also INTERLOCK, JERSEY, KNITTED FABRIC, WEFT-KNITTED FABRIC.

End uses: casual wear, T-shirts, dresses, trousers and jackets.

PLAID *see* CHECKS, TARTAN.

PLAIN KNIT FABRIC A general term for any weft-knitted fabric that is knitted in a plain knit structure. Plain knit fabric is a single jersey fabric that is characteristically smooth on the technical face side and has horizontal rows of loops on the technical back. It has more horizontal stretch than vertical stretch and so fits body shapes well. Plain knit is one of the four primary weft-knit base structures (the others are rib, interlock and purl). Once cut, plain knit fabrics are prone to curling at the edges and, like all weft-knitted fabrics, they can unravel.

Plain knit fabrics may be knitted using any fibre type or thickness of knitting yarn, and a very wide range of weights and qualities is produced. Elastane fibres are frequently incorporated into the fabric to increase its stretch and recovery properties. Plain knit fabric may be knitted by hand, or on any kind of weft-knitting machine using one set of needles on a single needle-bed. It is an extremely versatile knitted structure, and a large amount of plain knit fabric is produced for a very wide range of end uses. 'Stockinette' is an old-fashioned term for plain knit fabric that is no longer commonly used. Examples of plain knit fabrics or fabrics that incorporate this structure in part are accordion fabric, Balbriggan, fairisle, fleece fabric, fur fabric, laid-in fabric (weft-knitted), plush (weft-knitted), polar fleece and terry fabric (weft-knitted).

See also JERSEY, KNITTED FABRIC, WEFT-KNITTED FABRIC.

End uses: T-shirts, sweaters, cardigans, dresses, sportswear, jackets, scarves, hats, gloves, nightwear, children's wear, lingerie, underwear, stockings, tights and socks.

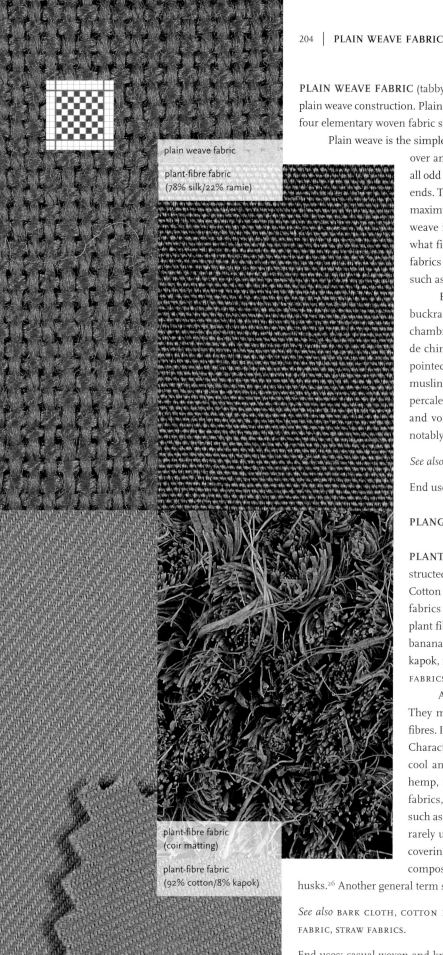

plain weave fabric

plant-fibre fabric
(78% silk/22% ramie)

plant-fibre fabric
(coir matting)

plant-fibre fabric
(92% cotton/8% kapok)

PLAIN WEAVE FABRIC (tabby) A general term for any woven fabric that is woven in a plain weave construction. Plain weave is sometimes also known as 'tabby'. It is one of the four elementary woven fabric structures (the others being sateen, satin and twill).

Plain weave is the simplest of all woven fabric constructions. The weft yarns pass over and under alternate warp yarns, the first row passing over all odd warp ends and the second row passing over all even warp ends. This sequence is repeated throughout the fabric. This is the maximum amount of interlacing possible in a woven fabric. Plain weave is therefore a very stable fabric construction, no matter what fibre or yarn count (thickness) is used. A huge variety of fabrics are woven in plain weave, ranging from very fine fabrics, such as chiffon, to much heavier fabrics, such as canvas.

Examples of fabrics woven in plain weave include batiste, buckram, bunting, calico, cambric, canvas, casement cloth, chambray, cheesecloth, chiffon, China silk, chintz, crash, crêpe de chine, cretonne, crinoline, duck, éponge, flannelette, four-pointed star check, georgette, gingham, grosgrain, lawn, mull, muslin, nainsook, ninon, organdie, organza, osnaburg, ottoman, percale, pongee, poplin, sailcloth, seersucker, shantung, taffeta and voile. There are also many plain weave variations, most notably hopsack.

See also HOPSACK, WOVEN FABRIC.

End uses: all kinds of fashion and furnishing fabrics.

PLANGI *see* RESIST-DYED FABRICS.

PLANT-FIBRE FABRICS A general term for any fabrics constructed, in part or in whole, with any kind of natural plant fibre. Cotton and flax (linen fabric) are the most common; however, fabrics may be constructed from all kinds of different natural plant fibres. Some of the less common plant fibres are bamboo, banana fibre, coir, hemp (*see* HEMP FABRIC), jute (*see* HESSIAN), kapok, nettle fibre, pineapple fibre (pina cloth), raffia (*see* STRAW FABRICS), ramie (*see* RAMIE FABRIC) and sisal (*see* STRAW FABRICS).

All plant fibres are staple fibres that are spun into yarns. They may also be blended with, or used together with, other fibres. In this case, the percentage of each should always be stated. Characteristically, most plant-fibre fabrics used for apparel are cool and comfortable to wear next to the skin. They include hemp, ramie, bamboo and nettle fibre. Like cotton and linen fabrics, however, they tend to crease easily. Some plant fibres, such as jute, sisal and coir, are very coarse and durable. They are rarely used for apparel, but make excellent mattings and floor coverings, for example. Coco matting is one such coarse fabric, composed of thick yarns made from coir fibre from coconut husks.[26] Another general term sometimes used for plant-fibre fabrics is 'grass cloth'.[9, 17]

See also BARK CLOTH, COTTON FABRIC, HEMP FABRIC, HESSIAN, LINEN FABRIC, RAMIE FABRIC, STRAW FABRICS.

End uses: casual woven and knitted clothing of all kinds, curtains, upholstery, blinds, wall coverings, floor coverings, mats, bags, shoes, sacking, tents, rope, string, and carpet and linoleum backings.

plant-fibre fabric
(pineapple fibre)

plant-fibre fabric (jute)

plant-fibre fabric
(45% cotton/55% bamboo)

plant-fibre fabric (handprinted
Japanese bamboo fibre, C19th)

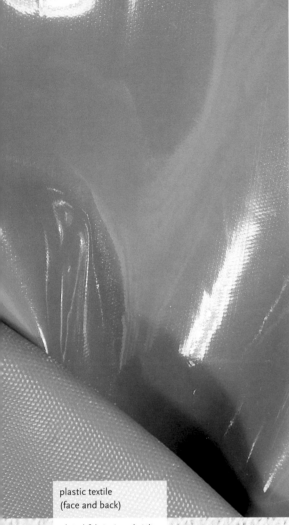

plastic textile
(face and back)

plated fabric (sandwich-
plated, face and back)

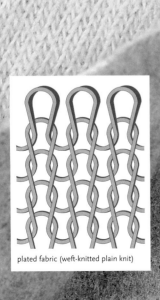

plated fabric (weft-knitted plain knit)

PLASTIC TEXTILES A general term for a range of plastic materials produced from chemicals for textile use. Characteristically, plastics are totally waterproof. For textile end uses, they are usually produced either as fibres or as fine polymer sheets, which can be made in any thickness. Plastics in sheet form are normally used as some form of protective or water-resistant layer. Plastics may also be applied as a coating to other fabrics.

All synthetic fibres, including acrylic, nylon and polyester, are thermoplastic in nature, and some fabrics made from continuous filaments in particular are very similar to plastic sheets. Plastic sheets are made in a variety of thicknesses from different materials. Thick plastic sheets are usually called 'plastic' or 'plastic sheeting', finer plastic sheets are usually called 'film', and extremely fine film is usually called a 'membrane'. The most common plastic or film sheets include cellophane (made from cellulose), vinyl (polyvinyl chloride or PVC), fluorofibre (polytetrafluoroethylene or PTFE), polypropylene and polyethylene. The finer plastic films and membranes are not very strong or stable and may be pulled out of shape very easily. They are therefore usually laminated to, or used together with, other fabrics. It is also possible to coat a base fabric with a thin layer of plastic, for example vinyl or polyurethane. A fluid plastic mixture is applied as a finishing treatment to one or both sides of the base fabric.

See also ACRYLIC FABRIC, COATED FABRIC, LAMINATED FABRIC, NEOPRENE, NYLON FABRIC, POLYESTER FABRIC, POLYMER MEMBRANE LAMINATES, POLYURETHANE, PVC, UMBRELLA FABRIC, WATERPROOF AND WATER-REPELLENT FABRICS.

End uses: (plastic sheeting) shower curtains, tablecloths, inexpensive weatherproof garments and packing materials; (films and membranes) waterproof laminates in all kinds of rainwear, ski wear and outerwear.

PLATED FABRICS Weft-knitted fabrics in which two yarns of different characteristics are knitted together simultaneously. One yarn features prominently on the face of the fabric, while the other features on the reverse.[25]

Any contrasting fibre types or yarn types may be used to knit plated fabrics. The plating yarn is the one that appears on the effect side of the fabric, and the other yarn is the ground yarn or back yarn.[38] There are a number of different variations, constructed as follows.

(i) *Cross-plated fabric*. The two different yarn types are plated so that they appear on one side of the fabric and then reverse with one another to appear on the other side, in different areas of the fabric.[25]

(ii) *Embroidery-plated fabric*. An additional plated yarn or yarns running in the lengthwise direction are superimposed onto the face side of a weft-knitted ground fabric, in variable but restricted areas only.[25, 38]

(iii) *Float-plated fabric*. This is a plated fabric in which the face yarn is floated on certain needles to allow the other yarn to show through to the fabric face.[25] Weft-knitted fishnet is an example of a float-plated fabric.

(iv) *Reverse-plated fabric*. This is a plated fabric in which the two different yarns are reversed on selected stitches within the same course to produce a fancy pattern effect.[25, 38]

(v) *Sandwich-plated fabric*. In this plated construction, the ground yarn is centrally positioned within the structure so that it is not visible on either the face or the back of the fabric. Polar fleece is an example of a sandwich-plated fabric.[25, 38]

Many 'comfort stretch' single jersey fabrics are made by plating stretchy elastane yarns into the fabric structure; *see* ELASTANE FABRIC, JERSEY, STRETCH FABRIC.

See also KNITTED FABRIC, PLUSH, POLAR FLEECE, PURL FABRIC, TERRY FABRIC, WEFT-KNITTED FABRIC.

End uses: all kinds of fancy knitwear, single jersey stretch fabrics, polar fleece and towelling fabrics.

pleated fabric (accordion pleats)

pleated fabric (knife pleats)

pleated fabric (woven plissé)

pleated fabric (woven plissé)

pleated fabric (woven plissé)

PLEATED FABRICS Fabrics in which there are (usually sharp) regular folds or creases, for decorative effect. Pleats may be made in woven or knitted fabrics. They usually run in the lengthwise direction and are extensible in the widthwise direction. Pleated effects give fabrics a three-dimensional quality.

It is possible to make pleats in woven, warp-knitted and weft-knitted fabrics as part of their construction. Pleats made in this manner are permanent. In addition, woven fabrics in particular may also be pleated by a special 'heat setting' finishing process. The pleats are pressed into the fabric using heat in a process similar to embossing. Pleats made in this manner will be permanent in fabrics made from thermoplastic fibres, such as polyester. In fabrics made with cellulosic fibres and cellulosic fibre blends, with the exception of triacetate, the pleats are usually either semi-permanent or impermanent. These fabrics may additionally be treated with resins and cured, either prior to the heat setting of the pleats or afterwards, in order to maintain the pleats for longer. Triacetate fabric, often in knitted jersey form, may be given permanent pleats and thus provides an alternative to permanently pleated synthetic polyester fabrics.

A true pleat is composed of two opposing folds flattened to form three layers of material. The top layer is visible in the garment, above the two other, underneath layers. Some fabrics described as pleats, for example accordion pleats and sunray pleats, are fabrics with crease patterns where the whole fabric is visible.[25] The different pleat effects that may be produced in a fabric are as follows.[25]

(i) *Accordion pleats*. These are narrow, regularly spaced pleats that may be folded up against each other, like the pleats of an accordion.

(ii) *Box pleats*. Two opposed pleats are folded so that they meet on the underside, producing flat vertical layers of fabric that stand proud against the under-layers.

(iii) *Cartridge pleats/crystal pleats*. These have small, rounded corrugations formed by a rotary pleating machine, which has rollers fitted with complementary dies similar to gears.

(iv) *Inverted pleats*. These are the opposite of box pleats. The two opposed pleats are folded so that they meet on the top of the fabric. The extra fabric layers form the partially visible under-layers.

(v) *Knife pleats*. These are single pleats with sharp folds. They lie flat on the fabric surface unless the fabric is extended.

(vi) *Sunray pleats*. These form a radial crease pattern, which is applied mainly to circular, half-circle or quarter-circle skirts.

'Plissé' is a term used to describe fabrics (usually woven) that have small pleats, folds or tucks (*plissé* is French for 'pleated' or 'crinkled'). Plissé is made by the same methods as pleated fabrics: by weaving pleats, folds and tucks into a fabric using special weave structures, or by ironing or pressing them into a fabric using heat. Suitable fabrics from which plissé may be made are plain weave cotton or polyester/cotton fabrics, such as print cloth and sheeting fabric. Plissé may also be made from the same grey cloth as calico, chintz, cretonne and percale, each being given a different finish.[19] In the United States, the term 'plissé' is also used to describe a woven blister fabric with a puckered or crinkled surface created by special finishing treatments, including embossing the fabric with hot rollers.[3] *See also* BLISTER CLOTH, CRÊPE, CRINKLE CRÊPE, CRINKLE FABRIC, EMBOSSED FABRICS. An exaggerated version of a warp-knitted bourrelet fabric is also sometimes known as 'plissé'. *See* BOURRELET.

See also POLYESTER FABRIC, TRIACETATE FABRIC.

End uses: (pleated fabrics) dresses, skirts, blouses, shirts, coats, jackets, bags, trims and garment details; (plissé) casual clothing (including blouses, skirts, dresses, shirts, jackets and beachwear), pyjamas, nightgowns, sportswear, children's clothes, lingerie, curtains and bedspreads.

PLISSÉ *see* PLEATED FABRICS.

plush (warp-knitted, printed, face and back)

plush (weft-knitted)

plush (woven)

PLUMETIS (*obs.*) A fine, sheer fabric made in wool or cotton, and produced on a swivel loom with small, feathery yarn tufts interspersed over a plain background.[9, 17]

PLUSH A term for a variety of fabrics with a long cut pile (of 3 mm or more) that is laid in one direction. The term 'plush' comes from French *peluche*, meaning 'shaggy', 'hairy'. Plush fabrics may be warp-knitted, weft-knitted or woven fabrics.

Plush fabrics may be made using a wide variety of different natural or man-made fibres, or combinations of these. Classic qualities include: a mohair warp pile against a cotton ground; silk and wool or wool blends; and acrylic pile against a nylon or polyester ground. (Seal plush is made with a silk pile to imitate sealskin.) Plush fabrics may be constructed by warp-knitting, weft-knitting or weaving, as described below. They may be piece-dyed in solid colours, yarn-dyed, or printed in a variety of different patterns. For example, some plush fabrics are printed to imitate animal skins. Sometimes they may also be crushed or embossed during finishing.

Warp-knitted plush can be made in several different ways.

(i) A series of pile yarns may be knitted-in or laid-in to a warp-knitted base mesh to form pile loops that stand proud of the rest of the fabric. The pile loops are then cut to produce a plush fabric. If left uncut, the fabric is called 'terry'; *see* TERRY FABRIC.

(ii) A double pile fabric, sometimes also called 'double plush', may be knitted on a double needlebar raschel warp-knitting machine on the face-to-face principle. Two separate ground fabrics are knitted face to face on each needlebar of the machine. They are connected by pile threads that knit on both needlebars. During finishing, the connecting threads are cut to produce two separate cut pile fabrics. Artificial lawn fabrics are produced in this manner.[38] Uncut double plush is sometimes also used as a spacer fabric to provide extra cushioning for car upholstery.[38] *See also* RASCHEL WARP-KNITTED FABRIC, SPACER FABRICS.

(iii) A two- or three-bar fabric can be knitted with long laps (of 4, 5, or 6 needle spaces) on the front bar. This is subsequently sheared and brushed to form the plush.

(iv) Warp-knitted plush may also be produced on a pile sinker (Pol) tricot machine. The pile loops are formed by the yarns on the front bar lapping over the additional sinker. Afterwards the fabric is sheared and brushed to form the plush. This fabric is used mainly for car upholstery.

Similar fabrics to warp-knitted plush include airloop fabric, loopraise and velour.

Weft-knitted plush is produced by knitting one yarn together with an extra 'plated' yarn in a plain knit construction. The extra yarn is made to form extended sinker loops, and may be knitted on every needle or on some needles only to form a pattern. This creates a surface pile of plush loops on the technical back of the fabric. The pile loops may be cut or uncut. The fabric is sheared and brushed to form the plush. If uncut, the fabric is called 'terry' (see TERRY FABRIC). The plated yarn loops are also sometimes cut and brushed to produce knitted velour, and, depending on the yarn used, fleecy effects are also possible (see POLAR FLEECE, VELOUR). Weft-knitted plush is constructed in a similar manner to weft-knitted laid-in fabric, but the loops are longer (see LAID-IN FABRIC).

Woven plush is an ancient fabric that has been woven since the Middle Ages.[5] It is constructed in a similar manner to a woven velvet fabric, but with a much longer, and slightly less dense, cut pile. The fabric is a warp pile fabric, the base of which is woven in plain weave (see VELVET). Woven plush may also be woven as a double cloth. With this construction method, two fabrics are woven face to face simultaneously. The warp pile ends are interchanged between both fabrics, and these connecting yarns are cut in the middle while the fabric is still on the loom, producing two separate fabrics. Characteristically, woven plush fabrics are given a special finish that presses the pile in one direction and gives the fabric a high lustre. Woven plush fabric made from wool was the original teddy bear fabric.[23] Plush is similar to woven pile velour and panne velvet but has a longer pile than either.

Poiret twill

polar fleece

polka dot fabric

See also COATING FABRIC, DOUBLE CLOTH, EMBOSSED FABRICS, FLEECE FABRIC, FUR FABRIC, KNITTED FABRIC, NAPPED FABRICS, PILE FABRICS, PLAIN KNIT FABRIC, PLATED FABRICS, VELVET, VELVETEEN PLUSH, WARP-KNITTED FABRIC, WEFT-KNITTED FABRIC.

End uses: dresses, leisure wear, children's wear, socks, coats, curtains, domestic upholstery, car upholstery, imitation furs, fleecy lining fabrics, hats, trimmings, soft toys (e.g. teddy bears), bed headboard coverings and paint roller covers.

POINT D'ÉSPRIT *see* NET.

POIRET TWILL A firm woven fabric with a steep, pronounced twill weave. It is a soft, medium-weight fabric with excellent drape, and is normally used for tailored goods. Poiret twill is woven with high-twist worsted wool yarns in a 3/1 twill weave structure. It is named after the French couturier Paul Poiret. Poiret twill is similar to gaberdine but finer and smoother.

See also TWILL FABRICS, WORSTED FABRIC.

End uses: tailored goods, including dresses and suits.

POLAR FLEECE A lightweight weft-knitted fleece fabric that is characteristically thick, soft and warm. It is a type of weft-knitted plush fabric (*see* PLUSH).

The fabric is weft-knitted with man-made microfibres in continuous filament form. It is knitted with a loop pile on both the face and the back, produced by knitting one yarn together with an extra plated yarn in a plain knit construction. The plated yarn is caused to sandwich-plate on the surface of both sides of the fabric and thus form the plush surface (*see* PLATED FABRICS). The microfibres of the plated yarn are raised onto the surface of the fabric during finishing to produce a soft, warm, napped surface.[25]

See also COATING FABRIC, FLEECE FABRIC, FUR FABRIC, KNITTED FABRIC, MICROFIBRE FABRIC, NAPPED FABRICS, PLAIN KNIT FABRIC, PLATED FABRICS, PLUSH, WEFT-KNITTED FABRIC.

End uses: coats, jackets, waistcoats, insulating linings (especially for coats and jackets), knitted sweatshirts, tracksuit bottoms and tops, sportswear, hats, gloves, scarves and toys.

POLKA DOT FABRIC A fabric, usually woven, that has been printed with an all-over pattern of small spots in a regular sequence. The pattern is a very crisp, precise one, often with only two sharply contrasting colours. The size of the spots may vary, but most polka dots are quite small.

A fine, smooth woven fabric is usually chosen as the print cloth in order to accentuate the crispness of the pattern. The fabric can be made from any fibre but is often cotton. The dot pattern is usually printed onto the fabric; however, where white or light-coloured polka dots against a dark background colour are required, the pattern is usually discharge printed. Some bandanna fabrics are patterned with polka dots; *see* BANDANNA.

See also DISCHARGE PRINTED FABRIC, PRINTED FABRIC.

End uses: dresses, blouses, children's clothes, nightwear and lingerie.

POLKA RIB *see* CARDIGAN RIB.

POLO CLOTH A high-quality, soft, heavyweight woven fabric, made from wool or wool and hair blended fibres. Characteristically, it is given a heavy nap finish on both sides. It is usually made in various shades of brown or camel.

Polo cloth is made from wool or wool blended with expensive hair fibres such as camel hair. Cheaper qualities may be made with wool and man-made fibres. It is woven

polo cloth

polyester fabric (example of woven fabric)

in plain, twill or hopsack weave structures, which become partially obscured by the finish. 'Polo' is the generic term for a heavy nap finish that produces a matt effect with little lustre.

See also COATING FABRIC, HAIR FABRICS, NAPPED FABRICS.

End uses: polo coats, jackets, caps and blankets.

POLO SHIRT FABRIC *see* PIQUÉ, WEFT-KNITTED.

POLYAMIDE FABRIC *see* NYLON FABRIC.

POLYESTER FABRIC A general term for any fabric constructed using polyester fibres or yarns. 'Polyester' is the generic term for a synthetic man-made polymer.[25] It may be produced in sheet form or in fibre form. For textiles, it is usually the fibres that are used.

The term 'polyester fabric' is used for fabrics of all different weights and constructions composed of 100% polyester fibres or yarns. Where polyester is used together with other fibres, the percentage of each should be stated. Polyester fibres are thermoplastic, or heat-sensitive, by nature, and they may be used in continuous filament form or chopped into shorter staple lengths and respun into yarns with different characteristics. Characteristically, polyester fabrics are strong fabrics with good abrasion resistance. Since they are thermoplastic, 100% polyester fabrics can be given permanent pleats, as can triacetate fabrics. Decorative shapes and patterns may also be laser-cut into them. Polyester fabrics have low absorbency, however, and may be prone to static build-up. Polyester staple fibres are therefore often blended with other staple fibres, particularly cotton, which reduces this effect. It is also possible to give polyester fibres a range of different properties by varying the manufacturing parameters. Modified polyester fibres are marketed under different brand names.

See also LASER-CUT FABRICS, PLEATED FABRICS, TRIACETATE FABRIC.

End uses: sportswear, leisure wear, fleeces, upholstery, furnishings, sheets, bedding, sewing threads, industrial textiles, sleeping bags, anoraks, luggage, bags, footwear and filling for duvets.

POLYMER MEMBRANE LAMINATES A range of textile laminates composed of one or more fabric layers (woven, knitted or nonwoven), with a thin polymer film or membrane laminated onto one of the layers. These composite or multi-component fabrics are both waterproof and windproof, but allow water vapour (perspiration) to pass through, making them breathable and comfortable to wear.

A polymer membrane is a very fine plastic film, about 0.02 mm thick (the thickness of domestic cling film). The two main types of polymer membrane, microporous and hydrophilic, are described below.

Microporous membranes have very fine micropores that allow water vapour (perspiration) to pass through them but are too small to allow liquids (i.e. water or rain droplets) through. The membrane is made from either polytetrafluoroethylene (PTFE) or polyurethane (PU). The pores are achieved by mechanical methods (*see* POLYURETHANE). PTFE is a synthetic polymer made from petrochemicals; in textiles, it is used mainly in microporous membranes. The brand-name product Teflon®, in the form of a fine microporous PTFE membrane, is used as a laminate for fabrics to make them waterproof and/or stain-resistant. GORE-TEX® fabric is perhaps the best-known product to use a Teflon microporous PTFE membrane.

Hydrophilic membranes (also called 'hygroscopic' or 'homogenous' membranes) are extremely thin solid membranes (12 microns or less) made from polyurethane or polyester-ether. The water vapour (perspiration) is able to pass through the membrane by

polymer membrane laminate (face fabric laminate, back and face)

polypropylene textile

a diffusion process (a natural process whereby gases pass from an area of high concentration to an area of low concentration). The thinner the membrane (10 microns is preferable), the higher the diffusion coefficient (i.e. the faster the moisture passes through). However, the passage of water vapour is still slower than with microporous membranes. As with microporous membranes, liquids (water or rain droplets) are too large to pass through. The advantage of this type of membrane, however, is that it has no micropores that could become blocked in use – by salt, dirt or adhesives, for example. Sympatex® is an example of a hydrophilic membrane. Water vapour passes through any laminated fabrics next to the membrane by wicking.

There are four main ways in which both microporous and hydrophilic membranes may be laminated to other woven, knitted or nonwoven fabrics with adhesives, in order to make a waterproof and/or weatherproof fabric composite.

(i) *Face fabric laminate.* The membrane is bonded to the back of a face fabric.

(ii) *Lining fabric laminate.* The membrane is bonded to a lining fabric.

(iii) *Three-layer laminate.* The membrane is bonded between a face fabric and a lining fabric to form a three-layer composite. GORE-TEX® fabric, which uses a microporous PTFE membrane, is an example of a three-layer laminated fabric; as such, it may be described as a poromeric fabric.

(iv) *Insert laminate.* The membrane is laminated to a knitted or nonwoven carrier fabric. This will then act as a sew-in layer between an outer fabric and a lining fabric.

See also HIGH-TECH TEXTILES, LAMINATED FABRIC, MOISTURE TRANSPORT TEXTILES, MULTI-COMPONENT FABRICS, PLASTIC TEXTILES, POLYURETHANE, TEFLON®, WATERPROOF AND WATER-REPELLENT FABRICS.

End uses: waterproof clothing of all kinds, including rainwear, anoraks, trousers, ski wear, rugged outdoor wear, active sportswear, sleeping bags and tents.

POLYPROPYLENE TEXTILES A general term for textiles made with polypropylene. Polypropylene is a polyolefin – a synthetic man-made polymer[25] that may be produced in sheet or fibre form. It is normally the fibres that are used for textiles.

Polypropylene may be the sole constituent of a textile, or it may be used together with other fibres or materials. In the latter case, the percentage of each fibre should be stated. Polypropylene fibres are thermoplastic or heat-sensitive by nature, and they may be used in continuous filament form or chopped into shorter staple lengths and spun into yarns with various characteristics. Polypropylene materials are known for their strength and good abrasion resistance. However, they have low absorbency and can be prone to static build-up. Polypropylene is the most hydrophobic (naturally moisture-resisting) of all commercial fibres. It is possible to give polypropylene fibres a range of different properties by varying the manufacturing parameters. Modified polypropylene fibres are marketed under different brand names.

See also ANTIMICROBIAL FABRIC, FUR FABRIC, LAMINATED FABRIC, MOISTURE TRANSPORT TEXTILES, NANOMATERIALS, PLASTIC TEXTILES.

End uses: moisture transport textiles, carpets, laminated fabrics, fur fabrics, nonwoven textiles, upholstery, ropes, luggage, shoe components, interlinings, waddings, filters and industrial textiles.

POLYTETRAFLUOROETHYLENE (PTFE) *see* POLYMER MEMBRANE LAMINATES.

POLYURETHANE (PU) A synthetic elastomer that is used in textiles in various forms: in fibre form, as fine polymer sheets made in any thickness, as a coating applied to other fabrics, or as foam. Characteristically, polyurethane is a totally waterproof material. It is therefore often used to provide some form of protective or water-resistant layer.

polyurethane coated fabric
(face and back)

pongee

The different forms in which polyurethane is used in textiles are as follows.
(i) *Polyurethane fibres.* Elastane and spandex are fibres made from polyurethane. *See* ELASTANE FABRIC.

(ii) *Polyurethane sheets.* Polyurethane sheets are made in a variety of thicknesses, mainly for use as water-protective barriers. Very fine polyurethane membranes may be laminated onto woven, knitted or nonwoven fabrics to make them both waterproof and windproof. *See* POLYMER MEMBRANE LAMINATES.

(iii) *Polyurethane-coated fabric.* Any fabric, woven, knitted or nonwoven, may be given a synthetic polyurethane coating. The polyurethane is applied to the textile in the form of a fluid mixture, by a blade, a roller, or by spraying it onto one or both sides of the fabric. The polyurethane mixture may contain a coloured pigment or it may be colourless. Both the amount of coating applied and the degree of penetration of the mixture is controlled in order to produce different fabrics. The base fabric provides strength and stability, and the polyurethane coating gives the fabric protective properties against such external factors as water, chemicals, oil or abrasion. Aeroplane fabrics are sometimes coated with polyurethane. Heavy polyurethane-coated fabrics are also used as industrial tarpaulins. *See also* COATED FABRIC.

(iv) *Polyurethane foam.* Polyurethane is also used to make thin layers of lightweight foam that may be laminated to other fabrics by heat fusing. The foam acts as an effective insulator and provides cushioning. This type of laminate is particularly useful for shoes and accessories. *See* FOAM, LAMINATED FABRIC, SUEDE CLOTH.

See also PLASTIC TEXTILES, PVC, WATERPROOF AND WATER-REPELLENT FABRICS.

End uses: (coated fabrics) outerwear, anoraks, apparel, sportswear, umbrellas, shoe uppers, mattress covers and industrial tarpaulins.

POLYVINYL CHLORIDE *see* PVC.

PONGEE Originally a slippery, lightweight, plain woven fabric made with wild tussah silk yarns. These give the fabric a characteristic coarse, irregular, slubbed appearance. It drapes well and frays fairly easily. Nowadays pongee fabrics may also be made with cotton or man-made fibres, but they still retain the look and handle of the original fabric.

The term 'pongee' comes from Chinese *pen-chi*, meaning 'home-loomed' or 'woven at home'.[3] Traditionally pongee was a lightweight plain woven silk fabric that was handwoven in northern China using wild tussah silk yarns (from wild silkworms that feed on oak leaves).[3] Nowadays pongee may be hand-woven or machine-woven using silk, acetate, triacetate, nylon, polyester or other fibres. The warp is usually finer than the weft, and the slubs in the weft yarn give the fabric its characteristic appearance. The fabric is woven in plain weave and it may be piece-dyed or printed. Traditional pongee fabrics may also be produced in their natural honey or ecru colours.

An imitation pongee fabric is also made with fine mercerized cotton yarns. A typical cotton pongee fabric construction is 8 to 6 tex warp sett at 38 to 43 ends per cm and 8 to 6 tex weft woven at 38 to 43 picks per cm.[26] Cotton pongees may also be mercerized and dyed in the piece, and they are often schreinered to give the fabric lustre. Pongee is a similar fabric to honan and shantung. It is lighter in weight than shantung.

See also SILK FABRIC.

End uses: blouses, dresses, women's suits, shirts, curtains, lining fabric, nightdresses and scarves.

POODLE CLOTH A general term for a knitted or woven fabric that has loops of yarn on the surface. It is normally used to describe thick, medium- to heavyweight curly pile fabrics.

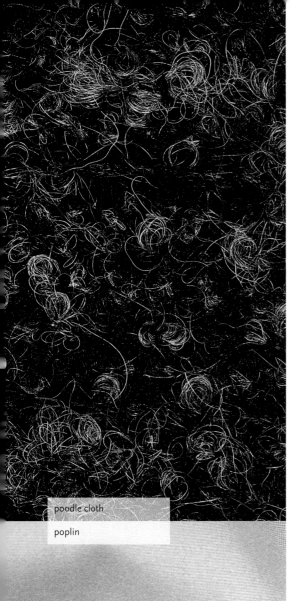

poodle cloth

poplin

Poodle cloth is normally constructed using a special looped yarn like a bouclé yarn, or by forming an ordinary yarn into a loop pile structure. The looped yarn is firmly constructed into a base fabric, which may be woven or knitted. Mohair, worsted or woollen yarns are normally used as the pile yarns, with mohair usually employed in the higher-quality fabrics since it gives the most lustre. The ground fabric may be made from a wide variety of fibres, including man-made fibres, cotton, worsted, wool and silk. Poodle cloth may be constructed in several different ways.

(i) *Woven warp pile poodle cloth.* The pile warp is lifted over wires at regular intervals during weaving against a firmly woven ground of plain weave. When the wires are removed, a mass of curly loops is formed on the surface of the fabric.

(ii) *Woven weft pile poodle cloth.* Extra weft yarns are floated across the surface of a firmly woven ground of plain weave at regular intervals. The texture may be emphasized by using a non-shrink extra weft yarn, such as mohair, and a yarn that shrinks in the ground fabric, such as botany wool. When the cloth is finished after weaving, the botany fabric shrinks but the mohair does not. The mohair yarns therefore form longer loops on the surface of the fabric. *See also* EXTRA WARP AND EXTRA WEFT FABRICS.

(iii) *Warp-knitted poodle cloth.* Like plush, warp-knitted poodle cloth may be knitted as a two- or three-bar fabric with long underlaps (of 4, 5 or 6 needle spaces) on the front bar to produce a loop pile. Yarns such as triacetate are used. Afterwards the loop pile is brushed to tease out the fibres and produce a curly pile. The fabric may be jet dyed. Alternatively, a thick, curly yarn may be attached to the surface of a ground fabric by the fine threads on one set of guide bars while the ground fabric is knitted on different guide bars.

(iv) *Weft-knitted poodle cloth.* A thick curly yarn is laid-in against a plain knit base fabric.

Similar fabrics to poodle cloth include astrakhan fabric, bouclé fabric, éponge, Montagnac, ratiné and terry fabric.

See also COATING FABRIC, FUR FABRIC, PILE FABRICS.

End uses: overcoats, jackets, collars, hats and bags.

POPLIN A very closely woven fabric with fine warp-faced ribs running in the weft direction. It is a lustrous, hard-wearing fabric, but may crease easily and be susceptible to seam pucker owing to its dense construction. It is a medium-weight fabric.

Originally poplin was woven with an organzine silk warp and a hard-twisted worsted weft. Today this type of poplin fabric is sometimes called 'Irish poplin'. Nowadays poplin is most likely to be woven with fine mercerized cotton yarns in both the warp and weft. It may also be woven in man-made fibres such as polyester or viscose and blends. Poplin is woven in plain weave using fine, highly sett two-fold warp yarns and two-fold weft yarns that are either of the same thickness or only marginally thicker. In a good-quality poplin fabric there will be at least twice as many warp ends per centimetre as weft picks. It is this imbalance of yarns that causes the weftways ribs.

Poplin may be woven in a wide variety of different weights and qualities, but typical cotton poplin fabric constructions are as follows:

- 14/2 tex combed and gassed Egyptian cotton warp sett at 60 ends per cm and 60 tex cotton weft woven at 14 picks per cm[26]
- 16 tex cotton warp sett at 48 ends per cm and 18 tex cotton weft woven at 24 picks per cm[25]

A typical Irish poplin fabric construction is:

- 5 tex (two-fold) organzine silk warp sett at 80 ends per cm and 68/3 tex genappe (or gassed) worsted weft woven at 14 to 22 picks per cm[26]

A typical poplin shirting fabric construction is:

- 10/2 tex warp sett at 54 ends per cm and 12/2 tex weft woven at 28 picks per cm[26]

Poplin may be piece-dyed, yarn-dyed or printed; it may also be given a resin finish to make it resistant to light rain or showers. There is a range of warp rib fabrics that are characterized by the size and prominence of their ribs. In increasing order of rib size, these are: broadcloth, poplin, taffeta, poult, faille, bengaline and grosgrain. Poplin is similar also to percale, especially in terms of weight. Poplin is a suitable fabric from which to make moiré fabrics, by giving it a moiré finish (*see* MOIRÉ FABRIC). The name 'poplin' comes from the French word *popeline*, which was the name of an ecclesiastical fabric made in the papal city of Avignon in southern France.[3]

See also COTTON FABRIC; RIB FABRICS, WOVEN; SHIRTING FABRICS; WATERPROOF AND WATER-REPELLENT FABRICS.

End uses: dresses, shirts, blouses, pyjamas, children's clothes, raincoats and jackets, occasion wear, women's suits, lining, trimmings and curtains.

POULT A closely woven, crisp fabric with smooth, rounded warp-faced ribs running in the weft direction. It is a lustrous, stiff fabric with a 'rustle', and it is prone to creasing and fraying. Poult is a medium-weight fabric (weighing approximately 140 g/m²).

Originally poult was always woven in silk and was known as 'poult-de-soie', but nowadays it is also woven in a variety of continuous filament man-made fibres, including polyester, acetate, triacetate, viscose or blends. Poult is woven in plain weave using fine highly sett warp yarns and a slightly thicker weft yarn, which causes the fabric to have weftways ribs. There are usually approximately three times as many ends as there are picks in this fabric. Poult may be woven in a wide variety of different weights and qualities, but a typical dress-weight poult fabric construction is as follows: 8.3 tex warp sett at 80 ends per cm and 22 tex weft woven at 22 picks per cm.[25] Poult is usually piece-dyed, but it may also be yarn-dyed or printed.

There is a range of warp rib fabrics characterized by the size and prominence of their ribs. In increasing order of rib size, these are: broadcloth, poplin, taffeta, poult, faille, bengaline and grosgrain. However, as many of them are woven in a variety of different weights, they can be hard to distinguish. Of all the woven rib fabrics, poult is most similar to taffeta, since they are both stiff and rustly, but poult is slightly heavier and has more pronounced ribs. Poult is a suitable fabric from which to make moiré fabrics, by giving it a moiré finish (*see* MOIRÉ FABRIC). The name 'poult' comes from the word 'padua-soy', which means 'silk fabric from Padua', the town in northern Italy where it was first woven.[3]

See also RIB FABRICS, WOVEN.

End uses: formal dresses, coats, wedding gowns, occasion wear, women's suits, millinery, linings, trimmings and curtains.

POWER NET A common warp-knitted stretch net fabric. Power net is the classic control fabric: it contains a high percentage of elastane fibres or yarns, which give it sufficient stretch and recovery for it to be used for body support and control garments. Power net fabrics are typically used for foundation wear, such as brassieres, girdles and corsets. Good moduli, or control, may be achieved with these fabrics, but lightweight versions with fine elastane fibres are also made for sheer lingerie. The fabric can look quite solid until stretched, when the openings in the net appear. It has good stretch both widthways and lengthways, and weights vary from 50 g/m² to 300 g/m².

poult

power net (raschel, face and back)

power net

Prince of Wales check

print cloth

The fabric is a raschel stretch fabric knitted on a raschel warp-knitting machine. It is knitted on four half-set guide bars (threaded one end in, one end out), the front two bars producing a net while the remaining two bars lay in an elastomeric yarn.[25, 38] The elastane yarns are trapped by the net stitches and, since they are under high tension, this causes the fabric to compact very strongly. In finishing, the fabric may be steamed and dried to produce maximum compaction and power, or it may be heat-set, which allows modification of the finished characteristics. Point d'ésprit effects may also be achieved with additional guide bars (*see* NET).

See also ELASTANE FABRIC, ELASTOMERIC FABRIC, KNITTED FABRIC, MESH FABRICS, NET, RASCHEL STRETCH FABRICS, SHEER FABRICS, STRETCH FABRIC, WARP-KNITTED FABRIC.

End uses: foundation wear, bras, girdles, corsets and lingerie.

PRINCE OF WALES CHECK A woven fabric that is traditionally made in wool in a distinctive check pattern. It is a district check fabric and originated in Scotland. The pattern is made with a colour and weave effect, which is created by combining a 2/2 twill weave structure with yarn-dyed stripes of alternating dark and light colours in both the warp and the weft. A fine overcheck is laid over the top of this. Prince of Wales check is woven in a variety of weights, ranging from light suiting weights to heavy overcoating weights. It is sometimes mistaken for Glen Urquhart check; they are exactly the same, except that the Prince of Wales check has a fine outline overcheck.

The original Prince of Wales check was a very large-scale check fabric with a 9-inch repeat. It had bold red or brown checks against a cream ground with a grey overcheck (a larger outline check overlaid ontop).[12] This Prince of Wales check was originally woven for Edward VII of England when he was Prince of Wales; however, when Edward VIII (later Duke of Windsor) became Prince of Wales in the early 20th century, he favoured a black and white Glen Urquhart check fabric. This has led to much confusion between the two fabrics. Today it is generally agreed that a Prince of Wales check is the same as a Glen Urquhart check, but with a fine overcheck. Prince of Wales check is usually woven with either wool or worsted wool yarns in a 2/2 twill weave structure. The yarns are arranged 4 dark / 4 light in sections that alternate with other sections that are arranged 2 dark / 2 light, in both the warp and weft directions. This produces alternating panels of houndstooth check and Guards check. A larger outline overcheck, usually in a contrasting colour, runs through the middle of the 2/2 section in both warp and weft directions.

See also CHECKS, COLOUR AND WEAVE EFFECTS, DISTRICT CHECKS, GLEN URQUHART CHECK, GUARDS CHECK, HOUNDSTOOTH CHECK, TWILL FABRICS.

End uses: men's and women's suits, jackets, trousers, skirts, coats, caps and hats.

PRINT CLOTH A general term for a range of fabrics, usually made from cotton or polyester/cotton, that are suitable base fabrics for printing. Print cloths are woven in various weights in simple weave structures, such as plain weave, twill or sometimes satin weave. Common print cloths include cotton broadcloth, calico, chintz, crash, oatmeal crêpe, cretonne, lawn, osnaburg, percale, percaline and sheeting fabric.

See also COTTON FABRIC, PLEATED FABRICS, PRINTED FABRIC, TOILE DE JOUY, WIGAN.

End uses: base cloths for printing all kinds of fashion and furnishing fabrics.

PRINTED FABRIC A general term for any fabric (knitted, woven, nonwoven or lace) that has been patterned with designs or motifs on its surface by the application of a colourant, usually in a thickened form such as paste or ink. Pressure is normally used to push the colour onto the fabric. The range of patterns that may be printed is virtually limitless.

printed fabric
(block-printed silk)

printed fabric (digitally
printed cotton)

Any kind of fabric may be printed, but the general term 'print cloth' is applied to a range of woven cotton fabrics that are consistently used as base cloths for many printed fabrics (*see* PRINT CLOTH).

Textile printing is a very ancient art that has been widely practised in different cultures. Through history a number of different printing techniques have been developed. The visual effect of most of these is very similar, with small variations. Today the majority of printed fabrics are printed by the methods described below. Other methods include stencilling, copper plate printing and engraved copper roller printing.

(i) *Rotary screen printing.* The pattern to be printed is applied to a rotary mesh screen by a photographic technique using soluble, light-sensitive chemicals. The screen is treated to block some areas of the mesh and to leave other areas exposed. The print paste is pumped into the centre of the rotary screen and then pushed through the open mesh areas to print the pattern onto the continuously moving fabric underneath. A separate rotary screen is required for each colour to be printed. This is a high-speed method of printing.

(ii) *Flat-bed screen printing.* A man-made fibre mesh is stretched over a metal or wooden frame. The print design is applied to the screen in the same manner as for rotary screen printing. A separate screen is required for each colour. The pattern is printed onto sections of the fabric; if printed fabric lengths are required, the pattern sections all need to align. This method is useful for printing fabric squares, such as scarves.

(iii) *Digital printing.* Digital printing is carried out using digital ink-jet printing machines. Print heads containing many fine nozzles squirt fine droplets of different-coloured inks onto a pre-treated fabric. The fabric is pre-treated with different chemicals, depending on the type of dyestuff to be used and the fibre content of the fabric. This method is particularly good for sampling and short runs, as it is quick and easy, but the image definition is not always as sharp and clear as with other methods.

(iv) *Heat transfer printing.* The pattern is first printed with special heat-sensitive disperse dyestuffs onto paper by screen printing. It is then transferred onto fabric from the printed paper in a heat transfer printing press. Under specific conditions of high temperature, pressure and appropriate timing, the dyes will 'sublime' and transfer onto the fabric, for which they have a greater affinity than paper.

(v) *Wooden block printing.* In some parts of the world (India, for example), certain fabrics are still printed by the ancient art of wooden block printing. The pattern is hand-carved onto wooden blocks, which are then coated with thickened dye paste that is stamped onto the fabric. A separate block is required for each colour. *See* KHADI.

(vi) *Resist printing.* Fabric printed with a resist printing paste (a mechanical or chemical resist material) is subsequently dyed to produce a white pattern against a coloured ground. If dyes are added to the resist printing paste, the patterned areas may also be coloured. It is difficult to distinguish between resist printed and discharge printed fabrics. *See also* RESIST-DYED FABRICS.

(vii) *Discharge printing. See* DISCHARGE PRINTED FABRIC.

Similar effects to printing may also be produced by resist-dyeing. Examples of printed fabrics include bandanna, chintz, cretonne, paisley, polka dot fabric and toile de Jouy.

See also DISCHARGE PRINTED FABRIC, DYED FABRICS, MICROENCAPSULATED TEXTILES, PRINT CLOTH, RESIST-DYED FABRICS, WARP-PRINTED FABRIC.

End uses: all kinds of fashion and furnishing end uses.

PRUNELLA (*obs.*) A fine, lightweight worsted woven fabric, woven in a 2/1 twill weave in solid colours. 'Prunelle twill' is the name of the ordinary 2/1 warp twill weave.[2, 4, 36]

PRUNELLE TWILL *see* TWILL FABRICS.

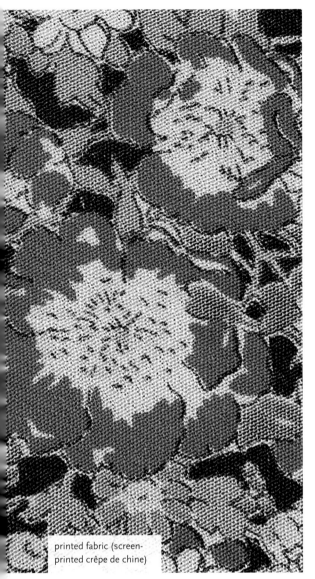

printed fabric (screen-printed crêpe de chine)

punto-di-Roma
(face and back)

purl fabric

PUNTO-DI-ROMA A weft-knitted, non-jacquard double jersey fabric. It is a double layer fabric based on an interlock structure and is therefore a firm, stable knitted construction.

The name 'punto-di-Roma' includes a reference to the city of Rome, which is famous for fine knitted fabrics. Punto-di-Roma is knitted in many weights and qualities, using all kinds of fibres and yarns; elastane is frequently included to increase stretch. The fabric is usually knitted on a double jersey knitting machine that has two needle-beds. The knit construction is composed of four different weft courses that repeat throughout the fabric. The first two rows are knitted in interlock structure on both needle-beds. The third row is of plain knit structure, knitted on the front bed only, and the fourth row is of plain knit structure, knitted on the back bed only (that is, rows 3 and 4 form a tubular knit). Visually this creates a reversible fabric in which courses of small stitches alternate with courses of larger stitches on both sides. The top arcs of the larger stitches adjacent to one another are not in alignment.[38] This fabric is very similar to Milano rib (full Milano).

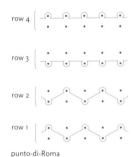

row 4

row 3

row 2

row 1

punto-di-Roma

See also INTERLOCK, JERSEY, KNITTED FABRIC, WEFT-KNITTED FABRIC.

End uses: general knitwear.

PURL FABRIC A general term for any weft-knitted fabric that is knitted in a purl structure. In purl fabrics, both face and back stitches occur in at least one wale, and sometimes in all of the wales. Purl fabrics are usually fairly chunky and, when they are not extended lengthwise, they often show only back loops on both the face and reverse of the fabric.[38] Purl is one of the four primary weft-knit base structures (the others are interlock, plain knit and rib), and it can be knitted by hand or on a special purl knitting machine. The widthwise extensibility of purl fabric is approximately the same as that of plain knit fabric, but its lengthwise extensibility is approximately twice as great. Its extensibility makes it a highly suitable fabric for close-fitted garments.

The purl knitting machine is a complex knitting machine; it has two needle-beds in which the needle tricks, containing double-headed latch needles, are aligned with one another. The needles can knit in either of the opposed needle-beds controlled by 'sliders' by the process called 'gating' or 'purl gating'. The complex nature of purl knitting machines makes them unsuited to high-speed production, so they are normally used for knitting garments rather than continuous lengths of fabric.

The knitting sequence may be varied to produce different end results.
(i) *1 × 1 purl fabric (plain purl fabric)*. A single course of back loops alternates with a single course of face loops.
(ii) *2 × 2 purl fabric*. Two courses of back loops alternate with two courses of face loops.
(iii) *3 × 3 purl fabric*. Three courses of back loops alternate with three courses of face loops.
(iv) *Fancy purl fabric*. This is a general term for a variety of fabrics in which a pattern is formed by various combinations of back and face loops. Fancy purl fabrics are sometimes also called 'links-links'.
(v) *Plated purl fabric*. This is a purl-based fabric containing two yarns, one forming the back loops on both sides of the fabric and the other being hidden on the inside and visible only when the fabric is stretched lengthwise.[38] *See* PLATED FABRICS.

See also KNITTED FABRIC, MOSS-STITCH FABRIC, WEFT-KNITTED FABRIC.

End uses: sweaters, jackets, scarves, hats and leisure wear, including close-fitted garments.

purl fabric (1 × 1 purl)

PVC (expanded vinyl)

PVC-coated fabric (printed cotton)

pyjama fabric

PVC (polyvinyl chloride, vinyl) A synthetic elastomer manufactured from petrochemicals. Its full name is polyvinyl chloride, but it is more commonly known by the shortened versions 'PVC' or' vinyl'. Characteristically, PVC is a totally waterproof material. It is therefore often used to provide some form of protective or water-resistant layer. It is used in textiles in various forms: in fibre form (a type of chlorofibre); as fine polymer sheets, made in a variety of qualities and thicknesses, mainly for use as water-protective barriers; or as coatings applied to other fabrics.

PVC-coated fabrics are often shiny and plastic in appearance. Any fabric, woven, knitted or nonwoven, may be given a synthetic PVC coating. The base fabric provides strength and stability, while the PVC coating gives it protective properties against such external factors as water, chemicals, oil or abrasion. The PVC is applied to the textile in the form of a fluid mixture, either by a blade or a roller, or by spraying it onto one or both sides of the fabric. The PVC mixture may contain a coloured pigment or it may be colourless. Both the amount of coating applied and the degree of penetration of the mixture are controlled, in order to produce different fabrics. For example, upholstery fabrics are made from expanded vinyl, which is softer and more flexible than ordinary PVC. These fabrics are sometimes called 'leather-cloth' or 'leatherette'.

See also COATED FABRIC, LEATHER-CLOTH, PLASTIC TEXTILES, POLYURETHANE, WATERPROOF AND WATER-REPELLENT FABRICS.

End uses: curtains, awnings, window blinds, upholstery, book covers, floor and wall coverings, shower curtains, tablecloths, aprons, hats, waterproof apparel, raincoats, protective wear, luggage, car hoods, and shoe uppers and liners.

PYJAMA FABRIC A general term for a range of light- to mid-weight, mostly woven fabrics, usually made from cotton. They are hard-wearing fabrics that are typically woven in coloured stripes or checks and used for pyjamas and nightgowns.

Pyjama fabrics are usually woven with soft, carded cotton yarns in a plain weave fabric structure. They are usually colour-woven with multicoloured stripe and check patterns, or they may be piece-dyed and/or printed after weaving. In finishing, the surface of the fabric is sometimes raised to form a nap on the face side, which obscures the weave structure beneath and gives the fabric a soft, warm handle. Examples of pyjama fabrics finished in this way are flannelette and winceyette. In some countries, including the UK, there is a legal requirement for children's nightwear to be made flame-resistant, either by using inherently flame-resistant materials or by applying a durable flame-retardant finish in accordance with the relevant standards. Pyjama fabric or pyjama check is a similar-looking fabric to dimity, but it is colour-woven and made with carded yarns, and is also slightly thicker.

See also CHECKS, FLAME-RESISTANT TEXTILES, NAPPED FABRICS, STRIPES.

End uses: pyjamas, nightgowns, shirts, blouses, children's clothes, and sheets.

QUEEN'S CLOTH (*obs.*) A fine cotton shirting bleached after weaving, made in Jamaica, in the West Indies.[9]

QUEENSCORD A firm, stable warp-knitted fabric with a slight vertical cord effect.

Queenscord is knitted on a two-bar tricot warp-knitting machine. The construction is made with full-set threading in both guide bars. The fabric is knitted in a stable, rigid construction that makes it useful as a scrim or backing fabric for laminated fabrics. This is achieved

queenscord (scrim)

quilted fabric

quilted fabric

by the front guide bar chaining continuously on the same needle to make short pillar stitch underlaps. This makes a rigid mesh with the back bar underlaps, which underlap three or four needle spaces. In appearance the fabric has a slight cord effect created by the pillar stitches, with inclined overlap stitches in between.[25, 31] Queenscord is a similar fabric to warp-knitted locknit and warp-knitted sharkskin, but it is more rigid than either.

See also KNITTED FABRIC, LAMINATED FABRIC, LOCKNIT, SCRIM, SHARKSKIN, TRICOT, WARP-KNITTED FABRIC.

End uses: backing fabric for laminated fabrics.

QUILTED FABRIC A multi-component fabric composed of an outer or face fabric, a layer of wadding, and sometimes also a backing fabric. The two- or three-layer composite is usually held together with rows of machine stitching, or sometimes the layers are fused together with heat or chemicals. This gives the fabric a padded appearance. Quilted fabrics are lightweight fabrics that are characteristically thick, bulky and warm.

The outer fabric layer is usually a plain woven fabric made from cotton, polyester/cotton, viscose or nylon. It is frequently printed, but sometimes the machine stitching provides a pattern. For some quilts, especially those used in bedding, patchwork fabrics are used as the outer fabric layer. The wadding layer is usually lightweight polyester and is available in a wide range of thicknesses. Foam or down are also sometimes used. The backing fabric is usually a cheaper plain fabric, such as a thin cotton or polyester (e.g. cheesecloth) or warp-knitted nylon (tricot). However, for reversible quilted fabrics, a better-quality fabric is selected.

Most quilted fabrics are stitched together with sewing thread. The composite layers are held together with parallel rows of machine stitching, or they may be stitched together in any number of different patterns, such as wavy lines or diamonds. Sometimes the stitching follows the outline of printed motifs. Twistless nylon monofilament thread is often used, since it is particularly strong and transparent. Lock-stitch is the most usual stitch type used.

'Trapunto' is the name of an Italian form of quilting in which the quilting is confined to particular motifs or areas of the fabric. 'Pinsonic quilting' is made by fusing composite layers of thermoplastic fibre fabrics together in patterned areas, using the heat generated by the vibrations of ultrasound (ultra high-frequency sound). Composite fabric layers may also be bonded together in patterned areas using chemical adhesives.

Sometimes the quilted effect is accentuated during finishing by the controlled shrinkage of the backing fabric. Fabrics that have a quilted appearance but are made by other means include Marseilles, matelassé and woven piqué. Quilted fabric should not be confused with 'quilt', which is a general term for a wide variety of bed coverings constructed in many different ways.

See also COATING FABRIC, LAMINATED FABRIC, MULTI-COMPONENT FABRICS, PATCHWORK, WADDING.

End uses: dressing gowns, bed jackets, coats, winter jackets, anoraks, ski wear, snow suits, body warmers, collars, hoods, duvets, quilts, bedspreads, cushions, mattresses and upholstery fabrics.

RABBIT-HAIR FABRIC *see* ANGORA FABRIC.

RADIUM A densely woven fabric that is characteristically highly lustrous and crisp, with a smooth, soft handle.

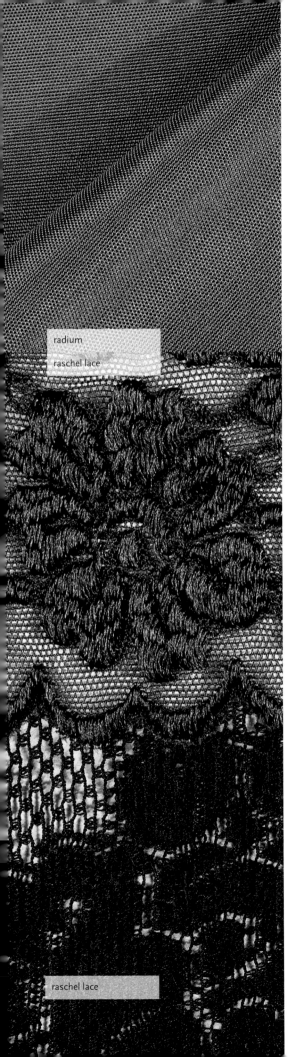

radium

raschel lace

raschel lace

Originally radium was a half crêpe fabric, woven with silk yarns (untwisted silk in the warp and alternate picks of 'S' and 'Z' twist yarns in the weft). Nowadays radium is also made with continuous man-made filament yarns, including viscose, acetate and triacetate. It is woven in a closely sett plain weave structure, with highly twisted weft yarns. Radium is usually a colour-woven fabric in which the weft yarns are of a different colour from the warp yarns. This creates a shot effect when the light catches the fabric at different angles. Radium is similar to woven crêpe fabric and taffeta. It has the crispness of taffeta but drapes like a crêpe fabric.

See also PLAIN WEAVE FABRIC, SHOT FABRICS, SILK FABRIC.

End uses: lingerie, dresssing gowns, dresses, blouses and linings.

RAFFIA *see* STRAW FABRICS.

RAMIE FABRIC A general term for any fabric constructed with ramie fibres or yarns. Ramie is a bast fibre obtained from the stem of the *Boehmeria nivea* plant (belonging to the nettle family), which grows in northern India and China.[25]

Ramie fibres are staple fibres that are spun into yarns, and they are often blended together with other staple fibres. The term 'ramie fabric' is used for fabrics of a range of different weights and constructions composed of 100% ramie fibres or yarns. In fabrics where ramie is used together with other fibres, the percentage of each should be stated. Characteristically, ramie fabrics are soft, strong fabrics with an irregular surface texture and a linen-like appearance.

See also PLANT-FIBRE FABRICS.

End uses: casual clothing and knitwear.

RASCHEL LACE The generic name for warp-knitted lace fabrics made on a raschel lace warp-knitting machine. A raschel lace machine has many more guide bars (up to 78) than a standard raschel machine, in order to produce intricate lace patterns. It is the cheapest way of producing a lace fabric, and these lace fabrics are mass-produced in a wide range of different weights and qualities, ranging from lightweight and transparent to heavy and dense. Characteristically, raschel lace fabrics are flat lace fabrics in which patterning yarns or threads are superimposed on a mesh-like ground structure.[38] Both stretch and non-stretch lace fabrics are produced in a wide variety of intricate patterns for apparel, furnishings and household textiles.

Raschel lace is often knitted with continuous filament polyester yarns or, if stretch lace is being produced, with nylon and elastane. The ground structure can be locknit, pillar inlay, tulle, three-bar voile or marquisette, or it can be achieved by means of a jacquard attachment.[38] Patterns and design motifs are produced in the fabric by the superimposed patterning yarns or threads. These may be knitted-in, tucked-in by means of a fall-plate (a thin metal blade attached to a bar and capable of extending the full width of the machine)[31] or laid-in using multiple guide bars.[38] When the decorative threads are laid-in, the background net and the patterned areas are constructed simultaneously.[11] Raschel lace fabrics may be made in different colours or they may be printed. They are also frequently cross-dyed, using nylon, polyester and viscose, for example.

See also KNITTED FABRIC; LACE; LACE, KNITTED; MESH FABRICS; NET; RASCHEL WARP-KNITTED FABRIC; WARP-KNITTED FABRIC.

End uses: lingerie, blouses, evening wear, dresses, trims, curtains, tablecloths and bedspreads.

raschel stretch fabric
(lockstitch, face and back)

raschel stretch fabric
(tecnet)

raschel stretch fabric
(sleeknit, face and back)

RASCHEL STRETCH FABRICS Warp-knitted fabrics that include elastomeric fibres and are made on a raschel warp-knitting machine. They are characteristically very stretchy fabrics, and most are 'power stretch fabrics' that provide high modulus (or degree of control) and a comfortable stretch; they are made for control applications such as bras and corsetry. Some raschel stretch fabrics are lighter in weight and are used for lingerie and swimwear. The stretch fabric trade uses the term 'raschel stretch fabrics' (or 'stretch raschel') to distinguish them from stretch tricot or locknit fabrics knitted on tricot machines, which are mostly fine 'comfort stretch fabrics' in which the elastane is knitted into the fabric construction (*see* STRETCH FABRIC).

To make raschel stretch fabrics, elastane or other elastomeric yarns are 'laid-in' into the fabric construction to provide the stretch. This method allows the inclusion of much thicker stretch yarns than the tricot machine allows, and it is therefore possible to produce the more elastic power stretch fabrics. In raschel stretch fabrics the elastane yarn 'floats' within the construction and is trapped in position by the non-stretch yarn, usually nylon or polyester. It is either caught by the underlaps or trapped between the loops and the underlaps, depending on the construction. Owing to the construction, the stretch is mainly in the warp direction.

Much of the fabric knitted on raschel machines is stretch fabric, and there are various types constructed in different ways.

(i) *Lockstitch*. Not to be confused with locknit, lockstitch is a two-bar raschel construction knitted with a ten-course pattern repeat that gives a textured appearance rather than a net. The back guide bar is threaded with coarse elastane that is fed under tension. The front guide bar knits nylon and traps the elastane within its stitches as it is laid-in. This fabric, together with tecnet and tecsheen, is sometimes called by the general term 'satinette', but this does not imply that it is satin in character.

(ii) *Tecnet/tecsheen*. These fabrics are more sophisticated versions of lockstitch, offering a smoother surface and a degree of lustre. There are several different constructions, most of them two-bar, but some, for technical reasons, use three or four guide bars. As with most raschel fabrics, the back guide bar is threaded with elastane under tension that lays-in into a nylon construction that is knitted on the front guide bar(s). These fabrics, together with lockstitch, are sometimes called by the general term 'satinette', but this does not imply that they are always satin in character.

(iii) *Sleeknit*. This fabric was originally patented, and it is a three-bar raschel fabric of unusual construction. The back guide bar lays in elastane, but the full-set front and centre guide bars alternately knit and lay-in a modified locknit stitch so that only one bar is knitting on each course. This produces a fabric with a very smooth surface and good stretch and control properties. If lustrous yarns are used, a satin effect may be produced. However, if the fabric is not carefully constructed and finished, the elastane yarns can slip in the fabric during wear. Lightweight versions of this fabric are used for brief backs and swimwear. A more lustrous 'mirror satin' fabric may also be produced on raschel machines. *See* SATIN, WARP-KNITTED.

(iv) *Weftloc*. Weftloc is knitted on a patented modified raschel weft-insertion machine. An elastane weft is laid across the full width of the machine and an elastane warp is laid-in. One full set guide bar binds the warp and weft together. The fabric has good modulus (control properties) and good stretch in both directions; however, it is expensive due to the high elastane content.

(v) *Triskin*. Triskin was developed in an attempt to create the effect of weftloc on a standard elastic raschel machine. It combines a two-way stretch with good two-way modulus (control properties). This is achieved by knitting nylon in the front guide bar and laying-in elastane on both the centre and back guide bars. The back guide bar lays-in a coarse elastane yarn, essentially in the warp direction. The centre guide bar lays-in a finer elastane yarn in a zigzag manner, essentially in the horizontal direction. This gives width stretch and modulus. Triskin is expensive owing to the high elastane content, which can be up to 50%, but it is very effective.

Examples of other warp-knitted raschel fabrics include power net and satin (warp-knitted).

See also ELASTANE FABRIC, ELASTOMERIC FABRIC, KNITTED FABRIC, LAID-IN FABRIC, LOCK-NIT, NET, POWER NET, STRETCH FABRIC, TRICOT, WARP-KNITTED FABRIC.

End uses: bras, corsetry, sportswear, lingerie, swimwear, some outerwear, and medical textiles (especially burn-relief garments).

RASCHEL WARP-KNITTED FABRIC A generic term used for all different kinds of warp-knitted fabric knitted on a raschel warp-knitting machine, ranging from sheer, lightweight fabrics to heavyweight fabrics. Both single and double layer fabrics are produced, on single-bar and double-bar raschel machines respectively.

Raschel fabrics are mainly knitted using nylon or polyester continuous filament yarns. Elastane or other elastomeric fibres, such as PBT yarns, are also often incorporated since many of the fabrics knitted on raschel machines are stretch fabrics. Raschel warp-knitted fabrics broadly fall into four main categories:

- stretch apparel (*see* RASCHEL STRETCH FABRICS)
- lace (*see* RASCHEL LACE)
- technical fabrics, including fabrics produced on double needlebar machines for tubular double plush and spacer fabrics (*see* PLUSH, SPACER FABRICS)
- fabrics produced on multiaxial and weft-insertion machines (*see* LAID-IN FABRIC, STITCH-BONDED FABRIC, WARP-KNITTED FABRIC)

See also KNITTED FABRIC, WARP-KNITTED FABRIC.

End uses: bras, corsetry, sportswear, lingerie, swimwear, outerwear, blouses, evening wear, dresses, leisure wear, trims, curtains, tablecloths, bedspreads, medical textiles, and domestic and car upholstery.

RATINÉ A rough, textured fabric that is woven or knitted using fancy textured yarns. A similarly textured fabric, produced by applying a special finishing process to fabrics woven with ordinary yarns, is sometimes also called 'ratiné'.

The term 'ratiné' comes from the French, meaning 'covered with a curly nap'; however, ratiné is thought to have first been made in Italy in the 17th century.[3] Ratiné fabrics may be made from a variety of different fibres, including wool, cotton, silk, viscose, acetate, polyester, nylon or blends of these. A traditional heavyweight woven ratiné fabric is made with thick, fancy twisted woollen yarns. These spiral or loop yarns with knots or nubs are used in both the warp and the weft. The fabric is usually woven in an open-sett plain weave or plain weave variation, to produce a spongy, bulky fabric that is typically used for overcoats. In less expensive versions of the fabric, the fancy yarns are used in the weft only. This type of ratiné fabric is similar in appearance to chinchilla fabric.

A lighter-weight, soft woven cotton ratiné fabric is also made, using fancy cotton gimp or spiral yarns. These yarns may be used in both the warp and the weft, or in the weft only. The fabric is usually woven in a fairly open-sett plain weave construction. This fabric is typically used as a ladies' dress or suiting fabric. Typical woven cotton ratiné fabric constructions are: 125 tex spiral yarn in warp sett at 7 to 8 ends per cm and 125 tex spiral yarn in weft woven at 7 to 8 picks per cm; or 74/2 to 30/2 tex ordinary soft-spun cotton

raschel stretch fabric
(triskin, face and back)

raschel warp-knitted fabric

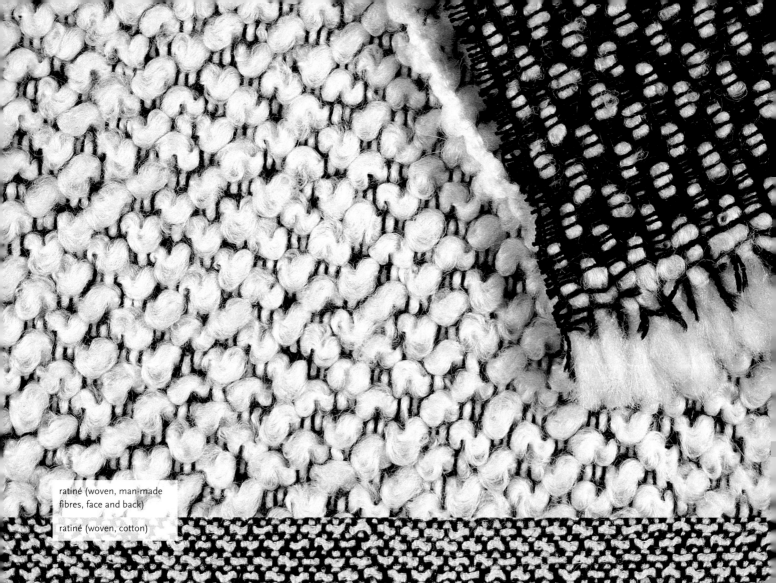

ratiné (woven, man-made fibres, face and back)

ratiné (woven, cotton)

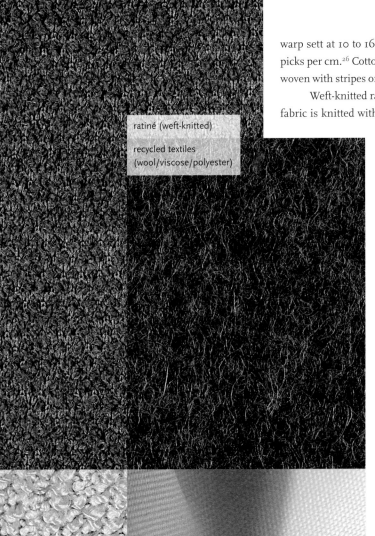

ratiné (weft-knitted)

recycled textiles
(wool/viscose/polyester)

reflective fabric

ratiné (weft-knitted)

warp sett at 10 to 16 ends per cm and 170 to 130 tex cotton spiral weft woven at 7 to 10 picks per cm.[26] Cotton ratiné fabrics may be bleached, piece-dyed in solid colours, colour-woven with stripes or checks, or printed. Cotton ratiné is a type of sponge cloth or éponge.

Weft-knitted ratiné fabrics are also made, in imitation of woven ratiné. Usually the fabric is knitted with fancy textured yarns in a simple knit structure such as plain knit. Similar fabrics to ratiné include bouclé fabric, chinchilla fabric, poodle cloth and terry fabric.

See also COATING FABRIC, ÉPONGE, SPONGE CLOTH.

End uses: overcoats, furnishing fabrics, and ladies' dress and suiting fabrics.

RAW SILK *see* SILK FABRIC.

RAYON *see* VISCOSE FABRIC.

RECYCLED TEXTILES A general term for any textiles made by recycling discarded textile products. An enormous amount of textile products, clothing in particular, is discarded. Some of this is collected and sorted for reuse; some items are redistributed and sold as second-hand clothing; and some items are sent to recycling or 'flocking' mills for the fibres to be reclaimed and recycled into new products. Textiles made from both natural and man-made fibres can be reclaimed and recycled.

Clothing and textiles made from natural fibres have been recycled for many years. Items sold to the specialist recycling mills are first graded according to fibre type and colour. Wool fabrics are then shredded into fibrous material. 'Shoddy' is the term for the waste fibres reclaimed from knitted or loosely woven fabrics. 'Mungo' is the term for the waste fibres reclaimed from hard-woven fabrics, milled fabrics or felt. Reclaimed fibres are usually carded to clean them, after which they are either used for padding materials or spun into new yarns. Sometimes reclaimed fibres are blended with other fibres, which may be new fibres or different reclaimed fibres, before being made into fabric. Recycled fabrics include felt, blankets and fabrics for new garments. Examples of fabrics containing recycled wool fibres include angola flannel (*see* FLANNEL), fearnought, felt and Ulster. Cotton, silk and hemp fibres are graded and used to make cleaning cloths, or they may be used in the manufacture of paper. Natural fibres that are not recycled are biodegradable, but wool fibres produce methane as they decompose. Cellulosic man-made fibres are also biodegradable, but synthetic fibre products are not. Some synthetic materials, however, can be recycled, and these are either re-spun into new fibres or used to make other plastic products.

See also FEARNOUGHT, FELT, FLANNEL, ULSTER.

End uses: felt, cleaning cloths, blankets and fabrics for casual wear garments.

REFLECTIVE FABRICS Fabrics coated with thousands of tiny microscopic reflective lenses. This creates a highly reflective surface that will return light projected in its direction back to the original source. Reflective fabrics are used mainly for protective clothing that increases the visibility of the wearer in the dark.

regatta
regence

regina (face and back)

The reflective lenses are bonded to a variety of different, mostly durable, fabric backings. They are able to reflect light entering both directly and at angles. Lenses bonded with heat-activated adhesives are usually formed into transfer films, which may then be laminated or embossed onto backing fabrics to form an all-over reflective fabric. Transfer films may also be cut to form patches, trims, logos and tapes, which can also be laminated or embossed onto other fabrics or garments. Most of these reflective fabrics are waterproof. It is also possible to screen print the reflective lenses, suspended in an ink or paste, onto a fabric. Reflective fabrics may also be sewn onto other fabrics. They can be hand-cut, die-cut, slit or guillotined. 3M™ Scotchlite™ Reflective Material is the registered brand name of one reflective material. Holographic fabrics used as decoration are similar to reflective fabrics used for protective clothing.

See also COATED FABRIC, EMBOSSED FABRICS, HOLOGRAPHIC FABRICS, LAMINATED FABRIC.

End uses: outerwear garments for emergency service workers, rescue workers' uniforms, sportswear, cyclists' and motorcyclists' clothing, children's protective wear, protective or decorative apparel, luggage and shoe uppers.

REGATTA A fine, striped, colour-woven cotton fabric. The warpways stripes of equal width are composed of a single colour alternating with white; the most common colour combination is blue and white stripes. It is a strong fabric that weighs about 180 g/m².

Regatta is woven with good-quality cotton yarns in a 2/1 warp-faced twill weave structure. The fabric is woven with a white or undyed weft yarn. In less expensive versions of the fabric, the stripes may be printed. A typical cotton regatta fabric construction is as follows: 27 tex cotton warp sett at 32 ends per cm and 33 tex cotton weft woven at 24 picks per cm;[26] or 30 tex cotton warp sett at 30 ends per cm and 33 tex cotton weft woven at 25 picks per cm.[25] Regatta is a similar fabric to galatea but is heavier in weight. It is also similar in both texture and weight to Harvard.

See also SHIRTING FABRICS, STRIPES, TWILL FABRICS.

End uses: shirts, dresses, blouses, nurses' uniforms, aprons, working clothes and protective garments.

REGENCE A very soft, lustrous silk fabric, woven in a warp-faced weave structure similar to a satin weave but with a very faint horizontal rib effect. It has good drape and is used for men's neckties.

The traditional regence fabric is woven entirely in silk, but it is also made with a silk warp and a viscose or acetate weft. The warp yarns are very highly sett so that they form the smooth face of the fabric. Regence is sometimes patterned with cross-wise stripes.

See also SILK FABRIC, TIE FABRIC.

End uses: men's neckties.

REGINA A fine lightweight, twill woven fabric made with cotton yarns. It weighs about 100 g/m².

Regina is woven with good-quality cotton yarns, either singles or two-fold yarns, in a 2/1 warp-faced twill weave structure. There are approximately twice as many warp ends as weft picks. It may be yarn-dyed, piece-dyed or colour-woven. A typical cotton regina fabric construction is as follows: 7 to 10 tex cotton warp sett at 57 ends per cm and 7 to 10 tex cotton weft woven at 28 picks per cm.[25]

See also COTTON FABRIC, SHIRTING FABRICS, TWILL FABRICS.

End uses: shirts, dresses and blouses.

RELIEF FABRIC *see* BLISTER CLOTH.

REPP A woven fabric that has a characteristic pronounced rib effect, composed of alternating thick and fine ribs running either horizontally across the width of the fabric (mainly in furnishing fabrics), or vertically down the length of the fabric parallel to the selvedge (the type traditionally used for tie fabrics). The ribs running horizontally usually form very pronounced ridges in the fabric, while ribs in the vertical direction tend to be smoother and flatter. All repp fabrics are very hard-wearing but they are prone to fraying. Repp is made in a wide range of different weights and qualities, ranging from lightweight to heavyweight, depending on the end use.

Repp fabrics may be woven in any fibre, including cotton, silk, worsted or man-made fibres and blends. It is usually either yarn-dyed or piece-dyed. Moiré fabrics are also sometimes made from repp fabrics by giving them a moiré finish (*see* MOIRÉ FABRIC). Repp effects in the horizontal direction are warp-faced, composed of a great number of highly sett warp yarns. Repp effects in the vertical direction are weft-faced, composed of a great number of highly sett weft yarns. These two kinds of repp fabric, (horizontal) warp-faced repp and (vertical) weft-faced repp, are described in detail below.

Warp-faced repp is made with two warps and two wefts, both of which are composed of alternating coarse and fine yarns. Characteristically, there is a much greater number of warp ends per centimetre than weft picks. Repp is woven in plain weave in sequence, so that the coarse warp ends are raised over the coarse weft picks and the fine warp ends are raised over the fine weft picks. The fine warp yarns are often more heavily tensioned than the coarse ones. This produces a fabric that has alternating thick and fine horizontal ribs. The fine horizontal ribs not only accentuate the thicker horizontal ribs, but also bind the fabric into a more secure construction, preventing the yarn slippage that is apparent in some other rib woven fabrics. Less expensive repp fabrics – épingle, for example – are also made with one warp and one weft, but still with the same rib effect. Woven rib fabrics of all kinds are similar to repp fabrics and may be made more cheaply, but their construction is not always as secure and they are not usually as hard-wearing. Cannelle and cannetille are examples of warp-faced repp fabrics.

Weft-faced repp is usually made with one warp and one weft. Characteristically, the weft yarns are very highly sett so that they cover the warp yarns entirely. This repp fabric is woven in a stitched plain weave variation, in which the weft yarns float over regular groups of warp yarns to form vertical cords or colums of weft floats on the face of the fabric. This produces a stable construction that is widely used for men's silk neckties. Repp is the traditional construction for regimental stripe ties, and there are hundreds of traditional patterns. The repp structure is also used in jacquard woven ties. The repp construction emphasizes the silk weft yarns and produces a soft, lustrous and luxurious surface with strong colour effects.

See also CANNELLE; CANNETILLE; ÉPINGLE; RIB FABRICS, WOVEN; TIE FABRIC.

End uses: upholstery, curtains and bedspreads (heavyweight repp, usually made in cotton and/or man-made fibres); men's and women's suits (medium-weight repp, usually made in worsted wool); and men's neckties and shirts (lightweight repp, usually woven in silk, cotton or man-made fibres).

RESIST-DYED FABRICS Dyed fabrics in which a pattern is produced by protecting selected areas of the fabric with a resist, so that the protected areas remain undyed and form a pattern against the dyed background. Either the fabric or the yarns used to make the fabric may be resist-dyed.

The fabric or yarns may be either fully or partially covered with liquid-resistant bindings, treated with a protective resist material, or manipulated in some other way (e.g. folding, tying), so that the protected areas form a (usually predetermined) pattern. When

repp (warp-faced)

repp (weft-faced)

resist-dyed fabric (Japanese)

resist-dyed fabric (plangi)

the fabric or yarns are dyed, the areas protected by the resist remain undyed. This produces a fabric that characteristically has a pale-coloured pattern against a darker dyed background colour. Many different kinds of resist material may be used, including wax, resin and resist chemicals. They all produce different effects and characteristics in a fabric. There are various kinds of resist-dyed textiles. Plangi, shibori and tritik are described below; for further examples, *see* BANDANNA, BATIK, CHINÉ FABRICS, IKAT, TIE-DYED FABRIC.

Other methods used to resist dye penetration involve the manipulation of the yarns or fabric. The yarns may be knotted or tied with resist materials, or the fabric may be manipulated by tying, knotting, plaiting, folding, pleating or sewing. For folding or pleating, the fabric must be very compact in order to resist the penetration of the dye. After dyeing, the fabrics are opened out and the pattern is revealed on the flat surface. 'Tritik' is the name of a method for making a resist by sewing. A thread is stitched through a fabric and then gathered very tightly along the line of the thread; the resulting folds resist the penetration of the dye and produce a fabric that is patterned with a line of undyed dots.

Different cultures have developed their own characteristic styles of resist-dyed fabrics, and traditional patterns and fabrics are known by different names in different parts of the world. For example, in Indonesia, the term 'plangi' (meaning many-coloured) is used to describe fabrics patterned by tying small objects into the fabrics and subsequently dyeing them. In India, the terms 'bandanna' and 'chunri' are used to describe resist-dyed textiles.[33] 'Shibori' is a Japanese term that is used generally for both a variety of resist-dyeing processes and the fabrics produced. The term is usually applied to a particular group of resist-dyed textiles that have been manipulated into three-dimensional structures by any of the following methods: folding, crumpling, stitching, plaiting, plucking or twisting the cloth. These are 'shaped resist-dye' methods that make use of the cloth itself, and the three-dimensional nature of the fabric is retained after selective dyeing.[39] Similar effects to resist-dyeing may be produced by discharge printing, resist printing (*see* PRINTED FABRIC), space-dyeing and warp printing.

See also DISCHARGE PRINTED FABRIC, DYED FABRICS, PRINTED FABRIC, SPACE-DYED FABRIC, WARP-PRINTED FABRIC.

End uses: dresses, blouses, scarves, shirts, T-shirts, tunics, dressing gowns, curtains and furnishing materials.

REVERSIBLES *see* DOUBLE CLOTH.

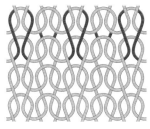

rib fabric, knitted (1 × 1 rib)

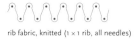

rib fabric, knitted (1 × 1 rib, all needles)

rib fabric, knitted (2 × 2 rib)

RIB FABRICS, KNITTED A general term for any weft-knitted fabrics that are knitted in a rib structure. Knitted rib fabrics characteristically have raised vertical wales or ribs on both sides. Rib is one of the four primary weft-knit base structures (the others are interlock, plain knit and purl), and it may be knitted by hand or on a weft-knitting machine. It is a highly extensible fabric in the weft direction and is widely used to make the edges and openings of knitted garments, for example neck collars, sleeve cuffs, welts and sock tops.

Knitted rib fabrics may be knitted using any fibre or yarn type and in all weights. The fabric is knitted on double-bed knitting machines with two sets of alternating single-headed needles. The vertical ribs on one side of the fabric are composed of face stitches that are knitted on one needle-bed. These alternate with the sunken wales composed of the back stitches of the ribs that are knitted on the second needle-bed. This produces the double-faced rib fabric.

The simplest rib structure is 1 × 1 rib fabric, which is a balanced structure composed of alternating single vertical ribs, one on the face and one on the back of the fabric. This fabric, also known as 'all needle rib', is knitted on all the needles on both needle-beds, which are set in zero rack position. In fine 1 × 1 ribs, the fabric can have the appearance of the technical face of a plain knit fabric on both sides, until it is extended horizontally, when the rib construction is seen more clearly. A variation of this fabric, also called

rib fabric, knitted (1 × 1 rib)

rib fabric, knitted (2 × 2 rib)

rib fabric, woven (warp rib)

rib fabric, knitted (2 × 2 rib)

'1 × 1 rib', is also knitted on alternating needles from both needle-beds, but on every other needle. The needle-beds are set in half-rack position. This is a half-gauged 1 × 1 rib. Other common balanced rib structures include 2 × 2, 3 × 3 and 4 × 4 ribs.

Rib structures may also be irregular, for example 2 × 1, 2 × 3 or 3 × 1. They may also be knitted in combination with one another: for example, sections of a 1 × 1 rib may alternate with sections of a 2 × 2 rib. There are a huge number of possible combinations, including the following examples:[38]

- English rib: a 2 × 2 rib in which the two needle-beds are set in half-rack position. Two adjacent wales of face stitches alternate with two adjacent wales of reverse stitches in the repeat.
- Swiss rib: a 2 × 1 rib in which the two needle-beds are set in zero rack position. Two adjacent wales of face stitches alternate with one wale of reverse stitches in the repeat.
- Derby rib: a 6 × 3 rib in which six adjacent wales of face stitches alternate with three adjacent wales of reverse stitches in the repeat.
- broad rib: a general name for a rib fabric in which broad sections of three or more adjacent wales of either face or back stitches are alternated.
- Richelieu rib: a rib-based fabric in which the rib effect appears on one side of the fabric only.

When the rib structure is used as rib borders at the edges of garments, it is possible to knit this integrally. The rib border is knitted on two needle-beds of the knitting machine and then all the stitches are transferred over to one needle-bed only and knitted in a plain knit construction to make the main body of the garment. Weft-knitted rib structure is also the base for a whole range of other weft-knitted fabric structures. Knitted fabrics based on rib structures include cable stitch fabric, cardigan rib (full and half cardigan), eight-lock, interlock, Milano rib (half-Milano and full Milano) and double piqué fabrics (see PIQUÉ, WEFT-KNITTED). A mock rib fabric is produced by inlaying elastomeric yarns into a plain knit base structure. This is sometimes used to make sock tops, for example.[38] One-sided or single-faced rib fabrics called 'single jersey cord' are also made on single-bed knitting machines using a single set of knitting needles. The face side of this fabric is similar in appearance to a knitted rib fabric. See SINGLE JERSEY CORD.

See also KNITTED FABRIC, LAID-IN FABRIC, WEFT-KNITTED FABRIC.

End uses: garment edges (including neck collars, sleeve cuffs, welts and sock tops); also cardigans, sweaters, dresses, T-shirts, socks, underwear, lingerie, sportswear and leisure wear.

RIB FABRICS, WOVEN A general term for woven fabrics that have a pronounced rib or cord effect running in either the weft or the warp direction. A warp rib fabric is a woven fabric that has a warp-faced rib effect that runs horizontally across the width of the fabric, from selvedge to selvedge. A weft rib fabric is a woven fabric that has a weft-faced cord effect running vertically down the length of a woven fabric, parallel to the selvedge; some weft rib fabrics are better known as 'cord fabrics'.

Warp rib fabrics have a greater number of warp ends per centimetre than weft picks. The fabric is woven in plain weave with either one very thick weft yarn or two or more yarns weaving as one. The ribs are formed by the warp yarns bending around the weft yarns, which remain more or less straight. The weft yarns are usually completely covered by the warp yarns, which form the ribs across the width of the fabric. Examples of warp rib fabrics include bengaline, broadcloth, faille, grosgrain, some moreen fabrics, ottoman rib (see OTTOMAN), Petersham (see NARROW FABRICS), poplin, poult, ribbed satin (see SATIN,

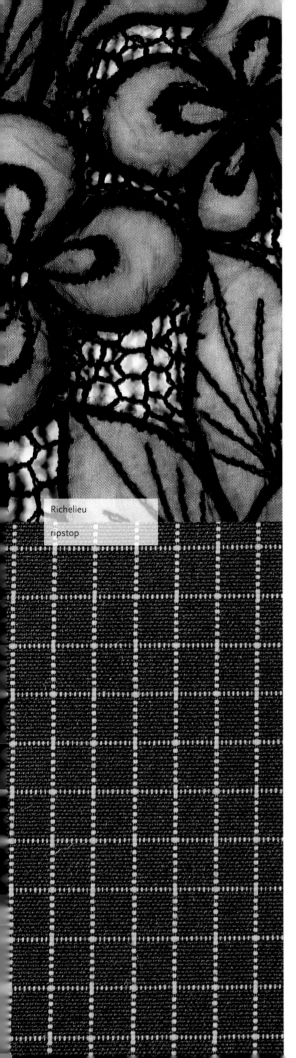

Richelieu

ripstop

woven) and taffeta. Similar fabrics to warp rib fabrics include piqué, repp, cannelle and cannetille. All four have ribs running horizontally across the width of the fabric, but they are constructed in more secure weave structures, which are less likely to slip.

Weft rib fabrics have a greater number of weft picks per centimetre than warp ends. The fabric is woven in plain weave with two or more warp ends weaving as one. The cords are formed by the weft yarns bending around the warp yarns, which remain more or less straight. The warp yarns are usually completely covered by the weft yarns, which form the cords running down the length of the fabric. Examples of weft rib fabrics include épingle, faille, some fustian fabrics, grosgrain, hair cord, Mogador, some moreen fabrics, ottoman cord (see OTTOMAN) and royal rib. See also CORD FABRICS.

The yarns in rib woven fabrics can be prone to slippage in the direction of the straight yarns unless the fabric is well constructed. Moiré fabrics may be made from woven rib fabrics by giving them a moiré finish. See MOIRÉ FABRIC.

End uses: all kinds of fashion and furnishing fabrics.

RIB VELVET *see* CORDUROY.

RICHELIEU A type of openwork, embroidered fabric. It is a crisp, medium-weight fabric, consisting of embroidered designs on a backing fabric.[2] These are often geometric and may include areas of cutwork.

Both the backing fabric and the embroidery yarns may be made from any fibre, including cotton, viscose, polyester, modal or a mixture of fibres.[2] The embroidery yarns may be in matching or contrasting colours to the backing fabric. They are stitched so that they form padded outlines on the backing fabric, in imitation of some lace fabrics.[36]

See also EMBROIDERED FABRICS, LACE.

End uses: blouses, dresses and garment detailing (including yokes and pockets).

RICHELIEU RIB FABRIC *see* RIB FABRICS, KNITTED.

RIPSTOP A general term for any kind of woven fabric that incorporates reinforcement yarns or ripstop yarns interwoven at regular intervals in order to increase the resistance of the fabric to ripping or tearing.

Ripstop fabrics are usually woven in a simple plain weave fabric construction. The reinforcement yarns are usually thicker and stronger than the yarns used throughout the rest of the fabric. They are positioned at regular intervals in both the warp and weft directions, usually forming a small-scale grid pattern in the fabric, although other geometric patterns are also woven. The reinforcement yarns may be the same colour as the fabric, or sometimes are used as a feature in a different colour in order to accentuate the pattern.

Ripstop constructions are most often used in lightweight fabrics where strength is an essential requirement, particularly those made with nylon or polyester. However, ripstop reinforcement can also be incorporated into heavier fabrics where extreme durability is a requirement, such as those used in the manufacture of heavy-duty luggage. Many ripstop fabrics are also either water-repellent or waterproof.

See also AEROPLANE FABRIC, WATERPROOF AND WATER-REPELLENT FABRICS.

End uses: parachutes, hot air balloons, waterproof clothing of all kinds (including rainwear, anoraks, ski wear and rugged outdoor wear), active sportswear, sleeping bags, tents, heavy-duty luggage, wind socks for airfields, kites, flags, banners and many other applications that require a strong lightweight fabric.

ROMAINE *see* CRÊPE ROMAINE.

royal rib, woven

rubber (sheeting)

ROUGH BROWNS (*obs.*) A linen fabric of poor quality in the loom state.[3, 36]

ROYAL RIB, KNITTED *see* CARDIGAN RIB.

ROYAL RIB, WOVEN A woven weft rib fabric that has a characteristic weft-faced cord effect running vertically down the length of the fabric, parallel to the selvedge. It is a type of cord fabric.

Royal rib is traditionally an all-cotton fabric. The vertical cords are made thick by having two or more warp ends drawn through each heald and reed space and weaving as one. There are a much greater number of weft picks per centimetre than warp ends. The fabric is woven in plain weave, the weft yarns bending around the thicker warp yarns, which remain more or less straight. The warp yarns are usually completely covered by the weft yarns, which form the cords running down the length of the fabric.

Royal rib is usually piece-dyed. Different qualities are made, but one typical royal rib fabric construction is 23 tex cotton warp sett at 28 ends per cm and 16 tex cotton weft woven at 56 picks per cm.[26] Royal rib fabrics can be prone to slippage in the direction of the straight yarns unless the fabric is well constructed. Royal rib is similar to a weft rib moreen fabric.

See also CORD FABRICS; COTTON FABRIC; RIB FABRICS, WOVEN.

End uses: casual trousers, skirts, jackets, shirts and furnishing fabrics.

RUBBER A very stretchy and totally waterproof material that is made from latex, a milky white juice extracted from many species of plants and trees grown in tropical countries. It is also possible to make rubber from the juice of the dandelion plant and of greater celandine, but yields are low in comparison to tropical plants.[3]

Rubber may be used in textiles in several different forms.

(i) *Rubber sheeting.* Rubber in sheet form may be produced in different thicknesses and colours. It may be flat, or it may have a textured surface to give it non-slip properties. It is used for items such as wetsuits, shoes, accessories, industrial textiles, mats and floor coverings.

(ii) *Rubber fibres.* Rubber may be manufactured into fibres, which are used together with other fibres to make stretchy knitted and woven fabrics. Both natural and synthetic rubber are used to make continuous filament rubber fibres. Synthetic rubber is manufactured from the fibre-forming substances that are contained in natural rubber. The rubber is usually wrapped with an outer covering of other fibres (e.g. cotton, nylon or polyester); sewing elastic is made in this way. Rubber may also be core-spun with an outer covering of other fibres, usually nylon or polyester. Rubber fibres have, however, largely been replaced by elastane fibres nowadays. Elastane is a man-made synthetic fibre that is also inherently stretchy, like rubber. *See* ELASTANE FABRIC.

(iii) *Rubber coating.* Rubber may be used as a coating, applied in liquid form to constructed fabrics of all kinds to make them waterproof, to give them protective qualities, or to create a durable non-slip surface. The whole fabric may be coated with rubber, or it may be applied to selected areas only. The Scottish chemist Charles Macintosh was the first to produce a waterproof fabric by laminating two cotton fabrics together with a rubber solution made from naphtha and rubber. His process was patented in 1823. The term 'mackintosh' is still used today to describe any type of waterproof raincoat.[3] Latex or liquid rubber may also be used to coat sturdy woven base fabrics, to produce heavy-duty waterproof clothing.[23] (*See* WATERPROOF AND WATER-REPELLENT FABRICS.) Rubber applied to a fabric in a dot formation (or in various other shapes) both strengthens the fabric and provides a durable non-slip surface. These fabrics are used for items such as slipper socks, gardening and work gloves, and workwear generally.

(iv) *Foam.* Rubber is used to make thin layers of lightweight foam that may be laminated to other fabrics. The foam acts as an effective insulator and provides cushioning. This type of laminate is particularly useful for shoes and accesssories. *See* FOAM.

rubber (dots)

sailcloth

Neoprene is a man-made synthetic elastomer that is a similar material to rubber and was developed as a substitute for it. *See* NEOPRENE.

See also COATED FABRIC, ELASTANE FABRIC, LAMINATED FABRIC, STRETCH FABRIC.

End uses: waterproof clothing, raincoats, wellington boots, rubber gloves, wetsuits, protective clothing, slipper socks, gardening and work gloves, workwear, shoes, accessories, industrial textiles, mats, floor coverings and elasticated stretch garments.

RUSSELL CORD (Russel cord) *see* CORD FABRICS.

RUSSIAN CORD A woven fabric in which raised vertical cords are produced down the length of the fabric by leno weaving. The colour of the raised cord stripes usually contrasts strongly with the background colour.

Instead of using the doup ends to make an open mesh structure, coloured leno or crossing ends are traversed on successive picks, from side to side of thick, standard ground ends. This creates solid warpways stripes with the majority of the coloured or effect yarns on the face of the fabric. Normally there are two ribs in the vertical cords produced.[26]

See also CORD FABRICS, LENO FABRIC.

End uses: shirts and dresses.

RUSSIAN TWILL *see* TWILL FABRICS.

SAILCLOTH A tightly woven cotton or linen fabric. Sailcloth is a strong, stiff, hard-wearing fabric that is prone to creasing and does not drape well. Sailcloth was originally made for use as yacht and ship sails, and so was given special finishing treatments in order to shrink and strengthen the fabric, making it less air-permeable and more waterproof. Nowadays it is no longer normally used as yacht sails, but has a wide range of fashion end uses (see list below). Modern fabrics used to make yacht sails are usually made from strong but lightweight nylon, polyester or aramid fibres. The fabrics may include ripstop threads to enhance tear resistance, they may be coated with various finishes, or they may be laminated, for example with thin polymer films to aid dimensional stability.

Traditional sailcloth is a medium- to heavyweight fabric made from high-twist, two-fold cotton or linen yarns. Nowadays it is also made from viscose, nylon, polyester or blends (most usually polyester/cotton). The fabric is woven in a close-sett plain weave or a 2/1 hopsack weave construction. It is usually either colour-woven in solid colours or piece-dyed. It is often finished with resin treatments, which give it a hard, stiff handle. Sailcloth is a similar fabric to canvas, duck and Holland, but it is lighter in weight than any of them.

See also HOPSACK, RIPSTOP.

End uses: hard-wearing trousers, dresses, shirts, children's clothes, summer jackets and suits, rainwear, uniforms, curtains and luggage.

SALISBURY FLANNEL *see* FLANNEL.

SAND CRÊPE *see* CRÊPE.

SANGLIER (*obs.*) A closely woven, plain weave fabric made from worsted and/or mohair; it had a rough, wiry surface. It was originally woven in France, *sanglier* being the French word for 'wild boar'.[5, 36]

sarsenet

sateen (back and face)

5-end sateen

8-end sateen

SARSENET (sarsonet, sarcenet) A woven lining fabric. There are two main qualities: a lightweight quality used in millinery, and a heavier-weight silk or cotton fabric.

The lightweight sarsenet (originally spelt sarcenet) is a thin, soft, sheer fabric, like a net or veiling, and is used as a lining in millinery. Traditionally it was plain woven in silk, but it is also woven in nylon and polyester. The name derives from the Arab Saracens who originally made and used the fabric for head-dresses. Sarsenet was first used in England in the 13th century.[36] A heavier sarsenet fabric is also woven in silk or cotton in a plain weave construction. The fabric is piece-dyed and calendered in finishing to give it a lustrous surface on the face side.

See also LINING FABRIC, PLAIN WEAVE FABRIC, SHEER FABRICS, STRAW FABRICS.

End uses: millinery fabric, linings, ribbons and veils.

SATEEN A woven fabric made in a sateen weave construction. Sateen is one of the four elementary woven fabric structures (the others being plain weave, satin and twill). Sateen is a completely weft-faced weave structure, which has long weft floats and infrequent binding points that are arranged in a regular all-over manner, so as to avoid diagonal twill lines in the fabric. Because of the few binding points, the weft yarns are able to pack very tightly together, creating a characteristically very dense, smooth, flat and lustrous fabric. Sateen is principally used as a lining for both garments and curtains. It is not a particularly hard-wearing fabric and is prone to yarn slippage.

The face side of sateen fabric, which consists almost entirely of weft floats, is the complete opposite of the reverse side, which consists almost entirely of warp floats (rather like a satin weave). However, sateen is not an exact reverse of a satin fabric because in a sateen fabric there are usually far more weft picks per centimetre than warp ends. This accounts in part for the predominance of weft yarns on the surface. Sateen weave is used to construct a wide range of weights and qualities of fabric, suited to different end uses. For example, sateen curtain lining fabric is usually made from mercerized cotton or polyester/cotton yarns. The weft yarns are thicker than the warp yarns and less highly twisted (i.e. medium twist), in order to accentuate their lustre. The result is a soft, lustrous, loosely constructed fabric that is usually made in natural tones, bleached, or dyed in solid colours. Occasionally it is printed. The fabric is often given a schreiner finish to improve cover and enhance the lustre. In addition, the striped cotton suit linings used by tailors are often made in sateen weave construction.

Most sateen fabrics are woven in a 5-shaft sateen construction (with five weft picks in the repeat), and some are woven in an 8-shaft sateen construction (with eight weft picks in the repeat). Different effects may be produced in the fabric by varying the direction of the yarn twist in relation to the direction of the sateen twill. There are several different variations. When the direction of the twill is the same as that of the twist of the weft yarns, a sateen fabric with an irregular appearance is produced. In French sateen, the direction of the twill (running from bottom left to top right) is the opposite to that of the twist of the weft yarns, producing a sateen fabric with a prominent, clear, distinct twill effect. In ordinary sateen, the direction of the twill (running from bottom right to top left) is the opposite to that of the twist of the weft yarns, producing a sateen fabric with a fairly prominent, clear twill effect, but not as prominent as in French sateen.[4]

Fabrics that are woven either in a sateen weave construction or in a construction based on a sateen weave include beaverteen, brocade, brocatelle, clip spot, damask, extra warp and extra weft fabrics, façonné, fleece fabric, fustian fabrics, imperial sateen, Italian, lancé, moleskin fabric and swansdown.

See also LINING FABRIC, WOVEN FABRIC.

End uses: lining for garments and curtains, suit linings, upholstery, curtains, mattress covers and theatrical costumes.

SATIN, WARP-KNITTED A satin fabric that is knitted on a warp-knitting machine. It is similar in appearance to woven satin, but its surface is less smooth and compact.

Warp-knitted satin is knitted on two guide bars with long front-bar underlaps, which produces a smooth fabric surface on the technical back of the fabric. This then becomes the face side of the fabric in use. Most non-stretch satin fabrics are knitted on high-speed tricot machines. Fabrics may be solid in colour or they may be subsequently printed. Tricot-knitted satin fabric is also often given a schreiner finish to improve lustre and increase the cover.[19] Stretch satin fabrics are knitted on raschel warp-knitting machines in order that the elastane may be 'laid-in' under adequate tension. Warp-knitted mirror satin is produced in this manner. It is noted for its smooth, lustrous appearance and is widely used for lingerie. It has good warp stretch but does not have particularly good modulus (control properties). It is normally produced using three guide bars, using a fine, high-quality nylon yarn in two of them and elastane in the third.

Warp-knitted fabrics knitted in a satin construction may also be brushed and cropped to produce a suede-like surface. These fabrics are usually knitted with cupro, nylon or polyester yarns, and the fabric is knitted with floats on the technical back. *See* SUEDE CLOTH.

satin, warp-knitted
(mirror satin, back and face)

satin, warp-knitted
(stretch satin, face and back)

See also KNITTED FABRIC; RASCHEL STRETCH FABRICS; SATIN, WOVEN; TRICOT; WARP-KNITTED FABRIC.

End uses: dress fabric, lingerie, outerwear fabrics and sheets.

SATIN, WOVEN A woven fabric made in a satin weave construction. Satin is one of the four elementary woven fabric structures (the others being plain weave, sateen and twill). Satin is a completely warp-faced weave structure that has long warp floats and infrequent binding points that are arranged in a regular all-over manner, so as to avoid diagonal twill lines in the fabric. Because of the few binding points, the warp yarns are able to pack very tightly together, creating a characteristically very dense, smooth, flat and lustrous fabric with a reflective surface and excellent drape.

The term 'satin' is thought to have come from the seaport town in south-eastern China known as Zaytoun (now called Chuanchou), from where fabrics were shipped.[3] Satin fabrics were traditionally made from silk, but nowadays they are woven in a wide variety of fibres. Highly lustrous warp yarns (mainly continuous filament) are usually selected in order to exploit the smooth, dense nature of the fabric surface. Fibres used include silk, acetate, viscose, nylon, polyester, mercerized cotton and blends of these. Slightly less lustrous satin fabrics may also be made with wool yarns. These fabrics are typically used as suiting fabrics.

The face side of satin fabric, which consists almost entirely of warp floats, is completely opposite to the reverse side, which consists almost entirely of weft floats (rather like a sateen weave). However, satin is not an exact reverse of a sateen fabric because in a satin fabric there are usually far more fine warp ends per centimetre than the slightly thicker weft picks (at least twice as many). This, combined with the warp-faced satin weave structure itself, results in a fabric with a predominance of warp yarns on the surface of the fabric. The satin weave structure characteristically has long floats of warp yarns that cover the weft yarns. Each warp end interlaces only once per repeat, which is over at least five

satin, woven

8-end satin

5-end satin

ends and sometimes as many as twelve ends. The two most common satin weave structures are a 5-end satin (with five warp ends in the repeat) and an 8-end satin (with eight warp ends in the repeat).

Satin fabric is woven in a very wide range of different weights and qualities according to its many end uses (see the list below). The heaviest, most luxurious satin fabric is probably duchesse satin. Fabrics that are woven either in a satin weave construction or in a construction based on a satin weave include the following, discussed in separate entries elsewhere: amazon, atlas (woven), beaver cloth, some blackout fabrics, traditional blazer cloth, brocade, brocatelle, buckskin fabric, charmante satin, charmeuse, clip spot, some crêpe fabrics (crêpe-back satin, faille crêpe, crêpe meteor), damask, doeskin fabric, some drill fabrics, duchesse satin, duvetyn, Eskimo cloth, extra warp and extra weft fabrics, façonné, Frenchback, grandrelle shirting, Madras shirting, messaline, peau d'ange, peau de cygne, peau de soie, serge (Frenchback serge), some ticking fabrics, some tie fabrics, Venetian and zibeline. A number of other traditional satin fabrics are discussed below. Satin is a suitable base fabric for embroidery; *see also* EMBROIDERED FABRICS.

ANTIQUE SATIN A heavy satin fabric with a dull lustre, usually woven with smooth warp yarns on the technical face side and slub or uneven weft yarns on the technical back. It is a reversible fabric, but it is often used with the technical back as the face side, especially with furnishing fabrics.

BARONET SATIN A highly lustrous satin fabric, woven with high-lustre viscose warp yarns and cotton weft yarns, and dyed in bright colours.

BRIDAL SATIN A smooth, lustrous, heavy satin woven fabric used for wedding gowns.

CHAMOIS SATIN A satin fabric that is finished to give a soft, semi-lustrous surface like that of a suede fabric.

CIRÉ SATIN A satin woven fabric that is given a ciré finishing treatment (*see* CIRÉ). This produces a stiff, leather-like fabric with an extremely high lustre. Ciré satin fabrics are often dyed in metallic colours.

COTTON SATIN A satin woven fabric made from cotton, which is often mercerized; it is typically used for shirts, dresses, sheets and lining fabrics.

DOUBLE SATIN (double-face satin) An expensive satin fabric that is woven as a double cloth, with satin weave on both sides. Both sides of the fabric are lustrous, and the weft is completely hidden on the inside. Each side of the fabric may be a different colour. It is used mainly for lingerie and ribbons. *See* DOUBLE CLOTH, PEAU DE SOIE.

EMBOSSED SATIN (hammered satin) A heavyweight satin fabric with an embossed pattern; it is typically used for evening wear wedding gowns. *See* EMBOSSED FABRICS.

FARMER'S SATIN A lustrous, durable lining fabric made with a cotton warp and worsted, viscose or cotton weft yarns. It is used as a lining fabric for men's suits.

HAMMERED SATIN see **embossed satin** above.

bridal satin

double satin
(double-faced)

embossed satin

cotton satin

PAILLETTE SATIN A satin fabric with a characteristic iridescent colour effect created by alternating two contrasting colours in the warp. It is woven in a 5-end satin weave construction and is a relatively thin, inexpensive quality of satin fabric.

PANNE SATIN A highly lustrous, heavy satin fabric that is traditionally made with silk yarns and given a stiff, lustrous finish by very heavy roller pressure. The term 'panne' is descriptive of this highly lustrous finish. Panne satin is used especially for evening wear.

satin stripe

ribbed satin

satin stripe

slipper satin

RIBBED SATIN A fabric with alternating stripes of rib and satin weave. It is sometimes given a moiré finish. *See also* MOIRÉ FABRIC; RIB FABRICS, WOVEN; STRIPES.

SATIN-BACK A double cloth fabric in which the backing fabric is woven in a satin weave construction. *See* DOUBLE CLOTH.

SATINET (satinette) A fabric woven in a 4-end (i.e. with four warp ends in the repeat) irregular satin or sateen weave structure. It is based on a broken twill weave structure.

SATIN MERVEILLEUX A soft satin fabric woven in a 7-end satin weave construction. It is usually woven with silk yarns and often has a shot colour effect (created by alternating two contrasting colours in the warp).

SATIN ROYALE A double-faced satin fabric woven in silk with satin weave on both sides. The lustre is further enhanced during finishing to produce an extremely lustrous and luxurious fabric. *See* DOUBLE CLOTH.

SATIN STRIPE A fabric that has lustrous satin woven stripes alternating with contrasting stripes woven in a different weave structure (e.g. sateen), with a different thickness of yarn or in a different colour. *See also* STRIPES.

SHOE SATIN see **slipper satin** below.

SLEAZY SATIN A thin, inexpensive but soft and lustrous satin fabric that is used mainly as a lining fabric. It is usually made from acetate or acetate and viscose.

SLIPPER SATIN (shoe satin) A densely woven satin fabric that is made from good-quality yarns and is therefore very hard-wearing. It was originally made for ladies' evening shoes and ballet shoes, with silk warp yarns and cotton weft yarns. This gives the fabric a silk face and a cotton back. It is now also made with man-made fibres, and it is available in a wide range of colours, including multicoloured jacquard designs. Slipper satin is traditionally woven with at least 120 ends per cm and enough picks to ensure a well-constructed fabric.[25] A typical slipper satin fabric construction using acetate yarns is: 67 dtex warp sett at 130 ends per cm and 44 dtex weft woven at 38 picks per cm.[25]

See also SATIN, WARP-KNITTED; WOVEN FABRIC.

End uses: upholstery, curtains, mattress covers, sheets, shoe uppers, ballet shoes, dresses, blouses, suits, jackets, trousers, men's neckties, tuxedo lapels, shirts, wedding dresses, evening wear, lingerie, ribbons, linings and trims.

Saxony

scrim (woven)

SATIN CRÊPE *see* CRÊPE.

SATINET *see* SATIN, WOVEN.

SATINETTE, WARP-KNITTED *see* RASCHEL STRETCH FABRICS.

SATINETTE, WOVEN *see* SATIN, WOVEN.

SAXONY A soft woven fabric made with good-quality woollen or worsted yarns. The term refers to the quality of the fabric rather than to its construction. It has a similar look to tweed, but it is softer. Saxony is known for being a good-quality, hard-wearing woollen fabric.

The name comes from the province of Saxony in northern Germany, where this fabric was originally woven from local wool for use as overcoats. It is now woven in many different countries, using good-quality botany yarns made from fine merino wool spun on the woollen system. Saxony is woven in simple weave structures such as plain weave or twill, in many different weights and qualities. It may be woven in plain colours, in small dobby woven check designs, or with tweed effects. It is usually milled and raised during finishing to give it a soft, smooth nap. Saxony is a similar fabric to West of England fabric and also to tweed, but it is made from finer, softer wool than tweed.

See also COATING FABRIC, DOBBY FABRIC, NAPPED FABRICS, TWEED.

End uses: suits, jackets, coats, caps and hats.

SAY (saye) (*obs.*) A fine twill woven fabric made from worsted wool, similar to wool serge. It was originally dyed black and used as shirtings. It was made in England (at Sudbury, in Suffolk) and in Holland.[3, 36]

SCHAPPE SILK *see* SILK FABRIC.

SCOTTISH TWEED (Scotch tweed) *see* TWEED.

SCRIM A general term for a lightweight base cloth that may be woven or warp-knitted and that is normally used as a backing fabric for other fabrics in order to give them added dimensional stability and/or strength. There are many different quality scrims, ranging from sheer, open-sett fabrics to heavier semi-sheer or opaque fabrics. Scrim fabrics may be sewn or laminated onto other fabrics; *see* LAMINATED FABRIC.

Most woven scrims belong to the muslin family of fabrics. They may be made from any low-grade fibre, but jute, hemp or cotton are often used. Woven scrim is usually woven in an open-sett plain weave or a simple leno fabric construction, and it is usually given a stiffening finish. Fabrics that are similar to woven scrim and also belong to the muslin family of fabrics include bolting cloth, book cloth, buckram, bunting, butter muslin, cheesecloth, crinoline, étamine, gauze, mull and tarlatan.

Warp-knitted scrim is sometimes a cheaper option than a woven scrim fabric. Warp-knitted scrims are usually lightweight fabrics, knitted in nylon or polyester. Suitable fabrics include locknit (warp-knitted), queenscord, sharkskin (warp-knitted) and tricot.

Fabrics that are sometimes supported by scrim include fur fabrics, needlefelt and nonwoven fabrics of various kinds.

See also FELT, KNITTED FABRIC, LAMINATED FABRIC, LENO FABRIC, LOCKNIT, MUSLIN, NON-WOVEN FABRIC, SHEER FABRICS, WARP-KNITTED FABRIC.

End uses: bandages, backing fabric for garments, backing fabric for upholstery and curtains, backing fabric for paper used in packaging, reinforcing fabric for plaster sculptures and support fabric used in millinery.

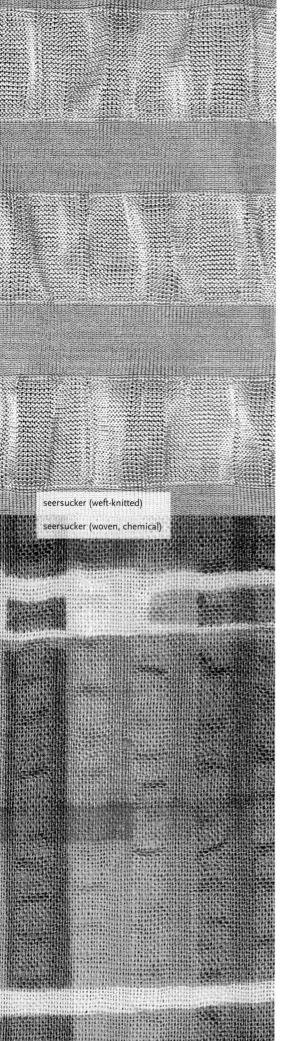

seersucker (weft-knitted)

seersucker (woven, chemical)

SEA ISLAND COTTON *see* COTTON FABRIC.

SEERLOOP *see* SEERSUCKER.

SEERSUCKER A woven fabric that has characteristic puckered or blistered areas contrasting with areas of flat, smooth fabric. Seersucker is usually woven in vertical stripe patterns of various widths – that is, puckered stripes alternating with flat woven columns; however, it may also be arranged in check formation, which is sometimes called 'seersucker gingham'. Because of the puckered effect of the fabric, creases do not show, and seersucker does not normally need ironing. Knitted seersucker fabrics are also made in imitation of woven seersucker fabric.

The word 'seersucker' comes from Persian *shir o shakkar*, meaning 'milk and sugar', the contrast between the two reflecting the two textures of the fabric.[3] Seersucker fabric may be woven in a wide variety of weights and qualities and using any fibres. However, the most common traditional seersucker is probably a mid- to lightweight cotton fabric. It is normally woven in plain weave. Seersucker may be dyed in solid colours, it may be printed, or it may be colour-woven with multicoloured stripes or checks integrated with the puckered areas.

A true seersucker fabric is produced by weaving the puckered effect into the fabric. Stripes of warp yarns are arranged on two different weaving loom beams for weaving. The beam containing the warp ends for the puckered stripes are fed to the loom at a faster rate than the beam containing the warp ends for the flat woven stripes. During weaving, as the weft yarns are beaten up, the more slackly tensioned warp yarns are woven into the fabric at a faster rate than the normally tensioned sections, causing the fabric to pucker in these areas. This effect is fixed as a permanent, inherent characteristic of the fabric.

Similar effects may also be produced, often more cheaply, by the application of various permanent or semi-permanent finishing treatments to a woven fabric. For example, stripes of a resist solution can be printed onto a cotton fabric to protect these areas. The fabric is then immersed in a solution of caustic soda, which causes the unprotected areas to shrink. The areas that were protected from the chemical by the resist material, which is removed afterwards, will be the areas that pucker. These fabrics are called by various names, including 'seersucker', 'seersucker effect fabrics', 'blister cloth' and 'crinkle crêpe'. In the United States seersucker effect fabrics are sometimes called 'crinkle fabric'. *See also* BLISTER CLOTH, CRINKLE CRÊPE, CRINKLE FABRIC.

Crimps are woven seersucker fabrics of a particular kind, in which two different counts of warp yarn are placed in small groups across the width of the fabric. Each is contained on different weaving loom beams. During weaving, the thicker warp yarns are tensioned more slackly so that they are woven into the fabric at a faster rate than the ground ends, causing these areas to crimp and pucker. The crimped areas may be the same colour as the ground fabric or a different colour.[36] Crimps can also be produced by mixing botany wool and mohair yarns in a fabric. The crimp effect is produced during finishing by the differential shrinkage of the two yarns.[36]

Seerloop is another variant, in which thicker warp yarns are placed either singly or in small groups across the width of the fabric. These yarns are contained on a different

seersucker (woven)

sequinned fabric

serge

serge (Frenchback)

weaving loom beam from the finer yarns of the ground fabric. They are tensioned more slackly, so that they are woven into the fabric at a faster rate than the ground ends, causing the yarns to form loops on the surface of the fabric. The loops are spaced at regular intervals down the length of the fabric and may be the same colour as the ground fabric or a different colour.[10]

Knitted seersucker fabrics are usually weft-knitted single jersey fabrics composed of alternating sections, knitted in contrasting yarns and/or contrasting knit structures: for example, sections of plain knit alternating with sections knitted in double cross tuck stitch.

End uses: casual clothing, including shirts, blouses, dresses, skirts, summer jackets, trousers, shorts, beachwear, children's wear, pyjamas and nightgowns; also lingerie, aprons, tablecloths, bed linen, bedspreads, curtains and (for wool seersucker) suitings.

SEQUINNED FABRICS A general term for fabrics of any kind that are decorated with sequins. Sequins are very small, usually round shiny discs that are used as decorative dress trimmings to give fabrics sparkle.

Any fabrics may be decorated with sequins, including woven, knitted, nonwoven or lace fabrics. However, those chosen are usually fine, costly fabrics, such as tulle or crêpe fabrics, that are typically used for glamorous evening wear garments. The sequins may be made from metal, plastic, plastic-coated metal or metal-coated plastic, and are usually just 2–4 mm in diameter. Sequins are produced in solid colours, including gold, silver and most other colours. They may also be patterned with holographic images for extra sparkle. *See* HOLOGRAPHIC FABRICS.

Most sequins are either hand- or machine-embroidered onto the backing fabric. Attaching them with adhesive is not usually a secure enough method for sustained use. Fabrics and garments may be decorated with sequins over the whole of their surface, producing a very shiny effect similar to a lamé fabric, or they may be sewn onto selected areas only.

See also BEADED FABRICS, EMBROIDERED FABRICS, LAMÉ, METALLIC FABRICS.

End uses: evening wear, bridal wear, wedding veils, theatrical costumes, ballet costumes, leotards, swimwear, shoes, purses and evening bags.

SERGE A densely woven, piece-dyed fabric, woven in twill weave and traditionally made from worsted wool yarns. It is a particularly hard-wearing fabric, with excellent drape and a smooth face that characteristically becomes shiny with wear.

Serge is a very ancient fabric. The name is thought to derive from Latin *serica*, meaning 'silk', suggesting that the fabric may have contained silk at one time.[3] During the 12th century, a very fine-quality serge fabric was made that was known as 'say' or 'saye'.[3] Although serge fabric today is usually made from worsted wool, it is also sometimes made from wool or wool blended with other fibres, and occasionally it is also made from other fibres, including cotton, silk, viscose and synthetic fibres and blends.

Characteristically, the yarns are highly twisted, and the fabric is closely sett in a more or less square cloth construction (i.e. with the same number of warp ends and weft picks). It is these features that make serge such a hard-wearing fabric. The strongest serge fabrics use either two-fold or three-fold yarns in both the warp and weft. Other qualities are woven with two-fold yarns in the warp and singles yarns in the weft, or with singles yarns in both the warp and the weft. Serge

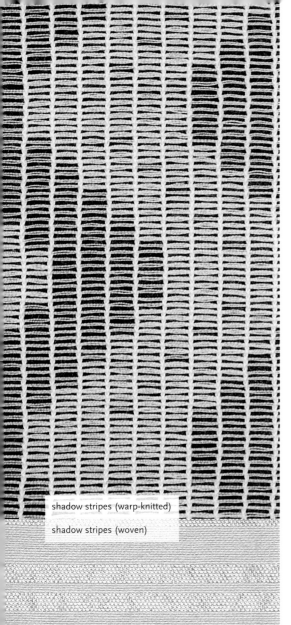

shadow stripes (warp-knitted)

shadow stripes (woven)

is usually woven in a balanced 2/2 right-hand twill weave construction (i.e. running from bottom left to top right). However, 3/3 twills or other twills are also sometimes used. The square construction of the fabric gives the twill diagonal an angle of 45°. Serge is given a clear finish (i.e. it is lightly milled and raised so that there are few protruding fibres and the yarns and weave structure are clear and distinct).

Most serge fabrics are medium-weight fabrics; however, many different qualities are made. The quality depends on how closely sett the warp and weft yarns are and on the type of yarns used. The handle of the fabric varies with the different qualities of wool used. For example, botany wool or 'botany twill' serges are softer and more luxurious in handle than serges made from cross-bred wools, which are firmer and rougher.

Variations of the traditional serge fabric include the following. French serge is a particularly good-quality serge fabric that is used extensively for tailored clothing, especially women's wear. It is made from a fine, soft worsted wool. Frenchback serge is a backed fabric consisting of two fabric layers woven together with a single weft. The face side, woven in twill weave, is the serge fabric, and the back is usually woven in a satin weave. Frenchback serge is therefore a much heavier serge fabric, almost twice the weight of French serge. It is used for men's wear and for women's suits and trousers. (*See* BACKED FABRIC, FRENCHBACK.) Imperial serge is a lightweight coating fabric, similar to imperial cloth but woven more loosely and therefore softer. Navy serge is a very strong, hard-wearing serge fabric that is traditionally used for US navy uniforms; it is sometimes called 'navy cloth'. Storm serge is a heavier-quality serge fabric, made with thicker than normal yarns. It is coarse and wiry in handle. Other variations of serge or fabrics similar to serge include cassimere, imperial cloth and gaberdine. Serge fabrics may also be piece-dyed to produce khaki fabrics. The following terms may be noted: 'silk serge', an alternative name for surah; and 'serge de Nîmes', from which the name 'denim' is thought to be derived (denim being a cotton twill fabric originally made in Nîmes, France).

See also BOTANY TWILL, COATING FABRIC, TWILL FABRICS, WOOL FABRIC, WORSTED FABRIC.

End uses: men's suits, men's and women's tailored wear, coats, school uniforms, military uniforms, trousers and skirts.

SERPENTINE CRÊPE *see* CRÊPE.

SHADOW STRIPES AND CHECKS Fabrics with an illusive shadow effect in the same colour as the ground colour. They have a subtle two-tone appearance. Most are woven, although similar effects may also be produced in some knitted fabrics, especially warp-knits.

Most woven shadow stripe fabrics are made by arranging the warp yarns into alternate sections of 'S' and 'Z' twist yarns. When dyed, light is reflected at different angles by the alternating sections of the woven fabric, and it is this that creates the shadow effect. Shadow stripes may also be made in the horizontal direction of a fabric by weaving alternate sections of 'S' and 'Z' twist weft yarns. When alternate sections of 'S' and 'Z' twist yarns are arranged in both the warp and the weft, shadow checks are produced. The fabric may be woven in any weave structure, and the shadow effect is clearly visible in plain and twill woven fabrics; however, it is most prominent when warp-faced twill weaves or satin weave structures are used. Usually either the 'S' twist or the 'Z' twist yarns are tinted with a fugitive dye during manufacture, so that the difference between the two yarns is obvious; this tint is removed from the fabric during finishing.

Shadow effects may also be created in woven fabrics in a number of other ways. (i) Shadow stripe effects may be achieved in plain woven lustre fabrics by varying the denting of the warp yarns in alternate sections: for example, one section dented with two ends per dent, alternating with the next section dented with one end per dent. Some pekin stripe fabrics and striped voile fabrics are made in this way. In high-lustre weft fabrics, an effective shadow check fabric may also be made by denting the ends irregularly and then weaving the fabric with alternate sections of 'S' and 'Z' twist weft yarns. *See* BRAD-FORD LUSTRE FABRICS, PEKIN, VOILE.[26]

(ii) Fine woven fabrics may be printed with a pattern that is the same colour as the base fabric (e.g. white on white). Shadow organdie (*see* ORGANDIE) is an example of a fabric made in this way.

(iii) The warp yarns may be printed prior to weaving. *See* WARP-PRINTED FABRIC.

(iv) Shadow stripes may be made by arranging alternate sections of yarns: using yarns of varying counts, with varying amounts of twist, or with variations in brightness and lustre.

(v) Variations in the weave structures used in the different sections can also produce a similar effect: for example, by reversing the direction of a regular satin weave structure or by varying the length of the warp floats in the different sections.[26] Fabrics woven in a herringbone weave structure can also sometimes create a shadow effect; however, they are not considered to be true shadow weave fabrics.[5]

In warp-knitted fabrics, shadow effects can be created by the following methods:
- knitting extra yarns of the same colour as the ground colour at intervals to form a pattern
- printing the knitted fabric with a pattern of the same colour
- space-dyeing the yarns with a different shade in the same colour
- using lustre-variant yarns to form stripes in the warp, for example lustrous or bright trilobal yarns (yarns made with a three-sided cross-section in order to increase light reflectance) and matt or semi-matt yarns.

See also CHECKS, OMBRÉ, SPACE-DYED FABRIC, STRIPES.

End uses: sheer curtains, lingerie, blouses, scarves and ladies' evening wear.

SHAKER FLANNEL *see* FLANNEL.

SHALLOON (*obs.*) A woven fabric made from cross-bred worsted yarns and woven in 2/2 twill. It was used as a lining fabric for coats and uniforms.[10, 25]

SHAMMY CLOTH *see* CHAMOIS CLOTH.

SHANTUNG A plain woven fabric that is traditionally made with uneven tussah silk yarns, giving the fabric a crisp, irregular surface texture that is most apparent in the weft direction. It is often made using the natural silk yarns that range in colour from ecru to brown, and it is usually a medium-weight fabric.

Shantung takes its name from the province of Shantung in northern China, where it was originally woven on hand-looms using raw tussah silk yarns. This is a type of wild silk obtained from the cocoon of the wild silkworm *Antheraea mylitta*,[36] and its imperfections give it a characteristic slubby and uneven texture. Nowadays the look is imitated using man-made fibres (particularly acetate and viscose) or cotton instead of the silk; the yarns are spun with deliberate irregularities and are used mainly in the weft. Sometimes yarns of different counts are also used in the weft to emphasize the irregular surface texture. Shantung is woven in plain weave structure and is either made using the natural brown-coloured silk yarns or dyed in solid colours.

A typical shantung fabric construction is 17 tex warp sett at 30 ends per cm and 17 tex weft woven at 29 picks per cm.[26] Similar fabrics to shantung include honan and pongee, which both originate from different districts in China. Shantung is heavier and rougher than pongee and, unlike honan, uses slub yarns in the weft only. Shantung is sometimes called 'tussore', which is the Indian name for a very similar fabric (*see* TUSSORE). A number of variations of shantung are discussed below.

ANTIQUE SHANTUNG A shantung fabric made with warp yarns dyed in one colour and woven with weft yarns dyed in a contrasting colour. This produces a 'shot' colour effect in

shadow checks (woven)

shantung

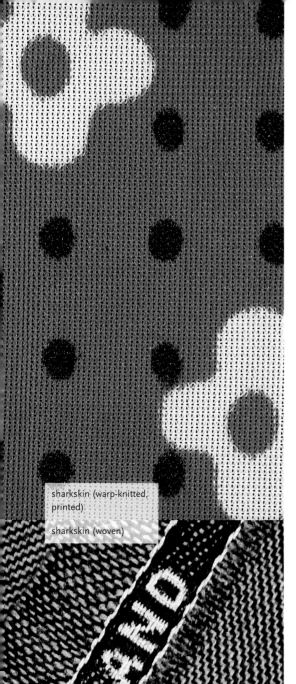

sharkskin (warp-knitted, printed)

sharkskin (woven)

the fabric, where the colour appears to change due to different light reflections when the fabric is moved. *See* SHOT FABRICS.

COTTON SHANTUNG A shantung fabric made using irregular cotton slub yarns. It is similar in appearance and weight to silk shantung and is sometimes called 'Himalaya'. It is used mainly for curtains and bedspreads.

DOUPION SHANTUNG A shantung fabric made with silk yarns obtained from double cocoons. It is the heaviest and most expensive shantung fabric produced. *See* DOUPION.

NYLON SHANTUNG A shantung fabric usually made with filament yarns of nylon in the warp and spun nylon yarns in the weft. It is quite a stiff fabric.

SHANTUNG TAFFETA A silk shantung fabric in which the natural gum of the silk is not removed after weaving, giving the fabric a crisp handle, similar to that of taffeta.

SPUN-SILK SHANTUNG A shantung fabric made with irregular slub yarns formed by spinning short, staple silk fibres.

VISCOSE SHANTUNG A shantung fabric that is usually made with filament yarns of acetate in the warp and spun viscose yarns in the weft.

See also PLAIN WEAVE FABRIC, SILK FABRIC.

End uses: dresses, blouses, shirts, women's lightweight suitings, occasion wear, scarves, curtains and bedspreads.

SHARKSKIN A term used for three different types of fabric:
(i) A high-quality, medium-weight woven fabric made with worsted yarns. It is very smooth and fine in texture and very hard-wearing, and it is used as a lightweight summer suiting fabric.
(ii) A lightweight, crisp and not very durable fabric, woven using acetate, viscose, triacetate or sometimes cotton yarns. It is used mainly for women's wear and sportswear, and is completely different from (i).
(iii) A warp-knitted sharkskin fabric.
     The three types of fabric are discussed in detail below.
(i) The traditional worsted sharkskin is woven with worsted yarns, usually in a very fine, balanced 2/2 twill weave construction. Yarns of two different colours, usually dark and light, are alternated in both the warp and the weft (either 1 and 1 or 2 and 2), producing a small step pattern in the fabric. This arrangement of coloured yarns produces diagonal stripes of colour that slope up to the left, in the opposite direction from the twill lines, which slope up to the right. Sometimes checked and striped designs are made; the fabric is sometimes also made using silk yarns or yarns of other fibres and blends. This type of sharkskin is intended to be worn in the summer or in hot climates, and may be described as a 'tropical suiting fabric'. *See* TROPICAL SUITING.
(ii) The second type of woven sharkskin fabric is woven using de-lustred continuous filament acetate, viscose, triacetate or sometimes cotton yarns. It is usually woven as a solid-colour fabric in either a plain weave or a hopsack weave construction. This fabric is dull in appearance owing to the use of de-lustred yarns.
(iii) Warp-knitted sharkskin fabric is knitted on a two-bar tricot warp-knitting machine. The construction is made with full-set threading in both guide bars. The back guide bar underlaps three or four needle spaces, and the front guide bar underlaps one needle space in the opposite direction. This produces a fabric similar to locknit, but heavier and more rigid; it is useful as a print base cloth and a scrim or backing fabric for laminated fabrics. The technical back is used as the effect side.[25, 31] *See* KNITTED FABRIC, LAMINATED FABRIC, LOCKNIT, QUEENSCORD, SCRIM, TRICOT, WARP-KNITTED FABRIC.

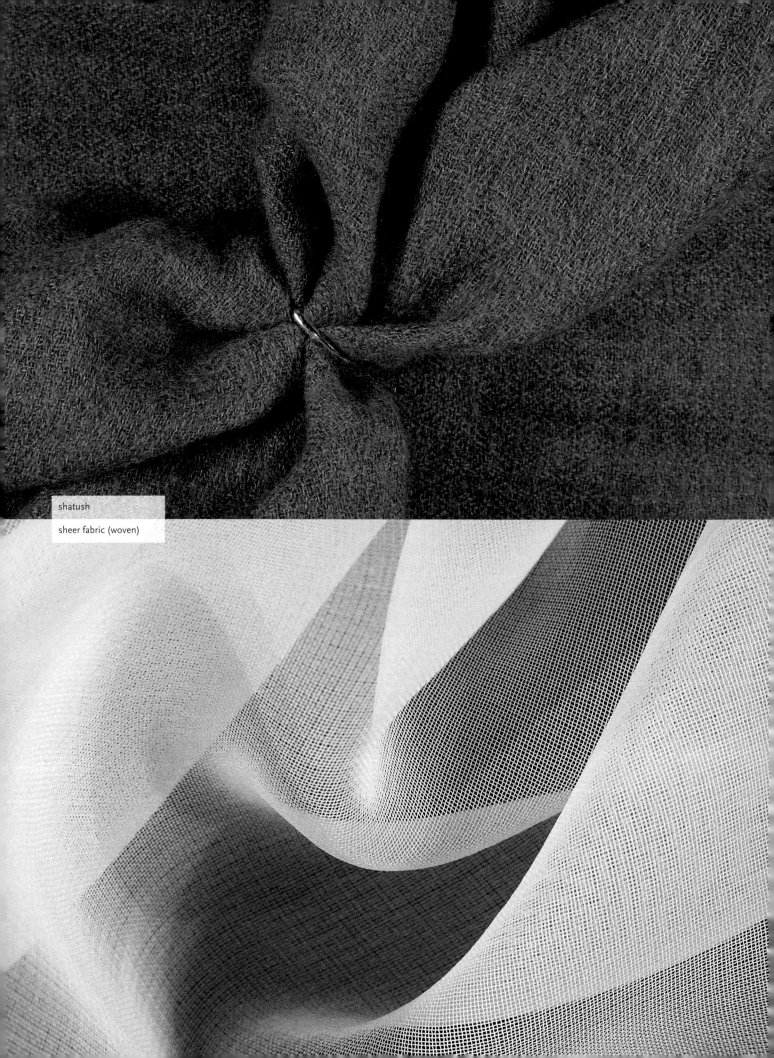

shatush

sheer fabric (woven)

End uses: (i) men's lightweight summer suiting fabric; (ii) women's wear, especially summer suits, uniforms and sportswear; (iii) print base cloth and backing fabric for laminated fabrics.

SHATUSH A fabric that is hand-woven from the hair of the wild cashmere goat *Capra aegagrus*, which is found in Kashmir and on the upper slopes of the Himalayas. This type of cashmere fibre is classed as a speciality hair fibre; since its supply is so limited, demand has made shatush one of the rarest, finest and most expensive fabrics in the world. In India, shatush is the most prized of luxury fabrics.

The fine fibre comes from the long, fine, white or silver-grey neck hair of the wild goat. It is spun into yarn and hand-woven into extremely fine, warm fabrics that are used as shawls. Shatush is usually woven in simple weave structures such as plain, twill or reverse twill weaves. The fibres and yarns are so fine that it is said a shawl 54 inches (137 cm) wide may be pulled through a wedding ring. (These shawls are therefore often called 'ring shawls'.) The name 'shatush' comes from the Persian words *shah*, meaning 'ruler', and *toosh*, meaning 'cloth'; it therefore translates as 'king's cloth'.

See also CASHMERE CLOTH, HAIR FABRICS, WEDDING RING FABRICS.

End uses: shawls and scarves.

SHEER FABRICS A general term for fabrics that are very thin, fine, lightweight and translucent or diaphanous in quality. The term 'sheer' may be applied to woven, knitted, nonwoven or lace fabrics.

Sheer fabrics may be constructed using any fibre types; however, the yarns used are usually very fine. Simple fabric constructions are used: most woven sheers are woven in plain weave, for example. Examples of sheer fabrics include bolting cloth, challis, chiffon, some clip spot fabrics, crêpe chiffon, some devoré fabrics, some gauze fabrics, georgette, gossamer, grenadine, Malines, marquisette (warp-knitted and woven), micromesh, Milanese (warp-knitted), mousseline, mull, some muslin fabrics, net, ninon, organdie, organza, power net, sarsenet, some scrim fabrics, some shadow stripes and checks, tulle, veiling, voile and zephyr. The term 'tissue' is also sometimes used in a general sense to describe lightweight, woven fabrics that have a diaphanous quality, but it is normally reserved for the slightly stiffer sheers that have a more papery feel. (*Tissue* is also the French word for 'woven fabric'.)

End uses: sheer curtains, evening wear, bridal wear, blouses, veiling, lingerie, scarves, hosiery and trims.

SHEETING FABRIC A general term for a wide range of both woven and warp-knitted fabrics made in a variety of widths (from 140 to 300 cm) and in all weights (light, medium and heavy), and used as bed coverings.

Originally woven sheeting fabrics were made using either linen yarns (hence the term 'bed linen') or cotton yarns, and were known as 'Bolton sheeting' (after the town of Bolton, England, where much of it was traditionally woven). Nowadays most woven sheeting fabrics are produced using polyester/cotton yarns for easy care; however, sheets made from cotton, linen, silk, polyester and nylon are also available. The cotton yarns are mostly carded, but more expensive fabrics are made using combed cotton yarns.

Woven sheeting fabrics are normally woven in a closely sett plain weave or 2/2 twill weave fabric construction. More luxurious sheets are sometimes woven in satin weave. Sheeting fabrics may be colour-woven or printed, but the vast majority are woven unbleached and subsequently bleached white. Many are also piece-dyed in a wide variety of colours. Typical woven sheeting fabric constructions are:

- plain weave, 35 tex warp sett at 25 ends per cm and 33 tex weft woven at 23 picks per cm[25]

- plain weave, 33 tex warp sett at 18 ends per cm and 38 tex weft woven at 18 to 24 picks per cm[26]
- 2/2 twill weave, 21 tex warp sett at 24 ends per cm and 37 tex weft woven at 28 picks per cm[25]
- 2/2 twill weave, 49 to 42 tex warp sett at 18 to 20 ends per cm and 60 to 49 tex weft woven at 25 to 28 picks per cm[26]
- plain weave (raised), 30 tex warp sett at 28 ends per cm and 9 tex weft woven at 18 picks per cm[25]

Woven sheeting fabrics include Bolton sheeting, flannelette, osnaburg, percale and cotton satin (*see* SATIN, WOVEN). Flannelette sheeting fabrics are woven in plain weave using soft condenser-spun cotton yarns. Percale is the finest type of sheeting fabric woven using combed cotton yarns, and osnaburg is also sometimes used as a sheeting fabric. Wigan is a similar fabric to a sheeting fabric, but it is not usually woven in wide widths. Woven sheeting fabrics may also be used for book cloth, plissé and print cloth.

Warp-knitted sheeting fabrics include airloop fabric and loopraise. Both of these are usually made from man-made fibres such as nylon or polyester, and have a soft, low pile surface. Flat sheets are sometimes made from warp-knitted satin. *See also* AIRLOOP FABRIC; LOOPRAISE; SATIN, WARP-KNITTED.

See also BOOK CLOTH; FLANNELETTE; OSNABURG; PERCALE; PLAIN WEAVE FABRIC; PLISSÉ; PRINT CLOTH; SATIN, WOVEN; TWILL FABRICS; WIGAN.

End uses: bed coverings, including sheets, pillowcases, duvets and valances; also curtains, sleepwear, shirts, blouses, dresses and children's clothes.

SHEPHERD'S CHECK A colour-woven fabric with a characteristic small-scale check pattern made with a colour and weave effect. The pattern is created by arranging both the warp and weft yarns into narrow alternating dark and light sections or sections of contrasting colours. The fabric is then woven in a twill weave structure that, when combined with the colour sequence, gives the pattern a diagonal effect.

Shepherd's check was traditionally a woollen fabric woven in the Highlands of Scotland and worn as a plaid or cloak by local shepherds. The traditional colours used were black with ecru or white, or (more rarely) blue with ecru or white. Nowadays the shepherd's check pattern is woven in a wide range of contrasting colours, in all fibres and for a variety of end uses (see the list below). The yarns are arranged to form 6 mm squares of dark and light yarns in both the warp and the weft.[2] The colours may be arranged 4:4, 6:6 or 8:8, although a pattern of 6:6 is frequently used in order to differentiate this check from the similar-looking houndstooth check pattern. The fabric is then woven in a 2/2 twill weave structure. The dark and light colours must be correctly aligned with the order of the weave structure repeat in order to obtain the correct pattern. Fabrics may be patterned solely with shepherd's checks throughout, or the pattern may be used in sections of other district check fabrics in conjunction with other patterns.

Houndstooth check is a particular form of shepherd's check pattern that is constructed with coloured squares arranged 4:4. The two fabrics are very similar, but shepherd's check has larger checks. Pepita is also a variation of a shepherd's check fabric. Some sources claim that 'pepita' is a German term for shepherd's check designs in two colours;[36] for others, pepita is a shepherd's check without a jagged edge to the square.[13]

See also CHECKS, COLOUR AND WEAVE EFFECTS, DISTRICT CHECKS, HOUNDSTOOTH CHECK, TARTAN.

End uses: (wool fabric) shawls, caps, coats and casual jackets; (worsted fabric) men's suits, jackets and women's skirts; (cotton, silk and man-made fibre fabrics) shirts, children's clothes and furnishing fabrics.

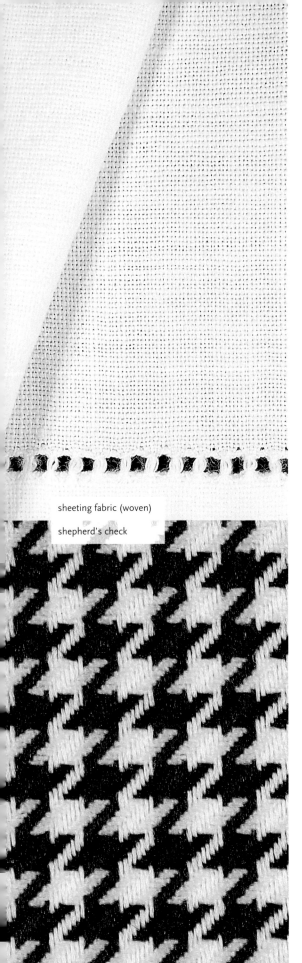

sheeting fabric (woven)

shepherd's check

Shetland fabric
Shetland tweed

shirting fabrics

SHETLAND FABRIC A general term, originally used for all types of knitted or woven fabric made from the wool of the Shetland breed of sheep, which is bred and reared on the Shetland Islands off the north-eastern coast of Scotland. The term is now also used more broadly, as described below. Shetland wool has a slightly coarse quality and handle, and Shetland fabrics are characteristically very warm and hard-wearing.

Originally the term 'Shetland fabric' was descriptive only of fabrics produced in the Shetland Islands from hand-spun yarns from the wool of the local Shetland sheep bred and reared on the islands. Nowadays the term is also used more widely to describe knitted or woven fabrics made from the wool of the Shetland breed of sheep in other locations in Scotland, and also to describe fabrics that are constructed using 100% new wool, spun on the woollen system, that have the quality and handle of the wool from the Shetland breed of sheep.[25] Shetland tweed is an example of a Shetland fabric.

See also TWEED, WOOL FABRIC.

End uses: sweaters, coats, jackets, trousers, and men's and women's suits.

SHETLAND TWEED A tweed fabric woven with special Shetland wool yarns, dyed at the fibre stage to give a characteristic soft, shaded colour effect. It was originally produced on the Shetland Islands, off the north-eastern coast of Scotland (hence the name).

The yarns for Shetland tweed were traditionally obtained by plucking, rather than shearing, the wool from Shetland sheep. This provided a much softer wool than is generally used in most other tweed fabrics and softness is one of its main characteristics.[11] The fabric is typically fibre dyed in soft browns, greys and greens, which reflect the colours of the local landscape. The fibres are carefully blended into yarns to produce the characteristic mixture or 'mélange' colour tones. The brown shade, often given the Shetland name of 'moorit', is very common. The fabric is traditionally woven in a 2/2 twill weave structure. A special finish is given to the fabric in order to obtain the full handle and benefit of the soft Shetland wool. The fabric is soap-scoured, lightly milled, and then blown rather than pressed in order to ensure that the natural look is not lost. This fabric is used mainly for sports jacketing.

See also MÉLANGE FABRIC, SHETLAND FABRIC, TWEED, WOOL FABRIC.

End uses: sports jackets and men's and women's suits.

SHIBORI *see* RESIST-DYED FABRICS.

SHIRTING FABRICS A general term for any fabrics used to make men's or women's shirts. However, the term is used mostly for men's woven shirting fabrics. They are usually light- to medium-weight fabrics that are hard-wearing in use.

Most shirting fabrics are fine woven fabrics, woven in plain or twill weaves and variations. Some shirting fabrics include fancy dobby weave structures, such as ribs, barathea, honeycomb, Bedford cords, crêpes, welts and piqués. Some shirting fabrics are also warp-knitted. Shirting fabrics may be made from all fibres and blends, but the most common are cotton, silk and polyester/cotton. Typically they are closely woven, strong and hard-wearing in use and have good washability. They may be bleached white, piece-dyed, colour-woven with stripes or checks, or printed with stripes, checks or other designs and motifs.

An example of a typical good-quality woven shirting fabric construction is plain weave, 27 tex warp sett at 22 ends per cm and 38 tex weft woven at 26 to 28 picks per cm.[26] Examples of shirting fabrics include chambray, cranky checks, dobby fabric, flannelette, galatea, grandrelle shirting, Harvard, herringbone shirting, some linen fabrics, Madras, Madras shirting, marcella, ottoman, Oxford, poplin shirting, regatta, regina, some cotton satin fabrics, some voile fabrics, winceyette, Zanzibar and zephyr.

See also CHECKS, DOBBY FABRIC, STRIPES.

End uses: shirts.

shot fabric

silence cloth

silesia

SHODDY *see* RECYCLED TEXTILES.

SHOT FABRICS (shots) Woven fabrics in which a shot effect (a two-tone colour effect) is created by using a solid colour in the warp and a different, contrasting or complementary colour in the weft. Shot fabrics (sometimes called 'shots') appear to change colour according to the angle of viewing. The colour effect is sometimes also called 'iridescent', 'changeable' or 'changeant' (a French term).

Shot fabrics are woven in all weights and qualities, using any type of fibre; however, the effect is probably most striking in closely sett, light- to medium-weight fabrics woven in plain weave. Lustrous yarns accentuate the effect as light is reflected from the textile. Shot fabrics are therefore traditionally woven with silk or lustrous man-made filament yarns. To achieve a shot effect, dyed yarns may be used or the fabric may be cross-dyed after weaving. The term 'shot' came into use because the colour change appears to 'shoot' along the yarns when the fabric moves.[23] The term 'iridescent' comes from the name of the Greek goddess Iris, the messenger of the gods; her symbol was a rainbow or the visible spectrum of colours.[23]

Many taffeta fabrics are woven with shot effects and described as 'shot taffeta'. Antique shantung, radium and solero are other examples of shot fabrics. Shot silk and shot lining fabrics are also typical examples of this type of fabric. Chameleon fabrics are a variation of shot fabrics in which three contrasting colours are woven together to produce the shot effect, rather than two. Nacré velvet is a further variation of a shot fabric, in which an iridescent effect is produced in a pile fabric (*see* VELVET).

See also CHAMELEON FABRIC, DYED FABRICS, RADIUM, SHANTUNG, SOLERO, TAFFETA.

End uses: evening dresses, blouses, linings and furnishing fabrics.

SHOWERPROOF FABRICS *see* WATERPROOF AND WATER-REPELLENT FABRICS.

SICILIAN *see* BRILLIANTINE.

SICILIENNE (*obs.*) A fabric woven with a silk warp and a fine cashmere weft.[3]

SILENCE CLOTH A thick, heavy woven fabric made with cotton yarns and strongly raised on both sides to make it dense and soft. It was originally used under tablecloths to minimize noise during dining, hence the name. Silence cloth is woven as a double-faced, double cloth fabric using carded cotton yarns. It is usually white in colour.

See also COTTON FABRIC, DOUBLE CLOTH, NAPPED FABRICS.

End uses: underlay for tablecloths, ironing boards and beds.

SILESIA A lightweight woven cotton fabric that has a smooth, lustrous, glazed face side and is used as a lining fabric. It is very hard-wearing.

Silesia is woven in a closely sett fabric construction with cotton yarns. Originally it was woven in plain weave, but now it is sometimes also woven in a 2/1 or 2/2 twill weave structure. It is usually piece-dyed, but it may also be colour-woven or printed with stripes. Silesia is heavily starched and given a calendered glaze finish, which produces a lustrous surface. An example of a typical silesia fabric construction is 2/2 twill weave, 27 tex warp sett at 24 ends per cm and 18 tex weft woven at 48 picks per cm.[26]

See also COTTON FABRIC, LINING FABRIC.

End uses: lining fabric and pockets for tailored garments.

SILK FABRIC A general term for any fabric constructed using silk yarns or fibres. Silk fabrics are known for their attractive high lustre, fineness, drape and soft, luxurious handle. Silk is the only natural fibre that is a continuous filament fibre. It is an animal fibre spun by the larvae of the silk moth in order to construct their cocoons.

The term 'silk fabric' is used for fabrics of all different weights and constructions composed of 100% silk fibres or yarns. Where silk is used together with other fibres, the percentage of each should be stated. Most silk fibre produced is cultivated silk, obtained from the larvae of the domesticated silk moth *Bombyx mori*. Silk produced from the larvae of other species of moth that are living in a wild or semi-domesticated state is termed 'wild silk'. There are a variety of fabrics produced using wild silk yarns: examples, discussed below, are **Assam silk**, **atlas silk** and **tussah silk**. 'Wild silk' is sometimes used as a general term for any of these fabrics. Both wild and cultivated silk are coated in a natural gum called sericin, which is usually removed by a process known as 'degumming'. The unprocessed continuous filaments or strands of silk, containing no twist and reeled directly from the cocoons, are called 'raw silk'.[25] Raw silk fibres may be used to construct fabrics, or the fibres may be twisted with other continuous filament fibres to produce thicker, more regular, cultivated silk yarns. Shorter staple lengths of either waste silk (the broken filaments from cultivated silk) or wild silk may be spun (twisted) into spun silk yarns. A number of examples of silk fabrics are described below.

ASSAM SILK (muga silk, moonga silk) A plain or hopsack woven silk fabric made with wild silk obtained from the cocoon of the wild silkworm genus *Antheraea*.[36] This type of silk is characteristically fawn or gold in colour and produces a good-quality, lightweight fabric with a rough surface. It is cultivated in the Assam region of India, whence it takes its name. Sometimes it is called 'muga silk'; 'muga' comes from the Sanskrit, meaning 'light brown'.[23] Assam silk fabrics are sometimes embroidered (*see* EMBROIDERED FABRICS).

ATLAS SILK A woven silk fabric made with wild silk obtained from the cocoon of the wild silkworm *Attacus atlas*. This type of silk is similar to **tussah silk** (see below) but darker in colour.[3] *See also* ATLAS, WOVEN.

CORAH SILK A lightweight silk fabric woven in India using natural, unwashed silk and afterwards washed to remove the natural gums, leaving the fabric creamy white in colour. Originally the fabric was made from wild silk, but now it is also made from cultivated silk. Corah silk is often subsequently dyed or printed. The term 'corah' comes from the Hindi word *kora*, meaning 'virgin'.[3]

INDIA SILK A hand-loomed woven silk fabric made mainly in India, but also elsewhere. It is a crisp fabric that is woven in plain weave, usually in solid colours, and has a slightly wrinkled appearance.[2]

MACCLESFIELD SILK A fairly crisp, textured silk fabric that was originally woven in Macclesfield, England. The term is used to describe the style of fabric, which is woven using highly twisted spun silk crêpe yarns, giving it a characteristic crêpe texture. Traditionally Macclesfield silks were striped or patterned with small jacquard woven motifs and used for men's neckties and women's classic shirts. They are hard-wearing fabrics that fray easily. *See also* TIE FABRIC, SPITALFIELDS.

NET SILK (nett silk) Silk fabric made with 'net silk' yarns. These are raw silk filaments that have been processed into yarns by twisting and/or folding, as opposed to spun silk yarns.[25] They have usually had their natural sericin removed by a degumming process. When dyeing, it is possible to obtain purer colours on degummed silk fabrics than on silk fabrics still 'in the gum'.

PARACHUTE SILK A very fine, strong silk fabric, woven with continuous filament silk yarns in plain weave. It was originally used to make parachutes during the World War II. Parachute fabric is now typically used for scarves and other fine clothing items.

Assam silk

parachute silk

SCHAPPE SILK Fabric made from spun silk yarns. Originally this term was used only when the spun silk fibres had been degummed by the schapping process (a fermentation process for partially removing the gum from silk waste fibres), but nowadays it is often used for fabrics made from all kinds of spun silk fibres.[25]

SILK NOIL A medium-weight silk fabric woven in plain weave with silk noil yarns. Silk noil yarns are spun from the short fibres discarded from the manufacture of higher-quality silk yarns. These waste yarns are spun on the condenser system to produce irregular silk noil yarns. Other fibres are also sometimes added. Fabrics woven with these yarns are characteristically textured with small flecks of fibre. Silk noil fabric is normally used for dresses and suits, or for curtains and furnishings. Bourette is an example of a fabric made using silk noil yarns. See BOURETTE.

TUSSAH SILK A general term for various woven fabrics made with wild silk obtained from the cocoon of the wild silkworm of the genus *Antheraea*. There are three types: *Antheraea mylitta* (largely Indian), *Antheraea pernyi* (largely Chinese) and *Antheraea yamamai* (largely Japanese).[25] Tussah silk yarn is a coarse, spun silk yarn with irregular slubs that is naturally ecru or yellowish beige to brown in colour. It is used to make pongee, shantung and tussore silk fabrics.

Fabrics traditionally made from silk include antung, atlas (woven), some barathea fabrics, silk bengaline, bombazine, bourette, silk broadcloth, some brocade fabrics, some brocatelle fabrics, cannelle, charmante satin, charmeuse, chiffon, China silk, some damask fabrics, doupion, duchesse satin, épingle, faille, foulard, Fuji, gazar, georgette, gossamer, grosgrain, habotai, honan, jappe, marquisette, messaline, Mogador, silk mousseline, ninon, organza, peau d'ange, peau de cygne, peau de soie, pongee, radium, regence, shantung, surah, antique taffeta, tsumugi, tussore and (silk) zibeline.

End uses: evening wear, wedding dresses, veils, blouses, dresses, scarves, suits, shirts, men's neckties, lingerie, nightwear, linings, hosiery, millinery, ballet shoes, bags, curtains and furnishings.

silk noil (dyed)
silk noil 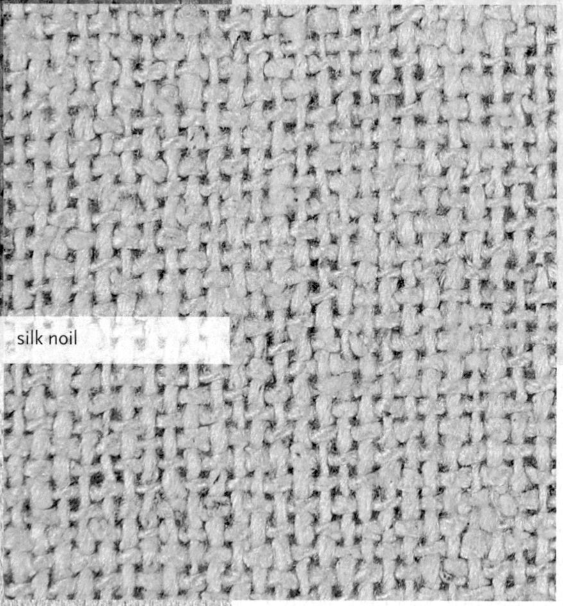
silk fabric (printed)

simplex

single jersey cord
(face and back)

SIMPLEX A general term for warp-knitted fabrics that are knitted on a simplex warp-knitting machine. This produces fine double-faced fabrics, which are the warp-knitted equivalent of weft-knitted double jersey fabrics. Simplex fabrics characteristically have a very smooth surface and good stretch properties in two directions. They are frequently used as a moulding for bra cups.

The simplex knitting machine is a fine-gauge knitting machine with two needle-bars and two guide bars. It produces a double layer fabric that is characteristically firmer, less extensible and therefore more stable than many other warp-knitted fabrics. Simplex fabrics are mainly knitted using nylon or polyester continuous filament yarns. Elastane or other stretch yarns, such as PBT yarns, are also often incorporated. This produces fabrics with greater stretch and control (modulus). Originally simplex fabrics were mainly knitted for gloves, often using cotton yarns. After knitting, the cotton was shrunk with caustic soda in a special finishing process and then sueded to produce a dense, suede-like surface.

See also ELASTANE FABRIC, KNITTED FABRIC, WARP-KNITTED FABRIC.

End uses: bras, lingerie, slips, foundation wear, form-fit garments and gloves.

SINAMAY *see* STRAW FABRICS.

SINGLE CLOTH *see* DOUBLE CLOTH.

SINGLE JERSEY *see* JERSEY.

SINGLE JERSEY CORD A single jersey weft-knitted fabric that has vertical ribs or cords on the face of the fabric and usually a smooth back. The face side is similar in appearance to a knitted rib fabric.

Most rib knitted fabrics are double jersey fabrics knitted on two needle-beds of a weft-knitting machine in order to produce ribs on both sides of the fabric. Since single jersey cord is a single jersey fabric knitted on one needle-bed of a weft-knitting machine, the vertical cords or ribs appear only on the face side of the fabric, and the back is normally either smooth or has weft floats in order to emphasize the cords on the face. Characteristically, therefore, single jersey cord does not have as much widthways stretch as a knitted rib fabric, and it has a definite face and back.

See also CORD FABRICS; JERSEY; KNITTED FABRIC; RIB FABRICS, KNITTED; WEFT-KNITTED FABRIC.

End uses: sweaters, dresses, T-shirts, underwear, sportswear and leisure wear.

SINGLE PIQUÉ *see* PIQUÉ, WEFT-KNITTED.

SISAL *see* STRAW FABRICS.

SLEEKNIT *see* RASCHEL STRETCH FABRICS.

SLIVER HIGH-PILE FABRIC *see* FUR FABRIC.

SMART TEXTILES 'High-tech' textiles that have been integrated with electronics or computer technology to make them electrically active, and that usually adapt to, or react with, their surrounding environment automatically. They usually have a specific function or feature incorporated into them.

Smart textiles have evolved from technology used in various 'electronic textiles' or 'e-textiles'. The first electronic textiles were electric blankets produced over eighty years

smart textiles
(electronic T-shirt)

solero (back and face)

ago.[34] Further developments in electronic textiles have included conductive textiles developed for a variety of 'passive' functions, such as static dissipation, electromagnetic interference and microwave attenuation.[40] Conductivity in textiles may be produced in both woven and knitted fabric constructions by incorporating very fine metal wires into the structure. Various metals have been used, including steel, nickel and silver. Thin, flexible conductive yarns have also been developed. Semi-conductive fabrics are also made by impregnating woven, knitted or nonwoven fabrics with carbon or metal powders, which are also conductive materials.[40] There are also conductive printing inks and metal-content surface coatings that will give fabrics conductive properties.[34]

Smart textiles take this technology further by making conductive textiles interactive with their environment. Smart textiles are able to sense and react to various external factors, such as temperature, pressure or electrical fluctuations, and to readjust themselves accordingly.[40] This has led to the development of various 'wearable electronics', but these can be very expensive. Because the technology is still so new and specialized, smart textiles have so far been developed mainly for specific market areas, some examples of which are discussed below.

(i) *Thermoregulation (temperature control)*. It is possible to maintain a constant temperature in garments made with conductive fabrics. Heating elements may be made out of either very fine wires or conductive yarns. A network of conductive material is incorporated into fabric structures to make low-voltage heat panels for use in garments, furnishing textiles or industrial textiles. The panels may be sewn into garments or onto sections of garments, or laminated onto other materials. These conductive textiles may be battery-powered, solar-powered or powered by body movements. Tiny batteries may also be built into glove fabrics and shoe soles in order to warm fingers and toes. End uses for these textiles include blankets, jackets, gloves, socks, diving suits, motorbike clothing, footwear, car seats and upholstery. Other thermoregulated materials include some microencapsulated textiles; *see* MICROENCAPSULATED TEXTILES.

(ii) *Healthcare and disability*. Biodegradable keyboards or other conductive structures may be incorporated into fabric and used in the healthcare industry for various applications: pressure detection on wound dressings; monitoring of body functions, such as heart rate, temperature and respiration; panic alarm buttons; remote control buttons; and products for people with special needs.

(iii) *Communication and entertainment systems*. Some garments are made with built-in electronic devices such as portable media players, mobile phones, remote controllers, earphones, headphones and digital cameras. Soft mechanical switches and touch-sensitive pads may also be built into electrically conductive fabric structures. This can provide fabric controls for media players and mobile phones. Some garments have been made to light up by the integration of electro-luminescent circuitry into textile structures. End uses for these textiles include children's novelty items and safety apparel.

See also HIGH-TECH TEXTILES.

End uses: sportswear, outerwear, children's novelty items, safety apparel, military textiles, medical textiles, thermoregulated textiles, furnishings and footwear.

SOLEIL *see* OTTOMAN.

SOLERO A woven fabric that is made in a variety of weights and qualities but is usually wool-based. Characteristically, it is woven with contrasting colours in the warp and weft, which gives it a subtle iridescent or 'shot' effect.

Solero is usually made with wool, worsted, mohair, silk, man-made fibres or combinations of these. Wool is normally used in the warp. Any combination of contrasting colours may be used, including black warp yarns and coloured weft yarns. The weft yarns are usually bold, bright, luminous colours. Solero is usually woven in plain or twill weaves.

space-dyed fabric
(weft-knitted)

space-dyed fabric (woven)

See also SHOT FABRICS, SUITING FABRIC, WOOL FABRIC.

End uses: suitings, ladies' wear, trousers, jackets and skirts.

SPACE-DYED FABRIC A general term for any fabric, knitted, woven or tufted, that is constructed using space-dyed yarns. Space-dyed yarns are variegated yarns produced by dyeing in sections along their length, with two or more, usually contrasting, colours. They may be coloured either at measured intervals along their length or randomly. When they are constructed into fabrics, a characteristic random pattern of streaky, multicoloured effects is produced.

There are various methods for producing coloured space-dyed yarns (many of them pioneered by the carpet industry from about 1946 onwards, with the introduction of tufted carpets and new technologies).
(i) Dyes may be applied to measured or random sections of yarns, in hank form, in package form, as single end yarns, or to warp yarns.[29, 35]
(ii) Space-dyed patterns may be printed onto yarns in sheet form or onto warp yarns.[29, 35]
(iii) Pre-knitted fabrics and pre-woven fabrics may be dyed in solid colours or randomly, and afterwards deconstructed to produce space-dyed yarns. These are then used to construct space-dyed fabrics.[29, 35]

Space-dyed yarns can also be used to create shadow stripes and checks; *see* SHADOW STRIPES AND CHECKS. Similar effects may also be produced in fabrics by ikat dyeing methods and by warp printing.

See also CHINÉ FABRICS, DYED FABRICS, IKAT, MARBLE CLOTH, RESIST-DYED FABRICS, WARP-PRINTED FABRIC.

End uses: fashion fabrics, furnishing fabrics and carpets.

SPACER FABRICS Knitted fabrics that consist of two fabric layers separated by a cushion of yarns with spaces in-between; either side may be used as the face side. Spacer fabrics were developed to replace foam trilaminates, which are expensive, not very environmentally friendly and sometimes prone to yellowing with degradation of the foam. Spacer fabrics may be either warp-knitted or weft-knitted, each type having its own special characteristics.

Weft-knitted spacer fabrics are knitted on a modified double jersey machine that knits separate single jersey fabrics on each machine bed and then links them together with (usually) a monofilament yarn, which is tucked into the stitches on both faces using special feeders. The space between the two fabrics may be varied to produce fabrics of different thicknesses, but this is limited to a few millimetres only. The monofilament yarns are sufficiently stiff to maintain the separation between the two fabric layers. Thinner, more spongy fabrics with less air space are also made using multifilament textured yarns. Elastane may be used in the fabric layers to produce a comfort stretch fabric or in order to facilitate moulding. Jacquard patterning is also possible.

Warp-knitted spacer fabrics are knitted on a double-needlebar raschel warp-knitting machine with at least six guide bars. Two guide bars produce a fabric on the front needlebar, and another two produce a fabric on the back needlebar. The remaining two guide bars link the two fabric layers together with

spacer fabric (weft-knitted, double-faced)

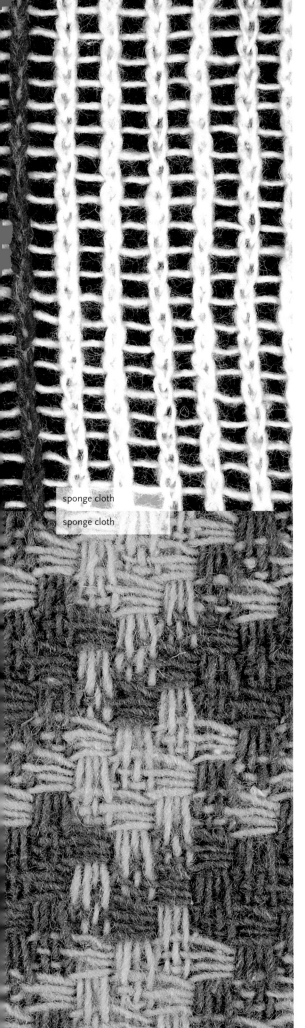

sponge cloth

sponge cloth

monofilament yarns. By modifying constructions and changing the needlebar separation, the fabric thickness can be varied from a few millimetres to several centimetres. One or both fabric layers are frequently knitted in a mesh construction to make the fabric more porous, and elastane can also be incorporated to add stretch. When spacer fabrics are used for car upholstery, air can be passed through the body of the fabric for heating and cooling purposes.

See also ELASTANE FABRIC; FOAM; JACQUARD FABRIC, KNITTED; KNITTED FABRIC; LAMINATED FABRIC; MULTI-COMPONENT FABRICS; RASCHEL WARP-KNITTED FABRIC; STRETCH FABRIC; WARP-KNITTED FABRIC; WEFT-KNITTED FABRIC.

End uses: (weft-knitted spacer fabrics) bra fabrics, sportswear and technical fabrics; (warp-knitted spacer fabrics) car upholstery, headliners, mattresses, overlays, pressure sore relief, wetsuits and bra cups.

SPANDEX FABRIC *see* ELASTANE FABRIC.

SPIDER SILK *see* GOSSAMER.

SPITALFIELDS (*obs.*) Fabrics with small geometric designs, made of silk or other fibres in a variety of weave structures and used for cravats and neckties. Spitalfields was a centre for silk-weaving in 16th-century England.[9]

SPONGE CLOTH A term used for several types of woven fabric that are characteristically soft, open-sett and bulky, with a spongy handle. There are three main types of sponge cloth that share these properties but are otherwise completely different fabrics, made for different end uses.

The three types of sponge cloth are described below.

(i) The original sponge cloth is a rough open mesh fabric, composed of coarse, folded warp yarns of low-grade cotton and woven in a leno weave structure or plain weave. These cloths are made to be absorbent and are used for cleaning cloths.[3, 4]

(ii) Another type of sponge cloth is woven in a 'sponge' weave structure, normally using soft yarns. There are several types of sponge weave, all of which group ends and picks together to produce a cellular construction with hollows and ridges, which creates a soft, spongy fabric. Weave structures include spot weaves, diamond effects, honeycomb weaves and variations and sateen-based weaves.[3, 25, 36] This fabric is used as an all-purpose household fabric for bedcovers, curtains and shawls. *See* HONEYCOMB, SATEEN.

(iii) The third kind of sponge cloth is made for dress fabrics. The term is used as a general one for a range of thick but lightweight open-textured woven fabrics that feel sponge-like. The texture is made by weaving the fabric with either loop yarns or other fancy textured yarns. The fabric is usually woven in plain weave with fancy yarns made from cotton, wool or viscose. This third type of sponge cloth is perhaps better known as 'éponge' (the French term for sponge). *See* ÉPONGE.

sponge weave

End uses: (i) cleaning cloths; (ii) all-purpose household fabric, used for bedcovers, curtains, bathrobes and shawls; (iii) dresses, ladies' suits, sportswear, lightweight coats and jackets, and furnishing fabrics.

STITCH-BONDED FABRIC (sew-knit fabric) A multi-component fabric whose components are held together by a series of interlooped warp-knitted stitches or vertical wales running along the length of the fabric. Stitch-bonding is a special form of warp-knitting that is used mainly for the manufacture of technical textiles, particularly composite and nonwoven textiles. The other component(s) of the fabric may be a fibre web or batt,

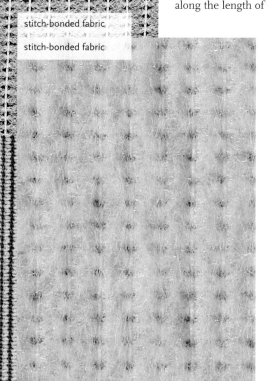

stitch-bonded fabric

stitch-bonded fabric

stitch-bonded fabric (weft insertion, warp stripe)

yarns or preformed fabric. This unique construction method produces fabrics that are extremely stable and often ribbed in appearance. All variations of stitch-bonded fabrics can be produced at very high speeds. Malimo is the generic term for a variety of stitch-bonded textiles that are constructed on Malimo stitch-bonding machines. Different types of stitch-bonding machines include Maliwatt, Malivlies, Kunit/Multiknit and Malipol. Each of these machines has been developed to knit different types of stitch-bonded fabrics, as discussed below.

Any fibres and yarns may be used to make stitch-bonded fabrics; however, strong synthetic fibres, often acrylic or modacrylic, are normally used, since these are best suited to the high-speed production methods. Stitch-bonded fabrics may be constructed in several different ways.

(i) A fibre web or batt is bonded together with the loop structure of warp-knit stitches. The warp-knitted stitches interlace through and around the fibre web along its length, which gives the fabric a corded appearance. Fabrics constructed in this manner may be stitch-bonded on Arachne and Maliwatt stitch-bonding machines, and on raschel warp-knitting machines.

(ii) On a Malimo stitch-bonding machine, the loop stitch structure of warp-knitting yarns along the length of the fabric entraps a series of laid-in yarns. The yarns may be laid-in in the warp direction, in the weft direction (weft insertion), or in both the warp and weft directions. Various Malimo fabrics are constructed in this manner. *See* Malimo.

(iii) A loop pile fabric is made by raising either warp-knit stitches or warp-direction laid-in yarns over 'sinkers' to form a loop pile. These loops are stitched into a base fabric, which may be knitted, woven, nonwoven or stitch-bonded. This produces a fabric with a pile on one side, which may be either cut or left uncut. Fabrics constructed in this manner may be stitch-bonded on Araloop and Malipol stitch-bonding machines.

(iv) The fabric is formed by using fibres within the fibre web or batt as the stitching loops. Fabrics constructed in this manner may be stitch-bonded on Arabeva and Malivlies stitch-bonding machines.

See also ACRYLIC FABRIC, FUR FABRIC, KNITTED FABRIC, LAID-IN FABRIC, MALIMO, MULTI-COMPONENT FABRICS, NONWOVEN FABRIC, PILE FABRICS, THREE-DIMENSIONAL TEXTILES, WARP-KNITTED FABRIC.

End uses: base materials for fibre-reinforced plastics, tablecloths, window blinds, semi-sheer curtains, upholstery fabrics, blankets, bedspreads, towels, outerwear fabrics (including fur-like coats), interlinings, linings, insulation materials, carpets, base fabrics for tufting, dishcloths and vegetable bags.

STOCKINETTE *see* PLAIN KNIT FABRIC.

STRAW FABRICS A general term for a range of fabrics and materials made from straw and used for making hats, bags, baskets, wall hangings, mats and floor coverings. For textile use straw is usually defined as the stalks of certain plants and sometimes also certain leaf fibres. Depending on the end use, straw fabrics may be heavy and closely constructed, or they may be lightweight, open structures.

Straw fabrics are made all over the world, but especially in China, the Philippines, South America and Africa. Most straw fabrics used in the making of hats are lightweight mesh-type fabrics, and characteristically they are able to be moulded into appropriate shapes. The straw is plaited or woven by hand. A variety of different fibres and constructions are used, some of which are outlined below.

straw fabric

stretch fabric

Parasisal is a fine, lightweight, high-quality natural straw made from sisal fibre, a pale cream-coloured fibre obtained from the leaves of the sisal plant (*Agave sisalana*).[25] It may be bleached or dyed, and it is characteristically woven in an open hopsack weave construction, which produces a fine straw fabric normally used for good-quality hats. Sisal straw fabric is also made with sisal fibre, but it is slightly coarser than parasisal and is usually woven in an open plain weave construction. Sinamay is made using Manila fibre (*Musa textilis*), also known as 'abaca', a plant grown in the Philippines.[25] 'Panama straw' is the name given to a type of straw woven in Ecuador, Peru and Colombia. It is a very resilient kind of straw and is used to make panama hats. It is usually bleached and may also be dyed in pale colours. (This fabric should not be confused with panama, panama canvas or panama suiting fabric; *see* PANAMA, PANAMA SUITING FABRIC.) Raffia is a fibre obtained from the leaves of the raffia palm (*Raphia ruffia*),[25] much of which comes from Madagascar. It is widely employed in the production of inexpensive casual straw hats, typically used as beachwear.

See also MESH FABRICS, PLANT-FIBRE FABRICS.

End uses: hats, baskets, bags, wall hangings, mats and floor coverings.

STRETCH FABRIC A general term for any fabric, knitted or woven, that is characterized by a greater degree of stretch and recovery than is normally the case. Elasticity is a characteristic property of some fibres, yarns and fabrics that allows them to stretch or elongate under tension and to recover to approximately their original length when released. The degree of stretch or elongation of a fabric can vary from 5% to 500% of the original length, but generally only fabrics with at least 15% elongation and recovery are described as stretch fabrics.

The combination of fibres, yarns and fabric construction will affect the degree of stretch a fabric will have. The majority of weft-knitted fabrics are inherently stretchy, for example, as are those containing crêpe and elastomeric yarns. Depending on the fabric construction and how the elastomeric yarns are incorporated, it is possible to achieve either one-way or two-way stretch in a fabric. If every yarn in the fabric construction is elastomeric, the fabric will be stretchy in all directions. According to the degree of stretch and recovery, stretch fabrics may be classified as 'comfort stretch fabrics' or 'power stretch fabrics'.

Comfort stretch fabrics stretch and recover within the range of approximately 15% to 30%, and they are used for everyday stretch garments that conform to body contours, such as stretch trousers, T-shirts, tights, sportswear and swimwear. Most of these fabrics are weft-knitted single jersey constructions or warp-knitted tricot fabrics. *See* JERSEY, TRICOT.

Power stretch fabrics usually stretch and recover within the range of 30% to 200%. They are typically used for items that compress and control the body shape (i.e. that provide good modulus), such as foundation wear, bras, active sportswear, stretch ski wear and surgical supports. These fabrics have a greater power of extension and a much faster recovery (snap-back) than comfort stretch fabrics, and may also be referred to as 'elastic fabrics'. In order to achieve this degree of stretch, the fabrics would usually contain a significant percentage of elastane, spandex, rubber, elastic, or other elastomeric fibres or yarns that have outstanding stretch and recovery properties. Most power stretch fabrics are warp-knitted, mainly on raschel machines. Note that the stretch fabric trade uses the term 'tricot' to describe stretch locknits with elastane, to distinguish them from stretch raschel fabrics. *See* LOCKNIT, POWER NET, RASCHEL STRETCH FABRICS, TRICOT.

See also ELASTANE FABRIC, ELASTOMERIC FABRIC, RUBBER.

End uses: casual wear, stretch trousers, T-shirts, tights, sportswear, swimwear, form-fit garments, foundation wear, bras, active sportswear, stretch ski wear and surgical supports.

straw fabric (raffia cut pile, African)

straw fabric (sinamay)

straw fabric (sisal)

straw fabric

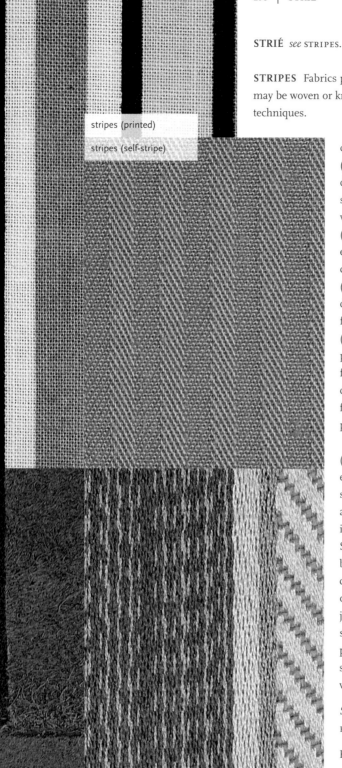

stripes (printed)

stripes (self-stripe)

stripes (strié)

suede (face and back)

STRIÉ *see* STRIPES.

STRIPES Fabrics patterned with a series of either vertical or horizontal lines. Stripes may be woven or knitted into a fabric, printed onto a fabric or created by special dyeing techniques.

To construct stripes as an integral part of the fabric, several different methods may be used, singly or in combination.

(i) Different-coloured yarns may be used in either the warp or the weft directions. By alternating two or more colours in the warp, lengthwise stripes are obtained. By alternating two or more colours in the weft, widthways stripes are obtained.

(ii) Textural stripes may be produced by alternating different yarns in either the warp or the weft direction. Fancy yarns or yarns of different counts (thicknesses) may be used.

(iii) Textural stripes may also be produced by weaving or knitting different sections of the fabric (in either warp or weft direction) in different fabric structures.

(iv) Woven union fabrics may be made in which different yarns composed of different fibres are arranged in stripe sections. When these fabrics are piece-dyed, the fibres in the different sections take the dye differently, producing stripes that are characteristically coloured in different tones of the same colour. This is an inexpensive method of producing coloured stripes in a fabric. *See* UNION FABRIC.

A striped fabric in which the stripes are all the same colour (made by varying the weave structure in sections) or a slightly different tone of the same colour is termed a 'self-stripe'. A fine random stripe or streaky effect in a woven fabric, usually in the warp direction and produced by dyeing the yarns in different tones of the same colour, is termed a 'strié'.[3] An unlimited variety of stripe patterns is possible. Some of the best-known stripe fabrics are as follows: blazer cloth, butcher cloth, canvas (awning stripes), chalk stripe (*see* PIN STRIPE), coutil, dimity, doria stripes, galatea, Glen stripe (*see* GLEN URQUHART CHECK), some grenadine fabrics, hairline, Harvard, hickory cloth, jaspé, some Madras fabrics, Madras shirting, morning stripe (*see* PIN STRIPE), some osnaburg fabrics, some Oxford fabrics, pekin, pin stripe, pyjama fabric, regatta, Russian cord, satin (ribbed satin), satin (satin stripe), shirting fabrics, ticking, velvet (pekin velvet), voile (striped voile) and zephyr.

See also COLOUR AND WEAVE EFFECTS, EXTRA WARP AND EXTRA WEFT FABRICS, OMBRÉ, SHADOW STRIPES AND CHECKS, UNION FABRIC.

End uses: all kinds of fashion and furnishing fabrics.

SUEDE The inner layer of the natural skin or hide of an animal, for example cowhide, goatskin, pigskin or sheep/lambskin. Thick animal hides can be split into layers. The outer layer of an animal skin or hide is called 'top-grain leather' or simply 'leather'. The inside split layer, or flesh side, is called 'suede'. The skin is preserved and softened in a process called 'tanning'. It may also be brushed or napped on one or both sides to enhance its softness. Suede is known for its characteristic soft, supple and pliable handle. It is, however, not easy to care for as it is prone to staining and can take on permanent creases, scratches or scuffs. The term 'suede' comes from the French name for Sweden, which at one time was known for producing fine kidskin suede gloves.[23]

The term 'chamois' is sometimes used instead of suede to describe the softest, innermost split layer of the hide of various animals. Strictly, however, chamois leather is the skin of the chamois (a species of antelope), which is very soft and similar to suede (*see also* LEATHER).

See also CHAMOIS CLOTH, FUR FABRIC, LEATHER, SUEDE CLOTH.

End uses: gloves, jackets, coats, shoes and bags.

SUEDE CLOTH A fabric made in imitation of real suede; it may be woven, warp-knitted, weft-knitted or nonwoven. It is usually given a special finish to one or both sides, to give it the smooth, soft, luxurious handle of real suede. Unlike real suede, however, most suede cloth is washable and quite hard-wearing.

There are many different types of suede cloth, which may be made in any weight or construction using any type of fibre, although cotton, wool and polyester are probably the most frequently used, particularly polyester microfibres. Woven, knitted, nonwoven and flocked suede cloth are discussed below.

Woven suede cloth is usually woven in a plain or twill weave structure. Suede cloth made with man-made continuous filament fibres, including microfibres, is usually sanded or emerized during the finishing process in order to break the surface filaments, creating a resemblance to the surface of real suede. If spun yarns are used, the fabrics are usually brushed or napped to raise the surface fibres, and then cropped close to the fabric surface to produce a soft, flat fabric.[23] This finishing treatment may be applied to one or both sides of the fabric. Cotton suede cloth, duvetyn and flannelette may all be converted from the same grey cloth, but suede cloth and duvetyn are sheared closely.[19] Duvetyn is sometimes mistakenly called suede cloth, but it is lighter in weight than suede cloth. *See* NAPPED FABRICS.

Warp-knitted suede cloth is made by warp-knitting a base fabric with cupro, nylon or polyester. The fabric is knitted with a float structure such as satin or loopraise on the technical back, or an overfed pile (like airloop fabric). This is subsequently brushed and cropped, or sueded, to produce the soft surface. It can be jet-dyed before or after sueding, depending on the finish desired. *See* AIR-LOOP FABRIC; KNITTED FABRIC; LOOPRAISE; SATIN, WARP-KNITTED; WARP-KNITTED FABRIC.

Nonwoven suede cloth is made by needle-punching a web of microfibres (usually polyester) together with a resin coating and polyurethane foam. Alternatively, a web of microfibres may be impregnated with polyurethane.[13] Polyurethane impregnation is common in many of the leather suedes, and it is usually carried out after brushing and before sueding. Alcantara® is the well-known brand name of a nonwoven suede cloth used for car upholstery, interior furnishings and clothing. Nonwoven suede cloth may be dyed and finished. When used for upholstery, this fabric is sometimes laminated to a woven cotton fabric.[19] *See also* LAMINATED FABRIC, NONWOVEN FABRIC, POLYURETHANE.

Flocked suede cloth is also made. Here the soft suede surface effect is created by attaching a flocked pile of polyester fibre with adhesive to both sides of a soft man-made base fabric (often

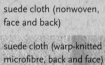

suede cloth (nonwoven, face and back)

suede cloth (warp-knitted microfibre, back and face)

suede cloth (woven)

suede cloth (weft-knitted)

suiting fabrics

suiting fabric (super 130's and cashmere)

viscose);[2] *see* FLOCKED FABRIC. Suede-look fabrics include beaver cloth, beaverteen, buck-skin fabric, doeskin fabric, duvetyn, all fustian fabrics, imperial sateen, moleskin fabric, suede flannel and swansdown.

See also CHAMOIS CLOTH, FUR FABRIC, LEATHER-CLOTH, SUEDE.

End uses: gloves, shoes, jackets, coats, suits, trousers, dresses, skirts, bags, coat and jacket linings, accessories, upholstery, curtains, wall coverings and automotive textiles.

SUEDE FLANNEL *see* FLANNEL.

SUITING FABRICS A general term for fabrics used to make both men's and women's suits. However, the term is used in particular for men's traditional woven suiting fabrics that are employed in tailoring. Most are hard-wearing, medium-weight fabrics within the range of 240–400 g/m².

Most traditional men's suiting fabrics are woven fabrics, constructed using fine wool or worsted yarns in simple weave structures such as plain, twill or herringbone. Spe-ciality hair fibres such as cashmere, vicuña or mohair are sometimes added for a luxurious handle, and man-made fibres are sometimes included for extra strength. The fabrics are often dark in colour; they may be a single colour throughout, or colour-woven with stripes, checks or small dobby patterns. The quality of the fabric is determined by the quality of wool used to make it, the highest quality being merino wool, which produced in many parts of the world but most notably in Australia. The fineness or diameter of wool fibres is measured by their micron value. The lower the micron value, the finer the fibre. Finer fibres result in finer yarns, which are used to produce the finest, highest-quality suiting fabrics; these have a soft handle, high lustre and excellent drape. Suiting fabrics are also given quality ratings whereby the higher the number, the finer and higher quality the fabric, as the following examples show:

- Super 100's and super 110's are made from 'fine' wool fibres with diameters of 18.75 microns or less and 18.25 microns or less, respectively.
- Super 120's and super 130's are made from 'superfine' wool fibres with diameters of 17.75 microns or less and 17.25 microns or less, respectively. The wool is usually obtained from the very soft neck hairs of merino sheep. This is a top-quality wool from which very fine, hard-wearing suiting fabrics are made.
- Super 140's and Super 150's are made from 'extrafine' wool fibres with diameters of 16.75 microns or less and 16.25 microns or less, respectively.
- Super 160's and Super 170's are made from 'ultrafine' wool fibres with diameters of 15.75 microns or less and 15.25 microns or less, respectively.

The highest quality is super 200's, but this is very rare.

Other fabrics that can be used for suitings include Afgalaine, alpaca fabric, ama-zon, angora fabric, Bannockburn, barathea, barleycorn fabric, beaverteen, Bedford cord, bengaline, birdseye suitings, blazer cloth, Bolivia, botany twill, box cloth, Bradford lustre fabrics, brilliantine, broadcloth, camel-hair fabric, camlet, Canton, cashmere cloth, cas-simere, cavalry twill, chalk stripe (*see* PIN STRIPE), Cheviot, Coburg, corkscrew fabric, covert cloth, district checks, dobby fabrics, doeskin fabric, Donegal, drill, duck, flannel, Frenchback, Fresco, gaberdine, Glen Urquhart check, granada, Guards check, gunclub check, hairline, Harris tweed, herringbone, homespun, hopsack, houndstooth check, houndstooth stripe, imperial sateen, kersey, some linen fabrics, marengo, mélange lustre fabric, merino fabric, mohair fabric (mohair suiting fabrics), moleskin (cotton moleskin for suitings), morning stripe (*see* PIN STRIPE), panama suiting fabric, pekin, pin stripe, pinhead check, piqué (woven), Poiret twill, Prince of Wales check, repp, Saxony, seer-sucker (wool seersucker for suitings), serge, sharkskin, shepherd's check, Shetland fabric, Shetland tweed, Sicilian (*see* BRILLIANTINE), solero, suede cloth, tartan, Tattersall check, thornproof tweed, tricotine, tropical suiting, tweed, velvet, Venetian (wool), vicuña fabric,

surah (printed)

swansdown (face and back)

West of England fabrics, whipcord, many wool fabrics and many worsted fabrics.

See also CHECKS, COLOUR AND WEAVE EFFECTS, DOBBY FABRIC, FELTED FABRIC, HAIR FABRICS, NAPPED FABRICS, WOOL FABRIC, WORSTED FABRIC, STRIPES.

End uses: men's and women's suits, jackets, trousers and skirts.

SURAH A soft, supple woven fabric constructed in a twill weave, originally from silk yarns. Characteristically, it is a very soft, smooth fabric with good drape and obvious twill lines. It is not very hard-wearing and is prone to creasing, fraying and seam slippage.

Surah is traditionally woven with roughly spun silk yarns, but it is also woven using man-made filament yarns, including viscose, polyester, acetate or triacetate. The fabric is woven in a balanced 2/2 twill weave structure. It may be piece-dyed, but more often is either yarn-dyed or printed with small-scale motifs and patterns against contrasting backgrounds. The name 'surah' comes from the port city of Surat in north-western India, from where the fabric was originally exported.[3]

There are a number of variations of surah fabrics. Surah chevron is similar in weight and quality to regular surah fabric, but it is woven in a herringbone weave structure rather than twill. Ecossais quadrille is a surah fabric that is colour-woven with Scottish tartan patterns. Surah gros cole is a heavyweight version of a surah fabric that is woven using thick closely sett yarns and finished with a high lustre on both sides. It may be used for furnishing fabrics as well as fashion fabrics. Surah is sometimes also called 'silk serge'. It is a similar fabric to foulard but heavier.

See also SILK FABRIC, TWILL FABRICS.

End uses: dresses, blouses, scarves, lingerie and linings.

SWANSDOWN A woven cotton fabric with a very heavily wefted face side that has been raised to give the fabric a characteristic downy appearance similar to the soft down of a swan (hence the name). It belongs to the group of fabrics known as 'fustians'.

Swansdown is usually woven with cotton yarns in a weave structure based on a 5-end sateen. Ordinary swansdown is woven with a 2 and 3 weft Venetian weave structure.[26] This weave structure has a large number of weft picks, which gives the fabric a weft-faced surface on both sides. The fabric is usually woven as grey cloth, using a soft rove weft yarn, and afterwards bleached or piece-dyed. The weft face on one or both sides of the fabric may then be raised or napped to give the fabric its characteristic downy appearance.

Typical swansdown fabric constructions are as follows: 33 tex warp sett at 19 ends per cm and 40 tex weft woven at 62 picks per cm;[26] or 30 tex warp sett at 25 ends per cm and 25 tex weft woven at 50 picks per cm.[25] Swansdown is a similar fabric to imperial sateen but is lighter in weight. It is also similar to beaverteen, Canton, flannelette, moleskin fabric and winceyette.

See also FUSTIAN, NAPPED FABRICS, SATEEN, SUEDE CLOTH, VENETIAN.

End uses: nightgowns, pyjamas, underclothing, linings, interlinings, pockets and baby clothes.

SWISS DOUBLE PIQUÉ *see* PIQUÉ, WEFT-KNITTED.

SWIVELS *see* BROCHÉ.

SYMPATEX® *see* POLYMER MEMBRANE LAMINATES.

TABARET (*obs.*) A silk dress fabric woven in alternate satin and watered silk (moiré) stripes, with coloured yarns in the moiré sections.[3, 36]

taffeta

taffeta (jacquard)

TABBY *see* PLAIN WEAVE FABRIC.

TABINET (*obs.*) A woven fabric made with a yarn-dyed silk warp and a fine grey worsted weft. It was similar to poplin and was usually given a moiré finish.[36]

TAFFETA A fine, crisp and lustrous woven fabric with warp-faced ribs running in the weft direction. Characteristically, it has a crisp, paper-like quality; it generally drapes well, but may crease and fray easily. It is available in a range of different weights and qualities, from light- to medium-weight. Taffeta dates from medieval times[3] but is still used very widely today.

The term 'taffeta' comes from Persian *tafta*, meaning a 'glossy twist'.[3] Taffeta was originally woven with highly twisted, lustrous silk filament yarns. Nowadays it is usually woven with highly twisted, lustrous man-made continuous filament yarns, such as acetate, triacetate, nylon, viscose, polyester or blends of these. It can also be made in cotton, wool or blends. It is the high twist of the yarns that gives the fabric its characteristic crisp handle. Taffeta is woven in plain weave using fine, closely sett warp yarns and slightly thicker weft yarns. There are a greater number of warp ends per centimetre than weft picks, and this produces the weftway ribs. It is usually woven in plain colours, but sometimes it is colour-woven with stripes or checks, or it may be printed. Taffeta is often given a stiff finish of size to increase its stiffness and to give it rustle. The size may be non-durable, in the form of water-soluble gelatin or gum, or durable, in the form of resins that are not removable by water or dry-cleaning fluids. Taffeta is also a suitable fabric from which to make moiré fabrics, by giving it a moiré finish (*see* MOIRÉ FABRIC). Variations of the basic taffeta fabric are described below.

ANTIQUE TAFFETA A taffeta fabric that is usually particularly heavy and stiff, and is traditionally woven with silk doupion slub weft yarns; it is also woven with man-made slub weft yarns. Sometimes it has a 'shot' effect (see **shot taffeta** below), and it is normally used as curtain fabric. *See also* DOUPION, SILK FABRIC.

CHAMELEON TAFFETA A taffeta fabric with a three-colour 'shot' effect achieved by weaving three different, contrasting colours together: one in the warp and two in the weft, which are woven together in the same shed. This produces a very luxurious taffeta fabric whose colour appears to change when the fabric is moved and the light is reflected differently. It is a variation of **shot taffeta** (see below). Fabrics with this effect are also described as 'iridescent' or 'changeant' (from French). *See also* CHAMELEON FABRIC, SHOT FABRICS.

FAILLE TAFFETA A taffeta fabric with a more pronounced rib effect than ordinary taffeta, similar to a faille fabric. *See* FAILLE.

JACQUARD TAFFETA A fabric in which jacquard woven motifs are incorporated into a (usually) taffeta woven ground fabric. *See* JACQUARD FABRIC, WOVEN.

MOIRÉ TAFFETA A taffeta fabric that has been given a moiré finish. *See* MOIRÉ FABRIC.

PAPER TAFFETA A lightweight taffeta fabric given a special, usually durable finish whereby the fabric is treated with lacquer to give it a very crisp, paper-like handle and rustle.

PIGMENT TAFFETA A taffeta fabric woven with pigment-coloured yarns or de-lustred viscose filaments with little or no twist. This produces a dull, matt fabric, without lustre. It is not a crisp fabric.

POMPADOUR TAFFETA A taffeta fabric that usually has large floral designs (or sometimes stripes) woven in velvet or another pile weave against a taffeta ground fabric. It is thought to have been named after Madame de Pompadour, the mistress of Louis XV of France. Seldom seen nowadays, except in museums, pompadour taffeta was usually woven in silk in bright, rich colours and was a very luxurious variation of a taffeta fabric.[5]

SHOT TAFFETA (taffeta glacé) A taffeta fabric woven with one colour in the warp and a completely different, contrasting colour in the weft. This produces a very luxurious taffeta fabric whose colour appears to change when the fabric is moved and the light is reflected differently. The effect is accentuated by the use (as is usual for taffeta fabrics) of highly lustrous yarns. Fabrics with this effect are also described as 'iridescent' or 'changeant' (from French). *See also* SHOT FABRICS.

TISSUE TAFFETA The lightest-weight taffeta fabric, so fine that it is almost transparent. Tissue taffeta is used mainly as a lining fabric or for lingerie.

There is a range of weft-ribbed fabrics characterized by the size and prominence of their ribs. In increasing order of rib size, these are: broadcloth, poplin, taffeta, poult, faille, bengaline and grosgrain. However, since many of them are woven in a variety of different weights, they are sometimes hard to distinguish. Of all the rib woven fabrics, taffeta is most similar to poult, as they are both stiff, rustly fabrics, but taffeta is slightly lighter in weight and has less pronounced ribs. Gros de Londres, a variation of grosgrain, is also a stiff, rib woven fabric, but it is heavier in weight and has more pronounced ribs than either taffeta or poult. Taffeta may be used to produce ciré fabric; *see* CIRÉ.

See also PLAIN WEAVE FABRIC; RIB FABRICS, WOVEN; SILK FABRIC.

End uses: dresses, bridal wear, evening dresses, women's suits, blouses, lining, trimmings, lingerie, theatrical costumes, hats, bags, curtains, upholstery, lampshades and umbrellas.

TAMISE *see* BATISTE.

TAMMY *see* BUNTING.

TANA LAWN *see* LAWN.

TAPA CLOTH *see* BARK CLOTH.

TAPESTRY A hand-woven fabric, often large in size and usually figured with pictorial designs and images. Yarns are inserted as required to make the pattern. Tapestries have been woven since at least the 13th or 14th centuries. The early European tapestries were usually large, heavy fabrics or hangings, predominantly made from wool, which depicted stories or significant historical events. They were woven by hand, and with their complex images often took many years to complete. Tapestries are seldom woven in this manner today; but these early tapestries were really the forerunners of modern jacquard woven fabrics, and the tapestry look is often imitated in jacquard woven fabrics used for furnishings. Such fabrics are called 'tapestry jacquards' (*see* TAPESTRY JACQUARD). Examples of hand-woven tapestries that are currently produced include kilim and dhurrie (*see* KILIM).

The term 'tapestry' is thought to have come from French *tapis*, meaning 'carpet' or 'table covering'.[3] Tapestries were usually constructed from a single-coloured warp of wool, cotton or linen, and from a series of different-coloured woollen weft yarns. The weft yarns did not pass from selvedge to selvedge, but were interlaced with the warp yarns only in the areas where they were required to form the pattern. In most early tapestries, there were more weft picks per centimetre than warp ends, so when the fabric was woven in a plain weave structure, a characteristic weft-faced fabric was produced. Some fabrics, however, were woven in more balanced plain or twill weave fabric structures, and some were warp-faced fabrics. The following text describes different construction techniques for forming the tapestry woven pattern and for making the joins or edges between adjacent areas of colour.

tapestry
(Flemish C17th, detail)

tapestry jacquard

(i) *Slit tapestry*. The weft yarns of adjacent colours were each woven into separate groups of warp yarns, leaving a slit in the warp direction between the two areas of colour. As there would also usually be horizontal and diagonal lines in the pattern, this effect could be minimized.

(ii) *Toothed tapestry or single dovetailed tapestry*. The weft yarns of adjacent colours were turned alternately around the same warp end. This resulted in a neat integration of the two colours at the point where they met.

(iii) *Interlocked tapestry*. The weft yarns of adjacent colours were interlocked around each other, either around the same warp end or around adjacent warp ends. The lock made between the two weft yarns could be either a single interlock or a double interlock. This construction produced a strong bond between the adjacent areas of colour.

(iv) *Dovetailed tapestry*. The weft yarns of adjacent colours were turned in groups of two or more, alternately around the same warp end. This produced a visual dovetailed effect at the edges of adjacent colour areas, which was a characteristic feature of many early tapestry fabrics.

(v) *Reinforced tapestry*. Tapestry fabrics could be made stronger and more stable by weaving one weft pick every so often, across the entire fabric from selvedge to selvedge.

(vi) *Inserted tapestry*. Tapestry woven motifs were inserted, in sections only, into a fabric that was mainly woven in a single weave structure throughout, from selvedge to selvedge. When the warp yarns were not required to weave the tapestry woven sections on the face of the fabric, they were left to float on the back of the fabric.

'Gobelin' is the name given to a number of famous large, pictorial tapestries produced at the Gobelin tapestry weaving factory in Paris from the 16th century onwards. The Gobelin tapestries produced at this time were renowned as the finest tapestries made. They required considerable time and skill to produce and were very expensive.[36] The Gobelin factory was originally founded as a dye works by Gilles and Jean Gobelin in 1450. It did not begin to produce the famous tapestries until the 16th century but retained the original name of Gobelin.[30] Gobelin tapestries are no longer made, but antique ones can still be bought.

See also EMBROIDERED FABRICS; FIGURED FABRIC; JACQUARD FABRIC, WOVEN; KILIM; PAISLEY; TAPESTRY JACQUARD.

End uses: wall hangings, floor coverings, rugs and ceiling hangings.

TAPESTRY JACQUARD A general term for a heavyweight jacquard woven fabric, typically with multicoloured, figured or pictorial patterns woven throughout the fabric. The designs often imitate the look of hand-woven tapestries. Tapestry jacquards are usually densely woven, durable, flat fabrics that are used mainly for upholstery.

Tapestry jacquards are usually woven on jacquard power looms and occasionally on jacquard hand-looms. In these fabrics, unlike in the early hand-woven tapestries, the weft yarns weave from selvedge to selvedge, and it is the jacquard mechanism that creates the design. They are complex, multicoloured jacquard woven fabrics, consisting of two or more warps and two or more weft yarns, which may be of the same or different fibres. They employ compound weave structures in order to gain the maximum number of colours in the design. The patterns or figures are made with the different warp or weft colours in conjunction with contrasting weave structures. Sometimes a fine binder warp and weft may also be incorporated in order to produce a firmer structure. In some tapestry jacquard fabrics, the design is clearer on one side of the fabric than the other. They are therefore not always reversible fabrics.

See also FIGURED FABRIC; JACQUARD FABRIC, WOVEN; TAPESTRY; VELVET.

End uses: upholstery, curtains, bedspreads, cushion covers, wall hangings, table coverings, handbags, luggage and (occasionally) jackets and coats.

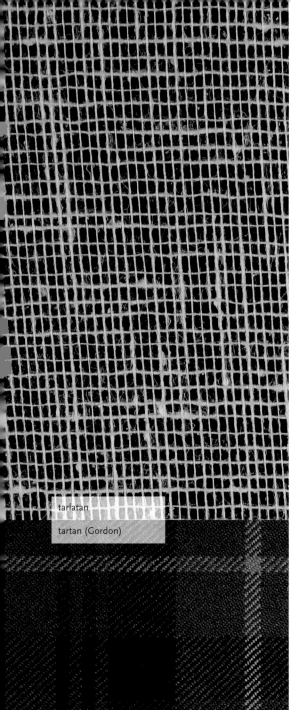

tarlatan

tartan (Gordon)

TAPESTRY VELVET *see* VELVET.

TARLATAN A stiffened muslin or gauze-type fabric. It is a very open-sett plain woven cotton fabric that is stiffened or glazed on one side. It is a lightweight, transparent fabric with a rough handle.

Tarlatan is woven in a plain weave fabric construction with carded or combed cotton (or occasionally linen) yarns. It is usually piece-dyed in solid colours and finished with a heavy starch size to make it stiff. Sometimes it is glazed on one side. Tarlatan is a similar fabric to cheesecloth, gauze and net. It is also similar to scrim, except that it is woven with much finer cotton yarns. Alternative spellings of the name (tarltan, tarlaton, tarlatane) are sometimes used, and tarlatan is sometimes also called 'Argentine cloth'.[3]

See also MUSLIN, PLAIN WEAVE FABRIC.

End uses: millinery, interlinings, stiffening for belts and waistbands, theatrical or fancy-dress costumes, curtains, linings, display fabric and packaging fabric.

TARPAULIN *see* CANVAS.

TARTAN A medium-weight colour-woven fabric that is traditionally woven with wool yarns in a wide variety of both simple and elaborate traditional check patterns. Tartan is the fabric from which Scottish kilts are made. There are many different tartan check patterns, which were originally developed by the Scottish clans (communities of interrelated families) in the Highlands of Scotland, each clan having its own distinct design. Many clans also have more than one tartan, with each traditionally used for different occasions (e.g. hunting, mourning, or 'dress' tartan for special occasions). Today there are 3,700 different clan tartans, each design being registered with the Scottish Tartans Authority.[46]

Traditional tartan fabrics are woven with yarn-dyed woollen or worsted yarns in a 2/2 twill weave construction. The fabric is woven as square cloth (i.e. with the same number of yarns per centimetre in both warp and weft). Bold stripes of coloured yarns are arranged in the same sequence in both the warp and the weft and, when woven, the colours combine with one another to form solid blocks of colour and blocks of mixed colours. Most tartan designs are characterized by the reversing of specific coloured checks along both a vertical and horizontal axis, with the resulting pattern repeated across the fabric.

Tartan fabrics were originally made from local Scottish wool dyed with vegetable dyes. Nowadays the fabrics are dyed with synthetic dyestuffs, and the colours are much stronger and brighter. Characteristically, the yarns are dyed in solid colours, unlike the mixed colour tones of the Harris and Shetland tweeds. Similarly, there are now many variations of the traditional tartan fabric. For example, tartans are not always woven with local Scottish wool; they are also woven in different fibres, such as acrylic or wool/acrylic, wool/polyester, wool/silk or wool/cotton blends. Different weave structures have also been introduced, such as plain weave or crêpe weaves. Tartan is therefore available in a wide range of different weights and qualities. There are also many fabrics available that are similar in appearance to traditional tartan fabrics (that is, they have similar check patterns) but are not authentic tartan fabrics – these are check fabrics.

Authentic clan tartans follow traditional patterns in which specific colours are accurately woven in specified widths of warp and weft stripes. If a tartan is scaled down in size (for use in children's wear), then, to be authentic, the correct ratio of one colour to another must always be maintained. The fabric is made with an exact number of repeats of the colour scheme across the width of 67 to 70 cm, and the same tartan design may have 4, 6 or 8 repeats, depending on the scale of the design.[26] Typical tartan fabric constructions are as follows: 90 tex woollen warp sett at 16 ends per cm and 90 tex woollen weft woven at 16 picks per cm; or 27/2 tex botany worsted warp sett at 28 ends per cm and 27/2 tex botany worsted weft woven at 28 picks per cm.[26] The fabric may be raised during finishing to give it a nap, or it may be left smooth.

Although some Scottish tartans can be traced back to 1538,[3] the majority of clan tartans were products of the early 19th century and woven by the famous weaving firm of William Wilson & Sons, of Bannockburn, near Stirling (founded *c.* 1765).[37] The simplest form of tartan fabric uses only two colours woven in an equal check pattern. One of the best-known tartans is the Black Watch, the clan tartan of the Campbell family; it is a blue, green and black check fabric. Abercrombie is also a well-known tartan; it has a blue and black ground with a green and white overcheck.[2] Other examples include Royal Stewart (a tartan with a predominantly red ground and black, green, yellow, white and blue checks) and Gordon (a tartan with green, blue and black checks and a yellow overcheck).

The term 'plaid' is sometimes used for tartan fabric, particularly in the United States, where it may be used as a general term for any fabric with an elaborate check pattern. Care should be taken, however, to differentiate between authentic tartan fabric and ordinary check fabric. 'Plaid' is also the name for a piece of woollen fabric forming part of traditional Scottish dress. This was worn over the shoulder as a type of cloak or mantle. It was patterned with either a tartan design or a check pattern (such as a shepherd's check), and was secured by a leather belt and pinned to the left shoulder with a large brooch. The plaid was originally used as a garment by day and as a blanket by night.[3] Together with the tartan kilt, a modified form of plaid still forms part of traditional Scottish Highland dress today.

See also CHECKS, COLOUR AND WEAVE EFFECTS, DISTRICT CHECKS, NAPPED FABRICS, SHEPHERD'S CHECK, TWILL FABRICS.

End uses: kilts, trousers, shawls, pleated skirts, pinafore dresses, coats, jackets, shirts, suits, hats, scarves, dressing gowns, blankets, curtains, upholstery, bags, carpets and bagpipes.

TATTERSALL CHECK A colour-woven check fabric originally made from wool. The traditional fabric is a small-scale check fabric with a white ground and small red and black overchecks.[44] It is usually a heavyweight fabric. Lighter-weight qualities made for shirts are more common nowadays. These are made in cotton or cotton/wool blends, and are colour-woven with window-pane overchecks in a variety of different colours, usually against a light ground.

Tattersall checks are smaller-scale versions of horse-blanket checks. It is thought that horse dealers associated with the London racehorse auctioneer company Tattersalls liked the bold horse-blanket designs and so adapted them for coating fabrics.[3] Although Tattersall check was originally made in wool, it is now also made with other fibres, including wool/silk blends, cotton, cotton/wool blends and man-made fibres. Tattersall check is usually woven in twill weave and is made in a variety of different check sizes and colour variations; typically, however, thin warpways and weftways stripes in bright colours form small-scale, window-pane outline overchecks against a contrasting white ground. The wool fabric is lightly milled during finishing to give it a soft handle. Heavyweight Tattersall check is a similar fabric to kersey.

See also CHECKS, COATING FABRIC, HORSE-BLANKET CHECK, TWILL FABRICS.

End uses: overcoats, jackets, suits, men's neckties, hats, caps and shirts.

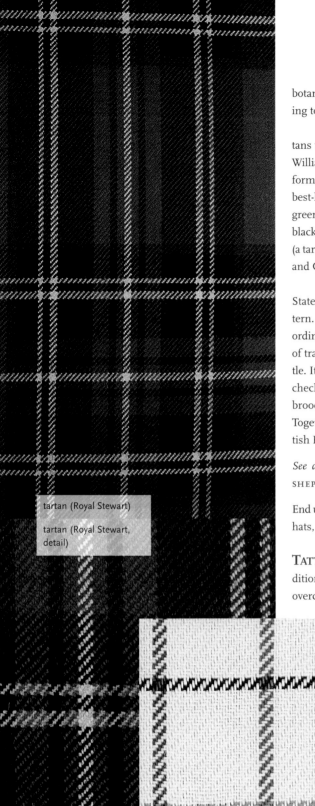

tartan (Royal Stewart)

tartan (Royal Stewart, detail)

Tattersall check

tatting

tea towelling

TATTING An openwork fabric that is similar to lace, but usually coarser. It is made by tatting, a very similar process to making lace by hand.

Tatting evolved in the mid-19th century from the art of knotting.[5] It is made by hand, using a small shuttle containing thread that may be of varying thicknesses. Tatting may be made from any fibres, including wool, cotton, silk, flax or man-made fibres, but the thread or yarn is usually tightly twisted in order to accentuate the loop structure of the fabric. The shuttle is worked to form a series of small knots, all tied together in circles or along a foundation thread. The type of knot used is the 'lark's head'.[5] The lacy pattern is formed by the loops of thread between the knots. The name 'tatting' is derived from 'tat-tie', meaning an Indian matting, which it resembles.[36]

See also CROCHET, LACE.

End uses: trims, edgings and table mats.

TEA TOWELLING A general term for a range of absorbent woven fabrics that may be used as tea towels, or tea cloths, for the drying of crockery. They are typically strong and hard-wearing. Fabrics suitable for use as tea towelling (discussed in separate entries) include birdseye, crash, damask, diced weaves, glass cloth, honeycomb, huckaback and terry fabric.

See also TOWELLING.

End uses: tea towels or tea cloths.

TECNET (tecsheen) *see* RASCHEL STRETCH FABRICS.

TEFLON® The brand name of a fluoropolymer treatment used to give special properties to all kinds of goods. For textile use it may be produced as fine polymer membranes or applied as a coating to other fabrics. Teflon is characteristically a water-resistant material and so is often used to provide some form of protective or water-resistant layer.

Teflon is widely known as a non-stick coating for cooking pots and pans. However, it is also used, in the form of a fine, microporous polymer membrane, as a laminate for fabrics to make them waterproof and/or stain-resistant. GORE-TEX® fabric is perhaps the best-known product to use a Teflon microporous membrane. Teflon may also be applied as a coating to any fabric, woven, knitted or nonwoven, to make it waterproof and stain-resistant. The coating is applied to the textile in the form of a fluid mixture, either by a blade or a roller, or by spraying it onto one or both sides. The mixture may contain a coloured pigment or it may be colourless. Both the amount of coating applied and the degree of penetration of the mixture are controlled in order to produce different fabrics.

See also COATED FABRIC, OIL CLOTH, POLYMER MEMBRANE LAMINATES, WATERPROOF AND WATER-REPELLENT FABRICS.

End uses: curtains, awnings, window blinds, upholstery, floor and wall coverings, car upholstery, tablecloths, aprons, hats, waterproof apparel, raincoats, protective wear, luggage, bags and footwear.

TERRY FABRIC A soft loop pile fabric made specifically to absorb moisture. It is constructed with uncut loops on either one or both sides of the fabric. Characteristically, therefore, it is a very absorbent, heavy, bulky fabric. It is sometimes also called 'terry towelling' or 'Turkish towelling'.[2] Terry fabric was traditionally a woven fabric, but it may also be warp-knitted or weft-knitted. It is made in different thicknesses, qualities and weights. The loop pile is prone to snagging and may shed lint, but terry fabrics do not need ironing.

Teflon® (Teflon coating)

terry fabric (jacquard knitted)

terry fabric (terry velour)

terry fabric (weft-knitted, face and back)

terry fabric (woven)

The term 'terry' comes from French *tirer*, meaning 'to pull', because at one time Turkish towelling was made by pulling out the pile loops by hand.[23] Terry fabric is traditionally constructed with 100% carded and folded cotton yarns, but nowadays man-made fibres, such as polyester, viscose, nylon or blends, may also be used in the base fabric. Cotton is normally used for the pile yarns as this is the most absorbent and hard-wearing. For example, cotton/polyester terry fabrics have a base fabric of either cotton/polyester or only polyester and a pile of 100% cotton yarns. Terry fabrics may be piece-dyed in solid colours, yarn-dyed, or printed in a variety of different patterns. They may be constructed by any of the methods described below.

Woven terry fabric is a warp pile fabric. Loops may be formed on one or both sides of the fabric, but the best-quality fabric has loops on both sides and a flat woven selvedge. The loops are woven very closely together and are firmly constructed into the backing fabric. With lower-quality terry fabrics, the loops are woven less closely and may be easily caught and pulled. Terry fabrics are woven on dobby looms or, to produce more complex patterns, on jacquard looms. Some looms weaving terry fabrics can be set up to weave two or more towel widths side by side. Terry fabric is a slack-tension fabric, like seersucker, and is constructed with two warps. The ground warp is kept under a constant tight tension, and the tension of the pile warp is loosened at regular intervals during weaving. Two or three weft yarns are inserted into the fabric, leaving a gap between them and the fabric already woven. When a third or fourth weft yarn is inserted, the pile warp is simultaneously slackened according to the height of the desired pile loop. The pile is formed when this weft yarn is beaten into place against the fell of the cloth. It pushes the slack warp yarns into loops and secures them into position in the backing fabric, which is usually woven in a firm plain weave construction. Patterns may be made by varying the size of the pile loops, by weaving the pile loops only in parts of the fabric, and by using different colour combinations. Other loop pile fabrics similar to terry fabric include astrakhan fabric, frisé, grospoint and moquette. *See also* COTTON FABRIC, PILE FABRICS, TOWELLING.

Terry poplin is a variation of woven terry fabric. It is woven with a silk warp and a worsted weft. The warp yarns are arranged alternately, with one warp end tightly tensioned and one terry warp end under slack tension. When the fabric is woven, the terry ends form a series of minute loops all over the fabric surface.[36]

Terry velour is a woven terry fabric in which the pile loops are sheared and brushed. This produces a velour fabric with a luxurious velvety handle and appearance. This fabric is, however, less absorbent than the loop pile terry fabric. Terry velour is sometimes also called 'cropped terry pile' or 'sheared terry pile'.[25] Plush, velour and velvet fabrics are all made in a similar manner to terry velour, but the height of the loop pile varies with each and the loop pile of each is cut to produce different cut pile surfaces. *See also* PLUSH, VELOUR, VELVET.

Warp-knitted terry fabric is a knitted loop pile fabric in which the ground construction is usually made with man-made continuous filament yarns and the pile loops with cotton yarns. Terry fabrics are knitted on a tricot warp-knitting machine, with half-set guide bars where only alternate guides carry the yarns. A single-sided pile fabric is made by laying-in elongated yarns into a ground construction to form loops. The pillar and inlay ground fabric is knitted on alternate knitting needles on the front two guide bars. The pile is formed on the back guide bar by laying-in the pile yarn into the ground fabric and then passing the loops around the unoccupied needles to form extended pile loops on the technical face of the fabric.[38] A double-sided pile fabric is made in a similar manner, on a four-bar tricot machine. The middle two guide bars knit the pillar and inlay

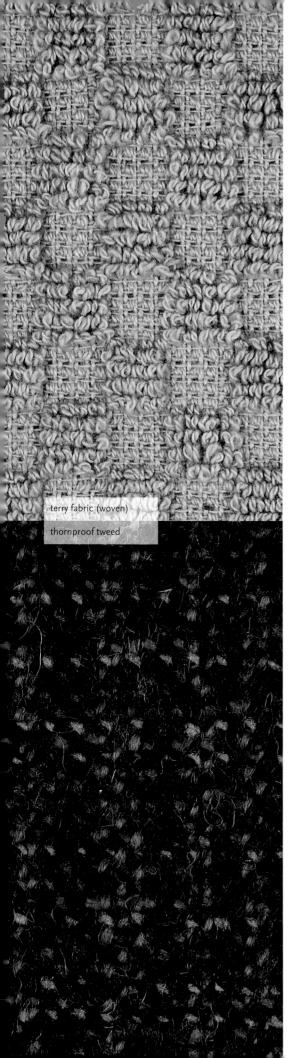

terry fabric (woven)

thornproof tweed

ground fabric. The front and back guide bars pass the pile yarn around the unoccupied needles to form loops on both the face and back of the fabric. The pile yarn is laid-in on the technical face side and knitted-in on the technical back.[38] Warp-knitted terry fabric may also be made by over-feeding the pile yarn. In warp-knitted terry fabric constructions, the loops are bound in more securely than in woven terry constructions and cannot pull out. *See also* KNITTED FABRIC, LAID-IN FABRIC, WARP-KNITTED FABRIC.

Weft-knitted terry fabric is a weft-knitted loop pile fabric that can be produced in two different ways:

(i) It can be produced by laying-in an extra yarn that is elongated into yarn loops and secured in a plain knit base construction.

(ii) It can be made by knitting one yarn together with an extra 'plated' yarn in a plain knit construction. The extra yarn is made to form extended sinker loops and may be knitted on every needle, or on some needles only, to form a pattern. This forms a surface of pile loops on the technical back of the fabric.

Pile loops on both sides of the fabric are produced either by knitting elongated sinker loops on both sides of the fabric or by knitting elongated sinker loops on one side and elongated laid-in stitches on the other. This fabric is called 'double-sided weft-knitted terry fabric'.[38] *See also* KNITTED FABRIC, LAID-IN FABRIC, PLAIN KNIT FABRIC, PLATED FABRICS, WEFT-KNITTED FABRIC.

There are also various loop yarn fabrics that are woven and knitted in imitation of terry fabric. A loop yarn fabric looks similar to a terry fabric, but it is usually a single cloth fabric that is either woven or knitted with a loop yarn, usually in the weft direction. This gives the appearance of a loop pile. Frotté is a soft, voluminous loop yarn fabric that is woven in imitation of terry fabric. It is a cheaper but less durable version of terry fabric. Other examples of loop yarn fabrics include bouclé fabric and éponge.

End uses: bath, beach and hand towels; flannels; tea towels; nappies; bath and swimming robes; casual clothing; slippers; bathroom accessories; and bar counter mats.

TEXI-PIQUÉ A weft-knitted, non-jacquard double jersey fabric knitted on an interlock basis. It has tuck stitches on both sides of the fabric.

The knit construction is composed of six different weft courses that repeat throughout the fabric. Rows 1, 2, 4 and 5 are knitted in interlock structure on both needle-beds. Courses 3 and 6 are knitted in tuck stitches on the alternate staggered needles on both needle-beds. This produces tuck stitches on both sides of the fabric.[38]

See also INTERLOCK; JERSEY; KNITTED FABRIC; PIQUÉ, WEFT-KNITTED; WEFT-KNITTED FABRIC.

End uses: casual wear, T-shirts, dresses, trousers and jackets.

row 6

row 5

row 4

row 3

row 2

row 1

texi-piqué

THORNPROOF TWEED A classic Scottish woven tweed fabric with a characteristic 'pepper and salt' colouring style in which the fabric appears to be sprinkled with different contrasting colours. Traditional thornproof tweed is a thick, rough woollen fabric that is warm, strong and very hard-wearing. It is a medium- to heavyweight fabric.

Thornproof tweed is woven with Cheviot-quality woollen yarns (wool from the Cheviot breed of sheep). In order to produce the pepper and salt colouring, two singles yarns in different colours are folded or twisted together. They may be two contrasting colours or two colours of similar tones; however, as the colour intensity of the individual yarns is greatly reduced once they are woven into the fabric, highly contrasting shades are usually selected. The fabric is woven in plain weave, and it is the combination of fancy

three-dimensional
textile (spacer fabric)

ticking

yarn and weave structure that produces the colour effect. Different colour combinations may also be used in both warp and weft in order to enhance the random colour mix.

The yarns for thornproof tweeds are more highly twisted than those used in other tweed fabrics, and the fabric is also quite highly sett. This produces a smooth, dense, firm fabric for outdoors wear that is resistant to the penetration of thorns and natural vegetation. It is from this quality that the fabric derives its name. Thornproof tweed is thought to have first been used in about 1870 when troops fighting in the Red River Rebellion in Canada were clothed in fabric that resisted thorns.[36] Thornproof tweed is finished with a minimum finishing treatment that maintains its rough handle. It is a similar fabric to Bannockburn.

See also COATING FABRIC, PLAIN WEAVE FABRIC, TWEED, WOOL FABRIC.

End uses: coarse wool suiting, sports jackets, coats, trousers and skirts.

THREE-DIMENSIONAL TEXTILES A general term for textiles made with special three-dimensional constructions. Three-dimensional textiles include fabrics made with various woven, warp-knitted, weft-knitted and stitch-bonded constructions. These textiles are characteristically more stable than most other fabric constructions. They are usually pliant and flexible and do not fray or unravel, and they are equally resilient in all directions.

Woven three-dimensional fabrics are woven on a special weaving loom that produces a fabric composed of yarns interlaced in the vertical, horizontal and diagonal directions. This is a particularly secure, stable fabric construction. Three-dimensional knitted fabrics include spacer fabrics, which consist of two fabric layers separated by a cushion of yarns with spaces in between. Spacer fabrics may be warp- or weft-knitted, and they vary in thickness from a few millimetres to a few centimetres thick; *see* SPACER FABRICS. In addition, some warp-knitted multiaxial and biaxial fabrics form three-dimensional constructions; *see* LAID-IN FABRIC. Many stitch-bonded fabrics are also made in three-dimensional constructions, including some Malimo fabrics; *see* MALIMO, STITCH-BONDED FABRIC.

End uses: sportswear, medical textiles, bra fabrics/cups, car upholstery, mattresses, filters and technical textiles of various kinds.

TIBET (thibet, Tibet cloth) (*obs.*) A term used for two different types of fabric:[9]
(i) A heavyweight wool dress or coating fabric with a soft, smooth surface, woven in twill weave.
(ii) A goat-hair fabric, similar to camlet.

TICKING A type of striped woven fabric originally used for mattress covers and similar end uses. Characteristically, mattress tickings are very strong, stiff, durable warp-faced woven fabrics that have a white or ecru background and combinations of thick and thin colour-woven stripes in the warp direction. Most tickings are heavyweight fabrics, but some are made in lighter weights for fashion end uses.

Ticking is traditionally made from tightly twisted 100% carded cotton yarns or 100% linen yarns, or sometimes it has a cotton warp and a linen weft. Nowadays blends with man-made fibres, usually polyester, are also common. The warp yarns are very closely sett and arranged with varying stripe widths, usually of white with one other colour. Black/white, blue/white, navy/white, brown/white or red/white are typical colour combinations. The weft is usually white or ecru in colour and has less twist than the warp yarns.

Ticking is usually woven in a 2-, 3- or 4-end warp-faced twill weave, a 5- or 8- end satin weave or a herringbone weave structure. It is woven so densely in order to make it down-proof. Although colour-woven stripe designs are traditional, ticking is also available in plain solid colours or woven with damask jacquard designs. More rarely it might be printed. Ticking may be mercerized or schreinered to increase its strength and lustre, and/or given a water-repellent finish. An example of a typical 2/1 twill linen ticking fabric construction is 56 tex warp sett at 28 ends per cm and 75 tex tow weft woven at 19 picks per cm.[26] An example of a typical 5-end satin cotton ticking fabric construction is 60 tex warp sett at 30 ends per cm and 50 tex weft woven at 22 picks per cm.[26]

The term 'ticking' comes from Latin *theca*, meaning a cover or case of cotton or linen.[3] At one time ticking was known as 'inlet', 'bedstout' or 'bed tick', but these terms are now rarely used. The term 'Limoges' is used for brightly coloured tickings with a hard glazed surface that were originally made in France.[3] Similar fabrics to ticking include drill, florentine, hickory cloth and jean.

See also DAMASK; HERRINGBONE; SATIN, WOVEN; STRIPES; TWILL FABRICS.

End uses: mattress covers, bolster covers, pillow coverings, duvet cases, cushion covers, upholstery, deckchair seats, curtains, bags, casual clothing, overalls, workwear, women's trousers and jackets.

TIE-DYED FABRIC A resist-dyed fabric with characteristic tie-dyed patterns, often with blurred edges. The resist is made by tying and/or knotting selected areas of the fabric prior to dyeing, usually in a predetermined pattern. When the fabric is subsequently dyed, the areas covered with the ties or hidden behind the knots will remain undyed. It is the undyed areas of fabric that form the pattern against the dyed ground.

Woven fabrics made from cotton are normally used to make tie-dyed fabrics, since they are easy to tie, knot and dye, but fabrics made from other fibres, especially silk and viscose, can also be tie-dyed. The patterns are determined by the manner in which the fabric is tied, and there are many different types of tying techniques, each producing different kinds of patterns and effects. The fabric itself may be tied into different knots, or separate ties may be applied to it: for example, string, yarn, thread, bast fibres, leaves, strips of cloth or other materials. Sometimes seeds, nuts or pebbles are tied inside the fabric. After dyeing, the ties and/or knots are removed, and these areas will be either undyed or partially dyed, depending on how far the dye was able to seep into them. The patterns produced characteristically have blurred edges where the dye was able to penetrate the fabric only partially.

Tie-dyeing techniques have been used for centuries in many parts of the world for patterning apparel fabrics, notably in parts of Africa and Asia. Traditionally made bandanna fabric is an example of a tie-dyed fabric. Other resist-dyed fabrics that can have similar effects to tie-dyed fabrics include batik, plangi, shibori and tritik.

See also BANDANNA, DYED FABRICS, RESIST-DYED FABRICS.

End uses: dresses, blouses, scarves, shirts, T-shirts, tunics, dressing gowns and curtains.

TIE FABRIC A general term for any fabric used to make men's neckties. Tie fabrics are usually medium-weight fabrics.

Most tie fabrics have traditionally been made from silk and, to a lesser extent, from wool or cotton. Nowadays they are also made from acetate, polyester, viscose and blends of these with natural fibres. Tie fabrics are usually narrow woven fabrics and may be constructed in all kinds of small-scale weave structures, including plain, twill, satin or herringbone weaves, small geometric dobby woven designs or small-scale jacquard woven motifs. They may be piece-dyed, colour-woven or printed, and they often have stripes or checks. Examples of tie fabrics include barathea, challis, some chiné fabrics, many dobby fabrics, épingle, faille, many figured fabrics, foulard, grenadine, grosgrain, some ikat fabrics, many jacquard fabrics (*see* JACQUARD FABRIC, WOVEN), Macclesfield silk (*see* SILK FABRIC), Mogador, natté, ottoman, regence, many repp fabrics, various rib woven fabrics, many silk fabrics and some Tattersall check fabrics.

tie-dyed fabric

tie fabric (worsted)

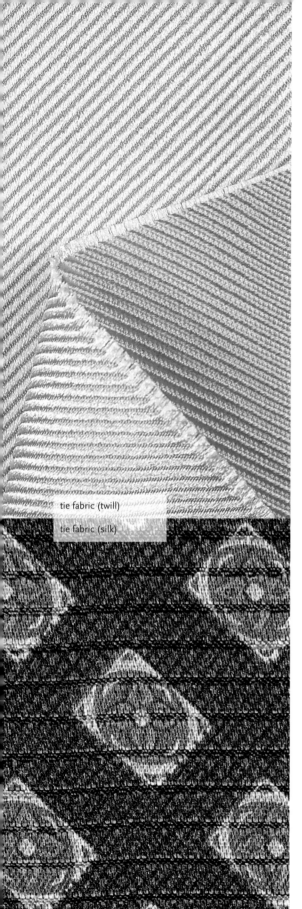

tie fabric (twill)

tie fabric (silk)

See also CHECKS; COLOUR AND WEAVE EFFECTS; DISCHARGE PRINTED FABRIC; DOBBY FABRIC; HERRINGBONE; MOIRÉ FABRIC; PLAIN WEAVE FABRIC; PRINTED FABRIC; SATIN, WOVEN; SPITALFIELDS; STRIPES; TWILL FABRICS.

End uses: men's neckties, cravats and scarves.

TIFFANY (obs.) A very fine silk gauze fabric used for trimmings.[3, 36]

TISSUE see SHEER FABRICS.

TISSUE FAILLE see FAILLE.

TISSUE GINGHAM see GINGHAM.

TISSUE TAFFETA see TAFFETA.

TOBACCO CLOTH see CHEESECLOTH.

TOILE DE JOUY A type of printed fabric with a characteristic style of pattern. Toile de Jouy fabrics were first produced in France in the 18th century, and were originally cotton, linen or silk woven fabrics that were printed with the characteristic fine engraved lines produced by etched copper plates. Typically, floral or scenic designs would be printed in a single colour against a light cream or white-coloured background. Nowadays the term 'toile de Jouy' is usually applied to fabrics screen-printed with similar floral or scenic designs from the 18th century onwards, often copied directly from original toile de Jouy fabrics.

'Toile' comes from the French for 'cloth', and is often used to refer to plain or twill woven linen fabrics.[10] Jouy is the name of a village near Versailles, in France, and therefore 'toile de Jouy' means 'cloth of Jouy'. In the later 18th century, hand-painted and hand-printed cotton fabrics imported from India were hugely popular in Europe, where nothing similar was being produced – until, in 1759, Christophe Philippe Oberkampf, a German, established his famous printing factory in Jouy. He pioneered many new fabric printing developments, including the use of etched copper plates; many of his fabrics were printed using these, usually in a single colour. This produced the characteristic style of fine engraved lines and subtle colours, and they often had a large repeat area.[5] At one time the term 'toile de Jouy' was used only for the printed fabrics produced in the village of Jouy, but nowadays the term refers more to the style of printed pattern. Modern-day print cloths used for toile de Jouy are usually light- to medium-weight fabrics made from carded cotton or cotton blends and woven in plain weave. Occasionally they may also be woven in satin or sateen weave.

See also PRINT CLOTH, PRINTED FABRIC.

End uses: furnishing fabrics, bed linen, tablecloths, accessories and, occasionally, dresses and blouses.

TOWELLING A general term for a range of different fabrics that may be used as towels. Most towelling fabrics are woven, but some are also knitted. Their main characteristic is that they are very absorbent; they are usually also very strong and hard-wearing.

Woven towelling fabrics are often made in narrow widths. As the specific purpose of towels is to dry things, they are typically made using absorbent materials such as cotton. They are also constructed in ways that allow for maximum absorption, for example with pile loops or three-dimensional weave structures. There are many different types of towelling fabric, including birdeye, crash, damask, diced weaves, frotté, glass cloth, honeycomb, huckaback, tea towelling and terry fabric. There is also a machine-knitted

tie fabric (jacquard)

toile de Jouy

towelling

tricot (back and face)

tricot (face and back)

towelling fabric, which is made with loops on one side and is used for stretch sheets and clothing.[3]

End uses: bath towels, bathrobes, flannels, slippers, casual clothing, tea towels and sheets.

TRACKSUIT FABRIC *see* FLEECE FABRIC.

TRIACETATE FABRIC A general term for any fabric constructed with fibres or yarns made from triacetate. 'Triacetate' is the generic term for a regenerated man-made material made from cellulose.[25] It may be produced in sheet form or in fibre form. To make clothing and furnishing fabrics, it is usually the fibres that are used.

The fibres may be used in continuous filament form or they may be chopped into shorter staple lengths and respun into yarns with different characteristics, sometimes blended with other staple fibres. The term 'triacetate fabric' is used for fabrics, of all different weights and constructions, composed of 100% triacetate fibres or yarns. Where triacetate is used together with other fibres, the percentage of each should be stated. Modified triacetate fibres are marketed under different trade names. Triacetate fabric, often in knitted jersey form, may be given permanent pleats and thus provides an alternative to permanently pleated, synthetic polyester fabrics.

See also PLEATED FABRICS, POLYESTER FABRIC.

End uses: dresses, skirts, blouses and furnishing fabrics.

TRICOLETTE (*obs.*) A fine, lustrous weft-knitted fabric used for underwear, lingerie and dresses. First made in 1924, it was the first knitted fabric made using viscose rayon continuous filament yarns.[9]

TRICOT A generic term for any kind of warp-knitted fabric knitted on a tricot warp-knitting machine, ranging from sheer, lightweight fabrics to heavyweight fabrics. Typically, however, tricot fabrics are lightweight, characterized by vertical wales on the technical face and horizontal ribs on the technical back. The name 'tricot' comes from the French for 'knitted fabric' or 'sweater'.

Tricot fabrics are valued as particularly stable fabrics: the common constructions will not ladder or unravel (the French term for them is *indémaillable*). In addition, many stretch fabrics are knitted on tricot machines – most being comfort stretch fabrics in which elastane yarns are knitted into the fabric construction. The stretch fabric trade uses the term 'tricot' for stretch locknits with elastane, to distinguish them from stretch raschel fabrics knitted on raschel machines, which are mostly power stretch fabrics in which the elastane is laid-in. *See* RASCHEL STRETCH FABRICS.

Originally tricot was made only in silk, but nowadays it is usually made with man-made coninuous filament yarns, especially nylon, polyester and acetate. Occasionally cotton or viscose is used, and elastane is often included to add stretch. Without elastane, the stretch can vary between high and negligible depending on the construction, but it is usually in the width direction. Single tricot, double tricot and stretch tricot are discussed below.

Single tricot is knitted with one fully threaded guide bar lapping alternately left and right by one needle space on one set of needles.[38] It is the simplest construction possible on a warp-knitting machine, but it is never normally used on its own commercially since it has little stability and cover, and can split in the length. It is widely used, however, as the base structure for other constructions, including locknit, loopraise, reverse locknit, sharkskin and many other plain and patterned fabrics.

Double tricot is a two-bar version of single tricot. Each of the two full-set guide bars makes a 1 and 1 lapping movement in opposite directions.[25] This construction makes a very stable, lightweight fabric that overcomes most of the shortcomings of single tricot,

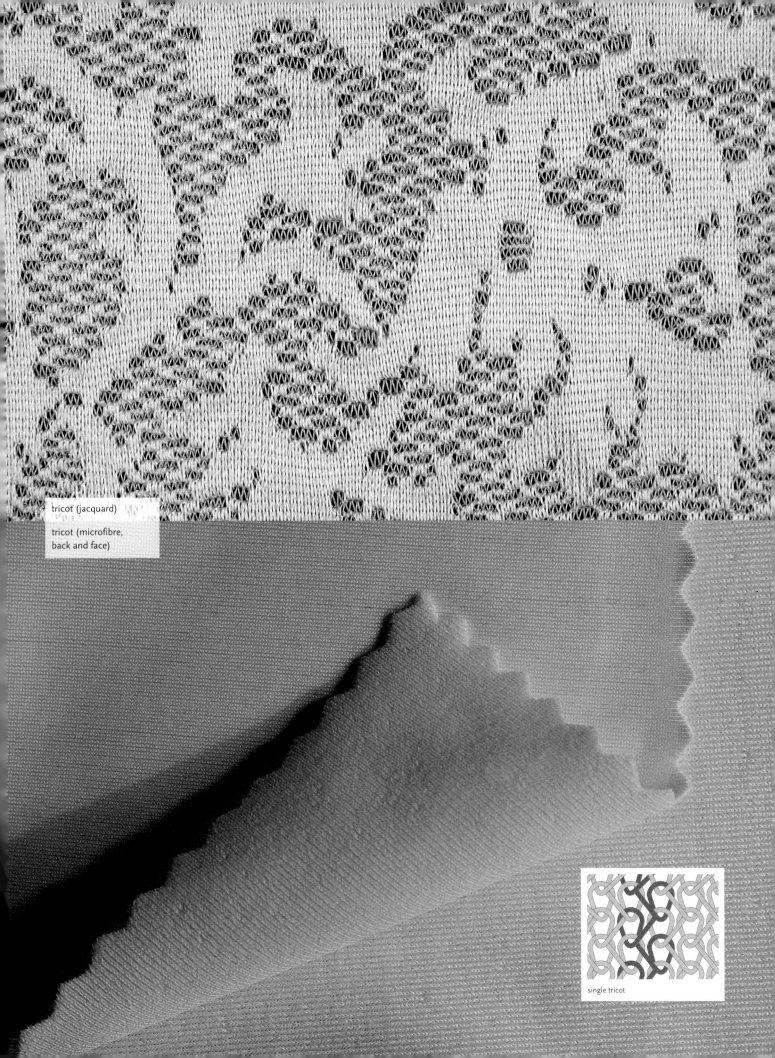

tricot (jacquard)

tricot (microfibre,
back and face)

single tricot

tricotine (face and back)

tropical suiting

with the exception of the tendency to split. Like single tricot, double tricot is commonly used as a ground for fancier fabrics. Stripes, textures or patterns may be incorporated into the fabric, for example, or it can be used as a base for velour or plush.

Stretch or elastomeric tricot fabrics are usually locknit fabrics or sometimes mesh fabrics. The stretch is produced by replacing the back bar yarn with a fine elastane yarn under high tension. The elastane yarn is knitted into the fabric structure in a similar manner to the non-stretch yarn knitting on the front bar. This fully locks it into position, and it is mostly hidden in the centre of the fabric, causing the fabric to compact very strongly in both directions. In finishing, this compaction is controlled to produce the required weight, width and stretch. Unlike normal locknit fabrics, which have some widthways stretch, these elastomeric versions will have very high warpways stretch as well as good widthways stretch. They are used for closely fitting comfort stretch garments, such as swimwear, lingerie, sportswear and outerwear. *See also* ELASTANE FABRIC, ELASTOMERIC FABRIC, LOCKNIT, STRETCH FABRIC.

Tricot fabrics such as locknit and satin are often given a schreiner finish to improve lustre and to increase the cover.[19] Because of their stability, light weight and low cost, tricot fabrics are also widely used as scrims or backing fabrics for many different kinds of laminated fabrics.

See also KNITTED FABRIC; LAMINATED FABRIC; LOCKNIT; NET; SATIN, WARP-KNITTED; SCRIM; SHARKSKIN; WARP-KNITTED FABRIC.

End uses: dresses, blouses, shirts, lingerie, nightwear, bridal wear, evening wear, gloves, casual clothing, laminated fabrics, lining fabric, upholstery and sheets; (stretch tricot) swimwear, lingerie, sportswear and outerwear.

TRICOTINE A term given to various woven fabrics that are usually constructed in twill weaves. Tricotine is a very hard-wearing, durable fabric.

The most common tricotine fabric is woven in a warp-faced, double twill weave forming steep double twill lines on the face side. Traditionally it is woven using closely sett woollen or worsted yarns, and it is usually piece-dyed and given a clear finish. An example of a typical tricotine fabric construction is 34/2 tex botany warp sett at 20 ends per cm and 28 tex worsted weft woven at 20 to 24 picks per cm.[26]

Although it is traditionally woven with highly twisted woollen or worsted yarns, tricotine may also be woven using other natural or man-made fibres. Other qualities, for example, include a weft-faced tricotine fabric woven in twill weave with a cotton warp and a worsted weft, and a plain weave fabric woven with a silk warp and a cotton weft, showing fine horizontal rib lines.[25, 26] Tricotine is a very similar fabric to cavalry twill and elastique. In the United States, the terms 'cavalry twill', 'elastique' and 'double twill tricotine' are sometimes used interchangeably.

See also TWILL FABRICS.

End uses: trousers, coats, suits and uniforms.

TRISKIN *see* RASCHEL STRETCH FABRICS.

TRITIK *see* RESIST-DYED FABRICS.

TROPICAL SUITING A general term for a range of woven, lightweight summer suiting fabrics weighing in the region of 160–240 g/m² and suitable for wear in summer or in hot climates.

Tropical suiting fabrics may be made in a variety of different fibres and weave structures. Appropriate fibres and blends include very fine worsted wool, wool/polyester, wool/viscose and wool/cotton. The fibres are usually highly twisted in order to produce

tsumugi

tufted fabric

very fine but strong yarns, which in turn produce strong, lightweight fabrics. Plain weave is probably the most frequently used weave structure, and the fabric is woven with a medium sett – just enough to produce a firm construction, but open enough for breathability. Plain woven fabrics made from worsted wool in this manner are sometimes called 'tropical worsted'. The yarns are highly twisted in order to achieve the fineness and lightness of the fabric. Tropical worsted is a very lightweight worsted fabric, usually woven in light colours like beige and white. The fabric is usually given a clear finish. Tropical worsted pleats and creases very well.[2] Fabrics suitable for use as tropical suiting include Fresco®, panama suiting fabric and sharkskin. Cotton fabrics used to make summer suits may also sometimes be described as 'tropical suiting'. Such fabrics include coutil and duck.

See also PLAIN WEAVE FABRIC, WORSTED FABRIC.

End uses: men's and women's summer-weight suits and coats.

TSUMUGI Woven silk fabrics that have traditionally been woven by hand in central Honshu, Japan, for many centuries.[17] They are very hard-wearing silk fabrics used for kimonos and other traditional garments.

Tsumugi are traditionally woven by hand using yarns hand-spun from waste silk fibres. The fabric has a slightly coarse, homespun appearance.[17] It is often patterned in some way, and it may be dyed, printed or colour-woven with stripes or checks. Since the fabric is so durable, in Japan it has always been used for everyday clothes and working clothes rather than for occasion wear like most other silk fabrics.

See also SILK FABRIC.

End uses: kimonos and other Japanese traditional clothing.

TUFTED FABRIC A pile fabric that is made either by densely knotting lengths of yarn into a warp by hand or, more usually, by inserting pile yarns with needles into a backing material that is usually a pre-made fabric. The pile may be left uncut to form pile loops, or it may be cut to form open tufts. Some carpets are made by the process of tufting.

All kinds of fibres may be used for tufting, including natural and synthetic fibres. Tufting may be done all over the backing fabric, or just in localized areas to form a pattern. The tufting is done by a series of needles, each carrying a yarn being fed from spools. The whole process is controlled by computer. The tuft density is determined by the number of needles carrying yarns per square centimetre, and the tuft height may also be varied. The needles punch the pile yarns through into the backing fabric, and hooks underneath the fabric hold each loop in place until the needles pull back again. The pile is secured in place during the finishing process when the pile yarns untwist and open out (blooming) and the backing fabric shrinks, thus trapping the yarns in place. The back of the backing fabric of many tufted fabrics is also back-coated with latex or similar material to further secure the pile.

Many different types of backing material may be used, ranging from very fine to very heavy in weight. It may be woven, knitted, nonwoven or stitch-bonded. Sometimes two backing materials may be used for extra strength and durability. In this case the pile yarn is inserted through the primary backing material, and a secondary backing material, for example hessian or foam, is then bonded onto the back of this in a separate process. Tufting is a cheaper method of producing a pile fabric than making woven or knitted pile fabrics, as it is extremely fast and less labour-intensive; however, the tufts may not always be as firmly secured in the base fabric as in more conventional methods. Examples of tufted fabrics include candlewick, carpet and some fur fabrics.

See also COATED FABRIC, MULTI-COMPONENT FABRICS, PILE FABRICS, STITCH-BONDED FABRIC.

End uses: carpets, rugs, mats, bags, blankets, upholstery, bedspreads, fur fabrics and coat linings.

tulle (metal-embroidered)

tussore

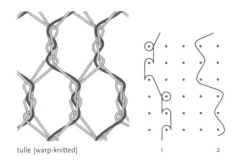

tulle (warp-knitted)   1   2

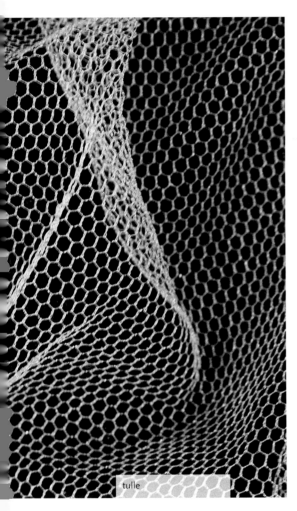

tulle

TULLE A very fine, lightweight net fabric characterized by a fine hexagonal mesh structure. It may be made on a lace machine or warp-knitted. Characteristically, tulle is a fine, sheer, soft, transparent fabric with excellent drape. However, it is also sometimes stiffened with starch, for use in millinery, petticoats and ballet costumes.

Tulle is traditionally made from fine silk yarns, but less expensive versions may also be made using cotton, viscose or nylon. The classic tulle fabric is made on lace machines. Tulle has been manufactured by machine in England since 1768.[3] Before this time it was a handmade lace fabric. When the bobbinet lace machine was invented in 1809, tulle was made on this machine, which constructed the fabric with a distinctive fine hexagonal mesh. Tulle was first manufactured in France on the bobbinet machine in 1817, in the town of Tulle, from which the fabric takes its name.[3] Nowadays tulle is mass-produced in piece form (as a wide fabric) on the Leavers lace machine, or it may be made as a narrow fabric edging.[3] It is also a suitable base fabric for embroidery. These are several different variations of the classic tulle fabric: tulle crinoline, a pleated tulle fabric made with a graduated sized mesh; tulle grec, a tulle fabric with a larger-sized mesh; and tulle grenadine, which has alternate rows of black and white mesh.[3]

Warp-knitted tulle fabrics with a fine, hexagonal mesh may also be constructed on both raschel and tricot warp-knitting machines (warp-knitted tulle). Two guide bars are used to make the structure. Pillar stitches are alternated with tricot stitches on the front guide bar and both are reinforced by laid-in yarns supplied by the back guide bar.[38] When the laid-in yarn is an elastomeric yarn, the fabric is known as 'elastic tulle net'.[38] Imitation tulle may be made by weaving very fine yarns in a very open-sett plain weave construction. *See also* GAUZE, NET. Tulle is a very similar fabric to Malines or Malines lace. It is also sometimes called 'illusion', being so fine that it is barely seen.[9]

See also EMBROIDERED FABRICS; FISHNET; KNITTED FABRIC; LACE; LACE, KNITTED; LAID-IN FABRIC; MESH FABRICS; NARROW FABRICS; RASCHEL LACE; SHEER FABRICS; TRICOT; WARP-KNITTED FABRIC.

End uses: bridal wear, veils, evening wear, dress trims, millinery, ballet costumes, petticoats under evening dresses and ground fabric for embroidery.

TUSSAH SILK *see* SILK FABRIC.

TUSSORE A fairly thick woven fabric made from tussah silk, a type of wild silk obtained from the cocoon of the wild silkworm *Antheraea mylitta*.[36] Tussah silk is naturally ecru or yellowy beige to brown in colour, and the yarns characteristically have slubs that give a stiff, coarse, uneven texture to the fabric.

Since most wild silk cocoons cannot be reeled, the silk fibre is usually spun. It is sometimes also used together with cotton or wool. The fibre is also not easily dyed and is therefore usually left in its natural colour. Tussah silk may be knitted or woven. If woven, it is usually woven in a plain or hopsack weave structure. Tussore silk fabric was originally made in Bengal, and today most tussore silk comes from Manchuria and India.[5] The words 'tussore' and 'tussah' come from Hindi *tasar*, originating from the Sanskrit *tasara*, meaning 'shuttle'.[3] At one time tussore fabrics were also made in cotton yarns and dyed and mercerized to imitate the silk fabric. An example of a cotton tussore fabric construction is: plain weave (warp rib): 30 tex cotton warp sett at 36 ends per cm and 50 tex cotton weft woven at 14 picks per cm.[26] Tussah silk can also be spun into much finer yarns, and in this form it is used to make pongee and shantung fabrics. Tussore is sometimes called 'shantung', which is the Chinese name for a very similar fabric (*see* SHANTUNG).

See also SILK FABRIC.

End uses: suits, dresses, skirts, shirts, blouses, coats and furnishings.

tweed

furnishing tweed

novelty tweed

TWEED Originally the name of a rough, hairy, heavyweight woven fabric that was made from wool and used as outerwear; now a term used for a wide range of rough-textured, medium- to heavyweight woollen fabrics, most of which have characteristic 'mélange' or mixed colour effects as opposed to solid colourings. For example, different-coloured fibres may be blended together during the spinning process, and/or marl yarns (two-fold yarns composed of two singles yarns dyed in contrasting colours) may be used. This produces fabrics with tonal or multicoloured effects (*see* MÉLANGE FABRIC). Other tweed fabrics may be solid in colour, striped or checked, or they may combine various colour and weave effects. Tweed fabrics are traditionally very strong, warm and hard-wearing woollen fabrics, but their rough surface texture means that they usually need to be lined in order to be worn next to the skin.

Tweed fabrics were originally handmade woollen fabrics, woven on the banks of the river Tweed in the Borders region between England and Scotland. It is said that the name came into use through the misunderstanding of a London cloth merchant in about 1840: a consignment of fabric from the area, woven in a twill weave, was labelled 'tweel' (the Scottish term for twills), and this was misread as 'tweed'.[8] These fabrics have been known as tweeds ever since. Nowadays tweed fabrics are almost all woven on industrial power looms, with the notable exception of Harris tweed, which is still woven by hand.

Tweed fabrics are traditionally made from carded virgin wool, much of which is Cheviot (from the Cheviot breed of sheep) or New Zealand cross-bred. Both are noted for their strength, durability and rather rough handle.[8] Cheaper tweed fabrics are woven using recycled or cheaper wool qualities. If man-made fibres are included, or if a tweed fabric is imitated using man-made fibres, this should be stated. Tweed fabrics may be woven in a variety of different weave structures, including plain, twills and herringbones; however, 2/2 twill is probably the most traditional (*see* TWILL FABRICS). Tweed fabrics are often milled during finishing in order to close up the fabric and increase the warmth. There are many different types of tweed fabrics. A number of these are discussed below; *see also* BAN-NOCKBURN, CHEVIOT, DONEGAL, HARRIS TWEED, SHETLAND TWEED, THORNPROOF TWEED.

CAMBRIAN TWEED A general term for woollen tweed fabrics originating in Wales. They are made using wool from the local breeds of sheep. The yarns may be dyed, or fibres in their natural wool colours (white, grey and black) might be blended together. The fabrics are most often woven in plain weave, hopsack or herringbone weave structures.[2]

FURNISHING TWEED A tweed similar in appearance to the dress-weight tweeds, but made from thicker, heavier yarns and used for upholstery and occasionally for curtains. Such fabrics are usually constructed to give maximum resistance to wear, using strong wool fibres such as Scottish Cheviot and New Zealand cross-bred. The yarns are hard-twisted to make them strong and durable. The fabric is then woven in a firm, stable weave structure such as plain weave or a variation (e.g. granite weave), and finished by scouring and milling, both of which ensure a strong, durable fabric construction.

GAMEKEEPER TWEED A thick, rough woollen fabric that is warm, strong and very hard-wearing. It is a medium- to heavyweight fabric, woven in colours that allow the wearer to blend in with the natural tones of the British countryside. It was traditionally worn by gamekeepers, hence the name. *See also* COVERT CLOTH.

HEATHER TWEED A tweed woven with 'heather' yarns, produced by the blending together of a range of different pink- and purple-coloured fibres during the spinning process. Weaving these yarns into a fabric produces a diverse range of subtle tones, similar to the colours of heather. The term is therefore a general one, probably originating in Scotland. *See* MÉLANGE FABRIC.

IRISH TWEED A general term for many different types of woollen tweed fabric originating in Ireland. Tweed fabrics have been woven in Ireland since at least the 12th century.[3]

The best known are Blarney, Connemara and Donegal (*see* DONEGAL). Connemara tweed is similar to Donegal tweed, but it tends to be brighter in colour.[3]

JACOB TWEED A tweed fabric woven using wool from the piebald or spotted four-horned Jacob sheep. Wool from this breed contains different shades that range from very dark brown to ecru. In quality the wool is similar to Cheviot, so it produces a strong, durable woven fabric in mottled colours.[3]

gamekeeper tweed

knickerbocker tweed

KNICKERBOCKER TWEED A rough-faced fabric made with wool and cotton yarns containing coloured neps, which give the fabric a grainy surface texture. The fabric was traditionally used for sportswear, and the name probably derives from the garment it was used for – knickerbockers or plus fours.

LOVAT TWEED A woollen tweed fabric produced in lovat (greeny-grey) shades and often used as an overcoating fabric.[2]

NOVELTY TWEED A general term normally used for very fancy tweed fabrics. These decorative fabrics may have a variety of different features, including multicoloured effects, yarns of different counts, fancy yarns (e.g. bouclés, slubs, knops, marls, gimps and snarls) and fancy weave structures. They may also feature special colour and weave effects. *See* COLOUR AND WEAVE EFFECTS.

PEPPER AND SALT TWEED A term sometimes used to describe either Bannockburn tweed or thornproof tweed, since their colourings are similar in appearance to the speckled effect of pepper and salt.

SCOTTISH TWEED (Scotch tweed) A general term for many different types of woollen tweed fabric originating in Scotland. Characteristically, the fibres or yarns are dyed to give mixed colour effects, unlike the solid colours of Scottish tartan fabrics. For example, different colour fibres may be blended together during the spinning process (fibre dyed) and/or marl yarns (two-fold yarns composed of two singles yarns dyed in contrasting colours) may be used. This produces fabrics with soft tonal or multicoloured effects. The best-known Scottish tweeds are Bannockburn, Cheviot, Galashiels or Gala (from the Scottish town of Galashiels), Harris tweed, **heather tweed** (see above) and Shetland tweed. Other Scottish tweeds include Bute, Craiganputtach and Glengarry. *See* BANNOCKBURN, CHEVIOT, HARRIS TWEED, SHETLAND TWEED.

WEST OF ENGLAND TWEED A tweed woven with good-quality, medium-spun botany yarns made from fine merino wool and spun on the woollen system into many interesting colour blends. This tweed is known for its fine, soft, supple handle and is traditionally patterned with a windowpane check or stripe in a contrasting colour to the background. The checks are often highlighted with threads of mercerized cotton. West of England tweeds were originally woven in the Cotswolds area of England.[2] *See also* WEST OF ENGLAND FABRICS.

West of England tweed

heather tweed

Other tweed fabrics include Linton and Manx. Saxony is a similar fabric to tweed, but is made from finer, softer wool.

See also COATING FABRIC, DYED FABRICS, HOMESPUN, MARL FABRIC, WOOL FABRIC.

End uses: overcoats, suits, jackets, sports jackets, trousers, skirts, hats and caps; (furnishing tweed) upholstery and occasionally curtains.

TWILLETTE *see* BLUETTE.

TWILL FABRICS (diagonals) A general term for woven fabrics that are woven in a twill weave construction. Twill is one of the four basic or elementary woven fabric structures (the others are plain weave, satin and sateen). Characteristically, it produces diagonal lines on the face of the fabric. These are formed by warp floats, weft floats or a combination of both. Twill fabrics may be woven in any weight, thickness and quality, and there are a large number of both traditional and modern fabrics that are woven in twill weaves. Other names for twill fabrics are 'diagonals' (used collectively) and 'croisé' (a French term).[36]

Through the use of twill weaves, fabrics can be made heavier than with plain weave.[36] Twill weaves are therefore normally used for any fabric that is particularly hard-wearing, such as drill and denim. The thickness and character of the twill lines are determined by the type of fibre and yarn used. Some twills are very prominent, while others may be quite obscured. In addition, there are a number of twill weave variations, described below.

(i) *Even and uneven twills.* In an even or balanced twill weave, an equal number of warp and weft floats are seen on both the face and the back of the fabric. This is because the fabric is constructed with the same number of warp floats passing over weft picks as vice versa. Examples of even twills are 2/2, 3/3, 4/4 and so on. Fabrics woven in balanced twills include foulard, houndstooth check, serge and sharkskin. Uneven warp-faced twills are produced in which there is a predominance of warp floats over weft floats. Examples of uneven warp-faced twills are 2/1, 3/1, 4/1, 3/2, 4/2, 4/3 and so on. A 2/1 twill is sometimes called a 'prunelle twill'. Fabrics woven in uneven warp-faced twills include cavalry twill, chino, covert cloth, denim, drill, gaberdine and jean. Uneven weft-faced twills are produced in which there is a predominance of weft floats over warp floats. Examples of uneven weft-faced twills are 1/2, 1/3, 1/4, 2/3, 2/4, 3/4 and so on. An example of a fabric woven in an uneven weft-faced twill is bluette.

(ii) *The angle of the twill diagonal.* The angle of the twill diagonal is determined by the type of yarn used and by the sett of both the warp and the weft yarns. If there are the same number of warp and weft yarns per centimetre, the twill will run at an angle of 45°. This is called a 'regular twill'. If there are more warp ends per centimetre than weft picks, the result is a 'steep twill' in which the twill angle is closer to the vertical. Cavalry twill, Poiret twill and whipcord are examples of fabrics woven in a steep twill weave. If there are more weft picks per centimetre than warp ends, the result is a 'reclining twill' in which the twill angle is closer to the horizontal. Bluette, cantoon and merino fabric are examples of reclining twill fabrics.

(iii) *Twill direction.* In most twill fabrics, the twill lines run from bottom left to top right (called 'twill right' or 'right-hand twill'), but there are some, for example drill, in which the twill lines run from bottom right to top left (called 'twill left' or 'left-hand twill'). The twill direction may also be described by making an analogy with the twist direction in yarns. Twill right would therefore be a 'Z' direction twill, and twill left an 'S' direction twill.

(iv) *Reversed and broken twill weaves.* By reversing the direction of the twill diagonal in different areas of a fabric, a large variety of different pattern effects collectively known as reversed twill weaves are produced. Diamond patterns, zigzags or chevrons can be created in this way. Waved twill weaves produce a zigzag effect in the fabric. Broken twill weaves are made by shifting the twill diagonal in sections so that the diagonal does not run continuously across the fabric, but rather produces vertical stripes of twill weave. Melton is an example of a fabric that is traditionally woven in a broken 2/2 twill weave structure.

twill fabric (2/2 twill)

twill fabric (3/1 twill, back and face)

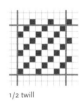

1/2 twill

1/3 twill

2/1 twill

2/2 twill

3/1 twill

twill fabric (waved or reverse twill weave)

twill fabric (wavy twill)

Tyvek®

Reversed broken twill weaves are produced by 'cutting and reversing' alternate vertical sections of a broken twill weave. This produces a characteristic vertical 'break' or 'cut' in the fabric along the vertical line where it is reversed. Herringbone is an example of such a fabric. Reversed twill or waved twill weaves that produce a zigzag effect in the fabric should not be confused with herringbone structures, which are reversed broken twill weaves. *See* HERRINGBONE, MELTON.

(v) *Fancy twill weaves.* Many fancy weave structures are based on twill weaves, and all have their own special characteristics. They include variations to the width of the twill diagonal, and various transposed twills in which corded effects are produced along the twill diagonal. One example is Russian twill, a broken twill weave in which a regular 2/2 twill is reversed every two ends to produce a small-scale herringbone-type structure.[25] Another example is Campbell twill (also called 'Mayo twill'), a special weave structure in which a fancy twill weave repeating over eight ends and picks is transposed every two ends to produce a corded effect along the twill diagonal. It is traditionally woven using wool yarns.[26, 36]

(vi) *Colour and weave effects.* Twill fabrics may be woven in one solid colour or with different stripe and check patterns. When contrasting colours are combined with the weave structure, many interesting colour and weave effects may be produced. Houndstooth check is an example of such a fabric.

The following are examples of classic twill weave fabrics: Albert twill, Bannockburn, blanket cloth, bluette, Bolivia, botany twill, box cloth, buffalo check, cadet cloth, some Canton flannel fabrics, cantoon, cassimere, cavalry twill, charmelaine, some Cheviot fabrics, chino, Coburg, corkscrew fabric, some coutil fabrics, covert cloth, denim, district checks, drill, duffel, dungaree, duvetyn, elastique, some flannel fabrics, florentine, flushing, foulard, frieze, gaberdine, galatea, Glen Urquhart check, granada, Guards check, gun club check, Harvard, Henrietta, hickory cloth, houndstooth check, imperial cloth, jean, kasha, kersey, khaki, some melton fabrics, merino fabric, middy twill (*see* jean), pilot cloth, Poiret twill, Prince of Wales check, regatta, regina, serge, sharkskin, shepherd's check, Shetland tweed, silesia, surah, tartan, ticking, tricotine, many tweed fabrics, whipcord and (silk) zibeline.

See also COLOUR AND WEAVE EFFECTS, HERRINGBONE, WOVEN FABRIC.

End uses: all kinds of fashion and furnishing fabrics.

TYVEK® The registered brand name of a paper-like nonwoven material that is sometimes also known as 'envelope paper'. It is a strong, durable, lightweight material that has qualities of paper, film and fabric. It was originally developed for protective clothing and is often white in colour.

Tyvek is made from a synthetic spunbonded polyolefin material. Very fine, continuous, high-density polyethylene fibres are flash-spun and laid randomly as a web. They are then bonded together using heat to melt the fibres and pressure to fuse them together. Different qualities are produced by varying the spinbonding conditions. Tyvek is strong and difficult to tear, but it is easily cut. It is liquid-resistant but vapour-permeable, which makes it suitable for providing protection against all kinds of different agencies but also comfortable to wear. It is possible to both write and print on it.

See also NONWOVEN FABRIC, WATERPROOF AND WATER-REPELLENT FABRICS.

End uses: protective clothing, disposable clothing, overalls, lab coats, jumpsuits, aprons, gloves, envelopes, labels, medical and industrial packaging, CD/DVD sleeves, car covers and groundsheets.

Ulster

umbrella fabric

union fabric (linen warp 60%/ viscose weft 40%)

union fabric (linen warp 50%/ cotton weft 50%)

ULSTER A thick, heavy woven fabric, originally made from wool; it is finished with a long nap that is flattened and lies in one direction, and is used for overcoats.

Ulster was originally made using a woollen warp and shoddy weft yarns (yarns made from recycled wool fibres).[36] Now it is also made using a variety of other fibres. The yarns are usually dyed in solid, dark colours (typically black, brown and navy). The warp yarns are twisted in the 'Z' direction, and the weft yarns in the 'S' direction.[17] When the fabric is woven in a fairly open weave, this produces a firm construction. The fabric is napped during finishing and the fibres laid flat in one direction. The name 'Ulster' probably derives from the Irish town of that name. At one time Ulster was used for travelling cloaks, but now it is used mainly as a coating fabric.[2] Ulster is a similar fabric to zibeline, but it is not as lustrous.

See also COATING FABRIC, NAPPED FABRICS, RECYCLED TEXTILES.

End uses: overcoats.

UMBRELLA FABRIC A general term for a range of fine, lightweight woven fabrics that are used to make umbrellas. Sometimes plastics are also used. Most woven umbrella fabrics are made in plain colours for cost reasons, but some are also printed with patterns; at one time, some umbrella fabrics were made with fancy woven borders, but this is rarely seen nowadays.[4]

Umbrella fabric may be woven with cotton, silk, viscose or nylon yarns, or mixtures of these. Continuous filament nylon is probably the most used as it is lightweight and naturally water-repellent. Fine nylon yarns are very closely sett and woven in a tight plain weave construction. Occasionally twill or satin weaves are also used. This produces a very lightweight but firm and strong fabric that is often back-coated with a water-repellent finish before being stretched over umbrella frames. Some ciré-finished fabrics are also used as umbrella fabrics (*see* CIRÉ). At one time, a fine, lightweight woven fabric called 'gloria' was made as an umbrella fabric. Gloria was woven in plain weave using cotton, silk or nylon yarns.[2]

See also COATED FABRIC, PLASTIC TEXTILES, WATERPROOF AND WATER-REPELLENT FABRICS.

End uses: umbrella coverings.

UNBROKEN LOOP *see* LOOPRAISE.

UNION FABRIC A general term for a woven fabric that is made with a warp of one kind of fibre and a weft of another. The percentage of each fibre is normally stated. Union fabrics are made to provide different fabric qualities and also sometimes to reduce costs by using a cheaper yarn in part of the fabric.

Originally the term 'union fabric' was used for fabrics made with a cotton warp and a woollen weft, or with a linen warp and a cotton weft.[25] Fabrics woven with yarns containing different fibres and arranged in stripe sections are also sometimes called union fabrics. When these fabrics are dyed, the fibres in the different sections take the dye differently, producing stripes that are characteristically coloured in different tones of the same colour. This is a cheap method of producing coloured stripes in a fabric. At one time such fabrics were used as men's working shirts, which were worn with white detachable collars and cuffs made from cardboard or celluloid.[2] Examples of union fabrics include some Albert twill fabrics, some alpaca fabrics, some astrakhan fabrics, bark crêpe, brilliantine, some Canton fabrics, Coburg, some crash fabrics, domet, some flannel fabrics, some gaberdines, glass cloth, granada, Henrietta, some melton fabrics, panama suiting fabric, wincey and zephyr flannel (*see* FLANNEL).

See also COTTON FABRIC, LINEN FABRIC, STRIPES, WOOL FABRIC.

End uses: all kinds of fashion and furnishing end uses.

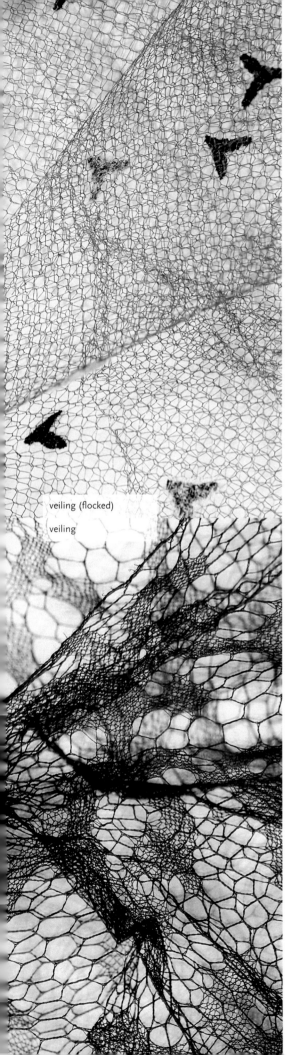

veiling (flocked)

veiling

UV PROTECTIVE FABRICS (ultraviolet protective fabrics) Fabrics that protect against harmful UV (ultraviolet) rays from the sun. This protection can be achieved in different ways. (i) *Traditional protective fabrics.* Some fibres are better at absorbing UV rays than others. Wool absorbs almost all UV rays. Synthetic fibre fabrics (polyester and some nylon fabrics) are also very good, and cotton absorbs approximately 90% of the harmful rays.[34] In addition, any densely woven or knitted fabric in dark colours will naturally protect against any harmful rays from the sun; heavier-weight fabrics are more effective. It is worth noting that the traditional garments worn in many hot countries are often made from densely woven fabrics in dark colours.

(ii) *UV-absorbing dyes.* Certain dyes absorb UV rays; these can be applied to fabrics in solution form or incorporated into printing inks and printed onto fabrics. These dyes may be applied to fabrics of all weights, including heavy fabrics like awning materials.

(iii) *UV absorbers.* UV absorbers are like tiny, colourless dye particles. They are found in suncreams and may also be applied to fabrics, either as a solution or by printing them on.

(iv) *Special finishes.* Finishes containing special reflective particles may be applied to a fabric. For example, ceramic particles will deflect harmful rays: they can be incorporated into a synthetic fibre during its manufacture or applied as a surface finish.

End uses: children's clothing, swimwear, beachwear, outdoor clothing, window blinds, awnings and tents.

VEILING A general term for a sheer, usually open mesh fabric that is used for bridal veils or for veils in millinery. All kinds of lightweight fabrics may be used: lace and net fabrics in particular, or fine, sheer woven fabrics.

Veiling is made from fine fibres of any kind, but particularly from continuous filament fibres, including silk, viscose, acetate and nylon. If woven, the fabric is usually woven in a simple, fairly open-sett, plain weave construction. It may be a plain fabric or it may be ornamented: embroidered, decorated with beads or sequins, or flocked with ornamental dots or other patterns, for instance. (*See* APPLIQUÉ FABRIC, BEADED FABRICS, EMBROIDERED FABRICS, FLOCKED FABRIC, SEQUINNED FABRICS.) Fabrics that may be used for veiling include gauze, gossamer, lace, malines, net, some silk fabrics, tulle and voile.

See also SHEER FABRICS.

End uses: bridal veils, face veils and hat veils.

VELCRO® *see* NARROW FABRICS.

VELOUR A term used for several different types of pile fabric that may be woven, warp-knitted or weft-knitted; the term is also used for a napped woven fabric that was the original velour fabric. Originally velour was a thick woven fabric made in good-quality wool and given a soft, dense nap finish on the face side;[2] this napped velour fabric was traditionally used for overcoats and is still made today. The name derives from Latin *villosus*, meaning 'hairy',[3] and is the French term for velvet.[2] Napped velour, woven pile velour, warp-knitted velour and weft-knitted velour are discussed in detail below.

Napped velour is traditionally a heavy, top-quality coating fabric. It is a thick, heavy woven fabric traditionally made using good-quality wool. Nowadays the best qualities are still made with 100% wool, but there are many other qualities made with all types of fibre, including synthetic mixes. The fabric is woven in a twill or satin weave structure and finished with a heavy nap finish on the face side. This lays all the surface fibres in one direction and gives the fabric a smooth appearance. Napped velour is a similar fabric to duvetyn but has a thicker, longer nap, and the weave structure remains visible. *See also* NAPPED FABRICS.

Woven pile velour has a short, closely cut warp pile and may be made from cotton, wool, silk, mohair or man-made fibres and blends. Most woven pile velours are made from cotton

velour (cord, warp-knitted tricot)

velour (warp-knitted, face and back)

velour (warp-knitted tricot)

and used mainly as furnishing fabrics. There are three ways of constructing woven velour:

(i) The fabric is woven as a double cloth, with a pile warp and a warp for the backing fabric. To make the pile, the pile warp yarns are lifted over wires at regular intervals during weaving to produce raised pile loops. The wires have blades attached to them; when the wires are removed after weaving, the blades cut the pile loops and the cut pile is formed. The pile loops are woven very closely together and are firmly interwoven into the backing fabric. The backing fabric may be woven in plain, twill or satin weave. After weaving, the tops of the loops are cut and the pile is laid in one direction, which gives a smooth surface.

(ii) Woven velour may also be made on the 'face-to-face principle', like some velvet fabrics. With this method, two velour fabrics are woven face to face simultaneously. The warp pile ends are interchanged between both base fabrics, and the connecting yarns are cut in the middle by a knife while the fabric is still on the loom, producing two separate velour fabrics.

(iii) The pile is formed on the 'terry' principle, whereby excess yarn is fed in to make the pile. This fabric is known as 'terry velour'. Essentially it is a terry fabric that has the tops of its pile loops sheared in order to produce a soft pile surface. It is used for upholstery, towels, dressing gowns and beach robes. *See* TERRY FABRIC.

Woven pile velour is similar to both velvet and velveteen but is a much heavier fabric. Its pile is made of thicker yarns and is much deeper and denser than in those two fabrics. It is also similar to plush, but plush has the longer pile.

Warp-knitted velour is a pile fabric that looks similar to a woven velour. The majority of knitted velour is warp-knitted, since this makes the most secure base structure and is the cheapest method of producing a knitted pile fabric that can be easily cropped afterwards. Warp-knitted velour is mostly made using man-made fibres (especially polyester) on a two- or three-bar warp-knitting machine, using a long lapping motion on the front bar to create a float. This is subsequently raised and cropped in a special finishing process to produce a fine, high pile surface. Traditionally acetate or triacetate filament yarns are used in the pile to create a lustrous surface that is easily raised. A high-quality warp-knitted velour fabric with a dense, vertical pile is sometimes known as '[warp-knitted] velvet' (*see* VELVET). Similar fabrics to warp-knitted velour include airloop fabric, loopraise and plush.

Weft-knitted pile velour fabrics are knitted in piece form on circular knitting machines so that they may be easily raised and cropped afterwards. Weft-knitted velour may also be constructed in three different ways, similar to those used to construct woven velour:

(i) By using special circular knitting machines, which have 'pile fingers' or 'pile points' that allow the pile to be formed.

(ii) By using double-bed circular knitting machines, which knit two fabrics simultaneously. These are knitted on the 'face-to-face' principle. With this construction method, two velour fabrics are knitted face to face simultaneously. The pile yarns are interchanged between both base fabrics, and these are cut in the middle with wires while the fabric is being knitted. This produces two separate knitted velour fabrics.

(iii) By using regular circular knitting machines and feeding in excess yarn to make the pile. Weft-knitted velour is sometimes also called 'jersey velour', and it is used for sweatshirts and sportswear. It is a similar fabric to weft-knitted plush, which has had its loops cropped to produce a velour fabric.

Also called 'velour' is a felt-like fabric made from rabbit hair, which is given a long, lustrous, hairy nap finish and used to make hats.[25] Similar fabrics to velour include chenille fabric, plush, velvet and velveteen.

See also DOUBLE CLOTH, KNITTED FABRIC, NAPPED FABRICS, PILE FABRICS, WARP-KNITTED FABRIC, WEFT-KNITTED FABRIC.

End uses: (napped velour) men's and ladies' coats, jackets and suits; (woven pile velour) upholstery and curtains; (terry velour) upholstery, towels, dressing gowns and beach robes; (warp- and weft-knitted velour) sweatshirts, leisure wear, children's wear, sportswear, dressing gowns, slippers and coverings for bedheads.

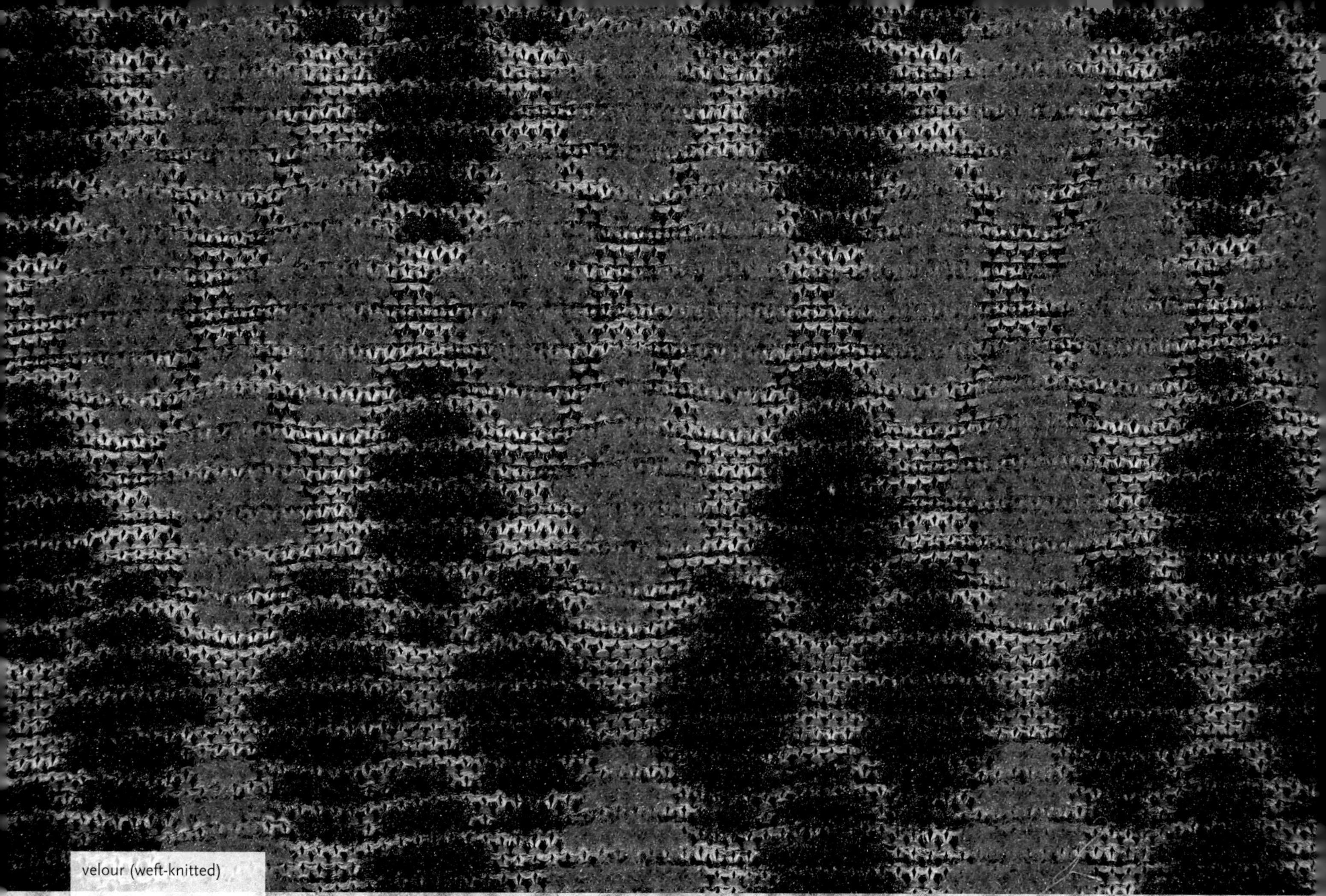

velour (weft-knitted)

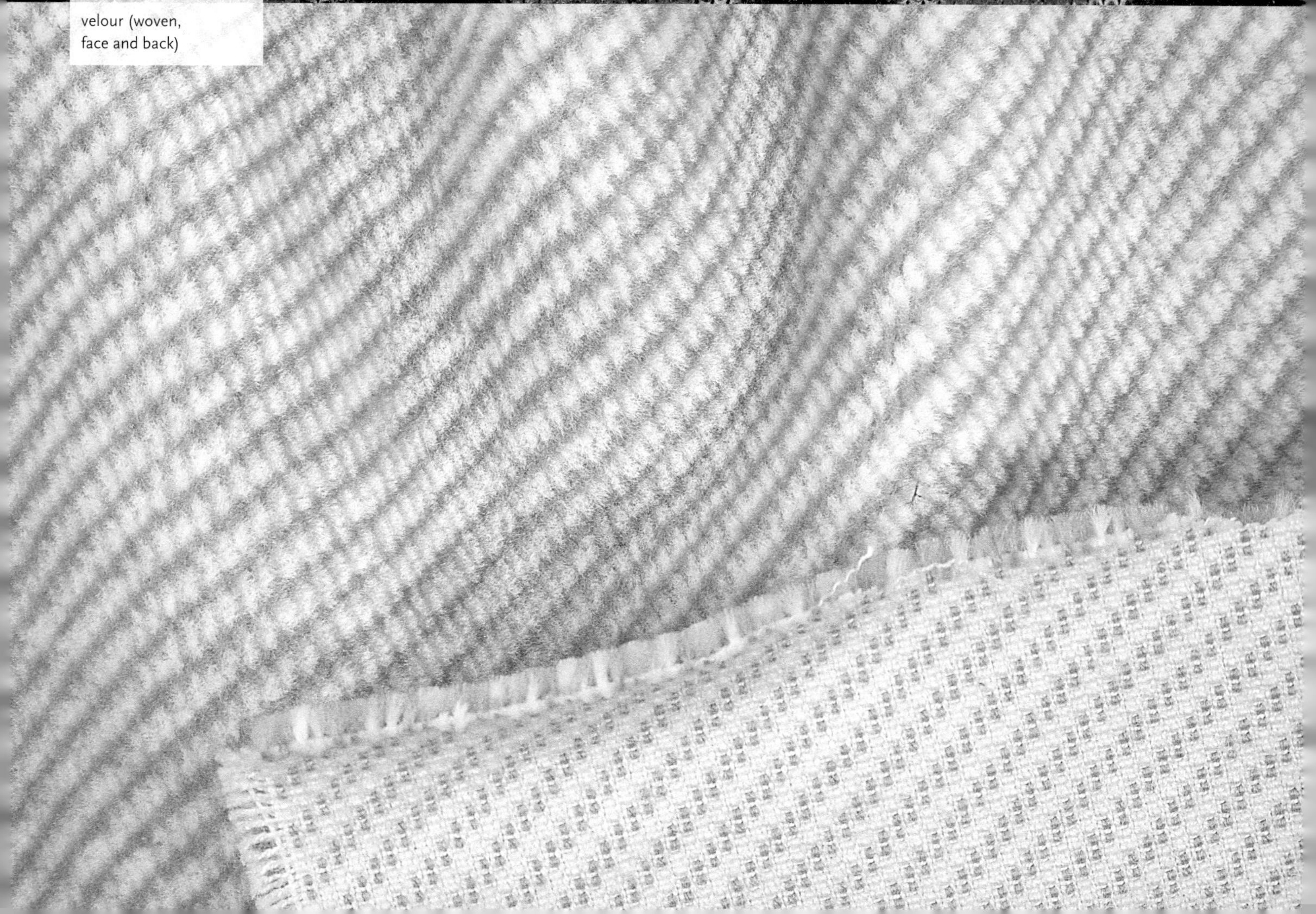

velour (woven,
face and back)

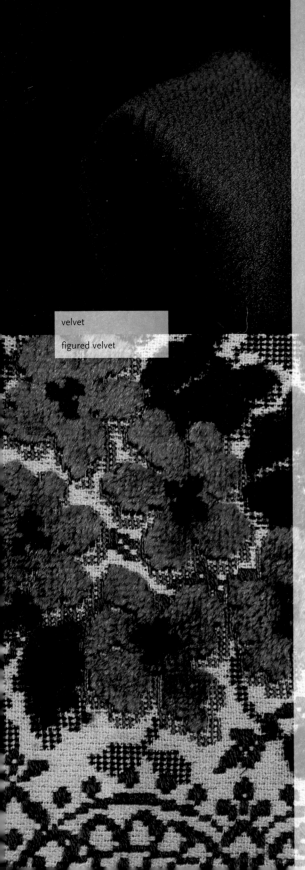

velvet

figured velvet

VELVET A woven fabric with a short, cut warp pile on the face side of the fabric. The pile yarns are made with an extra set of warp yarns. They are firmly bound into the structure of a ground or base fabric, made with a different set of yarns, which holds them in position. The cut ends of the pile warp form tufts on the surface of the fabric and are so closely sett to one another that they form a very soft, lustrous surface texture across the entire face of the fabric. Velvet is a heavy, rich, luxurious fabric that has been woven since at least the Middle Ages, when it was widely used by both royalty and the church as a status symbol. These classic 'solid' velvet fabrics are produced in many different weights and qualities, but there are also many different variations of this fabric (described below). When sewing velvet, care should be taken that pattern pieces are all cut in the same direction, since light can reflect differently from surfaces placed at different angles from one another. Velvet is usually best cleaned by dry-cleaning.

The term 'velvet' comes from Latin *vellus*, meaning 'a fleece'.[3] Velvet is a woven warp pile fabric in which the pile was originally made from silk and the ground fabric from cotton. Nowadays both pile and base fabric are woven in many different types of fibre, including silk, cotton, nylon, acetate, viscose, mohair, polyester or modal. Lustrous yarns, however, are often used for the pile warp, and these yarns are usually thicker than those used in the base fabric. There are three different ways in which a velvet fabric may be constructed:

(i) The fabric may be woven with two separate warps: a pile warp and a warp for the backing fabric. The backing fabric is usually woven in a firm plain weave construction. To make the pile, the pile warp yarns are lifted over wires at regular intervals during weaving to produce raised pile loops. The length of pile is determined by the size of the pile wire. The wires have blades attached to them; when they are removed during weaving, the blades cut the pile loops and the cut pile is formed. The pile loops are woven very closely together, but one to three weft yarns are always inserted into the backing fabric between the raising of each pile loop, to ensure that the pile tufts are firmly anchored into the backing fabric. With this method of weaving velvet, it is also possible to weave surface variations into the fabric: for example, some loops may be cut, while others are left uncut.

(ii) The fabric is constructed in the manner described in (i) above, but the wires do not have blades attached to them. Instead, the pile loops are cut with a 'trevet' (a small hand-held instrument with a sharp blade for cutting the pile of hand-woven velvets in the loom).[25] With this method of weaving velvet, it is also possible to weave surface variations into the fabric.

(iii) Cut pile velvets may also be made on the 'face-to-face' principle, like some carpets. With this construction method, two velvet fabrics are woven face to face simultaneously. The warp pile ends are interchanged between both base fabrics, and the connecting yarns are cut in the middle by a knife while the fabric is still on the loom, producing two separate velvet fabrics. It is not possible to weave surface variations into the fabric using this method.

The quality of the fabric is determined by the density of the pile tufts and the manner in which they are anchored into the base fabric. They may be bound into the backing fabric to form a 'V'-shaped attachment, where they loop around a single weft pick in the backing fabric that holds them in place. A firmer, more secure attachment of the pile into the backing fabric is made, in which it is held in position by three consecutive weft picks weaving in the backing fabric. This forms the pile tufts into 'W' shapes, which are clearly seen if they are pulled out of such a fabric. The 'W'-shaped binding arrangement produces a more stable, harder-wearing velvet fabric in which the pile is less likely to shed.

After weaving, the cut pile velvet fabric is trimmed during finishing with rotating blades working on the same principle as a lawn mower. This produces a regular pile surface throughout the fabric and determines the height of pile. In a true velvet, the pile is not longer than 3 mm ($^1/_8$ in.).[13] Anything longer would be described as plush (*see* PLUSH). Finally, after trimming, the velvet is brushed to raise and open the pile tufts, and steamed

crushed velvet (printed)

antique velvet

cord velvet

cotton velvet

to produce a soft surface lustre. Velvet may be yarn-dyed or piece-dyed in solid colours, yarn-dyed in multicolours or printed with many different patterns. It may also be woven with a jacquard pattern. There are many special finishes that may be applied to velvet, such as crush-resistant, water-repellent and soil-resistant finishes. Many finishes produce different effects in the fabric: velvet may be crushed or embossed, for example.

All these variations produce many different types of velvet, each with its own unique characteristics. These are described below.

ANTIQUE VELVET (slub velvet) A velvet fabric woven with occasional slub weft yarns, which produces an uneven surface similar to those made in earlier centuries.

BAGHEERA VELVET An uncut velvet fabric that has short, closely sett loops. It has a rough, pebbly surface texture and is crush-resistant. It is usually piece-dyed and used as outerwear or evening dresses.

BROCADE VELVET A velvet fabric in which the pile is sheared at different heights to produce a pattern. All kinds of patterns may be formed, including stripes, checks or florals. *See* BROCADE.

CHIFFON VELVET A very lightweight, soft, silky velvet fabric that has excellent drape. It has a very short cut pile, usually made from silk or viscose. Chiffon velvet is used for evening dresses, scarves and wraps. (Since chiffon is the lightest of fabrics, the term 'chiffon' is often used to describe the lightest qualities of other types of fabric too. *See* CHIFFON.)

CISELÉ VELVET A figured velvet fabric in which a pattern is formed by cutting only some of the pile. The rest is left uncut in loop form. Ciselé velvet was very popular in 19th-century England. The term 'ciselé' is French for 'chiselled'.[9] *See* FIGURED FABRIC.

CORD VELVET A velvet fabric with alternating vertical sections of backing fabric and velvet, which form raised ridges or cords.

COTTON VELVET A velvet fabric made using cotton yarns for both the pile and ground. It is usually woven as two fabrics weaving face to face. When the fabrics are cut after weaving, two cotton velvet fabrics with a short, soft pile are produced. This is a less luxurious but harder-wearing fabric than other velvets. It is used for more casual clothing, such as trousers, jackets, suits and furnishings.

CRUSHED VELVET A normal, solid velvet fabric in which the pile is pressed flat or crushed in different directions during finishing to produce an irregular reflective surface. To do this, the moist fabric is passed between heated rollers under pressure.

CUT VELVET In its most frequent use, a general term for cut pile velvet fabrics (as opposed to loop pile velvet fabrics); but it is also a term for a type of very fine, jacquard woven figured or brocade velvet, in which velvet motifs form a pattern against a (usually) very

nacré velvet (crushed)

panne velvet (woven and printed)

lightweight ground fabric such as chiffon. At one time the pile would have been cut away to expose these areas of ground fabric, but nowadays the pile is more likely to be burnt out using chemicals. Cut velvet is used for scarves, blouses and evening dresses. See **brocade velvet** (above), **façonné velvet** (below), **figured velvet** (below). *See also* FIGURED FABRIC.

DEVORÉ VELVET (burn-out velvet) see **façonné velvet** (below).

EMBOSSED VELVET A velvet fabric in which a pattern is made in the pile yarns by embossing. Heated, deeply engraved rollers are heavily pressed onto the surface of the fabric. This crushes the pile in some places and leaves the uncrushed areas standing proud. The effect is not permanent and will gradually reduce. *See* EMBOSSED FABRICS.

ÉPINGLE VELVET A fine, soft velvet fabric that is patterned with pin-like velvet cords. *See* ÉPINGLE.

FAÇONNÉ VELVET A velvet fabric in which a pattern is made by chemically burning away selected areas of the pile to reveal the base fabric beneath. In this process, called 'devoré' or 'burn-out', the chemicals burn away the pile fibres but not the ground fabric, which is made from fibres resistant to the chemical. (The fabric is also called 'devoré velvet' or 'burn-out velvet'.) An example of appropriate fibres would be natural fibres (e.g. cotton) for the pile warp and man-made fibres (e.g. nylon) for the base fabric. *See* DEVORÉ FABRIC.

FIGURED VELVET A jacquard woven velvet in which figures or patterns are made in the fabric by combining two or more of the following features: areas of cut pile, areas of uncut pile, pile in varying heights, and areas of backing fabric woven in different weave structures (for example satin and/or plain weave).

GENOA VELVET A complex figured, decorative fabric that has a satin woven ground fabric and a multicoloured pile. The pile may be cut or uncut.[2]

JARDINIÈRE VELVET A velvet fabric in which a velvet pile is characteristically woven in selected areas to form a pattern against a satin background weave.[5]

LYONS VELVET A high-quality, thick velvet fabric that has a crisp, rigid handle. The fabric has a stiff, erect, high pile and was traditionally made from silk yarns with the backing fabric made from silk, linen, cotton or viscose. The term 'Lyons' comes from the French city of Lyon, presumably where it was first made. Lyons velvet is used for coat collars, suits, coats, dresses and curtains, and in millinery.

MILLINERY VELVET A velvet fabric similar to **Lyons velvet** (see above), but made in narrow widths for hats.[9]

MIRROR VELVET see **panne velvet** below.

NACRÉ VELVET A velvet fabric in which the base fabric is woven in one colour and the pile in a different, usually contrasting colour. This produces an interesting iridescent colour effect in use, after which it was named: *nacré* means 'pearly' in French. Nacré velvet is used for specialist products such as evening wear. *See also* SHOT FABRICS.

PANNE VELVET A velvet fabric that has a longer pile than ordinary velvet but a shorter pile than plush.[3] Traditionally the ground warp was made from good-quality two-fold cotton yarns and the pile warp from spun silk. The weft was made from two-fold cotton. The weave was constructed so that there were two ground ends to one pile and three ground weave picks to one pile wire. Panne velvet has been made in this quality and construction since the Middle Ages, when the best quality came from Italy and later from France.[36] More recently panne velvet has been made using a variety of different fibres, including man-made fibres and wool. The pile is characteristically laid in one direction and steam-pressed flat under the pressure of heavy rollers during finishing. This gives the fabric a very high lustre, so that it has an almost reflective quality.[25] It is a shimmery or mirror-like fabric, and is sometimes called 'mirror velvet' or 'paon velvet'.[3, 36] Lighter-weight panne velvet fabrics are called 'pannette' or 'chiffon velvet' (see **chiffon velvet** above). *See also* PLUSH.

PEKIN VELVET A velvet fabric that is woven with coloured stripes. *See* PEKIN.

RING VELVET A very fine, lightweight velvet that is no longer made; it was said that a piece 36 inches (91 cm) wide could be pulled through a wedding ring.[36]

TAPESTRY VELVET A jacquard woven fabric in which sections of velvet and tapestry are combined to produce a complex figured fabric. It is used mainly for furnishings. *See* TAPESTRY JACQUARD.

TERRY VELVET A loop pile velvet fabric. The loops are formed with wires as described in (i) above, but the wires have no blades attached and therefore do not cut the loops when they are removed. It is similar to terry fabric but made using a variety of different fibres. *See also* TERRY FABRIC.

TRANSPARENT VELVET An extremely lightweight, soft, silky velvet fabric with excellent drape. It is lighter in weight than chiffon velvet. It is usually made from fine 100% silk, or the pile yarns are viscose or nylon and the base fabric is viscose or acetate. Transparent velvet is used for evening dresses and negligees.

UTRECHT VELVET A heavyweight velvet fabric used for upholstery. The pile is traditionally mohair, and this is packed very tightly together and firmly anchored into the base fabric (typically cotton) with a 'W' binding arrangement.[25] Characteristically, this produces an extremely thick, dense velvet fabric that is very hard-wearing. Utrecht velvet was first woven in Utrecht, Holland, in the 17th century, by Daniel Havart, a French political refugee.[5]

WARP-KNITTED VELVET A pile fabric that looks similar to woven velvet. It is a higher-quality version of a warp-knitted velour fabric; it is made in a similar manner, but has a denser, more vertical pile. *See* VELOUR.

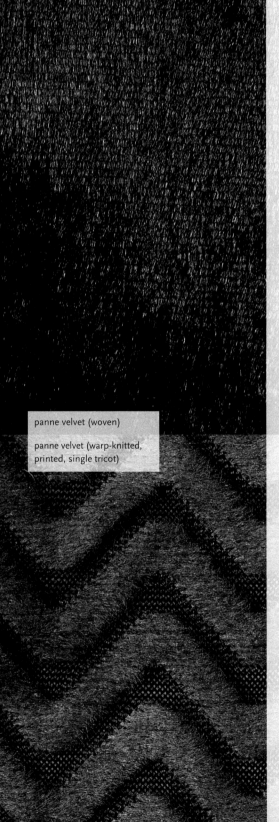

panne velvet (woven)

panne velvet (warp-knitted, printed, single tricot)

panne velvet (weft-knitted)

WEFT-KNITTED VELVET A weft-knitted pile fabric made in imitation of woven velvet. Like warp-knitted velvet, it too is a higher-quality version of a weft-knitted velour, with a denser pile. *See* VELOUR.

Similar fabrics to velvet include chenille fabric, plush, velour and velveteen. The process of flocking also produces a similar effect to velvet (*see* FLOCKED FABRIC). 'Rib velvet' is a rarely used name for corduroy; however, unlike velvet, which is a warp pile fabric, corduroy is a weft pile fabric (*see* CORDUROY). *See also* COATING FABRIC, PILE FABRICS.

End uses: a very wide range of end uses, including coats, evening wear, suits, dresses, trousers, jackets, shoes, curtains, upholstery, scarves, wraps, hats and trimmings.

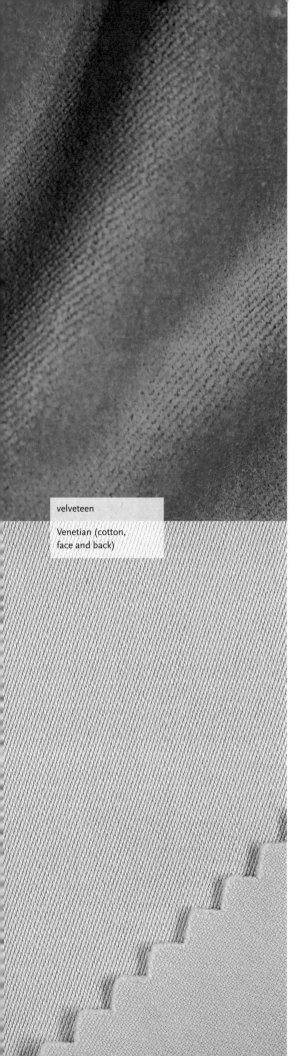

velveteen

Venetian (cotton, face and back)

VELVETEEN A woven fabric with a short cut weft pile on the face side of the fabric. It is a very similar fabric to velvet, but the pile is made with an extra set of supplementary weft yarns rather than warp yarns. The weft floats are firmly bound into the structure of a ground or base fabric made with a different set of yarns that holds them in position. They are cut after weaving to form the pile, which characteristically slopes at a slight angle to the base fabric, creating a subtle sheen on the face of the fabric.[3] Velveteen has more body and less drape than velvet.[19] It is made in different weights and qualities, but it is usually a thick, heavy fabric. As with velvet, when sewing the fabric, care should be taken that pattern pieces are all cut in the same direction, as light can reflect differently from surfaces placed at different angles from one another.

Traditionally velveteen is woven with cotton yarns; it is sometimes incorrectly referred to as 'cotton velvet', but it is a weft pile fabric made from cotton, whereas true cotton velvet is a warp pile fabric made from cotton. Velveteen was first produced in Manchester, England, in the early 18th century.[3] The name 'velveteen' indicates that it was seen as a variation of a velvet fabric, in the same way that sateen is a variation of a satin fabric. The best-quality velveteen is woven with combed, mercerized cotton yarns in both the supplementary weft and base fabric. It is also woven with carded cotton yarns, cotton and man-made fibre blends, and occasionally viscose.

Velveteen is woven in the same way as corduroy. The pile is produced by floats of supplementary weft yarns that float over the top of a tightly woven ground weave made with a separate set of yarns. The supplementary weft is interlaced with the ground weave at binding points that are spread equally throughout the length of the fabric. Owing to the positioning of the binding points and their close proximity to one another, when the floats in-between are cut after weaving, they form a very soft, lustrous surface texture across the entire face of the fabric, unlike the vertical columns of corduroy. The ground weave that makes the base cloth is usually plain or twill weave in construction. These fabrics are sometimes termed 'plain-back' or 'twill-back'. The quality of the fabric is determined by the number of weft yarns per centimetre, as this forms a denser pile and a more stable, durable fabric. When twill weave is used, it is possible to weave in a higher number of supplementary weft picks.[19]

The floats are cut either by hand, or in a special cutting machine with guides that lift the individual floats and revolving knives that cut them. As the rows of floats are so close, alternate rows are cut with each insertion into the machine, and the fabric must therefore be passed through the machine twice.[19] Velveteen is mostly piece-dyed, but it may also be colour-woven and/or printed. It may also be jacquard woven with figured patterns. During finishing, the cut weft is trimmed to produce a uniform height, brushed to raise and open the pile tufts and steamed to produce a soft surface lustre. The pile may also be waxed in order to increase its lustre.[17]

Velveteen plush is a variation with a slightly longer pile than normal velveteen; it is therefore a softer, more lustrous and luxurious fabric. Another variation is hollow-cut velveteen, which has grooves in the pile; these are either formed in the fabric construction or cut into the pile after weaving. Velveteen fabrics are also sometimes cut to give a corduroy appearance.[25] Velveteen belongs to the group of fabrics known as 'fustians'. It is also similar to chenille fabric, plush, velour and velvet.

See also COATING FABRIC, COTTON FABRIC, CORDUROY, PILE FABRICS.

End uses: dresses, coats, trousers, suits, curtains, upholstery, bedspreads and trimmings.

VENETIAN Originally a highly lustrous satin woven fabric made in Venice from silk yarns;[2] more often nowadays a fabric made in imitation of the silk fabric using other fibres. The main qualities are a cotton Venetian and a wool Venetian. Both are woven in either satin weave or variations, and both have a lustrous face side. In addition to the silk, cotton and wool qualities, Venetian is also sometimes woven with man-made fibres and blends.

Venetian (wool, face and back)

Cotton Venetian is traditionally woven with a warp made from combed, gassed Egyptian cotton. The yarns are usually two-fold and twisted in the same direction as the diagonals formed by the weave structure. The weft is a singles yarn of any quality. The fabric is woven grey, in an 8-end satin weave construction. Afterwards it is either piece-dyed or bleached, and mercerized and schreinered to produce a highly lustrous surface.[26] A typical cotton Venetian fabric construction is 20/2 to 14/2 tex warp sett at 58 to 66 ends per cm and 24 to 16 tex weft woven at 32 to 42 picks per cm.[26] Cotton Venetian is sometimes confused with Italian. They are very similar fabrics, but Venetian is woven in a satin weave structure while Italian is woven in a sateen weave structure. They are both lining fabrics. Cotton Venetian is also a similar fabric to Albert twill. *See also* ITALIAN; LINING FABRIC; SATIN, WOVEN.

Wool Venetian is woven using either wool or worsted yarns in the warp and woollen yarns in the weft. It is woven in a 5-end satin weave construction or a modified satin weave. During finishing it is milled, lightly raised and cropped. This reveals the fine, steep diagonal lines of the weave structure. Wool Venetian is usually dyed in solid colours. It was formerly the traditional fabric worn by Muslims when visiting Mecca.[2] Wool Venetian is a similar fabric to blazer cloth. When woven with warp stripes, it is sometimes also called 'blazer cloth', because both fabrics use the same satin weave structure. *See* BLAZER CLOTH.

Heavier-weight Venetian fabrics are used as overcoatings; they are similar to covert cloth. Lighter-weight Venetians are similar to amazon.

See also COATING FABRIC; SATIN, WOVEN; SWANSDOWN.

End uses: (cotton and silk Venetian) linings, dresses, jackets, curtains and cushion covers; (wool Venetian) men's suits, jackets, coats, trousers, skirts and upholstery.

Venetian (silk, face and back)

vicuña fabric

VICTORIA LAWN *see* LAWN.

VICUÑA FABRIC A general term for any fabric constructed with yarns made from vicuña hair. Vicuña hair is a natural animal fibre from the fleece of the vicuña (*Lama vicugna*, or *Vicugna vicugna* in some classification systems), a relative of the llama that lives in mountainous regions of South America. Vicuña is classed as a speciality hair fibre. Strictly speaking, the term 'vicuña fabric' should be applied only to fabrics made from 100% vicuña fibre; however, sometimes it is also applied to fabrics composed partly of vicuña and partly of another fibre – in this case, the percentages of each fibre should always be stated. Characteristically, vicuña is the colour of dark tobacco, and it is the finest hair fibre in the world.[36] It is a very valuable and extremely expensive fibre because of the limited supply. Vicuña fabric is a warm, soft fabric that has a high natural lustre.

Since vicuña is such an expensive fibre of limited availability, it is usually mixed with other fibres, especially wool. Sometimes a small percentage of nylon may also be added for extra strength. Vicuña is mostly used in the making of soft, lustrous woven coating fabrics. One quality is traditionally made as either a backed or double cloth fabric. The warp is worsted or worsted/vicuña, and the weft is wool or wool/vicuña. The fabric is woven with a 2/2 twill face

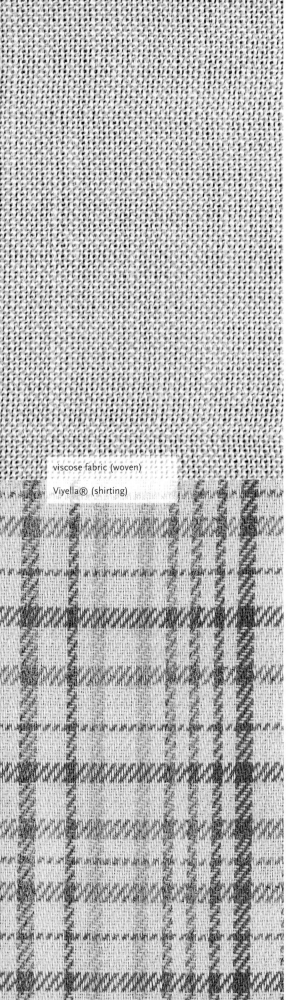

viscose fabric (woven)

Viyella® (shirting)

weave and a plain back, with the yarns arranged 2 face to 1 back in both the warp and weft. It is woven in the following construction: 35/2 tex warp sett at 36 ends per cm and 54 tex weft woven at 32 picks per cm.[26] Kasha and Montagnac are examples of fabrics sometimes woven from vicuña hair.

See also BACKED FABRIC, COATING FABRIC, DOUBLE CLOTH, HAIR FABRICS.

End uses: overcoating, dresses, suits, jackets, shawls and scarves.

VILENE® *see* INTERLINING.

VINYL *see* PVC.

VISCOSE FABRIC A general term for any fabric constructed with viscose fibres or yarns. Viscose is the generic term (as defined by the International Organization for Standardization) for a regenerated manufactured fibre made from cellulose, obtained by the viscose process. The generic term for this fibre in the United States is 'rayon'.[25]

The fibres may be used in continuous filament form, or they may be chopped into shorter staple lengths and respun into yarns with different characteristics, sometimes blended with other staple fibres. The term 'viscose fabric' is used for fabrics of a range of different weights and constructions composed of 100% viscose fibres or yarns. Where viscose is used together with other fibres, the percentage of each should be stated. Characteristically, viscose fabrics have excellent drape and a soft handle, and they are particularly absorbent. However, they have poor abrasion-resistance and low wet and dry strength; they also crease fairly easily. Viscose may be brushed to make it softer and warmer, and it is often combined with other fibres in a fabric. It is also possible to give viscose fibres a range of different properties by varying the manufacturing parameters. Modified viscose fibres are marketed under different brand names.

End uses: dresses, skirts, lingerie, blouses, underwear, thermal underwear, sleepwear, linings and curtains.

VIYELLA® The registered brand name of a woven fabric that was originally made with blended yarns consisting of 55% merino wool and 45% long staple cotton, but is now also made in several variants. The classic fabric is woven in twill weave and is characteristically a soft, durable fabric. A variety of different Viyella fabrics are produced today.

Registered in Britain in 1894, Viyella was the world's first fabric to be branded – an innovative idea at the time. The fabric is named after a valley in Derbyshire called Via Gellia, where the weaving mill that first produced it was located. The first garments to be made in Viyella were men's shirts and nightshirts. Each garment manufacturer was required to put the Viyella brand name on the garments directly when selling them to retailers. Later, knitted Viyella products were also made. Until recently, most of the classic grey shirts used as part of English school uniforms were made with Viyella.

End uses: men's shirts, nightshirts, women's blouses, nightdresses, skirts, school uniform shirts and sheets.

VOILE A very fine, sheer, lightweight fabric that is woven in plain weave. It is made with high-twist yarns from a variety of different fibres, both natural and man-made, which characteristically give it a crisp, wiry handle. Voile is a soft fabric with good drape and lustre.

The name 'voile' is the French word for 'veil', and voile fabric is so called because it was originally used as a veiling fabric.[3] Voile is woven in a range of different qualities from many different fibres, including combed cotton, worsted wool, silk, viscose, polyester, polyester/cotton and nylon. Of these, cotton voile is perhaps the most common.

voile (printed)

voile (printed, embroidered)

Voile is constructed with high-twist voile yarns. To make a voile yarn, the fibres are highly twisted together – more so than in normal yarns, but less than in crêpe yarns.[27] This produces a smooth, 'rounded' singles yarn. Two-fold voile yarns are then made by taking two singles voile yarns and plying these together in the same twist direction as the singles twist. This produces a fine, 'hard', strong yarn, which gives the fabric its characteristic crisp handle. The better-quality cotton voile yarns are also gassed or singed to remove loose fibres.[4]

The fabric is woven in a square, open-sett plain weave, usually with just a single end per dent in the reed. As the weave structure is so open, it is important that voile fabrics have firmly woven selvedges, and these are made by cramming yarns into the reed at the sides of the fabric for a width of 1.25 cm or more.[26] It is the quality of the yarns that gives the fabric its characteristic crisp handle. The highest-quality voile fabrics are made with two-fold yarns in both the warp and the weft. 'Mock voile' is the term given to a softer, less strong voile fabric that is woven using singles voile yarns in both the warp and the weft.[4, 25] This fabric is sometimes starched to enhance the crisp handle, but this will eventually wash out. Voile may be bleached white, piece-dyed, colour-woven with stripes or checks, or printed.

Typical cotton voile fabric constructions are:
- R15/2 tex warp sett at 23 ends per cm and R15/2 tex weft woven at 22 picks per cm (70 g/m²)[25]
- 24/2 tex warp sett at 14 ends per cm and 24/2 tex weft woven at 15 picks per cm[26]
- 12/2 tex warp sett at 23 ends per cm and 12/2 tex weft woven at 22 picks per cm[26]

Cotton voile is a similar fabric to organdie but it is coarser. It is also a similar fabric to gazar, organza, silk mousseline (see MOUSSELINE) and ninon.

Other qualities of voile are woven in nylon, polyester and wool. A typical nylon voile fabric construction is 56 dtex warp sett at 40 ends per cm and 56 dtex weft woven at 36 picks per cm.[25] Polyester voile, woven with polyester yarns, is produced as a fine, sheer curtaining fabric. These curtains, often called 'sheers', are soft and have good drape; see SHEER FABRICS. For worsted wool voile, a typical fabric construction is 110/3 tex warp sett at 9 ends per cm and 110/3 tex weft woven at 9 picks per cm.[26] Worsted wool voile is a very similar fabric to challis and wool batiste, but it is heavier than challis and lighter and more open-sett than batiste. See also BATISTE, CHALLIS.

The classic plain voile fabric may also be used as a background construction for other, more complex patterned fabrics. For example, it may be patterned with different kinds of clip spots (clip spot voile). It is a suitable base fabric for dotted Swiss fabrics, and also for embroidery (embroidered voile), with the embroidery yarns producing a high raised pattern against the fine voile ground fabric. See CLIP SPOT, DOTTED SWISS, EMBROIDERED FABRICS.

Woven variations of voile include various stripe and shadow stripe effects. Leno voile is one example: a plain weave, cotton voile with striped sections of the fabric woven in an open leno weave construction, which creates a subtle contrasting pattern against the rest of the fabric (see LENO FABRIC). Woven striped voile may also be achieved very simply by cramming more than one warp end into sections of the reed at intervals. This results in vertical warpways stripes in which the fabric is more closely woven than the rest of the fabric, an effect sometimes called a 'shadow stripe'. The same effect may be produced in the weft direction also, by weaving horizontal sections of weft yarns more closely together at intervals. More pronounced stripes, such as satin woven stripes, may be produced with the addition of extra warp and extra weft yarns. See EXTRA WARP AND EXTRA WEFT FABRICS, SHADOW STRIPES AND CHECKS.

See also PLAIN WEAVE FABRIC, SHEER FABRICS.

End uses: dresses, blouses, lingerie, nightwear, shirts, veils, scarves, trims, millinery, children's wear and sheer curtains.

wadding (cotton batting)

wadding (polyester)

WADDING A general term for a range of materials that are generally used for padding (as in quilting, for example), for stuffing, or as a packing material.[25] Wadding is usually a thick sheet of fibres that may or may not be bonded together. It is available in different thicknesses, but most waddings are bulky, lightweight nonwoven materials. When used in garment or fabric constructions, a layer of wadding provides warmth and comfort, and sometimes acts as a protective cushioning layer.

Wadding may be made from a variety of different fibres, including cotton, polyester, polyester/cotton blends or sometimes wool. Polyester wadding is the firmed and most springy of these. Wadding is used in quilting and patchwork quilting as a layer of insulation between a top fabric layer and a bottom fabric layer or backing material. Usually the layers are stitched together. It is assembled similarly for garments, and many padded jackets and coats are made in this manner, primarily for warmth. In tailoring it is used as a padding material (for shoulder pads, for example), and in upholstery it is used for stuffing items such as sofas and cushions. A fleecy, nonwoven material known as 'batting', made from cotton, polyester or a blend of the two, is used for similar purposes to other wadding fabrics. Similar fabrics to batting include bump cloth and domet. Both similar, but they are woven fabrics, and therefore stronger and more stable.

See also NONWOVEN FABRIC, PATCHWORK, QUILTED FABRIC.

End uses: padded jackets, coats, quilts, upholstery, cushions and shoulder padding in tailored garments (especially jackets and coats).

WAFFLE *see* HONEYCOMB; PIQUÉ, WOVEN.

WAFFLE PIQUÉ *see* MARCELLA; PIQUÉ, WOVEN.

WARP CRÊPE *see* CRÊPE.

WARP-KNITTED FABRIC The generic term for knitted fabrics composed of knitted loops, formed by constructing the individual warpwise yarns that run the length of the fabric, parallel to the selvedge, into the knitted loops. At intervals, these yarns are interlinked with adjoining wales to connect them all together and to form the knitted fabric. The connecting yarns are known as 'underlap'. The side where the knitted loops are prominent is known as the 'technical face', and the side where the underlaps are prominent is known as the 'technical back'.[25]

Warp-knitted fabrics are constructed on warp-knitting machines. There are three main types: raschel, tricot and simplex. Tricot machines and single-bar raschel machines have a single needlebar and knit single layer fabrics. Simplex machines and double-bar raschel machines have two needlebars and knit double layer fabrics. The main difference between the tricot and raschel machines is that on tricot machines the fabric is removed from the machine horizontally, while on raschel machines it is removed vertically downwards, facilitating the inclusion of much coarser stretch yarns than the tricot machine allows. With all warp-knitting machines, all the machine needles across the width of the machine form loops simultaneously to make a fabric. A sheet of warp yarns run the length of the

warp-knitted fabric (face)

warp-knitted fabric (back)

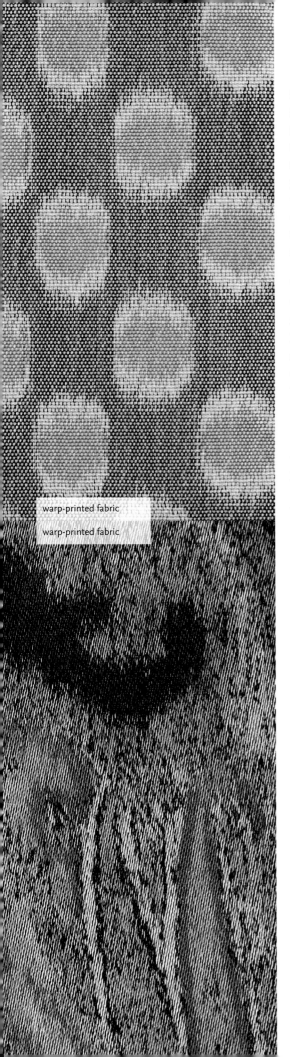

warp-printed fabric

warp-printed fabric

fabric, and each one is simultaneously formed into loops by separate machine needles in a similar manner to crochet, where each yarn is looped through a series of previously formed loops. These warp yarn chains are then interlinked with one another to form the knitted fabric. Characteristically, therefore, the majority of loops are formed substantially along the length of the fabric. In some warp-knitted fabrics, additional weft yarns are incorporated to reinforce the construction or to introduce different effects. In weft-insertion fabrics, which are knitted on special weft-insertion warp-knitting machines, weft yarns are inserted across the entire fabric width, each being held in position between the knitted loops and the underlaps of each wale. *See* LAID-IN FABRIC, STITCH-BONDED FABRIC.

Examples of warp-knitted fabrics include airloop fabric, atlas (warp-knitted), bouclette, bourrelet (warp-knitted), crêpe (warp-knitted), fishnet (warp-knitted), lace (knitted), laid-in fabric (warp-knitted), locknit, loopraise, marquisette (warp-knitted), mesh fabrics, milanese (warp-knitted), net (warp-knitted), piqué (warp-knitted), plush (warp-knitted pile fabric), power net, raschel lace, raschel stretch fabrics, raschel warp-knitted fabric, satin (warp-knitted), scrim (warp-knitted), simplex, spacer fabrics (warp-knitted), suede cloth (warp-knitted), terry fabric (warp-knitted), tricot, tulle (warp-knitted) and velour (warp-knitted pile fabric).

See also CROCHET; JACQUARD FABRIC, KNITTED; LACE; STITCH-BONDED FABRIC.

End uses: dresses, blouses, shirts, swimwear, lingerie, corsetry, bras, nightwear, sportswear, outerwear, bridal wear, evening wear, gloves, casual clothing, laminated fabrics, lining fabric, upholstery, sheets and automotive textiles.

WARP-PRINTED FABRIC A general term for a woven fabric in which the warp yarns are printed prior to weaving. The printed warp yarns move slightly during the subsequent weaving process and are also partially obscured by the weft yarns; this produces a pattern in the fabric that is characteristically diffuse and shadowy, with staggered or feathery edges.

Warp-printed fabrics may be woven using any fibres, but the yarns are usually very fine in order to emphasize the warp print. Traditionally silk was often used. Warp-printed fabrics may also be woven in any weave structure, although plain and satin weaves are common since, again, these show off the printed pattern the best. Examples of warp-printed fabrics are shadow cretonne (*see* CRETONNE), some delaine fabrics, some gros de Londres fabrics (*see* GROSGRAIN), some jaspé fabrics and marble cloth. Warps printed with stripes or checks are sometimes called 'shadow stripes' or 'shadow checks' (*see* SHADOW STRIPES AND CHECKS). Patterned fabrics with similar visual effects to warp-printed fabrics include chiné fabrics, ikat, resist-dyed fabrics and space-dyed fabric.

See also PRINTED FABRIC.

End uses: evening wear, blouses, dresses, curtains and upholstery.

WARP RIB FABRICS *see* RIB FABRICS, WOVEN.

WATERPROOF AND WATER-REPELLENT FABRICS A general term for any fabrics resistant to penetration by water. Fabrics that are fully resistant to penetration by water are described as 'waterproof',[25] while fabrics that resist water only partially or only for a limited time are termed 'water-repellent', 'water-resistant' or 'showerproof'.

Waterproof fabrics can be produced in several different ways:
(i) *Waterproof materials.* Some materials are naturally waterproof, for example rubber and plastic materials of various kinds. *See* PLASTIC TEXTILES, RUBBER.

water-repellent fabric

wedding ring fabric
(baby Altai scarf)

(ii) *Protective coatings.* Woven, knitted or nonwoven fabrics may be coated with various waterproof materials to make them completely impervious to rain, water or snow. The gaps in the fabric construction are completely blocked by the coating material, which acts as a barrier to all liquids and air. Examples of waterproof coatings include rubber, polyurethane (PU), polyvinyl chloride (PVC), Teflon®, wax, and oil compounds. Fabrics coated with these materials are excellent for many end uses; however, when used in clothing, many coatings have the disadvantage that they are not breathable – that is, they do not allow water vapour or perspiration to evaporate away from the inside of the garment. This can make such waterproof garments clammy and uncomfortable to wear. Only microporous coatings have pores fine enough to allow water vapour and air to pass out, while preventing the larger water droplets from coming in. *See* COATED FABRIC.

(iii) *Laminating.* Many laminated fabrics are also completely waterproof, especially if they have been laminated to thin waterproof films or polymer membranes, such as a Teflon® polymer membrane. Although these are usually more expensive than coated fabrics, their advantage is that they have various in-built systems that allow them to be both waterproof and breathable. *See* LAMINATED FABRIC, POLYMER MEMBRANE LAMINATES, TEFLON®.

Macintosh fabric is the name of a waterproof fabric now no longer made.[2, 36] Named after its inventor, the Scottish chemist Charles Macintosh, it consisted of two cotton fabrics laminated together with a rubber solution made from naphtha and rubber. The process was patented in 1823 and, among other things, this fabric was used to make raincoats. The fabric was not breathable and the rubber was not very durable, but 'mackintosh' is now a generic term for waterproof coats of all kinds, irrespective of what they are made from.[2] Examples of waterproof fabrics include some coated fabrics, leather-cloth, neoprene, oil cloth, oilskin, plastic textiles, polymer membrane laminates, polyurethane (PU), PVC, ripstop, rubber and Teflon®.

Water-repellent (or showerproof) fabrics are usually woven fabrics that have been made partially repellent to water – that is, capable of delaying the absorption and penetration of water into the fabric. They too can be produced in several different ways:

(i) *Water-repellent materials.* Some materials are naturally water-repellent. For example, wool is a naturally water-repellent fibre, as are nylon and polyester. Tyvek, a nonwoven fabric made from a synthetic spunbonded fibre, is a breathable, water-resistant material used for protective clothing (*see* TYVEK®).

(ii) *Fabric construction.* Closely woven fabric constructions can also provide resistance to water penetration. Very closely sett fabric constructions are difficult for water droplets to penetrate – for instance a densely woven plain weave fabric with maximum interlacings, such as canvas, gaberdine, umbrella fabric or closely woven microfibre fabrics. These are all highly water-repellent, but still breathable or water-vapour permeable. These fabrics are often used for showerproof garments.

(iii) *Protective finishes.* Fabrics may be treated with various natural and chemical finishes to make them resistant to water. For example, a base fabric of lightweight but densely woven cotton or polyester/cotton, such as poplin, may be given a special water-repellent finish by spraying it with latex or a chemical finish on the reverse side. Unlike waterproof coatings, water-repellent finishes usually coat just the surface fibres on the fabric and do not completely fill the gaps in the fabric construction. These fabrics are therefore still breathable and allow water vapour and air to pass through the structure. Chemical finishes include silicone compound finishes, fluoro-textile finishes or ciré finishes. *See* CIRÉ. Examples of water-repellent fabrics include canvas, some ciré-finished fabrics, some coated fabrics, gaberdine, microfibre fabric, showerproof poplin, ripstop, Tyvek and umbrella fabric.

End uses: raincoats, anoraks, jackets, cagoules, ski wear, rugged outdoor wear, sportswear, hats, gloves, umbrellas, aprons, protective clothing, tents, awnings, footwear, rucksacks and heavy-duty luggage.

weft-knitted fabric (face)

weft-knitted fabric (back)

WEDDING RING FABRICS A general term for a small group of extremely fine, usually hand-woven fabrics made from rare, natural speciality hair fibres such as cashmere. The best-known wedding ring fabric is probably shatush, which comes from India. It is made from a particular type of cashmere goat hair so fine that the fabric may be pulled through a wedding ring. *See* CASHMERE CLOTH, SHATUSH.

Wedding ring fabrics are also made with the hair from other types of goat, many of which are so rare that they are protected species. The fibres are spun into yarn and hand-woven into extremely fine, warm fabrics, which are used as scarves and shawls. Wedding ring fabrics are usually woven in simple weave structures such as plain, twill or reverse twill weaves. These are speciality hair fabrics. Since the supply of the fibres is so limited, wedding ring fabrics are some of the rarest, finest and most expensive fabrics in the world. The illustration opposite shows a scarf woven from baby Altai hair – the hair of a young kid goat of the Altai Mountain breed, which is reared on farms in the Gorno-Altai region of Russia. The fibre is softer, finer and whiter than that from the adult goat.

See also HAIR FABRICS.

End uses: scarves and shawls.

WEFT-INSERTION FABRIC, WARP-KNITTED *see* WARP-KNITTED FABRIC.

WEFT-KNITTED FABRIC The generic term for knitted fabrics constructed from yarns that are formed into loops substantially across the width of the fabric. Each weft thread is fed more or less at right angles to the direction in which the fabric is produced.[25] Weft-knitted fabrics may be knitted by hand using hand knitting needles, or on a weft-knitting machine.

To make the weft-knitted fabric, the yarn is formed into an interconnecting loop construction by looping it through a series of previously formed loops. There are two main kinds of weft-knitting machines: flat knitting machines (single- or double-bed), and circular knitting machines (single- or double-bed). All weft-knitting machines form the loops in each weft course successively, one at a time, in sequence. Flat knitting machines can knit fabric lengths or knit garments integrally in order to make fully-fashioned garments. Most circular machines are high-speed machines that produce fabric lengths in tubular form. After knitting, the fabric is either used in tubular form or cut to make flat fabric pieces from which garment pieces may then be cut to pattern, to make 'cut-and-sewn' garments. There are four main weft-knitted structures that form the base structure for most weft-knitted fabrics. These are plain, rib, interlock and purl.

'Jersey' is a generic term that is applied to all types of weft-knitted fabric. Knitted fabrics produced by weft-knitting include accordion fabric, Aran fabric, Argyll, blister cloth (knitted), bourrelet (weft-knitted), cable stitch fabric, cardigan rib (full and half cardigan), crêpe (weft-knitted), double jersey (see JERSEY), eight-lock, fairisle, fishnet (weft-knitted), fleece fabric, intarsia, interlock, jacquard fabric (knitted), lace (knitted), laid-in fabric (weft-knitted), micromesh, Milano rib (half-Milano and full Milano), moss-stitch fabric, piqué (weft-knitted), piquette, plain knit fabric, plated fabric, plush (weft-knitted pile fabric), polar fleece, punto-di-Roma, purl fabric, rib, single jersey (*see* JERSEY), single jersey cross-tuck, single jersey cord, spacer fabrics (weft-knitted), terry fabric (weft-knitted), texi-piqué and velour (weft-knitted pile fabric).

See also JACQUARD FABRIC, KNITTED; JERSEY.

End uses: T-shirts, sweaters/pullovers, cardigans, dresses, sportswear, jackets, scarves, hats, gloves, nightwear, children's wear, lingerie, underwear, stockings, tights and socks.

WEFTLOC *see* RASCHEL STRETCH FABRICS.

WEFT RIB FABRICS *see* RIB FABRICS, WOVEN.

WEST OF ENGLAND FABRICS A general term for a range of very high-quality woven fabrics made from wool, whose main characteristic is their very soft, supple handle. The term therefore refers more to the quality and handle of fabric than to a particular fabric type. Included in this group are beaver cloth, blanket cloth, doeskin, West of England flannel (*see* FLANNEL) and West of England tweed (*see* TWEED).

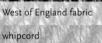

West of England fabric

whipcord

The name comes from the area where these fabrics were originally woven – the Cotswolds region in the west of England. The fabrics are usually woven with good-quality, medium-spun botany yarns made from fine merino wool and spun on the woollen system. Many interesting colour blends are produced. The different West of England fabrics are each constructed in their own unique way, but they are all given special finishing treatments in order to produce their characteristic soft handle, which is similar to that of Saxony.

See also COATING FABRIC, FLANNEL, TWEED.

End uses: men's suits, trousers, jackets and coats.

WHIPCORD A densely woven fabric that is constructed in a prominent, steep twill weave. Traditionally it is woven using bulky, closely sett woollen or worsted yarns. Characteristically, this forms pronounced raised, ribbed twill diagonals that look like the cord of a whip. Whipcord is a medium- to heavyweight fabric that is very hard-wearing and durable.

Although it is traditionally woven with highly twisted woollen or worsted yarns, whipcord is also woven with cotton, man-made fibres or natural/man-made fibre mixes. The two-fold or three-fold warp yarns are closely sett, with many more warp ends per centimetre than weft picks. Whipcord may be woven in any of a number of special right-hand, steep twill weaves with longish warp floats, known as 'whip cords'. This produces a warp-faced twill line that is steeper than normal (often a 63° steep twill). The twill line is emphasized further by the twist direction of the warp yarns, which are twisted in the opposite direction to that of the twill weave.[26] Whipcord is usually piece-dyed, and wool fabrics are given a clear finish. Some cotton whipcords are given a nap finish on the back. Whipcord is a similar fabric to cavalry twill, covert cloth, elastique, gaberdine and tricotine, but it has a steeper, more prominent twill than any of these. Whipcord is sometimes also known as 'artillery cloth' or 'artillery twill'.[3]

See also COATING FABRIC, NAPPED FABRICS, TWILL FABRICS.

End uses: trousers, riding breeches, overcoats, suits, sports clothes, uniforms and upholstery.

whipcord

WIGAN A woven cotton fabric that is made in plain or twill weave and is of low to medium quality. It is a medium-weight fabric that traditionally weighs about 135 g/m².[25] Its main use is as a backing or lining fabric, both for the insides of garments and in shoes and boots.

Wigan is woven as grey cloth in plain or 2/2 twill weave and is either used undyed or piece-dyed in dark colours. It is usually starched and calendered in finishing, which gives it a dull appearance. Typical Wigan fabric constructions are:

• 25 tex warp sett at 17 ends per cm and 31 tex weft woven at 23 picks per cm (127 g/m²)[25]
• plain woven, 50 tex warp sett at 16 ends per cm and 50 tex weft woven at 25 picks per cm[26]

Wigan

wincey

winceyette (printed)

- 2/2 twill, 42 tex warp sett at 18 ends per cm and 42 tex weft woven at 33 picks per cm[26]

Wigan is a similar fabric to a sheeting fabric or print cloth, but it is not usually available in such wide widths.[2]

See also CASEMENT CLOTH, LINING FABRIC.

End uses: casement cloths, interlinings, shoe and boot linings, backing fabric or interfacing for men's jackets and coats.[2]

WILD SILK *see* SILK FABRIC.

WILTON *see* CARPET.

WINCEY (winsey) A fine, lightweight woven fabric that is traditionally made from cotton and wool and weighs about 136 g/m².[25] It has a soft, fibrous surface and is known for its warmth and comfort.

Wincey was originally a union fabric, made with a cotton warp and a woollen weft; it is also made with mixture yarns containing wool. It is usually woven in a plain weave structure as grey cloth and subsequently bleached and dyed. It may also be colour-woven with dyed yarns, either in solid colours or with stripes and checks. Sometimes it is also printed. In finishing, the surface of the fabric is raised on one or both sides. This obscures the weave structure beneath and gives the fabric its soft, warm handle. An example of a typical plain woven wincey fabric construction is 23 tex bleached cotton warp sett at 25 ends per cm and 56 to 49 tex weft (containing 40% wool) woven at 20 to 22 picks per cm.[26]

Along with the names 'linsey-wolsey' (*see* LINSEY) and 'kersey', the terms 'wincey' and 'winsey' probably originated as word plays, mixing the words 'linen' and 'wool' with the names of Lindsey and Kersey, the two villages in Suffolk, England, where these fabrics were originally produced.[3] Wincey is a similar fabric to both flannelette and winceyette but, unlike these all-cotton fabrics, it contains wool and is therefore a warmer fabric. At one time, like them, it was used for warm pyjamas and underclothes. It is also similar to flannel, but it is much finer in texture than even baby flannel.[25]

See also NAPPED FABRICS, UNION FABRIC.

End uses: shirts and blouses.

WINCEYETTE A light- to medium-weight cotton fabric that characteristically has a soft, fibrous surface and is known for its warmth and comfort. It is prone to pilling, creasing and abrasion, but is relatively cheap and has good washability. Winceyette is a very similar fabric to flannelette, but it is lighter in weight, traditionally weighing 136–170 g/m².[25]

Winceyette is traditionally woven with cotton yarns in the warp and thick, low-twist cotton yarns in the weft. Sometimes other fibres, such as viscose, may be included in the weft – if so, this should be stated. Winceyette may be woven in plain weave, double-end plain weave or twill weave. In finishing, the surface of the fabric is raised on one or both sides. This obscures the weave structure beneath and gives the fabric its soft, warm handle. The nap is produced almost entirely from the soft, low-twist weft yarns. Winceyette is usually woven as grey cloth and subsequently bleached and dyed. It may also be colour-woven with dyed yarns, either in solid colours or with stripes and checks. Sometimes it is also printed. Similar fabrics to winceyette include Canton flannel, flannelette, swansdown and wincey (or winsey).

See also COTTON FABRIC, NAPPED FABRICS, PYJAMA FABRIC.

End uses: pyjamas, nightgowns, sheets, pillowcases, shirts, underwear, children's clothes, linings and gloves.

WITNEY *see* BLANKET CLOTH.

WOOL CRÊPE *see* CRÊPE.

WOOL FABRIC A general term for any fabric constructed with wool fibres or yarns. Wool is a natural animal fibre. It is the hair from sheep (*Ovis aries*), of which there are hundreds of different breeds.

Wool fibres are staple fibres that are spun into yarns; they are sometimes blended together with other staple fibres. The term 'wool fabric' is used for fabrics of a range of different weights and constructions composed of 100% wool fibres or yarns. Where wool is used together with other fibres, the percentage of each should be given. Fabrics containing both wool yarns and yarns made from a different fibre or fibres are described as 'wool union fabrics'. *See* UNION FABRIC.

Wool fabrics are perhaps best known for their warmth and they are widely used for all kinds of apparel, particularly winter and cold weather garments, and for blankets. They have a soft, hairy surface texture, the character of which is largely determined by the finish of the fabric. There are numerous different finishes for wool fabrics, each of which can produce an entirely different appearance and handle. Characteristically, wool is also inherently flame-resistant, and wool fabrics are therefore also widely used for furnishings and carpets.

After being graded according to their quality (whiteness, fineness, regularity, etc.), wool fibres are divided into two main groups according to their staple length. The longer staple fibres are used to make worsted yarns and fabrics (*see* WORSTED FABRIC). The shorter staple fibres are used to make 'woollen' yarns and fabrics. These are produced on the condenser system. They are carded prior to spinning, which produces lofty, hairy yarns that may be knitted, woven or used in nonwoven fabrics. Woollen yarns and fabrics are generally thicker and less strong than worsted yarns and fabrics but, because of their bulkiness, they are usually warmer.

Some common wool terms are explained in the following text.

- Botany wool is a term applied to tops, yarns and fabrics made from merino wool.[25] The name comes from Botany Bay, Australia, from where much of the world's merino wool is shipped (see also merino wool, below).
- Cool Wool™ is a trademark owned by The Woolmark Company Pty Ltd, and is sometimes used on specified apparel products as a quality symbol. The term describes fine, lightweight knitted and woven apparel fabrics that weigh less than 220 g/m² and are made from 100% virgin wool (see below). Suitable fibre diameters and yarn counts are both specified, and the yarns are spun on the worsted system. *See* WORSTED FABRIC.
- Lambswool is the soft wool obtained from lambs (young sheep prior to their weaning), irrespective of the breed of sheep. It has been common practice in the trade to apply this term to 100% virgin wool goods of which at least one third is lambswool.[25]
- Merino wool is wool from the merino breed of sheep, which were originally native to Spain. This top-quality wool is noted for its softness, fineness and whiteness; it is among the finest of wools, with a fibre diameter usually of 24 microns or less. Merino sheep were exported from Spain from the late 1700s and are now bred in many parts of the world. Well-known types of merino are Australian, Rambouillet, Vermount, South African and Saxony. The term 'merino' is now almost synonymous with 'fine wool'.[25] See above for botany wool. *See also* MERINO FABRIC.
- Recovered wool fibres are fibres from waste and discarded wool textiles that are collected and recycled into new yarns and fabrics. This is done because there is not normally enough virgin wool available to meet demand. Some virgin wool is sometimes added. *See* RECYCLED TEXTILES.
- Shetland wool is wool from the Shetland breed of sheep, native to the Shetland Islands of Scotland. Strictly used, the term applies only to fabrics woven from wool from this breed. *See* SHETLAND FABRIC.

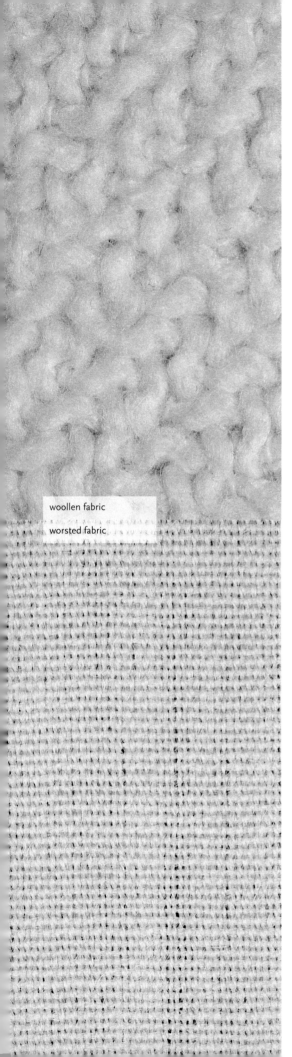

woollen fabric

worsted fabric

- Super 120's, super 100's and so on are references to the fineness or diameter of wool fibres and the fabrics made from them. They are a quality reference for suiting fabrics. *See* SUITING FABRICS.
- Virgin wool (also called 'new wool') is new wool from the sheep. It has not been previously used, unlike recovered wool fibres, which have been recycled to make new yarns and fabrics.
- The Woolmark symbol is a registered trademark owned by The Woolmark Company Pty Ltd; it is recognized worldwide as a quality symbol on all kinds of clothing and interior textile products made from wool. It is an endorsement of quality for the consumer. Manufacturers whose products comply with the fibre content and quality specification of The Woolmark Company are granted a licence to use the Woolmark symbol on their products.

Classic fabrics traditionally made from wool include Afgalaine, albatross, Albert cloth, amazon, astrakhan fabric, baize, Bannockburn, beaver cloth, billiard cloth, blanket, blazer cloth, Bolivia, botany twill, (wool) bouclé fabric, (wool) broadcloth, buffalo check, cadet cloth, cassimere, (wool) crêpe, cavalry twill, (wool) challis, charmelaine, Cheviot, corkscrew fabric, covert cloth, delaine, district checks, doeskin fabric, Donegal, duffel, (wool) duvetyn, (wool) éponge, étamine, flannel, flushing, Fresco®, frieze, (wool) gaberdine, Glen Urquhart check, granada, Guards check, gunclub check, Harris tweed, homespun, horse-blanket check, houndstooth check, imperial cloth, kasha, kersey, loden cloth, marengo, melton, merino fabric, molleton, pilot cloth, Poiret twill, polo cloth, poodle cloth, Prince of Wales check, (wool) ratiné, Saxony, serge, sharkskin, shepherd's check, Shetland fabric, tartan, Tattersall check, thorn-proof tweed, tricotine, tropical suiting, tweed, Ulster, velour, West of England fabrics and whipcord.

See also FLAME-RESISTANT TEXTILES, SUITING FABRICS, WORSTED FABRIC.

End uses: an extremely wide range of different end uses, including coats, jackets, suits, jumpers, cardigans, dresses, blankets, carpets, and curtain and upholstery fabrics.

WOOLLEN FABRIC *see* WOOL FABRIC.

WORSTED FABRIC A general term for any fabric constructed with worsted wool fibres or yarns. Worsted yarns are fine, strong yarns made from the longer staple wool fibres that are carded and combed prior to spinning. Worsted fabrics are known for being hardwearing, durable fabrics. *See also* WOOL FABRIC.

Worsted wool fibres are staple fibres that are spun into yarns; they are sometimes blended with other staple fibres. The term 'worsted fabric' is used for fabrics of a range of different weights and constructions composed of 100% worsted wool fibres or yarns. In fabrics where worsted wool is used together with other fibres, the percentage of each should be given.

Traditionally most worsted fabrics are woven fabrics, and they are used mainly as men's suiting fabrics, but they also have other end uses (see list below). Worsted yarns and fabrics are generally finer, smoother and stronger than woollen yarns and fabrics. Many worsted fabrics are given a clear finish that leaves the weave structure and any colour effects clearly visible. The term 'worsted' comes from the English village of Worstead in Norfolk, where worsted fabrics have been woven since the 12th century.[23] Fabrics made from worsted wool include botany twill, some Bradford lustre fabrics, (worsted) challis, (worsted) flannel, some gaberdine fabrics, paddock (*see* GABERDINE), poirette twill, sharkskin, many suiting fabrics and tropical suiting.

See also SUITING FABRICS, WOOL FABRIC.

End uses: men's and women's suits, coats, jackets, trousers, skirts, dresses, upholstery fabrics and curtains.

WORSTED FLANNEL *see* FLANNEL.

WOVEN FABRIC The generic name for a constructed fabric that is formed by interweaving two sets of yarns at right angles to one another. This produces a firm, close fabric construction that maintains the relatively straight nature of the yarn, as opposed to a knitted fabric in which the yarn is formed into an interconnecting loop construction.

The yarns that run the length of the fabric, parallel to the selvedge, are collectively called the 'warp' (an individual warp yarn is called an 'end'). The yarns that interlace with the warp ends across the width of the fabric are collectively called the 'weft' (an individual weft yarn is called a 'pick'). Characteristically, most woven fabrics are very strong, stable fabrics that, if designed to do so, may provide maximum surface cover. They may be constructed on a hand weaving loom (machine) or on a power weaving loom, of which there are several different types. It is the order in which the warp and weft yarns are interlaced with one another, known as the 'weave structure', that produces the woven pattern in the fabric. Weaving looms may be fitted with different mechanisms to lift the warp ends and thus produce different woven effects in the fabric.

Dobby or tappet woven fabrics are woven on weaving looms that have either a dobby or a tappet patterning mechanism, as opposed to a jacquard mechanism. The majority of woven fabrics are produced on such looms. These are high-speed power looms that select and lift the warp yarns in regular sequences that repeat across the fabric width and down its length, enabling a wide variety of simple weave structures and pattern effects to be woven. There are four basic or elementary woven fabric structures: plain weave, twill, satin and sateen (described in separate entries). There are also many variations of each of these structures and countless other, less common weave structures. Entire fabrics may be woven in a single weave structure, or different weave structures may be used in combination to produce more complex patterns. Complex small-scale, geometric weave structures woven on dobby looms are often called 'dobby fabrics'. *See* DOBBY FABRIC.

Jacquard woven fabrics are woven using a jacquard patterning mechanism on a weaving loom, as opposed to a dobby or tappet mechanism. The jacquard mechanism allows any of the warp ends to be selected and lifted individually rather than in groups. This enables large-scale or complex patterns to be woven in a fabric. Woven jacquards usually incorporate more than one weave structure. They often have curvilinear motifs and sometimes they have pictorial designs. *See* JACQUARD FABRIC, WOVEN.

See also THREE-DIMENSIONAL TEXTILES.

End uses: all kinds of fashion and furnishing fabrics.

ZANZIBAR A colour-woven cranky check fabric. Traditionally made from cotton, it is composed of red, white and blue sections that form a squared check design. It is used for shirts.[4]

The cotton warp ends are woven in pairs together (i.e. there are two ends in one heald eye). The weft picks are also woven in pairs together (i.e. two weft picks are woven in one shed).[4] Stripes of red, white and blue are alternated in both the warp and the weft. The fabric is woven in various simple weave structures, such as plain weave or twills; these, when combined with the coloured warp and weft stripes, produce a variety of interesting colour and weave effects.

See also CHECKS, COLOUR AND WEAVE EFFECTS, CRANKY CHECKS, SHIRTING FABRICS.

End uses: shirts and dresses.

woven fabric (dobby)

woven fabric (jacquard, face and back)

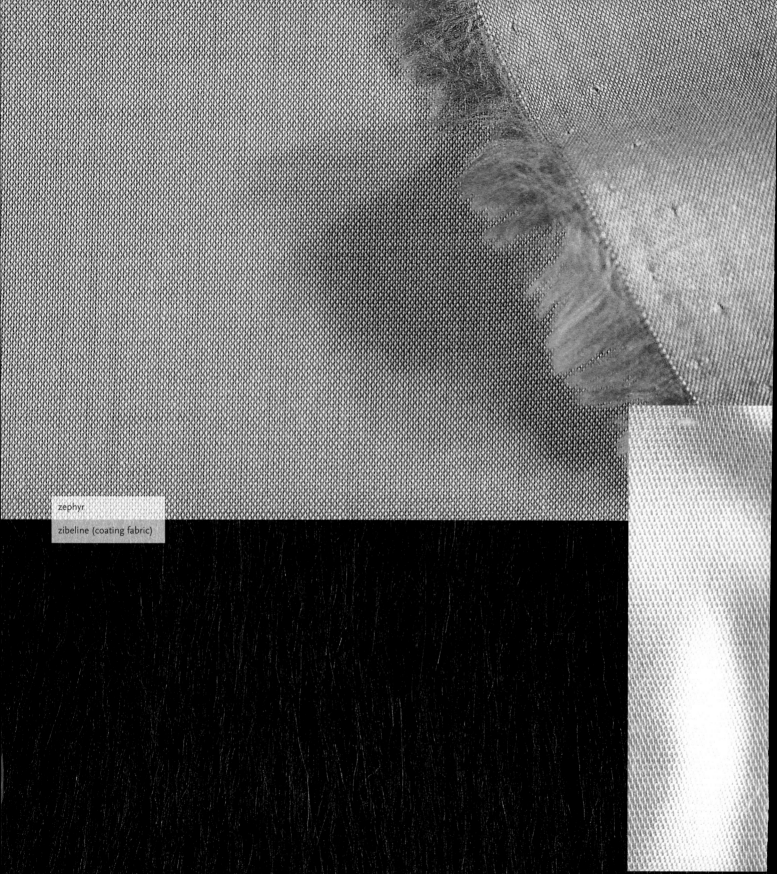

zephyr

zibeline (coating fabric)

ZEPHYR A fine, soft, lightweight colour-woven fabric that is woven in plain weave. It is woven in stripes and checks, usually in light, delicate pastel colours. A typical zephyr has coloured stripes on a white ground.[25] Sometimes thicker yarns (usually warp yarns) are inserted at regular intervals to give the fabric a corded surface texture.

Originally zephyr was made from 100% wool, but it is now woven in a range of different qualities, including cotton, wool, silk, viscose, polyester and mixtures of these.[5] The fabric is made from fine singles yarns in both the warp and the weft. Any thicker cord yarns are usually two-fold. This gives the fabric its light, sheer quality. The term 'zephyr' comes from Zephyrus, the name of the Greek god of the West Wind, and refers to the light, airy quality of the fabric.[5] When made from fine singles combed cotton yarns, zephyr is like a particularly lightweight version of a gingham fabric. This fabric is similar in weight to chambray, lawn and batiste. Zephyr is also similar to Madras, but it is lighter in weight and more subtly coloured.

See also CHECKS, PLAIN WEAVE FABRIC, SHEER FABRICS, SHIRTING FABRICS, STRIPES.

End uses: lightweight shirtings, blouses and dresses.

ZEPHYR FLANNEL *see* FLANNEL.

ZIBELINE A term used for two different types of fabric, both of a lustrous nature:
(i) A thick, heavy woven coating fabric that is traditionally made from wool. It is finished with a long, silky, waved nap on one side that is flattened and laid in one direction. This gives the fabric its characteristic high lustre. It is usually made in strong colours and is sometimes striped.
(ii) A stiff, lustrous, medium- to heavyweight silk fabric that is woven in twill weave in a variety of different qualities and used mainly for wedding gowns.

The two types of fabric are discussed in more detail below.
(i) The coating fabric zibeline is woven in imitation of the soft fur of the Siberian sable; no sable fur is used in its manufacture, however. Instead, zibeline is woven with lustrous worsted yarns from cross-bred sheep,[3] and may also include some man-made fibres such as acrylic.[2] Often speciality fibres, such as mohair, camel hair or alpaca, are used in the weft to enhance the appearance of the fabric. Zibeline is woven in a satin weave structure and is afterwards raised and cropped on one side to produce the long, lustrous nap. The fabric is then steamed, and the fibres laid flat in one direction. Sometimes the length of nap is varied in different sections of the fabric, which can produce crosswise ridges.[7] Zibeline coating fabric is usually dyed black, and sometimes a slight striping or ripple effect caused by the finish can be seen through the nap; this fabric is sometimes also called 'ripple cloth'.[3] This zibeline fabric is a similar fabric to Ulster but is more lustrous.
See also COATING FABRIC, FUR FABRIC, MOHAIR FABRIC, NAPPED FABRICS.
(ii) Silk zibeline is a stiff, densely woven fabric that is woven in twill weave. It is a luxurious, expensive fabric that is usually woven with white or cream-coloured yarns. It is produced in a variety of different weights, and its principal use is for wedding dresses.
See also SILK FABRIC, TWILL FABRICS.

End uses: (i) men's, women's and children's coats and jackets; (ii) wedding dresses, ball gowns and occasion wear.

zibeline (silk)

GLOSSARY

The Glossary is reproduced by kind permission of The Textile Institute.

back loop *see* knitted loop (2).

bast fibre Fibre obtained from the outer layers (bast layers) of the stems of certain plants.

batt (web) Single or multiple sheets of fibre used in the production of nonwoven fabric.

beam *see* weaving loom beam.

beetle To produce a firm, close and lustrous fabric of cellulosic material, particularly linen or cotton, by subjecting the damp material, batched on a wooden or metal beam or roller, to repeated blows of wooden or metal hammers.

bleeding Loss of colourant from a coloured material in contact with a liquor, leading to an obvious coloration of the latter, or of adjacent areas of the same or other materials.

blending (spinning) A process or processes concerned primarily with the mixing of various lots of fibres to produce a homogeneous mass. Blending is normally carried out to mix fibres that may or may not be similar in their physical or chemical properties, market values or colours. Blending is also used to ensure the consistency of an end product.

bouclé yarn *see* fancy yarns.

calender (1) A machine in which heavy rollers rotate in contact under mechanical or hydraulic pressure. The rollers may be unheated, or one may be a thick-walled steel shell that is heated internally. All rollers may rotate at the same surface speed or – for example in friction calendering – one highly polished and heated roller may rotate at a higher surface speed than the rest. In certain specialized machines (e.g. those for knitted goods), two adjacent rollers may be heated; or, in the case of a laundry calender, one roller may work against a steam chest shaped to the curvature of the roller.
(2) To pass fabric through a machine, as in (1) above, normally to smooth and flatten it, to close the intersections between the yarns or to confer surface glaze. Special calenders with an engraved heated roller imprint a pattern in relief (*see* emboss) or modify the fabric surface to give high lustre (*see* schreiner).
(3) When coating a fabric with rubber or plastics, to use such a machine with the rollers a certain distance apart, so that the rubber or plastics mass is attenuated to form a thin, uniform sheet, which is then pressed into a firm adhesion with one side of the fabric passing through. Sometimes this operation is referred to as 'calender spreading'.

circular knitting machine A knitting machine in which the needles are set radially or in parallel in one or more circular beds. Used without further qualification, the term generally refers to a weft-knitting machine of this type. For the other main type of weft-knitting machine, *see* flat knitting machine. (*See also* knitting machine.)

clear finish A type of finish on fabrics containing wool. The surface of the fabric is relatively free from protruding fibres, and the weave and the colours of the constituent yarns are clear and distinct. Examples of clear-finished fabrics include serge and many other worsted fabrics.

cloth A generic term embracing most textile fabrics. The term was originally applied to wool cloth suitable for clothing. It has now largely been replaced by the term 'fabric' (*see* fabric).

colour-woven (coloured woven) *see* yarn-dyeing.

combed yarn Yarn produced from fibres that have been carded (or prepared) and combed.

condenser spun Descriptive of yarn spun from slubbing (*see* slubbing).

continuous filament yarn (filament yarn) A yarn composed of one or more filaments that run essentially the whole length of the yarn. Yarns of one or more filaments are usually referred to as 'monofilament' or 'multifilament', respectively.

corkscrew yarn (spiral yarn) *see* fancy yarns.

cotton count (cc) A traditional English system of expressing the linear density (length per unit weight) of yarns, calculated by the number of 840-yard hanks per pound. It is an 'indirect yarn count system' in which the higher the count, the finer the yarn.

count of yarn *see* yarn count.

course In knitted fabric, a row of loops (i) across the width of a flat fabric, or (ii) around the circumference of a circular fabric. In weft-knitting, the course may be formed by one or more traverses of a feeder. Some fabrics knitted on two needle-beds have a different number of courses on one side of the fabric from the other.

cover (1) The degree of evenness of thread spacing. Good cover gives the effect of a uniform plane surface and cannot be obtained with hard-twisted yarns.
(2) The degree to which, in fabric finishing, the underlying structure is concealed by the finishing materials or treatments. *See also* grin.

crimped yarn *see* textured yarn.

crop *see* shear.

cross-bred (1) A term used to describe a sheep that is the progeny of parents from two different breeds.
(2) A term commonly used to describe wool coarser than 25 micrometres (μm) in diameter.

cross-dyeing The dyeing of one component of a mixture of fibres of which at least one is already coloured.

cupro The generic name of a manufactured fibre of cellulose obtained by the cuprammonium process. (The full name is cuprammonium rayon.) The generic name used in the United States is 'cupra fibre'.

curled yarn A yarn constructed or treated, or both, so as to produce a pile with a curled effect when used in a suitable fabric construction. *See also* fancy yarns, textured yarn, yarn.

decitex *see* tex system.

dent The unit of a reed comprising a reed wire and the space between adjacent wires. The spaces in the reed are dented with warp yarns to provide the sett of the warp yarns. *See also* reed, sett.

differential dyeing The dyeing of textiles containing differential dyeing fibres (or dye variant fibres): fibres of the same generic class that have potential dyeing properties different from those of the standard fibre.

dobby weaving loom *see* weaving loom.

double *see* fold.

drafting (1) The process of drawing out laps, slivers, slubbings and rovings to decrease the linear density.
(2) The order in which threads are drawn through heald eyes before weaving.

drape The ability of a fabric to hang in graceful folds (e.g. the undulating folds of a curtain or a skirt). If a fabric drapes well, it is said to have good drape. If there is little or no drape, the fabric is said to have poor drape, or it might be described as stiff.

dress-face finish A finish for wool fabrics characterized by a closely cropped surface and high lustre. The effect is produced partly by raising and cropping and partly by the highly regular lie of the fibres.

dtex *see* tex system.

ecru The natural colour of unprocessed textiles; descriptive of fibres, yarns or fabrics that have not been subjected to processes affecting their natural colour. (*See also* grey cloth.)

effect side The surface of a plain weft-knitted fabric intended to be used outermost on a garment or other construction. The surface opposite to this is usually called the 'reverse side'.

emboss To produce a pattern in relief by passing fabric through a calender, in which a heated metal roller engraved with the pattern works against a relatively soft roller built up of compressed paper or cotton on a metal centre. In practice any residual surface patterning generated on the relatively soft roller is removed by compression against a third small metal roller. *See also* calender.

emerizing A process in which fabric is passed over a series of rotating emery-covered rollers to produce a suede-like finish. A similar process is known as 'sueding' (*see* sueding).

end (warp end) In weaving, an individual warp thread.

ends per cm (EPC) The number of warp yarns per centimetre.

ends per inch (EPI) The number of warp yarns per inch.

fabric A manufactured assembly of fibres and/or yarns that has substantial surface area in relation to its thickness and sufficient cohesion to give the assembly useful mechanical strength. Fabrics are most commonly woven or knitted, but the term includes assemblies produced by felting, lace-making, net-making, nonwoven processes and tufting. *See also* material, textile.

face loop *see* knitted loop (2).

fancy yarns Yarns that differ from normally constructed single and folded yarns by way of deliberately produced irregularities in their construction. These irregularities relate to an increased input of one or more components, or to the inclusion of periodic effects, such as knops, loops, curls, slubs or the like. (*See also* curled yarn, textured yarn, yarn.) Examples of fancy yarns include the following.
- A bouclé yarn is a compound yarn comprising a twisted core with an effect yarn wrapped around so as to produce wavy projections

on its surface. (Bouclé yarns belong to the same group as gimp yarns and loop yarns. The effect is achieved by differential delivery of the effect component as compared with the core yarn, the former wrapping around the latter either tightly or loosely according to the amount of excess delivery and the doubling twist inserted. Generally speaking, bouclé yarns exhibit an irregular pattern of semicircular loops and sigmoid spirals; gimp yarns display fairly regular semi-circular projections; and loop yarns have well-formed circular hoops.)
- A gimp yarn is a yarn made of one or more strands twisted around a usually finer central ground yarn and overfed to form a clear spiral wrapping.
- A knop yarn is a yarn that contains prominent bunches of one or more of its component threads, arranged at regular or irregular intervals along its length.
- A loop yarn is a compound yarn comprising a twisted core with an effect yarn wrapped around it so as to produce wavy projections on its surface.
- A nepp yarn (also called a 'knickerbocker yarn' or 'knicker yarn') is a yarn in which the incidence of nep occurs at a relatively high level and is used purposely as decoration. It is made on the woollen system and shows strongly contrasting spots on its surface that are made either by dropping in small balls of wool at the latter part of the carding process or by incorporating them in the blend and setting the carding machine so that these small lumps are not carded out. Undesirably neppy yarns can, however, also constitute a fault. *See also* nep.
- A slub yarn is a yarn in which slubs are deliberately created to produce a desired effect. The yarn has thick and thin sections along its length.
- A snarl yarn is a compound yarn that displays snarls or kinks projecting from the core.
- A spiral yarn (or corkscrew yarn) is a plied yarn displaying a characteristic smooth spiralling of one component around the other. Spiral yarns include: (i) a plied yarn made up of two single ends or groups of ends of equal length containing 'S' and 'Z' twists respectively; (ii) a plied yarn produced by delivering one or more of its components at a greater rate (the shorter length forms the base, while the greater length of its companion(s) creates a spiral round it); (iii) a plied yarn made from two ends of equal length, one coarser than the other.

fell (cloth fell) The line of termination of the fabric in the loom formed by the last weft thread.

felting *see* milling.

fibre Textile raw material, generally characterized by flexibility, fineness and high ratio of length to thickness. (The US spelling is 'fiber'.) *See also* man-made fibre, natural fibre, regenerated fibre, synthetic fibre.

filament yarn *see* continuous filament yarn.

flat knitting machine A weft-knitting machine that has straight needle-beds carrying independently operated, usually latch, needles. Rib machines (V-type) usually have two needle-beds, which are opposed to each other in inverted 'V' formation; purl machines usually have two needle-beds horizontally opposed in the same plane. For the other main type of weft-knitting machine, *see* circular knitting machine. (*See also* knitting machine.)

fold (double, twist, ply) To combine yarns by twisting together two or more single yarns to form a folded yarn. *See also* singles yarn.

friction-calendering The process of passing fabric through a calender (*see* calender) in which a highly polished, usually heated, steel roller rotates at a higher surface speed than the softer (cotton- or paper-filled, for example) roller against which it works, thus producing a glaze on the face of the fabric that is in contact with the steel roller. The ratio of the peripheral speed of the faster steel roller to that of the slower roller is termed the 'friction ratio' and is normally in the range 1.5 to 3.0.

fulling *see* milling.

gassed yarn (singed yarn) A yarn that has been passed through a flame or over a heated element to remove unwanted surface fibres. A genappe yarn is a gassed worsted yarn.

gating (gaiting) The relative alignment of two sets of knitting elements, for example needles, on knitting machines. Two forms of needle gating (rib and interlock) are common and may be interchangeable on the same machine. Types of gating are:
- interlock gating – the opposed alignment of one set of needles with the other on a knitting machine
- purl gating – in weft-knitting, the opposed alignment of tricks of two needle-beds lying in the same plane, on a machine equipped with double-headed needles
- rib gating – the alternate alignment of one set of needles with the other on a machine equipped with two sets of needles arranged to knit rib fabrics

gauge (cut) (**1**) In knitting, a term giving a notional indication of the number of needles per unit length, along a needle-bed or needlebar, of a knitting machine. In current practice a common unit length of 1 'English' inch (25.4 mm) is used for all types of warp- and weft-knitting machines. For circular knitting machines, the length referred to is measured along the circumference of the needle cylinder. Such values are generally quoted to the nearest whole number (or to the nearest half if less than 5) and, in keeping with the present national and international use of the concept, written as 'E10', say, rather than as '10 needles/inch', or the older abbreviated form '10G'. Gauging systems other than these are also still used.
(**2**) A term specifying a dimension, usually thickness, of the needles or other loop-forming elements of a knitting machine.

genappe *see* gassed yarn.

gimp yarn *see* fancy yarns.

glaze To produce a smooth, glossy, plane surface on a fabric by heat, heavy pressure or friction. Glazing may be produced intentionally by a finishing process (e.g. friction calendering) or as a fault.

grandrelle yarn (twist yarn) A two-ply yarn composed of singles of different colour or contrasting lustre.

grey cloth (gray, greige) Descriptive of textile products before being wet-processed (e.g. bleached, dyed, printed or finished). Some, however, may contain dyed or finished yarns. In the linen and lace trades, the term 'brown goods' is sometimes used. *See also* ecru.

grin (grinning) A defect in a compound structure, for example a double cloth, in which one fabric can be seen 'grinning through' the other, as a result of bad cover. The term can be applied to compound woven and knitted structures, including pile fabrics. *See also* cover, grinny cloth.

grinny cloth A cloth with unsatisfactory cover. It is sometimes said to be grinning and is also known as hungry cloth. *See also* cover, grin.

handle (hand) The quality of a fabric or yarn assessed by the reaction obtained from the sense of touch. It is concerned with the judgment of roughness, smoothness, harshness, pliability, thickness, and so on.

hand-loom (hand weaving loom) *see* weaving loom.

heald (heddle) A looped cord, shaped wire, or flat steel stripe with an eye in the centre through which a warp yarn is threaded so that its movement may be controlled during weaving.

hydrophilic Having the property of absorbing moisture; water-attracting.

hydrophobic Having the property of resisting the absorption of moisture; water-repellent.

jacquard Term applied to a patterning device and mechanism used to select individual warp threads in weaving or warp-knitting, individual threads in lace making, and knitting elements in weft-knitting.

jacquard weaving loom *see* weaving loom.

knitted loop (**1**) A basic unit of warp-knitted fabric, consisting of a loop of warp yarn linked laterally with loops on one or both sides, linked within the same wale, or linked both laterally and within the same wale. The interlinking of the warp-knitted loop with other loops in order to form a fabric differs from that of the weft-knitted loop (see (2) below) in that sideways interlinking of the warp-knitted loop is achieved by lateral displacement of the warp yarns running along the length of the fabric, whereas the weft-knitted loop is interlinked with loops above and below. The main components of the warp-knitted loop are generally identical to those forming the weft-knitted loop, namely the curved needle loop at the top and the two inclined portions on either side. For some types of warp-knitted fabric, additional yarns may be inlaid in the structure, in either warp or weft directions, and held in place by the interlinking.
(**2**) A basic unit of weft-knitted fabric, consisting of a loop of yarn meshed at its base with a previously formed loop. At the point of mesh with the previously formed loop, a knitted loop is usually open but may be crossed. Component parts of the knitted loop may be identified as:
• back loop (reverse loop) – a knitted loop meshed through the previous loop towards the back of the fabric (away from the viewer)
• face loop (front loop, plain loop) – a knitted loop meshed through the previous loop towards the front of the fabric (towards the viewer)
• needle loop – the upper curved portion of a knitted loop
• sides (legs) – the parts of the knitted loop that connect the sinker and needle loops
• sinker loop – the lower curved portion of a knitted loop

knitting machine A machine for the production of fabrics, garments or yarns by warp-knitting or weft-knitting. The different types of warp- and weft-knitting machines are classified and named, primarily, according to (i) the type of fabric or garment they are intended to produce; (ii) the type of needle used; (iii) the form, arrangement and activation of their needles or needle-beds; (iv) the type of patterning control used; and (v) whether they are hand-operated or power-operated. *See also* circular knitting machine, flat knitting machine.

knop yarn *see* fancy yarns.

lapping movement In warp-knitting, the compound motion of the guide bars of warp-knitting machines that presents the threads to the needles so that loops can be formed. This compound motion consists in swinging motions of the guides at right angles to the needlebar, and lateral movements parallel to the needlebar. *See also* overlap, underlap.

loom *see* weaving loom.

loop yarn *see* fancy yarns.

man-made fibre (manufactured fibre) A fibre that does not occur in nature, although the material of which it is composed may occur naturally. (*See also* natural fibre.) The raw materials for the manufacture of fibres may be derived from:
• naturally occurring, non-fibrous materials (e.g. metal fibres from a variety of metals and their ores, glass fibre from silica and other minerals)
• natural polymers (e.g. rubber fibre from latex, viscose from wood cellulose, azlon from natural proteins; *see* regenerated fibre)
• synthesized polymers (e.g. the polyamides and polyesters; *see* synthetic fibre)
• other manufactured fibres, which then undergo further significant physical or chemical modification (e.g. carbon fibre made from acrylic or pitch fibres)

manufactured fibre *see* man-made fibre.

material A term often used as a synonym for fabric but also descriptive of, for example, leather and PVC, which are the subject of cutting and making-up operations. *See also* fabric, textile.

mélange printing (vigoureux printing) A printing process in which bands of thickened dye paste, with intervening blank areas, are applied across slubbings of wool or other fibres. The slubbing is subsequently steamed, washed and then combed to produce a very even mixture of dyed and undyed lengths of fibre.

mercerization The treatment of cellulosic textiles in yarn or fabric form with a concentrated solution of caustic alkali, whereby the fibres are swollen, the moisture regain, strength and dye affinity of the materials are increased, and their handle is modified. The process was discovered in 1844 and takes its name from its discoverer, John Mercer. The additional effect of enhancing the lustre by stretching the swollen materials while wet with caustic alkali and then washing off was discovered by Horace Lowe in 1889. The modern process of mercerization involves both swelling in caustic alkalis and stretching to enhance the lustre, to increase colour yield and cotton yarn strength.

microfibre (1) A fibre or filament of linear density below approximately 1 decitex. (Note, however, that some commercial fibres as coarse as 1.3 decitex are classified as microfibres by their producers.) Fibres finer than approximately 0.2 decitex are sometimes referred to as 'ultra-fine fibres' or 'ultra-fine microfibres'.
(2) For glass and other manufactured mineral fibres, a fibre or filament of a thickness less than approximately 3 micrometres (μm).

milling (fulling, felting) A finishing treatment that consolidates or compacts fabrics, usually fabrics that contain wool or other animal fibres. The treatment, which is usually given in a rotary milling machine or in milling stocks, produces relative motion between the previously wetted fibres of a fabric. Depending on the type of fibre, the structure of the fabric and variations in the conditions of milling, a wide range of effects can be obtained, varying from a slight alteration in handle to a dense matting with considerable reduction in area. The alternative term 'felting' used here to describe a finishing treatment should not be confused with the process of felting (i.e. the making of a nonwoven fabric) as discussed in the main text under FELT.

mixture yarn (ingrain yarn) A worsted yarn with a colour effect produced by blending together fibres of two or more colours.

modal The generic name of a manufactured fibre of cellulose obtained by processes giving a high breaking strength and a high wet modulus.

modulus The ability of a textile to maintain its integrity when stretched (i.e. to return to its original dimensions after being stretched). A stretch fabric that requires a large force to stretch it is said to have high modulus; it provides a degree of control in garments such as corsets.

monofilament yarn *see* continuous filament yarn.

multifilament yarn *see* continuous filament yarn.

nap (1) A fibrous surface produced on a fabric or felt by raising, in which part of the fibre is lifted from the basic structure. 'Nap' in this sense should be distinguished from 'pile' (*see* pile). The two terms are often used synonymously, but the practice of using them for different concepts is to be encouraged since it provides a means of distinguishing between them and thus avoiding confusion.
(2) A variant of 'nep', used in the flax-producing industry.
(3) In raw cotton, matted clumps of fibres that are entangled more loosely than those in neps (*see* nep).

napping *see* raising.

narrow loom *see* weaving loom.

natural fibre A fibre occurring in nature. Fibres are found in all three sectors of the natural world: animal (e.g. silk, wool); vegetable (e.g. cotton, jute); and mineral (e.g. asbestos).

needleloom A machine for producing needlefelt in which a needle beam (or beams) reciprocates vertically. Felting needles mounted on a board pass through a web or batt, which is supported between bed and stripper plates.

nep A small knot of entangled fibres. A local variation of the term, referring to flax, is 'nap'.

nepp yarn *see* fancy yarns.

organzine Silk yarn used as warp for weaving or for knitting, comprising single threads that are first twisted and then folded together two-, three- or four-fold, and then twisted in the direction opposite to that of the singles twist.

overlap Lateral movement of the guide bars on the beard or hook side of the needles in warp-knitting. This movement is normally restricted to one needle space. *See also* lapping movement.

parchmentizing A finishing treatment, comprising a short contact with, for example, sulphuric acid of high concentration, the aim of which is to produce a variety of effects, depending on the type of fabric and the conditions used, ranging from a linen-like handle to a transparent organdie effect. The treatment is applied mainly to cotton. Reagents other than sulphuric acid will also produce the effect.

PBT Polybutylene terephthalate. This is a fibre-forming substance related to polyester. In stretch textured form, it can give a fabric stretch and recovery properties similar to stretch nylon, but with better modulus.

pick (weft pick) (1) A single operation of the weft-inserting mechanism in weaving.
(2) A single weft thread in a fabric as woven. Note that a single picking operation in weaving may insert more than one pick (i.e. weft thread) in the fabric.
(3) To pass the weft through the warp shed in weaving.

picks per cm (PPC) The number of weft yarns per centimetre.

picks per inch (PPI) The number of weft yarns per inch.

piece-dyeing Dyeing of one or more pieces of fabric (piece-dyed fabrics are fabrics that have been coloured at the fabric stage).

pile A surface effect on a fabric formed by tufts or loops of yarn that stand up from the body of the fabric. 'Pile' should be distinguished from 'nap' (*see* nap (1)). The two terms are often used synonymously, but the practice of using them for different concepts is to be encouraged as it helps to avoid confusion.

pilling The entangling of fibres during washing, dry-cleaning or testing, or in use, to form balls or pills which stand proud of the surface of a fabric and which are of such density that light will not pass through them (so that they cast a shadow).

ply *see* fold.

power loom (power weaving loom) *see* weaving loom.

racking (shogging) In weft-knitting, the lateral movement of a needle-bed or point bar across a predetermined distance on a flat knitting machine. In warp-knitting, it is the lateral movement of a guide bar relative to the needlebar over a predetermined number of needle spaces (*see also* overlap, underlap).

raising (napping) The production of a layer of protruding fibres on the surface of fabrics by brushing, teazling or rubbing. The fabric, in open width, is passed over rotating rollers covered with teazles, fine wires, etc., whereby the surface fibres are pulled out or broken to give the required effect.

reed (sley) (1) A moving part on a weaving loom, consisting of several wires closely set between two slats or baulks, that may serve any or all of the following purposes: separating the warp threads; determining the spacing of the warp threads; guiding the shuttle or rapier (if applicable); and beating up the weft. *See also* dent, sett.
(2) To draw ends through a reed. (In the UK, this is also known as to 'sley', to 'bob the reed' or to 'enter the reed'.)

regenerated fibre A fibre formed from a solution of a natural polymer or of a chemical derivative of a natural polymer and having the same chemical constitution as the natural polymer from which the solution or derivative was made.

resist (1) A substance applied to a substrate to prevent the uptake of fixation of a dye in a subsequent operation. The substance can function by forming a mechanical barrier, by reacting chemically with the dye or substrate, or by altering conditions (e.g. pH value) locally so that development cannot occur. Imperfect preparation of the substrate may cause a resist as a fault.
(2) In printing plate or roller making, a coating of, for example, light-hardened gelatine that protects from the action of the etching solution those areas of the plate or roller that are not required to be etched.

resultant count (R) The actual count of a plied (folded) or cabled construction. This can be expressed in any count system. 'R' is used as an abbreviation.

reverse side *see* effect side.

roving A name given, individually or collectively, to the relatively fine fibrous strands used in the later or final processes of preparation for spinning.

sanding A process in which silk materials are subjected to the gentle abrasion of a sand-and-water mixture to produce a characteristic soft handle.

sanforizing A controlled compressive shrinkage process used principally for cellulosic fabrics. The trademark Sanforized® is owned by Cluett, Peabody & Co., Inc., and can be applied to fabrics that meet defined and approved standards of washing shrinkage.

Schiffli embroidery machine An embroidery machine consisting of a multiplicity of lockstitch sewing elements, working on a basic net or fabric that is attached to a frame movable vertically and horizontally according to the requirements of the pattern.

schreiner (1) To finish a fabric by passing it through a schreiner calender. The object of the process is to enhance the lustre of the fabric.
(2) Descriptive of a finish obtained by the process of schreinering (as in (1)).

scutching The mechanical operation of extracting flax or hemp fibres from the retted straw. The term is usually applied to processes that use rotating turbine blades to effect the separation of fibre from straw. (Retting is a chemical or biological treatment for flax or hemp, to render the fibre bundles more easily separable from the woody part of the stem.)

selvedge (selvage) When used without qualification, the term refers to the longitudinal edges of constructed fabrics. In woven fabrics, selvedges are often up to 20 mm wide and may differ from the body of the fabric in construction, in weave or both, or they may be of exactly the same construction as the body of the fabric and be separated from it by yarns of different colour. Selvedges may contain fancy effects or may have brand names or fabric descriptions woven into or printed on them, but their main purpose is to prevent fraying of the outside ends from the body of the fabric and to give strength to the edges of the fabric so that it will behave satisfactorily in weaving and subsequent processes.

sett (set, pitch, reed count) (1) A term used to indicate the density of ends or picks or both in a woven fabric, usually expressed as the number of yarns per centimetre. The state of the fabric at the time should be described (e.g. loom state or finished). In a high sett (or closely sett) fabric, there is a high number of yarns per cm; in a low sett (or open-sett) fabric, there is a low number of yarns per cm. *See also* square sett.
(2) The number of dents per unit width of reed. There have been many units in common use, for example: (i) the number of dents per inch; (ii) the number of dents per 2 inches; (iii) the number of groups of 20 dents per 36 inches; and (iv) the number of dents per 10 cm. The recommended unit is dents/cm. *See also* dent, reed.

shear (1) To cut the fleece from a sheep.
(2) (*also* crop) To cut a nap or pile to uniform length or height.
(3) (*also* crop) To cut loose fibres or yarn from the surface of a fabric after weaving.

shed (warp shed) The opening formed when warp threads are separated in the operation of weaving.

shogging *see* racking.

singles yarn (single yarn) A thread produced by one unit of a spinning machine or of a silk reel. *See also* fold.

sinker loop *see* knitted loop (2).

size A gelatinous film-forming substance, in solution or dispersion, applied normally to warps but sometimes to wefts, generally before weaving, to protect the yarns from abrasion in the healds and reeds and against each other; to strengthen them; and, by the addition of oils and fats, to lubricate them. The main types of size are carbohydrates and their derivatives, gelatin and animal glues. Other substances, such as linseed oil, polycyclic acid and polyvinyl alcohol, are also used.

sizing The application of size solution to textile yarns by immersion or by contact with a partially immersed roller; penetration of the yarn by size solution.

sley *see* reed.

sliver An assemblage of fibres in continuous form without twist.

slub An abnormally thick place in a yarn.

slubbing The name given, individually or collectively, to the fibrous strands produced during the stages of preparation for spinning, and also to strips of web from a condenser card that have been consolidated into a circular cross-section by rubbing.

slub yarn *see* fancy yarns.

snarl yarn *see* fancy yarns.

spinneret (spinnerette) A nozzle or plate provided with fine holes or slits through which a fibre-forming solution or melt is extruded in filament manufacture.

spiral yarn *see* fancy yarns.

square sett (square cloth) Descriptive of a fabric sett in which the number of ends per centimetre and the number of picks per centimetre are approximately equal. For practical reasons, the linear densities of warp and weft would normally be approximately the same in such a fabric. The contrasting term 'unbalanced sett' is descriptive of a fabric sett in which there is an appreciable difference between the numbers of ends and picks per centimetre. *See also* sett.

staple fibre A fibre of limited and relatively short length. Natural staple fibres range in length from a few millimetres (e.g. cotton linters) up to about a metre (e.g. some bast fibres). Manufactured staple fibres are produced over a similar range of lengths. They are normally prepared from extruded filaments by cutting or breaking into lengths suitable for the subsequent processing system or end use; they are also usually crimped.

staple length The distance between the ends of a staple fibre when measured under specified conditions.

stonewashed finish A finish obtained by vigorous tumbling of wet garments, usually made from denim, with stones derived from pumice or from synthetic, ceramic materials.

'S' twist yarn *see* twist direction.

sueding A mechanical finish that produces a soft, suede-like surface on the fabric. The fabric is passed over a series of rotating rollers covered in a sandpaper-like material. A similar process is known as 'emerizing' (*see* emerizing).

swivel weaving A method of weaving in which a figure is produced in a woven fabric by the introduction of additional weft threads into a base fabric to produce spot effects. The figuring yarn is fed from a series of small shuttles mounted over the top of the weaving surface.

synthetic fibre A fibre manufactured from a polymer synthesized from chemical elements or compounds, in contrast to a fibre made from naturally occurring fibre-forming polymers.

tanning The process of treating animal skins with chemicals to prevent decomposition and thus converting the material into leather.

tappet weaving loom *see* weaving loom.

teazle (teasel, teazel) The dried seed-head of the plant *Dipsacus fullonum* (Fullers' thistle) used to raise a pile or nap on certain fabrics. The machine used for this purpose is known as a 'teazle gig'.

technical back The surface of a plain weft-knitted fabric that consists wholly of back loops.

technical face The surface of a plain weft-knitted fabric that consists wholly of face loops.

tex system A system of expressing the linear density (mass per unit length) of fibres, filaments, slivers and yarns, or other linear textile material. The basic unit is tex, which is the mass in grams of one kilometre of the product. Multiples and sub-multiples recommended for use in preference to other possible combinations are: kilogram per kilometre, designated kilotex (ktex); decigram per kilometre, designated decitex (dtex); and milligram per kilometre, designated millitex (mtex). Tex is a recognized SI unit (SI is the Système International d'Unités). The tex system is a 'direct yarn count system' where the higher the count, the coarser the yarn.

textile A term originally designating a woven fabric, but now also applied (in the singular and plural forms) to fibres, filaments and yarns, natural and manufactured, and most products for which these are a principal raw material.

This definition embraces, for example, fibre-based products in the following categories: threads, cords, ropes and braids; woven, knitted and nonwoven fabrics, lace, nets and embroidery; hosiery, knitwear and made-up apparel; household textiles, soft furnishings and upholstery; carpets and other floor coverings; and technical, industrial and engineering textiles, including geotextiles and medical textiles. The term 'textile' may also be used adjectivally. *See also* fabric, material.

textured yarn A continuous filament, man-made fibre yarn that has been processed to introduce durable crimps, coils, loops or other fine distortions along the length of the filaments. *See also* curled yarn, fancy yarns, yarn.

toile (1) A French word for 'fabric'.
(2) Fabric of appropriate mass per unit area (i.e. weight) for the construction of prototype garments. Normally unbleached cotton cloth is used.
(3) A prototype garment cut out in toile (see (2)).

top (1) Sliver that forms the starting material for the worsted and certain other drawing systems (operations by which slivers are blended, doubled or levelled, and, by drafting, reduced to a sliver or a roving suitable for spinning). It is usually obtained by the process of combing, and is ideally characterized by the following properties: (i) the absence of fibres so short as to be uncontrolled in the preferred system of drawing; (ii) a substantially parallel formation of the fibres; (iii) a substantially homogeneous distribution throughout the sliver of fibres from each length-group present.
(2) The form or package in which sliver is delivered, for example ball top or bump top.

tow (1) Any substantially clean flax or hemp fibre of less than scutched length.
(2) In manufactured fibre production, an essentially twist-free assemblage of a large number of substantially parallel filaments.

tram A silk weft yarn comprising two or more ends of raw silk folded with 80 to 400 turns per metre (2–10 turns per inch).

tuck loop In knitted fabrics, a length (or lengths) of yarn received by a needle and not pulled through the loop of the previous course.

twist The twist level of a yarn is measured in turns per unit length. The term is used for both singles and folded yarns. In high-twist yarns, there is a high number of turns per unit length; in low-twist yarns, there is a low number of turns per unit length. A yarn that has a tendency to twist or untwist spontaneously is called a 'twist-lively', 'lively' or 'snarly' yarn.

twist direction The direction of twist inserted into a yarn. Twist is described as 'S' or 'Z' according to which of these letters has its centre inclined in the same direction as the surface elements of a given twisted yarn when the yarn is viewed vertically. In an 'S' twist yarn, the twist has been inserted in an anti-clockwise direction; in a 'Z' twist yarn, the twist has been inserted in a clockwise direction.

twist liveliness *see* twist.

twist yarn *see* grandrelle yarn.

unbalanced sett *see* square sett.

underlap (1) In warp-knitting, lateral movements of the guide bar made on the side of the needle remote from the hook or beard; the amount of this movement is limited only by mechanical considerations. *See also* lapping movement.
(2) The connection between stitches in consecutive courses in a warp-knitted fabric.

union yarn A yarn made by twisting together yarns of different fibres.

vigoureux printing *see* mélange printing.

wale A column of loops along the length of a knitted fabric.

warp The lengthwise yarns in a woven or warp-knitted fabric, parallel to the selvedge.

warp-faced Descriptive of a fabric that has been constructed with more warp ends than weft picks visible on the face of the fabric.

weaving loom (weaving machine) A machine used for producing fabric by weaving. Most looms are single-phase weaving machines in which the weft is laid across the full width of the warp sheet in a single phase of the working cycle. Some of the main types of weaving loom, classified according to the types of fabric they produce, are as follows.
• A broad loom is an extra-wide loom that can weave textiles in wider widths than most other fabrics, for example carpets.
• A dobby loom is a loom with a mechanism for controlling the movement of the heald shafts. It is required when the number of heald shafts or the number of picks in a repeat of the pattern, or both, are beyond the capacity of tappet shedding.
• A hand-loom (hand weaving loom) is a hand-operated machine for producing cloth by weaving. In some instances the shedding is performed by foot operation.
• A jacquard loom has a jacquard shedding mechanism attached to it, which allows individual control of up to several hundred warp threads and thus enables large figured designs to be produced.

- A narrow loom is smaller than a normal loom and weaves narrow fabrics such as ribbons and tapes.
- A power loom (power weaving loom) is a loom that is driven by a source of power such as an electric motor.
- A tappet loom is a loom where the control of the movement of the heald shafts in the weaving of simple constructions is by means of cams or tappets. Positive tappets raise and lower the heald shaft. Negative tappets move the heald shafts in one direction only and require another mechanism, usually springs, to return them. *See also* heald, shed, swivel weaving.

weaving loom beam (weaver's beam) A roller on each side of which large flanges are usually fixed so that a warp may be wound on it in readiness for weaving.

weft The transverse yarns in a woven or warp-knitted fabric, running from selvedge to selvedge.

weft-faced Descriptive of a fabric that has been constructed with more weft picks than warp ends visible on the face of the fabric.

wicking The penetration of liquids, under the influence of capillary forces, along or through a textile material, the textile element of a coated fabric, or along interstices formed by that element and the coating polymer of the coated fabric.

yarn A product of substantial length and relatively small cross-section consisting of fibres and/or filament(s) with or without twist. Note that assemblies of fibres or filaments are usually given other names during the stages that lead to the production of yarn (e.g. 'tow', 'slubbing', 'sliver' or 'roving'). Except in the case of continuous filament or tape yarns, any tensile strength possessed by assemblies at these stages is generally the minimum that can hold them together during processing. *See also* curled yarn, fancy yarns, textured yarn.

yarn count (count of yarn, yarn number) Methods of expressing the mass per unit length or the length per unit mass of a yarn. *See also* cotton count, tex system.

yarn-dyeing Dyeing at the yarn stage (in contrast to piece-dyeing, which is done at the fabric stage). Woven fabrics made with dyed yarns (in the warp, the weft, or both warp and weft) may be described as 'yarn-dyed' or 'colour-woven'.

'Z' twist yarn *see* twist direction.

REFERENCES

1 Burnham, Dorothy K. *A Textile Terminology: Warp and Weft*. London: Routledge & Kegan Paul, 1981.

2 Ladbury, Ann. *Fabrics*. London: Sidgwick & Jackson, 1979.

3 Hardingham, Martin. *The Illustrated Dictionary of Fabrics*. London: Studio Vista, 1978.

4 Hough, Walter. *Encyclopaedia of Cotton Fabrics* (4th edn). Manchester: John Heywood, 1927.

5 Jerde, Judith. *Encyclopedia of Textiles*. New York: Facts on File, 1992.

6 Elsasser, Virginia Hencken. *Textiles: Concepts and Principles* (2nd edn). New York: Fairchild, 2005.

7 Hollen, Norma, Saddler, Jane and Langford, Anna L. *Textiles* (5th edn). New York: Macmillan, 1979.

8 Fraser, Grace Lovat. *Textiles by Britain*. London: George Allen & Unwin, 1948.

9 Calasibetta, Charlotte. *Fairchild's Dictionary of Fashion*. New York: Fairchild, 1975.

10 Taylor, Marjorie A. *Technology of Textile Properties* (3rd edn). London: Forbes, 1994.

11 Miller, Edward. *Textiles: Properties and Behaviour in Clothing Use*. London: Batsford, 1992.

12 'Weave Directory', *World Review of Textile Design*, 1991, pp. xxxiii–xxxvi.

13 *Clothing Technology: From Fibre to Fashion* (2nd edn). Haan-Gruiten, Germany: Europa-Lehrmittel, 1999.

14 Joseph, Marjory L. *Essentials of Textiles* (3rd edn). New York: Holt, Rinehart & Winston, 1984.

15 Ostick, E. *Textiles for Tailors*. London: Tailor and Cutter, n.d.

16 Ostick, E. *Textiles for Tailors: What You Should Know about Cloth* (2nd rev. edn). London: Tailor and Cutter, n.d.

17 Corbman, Bernard P. *Textiles: Fiber to Fabric* (6th edn). New York: McGraw-Hill, 1983.

18 Lyle, Dorothy S. *Modern Textiles* (2nd edn). New York: Wiley, 1982.

19 Kadolph, Sara J., Langford, Anna L., Hollen, Norma and Saddler, Jane. *Textiles* (7th edn). New York: Macmillan, 1993.

20 Price, Arthur, Cohen, Allen C. and Johnson, Ingrid. *J. J. Pizzuto's Fabric Science* (7th edn). New York: Fairchild, 1999.

21 Patten, Marguerite. *The Care of Fabrics*. London: Ginn, 1971.

22 Gioello, Debbie Ann. *Profiling Fabrics: Properties, Performance and Construction Techniques* (Language of Fashion series). New York: Fairchild, 1981.

23 Humphries, Mary. *Fabric Glossary*. London: Prentice-Hall, 1996.

24 Scottish Woollen Publicity Council. *Scottish Wool Cloth Sample Book*. London: Dept of Education and Training, International Wool Secretariat, n.d.

25 *Textile Terms and Definitions* (11th edn). Manchester: Textile Institute, 2002.

26 Grosicki, Z. *Watson's Textile Design and Colour*. London: Butterworth, 1979.

27 Parker, Julie. *All about Cotton: A Fabric Dictionary and Swatchbook* (rev. edn) (Fabric Reference Series, vol. 2). Seattle: Rain City, 1998.

28 Wilson, Janet. 'The Flowering Tree Motif in Textiles'. Undergraduate dissertation, Manchester Polytechnic, 1978.

29 Wilson, Janet. 'An Investigation of Warp Printing by means of Heat Transfer'. MPhil thesis, Central School of Art and Design, London, in collaboration with Tootals Ltd, Manchester, 1983.

30 *The Hutchinson Encyclopedia* (1995 edn). Oxford: Helicon, 1994.

31 Spencer, David J. *Knitting Technology* (3rd edn). Cambridge: Woodhead, 2001.

32 Braddock, Sarah E. and O'Mahony, Marie. *Techno Textiles: Revolutionary Fabrics for Fashion and Design*. London: Thames & Hudson, 1999.

33 Larsen, J. L., Buhler, A., Solyom, G. and Solyom, B. *The Dyer's Art: Ikat, Batik, Plangi*. New York: Van Nostrand Reinhold, 1976.

34 Hibbert, Ros. *Textile Innovation: Interactive, Contemporary and Traditional Materials* (2nd edn). London: Line, 2004.

35 Fluss, K. H. 'Space-Dyeing: Survey of Methods', *Bayer Farben Revue*, no. 26, July 1976, pp. 20–28.

36 Textile Mercury. *The 'Mercury' Dictionary of Textile Terms*. Manchester: Textile Mercury, n.d. [c. 1950].

37 Peter MacDonald Tartan Design & Consultancy, 'A Short History of Tartan', September 1998, http://www.users.zetnet.co.uk/tartan/history.htm (viewed 10 Nov. 2009).

38 British Standard and International Organization for Standardization, BS ISO 8388:1998, 'Knitted Fabrics – Types – Vocabulary'.

39 Wada, Yoshiko Iwamoto. *Memory on Cloth: Shibori Now*. Tokyo: Kodansha International, 2002.

40 Anderson, Kim. 'Smart Textiles Update', August 2005, http://www.techexchange.com/thelibrary/smarttextiles.html (viewed 10 Nov. 2009).

41 Holme, Ian. 'Microencapsulation: The Changing Face of Finishing', *Textiles Magazine*, no. 4, 2004, pp. 7–10.

42 Gupta, Sanjay. 'Design Innovation and New Technologies', August 2005, http://www.techexchange.com/ thelibrary/designinnov.html (viewed 10 Nov. 2009).

43 Ploch, S., Böttcher, P., Scharch, D. *Malimo-Nähwirktechnologie*. Leipzig: Veb Fachbuchverlag, 1978.

44 Harrison, E. S. *Our Scottish District Checks*. Edinburgh: The National Association of Scottish Woollen Manufacturers, 1968.

45 Barber, E. J. W. *Prehistoric Textiles*. Princeton, N.J.: Princeton University Press, 1991.

46 Scottish Tartans Authority, http://www.tartansauthority.com.

BIBLIOGRAPHY

Albrecht, Wilhelm, Fuchs, Hilmar and Kittelmann, Walter (eds). *Nonwoven Fabrics: Raw Materials, Manufacture, Applications, Characteristics, Testing Processes*. Weinheim: Wiley-VCH, 2003.

American Fabrics and Fashions Magazine editors. *Encyclopedia of Textiles* (3rd edn). Englewood Cliffs, N.J.: Prentice-Hall, 1980.

Anderson, Kim. 'Smart Textiles Update', August 2005, http://www.techexchange.com/thelibrary/smarttextiles.html

Anstey, H. and Weston, T. *The Anstey Weston Guide to Textile Terms*. [n.p.]: Weston Publishing, 1997.

Baker, George Percival. *Calico Painting and Printing in the East Indies in the XVIIth and XVIIIth Centuries*. London: Edward Arnold, 1921.

Barber, E. J. W. *Prehistoric Textiles*. Princeton, N.J.: Princeton University Press, 1991.

Barker, A. F. and Midgley, E. *An Analysis of Woven Fabrics*. London: Scott, Greenwood and Son, 1914.

Blood, Janet and Sinclair, John D. *Rubber: Fun, Fashion, Fetish*. London: Thames & Hudson, 2004.

Brackenbury, Terry. *Knitted Clothing Technology*. Oxford: Blackwell Scientific Publications, 1992.

Braddock, Sarah E. and O'Mahony, Marie (eds). *Textiles and New Technology: 2010*. London: Artemis, 1994.

Braddock, Sarah E. and O'Mahony, Marie. *Techno Textiles: Revolutionary Fabrics for Fashion and Design*. London: Thames & Hudson, 1999.

Braddock, Sarah E. and O'Mahony, Marie. *Techno Textiles 2: Revolutionary Fabrics for Fashion and Design*. London: Thames & Hudson, 2005.

Brédif, Josette. *Toiles de Jouy: Classic Printed Textiles from France (1760–1843)*. London: Thames & Hudson, 1989.

British Standard and International Organization for Standardization, BS ISO 8388:1998, 'Knitted Fabrics – Types – Vocabulary'.

Bunnschweiler, David and Hearle, John (eds). *Polyester: 50 Years of Achievement*. Manchester: Textile Institute, 1993.

Buff, Regula. *Bindungslehre: Ein Webmusterbuch*. Bern: Verlag Paul Haupt, 1985.

Bühler, A. 'The Ikat Technique', *Ciba Review*, no. 44, 1942, pp. 1586–1611.

Bühler, A. 'Earliest Ways of Colouring, Primitive Dyeing Methods and Some Problems of Primitive Dyeing', *Ciba Review*, no. 68, 1948, pp. 2478–2508.

Bühler, A. *Ikat, Batik, Plangi: Reservemusterungen auf Garn und Stoff aus Vorderasien, Zentralasien, Südosteuropa und Nordafrika* (3 vols). Basel: Pharos Verlag H. Schwabe, 1972.

Buresh, Francis M. *Nonwoven Fabrics*. New York: Reinhold, 1962.

Burnard, Joyce. *Chintz and Cotton: India's Textile Gift to the World*. Kenthurst, NSW: Kangaroo Press, 1994.

Burnham, Dorothy K. *A Textile Terminology: Warp and Weft*. London: Routledge & Kegan Paul, 1981.

Calasibetta, Charlotte. *Fairchild's Dictionary of Fashion*. New York: Fairchild, 1975.

Clothing Technology: From Fibre to Fashion (2nd edn). Haan-Gruiten, Germany: Verlag Europa-Lehrmittel, 1999.

Cole, Drusilla. *Patterns: New Surface Design*. London: Laurence King, 2007.

Cole, Drusilla. *Textiles Now*. London: Laurence King, 2008.

Cole, Drusilla (ed.). *1000 Patterns*. London: A & C Black, 2003.

Collier, Ann M. *A Handbook of Textiles* (3rd edn). Exeter: Wheaton, 1980.

Commission of the European Communities. *Subcontracting Terminology: Textile and Clothing Sectors*. Luxembourg: Office for Official Publications of the European Communities, 1990.

Corbman, Bernard P. *Textiles: Fiber to Fabric* (6th edn). New York: McGraw-Hill, 1983.

Craig, Elizabeth. *Elizabeth Craig's Needlecraft*. London: Collins, 1947.

Cresswell, Lesley. *Textiles at the Cutting Edge*. London: Forbes, 2001.

De' Marinis, Fabrizio. *Velvet: History, Techniques, Fashions*. Milan: Idea Books, 1994.

Denny, Grace G. *Fabrics* (8th edn). Philadelphia: Lippincott, 1962.

Dillement, Thérèse de, *Encyclopedia of Needlework*. Mulhouse: DMC Library, n.d.

Dumville, J. and Kershaw, S. *The Worsted Industry* (4th edn). London: Pitman, 1947.

Earnshaw, Pat. *A Dictionary of Lace*. Aylesbury: Shire, 1982.

Earnshaw, Pat. *Bobbin and Needle Laces: Identification and Care*. London: Batsford, 1983.

Earnshaw, Pat. *Lace Machines and Machine Laces* (vol. 2). Guildford: Gorse, 1995.

Elsasser, Virginia Hencken. *Textiles: Concepts and Principles* (2nd edn). New York: Fairchild, 2005.

Emery, Irene. *The Primary Structures of Fabrics: An Illustrated Classification*. New York: Watson-Guptill, 1994.

Fluss, K. H. 'Space-Dyeing: Survey of Methods', *Bayer Farben Revue*, no. 26, July 1976, pp. 20–28.

Franck, Robert R. (ed.). *Silk, Mohair, Cashmere and Other Luxury Fibres*. Cambridge: Woodhead, 2001.

Fraser, Grace Lovat. *Textiles by Britain*. London: George Allen & Unwin, 1948.

Fung, Walter. *Coated and Laminated Textiles*. Cambridge: Woodhead, 2002.

Gale, Elizabeth. *From Fibres to Fabrics*. London: Mills & Boon, 1971.

Gioello, Debbie Ann. *Profiling Fabrics: Properties, Performance, and Construction Techniques*. (Language of Fashion series.) New York: Fairchild Publications, 1981.

Gioello, Debbie Ann. *Understanding Fabrics: From Fiber to Finished Cloth* (Language of Fashion series). New York: Fairchild, 1996.

Goerner, Doris. *Woven Structure and Design. Part 1: Single Cloth Construction*. Leeds: WIRA Technology Group, 1986.

Grosicki, Z. *Watson's Advanced Textile Design*. London: Butterworth, 1977.

Grosicki, Z. *Watson's Textile Design and Colour*. London: Butterworth, 1979.

Gupta, Sanjay. 'Design Innovation and New Technologies', August 2005, http://www.techexchange.com/thelibrary/designinnov.html.

Hardingham, Martin. *The Illustrated Dictionary of Fabrics*. London: Studio Vista, 1978.

Harrison, E. S. *Our Scottish District Checks*. Edinburgh: The National Association of Scottish Woollen Manufacturers, 1968.

Hatch, Kathryn L. *Textile Science*. Minneapolis/Saint Paul, Mich.: West, 1993.

Heylin, Hy. B. *Cottons, Linens, Woollens, Silks: How to Buy and Judge Materials*. Manchester: John Heywood, 1917.

Hibbert, Ros. *Textile Innovation: Traditional, Modern and Smart Textiles*. London: Line, 2002.

Hibbert, Ros. *Textile Innovation: Interactive, Contemporary and Traditional Materials* (2nd edn). London: Line, 2004.

Higgins, J. P. P. *Cloth of Gold: A History of Metallised Textiles*. London: Lurex, 1993.

Holker, J. R. *Bonded Fabrics*. Watford: Merrow, 1975.

Hollen, Norma, Saddler, Jane and Langford, Anna L. *Textiles* (5th edn). New York: Macmillan, 1979.

Holme, Ian. 'Microencapsulation: The Changing Face of Finishing', *Textiles Magazine*, no. 4, 2004, pp. 7–10.

Hongu, Tatsuya and Phillips, Glyn O. *New Fibers* (2nd edn). Cambridge: Woodhead, 1997.

Hough, Walter. *Encyclopaedia of Cotton Fabrics* (4th edn). Manchester: John Heywood, 1927.

Hoye, John. *Staple Cotton Fabrics*. New York; London: McGraw-Hill, 1942.

Hudson, Peyton B., Clapp, Anne C. and Kness, Darlene. *Joseph's Introductory Textile Science* (6th edn). New York: Holt, Rinehart and Winston, 1993.

Humphries, Mary. *Fabric Glossary*. London: Prentice-Hall, 1996.

Humphries, Mary. *Fabric Reference*. London: Prentice-Hall, 1996.

The Hutchinson Encyclopedia (1995 edn). Oxford: Helicon, 1994.

ICS Reference Library: Weave Glossary, Fabric Analysis, Weave Varieties, Colour Designs. Scranton, Pa.: International Textbook Company, 1906.

Irwin, John and Brett, K. B. *Origins of Chintz*. London: HMSO, 1970.

Jerde, Judith. *Encyclopedia of Textiles*. New York: Facts on File, 1992.

Joseph, Marjory L. *Essentials of Textiles* (3rd edn). New York: Holt, Rinehart and Winston, 1984.

Kadolph, Sara J., Langford, Anna L., Hollen, Norma and Saddler, Jane. *Textiles* (7th edn). New York: Macmillan, 1993.

Kaufman, Morris. *The History of PVC: The Chemistry and Industrial Production of Polyvinyl Chloride*. London: Maclaren & Sons, 1969.

Klapper, Marvin. *Fabric Almanac* (2nd edn). New York: Fairchild, 1971.

Krčma, Radko. *Nonwoven textiles*. Manchester: Textile Trade Press; Prague: SNTL Publishers of Technical Literature, 1962.

Krčma, Radko. *Manual of Nonwovens*. Manchester: Textile Trade Press; Georgia, Ga.: W. R. C. Smith, 1971.

Ladbury, Ann. *Fabrics*. London: Sidgwick & Jackson, 1979.

Larsen, J. L., Buhler, A., Solyom, G. and Solyom, B. *The Dyer's Art: Ikat, Batik, Plangi*. New York: Van Nostrand Reinhold, 1976.

Levey, Santina M. *Lace: A History*. [London]: Victoria and Albert Museum; Leeds: W. S. Maney and Son, 1983.

Lowry, Priscilla. *The Secrets of Silk: From Textiles to Fashion*. London: St John's Press, 2004.

Lubell, Cecil. *Textile Collections of the World. Vol. 1: United States and Canada; Vol. 2: UK and Ireland; Vol. 3: France*. London: Studio Vista, 1976.

Lyle, Dorothy S. *Modern Textiles* (2nd edn). New York: Wiley, 1982.

MacDonald, Peter. *The 1819 Key Pattern Book: One Hundred Original Tartans*. Perth: Jamieson and Munro, 1996.

McQuaid, Matilda. *Extreme Textiles: Designing for High Performance*. London: Thames & Hudson, 2005.

Mehta, Rustam Jehangir. *Masterpieces of Indian Textiles*. Bombay: D. B. Taraporevala, 1970.

Meller, Susan and Elffers, Joost. *Textile Designs: 200 Years of Patterns for Printed Fabrics*. London: Thames & Hudson, 1991.

Meredith, R. *Elastomeric Fibres*. Watford: Merrow, 1971.

Miller, Edward. *Textiles: Properties and Behaviour in Clothing Use*. London: Batsford, 1992.

Montgomery, Florence M. *Textiles in America, 1650–1870*. New York: Norton, 1984.

Nomachi, Katsutoshi. *Japanese Textiles* (Survey of World Textiles, no. 14). Leigh-on-Sea: F. Lewis, 1958.

Oelsner, G. H. *A Handbook of Weaves*. New York: Dover, 1952.

Okamura, Kichiemon. *Handicrafts of Okinawa: A Pictorial Record*. [Tokyo?]: Seidosha, 1964.

Ostick, E. *Textiles for Tailors*. London: Tailor and Cutter, n.d.

Ostick, E. *Textiles for Tailors: What You Should Know about Cloth* (2nd rev. edn). London: Tailor and Cutter, n.d.

Parker, Julie. *All about Cotton: A Fabric Dictionary and Swatchbook* (rev. edn) (Fabric Reference series, vol. 2). Seattle: Rain City, 1998.

Patten, Marguerite. *The Care of Fabrics*. London: Ginn, 1971.

Percival, Maciver. *The Chintz Book*. London: Heinemann, 1923.

Peter MacDonald Tartan Design & Consultancy, 'A Short History of Tartan', September 1998, http://www.users.zetnet.co.uk/tartan/history.htm.

Phillips, Janet. *The Weaver's Book of Fabric Design*. London: Batsford, 1983.

Picton, John and Mack, John. *African Textiles*. London: British Museum, 1979.

Ploch, S., Böttcher, P., Scharch, D. *Malimo-Nähwirktechnologie*. Leipzig: Veb Fachbuchverlag, 1978.

Powys, Marian. *Lace and Lace Making*. Boston, Mass.: Charles T. Branford, 1953.

Price, Arthur, Cohen, Allen C. and Johnson, Ingrid. *J. J. Pizzuto's Fabric Science* (7th edn). New York: Fairchild, 1999.

Price, Arthur, Cohen, Allen C. and Johnson, Ingrid. *J. J. Pizzuto's Fabric Science Swatch Kit* (7th edn). New York: Fairchild, 1999.

Reilly, Valerie. *Paisley Patterns: A Design Source Book*. London: Studio Editions; New York: Portland House, 1989.

Robinson, A. T. C. and Marks, R. *Woven Cloth Construction*. Manchester: Textile Institute; London: Butterworths, 1973.

Robinson, Stuart. *A History of Dyed Textiles*. London: Studio Vista, 1969.

Schoesser, Mary. *Silk*. New Haven, Conn.: Yale University Press, 2007.

Schwab, David E. *The Story of Lace and Embroidery*. New York: Fairchild, 1951.

Scottish Tartans Authority, http://www.tartansauthority.com.

Scottish Woollen Publicity Council. *Scottish Wool Cloth Sample Book*. London: Dept of Education and Training, International Wool Secretariat, n.d.

Seiler-Baldinger, Annemarie. *Textiles: A Classification of Techniques*. Bathurst, NSW: Crawford House, 1994.

Spencer, David J. *Knitting Technology* (3rd edn). Cambridge: Woodhead, 2001.

Spencer-Churchill, Henrietta. *Classic Fabrics*. London: Collins and Brown, 1996.

Storey, Joyce. *Textile Printing*. London: Thames & Hudson, 1974.

Storey, Joyce. *Dyes and Fabrics*. London: Thames & Hudson, 1978.

Strong, John H. *Foundations of Fabric Structure*. London: National Trade Press, 1946.

Tao, Xiaoming (ed.). *Smart Fibres, Fabrics and Clothing*. Cambridge: Woodhead, 2001.

Tattersall, C. E. C. *A History of British Carpets*. Leigh-on-Sea: F. Lewis, 1966.

Taylor, Marjorie A. *Technology of Textile Properties* (3rd edn). London: Forbes, 1994.

Textile Mercury. *The 'Mercury' Dictionary of Textile Terms*. Manchester: Textile Mercury, n.d. [*c.* 1950].

The Textile Recorder Year Book, 1941 issue.

Textile Terms and Definitions (11th edn). Manchester: Textile Institute, 2002.

Thompson, Francis. *Harris Tweed: The Story of a Hebridean Industry*. Newton Abbot: David and Charles, 1969.

Tomita, Jun and Tomita, Noriko. *Japanese Ikat Weaving: The Techniques of Kasuri*. London: Routledge & Kegan Paul, 1982.

Tortora, Phyllis G. and Collier, Billie J. *Understanding Textiles* (6th edn). Upper Saddle River, N.J.: Prentice Hall, 2001.

Tortora, Phyllis G. and Merkel, Robert S. *Fairchild's Dictionary of Textiles* (7th edn). New York: Fairchild, 1996.

Turner Wilcox, R. *The Dictionary of Costume*. London: Batsford, 1979.

Van Roojen, Pepin. *Batik Design*. Amsterdam: Pepin Press BV, 1996.

Wada, Yoshiko Iwamoto. *Memory on Cloth: Shibori Now*. Tokyo: Kodansha International, 2002.

Watkinson, Carol. *Fabrics Unravelled*. Durban: Fabrics Unravelled, 2003.

'Weave Directory', *World Review of Textile Design*, 1991, pp. xxxiii–xxxvi.

Welford, T. *The Textile Student's Manual* (4th edn). London: Pitman, 1957.

Wilson, Jacquie. *Handbook of Textile Design: Principles, Processes and Practice*. Cambridge: Woodhead, 2001.

Wilson, Janet. 'The Flowering Tree Motif in Textiles'. Undergraduate dissertation, Manchester Polytechnic, 1978.

Wilson, Janet. 'An Investigation of Warp Printing by means of Heat Transfer'. MPhil thesis, Central School of Art and Design, London, in collaboration with Tootals Ltd, Manchester, 1983.

Wingate, Isabel B. and Mohler, June F. *Textile Fabrics and their Selection* (8th edn). London: Prentice-Hall, 1984.

Wynne, A. *Textiles* (The Motivate Series: Macmillan Texts for Industrial Vocational and Technical Education). London: Macmillan Education, 1997.

LIST OF TRADEMARKS

The following trademarked terms have been used with the permission of the owners:

- Aertex® is the brand name of a woven cellular fabric produced by Aertex Ltd
- Alcantara® is the brand name of a fabric produced by Alcantara S.p.A.
- Barbour®
- Burberry Check® is the worldwide registered trademark of the Burberry Check owned by Burberry Ltd
- Cool Wool™ is a trademark owned by The Woolmark Company Pty Ltd
- Fresco®
- GORE-TEX®, GORE® and designs are registered trademarks of W. L. Gore & Associates.
- Harris Tweed®
- Kevlar® is the registered trademark of E. I. du Pont de Nemours and Company
- Lacoste®
- 'Liberty Tana lawn' is the registered trademark of Liberty Plc
- Lurex® is the registered trademark of the Lurex Company Ltd
- LYCRA® fibre is a trademark of INVISTA
- MILIUM® is the registered trademark of Milliken & Company
- Nomex® is the registered trademark of E. I. du Pont de Nemours and Company
- Sanforized®. The trademark Sanforized® is owned by Cluett, Peabody & Co., Inc.
- Scotchlite 3M™ and Scotchlite™ are trademarks of 3M
- Sympatex®
- Teflon® is the registered trademark of E. I. du Pont de Nemours and Company
- Tyvek® is the registered trademark of E. I. du Pont de Nemours and Company
- VELCRO® is the brand name of a narrow fabric used as fastening material, produced by VELCRO Ltd
- Vilene® is the registered trademark of Freudenberg Vliesstoffe KG
- Viyella® is the registered trademark of Viyella, part of the Austin Reed Group Plc

ACKNOWLEDGMENTS

I would like to express my sincere thanks to the following individuals and companies who have provided information and advised on the content of the text:

Chris Beever, University of Huddersfield

Jeni Bougourd, Senior Research Fellow, London College of Fashion, University of the Arts, London

Drusilla Cole, artist and author

Rosemary House, Des RCA

The team at Joseph H. Clissold, Bradford (Malcolm Campbell, Richard Chambers, Kenneth Forsyth and Ruth Crawshaw-Sykes)

Brian J. McCarthy, Director, TechniTex Faraday Ltd, Manchester

The Textile Institute, Manchester

Thames & Hudson, London

David Tooth, Chairman, Vanners, Sudbury, Suffolk

Nigel Whatmough

I would also like to thank the following individuals for their input and support:

Hazel Bidder, Associate Lecturer, London College of Fashion, University of the Arts, London

Alan Cannon-Jones, Principal Lecturer, London College of Fashion, University of the Arts, London

Ian Kerr, AV/Graphics, London College of Fashion, University of the Arts, London

Julie King, Head of Department of Fashion and Textiles, De Montfort University, Leicester

Wendy Malem, Dean of Enterprise and International Development, London College of Fashion, University of the Arts, London

Professor Roy Peach, Dean of the Graduate School, London College of Fashion, University of the Arts, London

Andrew Watson and The Photography Department, Central St Martin's College of Art & Design, University of the Arts, London

Professor Maureen Wayman, Pro-Vice-Chancellor and Dean of the Faculty of Art & Design, Manchester Metropolitan University, Manchester

I also offer my grateful thanks to the following companies and individuals who have provided information and fabric samples to photograph:

Acorn Fabrics (Cumbria) Ltd, Nelson, Lancashire

Aertex Ltd, Manchester

J. Barbour & Sons Ltd, South Shields, Tyne & Wear

Berwin & Berwin, London

Maureen and Tim Brennan

Brisbane Moss Corduroys, Todmorden, Lancashire

Emma Brown

Burberry Ltd, London

Joseph H. Clissold, Bradford, West Yorkshire

Jody and Rupert de Salis

Drummond Fabrics Ltd, Huddersfield, West Yorkshire

E. I. Du Pont de Nemours and Company, Wilmington, Del.

Elanbach, near Brecon, Powys

Freudenberg Vliesstoffe KG, Weinheim, Germany

Alison and Peter Gayek

June Tracy Gayek

Geoffrey (Tailor) Ltd, Edinburgh

Lynn Gordon

W. L. Gore & Associates (UK) Ltd, Livingston, West Lothian

A. W. Hainsworth & Sons Ltd, Stanningley, Pudsey, West Yorkshire

HFW Huddersfield Ltd, West Yorkshire

Hield Brothers Ltd, London

Holland & Sherry, Peebles, Borders

Hunt and Winterbotham, Huddersfield, West Yorkshire

Invista, Wichita, Kans.

James Hare Silks, Leeds, West Yorkshire

Suzanne Jarvis

Joshua Ellis & Co. Ltd, Batley, West Yorkshire

Karl Mayer Textilmaschinenfabrik GmbH, Chemnitz, Germany (Alexander Wegner)

Loden-Steiner, Steiner GmbH, Mandling, Austria

The Lurex Co. Ltd, London

Harriet Maack

The Marilyn Garrow Fine Textile Art Gallery, London (Lydia and Marilyn Garrow)

Minova Fabrics Ltd, Dewsbury, West Yorkshire (Dawn Whitehouse and Fred Barber)

Moxon Ltd, Huddersfield, West Yorkshire (Firas Chamsi-Pasha)

Cathy Noble

Parkland Fabrics Ltd, Huddersfield, West Yorkshire (Brian Leach)

Polartec, Lawrence, Mass.

Pongees Ltd, London

Kathleen Robinson

The Scottish Tartans Authority, Crieff, Perthshire

Sylvia Simpson

Jonathan Smith

Stephen Walters & Sons Ltd, Sudbury, Suffolk

Strella Fabrics Ltd, Nottingham, Nottinghamshire

Sympatex® Technologies GmbH, Unterföhring, Germany

Taylor & Lodge, Huddersfield, West Yorkshire

Vanners, Sudbury, Suffolk

Viyella, London

David Wilson

Doreen and Tony Wilson

Jacky Wilson

Jennifer Wilson

Lucy Wilson

The Wilton Carpet Factory, Wilton, Wiltshire

Philip Wong

The Woolmark Company Pty Ltd, Australia